MODELS OF MUSIC THERAPY
INTERVENTIONS IN SCHOOL SETTINGS

EDITOR

BRIAN L. WILSON
Western Michigan University
Kalamazoo, Michigan

EDITORIAL CONSULTANT

DAVID S. SMITH
Western Michigan University
Kalamazoo, Michigan

TECHNICAL ASSISTANCE

WORDSETTERS
Kalamazoo, Michigan

MODELS OF MUSIC THERAPY INTERVENTIONS IN SCHOOL SETTINGS

Second Edition

Edited by

Brian L. Wilson
School of Music
Western Michigan University

American Music Therapy Association, Inc.

The American Music Therapy Association is a non-profit association dedicated to increasing access to quality music therapy services for individuals with disabilities or illnesses or for those who are interested in personal growth and wellness. AMTA provides extensive educational and research information about the music therapy profession. Referrals for qualified music therapists are also provided to consumers and parents. AMTA holds an annual conference every autumn and its eight regions hold conferences every spring.

For up-to-date information, please access the AMTA website at www.musictherapy.org

ISBN: 1–884914–04–7

The American Music Therapy Association, Inc.
8455 Colesville Road, Suite 1000
Silver Spring, MD 20910

Phone: (301) 589-3300
Fax: (301) 589-5175
Email: info@musictherapy.org
Website: www.musictherapy.org

LIST OF PRINCIPAL CONTRIBUTORS

Mary S. Adamek, Ph.D., MT-BC
University of Iowa
Iowa City, Iowa

Mike D. Brownell, M.M., MT-BC
Private Practice
Ann Arbor, Michigan

Betsey K. Brunk, M.M.T., MT-BC
Southern Methodist University
Dallas, Texas

Kathleen A. Coleman, M.M.T., MT-BC
Private Practice
Grapevine, Texas

Cynthia M. Colwell, Ph.D., MT-BC
University of Kansas
Lawrence, Kansas

Carol L. Culton, Ph.D., MT-BC
Wartburg College
Waverly, Iowa

Alice-Ann Darrow, Ph.D., RMT
University of Kansas
Lawrence, Kansas

Jennifer K. DeBedout, M.M., MT-BC
Fulton County School System
Atlanta, Georgia

Laurie A. Farnan, M.M.T., WMTR, MT-BC
Central Wisconsin Center for the
Developmentally Disabled
Madison, Wisconsin

Amelia Greenwald Furman, M.M., RMT
Minneapolis Public Schools
Minneapolis, Minnesota

Susan C. Gardstrom, M.A., MT-BC
University of Dayton
Dayton, Ohio

Ned D. Gladfelter, M.M., MT-BC
The Pilot School
Wilmington, Delaware

Heather Schunk Grohe, M.M.E.
Adjunct ASL Instructor, De Anzo College
& San Jose City College
Freelance ASL Interpreter
San Jose, California

Lalah M. Hightower, MT-BC
Clayton County School System
Jonesboro, Georgia

Jane E. Hughes, M.A., MT-BC
Leon County Schools
Tallahassee, Florida

Marcia Earl Humpal, M.Ed., MT-BC
W. P. Day Early Childhood Center
Cleveland, Ohio

Faith L. Johnson, M.A.
Milwaukee Public Schools
Milwaukee, Wisconsin

Jihyun Kim
University of Kansas
Lawrence, Kansas

Michelle Lazar, MT-BC
Coast Music Therapy and Consulting
San Diego, California

Brenda J. Rice, M.M.E., MT-BC
Leon County Schools
Tallahassee, Florida

Judy Simpson, MT-BC
American Music Therapy Association
Silver Spring, Maryland

Angela M. Snell, MT-BC
Monroe County Intermediate School District
Monroe, Michigan

Amber Weldon-Stephens, M.Ed., MT-BC
Fulton County School System
Atlanta, Georgia

Brian L. Wilson, M.M., MT-BC
Western Michigan University
Kalamazoo, Michigan

TABLE OF CONTENTS

TABLE OF CONTENTS, CONTINUED

TABLE OF CONTENTS, CONTINUED

Section One:
Theoretical Issues

INCREASING ACCESS TO MUSIC THERAPY: THE ROLES OF PARENTS, MUSIC THERAPISTS AND AMTA

Judy Simpson

THE American Music Therapy Association's (AMTA) mission is to advance public knowledge of the benefits of music therapy and increase access to quality music therapy services in a rapidly changing world. Implementation of this mission is evident in all music therapy work settings throughout the United States. In special education settings, however, mission implementation can take on a life of its own. Due to the extensive process and multiple participants involved with developing a special education program, increasing access to music therapy services in this setting requires specific procedures to ensure success. It is not enough for AMTA as a professional association to simply distribute public relations brochures and referral lists of qualified therapists. An established method of response, involving parents, music therapists, and AMTA, is necessary when furthering the mission of advancing knowledge and increasing access to quality music therapy services.

This collaborative work with parents corresponds with concepts found within the Individuals with Disabilities Education Act (IDEA), which serves as a common denominator for development and implementation of all special education programs. Amendments made in 1997 to this important legislation offered positive changes to help ensure all children with disabilities have access to free appropriate public education. As a result of the IDEA amendments, the focus of the Individualized Education Program (IEP) shifted from procedural requirements for staff to educational results for each child. Recognizing the need for effective behavioral assessments and interventions to assist students experiencing behavioral barriers to learning was another improvement. In addition, the 1997 IDEA amendments emphasized the role of the parents on the IEP team, indicating a cooperative partnership between parents and school staff when designing and applying educational plans (106th Congress, 2000). Although parents have always held the assumed role of advocate, this new attention to enhancing the parents' position as "equal" members of the IEP team has helped parents feel more empowered to seek services for their children with special needs.

Parent Advocacy

As parents begin the search for effective educational interventions and treatments for their children, they often turn to the Internet for its quick supply of resource information. The increased use of the World Wide Web for special education networking among parents has had a significant impact on the number of inquiries AMTA has received about music therapy as a possible intervention. Since the IDEA revisions of 1997 redefined the role of parents in IEP development, parent advocacy seems to have made a noticeable impact on the outcome of many educational programs. Parents seek knowledge about all the educational services available that might benefit their children. This expanded role of the parent to not only deal with the day-to-day demands of raising a child with disabilities but also to monitor, direct, and ultimately fight for that child's educational rights can be overwhelming. Parents may either feel empowered by or enraged with the tasks before them. It is often at this point, the line between empowerment and frustration, that parents call upon AMTA for assistance in securing music therapy services for their child.

By the time parents contact AMTA through e-mail or phone calls, they have usually reviewed the association's website which has several categories of helpful information. Sections titled "Frequently Asked Questions," "Music Therapy with a Specific Population," and "Music Therapy in Special Education" (see Appendix A) have served to increase public awareness of who can benefit from music therapy. Once parents realize that music therapy is considered a related service under IDEA, they often begin to feel empowered once again in their fight for that free appropriate public education for their child. To assist those families who may be further along in their advocacy work, the "Researching Music Therapy" page offers help in finding related journal articles and other mentions of music therapy in the literature. In addition, the "How to Find a Music Therapist" section on the website allows parents to request referrals to qualified therapists practicing in specific geographic areas.

The following is an example of how parents may attempt to access music therapy for their children with special needs:

1. Parents locate AMTA website through a search on music therapy.
2. Parents read section titled, "Music Therapy in Special Education" and send e-mail message to AMTA requesting assistance in securing music therapy on their child's IEP.
3. AMTA staff determines level of information needed to address request. This may include:
   • Public relations material for the school district
   • Research articles related to the child's disability
   • Support letter addressed to school administrators
   • Copy of letter from the U.S. Department of Education clarifying music therapy as a related service under IDEA
   • List of qualified therapists in the area
4. AMTA staff maintains communication with parents and provides additional resources as needed.

It is important to remember that the primary advocacy role must be open to the parents.

The Clinician's Role in Advocacy

When music therapists call the national office requesting assistance in securing services for a child in their caseload, it is recommended that the therapist refer the child's parent or family advocate to AMTA directly for assistance. Moving the clinician out of a direct advocacy role for a specific child is a helpful procedural step, whether or not the therapist is employed by the school district. This step prevents any conflict of interest questions from the school and protects the integrity of any previous assessments or treatment documentation. Although the AMTA Code of Ethics clearly outlines professional conduct requirements, some schools may assert that a therapist will always advocate for music therapy interventions if the therapist stands to benefit financially from that recommendation.

Music therapists who are approached by a parent or advocate working on the family's behalf, and are requested to complete an assessment to determine if music therapy is necessary for a child to benefit from his/her special education program, should ask if they intend on asking the school to pay for the service. Many times, parents are unaware that music therapy is considered a related service and can be included on the IEP. It is recommended that the parents ask the school to provide a music therapy assessment as part of the IEP process to determine if the intervention would be an appropriate addition to the child's educational program. Following this method would require the school to contract with a music therapist to complete an assessment, utilizing school funds. If parents pay for an assessment privately, which is always their option, it is possible for the school district to refuse acceptance of the assessment results if they do not feel music therapy is necessary. Requesting the assessment from the school district first might possibly save time in the process of accessing services.

If the assessment does not indicate that the child needs music therapy in order to benefit from his/her special education program, music therapy is not recommended for inclusion on the IEP. This does not mean, however, that the child would not benefit on some level from music therapy. It simply means the service is not necessary for the child to reach the educational goals directly addressed on the IEP. Occasionally parents disagree with this decision because they feel their child needs the service. In this case, parents have the right to contract privately for music therapy, requesting private insurance reimbursement or simply paying for the service themselves. Those interventions would be provided outside of the school day.

It sometimes occurs that a music therapist begins providing services to a child with the parents paying privately. Over a period of time, the parents may learn that the school could be paying for the service. This can be an awkward situation as it can put the music therapist in the middle of a dispute between the parents and the school. Again, it is important for the parents to assume the role of advocate and approach the school, requesting an assessment to determine if music therapy is necessary for their child to benefit from his/her special education program. The school may want to contract with a different therapist for this assessment so as not to cloud the results by the rapport developed between the child and original therapist. If requested by the parents, the original therapist can offer assessment and treatment plan information to the school through participation in the child's IEP. It is not advised, however, that specific music therapy strategies be provided within this setting unless the IEP includes plans to add music therapy as a consultative service.

AMTA as Advocate

Recognizing the lead advocate role held by the parents and the supporting advocate role held by the music therapist, what role does AMTA play in the process of accessing services in special education settings? If comparing to parts portrayed in a movie, AMTA's advocate role would best be described as the cameo or special guest appearance utilized to support the existing players in the scene. Although the association has always offered advocacy assistance as part of its Strategic Plan, positive opportunities in recent years related to securing music therapy in special education settings have added to the success of these advocacy endeavors.

In the spring of 2000, after several months of communicating with different individuals within the Department of Education regarding barriers to music therapy services due to Individuals with Disabilities Education Act (IDEA) revisions and other factors, AMTA addressed concerns with the newly appointed Director of the Office of Special Education Programs (OSEP), Dr. Kenneth Warlick. A formal written request (see Appendix B) was submitted to Dr. Warlick in March 2000, seeking clarification about the inclusion of music therapy as a related service under IDEA.

AMTA also discussed this issue with Dr. Warlick directly. In addition, AMTA initiated verbal and written communication with the Office of Special Education and Rehabilitative Services (OSERS) Assistant Secretary Judith Heumann in April 2000 regarding this topic. The result of these advocacy efforts became evident on June 14, 2000, when AMTA received a letter of clarification from Dr. Warlick clearly stating music therapy is a related service under IDEA and those who provide music therapy must be appropriately qualified (see Appendix C).

This letter's purpose is to address difficulties experienced by parents throughout the country when attempting to access music therapy services within a special education setting. For example, a parent requests a music therapy assessment within an IEP meeting and the school representatives state one or more of the following:
"We don't do that here."
"We have music educators who can teach your child music."
"Our teachers include music in their classroom instruction."

"Music therapy isn't listed as a related service in the regulations."

These scenarios are not uncommon and are typically what parents might be facing when they begin looking for assistance and guidance in responding to the school. When the parents contact AMTA, either through the website, a family advocate, or a music therapist, several levels of response are offered, depending upon the situation. If the parents feel the school would benefit from direct contact with AMTA, staff request the name, title, and address of the IEP chair or school administrator involved so that a personalized introductory letter of support can be sent (see Appendix D). Along with this support letter, AMTA includes a copy of the letter from the U.S. Department for Education clarifying music therapy as a related service. Many times, this single communication is effective in encouraging the school to proceed with a music therapy assessment.

Unfortunately there are times when schools refuse to complete a music therapy assessment, no matter what type of supportive information has been offered. In some situations, the school may claim that the child is making too much progress and does not require any additional related services. It is then up to the parents to monitor the level of progress actually achieved through IEP goal documentation and utilize that information to pursue additional related services. If the school continues to deny the assessment, the parents must decide whether or not to pursue mediation or due process, which is their right under the law. Once again, it is important to remember the parents' roles as advocates for their child. The music therapist can offer accurate documentation and AMTA can offer support regarding how IDEA is interpreted, but the parents must decide how far to push the school for access to music therapy services.

A Parent's Perspective

On a personal note, it cannot be stressed enough the importance of respecting the parents in the process of developing a successful special education program. In reflecting on some of the most uncomfortable experiences in my life, I would have to say those moments were during IEP meetings for my daughter who is diagnosed with autism. Even when parents and staff come prepared with accurate documentation, realistic goals, and reasonable related service requests, the final product ultimately reflects the level of respect and professionalism demonstrated by the entire IEP team. I wish I could say that I felt respected during these IEP meetings. Unfortunately we tend to remember the negative feedback for a long time and, as a result, it places an unnecessary strain on communication between parents and school staff, to the detriment of the child involved.

As challenging as it might be at times, showing respect for the parents and the children is imperative when working within the special education setting. As with other members of the IEP team, music therapists must find the positive aspects of the interaction and build on a child's strengths instead of focusing on the child's limitations. It does not serve anyone's interests to constantly remind the parents of how many tasks a child cannot complete. Remember that you only see these children a few minutes a week while the parents are with them 24/7 and are well aware of their needs. Look for opportunities to stress the child's progress while setting realistic goals that can be achieved within the IEP time frame.

Once you have worked with children who have disabilities for any length of time, you automatically become their advocate. Build on that natural desire to defend them not necessarily to shelter them but to defend their rights as individuals. Protection of those rights within the educational setting is what IDEA has intended to provide all along. Know the rights of your clients and their parents as they search for effective related services within the special education system. Just as your role as music therapist doesn't start and stop with the "Hello" and Goodbye" songs in your sessions, your role as advocate can continue throughout your entire professional career. With parents, music therapists, and AMTA all working together in defined advocate roles, we will be able to celebrate the success of increased access to quality music therapy services.

References

Office of the Federal Register, National Archives and Records Administration. (1999). *Federal Register, Part II, Department of Education*. 64 FR 12548. Washington, DC.

106th Congress, 2d Session. (2000). *House Concurrent Resolution 399*. Washington, DC.

Appendix A

AMERICAN
MUSIC
THERAPY
ASSOCIATION

American Music Therapy Association, Inc.

8455 Colesville Road, Suite 1000, Silver Spring, MD 20910   (301) 589-3300   fax (301) 589-5175
email: amta@musictherapy.org   website: www.musictherapy.org

Music Therapy in Special Education

Music Therapy is considered a related service under the Individuals with Disabilities Education Act (IDEA).

When music therapy is deemed necessary to assist a child benefit from his/her special education, goals are documented on the Individual Education Plan (IEP) as a related service intervention.

Music therapy can be an integral component in helping the child with special needs attain educational goals identified by his/her IEP team.

Music therapy interventions can address development in cognitive, behavioral, physical, emotional, and social skills.   Music therapy can also facilitate development in communication and sensori-motor skills.

Music therapy can offer direct or consultant services as determined by the individual needs of the child.

Music therapists can support special education classroom teachers by providing effective ways to incorporate music into their academic curriculum.

Music therapy involvement can stimulate attention and increase motivation to participate more fully in other aspects of the educational setting.

Music therapy interventions apply the inherent order of music to set behavioral expectations, provide reassurance, and maintain structure for children with special needs.

Music therapy can adapt strategies to encourage a child's participation in the least restrictive environment.

4/00

Appendix B

AMERICAN
**MUSIC
THERAPY**
ASSOCIATION

Children with Disabilities in Need of Related Services: Music Therapy

1) <u>Music Therapy as a Related Service</u>
Since the revisions of March 1999, the note section listing music therapy as a related service was removed from the IDEA regulations. Although we have been advised to refer school administrators to *Attachment 1 to the final regulations, Analysis of Comments and Changes, published at 64 FR 12548 (March 12, 1999)*, this has not been effective in securing services for children referred for music therapy.

The American Music Therapy Association (AMTA) received over 200 calls in 1999 from parents, administrators and therapists requesting assistance in adding music therapy to a child's IEP. The recurring argument from school districts is "Music Therapy is not on the list so we don't have to pay for it." Referral to IDEA's intent of a "non-exhaustive" related services list has not been successful.

Desired Action
A letter of clarification from the Office of Special Education Programs stating Music Therapy is a related service under IDEA if it is deemed necessary to assist a child with a disability benefit from his/her special education.

2) <u>Difference Between Music Therapy and Music Education</u>
A common misconception of school administrators is that music educators can provide the same interventions as a music therapist. When an IEP team recognizes a child would benefit from music therapy, the team frequently argues that the music educator on staff will address the identified goals within the general music class. This concept would be analogous to stating that the Physical Education Teacher will address the Physical Therapy goals and thus the school does not need to provide Physical Therapy.

3) <u>Standard Qualifications</u>
The current standard of determining who is qualified to provide related services often falls under state criteria. Many times, this criteria demands education certification or licensure that is not available to board certified music therapists. Some schools argue that our national board certification credential is not accepted by the state and so they refuse to provide music therapy services in their schools. This demand for education certification is not always required of other related service personnel and yet those related services are not denied.

Desired Action
Within the letter of clarification regarding related services, recognition of Music Therapy's national board certification credential when identifying qualified personnel could remedy this disparity.

8455 Colesville Road

Suite 1000

Silver Spring. MD 20910

Phone (301) 589 – 3300

Fax (301) 589 – 5175

E-mail info@musictherapy.org

Appendix C

UNITED STATES DEPARTMENT OF EDUCATION

OFFICE OF SPECIAL EDUCATION AND REHABILITATIVE SERVICES

JUN - 9 2000

Ms. Andrea H. Farbman
Executive Director
American Music Therapy Association
8455 Colesville Road, Suite 1000
Silver Spring, Maryland 20910

Dear Ms. Farbman:

Your letter to Assistant Secretary Judith Heumann dated April 5, 2000, written on behalf of the American Music Therapy Association, regarding the provision of music therapy as a related service for students with disabilities has been referred to the Office of Special Education Programs (OSEP) for response.

Specifically, in your letter, you describe the many difficulties parents, advocates, and providers have experienced in securing music therapy services for students with disabilities as a related service under the Individuals with Disabilities Education Act (IDEA). Therefore, you seek a letter of policy clarification from OSEP regarding the requirements of Part B of IDEA (Part B) that would be applicable to (1) music therapy as a related service under Part B and (2) the standards for appropriate personnel to provide music therapy as a related service. The following is an explanation of the requirements of Part B that are relevant to these inquiries.

As to your first inquiry, under Part B, each State and its local school districts must ensure that a free appropriate public education (FAPE) is made available to all children with disabilities residing in the State in mandatory age ranges. FAPE includes, among other elements, special education and related services provided at no cost to parents in conformity with an individualized education program (IEP) that meets the requirements of 34 CFR §§300.340-300.350. 34 CFR §300.13. The term "related services" is defined as:

> ...[t]ransportation and such developmental, corrective, and other supportive services as are required to assist a child with a disability to benefit from special education, and includes speech-language pathology and audiology services, psychological services, physical and occupational therapy, recreation, including therapeutic recreation, early identification and assessment of disabilities in children, counseling services, including rehabilitation counseling, orientation and mobility services, and medical services for diagnostic or evaluation purposes. The term also includes

Our mission is to ensure equal access to education and to promote educational excellence throughout the Nation.

Page 2 - Ms. Andrea H. Farbman

school health services, social work services in schools, and parent
counseling and training.

34 CFR §300.24(a); see also 20 U.S.C. §1401(22). (Individual terms used
in this definition are defined in paragraph (b) of 34 CFR §300.24 of the
Part B regulations.)

The IDEA Amendments of 1997 make the focus of each disabled child's IEP the child's
appropriate involvement in the general curriculum, that is, the same curriculum as for
nondisabled students. 34 CFR §300.347(a)(1)-(2). Each child's IEP must contain,
among other components,

[a] statement of the special education and related services and
supplementary aids and services to be provided to the child, or on behalf
of the child, and a statement of the program modifications or supports for
school personnel that will be provided for the child--(i) to advance
appropriately toward attaining the annual goals; (ii) to be involved and
progress in the general curriculum...and to participate in extracurricular
and other nonacademic activities....
34 CFR §300.347(a)(3).

As a general matter, each child's IEP team, which includes the child's parents along with
school officials, makes the determination as to the instruction and services that are
appropriate for an individual child to enable that child to receive FAPE. 34 CFR
§§300.343-300.347. As is true regarding consideration of any related service for a
disabled child under Part B, individual determinations must be made in light of each
child's unique abilities and educational needs, and any instruction or services determined
by the IEP team to be necessary for the child to receive FAPE must be provided at public
expense and at no cost to the parents.

In the past, much confusion has arisen when a request is made for a child to receive a
related service not specifically identified in the statutory list of examples of related
services. It has been the Department's longstanding interpretation that "...[a]s under
prior law, the list of related services is not exhaustive and may include other
developmental, corrective, or supportive services (such as artistic and cultural programs,
art, music, and dance therapy), if they are required to assist a child with a disability to
benefit from special education in order for the child to receive FAPE." Analysis of
Comments and Changes, published as Attachment 1 to the final Part B regulations, 64
Fed. Reg. at 12548 (Mar. 12, 1999); incorporating the substance of the former Note 1 to
34 CFR §300.16; see also Notice of Interpretation, published as Appendix A to 34 CFR
Part 300, question 34, 64 Fed. Reg. at 12479..

Page 3 - Ms. Andrea H. Farbman

We recognize that music therapy may be appropriate and useful for some children with disabilities. This also is true with regard to the therapeutic services specified in the statutory and regulatory list of examples of related services. According to your inquiry, however, removal of note 1 to the prior regulations defining the term "related service" formerly at 34 CFR §300.16 is being interpreted by some school officials as relieving them of their responsibility to provide music therapy as a related service under any circumstances.

This misinterpretation is unfortunate. As noted in the preamble to the final Part B regulations published on March 12, 1999, "[a]ll notes in the NPRM related to the sections or subparts covered in these final regulations . . . [were] removed.... The substance of any note considered to provide clarifying information or useful guidance has been incorporated into the discussion of the applicable comments in the "Analysis of Comments and Changes" (see Attachment 1 to these final regulations). All other notes have been deleted." We continue to support our prior position that for some children, art, music, or dance therapy is to be identified in their IEPs as a related service if the IEP team, which includes the child's parents, determines that the particular therapy would be necessary for the child to benefit from special education and to receive FAPE.

If the IEP team determines that music therapy is an appropriate related service for a child, the team's determination must be reflected in the child's IEP, and the service must be provided at public expense and at no cost to the parents. However, let me emphasize that there is nothing in this clarification or in any statements in the discussion of comments and changes to the final regulations or in notes previously included in these regulations that would require that every disabled child receive music therapy as a related service regardless of the IEP team's determination as to whether the service is appropriate for the individual disabled child.

The second part of your inquiry raises several issues regarding the standards for, and type of, personnel who are qualified to provide music therapy as a related service. State and local educational agencies must ensure that students with disabilities receive appropriate instruction or services as reflected in their IEPs. 34 CFR §300.600. This means that any instruction or service for a child with a disability under Part B must be provided by personnel who meet appropriate State standards for qualified personnel, as that term is defined at 34 CFR §300.23 of the Part B regulations.

Music therapy and general music education are distinct disciplines and professions. School music educators therefore may not have the appropriate training to provide music therapy for a child with a disability. Part B requires States to have policies and procedures relating to the establishment and maintenance of standards for ensuring that personnel necessary to carry out the purposes of Part B are appropriately and adequately prepared and trained, and that the standards are consistent with any State-approved or recognized certification, licensing, registration, or other comparable requirements that

Page 4 - Ms. Andrea H. Farbman

apply to the profession or discipline in which a person is providing special education or related services. 34 CFR §300.136(b)(1)(i)-(ii). You indicated that there is a national credential for music therapists, based on a standard established by your organization, the American Music Therapy Association (AMTA). If the State has education certification or licensure standards that are not relevant or appropriately applicable to the qualifications of music therapists, it may wish to adopt an appropriate standard for providers of music therapy services. While States are not precluded from adopting an appropriate training credential for providers of music therapy services, such as that developed by your organization, the Part B regulations clarify that "[n]othing in [Part B] requires a State to establish a specified training standard (e.g., a masters degree) for personnel who provide special education and related services under Part B of the Act." 34 CFR §300.136(b)(3).

We hope that you find this explanation helpful. If we can be of further assistance, please contact Dr. JoLeta Reynolds at (202) 205-5507.

Sincerely,

Kenneth R. Warlick
Director
Office of Special Education Programs

Appendix D

Date

Dear Special Education Administrator:

The purpose of this letter is to support the provision of quality music therapy services for a child in your school district who may be in need of such services. We hope you will find this information useful in meeting the needs of this child and of any other child ever found to be in need of music therapy.

As you know, the original purpose of *IDEA* was to establish a statutory right of all children to a free, appropriate public education specifying special education and related services as the vehicles to provide support for the inclusion of students with disabilities in regular education classrooms. Related services are defined in the bill under Part B as those services deemed necessary to help the child benefit from special education. Appropriate related services are to be specified in the Individual Education Plan (IEP). Final regulations released in 1999 provide that the law's list of related services is not exhaustive and may include music therapy if it is required to assist a child with a disability to benefit from his/her special education. **Attachment 1 to the final regulations, Analysis of Comments and Changes, published at 64 FR 12548 (March 12, 1999).** A school district is required to supply those services that will enable a child to receive a free and appropriate special education (FAPE).

Qualified music therapists have been providing music therapy as a related service to literally thousands of children with disabilities in every state of the nation over the course of the twenty-five years since the passage of Public Law 94-142. If music therapy is deemed "necessary" to assist a child with a disability to benefit from special education it must be delivered at no cost to the parents.

Enclosed please find a copy of a policy interpretation letter from the U.S. Department of Education regarding music therapy as a related service under IDEA. Please feel free to contact our national office if any further clarification is needed.

Sincerely,

Andrea H. Farbman, Ed.D.   Judy Simpson, MT-BC
Executive Director   Government & Public Relations Associate

AMERICAN
MUSIC
THERAPY
ASSOCIATION

8455 COLESVILLE ROAD

SUITE 1000

SILVER SPRING, MD 20910

PHONE (301) 589 - 3300

FAX (301) 589 - 5175

E-MAIL INFO@MUSICTHERAPY.ORG

2

IN THE BEGINNING: A REVIEW OF EARLY SPECIAL EDUCATION SERVICES, AND LEGISLATIVE/REGULATORY ACTIVITY AFFECTING THE TEACHING AND PLACEMENT OF CHILDREN WITH SPECIAL NEEDS

Mary S. Adamek

THE availability of public education in the United States for students with disabilities continues to evolve and move in new directions. Before the 1880s, students who were disabled were not even considered to be eligible for public education. When public education became available for these students, a separate, segregated model was implemented. Currently the education system in the United States is moving towards an integrated educational system where the needs of the individual student are key in developing approaches to educate the child.

Early Years of Education

One of the first people to introduce the idea of educating persons with disabilities was an American physician named Benjamin Rush. Rush discussed this concept in the late 1700s, yet the first educational program for persons with disabilities was not established until 1817. This program, founded by Thomas Gallaudet, was at the American Asylum for the Education and Instruction of the Deaf and Dumb in Connecticut (Stainback, Stainback, & Bunch, 1989). Other programs for deaf, blind, and students with mental disabilities soon followed in various cities around the United States.

As early as the 1880s, compulsory school attendance for students with disabilities was being discussed among educators and some special programs continued to develop to service these students. By the early 1900s schooling had become the social norm for the majority of nondisabled children in the United States. Classes in most schools were designed to meet the needs of the average students, while those students who were below average were serviced in special programs by special teachers in asylums or government supported institutions. While some students with disabilities participated in public special education programs, many students with disabilities still were not receiving any educational services at this time.

Around 1910, the education of some students with disabilities was moved from the institutions to the public school setting, in the form of separate, segregated classrooms. The formation of segregated classes was initially met with great enthusiasm. Educators believed that separate classes would be favorable for special students, especially when otherwise faced with the option of educating students with disabilities in the regular classroom. They believed that separate classes could offer students with disabilities the benefits of a low teacher to student ratio, more individualized instruction, more academic success in a less competitive environment, and remedial instruction so that some children could return to the regular classroom (Winzer, 1993).

Between 1910 and 1930 the number of segregated classrooms in public schools increased dramatically. Allied professional and support services increased with the expansion of state and federal funding for special education services. This commitment on the part of the federal government was reinforced by the 1930 White House Conference on Child Health and Protection, a milestone in the field of special education. It was at this conference that special education received national recognition as a justifiable component of the educational system (Winzer, 1993).

The 1930s witnessed a decline in special education services for students with disabilities. Many factors contributed to this decline, including the fact that the entire country was struggling with the Great Depression. Other factors, including poorly trained teachers, ineffective curricula, and a low rate of success for students with disabilities, led to discouragement and pessimism about the future of special education (Winzer, 1993). Although it was the intent of educators at that time to provide equal access to education for students with disabilities, the reality was less effective than originally planned. Separate classes frequently served to eliminate a broad range of students described as atypical, defective, backward, recalcitrant, and mentally retarded. These students were subject to exclusion and sweeping segregation from the regular classroom.

By the 1940s the special education classroom had eroded to deplorable conditions and became as limiting and custodial as the earlier institutional settings. Children with vastly different disabilities were placed together in classes, teachers were poorly trained, and little effort was made to actually teach. The students were isolated and stigmatized by their placement in the segregated special education environment. Although the number of special classes and day programs for students with disabilities had increased since the early 1900s, the educational programs in residential institutions and asylums continued to educate the majority of these students through the mid 1900s (Stainback, Stainback, & Bunch, 1989).

Special education experienced another round of renewal in the 1940s and 1950s. Parent groups became more involved in special education, legislation expanded, and interest in the needs of the disabled individual were being considered by many education professionals. In addition, educators revised curricula to eliminate some of the repetitious drill from earlier programs to include more emphasis on social participation and job skills. For the first time in history, the public began to realize the need for equal opportunities for mentally retarded individuals. It was during this time that the ideals of due process, equal protection under the law, and protection from cruel and unusual punishment were established as basic constitutional rights for these citizens.

Awareness of equal rights for students who were mentally retarded extended into the public school classroom. Efforts were focused on improving and expanding public school services for students who were mentally retarded, and moving away from institutionalization and isolation.

> The net result of all these changes was huge expansions in numbers: between 1948 and 1968 the number of children in public school special education classes in the United States went from 357,000 to 2,252,000, or from 1.2 to 4.5 percent of the total enrollment in kindergarten to grade twelve. (Winzer, 1993, p. 376)

This expansion of special education continued during the 1960s due to increased federal and state support. The number of institutions for training special educators also increased from fewer than 40 in 1958 to more than 400 in 1976. In 1963 President Kennedy signed a law that expanded legislation to provide special education services for most children with severe disabilities. This legislation expanded the definition of which students should receive special education services. The new definition included not only children with mental retardation, but also children with speech, hearing or visual impairments, children having emotional disorders, and children with other health impairments.

Institutionalization of children with the most seriously disabling conditions continued into the 1960s. Many persons with severe mental retardation and severe behavior problems were housed in facilities that were underfunded and inhumane. Public outcry concerning the conditions under which many institutionalized individuals with mental retardation lived helped lay the groundwork for change. By the 1970s a movement to deinstitutionalize and normalize individuals with mental retardation into the community was in place throughout the country.

In the school setting, this effort toward normalization included an educational process that eventually became known as mainstreaming. The beliefs underlying this movement were that all children have individual differences, and these differences must be respected by members of the school community. Educational services had to be developed to meet the needs of each individual student. As normalization practices continued to expand, educators came to the understanding that all children had a right to a free, appropriate education. It was during this time that the educational system began to shift from servicing students with disabilities in segregated special education classes to educating students with disabilities in the regular education classroom setting supported by special education professionals (Winzer, 1993).

Since the beginning of the 20th century, the special education movement in the United States had made substantial progress in providing educational services to students with disabilities, yet by the 1970s there were still many problems to overcome. Funding for special programs was sometimes inadequate and difficult to obtain, identification and placement of students with disabilities was often inconsistent and inappropriate, and parental involvement was discouraged. In addition, special educators and regular educators were in competition for the limited funding that was available. These difficulties led to increased separation of the special education and regular education programs, with little cooperation between the two.

By 1975 there were approximately eight million children with disabilities in the United States. Approximately three million of these children were not receiving appropriate education in the public schools, and another one million were totally excluded from public school education. At that time in our history more than half of the children with disabilities in the United States were receiving inappropriate public school education, or none at all (Rothstein, 1990).

Early Years of Music in Special Education

Music has been an important part of the training and education of students who were deaf, blind and cognitively impaired since at least the early 1800s. Jean-Marc-Gaspard Itard (1775–1838) was one of the first people to utilize music in the diagnosis of hearing and speech impairment and to develop auditory discrimination skills. A student of Itard, Edouard Seguin (1812–1880) continued the work of his teacher and developed a methodology for using music to teach auditory and speech skills to cognitively impaired students (Solomon, 1980). Lowell Mason taught music at the Perkins School for the Blind in South Boston from 1832 until 1836. Mason taught vocal music and piano at the school. In the school's 1835 annual report, it was stated that music was an important part of the curriculum (Heller, 1987).

Two pioneers in the use of music for the deaf were William Wolcott Turner and David Ely Bartlett. These men published their accounts of teaching music to a student who was hard of hearing in an 1848 article that was printed in the *American Annals for the Deaf and Dumb*. This work began a trend that would later lead to current practices of teaching music to students who were deaf and hard of hearing (Darrow & Heller, 1985). By the late 1800s some schools for students who were deaf and blind utilized music as part of the curriculum, including singing, clapping, playing drums and other rhythm instruments, and playing simple instruments such as whistles and bells (Solomon, 1980).

For many years, music has been a part of the programming in institutions for children who are mentally retarded. Sheerenberger (1953) described how singing and rhythm activities were developed to meet the current needs of the children in an institutional setting. Music activities were also used to prepare the children for interactions with the community.

The use of music in early special education settings was primarily with children who were deaf, hard of hearing, blind, or mentally retarded. Early educators found music to be a reinforcing, valuable tool to enhance the accomplishments of the students and to facilitate learning. These practices are the foundation on which educators and therapists continue to expand the use of music in special education.

Solomon (1980) noted four themes that emerged from a study of the use of music in early special education settings. First, music was an important part of early attempts to train and educate children with disabilities. Second, singing has been used to involve children who did not speak, for proper breathing, and to improve articulation. Third, music activities have been used as diagnostic tools before the development of audiology equipment. And, fourth, music has been used in the education of deaf students since the early nineteenth century.

As educational opportunities increased for students with disabilities, so did the literature regarding the use of music in special education settings. Jellison (2000) compiled a content analysis of music research focusing on students with disabilities. This review cites research literature from 1975–1999 and documents the effectiveness of music as therapy for students with disabilities in special education settings.

Litigation and Legislative History Prior to PL 94-142

The racial desegregation decision in the 1954 *Brown v. Board of Education* was the first landmark in special education case law. This decision did not concern the rights of students with disabilities, yet it laid the groundwork for the future of integrated educational settings. In *Brown v. Board of Education* Chief Justice Warren ruled that educating black children separately from white children did not provide an equal educational experience, due to the stigma of being educated separately and the lack of interaction with children of other backgrounds (Rothstein, 1990). Not only did this decision bring an end to exclusionary educational policies toward racial minorities, it also paved the way for the elimination of exclusionary policies for students with disabilities. This case led to the determination by some educators that educating children in a segregated environment was adverse. Advocates for the rights of people with disabilities applied the principles of the Brown decision to eliminate policies that were discriminatory towards individuals with disabilities.

The right to a free and appropriate education for all children labeled as mentally retarded was established in the groundbreaking case *Pennsylvania Association of Retarded Citizens (PARC) v. Commonwealth* in 1971. In this class action law suit, the federal district court in Philadelphia overturned a Pennsylvania law that allowed the public schools the freedom to exclude children who were mentally retarded. Based on evidence documenting how these children could benefit from education, the *PARC* decision stipulated that children with mental retardation could not be excluded from schools, due process must be followed before a change of placement could occur, and integration was favored over segregated, restrictive placements (Weiner, 1985).

In 1972, one year after the *PARC* decision, the federal district court of Washington, D.C., went further to solidify the educational rights of children with disabilities. Following the principle that education was important for disabled individuals to live as independently as possible, the *Mills v. Board of Education* decision "mandated that due process include procedures relating to the labeling, placement, and exclusionary stages of decision making" (Rothstein, 1990, p. 3). Also included in these procedures was a right to a hearing, a right to appeal, and a right to access information. The *Mills* decision also dictated that the Washington, D.C., school district must educate students with disabilities, even if school district money was limited. The court said that students with disabilities should not suffer due to financial shortcomings any more that students who are not disabled (Weiner, 1985). While *PARC* established the right to a free and appropriate education for children with mental retardation, *Mills v. Board of Education* expanded the *PARC* decision to also include children with disabilities other than mental retardation. The *Mills* decision later provided the basic framework for PL 94-142.

A third milestone that paved the way for the rights of individuals with disabilities, and eventually Public Law 94-142, was the Rehabilitation Act, Section 504 which was passed in 1973. This Act, along with later amendments, guaranteed the rights of persons with handicaps in educational and employment settings, if those settings received support from the federal government (Stainback, Stainback, & Bunch, 1989).

Public Law 94-142

After the *PARC* and *Mills* decision, the Rehabilitation Act, Section 504, and pressure from parents, courts and legislators, Public Law 94-142 was passed in 1975 and became effective in 1977. This law, also called Education for All Handicapped Children Act of 1975, stipulated that no child can be denied free and appropriate education, and that education must take place in the least restrictive environment. The right to an education was extended to all children with handicaps, not just those children with mental retardation. In addition, the law proposed that this education was to take place in the least possible segregated environment.

PL 94-142 is basically a grant statute that assures the rights of the individual. Based on this law, a state can obtain federal funding to support the education of children with disabilities aged 3 through 21 if that state develops a plan to provide a free and appropriate public education to all children in the state who need special education services. This programming must emphasize special education and related services designed and implemented to meet the unique needs of the individual student. While there are many specific parameters and details of PL 94-142, the following are the basic underlying principles included in the law.

- Education must be provided for all children with disabilities.
- Programming must take place in the least restrictive environment.
- Education is to be appropriate and individualized to the needs of the child.
- Education must be provided free of charge.
- Parents have the right to be involved in the development of their child's education program.
- Procedural protections must be in place to ensure that the requirements are met (Rothstein, 1990).

Each state and school district must have a plan to ensure that all of the requirements of the law are being met. Other important areas of the law address parent involvement and consultation, due process, nondiscriminatory evaluation, confidentiality, and in-service training for teachers and other professional personnel.

Although the mandate to comply with the requirements of PL 94-142 applies only to states that seek federal funding to support special education, all states accept that funding and must therefore comply with the law. Public education institutions are also subject to the requirements of the 1973 Rehabilitation Act, which prohibits discrimination based on handicap and provides equal protection and due process stipulations.

Components of the Law

Individualized Education Program (IEP)

The law states that the education of a child with disabilities must be appropriate and individualized to the needs of the child. This is implemented through the Individualized Education Program (IEP) that is developed jointly by education and health care professionals, parents, and child advocates who are involved with the student. All students who are placed in special education must have an IEP (Gearheart, Weishahn, & Gearheart, 1992; National Council on Disability, 1989).

Procedures for writing the IEP vary from school district to school district, but P.L. 94-142 mandates that each IEP contain the following elements: assessment information about the individual's present level of functioning, long-term and short-term goals and objectives for the student, plans for initiation and duration of service, plans for specific educational services to be provided and to what extent the student will be involved in regular education, and criteria for evaluation of the student's progress. Most school districts develop their own standard format for writing the IEP. In addition to the required information, many districts include information concerning who is responsible for delivering services, specific methods and materials that will be used, and other information specific to the education of the child.

All professionals who are involved with the student are expected to participate on some level in the written plan and/or at the annual evaluation meeting. Regulations mandate that the people present at the writing of the IEP include: a school system representative who is familiar with due process involved in special education, the child's teacher, parents and/or guardians, and the student, when appropriate (Coleman, 1992). Other professionals who are involved in evaluation or ongoing service to the child may also be included in the IEP meeting, at the discretion of the parents or school personnel. This might include the school psychologist, speech and language pathologist, other special education teachers, music therapist, occupational therapist, physical therapist and legal experts such as attorneys or parent advocates (Lerner, 1988).

Least Restrictive Environment (LRE) and Mainstreaming

One of the fundamental principles of PL 94-142 is the idea of educating students with disabilities with nondisabled students to the greatest extent appropriate. The regulations in PL 94-142 concerning education in the "least restrictive environment" are interpreted differently by various local school districts. Educating a student in the least restrictive environment is often referred to as "mainstreaming," although this term was not actually mentioned in the statutory or regulatory language of the law (Rothstein, 1990). It is the responsibility of the state educational agency to ensure that each public agency establishes and implements appropriate procedures to meet the requirements. The law states:

(1) That to the maximum extent appropriate, handicapped children, including children in public or private institutions or other care facilities are educated with children who are not handicapped, and

(2) That special classes, separate schooling or other removal of handicapped children from the regular educational environment occurs only when the nature or severity of the handicap is such that education in regular classes with the use of supplementary aids and services cannot be achieved satisfactorily. (20 U.S.C. 1412(5)(B); 1414(a)(C)(iv)

The rationale for placing students in the least restrictive environment where education takes place along with nondisabled peers is based on several premises. One premise is that educating students with disabilities in segregated settings is inherently stigmatizing to the student. Also, there is a concern that there will be lower expectations for a disabled child in a separate class, and thus the child will not achieve what might be possible. Another important premise for integration is the value of interaction between disabled and nondisabled students working together.

The mandates concerning the least restrictive environment allow for a continuum of placement alternatives, but with the goal of providing individualized programming in the most appropriate setting. For the student with disabilities, this could mean placement ranging from the entire day spent in a regular education classroom (least restrictive), to residential treatment (most restrictive), and any number of options in between. The concept of least restrictive environment suggests movement from a more restrictive setting to a less restrictive, more integrated setting, whenever possible (Reynolds & Fletcher-Janzen, 1990). The philosophy is to provide services to the child in the least restricted environment that is appropriate for the individual child's needs, without causing undue disruption to the other children in the class (Rothstein, 1990). The vague parameters for this regulation have led to varying interpretations of the law by individual school districts.

Amendments to PL 94-142

Although the basic premise of PL 94-142 has remained the same, amendments have been added to the law in an effort to broaden and improve educational services for students with disabilities. When it was passed in 1975, PL 94-142 was referred to as the Education for All Handicapped Children Act (EAHCA).

After a series of amendments to the original act in the early 1980s, PL 94-142 came to be known as the Education of the Handicapped Act (EHA). Then in 1986, PL 99-457 amended the EHA to provide services for children with disabilities between the ages of 3 and 5, and it established new incentives for early intervention programs for children aged birth through 2. In 1990, PL 101-476 amended the EHA and it was renamed the Individuals with Disabilities Education Act (IDEA). IDEA retained the basic principles of PL 94-142, but made several changes in terminology. The term "disabilities" was substituted for the term "handicapped" in the new document. The new document also specifically requires service for children with listed disabilities, including mental retardation, autism, hearing impairment or deafness, visual impairment or blindness, serious emotional disturbances, specific learning disabilities, orthopedic impairments, speech or language impairment, and other health impairments. IDEA also listed specific services that should be made available to children when appropriate. Some of the services on this list include counseling services, medical services, audiology, occupational therapy, physical therapy, recreation, and speech pathology. While other services were listed, it was not intended to be an all inclusive list. Rather, the list was meant to be representative of a broad range of services and reflective of the intent of the law (Gearheart, Weishahn, & Gearheart, 1992).

Music Under PL 94-142

Music is valued in the American society. Participation in music is frequently a group activity, which provides for reinforcement, self-esteem and aesthetic experiences. All of these things promote the positive value of music. Music is also a highly normalizing activity in which people of all abilities can participate. Music is a means to bring together groups of people, and can be used to integrate special education and regular education students in schools (Alley, 1979). Music can facilitate academic learning, socialization, communication and behavioral skills (Jellison, 2000).

Mainstreaming in music education classes has been a widely used practice in the United States for the last 20 years. In many school districts it is commonplace for students to be placed in regular education music classrooms with nondisabled peers (Jellison & Gainer, 1995). One would hope that this type of placement is being made to provide the students with meaningful learning experiences and not to simply comply with the legislative mandates for inclusion with regular education. Even though mainstreaming or inclusion in the music classroom is a common practice, many music educators continue to feel unprepared to successfully meet the needs of the special needs students (Atterbury, 1986; Darrow & Gfeller, 1991; Gfeller, Darrow, & Hedden, 1990; Gilbert & Asmus, 1981). Music educators and music therapists must work together to develop appropriate experiences to enhance the social and academic skills of both special education and regular education students.

Although research on mainstreaming in music education is limited (Darrow, 1990), some researchers have found that children who are disabled and children who are not disabled seem to benefit from participating together in music classes (Force, 1983; Humpal, 1991; Kostka, 1993). Jellison, Brooks, and Huck (1984) found that positive social interactions in the integrated music classroom do not occur automatically. Positive social interactions between students with and without disabilities were found to be a function of the structure of the teaching environment and reinforcement, and not a result of the music instruction or music classroom experiences alone. Small cooperative groups with music as a reinforcement facilitated the most interactions between the students. In addition, when Jellison and Flowers (1991) interviewed students with and without disabilities concerning music preferences, music experiences, and music skills, they found similar responses from both groups of students. This knowledge of similarities among the students may function as a starting point for music educators to structure positive musical, social, and academic experiences for all of their students.

Music as a Related Service on the IEP

Under IDEA, each state and the local school districts must ensure that a free and appropriate public education (FAPE) is available to all children with disabilities who live in the state and who meet the mandatory age limits. FAPE includes special education services as well as related services that are provided to parents at no cost, and are included on the child's IEP. The list of related services noted in the law is not exhaustive and may include a variety of developmental, corrective or other supportive services such as speech-language pathology services, psychological services, physical and occupational therapy, medical services, and recreation therapy. These related services are decided upon by the IEP team and must be deemed necessary for the child to benefit from special education.

While neither music therapy nor music education is specifically mentioned in the law, Congress urged the use of arts therapies in the implementation of services of PL 94-142 (Alley, 1979). The Senate Report on PL 94-142 included the following statements about the arts:

> The use of the arts as a teaching tool for the handicapped has long been recognized as a viable, effective way not only of teaching special skills, but also of reaching youngsters who had otherwise been unteachable. The Committee envisions that programs under this bill could well include an arts component and, indeed, urges that local educational agencies include the arts in programs for the handicapped funded under this act. Such a program could cover both appreciation of the arts by the handicapped youngsters, and the utilization of the arts as a teaching tool per se. (Senate Report No. 94-168, 1975, p. 13)

In the implementation section, under Services-Program Options, the law itself states that:

> each public agency shall take steps to insure that its handicapped children have available to them the variety of educational programs and services available to non-handicapped children in the area served by the agency, including art, music, . . . (20 U.S.C. 1412(2)(A); 1414(a)(1)(C)

Music therapy services can enhance the education of a child with disabilities in the areas of academics, physical rehabilitation, self-help skills, emotional well-being, and social skills. These services can be provided in a variety of integrated to segregated settings to meet the individual needs of the students. Even though the law does not specifically mention music therapy services or mandate music for students with disabilities, the intent of the legislation was to ensure that students with disabilities receive the same educational experiences provided to students who are not disabled. It is important to be aware of the language of the law as cited above to support the case for music therapy and music education for students in special education programs. The Senate Report on PL 94-142 and the implementation section, under Services-Program Options, along with language from the recent letter of clarification from the U.S. Department of Education, Office of Special Education and Rehabilitative Services (see Chapter 1), should be cited by individuals who are interested in providing music therapy to students as a related service on the child's IEP. The intent of the law is clear. Music therapists must promote the addition and expansion of music therapy services in the schools in order to enhance the education of students with disabilities and to ensure that the individual student's rights are being preserved.

A quarter of a century ago, Alley (1977) stated that in order for music therapy to be a considered and accepted as an educational discipline, music therapists must provide services that are: "(1) unique enough to be viewed as complementary to, but not overlapping with, standard educational disciplines, (2) specific to educational objectives communicated in educational jargon, (3) accountable for pupil progress, and (4) competitive for available funding resources" (p. 50). These important factors must still be considered today when implementing music therapy services in educational settings.

References

Alley, J. M. (1977). Education for the severely handicapped: The role of music therapy. *Journal of Music Therapy, 14*, 50–59.

Alley, J. M. (1979). Music in the IEP: Therapy/education. *Journal of Music Therapy, 16*, 102–110.

Atterbury, B. W. (1986). A survey of present mainstreaming practices in the southern United States. *Journal of Music Therapy, 23*, 202–207.

Coleman, M. C. (1992). *Behavior disorders: Theory and practice* (2nd ed.). Boston: Allyn and Bacon.

Darrow, A. A. (1990). Research on mainstreaming in music education. *Update, 9*(1), 35–37.

Darrow, A. A., & Gfeller, K. (1991). A study of public school music programs mainstreaming hearing impaired students. *Journal of Music Therapy, 28*, 23–39.

Darrow, A. A., & Heller, G. N. (1985). Early advocates of music education for the hearing impaired: William Wolcott Turner and David Ely Bartlett. *Journal of Research in Music Education, 33*, 269–279.

Force, B. (1983). The effects of mainstreaming on the learning of nonretarded children in an elementary music classroom. *Journal of Music Therapy, 20*, 2–13.

Gearheart, B., Weishahn, M., & Gearheart, C. (1992). *The exceptional student in the regular classroom.* New York: Macmillan.

Gfeller, K., Darrow, A. A., & Hedden, S. (1990). On the ten-year anniversary of P.L. 94-142: The perceived status of mainstreaming among music educators in the states of Iowa and Kansas. *Journal of Research in Music Education, 38*, 90–101.

Gilbert, J. P., & Asmus, E. P. (1981). Mainstreaming: Music educators' participation and professional needs. *Journal of Research in Music Education, 29*, 283–289.

Heller, G. N. (1987). Ideas, initiatives, and implementations: Music therapy in America, 1789–1848. *Journal of Music Therapy, 24*, 35–46.

Humpal, M. (1991). The effects of an integrated early childhood music program on social interaction among children with handicaps and their typical peers. *Journal of Music Therapy, 28*, 161–177.

Jellison, J. (2000). A content analysis of music research with disabled children and youth (1975–1999): Applications in special education. In *Effectiveness of music therapy procedures: Documentation of research and clinical practice* (pp. 199–264). Silver Spring, MD: American Music Therapy Association.

Jellison, J., Brooks, B., & Huck, A. (1984). Structuring small groups and music reinforcement to facilitate positive interactions and acceptance of severely handicapped students in the regular music classroom. *Journal of Research in Music Education, 32*, 242–264.

Jellison, J., & Flowers, P. (1991). Talking about music: Interviews with disabled and nondisabled children. *Journal of Research in Music Education, 39*, 322–333.

Jellison, J., & Gainer, E. (1995). Into the mainstream: A case study of a child's participation in music education and music therapy. *Journal of Music Therapy, 32*, 228–247.

Kostka, M. (1993). A comparison of selected behaviors of a student with autism in special education and regular education music classes. *Music Therapy Perspectives, 11*, 57–60.

Lerner, J. W. (1988). *Learning disabilities: Theories, diagnosis, and teaching strategies.* Boston: Houghton Mifflin.

National Council on Disability. (1989). *The education of students with disabilities: Where do we stand? A report to the President and the Congress of the United States.* Washington, DC: National Council on Disability.

Reynolds, C., & Fletcher-Janzen, E. (Eds). (1990). *Concise encyclopedia of special education.* New York: John Wiley & Sons.

Rothstein, L. R. (1990). *Special education law.* White Plains, NY: Longman.

Senate Report No. 94-168, p. 13, 1975.

Sheerenberger, R. (1953). Description of a music program at a residential school for the mentally handicapped. *American Journal of Mental Deficiency, 57,* 573–579.

Solomon, A. L. (1980). Music in special education before 1930: Hearing and speech development. *Journal of Research in Music Education, 28,* 236–242.

Stainback, W., Stainback, S., & Bunch, G. (1989). Introduction and historical background. In S. Stainback, W. Stainback, and M. Forest (Eds.), *Educating all students in the mainstream of regular education* (pp. 3–14). Baltimore: Paul H. Brookes.

Weiner, R. (1985). *P.L. 94–142: Impact on the schools.* Arlington, VA: Capitol.

Winzer, M. (1993). *The history of special education: From isolation to integration.* Washington, DC: Gallaudet University Press.

3

CHANGING TIMES:
THE EVOLUTION OF SPECIAL EDUCATION

Brian L. Wilson

A FTER the implementation of PL 94-142 in the 1970s, many students (especially those with milder disabilities) were integrated into the mainstream for at least part of their education. However, many others with more severe disabilities remained in segregated classrooms or residential/day schools having little contact with regular education students. Before long, a number of educators, politicians, and parents began to question whether the stated intent of the law to educate as many children as possible in the "least restrictive environment" was being adequately addressed. It was their belief that even more children should receive all of their education in general education settings. These same critics argued that the special education system was becoming self-serving, frequently guilty of inflating or misdiagnosing the number of students requiring special services, and lacking in credible evidence for maintaining "separate but equal" educational opportunities. Further fanning the flames of reform were statistics showing that increasing numbers of students with disabilities continued to be taught in segregated, rather than integrated, settings even though the apparent intent of the federal law was essentially to do just the opposite (Gartner & Lipsky, 1987; Hallahan, Kauffman, Lloyd, & McKinney, 1988; Stainback & Stainback, 1984).

Interpreting the Federal Law

At the heart of this controversy are three components of the federal law that became particularly contentious during the 1980s and 1990s. This subsequently resulted in a number of interpretations being generated regarding how each aspect of the law should be implemented.

FAPE: Free, Appropriate, Public Education

Seen as one the centerpieces of the federal law by many, the FAPE clause has caused considerable confusion as to what exactly constitutes an "appropriate" educational experience. The lack of a precise definition has led to numerous cases of litigation, typically between parents and school districts, in an attempt to clarify the initial intent of this particular aspect of the law. In the early 1980s, the U.S. Supreme Court declared that education is appropriate when it involves a program of services that is developed in a procedurally correct manner, is individualized, and can reasonably be expected to provide the student with educational benefit The actual degree of benefit is to be determined on a case-by-case basis *except* for students who are placed in regular classrooms. In that particular situation, all necessary aids and services are to be provided to the student in order that he or she will be able to earn passing grades and legitimate passage from grade to grade (Crockett & Kauffman, 1999a).

It should also be noted that the Supreme Court did not define educational benefit as necessarily providing opportunities that were equal to those received by nondisabled students. In writing the majority opinion for the Court in the *Board of Education of Hendrick Hudson Central School District v. Rowley* (1982) case, Chief Justice Renquist emphasized the Congress had not intended to provide a "precise guarantee" but rather a "basic floor of opportunity" for disabled children. In effect, Congress had granted equal protection of disabled children but only by providing them with "equal access" and without anything additional that would serve to "maximize" their potential (Daugherty, 2001, p. 32; Siegel, 1994, p. 121). Put another way, the court ruled that the intent of PL 94-142 was to provide the opportunity for students with disabilities to receive "some" services, but not to guarantee a particular level of service.

LRE: Least Restrictive Environment

The categories of placement (i.e., regular class, resource room, separate class, separate school facility, residential facility, and homebound/hospital environment) that are identified in the federal law have remained basically constant starting with PL 94-142 in the 1970s and continuing through the latest reauthorization, IDEA 1997. As the push to educate more children with disabilities in the regular classroom setting has steadily increased, education scholars and researchers have voiced differing opinions as to whether or not the language in the law that indicates that students with disabilities should be educated with their nondisabled peers "to the maximum extent appropriate" actually means "to the greatest degree possible." More than just a difference in semantics, those embracing the latter phrase believe there is little reason why any child should be denied access to the general education classroom.

Although the setting where special learners receive educational services has become a hotly contested issue in many school districts over the past several years, Bateman (1996) contends that placement decisions should only be made after determination of each student's unique educational needs and the development of an individualized program of services to address them. The placement of the child should be determined *after* consideration of which instructional setting is best equipped to support the provision of an appropriate education. In other words, the "how" should come before the "where." Specifically, IDEA requires that "to the maximum extent appropriate" the school, whether public or private, must educate the child with disabilities with children who do not have a disability. The LRE requirement contained within IDEA further mandates that children be educated outside the regular classroom only when "the nature or severity of the disability is such that education in regular classes with the use of supplementary aids and services cannot be achieved satisfactorily" (Guernsey & Klare, 1993, p. 104). Therefore, it is the responsibility of those involved in making placement decisions to give full consideration to any potential harmful effect on the child or on the quality of services that the child requires when seeking the best learning environment for the special needs student. Although the LRE for some students might be the regular education classroom, it is not necessarily required nor even desirable in all cases. The LRE requirement must be viewed in light of the individual needs of the child; it should be addressed on a case-by-case basis without assuming that children with similar disabilities will automatically receive or benefit from the same placement recommendations.

Related Services

Once it has been determined that a child is eligible to receive special education services, an individualized education program (IEP) must be developed that is reflective of the child's unique educational needs. In order to provide the "basic floor of opportunity" for all students, the Supreme Court has also reasoned that specialized instruction and related services may be necessary in order for the student with disabilities to receive educational benefit. According to the law, related services are defined as "transportation and such developmental, corrective, and other supportive services as are required to assist a child with a disability to benefit from special education, and includes speech pathology and audiology, psychological services, physical and occupational therapy, recreation, including therapeutic recreation, early identification and assessment of disabilities in children, counseling services, including rehabilitation counseling and medical services for diagnostic or evaluation purposes" (Daugherty, 2001, p. 39). While music therapy and the arts in general are not mentioned specifically in this language, the notes section that accompanied this portion of the law did include music, art, and dance therapy among other possible related services. However, editorial revisions to IDEA 1997 (that went into effect in March 1999) removed the notes section presumably in deference to IDEA's intent that the listing of related services not be viewed as exhaustive. Unfortunately, this lack of specificity has resulted in many parents being told by their school districts that music therapy does not qualify as a related service since it is no longer mentioned by name. A subsequent request for clarification by AMTA regarding this matter has resulted in a document from the U.S. Office of Special Education and Rehabilitative Services (see Chapter 1) stipulating that music therapy must be provided at public expense and no cost to the parents if the child's IEP team determines that such service would be *necessary* for the child to benefit from special education.

Models for Change

Starting in the early 1980s the pressure to provide more integrated educational experiences and to limit the number of specialized education offerings gained increasing momentum. Over the next two decades different models were developed and introduced into the educational system with the primary goal being the integration of greater numbers of special learners into mainstream settings.

The Regular Education Initiative

The idea of a "merger" between special education and regular education gained national attention during a professional conference in 1985. Madeline C. Will, then Assistant Secretary for the U.S. Office of Special Education and Rehabilitative Services, told the special educators gathered at this meeting that the "so-called 'pull-out' approach to the educational difficulties of students with learning problems has failed in many instances to meet the educational needs of these students and has created, however unwittingly, barriers to their successful education" (Will, 1986, p. 412). Based on her conviction that the structure was not working as effectively as it should have been, Will issued a charge to special educators that an extensive self-examination of the entire special education delivery system was warranted. Relying heavily on the Adaptive Learning Environments Model (ALEM) developed by Margaret Wang and her colleagues (Wang, 1980; Wang & Birch, 1984), Will called for a partnership to be developed between general and special education that became more commonly known as the Regular Education Initiative (REI).

Grounded in the belief that a "dual system" of education was ineffective, Will (1986) further proposed the dismantling of the traditional dual system of education management in favor of the unification of special education with general education. This platform was strongly endorsed by the REI movement that supported a de-emphasis of educational segregation by promoting the development of one unified system of education to meet the unique needs of all children. The REI debate that followed challenged educators to reevaluate their current practices regarding the identification, instruction, and placement of all at-risk children and not just those with traditional disabilities. By doing so, proponents envisioned that a large percentage of children who were educationally disadvantaged would be able to receive support services through the use of large scale, full-time mainstreaming efforts instead of the more traditional case-by-case approach (Davis, 1990).

Opponents of the REI countered that any attempt to dismantle the dual education system before a new system was in place was premature and irresponsible. Without the means to assess and identify those with learning problems, they feared that the rights of the students with disabilities would be in jeopardy. Still others questioned the logic of assuming that the general education system, which was under increasing pressure to improve standardized test scores, could best accommodate the same students that previously failed in it. They argued that some students do require special education environments with teachers and others who have highly specialized skills and favorable attitudes toward individuals with disabilities (Braaten, Kauffman, Braaten, Polsgrove, & Nelson, 1988; Byrnes, 1990)

The Adaptive Learning Environments Model (ALEM)

The ALEM was developed in an effort to replace "pull-out" programs in regular schools, especially resource rooms and compensatory education programs. The overall goal is to provide successful school environments that maximize learning and mastery of academic subjects while the student concurrently gains confidence and develops coping strategies for the classroom (Wang, 1980). Among the primary components of the ALEM are the following:

1. Instruction is provided in general education settings on a full-time basis.
2. Support and services from specialists are delivered within the general education setting.
3. Academic skills are developed through the use of highly structured prescriptive learning based on built-in diagnostic procedures.
4. Students plan and manage their own learning in an open-ended, exploratory atmosphere that fosters social and personal development.
5. Educational plans are designed for each student to accommodate unique strengths and needs.
6. Flexibility is encouraged when arranging the learning environment.

Since its introduction, the ALEM has received a mixed review from the special education profession. While there is some evidence that placing students with disabilities into ALEM classrooms can positively influence their academic performance and social skills (Fuchs & Fuchs, 1988), the research reported by Wang and her associates has been criticized for serious methodological weakness, overemphasis on the physical placement of students rather than the content and success of their learning, and for not being subjected to the rigors of scientific research (Hallahan, Keller, McKinney, Lloyd, & Bryan, 1988). Consequently, attempts to enact large-scale full-time mainstreaming programs based on the efficacy of the ALEM have often been viewed as inappropriate given the limitations of the existing research base (Fuchs & Fuchs, 1988; Hallahan, Keller, et al., 1988; Keogh, 1990).

Full Inclusion

While the REI resulted in many children who had previously been in self-contained classrooms and separate schools being taught with regular education students, those with more severe disabilities were still frequently left behind. Advocates for this particular group of learners (e.g., The Association for Persons with Severe Handicaps [TASH]) asserted that all students should have access to the mainstream regardless of the severity of the student's disability. This desire to include all students in the regular classroom became more commonly known as the inclusive schools movement or full inclusion. Although there is no single, universally accepted definition, it is generally agreed that inclusion means providing appropriate educational experiences for any child, regardless of disability, in the same classroom, or at least the same school, that the student would attend if he or she did not have a disability (Lombardi, 1994). Whereas the REI suggests that regular classroom teachers be more accommodating and responsive to those students with disabilities who are already included for all or part of their day, full inclusion insists that all education services be provided in the regular classroom with support services brought into the room only as absolutely necessary. In effect the proponents of inclusion believe that the services should come to the student rather than bringing the student to the services.

While there are several important philosophical distinctions between the REI and full inclusion movement, the major difference has been the issue of placement. Those supporting full inclusion argue that all students with disabilities can have a more meaningful educational experience when taught with their nondisabled peers in the regular classroom during the entire school day. Advocates for the REI contend that consideration of the LRE must be secondary to, and balanced against, the primary objective of providing an appropriate education (Kauffman & Lloyd, 1995). Put another way, supporters of the REI believe that placement is *an* issue, while full inclusionists believe that placement is *the* issue.

A second major disparity between these two ideologies is the anticipated outcomes of the educational experience being provided to the special learner. Whereas those supporting the REI have maintained the importance of the acquisition of a knowledge base and skill development (Fuchs & Fuchs, 1994), full inclusionists tend to measure success in terms of social acceptance of special learners by both teachers and classmates. In fact, Snell (1991) concluded that one of the most important benefits resulting from integration of regular and special needs students was "the development of positive relationship and friendships between peers" (pp. 137–138).

A third philosophical difference is concerned with the appropriateness and necessity of maintaining a separate educational system for students with disabilities. Lipsky and Gartner (1991) summarized their position in favor of reducing special education by stating "the concepts of Least Restrictive Environment —a continuum of placements, and a cascade of services—were progressive when developed but do not today promote the full inclusion of all persons with disabilities in all aspects of societal life" (p. 52). Rather than attempting to reform special education, full inclusionists want to eliminate it. Although such action could signal the end of labeling practices, special education programs, and special classes, it is not intended to eliminate necessary support services; specialists and consultants would follow the special learner into the regular classroom. Ultimately, this could lead to greater numbers of students receiving services including those deemed to be "at risk" (Pearpoint & Forest, 1992).

Opponents of full inclusion see all of this as little more than the "dumping" of students with disabilities into regular classrooms. They contend that inclusion is basically a misguided effort to achieve a "normalized" environment for a group of students whose limited level of functioning has typically precluded them from being considered for placement in the regular classroom. Critics also question whether the presence of a number of specialists in the regular classroom will not disrupt ongoing classroom activities and further stigmatize the special needs student (Kauffman, 1989; Petch-Hogan & Haggard, 1999).

Determining Effectiveness

In order to evaluate whether any of the philosophical approaches to modify special education have led to greater success for disabled students or their nondisabled peers, scholars and researchers have looked at two major indicators (i.e., academic achievement and social outcomes) as primary measures of effectiveness. These attempts to quantify whether certain approaches are effective have sometimes been hampered by the highly charged and emotionally laden nature of the debate surrounding the placement of special education students. Some have characterized the resulting rhetoric as an ideological division in special education representing two camps: the "anointed" or "abolitionists" and the "benighted" or "conservationists" (Crockett & Kauffman, 1999a; Kavale & Forness, 2000). Those who advocate forcefully for full inclusion are usually included in the former groups while those who call for research validation and empirical verification of effectiveness are often identified with the latter groups. Without always having the empirical evidence to validate one particular philosophical position over another, many of the reformers of special education have, however unwittingly, drawn a "line in the sand" over the issue of inclusion resulting in an "us" versus "them" mentality.

Several of the efficacy studies comparing academic and/or social achievement of students with disabilities in general education placements to those in special classes have shown generally positive results. In their analysis of 261 studies comparing students with severe and profound disabilities in integrated placements with their peers in segregated placements, Halvorsen and Sailor (1990) concluded that students in integrated placements demonstrated greater socialization skills (e.g., fewer inappropriate behaviors, more independence, and increased communication skills) than those in more segregated settings. Other studies have reported similar outcomes, especially in relation to the development of appropriate social skills and successful interactions with nondisabled peers. Corbin (as cited in Lombardi, 1994) found that parents of special needs students who had been fully included in five different elementary schools reported greater improvement in both their children's academic and social learning when compared to their previous segregated settings. The teachers also reported that the regular education students maintained their academic performance, were understanding and accepting of the students with disabilities, and became role models for those students. In a study (Lombardi, Nuzzo, Kennedy, & Foshay, 1994) involving high-school age students there was a lower dropout rate, fewer classroom disturbances, and acceptable academic gains when students with disabilities were placed in regular classrooms. Peck, Donaldson, and Pezzoli (1990) interviewed 21 nondisabled high school students who had social experiences with peers with severe disabilities and found that those experiences resulted in improved self-concept, social-cognitive growth, reduced fear of human differences, and increased tolerance of other people. In addition, a longitudinal study of early elementary students reported increased reading achievement, decreased special-education referrals, reduced retention rates, and improved attendance when students were involved in "Success for All," a district-wide early intervention program serving large numbers of disadvantaged students (Madden, Slavin, Karweit, Dolan, & Wasik, 1993).

Critics charge that many of these studies are seriously flawed since mainstreamed participants rarely were determined by random assignments and tended to be stronger academically and/or socially at the beginning of the study (Fuchs & Fuchs, 1995; Hallahan & Kauffman, 1994). In other words, many of the studies showing favorable results for students included in regular education settings compared outcomes for individuals who were already socially and academically stronger at the outset to those of their lower performing peers still in special education settings with somewhat obvious results. Rogers (1994) further cautions that published studies extolling the benefits of inclusion generally reflect model programs "with adequate instructional support and with caring teachers who value each of their students sufficiently to assume that every child is challenged" (p. 4). Furthermore, although proponents of the inclusive schools movement claim that students with disabilities will achieve greater mastery of academic concepts and will demonstrate improvement in their social skills, opponents question whether the claims aren't based more on wishful thinking than research validation. Guetzloe (1999) contends that very few empirical studies have measured actual gains made in the regular classroom in either basic skills (viz., reading writing, speaking, and mathematics), social competence (viz., listening, asking for help, avoiding fights, or controlling aggression), or other content areas (viz., health, social studies, or foreign languages).

On balance, the efficacy studies that have been conducted over the past half century indicate that many special learners placed in integrated classrooms have performed as well as, and sometimes better than, their counterparts in self-contained settings, particularly when only social parameters are measured. However, closer examination of many of these studies reveals that there may be substantial variation in the results among the different groups of participants tested. Therefore, research where successful results are reported collectively for all students rather than by different ability levels or disability classifications should be interpreted with caution.

In reality, many school districts have placed children in regular classrooms with little or no expectation of grade level performance that is similar to their non-disabled peers and with only limited support provided, if any at all, to approach it (Crockett & Kauffman, 1999a). Advocates for full inclusion acknowledge that learners with severe intellectual limitations rarely obtain the same degree of academic success as students with mild or moderate impairments. To rectify this situation, they believe that fundamental changes need to be made in the very foundation of general education by de-emphasizing (or eliminating) a standard curriculum and knowledge base in favor of a more process-oriented approach to education (Stainback, Stainback, & Moravec, 1992). Using this approach, children would be encouraged to learn "as much as they can" in any given subject area without being held accountable through typical testing and evaluation procedures.

Although the existing special education structure has been sharply criticized for failing to help students achieve academically or socially (Gartner & Lipsky, 1987), it is unwarranted to conclude that special education programming over the past 30 years has been ineffective. In their meta-analysis synthesizing the findings from 50 efficacy studies, Carlberg and Kavale (1980) discovered that the area of disability appeared to be a primary indicator of how much students benefitted from their educational placement. They found that special class placement produced substantially better outcomes than regular class placement for students classified as learning disabled and behaviorally disordered/emotionally disturbed. However, regular classroom placement produced slightly better results than special class placement when all types of students were considered together and even more so when students with mild mental retardation were considered alone. Sindelar and Deno (1978) reported no discernable difference in academic improvement of children with mild mental retardation between resource and mainstream classes but did find that resource rooms were more effective than regular classrooms in improving the academic achievement of students with learning disabilities or emotional and behavioral problems. Similarly, Madden and Slavin (1983) found that students with more serious learning problems benefitted the most from placement in special classes.

Although studies of placement trends have yielded mixed results, experts generally concede that students with mild learning disabilities have been the most successful in transitioning from the special education setting to the regular classroom (Cronis & Ellis, 2000). According to data provided by the U.S. Department of Education, the percentage of students with disabilities educated in regular classrooms increased by 19.9% between 1986 and 1996 with the greatest increase (27%) for children with specific learning disabilities (Zera & Seitsinger, 2000). By the end of the 20th century, the U.S. Department of Education reported that about 95% of students with disabilities were being taught in regular schools with regular classrooms being the primary placement (i.e., 80% or more of the day) for approximately 55% of younger students (ages 6–11) with disabilities and 33% for older students (ages 12–17) with disabilities (Crockett & Kauffman, 1999a; Kavale & Forness, 2000). The data also indicate that students with learning disabilities are more likely to be placed in regular classrooms while students with mental retardation, autism, and multiple disabilities are more often placed in separate classes.

Full Inclusion or a Continuum of Placement/Service Options?

Without question, the notion of placing all students in regular classrooms can be financially beneficial and politically expedient. Many state governments, looking for ways to reduce spending, have expressed serious doubts as to whether the continued existence of a dual educational system (regular education and special education) is even necessary. Increasing numbers of parents of students with disabilities are also demanding that their children have as much contact as possible with their nondisabled peers in hopes of enhancing the probability that their children will learn more socially appropriate behaviors. On the other hand, some parents of nondisabled students wonder whether the presence of special learners in the regular classroom will consume an inordinate amount of the teachers' attention resulting in a diluted curriculum.

Several crucial issues will need to be addressed in order that the rights of all children are maintained and protected before the doors of the regular education classroom are completely opened to everyone. For example, will mechanisms be in place to assess and identify those who have significant learning problems ensuring that children with disabilities receive appropriate services? Should general educators be expected to address the needs of special learners with only limited preparation or assistance, if any at all? How will the negative attitudes and the lack of preparation of many general education teachers be sufficiently addressed so that the regular classroom is a place for success and not failure? Are effective strategies for teaching exceptional children in the general classroom readily available? Are special education students being placed in regular classrooms inappropriately, too soon, or too many at once? Will providing support services in the classroom actually further stigmatize the student with special needs? Will attempts to limit federal mandates, reduce administrative structure, and encourage local control of education (with concomitant reduction in federal funding) only serve to return the country to conditions that existed prior to the passage of PL 94-142?

Sorting through the rhetoric as to how and when special learners should be integrated into the mainstream can be a daunting task. Various groups advocating for students with disabilities have engaged in passionate discourse as to which philosophical approach is best for their constituency. While all interested parties in this national debate would probably agree that access to the mainstream is the ultimate goal for all students, not all parents of children with disabilities believe that regular classrooms in a neighborhood school are capable of providing relevant educational opportunities for their children. It would seem to be naïve and overly simplistic to assume that any single educational setting or teaching approach will be able to meet the needs of those students, regardless of their abilities or limitations. A review of position statements by 15 national associations representing different factions of children with disabilities found that the majority opinion favors maintaining a full continuum of placement and service options rather than offering only the single option of full inclusion (Verstegen & Martin, 1996). In other words, most advocates for the special learner continue to support the inclusion of exceptional children as stipulated in the least restrictive environment clause of the IDEA where inclusion in the general classroom is but one option out of several.

Obstacles to the Integration of Special Learners Into Regular Classrooms

Several of the major tenets of both the REI and full inclusion movement (e.g., working toward improved interaction between professionals, better coordination of services for students, looking for the most effective and economical methods of serving students with disabilities, identifying special learners only when necessary, and supporting research that will lead to the best possible instruction for all students) have received nearly universal endorsements among special education professionals. However, other components associated with these changes in the delivery system have been substantially more controversial and vigorously debated in the literature.

Will the push for integration in regular education settings and against labeling result in fewer students with disabilities receiving needed services?

Whether students receive services will depend to some extent on if they are even identified as needing those services. In the past, special education has been accused of exaggerating the number of students needing special services (Algozzine, Ysseldyke, & Christenson, 1983; Biklen & Zollars, 1986). Shepard (1987) has suggested that 90% of special education students are very mildly disabled, if at all, and indistinguishable from low achievers. Reynolds, Wang, and Walberg (1987) consider three fourths of special education students to be "judgementally handicapped" (p. 391).

In their review of the extant literature, Hallahan and Kauffman (1994) admit that labeling a person as disabled may lead others to view that individual differently. While most would find capricious labeling and increased stigmatization of children to be unpalatable, the problems associated with labeling may have been overstated. Labels can "help explain behavior that is out of the ordinary and lead to a better understanding and sensitivity toward the labeled person" (Hallahan & Kauffman, p. 502). Without labels, children may be erroneously accused of being "lazy" or "trouble-makers," when in reality their learning disabilities are the reason for their lack of achievement or disruptive behaviors. Braaten et al. (1988) argue that special learners, especially those with emotional and behavioral disorders, are often labeled by peers and teachers as deviant or different long before they are referred to special education. Furthermore, they contend that removing that label does not remove the problem. Many educators and parents are also concerned that financial support for needed services may be in jeopardy if learning problems are not identified in some manner. If there is not a system to determine learning problems it is not clear how appropriate educational programs can be designed, implemented, and funded.

Is it realistic to expect that general education teachers can and will accommodate the special needs of students with disabilities?

General and special educators often have mixed, and sometimes differing, reactions to the inclusion of special learners in regular education classrooms. These distinctions are apparently related to each group's perceived ability to implement inclusion as well as their perception of administrative support. While those advocating for the inclusion of greater numbers of special learners in the regular classroom may have assumed that their vision for reform would be embraced by regular educators, such has not necessarily been the case. In fact, what many have described as reform of special education has actually been a reform of general education. Unfortunately, the regular education teachers who are being asked to integrate increasing numbers of children with special needs into their classrooms have typically been given little opportunity to enter into the deliberations. In reality, the inclusion debate has largely involved faculty in institutions of higher learning, specifically faculty in special education, while K–12 educators/administrators have been given little opportunity to voice their opinions about proposed changes (Cronis & Ellis, 2000; Meese, 1994).

The following assumptions appear to be the foundation upon which a merger between general and special education has been predicated:

1. Students are more alike than different and can benefit from the application of education equally to all students. Distinguishing students as disabled/nondisabled has no educational purpose since atypical educational methods are not required to meet their needs.
2. Good teachers are good teachers, regardless of the student. They should be able to teach all students with only minor changes in teaching strategies and without the need for special training. Special education has become a convenient way for general educators to avoid their responsibility to teach all students.
3. All children can receive a quality education without the need to identify some students as different and without special programs, budgets, training programs, teachers, or classes. Special targeting of funds for special students is inefficient, confusing, and often abused for financial gain. The few students who may need some special services do not need to be formally identified to ensure that they receive appropriate services.
4. Education outside the regular classroom is not required for anyone. All students can be instructed and managed effectively in regular classrooms. Moreover, the separation of students from their ordinary chronological-age peers is an immoral, segregationist act that has no legitimate place in our free and egalitarian society.
5. Physically separate education is inherently discriminatory and unequal. The most important equity issue is the site, not the quality of instruction. (Kauffman, 1989; Kavale & Forness, 2000)

Research indicates that general education teachers often feel ill prepared to teach students with special needs, lack the skills in teaming and collaboration that are required for successful partnerships with special education personnel, and report that their school districts rarely provide inservice opportunities to help address these needs (Buell, Hallam, & Gamel-McCormick, 1999; Crockett & Kauffman, 1999b; Daane, Beirne-Smith, & Latham, 2000). Earlier studies investigating general classroom teachers' perceptions of more inclusive classrooms found that many teachers supported traditional programming (self-contained classrooms, pull-out programs) as the most effective way to address the needs of special education students (Coates, 1989; Davis & Maheady, 1991; Houck & Rogers, 1994; Semmel, Abernathy, Butera, & Lesar, 1991). In their review of 27 survey studies published between 1958 and 1995 involving over 9,000 teachers, Scruggs and Mastropieri (1996) found little change across the decades in the willingness of teachers to integrate special learners into regular classrooms. Only about one fourth of the respondents stated that mainstreaming most students with disabilities was desirable. Particularly unsettling was the authors' findings that, in two of the more recent (1994) studies, up to 80% of the teachers felt coerced toward accepting full inclusion. Even when teachers do support the integration of special learners into the regular classroom, they frequently report a lack of knowledge about the needs of these students and little understanding of the methods and materials that should be used in their education. This is a dichotomy similar to the one experienced with the implementation of PL 94-142. At that time, regular education teachers, while often philosophically supportive of the principles contained in the new law, remained generally resistant to the integration of disabled students in general classroom settings. Their resistance was not only attributed to such factors as the teachers' reported limited knowledge base, lack of experience of working with students with disabilities, and lack of technical support from specialists, but also to the reformers' failure to recognize that change of this magnitude affects the entire culture of the educational system.

There are some indications that the negative attitudes of regular educators to including special learners in their classrooms may be changing. In a recent survey of 174 general education teachers, those who had experience teaching in inclusive programs were generally more favorable toward several aspects related to inclusion than those who did not have special learners in their classrooms (McLeskey, Waldron, & So, 2001). In a smaller survey of recently graduated inservice teachers in Michigan, Snyder, Garriott, and Aylor (2001) reported that over half of the respondents to their survey reported a favorable change in their attitudes towards students with special needs partly because of their students' academic achievements and overall competency levels. Both studies seem to underscore the importance of providing opportunities for positive classroom interactions between regular education teachers and students with special needs.

Implications for Music Therapy/Music Education

Changes in the placement of, and educational services available for, students with disabilities have also had a direct effect on the music classroom. Music educators assigned to educationally segregated or integrated music classes have voiced concerns similar to those of their general education colleagues as how to best meet the needs of the children they have been asked to teach. Music educators report that they often feel inadequate about working with special learners, possibly due to very limited experience with exceptional students, a lack of administrative support, limited involvement in decisions regarding the placement of special education children in music classes, and little knowledge of appropriate methods for teaching integrated classrooms (Darrow, 1990; Frisque, Niebur, & Humphreys, 1994; Gfeller, Darrow, & Hedden, 1990; Gilbert & Asmus, 1981). Despite the fact that music teachers have fairly consistently reported to having little formal training to adequately prepare them for teaching in inclusive situations, there is evidence that their attitude towards teaching all children in the mainstream may be changing. In her survey of Texas music educators, Jellison (1992) found that a large majority (over 90%) felt positive about teaching students with disabilities whether in the regular classroom or in more traditional settings. It is important to note, however, that (a) most of the respondents taught only children with moderate disabilities, and (b) the majority thought that a music therapist rather than a music educator should be responsible for music instruction for students with disabilities. When preservice elementary education majors, preservice music education majors, and inservice music teachers were asked to indicate their perceptions regarding the integration of students with mental retardation in a regular music classroom, Jellison and Duke (1994) found that inservice teachers were more likely to consider the integrated classroom as being a potentially less successful placement for all students than did their preservice counterparts. However, the authors also found that all respondents were likely to view the inclusion of any child, whether disabled or not, more positively if the student exhibited appropriate social behaviors.

As in other general education settings, the criteria for evaluating the success of mainstreaming in music education may be based on the acquisition of functional knowledge, the development of social/interpersonal relationships, or both. Although the Music Educators National Conference discourages the placement of special learners in music classes for reasons other than music ability, administrators frequently place students with disabilities in music classes in order to satisfy mainstreaming mandates, because it is assumed that few prerequisite academic or behavioral skills are required, or simply because the child is known to "like music." As recently as the mid 1990s, a survey of music educators in Arizona revealed that the majority of respondents believed that most special needs students in general music, band, chorus, or string programs were placed there primarily because of student interest and for socialization purposes (Frisque et al., 1994).

The type and severity of a student's disability appears to be a factor correlated with both general and music educators' feelings about mainstreaming and willingness to include special learners in their classrooms. For example, regular educators in Illinois reported that they were more willing and able to integrate students with physical, speech and hearing impairments than they were those with moderate to severe developmental delays (Phillips, Allred, Brulle, & Shank, 1990). Music educators tend to be more positive toward the integration of students with less severe disabilities (e.g., learning disabilities, orthopedic problems) than they are towards those with more severe disabilities (multiple impairments, mental retardation, and emotional and behavioral disorders) into music classes (Gfeller, Darrow, & Hedden, 1990; Sideridis & Chandler, 1995; Wilson & McCrary, 1996). There is some evidence, however, that combining university instruction with practicum experience may be an effective way to improve the attitudes of practicing music teachers towards working with students with disabilities (Smith & Wilson, 1999).

The regular music classroom is not the only placement option available, nor is it always the most appropriate environment for the special learner. Music instruction can also be provided in the self-contained classroom or in separate facilities. Some special learners may be referred to a music therapist employed within the school system to help them master the musical and/or behavioral skills necessary to be successfully integrated into the music classroom. Such services can be provided individually, with disabled peers, or within the mainstreamed classroom. Students placed in music education classes may also be concurrently receiving music therapy services. Kostka (1993) and Jellison and Gainer (1995) have published case studies indicating that the acquisition of positive social and behavioral skills learned in music therapy appear to transfer to the music education setting.

Where Do We Go From Here?

Since the passage of the Education for All Handicapped Children Act (PL 94-142) in 1975, the structure of special education and the educational opportunities provided for individuals with disabilities have changed dramatically. Subsequent reauthorizations of PL 94-142/ IDEA, along with the passage of additional federal legislation (e.g., PL 99-457; Americans with Disabilities Act [ADA]) has further expanded and clarified the criteria as to who is qualified to (and should) receive special education services.

Without question, the number of children with special needs being taught in general education settings has increased substantially over the years. While many applaud the increasing numbers of special education students being taught in general education classrooms, others argue that such large-scale adherence to one specific ideology violates the basic tenets of the IDEA. Because the IEP requires *individualized* education programming, proponents for maintaining a continuum of services and placement options contend that it is naive and unethical to assume that all children will benefit from primarily one teaching method/strategy.

Yet the push to include even more students in the mainstream continues. The LRE clause, one of the centerpieces of PL 94-142 with its range of placements and services, is now being challenged in the courts. Increasingly, rulings are less likely to come down on the side of school officials or parents on the LRE issue when the recommendations are for more restrictive placements (Osborne & Dimattia, 1994). Today a school district's decision to place a student in anything less than a regular classroom setting will probably only be upheld in court if school officials or parents can demonstrate that sincere attempts at inclusion have failed or provide evidence to support the belief that an inclusive setting will not be the best choice for the student (Osborne & Dimattia, 1995).

To be responsive to these changes, music educators must continue to develop teaching strategies and curriculum models that ensure the success of all the students assigned to their classes. The following recommendations are suggested as music educators, often working in tandem with music therapists and other specialists, strive to provide the highest quality education for all students:

1. Keep the needs of the child paramount when decisions regarding placement must be made. Students who are recommended for inclusion should be provided with meaningful learning experiences and not placed in music classrooms simply to comply with political agendas.
2. Request support (from administrators and colleagues) in the form of relevant information (via workshops, inservice training, etc.) when asked to implement models of inclusion. Of all the support specialists, music therapists are perhaps in the best position to provide successful, music-based intervention strategies.
3. Ask for information resulting from IEP decisions. Since music educators rarely attend IEP meetings, they usually have little information about the students being placed in their classes and little influence over their decisions. Too often, music educators are "out of the loop" when placement decisions are made.
4. Realize that, like other general educators, music educators may feel overburdened and unfairly criticized for their perceived lack of response to sweeping changes in special education mandates. Become more assertive in asking for support (e.g., aide, consultants) when asked to implement mainstreaming programs.
5. Reform music education and teacher certification programs so that coursework addressing the unique role of music with special learners and hands-on experience with students who have disabilities is a requirement and not just an elective.

Whether the integration of the majority of special needs students into regular classes is a good idea or not is no longer the issue. Inclusion is now a reality in classrooms all over the country. Nevertheless, it should not be viewed as a panacea to cure all of the past ills of special education. Given the volume of evidence in the extant literature, it seems presumptuous and cavalier to assume that general educators have the ability to make needed instructional adaptations in their classroom for students with disabilities, and that those same students will automatically make a satisfactory adjustment to the regular class, without some type of support. Responsible inclusion requires careful and individualized planning before any student with disabilities is placed in a regular class. With adequate support from school administrators and related service personnel, both regular and special educators will be more willing and better prepared for their changing roles in meeting the needs of all of the students they have been asked to teach.

References

Algozzine, B., Ysseldyke, J., & Christenson. S. (1983). An analysis of the incidence of special class placement: The masses are burgeoning. *Journal of Special Education, 17,* 141–147.

Bateman, B. (1996). *Better IEPs.* Longmont, CO: Sopris West.

Bicklen, D., & Zolars, N. (1986). The focus of advocacy in the LD field. *Journal of Learning Disabilities, 19,* 579–586.

Board of Education of Hendrick Hudson Central School District v. Rowley, 458 U.S. 176, 102 S. Ct. 3034 (1982).

Braaten, S., Kauffman, J., Braaten, B., Polsgrove, L., & Nelson, C. (1988). The Regular Education Initiative: Patent medicine for behavioral disorders. *Exceptional Children, 55,* 21–27.

Bricker, D. D. (2000). Inclusion: How the scene has changed. *Topics in Early Childhood Special Education, 20*(1), 14–19.

Buell, M., Hallam, R., & Gamel-McCormick, M. (1999). A survey of general and special education teachers' perceptions and inservice needs concerning inclusion. *International Journal of Disability, Development, and Education, 46*(2), 143–156.

Byrnes, M. (1990). The Regular Education Initiative debate: A view from the field. *Exceptional Children, 56,* 345–349.

Carlberg, C., & Kavale, K. (1980). The efficacy of special v. regular class placement for exceptional children: A meta-analysis. *Journal of Special Education, 14,* 295–309.

Coates, R. (1989). The Regular Education Initiative and opinions of regular classroom teachers. *Journal of Learning Disabilities, 22,* 532–536

Crockett, J., & Kauffmann, J. (1999a). *The least restrictive environment: Its origins and interpretations in special education.* Mahwah, NJ: Lawrence Erlbaum Associates.

Crockett, J., & Kauffmann, J. (1999b). Taking inclusion back to its roots. *Educational Leadership, 56*(2), 74–77.

Cronis, T., & Ellis, D. (2000). Issues facing special educators in the new millennium. *Education, 120*(4), 639–648.

Daane, C., Beirne-Smith, M., & Latham, D. (2000). Administrators' and teachers' perceptions of the collaborative efforts of inclusion in the elementary grades. *Education, 121*(2), 331–339.

Darrow, A. A. (1990). Research on mainstreaming in music education. *Update, 9*(1), 35-37.

Daugherty, R. F. (2001). *Special education: A summary of legal requirements, terms and trends.* Westport, CT: Bergin & Gavey.

Davis, J., & Maheady, L. (1991). The Regular Education Initiative: What do three groups of education professionals think? *Teacher Education and Special Education, 14,* 211–220.

Davis, W. E. (1990). Broad perspectives on the Regular Education Initiative: Response to Byrnes. *Exceptional Children, 56,* 349–351.

Frisque, J., Niebur, L., & Humphreys, J. (1994). Music mainstreaming: Practices in Arizona. *Journal of Research in Music Education, 42,* 94–104.

Fuchs, D., & Fuchs, L. (1988). Evaluation of the Adaptive Learning Environments Model. *Exceptional Children, 55,* 115–127.

Fuchs, D., & Fuchs, L. (1994). Inclusive schools movement and the radicalization of special education reform. *Exceptional Children, 60,* 294–309.

Fuchs, D., & Fuchs, L. (1995). Special education can work. In J. M. Kauffman, J. W. Lloyd, D. P. Hallahan, & T. A. Astuto (Eds.), *Issues in educational placement: Students with emotional and behavioral disorders* (pp. 363–377). Hillsdale, NJ: Lawrence Erlbaum Associates.

Gartner, A., & Lipsky, D. (1987). Beyond special education: Toward a quality system for all students. *Harvard Educational Review, 57,* 376–395.

Gfeller, K., Darrow, A. A., & Hedden, S. (1990). Perceived effectiveness of mainstreaming in Iowa and Kansas schools. *Journal of Research in Music Education, 38,* 90–101.

Gilbert, J., & Asmus, E. (1981). Mainstreaming: Music educators' participation and professional needs. *Journal of Research in Music Education, 29,* 31–38.

Guernsey, T., & Klare, K. (1993). *Special Education Law.* Durham, NC: Carolina Academic Press.

Guetzloe, E. (1999). Inclusion: The broken promise. *Preventing School Failure, 43*(2), 92–98.

Hallahan, D., & Kauffman, J. (1994). Toward a culture of disability in the aftermath of Deno and Dunn. *Journal of Special Education, 27,* 496–508.

Hallahan, D., Kauffman, J., Lloyd, J., & McKinney, J. (1988). Introduction to the series: Questions about the Regular Education Initiative. *Journal of Learning Disabilities, 21,* 3–11.

Hallahan, D., Keller, C., McKinney, J., Lloyd, J., & Bryan, T. (1988). Examining the research base of the Regular Education Initiative: Efficacy studies and the adaptive learning environments model. *Journal of Learning Disabilities, 21,* 29–35.

Halvorsen, A., & Sailor, W. (1990). Integration of students with severe and profound disabilities: A review of the research. In R. Gaylord-Ross (Ed.), *Issues and research in special education* (pp. 110–172). New York: Teachers College Press.

Houck, C., & Rogers C. (1994). The special/general education integration initiative for students with specific learning disabilities: A "snapshot" of program change. *Journal of Learning Disabilities, 27,* 435–453.

Jellison, J. (1992). Music and students with disabilities: A preliminary study of Texas music educators' experiences, attitudes, and perceptions. *Texas Music Education Research*. Austin, TX: Texas Music Educators Association.

Jellison, J., & Duke, R. (1994). The mental retardation label: Music teachers' and prospective teachers' expectations for children's social and music behaviors. *Journal of Music Therapy, 31*(3), 166–185.

Jellison, J., & Gainer, E. (1995). Into the mainstream: A case study of a child's participation in music education and music therapy. *Journal of Music Therapy, 32,* 228–247.

Kauffman, J. (1989). The Regular Education Initiative as Reagan-Bush education policy: A trickle-down theory of education of the hard-to-teach. *Journal of Special Education, 23,* 256–278.

Kauffman, J., & Lloyd, J. (1995). A sense of place: The importance of placement issues in contemporary special education. In J. Kauffman, J. Lloyd, D. Hallahan, & T. Astuto (Eds.), *Issues in educational placement: Students with emotional and behavioral disorders* (pp. 3–20). Hillsdale, NJ: Lawrence Erlbaum Associates.

Kavale, D. A., & Forness, S. R. (2000). History, rhetoric, and reality: Analysis of the inclusion debate. *Remedial and Special Education, 21*(5), 279–296.

Keogh, B. (1990). Narrowing the gap between policy and practice. *Exceptional Children, 57,* 186–190.

Kochhar, C., West, L., & Taymans, J. (2000). *Successful inclusion: Practical strategies for a shared responsibility.* Upper Saddle River, NJ: Prentice Hall.

Kostka, M. (1993). A comparison of selected behaviors of a student with autism in special education and regular music class. *Music Therapy Perspectives, 11,* 57–60.

Lipsky, D., & Gartner, A. (1991). Restructuring for quality. In J. W. Lloyd, A. C. Repp, & N. N. Singh (Eds.), *The Regular Education Initiative: Alternative perspectives on concepts, issues, and models* (pp. 43–56). Sycamore, IL: Sycamore.

Lombardi, T. (1994). Responsible inclusion of students with disabilities. *Phi Delta Kappan, 75,* 7–39.

Lombardi, T., Nuzzo, D., Kennedy, K., & Foshay, J. (1994). Perceptions of parents, teachers and students regarding an integrated education inclusion program. *High School Journal, 77,* 315–21.

Madden, N., & Slavin, R. (1983). Effects of cooperative learning on the social acceptance of mainstreamed academically handicapped students. *Journal of Special Education, 13*(1), 32–37.

Madden, N., Slavin, R., Karweit, N., Dolan, L., & Wasik, B. (1993). Success for all: Longitudinal effects of a restructuring program for inner-city elementary schools. *American Educational Research Journal, 30,* 123–148.

McLeskey, J., Waldron, N., & So, T. (2001). Perspectives of teachers toward inclusive school programs. *Teacher Education and Special Education, 24*(2), 108–115.

Meese, R. (1994). *Teaching learners with mild disabilities: Integrating research and practice.* Pacific Grove, CA: Brooks/Cole.

Osborne, A., & Dimattia, P. (1994). The IDEA's least restrictive environment mandate: Legal implications. *Exceptional Children, 61,* 6–14.

Osborne, A., & Dimattia, P. (1995). Counterpoint: IDEA's LRE mandate: Another look. *Exceptional Children, 61,* 582–584.

Pearpoint, J., & Forest, M. (1992). Foreword. In S. Stainback & W. Stainback (Eds.), *Curriculum considerations in inclusive classrooms: Facilitating learning for all students* (pp. xv–xvii). Baltimore: Paul Brookes.

Peck, C., Donaldson, J., & Pezzoli, M. (1990). Some benefits nonhandicapped adolescents perceive for themselves from their social relationship with peers who have sever handicaps. *Journal of the Association for Persons with Severe Handicaps, 15,* 241–249.

Petch-Hogan, B., & Haggard, D. (1999). The inclusion debate continues. *Kappa Delta Pi Record, 35*(3), 128–131.

Phillips, W., Allred, K., Brulle, A., & Shank, K. (1990). The Regular Education Initiative: The will and skill of regular educators. *Teacher Education and Special Education, 13*(3–4), 182–186.

Reynolds, M., Wang, M., & Walberg, H. (1987). The necessary restructuring of special and regular education. *Exceptional Children, 53*, 391–398.

Robinson, C. (1994, November). *Choral music educators' beliefs about the causes of success and failure of mainstreamed students in music.* Paper presented at the National Association for Music Therapy annual conference, Orlando, FL.

Rogers, J. (1994). *Inclusion: Moving beyond our fears.* Bloomington, IN: Phi Delta Kappa.

Scruggs, T. E., & Mastropieri, M. A. (1996). Teacher perceptions of mainstreaming/inclusion, 1958–1995. A research synthesis. *Exceptional Children, 63*, 59–74.

Semmel, J., Abernathy, T., Butera, G., & Lesar, S. (1991). Teacher perceptions of the Regular Education Initiative. *Exceptional Children, 58*, 9–23.

Shepard, L. (1987). The new push for excellence: Widening the schism between regular and special education. *Exceptional Children, 53*, 327–329.

Sideridis, G., & Chandler, J. (1995). Attitudes and characteristics of general music teachers toward integrating children with developmental disabilities. *Update, 14*(1), 11–15.

Siegel, L. M. (1994). *Least restrictive environment: The paradox of inclusion.* Horsham, PA: LRP Publications.

Sindelar, P., & Deno, S. (1978). The effectiveness of resource programming. *Journal of Special Education, 12*(1), 17–28.

Smith, D., & Wilson, B. (1999). Effects of field experience on graduate music educators' attitude toward teaching students with a disability. *Contributions to Music Education, 26*(1), 33–49.

Snell, M. (1991). Schools are for all kids: The importance of integration for students with severe disabilities and their peers. In J. W. Lloyd, A. C. Repp, & N. N. Singh (Eds.), *The Regular Education Initiative: Alternative perspectives on concepts, issues, and models* (pp. 133–148). Sycamore, IL: Sycamore.

Snyder, L., Garriott, P., & Aylor, M. W. (2001). Inclusion confusion: Putting the pieces together. *Teacher Education and Special Education, 24*(3), 198–207.

Stainback, W., & Stainback, S. (1984). A rationale for the merger of special and regular education. *Exceptional Children, 51*, 102-111.

Stainback, W., Stainback, S., & Moravec, J. (1992). Using curriculum to build inclusive classrooms. In S. Stainback & W. Stainback (Eds.), *Curriculum considerations in inclusive classrooms: Facilitating learning for all students* (pp.65–84). Baltimore: Paul Brookes.

Verstegen, D., & Martin, P. (1996). *A summary of position statements on the inclusion of special education students in the general classroom and excerpts on funding from fifteen national associations.* (ERIC Document Reproduction Service No. ED 386 880)

Wang, M. (1980). Adaptive instruction: Building on diversity. *Theory into practice, 19*, 122–127.

Wang, M., & Birch, J. (1984). Comparison of a full-time mainstreaming program and a resource room approach. *Exceptional Children, 51*, 33–40

Will, M. (1986). Education children with learning problems. A shared responsibility. *Exceptional Children, 52*, 411–415.

Wilson, B., & McCrary, J. (1996). The effect of instruction on music educators' attitudes toward students with disabilities. *Journal of Research in Music Education, 44*, 26–33.

Zera, D. A., & Seitsinger, R. M. (2000). The oppression of inclusion. *Educational Horizons, 79*(1), 16–18.

4

RESEARCH ON MAINSTREAMING: IMPLICATIONS FOR MUSIC THERAPISTS

Alice-Ann Darrow
Cynthia M. Colwell
Jihyun Kim

Introduction

FROM the beginning of mainstreaming until today, the music classroom has served as a common placement for students with disabilities. Music educators were pioneers in the movement to integrate students with disabilities into the regular classroom (Atterbury, 1990; Graham & Beer, 1980). Too often, however, the placement of these students in the music classroom was due to administrators' misconception about the academic environment of the music classroom. They believed any student could be integrated into a class to sit and merely listen to music. Administrators were, and often still are (Goeke, 1994), unaware that music educators are responsible for implementing a structured curriculum that involves music reading, writing, creating, and listening as well as performance skills, such as singing and playing. In the early years of mainstreaming, music educators were given little or no training in adapting the music curriculum for students with disabilities. With the passage of the PL 94-142, the Education for All Handicapped Children Act in 1975, increasing numbers of students with disabilities were mainstreamed into the music classroom. As a result, academic specialists, such as music therapists, became more involved in school programs for students with disabilities.

The U.S. Department of Education has reported that over 70% of the students with disabilities in this country receive their instruction in the regular classroom (United States Department of Education, 1994). Part-time placement in the regular classroom was the most common until the recent movement toward the total integration of students with disabilities (Rodriguez & Tompkins, 1994). With this movement came the term *inclusion*. The National Association of State Boards of Education (1992) provides the following definition:

> Inclusion . . . means that students attend their home school with their age and grade peers. It requires that the proportion of students labeled for special services is relatively uniform for all of the schools within a particular school district, and that this ratio reflects the proportion of people with disabilities in society at large. Included students are not isolated into special classes or wings within the school. To the maximum extent possible, included students receive their in-school educational services in the general education classroom with appropriate in-class support. (p. 12)

Inclusive schools also adopt the zero rejection principle—no student can be denied access to academic programs on the basis of disability. Consequently, there has been increased enrollment of students with severe disabilities, such as those with autism and traumatic brain injuries, in regular music classes. The inclusion of these students has required special skills on the part of music educators. The total inclusion of students with disabilities into music classrooms has meant that music educators must be prepared to create a learning environment that varies with the needs and abilities of their students. Most pre-service music educators now receive some preparation regarding the characteristics and general education of students with disabilities. In most cases, however, this preparation does not include actual teaching experiences with students who have various disabilities or information regarding systematic and viable instructional strategies that facilitate the success of all students in a mainstreamed environment (Gfeller, Darrow, & Hedden, 1990).

As a result of the inclusion movement and the common placement of students with disabilities into regular music programs, the role of the music therapist has been redefined in many schools. As a part of their newly defined role, the school music therapist is often called upon to team teach with or to serve as a consultant to music educators. Though some school music therapists still work with students who have severe disabilities in self-contained classrooms, most work with students in multi-level groupings. Given the educational environment, the music therapist must be aware of and sensitive to instructional objectives that address not only therapeutic goals, but also the musical development of students with disabilities. Fortunately, many music therapy and music education goals overlap and both types of goals can often be met through similar classroom activities. Music therapists, along with other specialists, have been able to provide valuable information regarding the modification of materials and methodology often needed to support individual students in the mainstreamed music classroom.

The rapid movement toward inclusion has required that music therapists increase their knowledge of mainstreaming practices. There is a great deal that music therapists can learn from the related research literature. Mainstreaming research, both in the general classroom and in the music classroom, will be reviewed with implications given for music therapists. The final section of the chapter will include a bibliography of research related to students with specific communication, cognitive, sensory, physical, and social disabilities.

Mainstreaming Research in General Education

Mainstreaming is a difficult concept to study empirically. There are numerous problems that can complicate any comparative field investigation in education: finding equivalent teachers and students, eliminating teacher biases, maintaining equal school resources, changing services within the schools, and standardizing definitions between sites (Reynolds & Birch, 1988). There are several additional problems that make research in the specific area of mainstreaming difficult:

1. Lack of a valid source of measurement for effective mainstreaming;
2. The variety of disabilities often represented by single terms such as *disabled, handicapped, special,* or *exceptional*;
3. The variety of mainstreamed class configurations (ranging from few students with one disability to many students with various disabilities);
4. Lack of consensus regarding appropriate instructional objectives for the mainstreamed classroom;
5. Varying degrees of support services for educators in the mainstreamed classroom; and
6. Lack of specific information regarding the degree to which teacher attitude and preparation influence the effectiveness of mainstreaming. (Darrow, 1990, p. 35)

Despite these methodological problems, a number of researchers have attempted to examine mainstreaming practices and efficacy. The following research studies were selected for review because they (a) address problems of the mainstreamed classroom, (b) represent quality research, and (c) are applicable to both music therapy and music education. The research is organized by the four most commonly identified problems related to mainstreaming (Salend, 1994):

Varied Abilities in Mainstreamed Classes
Grading Mainstreamed Students
Teacher/Student Attitudes toward Mainstreamed Students
Efficacy of the Mainstreamed Setting

Varied Abilities in the Mainstream Classroom

One of the common complaints made by teachers of many mainstreamed classrooms is that the abilities of their students are too varied; consequently, group instruction is extremely difficult. Researchers have offered opposing opinions regarding the heterogeneous and homogeneous grouping of students for instructional purposes (Evertson, Sanford, & Emmer, 1981; Stallings, 1985). Slavin's (1987) review of the literature indicated that the differential use of both heterogeneous and homogeneous grouping could be beneficial for students as well as teachers. A study by Swank, Taylor, Brady, Cooley, and Freiberg (1989) highlighted the trade-offs in both kinds of classrooms. These researchers found that mainstreamed students exhibited fewer behavioral problems and spent more time on-task and with learning materials in heterogeneous classes; teachers, however, provided more direct and active instruction in homogeneous classes. One of the benefits of heterogeneous student grouping is the provision of peer models and the presence of peer pressure to conform. One of the benefits of homogeneous grouping of students, however, is that teachers can implement group lessons more easily. Espin, Deno, and Albayrak-Kaymak (1998) found that teachers in more homogeneous classrooms tended to design individualized program goals and objectives for the academic achievement of students with special needs. They more easily identify long-range goals and used more varied information about the skills currently owned by those students. Smaller homogeneous classrooms played a role as one of the prerequisites to implementing group lessons more with ease (Kostland, Wilkinson, & Briggs, 1997).

Compared to the homogeneous classroom, it is not surprising that teachers in heterogeneous classrooms face instructional challenges in satisfying the needs of students with varied levels of ability. However, despite those challenges in individualizing the instruction, it is believed that the heterogeneous grouping of students may maximize the academic and interpersonal benefits of implementing adaptive instructional strategies.

Effectively grouping students within a mainstreaming classroom may facilitate implementation of instruction as well as satisfy students' academic and social needs. Vaughn, Hughes, Moody, and Elbaum (2001) reviewed instructional grouping practices for students with learning disabilities and consequently provided important implications for several types of grouping patterns. They suggested that during reading instruction, the balanced use of grouping practices may help teachers meet the needs of all students, those with and without disabilities. These findings perhaps have implications for music reading as well.

Students in music programs are commonly placed in performing groups on the basis of their musical ability; hence, groups are titled beginning band, concert band, symphonic band, etc. Many mainstreamed students, because of physical or cognitive disabilities, are often difficult to place in ability-assigned groups. According to Vaughn et al. (2001), ability grouping may not be the utmost solution due to the following factors: (a) it may reduce self-esteem and motivation, (b) it may restrain friendship choices, and (c) it may increase the gap between the students with higher and lower levels of ability. Therefore, the research would suggest that there are advantages to placing students of varying abilities in the same group. The challenge for the music teacher or music therapist is to find ways of providing individualized or small group instruction.

Small group instruction is one grouping method that benefits students by allowing more opportunities to respond, and to garner feedback from other students and their teacher (Vaughn et al., 2001). Waldron and Van Zandt Allen (1999) suggest several tips for designing successful small group instruction:

1. Assign students with special needs to work with students of varying abilities who have a positive attitude toward those students.
2. Include only one student with special needs per group.

3. In the beginning of group work, teach students the way to work collaboratively before advancing to cooperative learning groups.
4. Form a group that remains together for certain periods of time (i.e., several weeks) to enhance the benefits for students with special needs, rather than constructing new groups for each project.
5. Provide the students with special needs with a sufficient preview of what will occur in class and the role of each student within his or her groups.
6. Provide additional environmental adaptations for students with physical disabilities.

A good mainstreaming teacher will also find ways to maximize the benefits of peer modeling, peer pressure, peer tutors, and cross-age tutors. Utley, Mortweet, and Greenwood (1997) state that peer-mediated instruction and interventions (PMII) bring positive outcomes not only in students' basic academic skills, but also in their interpersonal relationships and motivation levels. Maheady, Harper, and Mallette (2001) describe how different types of peer-mediated instruction and interventions have been utilized for improving the academic and behavioral outcomes for students with mild disabilities. They described two particular peer teaching methods, CSTS (Classwide Student Tutoring System) and NHT (Numbered Heads Together), and emphasized the positive effects of these two peer teaching programs on academic and behavioral outcomes for the students with mild disabilities.

Several studies suggest that students with disabilities should be provided an opportunity to be tutors as well as tutees, especially in the cross-age tutoring system (Vaughn et al., 2001; Waldron & Van Zandt Allen, 1999). Students with disabilities may gain greater benefits when they serve as tutors (Waldron & Van Zandt Allen, 1999). Kamps, Dugan, Potucek, and Collins (1999) examined the effect of a peer network system on the social interaction among students with autism and general education students. In their study, the researchers used older students with autism and typically developing students as tutors for first-grade students with academic deficiency in sight word recognition. The results indicated that the peer-network system not only increased the social interaction of students with autism, but also resulted in academic gains for the first-grade students. In addition, the students with autism viewed themselves as contributors to the academic gains of the first grade students, rather than perceiving themselves as in need of help.

In a study utilizing music and cross-age tutors, Madsen, Smith, and Feeman (1988) were concerned with tutees' academic success as well as tutors' improved self-esteem. In their study, older special education students with behavioral problems served as tutors for young academically deficient kindergartners. Results indicated positive gains for both tutors and tutees. The data from this study indicate several important and valuable strategies for music teachers and therapists working in the mainstreamed classroom:

1. Set the occasion for students to feel good about themselves. Students with behavioral problems are rarely in a position to receive recognition for good deeds and, hence, to feel good about themselves. Since these opportunities for recognition seldom occur by chance, they must be set up by the music teacher or therapist.
2. Make sure students with disabilities are given the opportunity to be tutors as well as to be tutored. Students with disabilities, like all other students, need to learn to assist others as well as to receive assistance. They also need to be recognized for their abilities rather than only for their disabilities.
3. Music serves as a valuable contingency for student participation, task completion, and as a teaching aid for academic work. Music's flexibility as well as its popular appeal make it a useful tool for the mainstreamed classroom.

Grading Mainstreamed Students

School music therapists are working in an educational environment that often requires them to assign grades to students for music learning and participation. Assigning grades in music is difficult for a number of reasons. The music therapist is usually working with many more students than the average classroom teacher; therefore, assessment and record keeping require a considerable amount of time. Music therapists must also decide if students are to be evaluated on the basis of musical skill, academic progress, effort, conduct, attendance, or any other number of related factors. If grades are determined by a combination of the aforementioned factors, each factor must represent a percentage of the final grade. Most music therapists have been trained to administer ongoing assessments of their students' progress; assigning grades, however, is a separate issue. Music therapists often feel uncomfortable assigning grades solely on the basis of musical or academic progress.

Researchers have found that music educators often have different educational objectives and grading practices for students with disabilities from those they have for students without disabilities (Frisque, Niebur, & Humphreys, 1994; Gfeller et al., 1990). Music therapists, like teachers, are often concerned about whether they should alter their established grading practices for students with disabilities. According to some authors (Bradley & Calvin, 1998; Christiansen & Vogel, 1998), many teachers question the effectiveness of alternative grading practices for the following reasons: (a) these adaptations may decrease the academic standards for all students, (b) they may violate the grading policies, and (c) it is not fair to students without disabilities. The issue of fairness in grading practice is one of great concern to students without disabilities. A study by Bursuck, Munk, and Olson (1999) revealed that students without disabilities often view alternative grading practices as unfair in that: (a) grading systems should be applied equally to every student, without exception, and (b) alternate grading practices may decrease the motivation of students with high achievement. Negative perceptions regarding alternative grading may influence teachers' decision to reject such grading practices (Bursuck et al., 1999).

Grading issues often receive little attention until students with disabilities are integrated into the general classroom (Lindsey, Burns, & Guthrie, 1984). A number of recent studies have addressed some of the aspects of grading (Donahue & Zigmond, 1990; Valdes, Williamson, & Wagner, 1990; Zigmond, Levin, & Laurie, 1985). These descriptive studies indicate that most mainstreamed students received lower grades and were not graded on the same criteria as their peers. There has been increasing demand to develop a grading system that integrates all students fully in large-scale assessments (Turner, Baldwin, Kleinert, & Kearns, 2000). A number of recent studies address adaptations in grading practice and provide helpful teacher strategies for making grading adaptations benefit all students (Bradley & Calvin, 1998; Elliott, Kratochwill, & Schulte, 1998; Erickson, Ysseldyke, Thurlow, & Elliott, 1998). Testing accommodations and alternate assessments are strategies that can be used to increase the participation of students with disabilities in assessments. Testing accommodations refer to alterations in presentation and response formats, timing or scheduling of tests, and setting of tests.

Elliott and colleagues (1998) emphasized the effectiveness of the Assessment Accommodation Checklist (AAC) designed to help teachers provide fair and effective assessment accommodations for students. These accommodations include provision of assistance prior to or during the assessment, extra testing time in scheduling, adaptations in testing environments, assessment directions, and changes in test format and content (Elliott et al., 1998). The alternate assessment system is designed for students whose disabilities are categorized as inappropriate for full inclusion in the large-scale assessments. Erickson and colleagues (1998) suggest several other models of alternate assessments such as performance task, portfolio development, information acquired from videotape, interviews, or direct observations. In addition, Bradley and Calvin (1998) provide several types of current grading practices that include letter and number grades, progress checklist, contracts, work samples, curriculum-based assessments, multiple grading, portfolio, and rubrics.

Several authors have reported on inclusive assessment programs being used in the state of Kentucky (Kearns, Kleinert, Clayton, Burdge, & Williams, 1998; Kleinert, Kennedy, & Kearns, 1999). According to Kearns and colleagues, the inclusive assessment system in Kentucky consists of three methods: (a) participation of students with mild disabilities in regular assessment without individualized accommodations; (b) participation of other students with disabilities in regular assessment with individualized accommodations; and (c) participation of students with severe disabilities in alternate assessment, such as alternate portfolio. Kleinert, Kennedy, and Kearns (1999) surveyed teachers of students assessed using alternate portfolio and found that teachers viewed the state's assessment system as beneficial not only for students' outcomes, but also for classroom programming.

There is a considerable body of research that deals with the nondiscriminatory assessment of students with disabilities, primarily for the purpose of determining service delivery (Bailey & Harbin, 1980; Fuchs & Fuchs, 1986; McLoughlin & Lewis, 1990; Marston & Magnusson, 1985). This research is related to intelligence testing, achievement testing, and disability diagnosis (Lewis & Doorlag, 1991). From this body of research and other sources related to best practices (Bradley & Calvin, 1998; Gearheart, Weishahn, & Gearheart, 1992; Salend & Duhaney, 2002; Smith, Polloway, Patton, & Dowdy, 1995), the following suggestions for grading students with disabilities are offered:

1. Consider brief narrative reports on students' progress rather than the assignment of letter grades.
2. Utilize cooperative assignment grades (e.g., grades for group compositions).
3. Investigate alternative procedures for evaluating assignments (e.g., singing a piece rather than playing it, or identifying the piece by name and composer).
4. Emphasize effort or the acquisition of new skills as the basis for grades.
5. Consider a point system for which students are offered or can self-select alternative options for earning points that determine their final grade.
6. Allow for alternative assignments related to music objectives (e.g., looking up information on the internet about Mozart as an alternative to playing his music).
7. Provide students with an opportunity to grade themselves and peers, especially in group activities.
8. Utilize pass/fail systems where minimum course competencies are specified.
9. Contract grading where students and teachers agree on a contract outlining the learning objectives, quality of the product, and the procedures for assessment.
10. Level grading where a numeric subscript indicates the level of difficulty at which the students' grades are based.

A recent music study by Johnson and Darrow (1997) found that students are also aware of some of the logistical problems associated with mainstreaming, such as assigning grades. Subjects in their study were positive about the inclusion of students with disabilities in their band programs; however, when subjects were presented statements such as, "Students with disabilities should have to audition like other students who want to be in band," or "Students with disabilities should be graded like other students," their views regarding mainstreaming became less clear. Students, like many teachers, may be in agreement regarding the philosophy underlying mainstreaming, but they are often bewildered when the philosophy is to be reflected in grade or chair (as in orchestra or band) assignments. The results of the Johnson and Darrow study suggest that inclusion may be like many other issues wherein people may agree on the idea but disagree, or are perhaps confused, regarding methods of implementation. No experimental studies could be found that explored the effects of differential grading on student achievement. Though such studies would be useful, the inherent ethical issues involved make such research difficult to carry out.

Teacher/Student Attitudes toward Mainstreamed Students

Teachers' and students' attitudes affect their behaviors; therefore, their attitudes toward mainstreaming have important implications for the classroom interactions of students with disabilities. One of the arguments against mainstreaming is that teachers and students often have negative attitudes toward mainstreaming; consequently, students with disabilities are often isolated and stigmatized. Early studies indicated that, indeed, many teachers were opposed to mainstreaming (Baker & Gottlieb, 1980; Stephens & Braun, 1980) and that students without disabilities often had negative attitudes toward classmates with disabilities (Altman, 1981; Horne, 1985). Fortunately, more recent research indicates that these attitudes are changing (Larrivee & Horne, 1991; Williams, Fox, Thousand, & Fox, 1990).

Attitudes toward students with disabilities are often affected by information. Various studies have examined the effect of information on subjects' attitude toward students with disabilities (Fiedler & Simpson, 1987; Handlers & Austin, 1980; Simpson, 1980). The findings of these studies indicate that information dispels misconceptions, clarifies misunderstandings, and decreases fears; consequently, attitudes improve. Studies concerned with improving attitudes toward disabled students have also indicated the feasibility of facilitating acceptance through social interaction (Amsel & Fichen, 1988) and personal conversations (Evans, 1976).

Attitudes toward students with disabilities can be affected by other variables such as a student's type and/or degree of disability, an individual's previous experience with a person who has a disability, and an individual's gender. Several recent studies have explored the relationship between these variables and teachers' or students' attitudes toward students with disabilities (Avramidis, Bayliss, & Burden, 2000; Cook, 2001; Ferguson, 1998; Hodge & Jansma, 2000). The findings of these studies include: (a) teachers' perceptions regarding the severity of a student's disabilities may affect their attitudes toward the student, (b) certain types of disabilities such as behavior and/or emotional difficulties may negatively influence teachers' attitudes more than other types of disabilities, (c) teachers or students who have previous experience interacting with students with disabilities show more positive attitudes (e.g., students who have participated in peer tutoring programs or other services for students with disabilities), and (d) female teachers or students show more positive attitudes toward students with disabilities than male teachers or students. According to these studies, attitudes toward students with disabilities may be improved by increasing: knowledge about different types of disabilities, teacher training on behavior management, experiences with students who have disabilities, and ongoing collaboration with other teachers involved in inclusion.

Teachers' effectiveness or perceptions of teacher-efficacy may be another factor that influences attitudes toward mainstreaming students with disabilities. Brownell and Pajares (1999) found that teachers who perceived themselves as competent in mainstreaming students showed more positive attitudes in including those students in their general classrooms. In a survey of high school general education teachers, Soodak, Podell, and Lehman (1998) found that teachers with a low sense of teaching efficacy tended to be less receptive to inclusion. The researchers suggested that collaboration with supportive personnel may be an effective strategy to increase teachers' sense of self-efficacy, which in turn may enhance teachers' positive responses toward students with disabilities. The findings of a study by Treder, Morse, and Ferron (2000) confirmed that effective teachers tend to be more willing to include students with disabilities than other teachers.

Music therapists can serve as positive role models to teachers. Their behaviors must reflect the attitude that all students are accepted and valued. Music therapists' attitudes toward mainstreaming play an important role in determining the success or failure of mainstreaming. Teaching students to appreciate and accept individual differences can also facilitate the successful mainstreaming of students with disabilities (Simpson, 1980). Research has indicated that when negative attitudes exist, positive attitudes can be fostered through a variety of attitude change strategies (Conway & Gow, 1988; Donaldson, 1980). Attitude change strategies have four basic goals: (a) to provide information about disabilities, (b) to increase students' and teachers' comfort level with students who have disabilities, (c) to foster empathy, and (d) to facilitate accepting behavior toward people with disabilities (Barnes, Berrigan, & Biklen, 1978, p. 19).

Disability simulation is one type of strategy to teach positive attitudes toward students with a disability. Jones, Sowell, Jones, and Butler (1981) found that a training program that included simulations to sensitize students to the needs and experiences of others with disabilities led to an increase in positive attitudes toward persons with disabilities. Simulation experiences introduce others to the problems encountered by individuals with disabilities and give insight into the reactions of other individuals who do not have disabilities. Clore and Jeffrey (1972) noted that attitude changes via disability simulations were long lasting.

A second strategy is to introduce to students highly successful individuals who have disabilities. Lazar, Gensley, and Orpet (1971) found that they could promote positive attitudes toward individuals with disabilities by instituting an attitude change program that included a unit on individuals with disabilities who have made significant contributions to society. Two examples of well-known and respected musicians with disabilities are Itzak Perlman and Ray Charles. It is important for students to be aware that individuals with disabilities often have extraordinary abilities.

Inviting guest speakers, showing films, and reading books (Greenbaum, Varas, & Markel, 1980; Litton, Banbury, & Harris, 1980) are additional ways in which students can learn about individuals with disabilities. Leung (1980) found that a literature program consisting of 10 short stories and discussions concerning individuals with disabilities increased the number of positive and neutral interactions among mainstreamed students and their regular classroom teachers and peers, while the number of negative interactions decreased. Salend and Moe (1983) compared the effects of two interventions on student attitudes: students were exposed to books about disabilities (a) by listening to the teacher reading them; and (b) by listening to the books with the teacher highlighting the main points to be learned through discussion, simulations, and explanations. The second intervention, which combined books and activities, resulted in significant changes in student attitudes toward persons with a disability.

Providing students and teachers with information on disabilities often promotes understanding. Information usually includes the characteristics and causes of disabilities, advocacy, and an awareness of negative attitudes and stereotypes directed toward individual disabilities (Simpson, 1980). Maras and Brown (2000) suggest caution when providing information since labeling or categorizing disabilities can imply stereotypes and, consequently, can result in negative attitudes toward students with disabilities. Additional research has indicated that other successful strategies, besides the provision of information, include reverse mainstreaming (McCann, Semmel, & Nevin, 1985), group discussions (Gottlieb, 1980), and continued communication between students and teachers without disabilities and those with disabilities (Salend & Knops, 1984).

Efficacy of the Mainstreamed Setting

An important body of research in the field of mainstreaming is related to the academic efficacy of the mainstreamed setting. A recent analysis of the mainstreaming literature indicates that much less attention has been given to the evaluation of student performance than to the assessment of teacher and student attitudes (Miller, Fullmer, & Walls, 1996). While teacher opinions regarding mainstreaming strongly influence practice (Smith et al., 1995), there is also research that has indicated a strong relationship between teachers' ratings of academic success and the social acceptance of students with disabilities as well as those students without disabilities (Roberts & Zubrick, 1993). As a result of their analysis of the mainstreaming literature, Miller et al. (1996) suggest greater attention be given to research that examines student academic achievement as well as specific instructional strategies.

Early efficacy studies were conducted by Dunn (1968), who reported data indicating damaging implications for segregated education. Based upon his data, Dunn concluded that students with mental retardation who were educated in special classes achieved no better academically than their peers educated in regular classrooms; and that in either setting, these students did not work up to their mental capacity. Furthermore, the higher their intellectual functioning, the less students liked special placements and the lower their self esteem. Based upon Dunn's early studies and others reviewed by Smith, Price, and Marsh (1986), researchers began to examine the efficacy of mainstreamed settings for students with disabilities.

No research has conclusively provided justification for serving students solely through mainstreamed programs; however, much of the work that has been done indicates that students do as well or better in integrated settings than they do in self-contained classrooms or other segregated settings. Some researchers have found that mainstreamed students' academic performance is improved by placement in the regular classroom and that their social interactions in the regular classroom were no different from the social interactions of their peers without disabilities (Madden & Slavin, 1983; Ray, 1986). An analysis of previous literature was conducted by Hunt and Goetz (1997) for the purpose of investigating the programs, practices, and outcomes for students with disabilities. Their analysis revealed that including students with disabilities did not negatively affect academic performances compared to groups that did not include students with disabilities. Moreover, it is believed that students with disabilities may achieve positive academic outcomes in inclusive settings (Hunt & Goetz, 1997). The inclusion of students with disabilities may affect not only their own achievements, but also the achievements of students without disabilities. Several studies have been concerned with the effect of inclusion on students both with and without disabilities. Stevens and Slavin (1991) analyzed studies that compared students with and without disabilities in achievement when cooperative learning was used in the classroom. They concluded that when cooperative learning instructional processes include individual accountability and group rewards, they are likely to have a positive effect on the achievement of students with and without disabilities.

Tapasak and Walther-Thomas (1999) evaluated the self-perceptions of academic and social competence of students with disabilities as well as those without disabilities in inclusive classrooms. The results of their study indicated that both students with and without disabilities at the primary level in inclusive classrooms showed significant increases in self-perceptions of academic and social competence. However, students without disabilities showed greater self-perception in academic competence than students with disabilities in older student groups. Salend and Duhaney (1999) reviewed studies related to the effect of inclusion programs for students with and without disabilities and their educators. Analyzing these studies led the researchers to conclude: (a) the effect on the academic outcomes of students with disabilities is varied depending on variables such as the quality of inclusive education programs and the amount of accommodations given to the academic and social needs of the students with disabilities; and (b) the students without disabilities received benefits from the inclusive program, including increased acceptance, understanding of individual differences, and development of friendships with students with disabilities. Peltier (1997), in his analysis of previous studies, listed several benefits from relationships between students with and without disabilities such as: (a) increased self cognition, (b) increased self-concept, and (c) increased responsiveness toward the needs of other students. These researchers (Salend & Duhaney, Peltier) were also concerned with the negative effect of inclusion, especially on the academic achievements of students without disabilities. They concluded that inclusive education has no negative effect on the academic achievement of students without disabilities. The data reported in these particular studies indicate four important implications for music therapists and teachers working with students of varied abilities:

1. Students must be accountable for their own work, implying that work must also be individualized to meet the needs of varying academic abilities.
2. Group rewards, given for the academic accomplishments of students with disabilities, foster an investment in classroom performance, and consequently, result in cooperation and shared learning.
3. Facilitating the friendships between students with and without disabilities may enhance cooperation and shared learning among these students.
4. The collaborative efforts of music therapists and music educators are required in developing the curriculum, solving problems, and, consequently, meeting the needs of all students.

In several earlier studies (Calhoun & Elliot, 1977; Guerin & Szatlocky, 1974; Haring & Krug, 1975; Macy & Carter, 1978) as well as later studies (Freeman & Alkin, 2000; Leinhardt, 1980; Madden & Slavin, 1983; Miller, Fullmer, & Walls, 1996; Wang & Birch, 1984), researchers found that students placed in mainstreamed settings showed significantly greater gains in achievement than their counterparts educated in self-contained special education classes. Wang, Anderson, and Bram (1985) performed a meta-analysis of 50 studies comparing regular and special education placements and found that, across all types of disabilities, results indicated not only that the academic and social performance of students with special needs in mainstreamed settings was superior to those students educated in special classes, but also that the students who were mainstreamed on a full-time basis performed better than their peers who were mainstreamed on a part-time basis. In their research, Wang et al. also examined program characteristics that are related to the effectiveness mainstreaming. They found that features commonly associated with successful mainstreaming programs were:

1. ongoing assessment of students' performance,
2. adaptive instructional strategies and materials,
3. individualized instruction,
4. cooperative learning arrangements,
5. student self-management strategies, and
6. use of consultation and instructional teaming.

These features of effective mainstreaming programs have important implications for music therapists working in schools. Music therapists can assist in the implementation of these identified characteristics by:

1. being knowledgeable about disability related assessment issues and advising music educators accordingly;
2. assisting music educators in the actual assessment of students with disabilities;
3. advising music educators regarding appropriate instructional strategies, adaptive technology, instructional materials, and musical instruments;
4. providing individualized instruction for students with disabilities when needed;
5. supervising cooperative learning arrangements in the music classroom;
6. devising and helping to implement student self-management strategies; and, most important,
7. serving as consultants to music educators and as members of instructional teams in the classroom.

There are researchers who have found no differences between students placed in segregated settings versus mainstreamed settings (Budoff & Gottlieb, 1976; Walker, 1974) or found that mainstreamed settings have not been effective placements for students with disabilities (Gottlieb, 1981; Gresham, 1982). Daane, Beirne-Smith, and Latham (2000) surveyed administrators, and general and special education teachers in order to investigate their perceptions toward inclusive education. The survey revealed that all three groups expressed their concerns about the low academic achievement of students with disabilities in mainstreamed settings. Some research data indicate that students with specific disabilities, such as those with learning disabilities and behavior disorders, perform better in the self-contained classroom (Carlberg & Kavale, 1980). Other researchers have found data that indicate students with even mild mental retardation need support in the regular classroom and that they are often less popular than their peers (Bryan & Bryan, 1978; Siperstein, Bopp, & Bak, 1978; Myers, 1976). Some professionals in the field of special education contend, however, that many of the problems associated with mainstreaming in these early studies have now been resolved (Reynolds & Birch, 1988). Zigler and Muenchow (1979) noted that school programs in the early years of PL 94-142 implemented the "least expensive" rather than the "least restrictive" alternative for students with disabilities. Several researchers have found that inconsistent findings in efficacy studies are also a result of the schools' failure to implement mainstreaming appropriately (Stainback, Stainback, Courtnage, & Jaben, 1985). Such failures in implementing appropriate mainstreaming were apparently from the lack of technical support, lack of information about individual needs, lack of a training program for collaboration, lack of trained individuals to provide support, and, finally, lack of financial support (Daane, Beirne-Smith, & Latham, 2000; Gibb, Allred, Ingram, Young, & Egan, 1999).

While the research on the efficacy of mainstreaming has reported varied results, there are substantial data to support the notion that students with disabilities can be successful in the music classroom. The key is for music therapists and music educators to work together to structure the classroom such that all students be successful, musically and personally. The work of several researchers indicate that collaboration, sharing expertise, and sharing resources is necessary for the successful inclusion of students with disabilities (Bauwens, Hourcade, & Friend, 1989; Idol & West, 1991). Most importantly though, music therapists and music educators must share a common goal that all students are accepted as individuals and that all students deserve the opportunity to have music as a part of their education.

Mainstreaming Research in Music Education

Mainstreaming in music education has a long and varied history. Music educators were integrating students with disabilities into the music classroom long before the term "mainstreaming" came into use. Research might indicate, however, that our experience with mainstreaming has not necessarily served us well. Music educators have expressed, with considerable consistency over the years, serious concerns regarding the mainstreaming of students with disabilities into the music classroom.

A recent issue of the *Music Educators Journal* (Damer, 2001b) was devoted to issues that music teachers face when working in inclusive classrooms. Damer (2001a) provided a succinct and clear overview of the laws from the 1975, PL 94-142 through to the current amendments of the original 1990, PL 101-476. Adamek (2001) addressed terminology related to the implementation of these laws: *normalization, partial participation, interdependence,* and *individuality;* and provided teachers with ideas for adaptations in six areas: participation level, difficulty level, level of support, input, output, and alternative goals. Bernstorf (2001) focused her attention on working with paraprofessionals and guided the music teacher on the different types of paras and cited specific ways in which they can be helpful in the music setting. In this special issue (Zdzinski, 2001) and in a later *MEJ* issue that same year (VanWeelden, 2001), two educators addressed inclusion at the secondary level. Zdzinski made adaptation suggestions in the following areas in an effort to encourage instrumental ensemble directors to include special learners: musical instruments, social environment, parental involvement, music, teaching techniques, and evaluation techniques. In a similar fashion, VanWeelden offered tips for success for choral music educators including planning ahead, classroom set-up, rehearsal modifications, promoting quality singing, and dealing with disruptions.

Although not research-based, this dedication of an entire issue of the *Music Educators Journal* to the issue of inclusive practices in music education sheds light on the fact that teachers remain concerned about this educational movement. A comprehensive article based on the special education research on mainstreaming and inclusion practices details 11 principles appropriate for the inclusive music classroom which can provide the framework for developing, selecting, adapting, implementing, and evaluating lessons and activities (Jellison, 1992). The author lists quality of life as the overarching principle followed by normalization; social valorization; natural proportion; transition; functional value; chronological age appropriateness; individual achievement and choice; participation and partial participation; advocacy, social interaction, and friendship; and collaboration and support systems. In Part 2 of the manuscript, Jellison gives suggestions for seven typical activities (i.e., small group participation) in the music classroom citing the underlying principles as support. In the final section of the manuscript, the author provides a series of questions that the music teacher can review to determine if the application of these principles is being implemented successfully.

Over 25 years have passed since the implementation of PL 94-142. Thousands of students with disabilities have passed through music classrooms. It is time to address some of the problems with mainstreaming that still exist for music educators. The key to solving these problems may be through the collaborative research efforts of music therapists and music educators. Music therapists and music educators are likely candidates for collaboration. Idol and West (1991) explain that "educational collaboration is an interactive relationship first, then a technique or vehicle for change . . . a tool for problem solving" (p. 87).

Professionals in the field of music education and music therapy have different areas of expertise. Music educators are well versed in music curricular issues and the musical development of children. Music therapists are especially knowledgeable about functional music as well as instructional issues and adaptive strategies related to persons with disabilities. The educational preparation of music therapists includes much of the information that music educators need to successfully integrate students with disabilities into the mainstreamed classroom. Their professional preparation includes information related to various disabilities, adaptive instructional strategies, assistive technology, and adapted music materials. Music therapists can provide valuable assistance to music educators regarding the instruction of students with disabilities.

Another key to identifying and solving mainstreaming problems is through research. Collaborative research between music therapists and music educators is perhaps our greatest hope for bringing students with disabilities into the mainstream of music education. The following review of related research should provide useful information concerning some of the problems related to mainstreaming in music education. The review includes studies that were published over the past 25 years in the music therapy and music education research journals. For those who wish to read additional research regarding mainstreaming, a number of doctoral dissertations and manuscripts have been written about mainstreaming practices in specific school districts or states (Brown, 1981; Damer, 1979; Gavin, 1983; Hawkins, 1991; Nocera, 1981; Shepard, 1993; Smaller, 1989; White, 1984). Most of the related studies that have been published in the major research journals are descriptive in nature. The descriptive research includes studies that describe the status of mainstreaming in music education, mainstreaming practices with students who have specific disabilities, and the attitudes of music teachers and students toward mainstreaming.

Status of Mainstreaming in Music Education

In examining the status of music mainstreaming, researchers have frequently found that music educators feel they are not adequately prepared to teach in the mainstreamed classroom (Atterbury, 1998; Frisque et al., 1994; Gfeller et al., 1990; Gilbert & Asmus, 1981). The ability to adapt educational procedures to the learning characteristics of students with disabilities often requires specialized educational preparation. Music educators' lack of preparation is unfortunate since research has indicated that disability-related information is positively related to teachers' attitudes and willingness to integrate students with disabilities into the regular classroom (Stephens & Braun, 1980).

In response to the research illustrating the concern of music educators about their level of preparation to teach in the mainstreamed classroom, two studies examined undergraduate programs. Heller (1995) surveyed music education teacher training institutions in the Great Lakes region of the United States. She sought to determine what training and experiences current methods instructors had received in their own undergraduate curriculum, how their programs are preparing preservice teachers to work in mainstreamed settings, and to discover what plans the faculty have for program change to address this issue. As suspected, those instructors with prior personal experience were more likely to include mainstreaming issues in their methods courses. Sixty-three percent of instructors reported that they did address mainstreaming topics in their courses, but only 40.8% had internal music requirements for working with special learners.

In a later study, Colwell and Thompson (2000) examined teacher training programs in music education to provide an overview of course offerings in Special Education available to Music Education majors. From each state, the catalogues from one Research Category 1, one state-funded regional, and one private institution were examined to determine (a) existence of a course in special education for music education majors, (b) department through which course was offered (nonmusic content or music content specific), (c) required or elective status of course, (d) course title and credit hours, and (e) reference to mainstreaming in music methods course descriptions. Results indicated that 74% of the schools did indeed have a course in special education available for music education majors with 86% of those schools requiring at least one course in the degree program. Sadly, only 30 of the 140 available courses were music content specific. Eighty-nine percent of the 110 noncontent courses were required, yet only 43% of the 30 content specific courses were required to graduate.

In an effort to improve undergraduate music education in the area of preparation for working with students with special needs, Hammel (2001) surveyed elementary music teachers and music methods instructors. She sought to identify what teacher competencies were essential for successful inclusion of students with special needs in the elementary general music class. Results of surveys, interviews, observations, and syllabi examination revealed 14 competencies deemed essential (i.e., acquaintance with various handicapping conditions, knowledge of IDEA, knowledge of appropriate materials for diverse learning abilities and styles, and ability to adapt material to provide for individual differences). The intent of the author is to use this information to develop a unit of study for implementation within the undergraduate teacher training program.

Three years after the implementation of Public Law 94-142 (The Education for All Handicapped Children Act), Gilbert and Asmus (1981) examined music educators' involvement with mainstreamed students, their knowledge of legislation concerning students with disabilities, and professional needs in developing and implementing music education programs for these students. A nationwide survey of general, instrumental, and vocal music educators revealed that 63% of the respondents were professionally involved with mainstreamed students, with significantly greater experience found at the elementary level. Despite this active involvement in mainstreaming, music educators expressed great concern regarding appropriate methods of teaching and evaluating these students. Music educators felt unprepared to meet the needs of special education students in the music classroom. Most states now require a college special education course for all education majors. Nevertheless, many music educators still feel that they are not effectively educating students with disabilities (Frisque et al., 1994).

Additional concerns were revealed in a later study by Atterbury (1986). A random sample of elementary music educators in the Southern Division of the Music Educators National Conference (MENC) responded that decisions and placements in elementary music were not supported by appropriate administrative assistance. Only 1% of the respondents actively participated in the development of mainstreamed students' Individualized Education Programs (IEPs). Furthermore, music educators said that they were often asked to accommodate too many mainstreamed students in the music classroom.

A later study of music educators in Kansas and Iowa (Gfeller et al., 1990) revealed little change in music educators' concerns regarding the mainstreamed classroom. More than 10 years after the passage of PL 94-142, music educators still reported an inadequate level of educational preparation and administrative support. Of greatest concern were the percentages of music educators who indicated mainstreamed students hindered the progress of other students (61%) and that special education students' music education needs would be better met in special classes (50%). A study by Frisque, Niebur, and Humphreys (1994) published nearly five years later, reported findings nearly identical to those of Gfeller et al. regarding the status of mainstreaming. Using the same survey, Atterbury (1998) compared the status of mainstreaming in Maine to that reported in the studies for Kansas, Iowa, and Arizona. Although many similarities exist, music teachers in Maine reported higher inclusion in the IEP process and more assistance from aides. These findings, along with those of Atterbury's earlier study (1986), would indicate that little has changed over the years since the implementation of PL 94-142.

In an effort to determine what adaptive teaching strategies for students with disabilities are used by elementary music teachers, Perkins (1996) examined a questionnaire completed by 166 teachers. After analyzing these results, she observed and interviewed four teachers to obtain further information. Strategies tended to fall in one of two categories, teaching behaviors strategies and pupil reinforcement strategies. Specific adaptations were noted when working with students with behavior disorders, communication disorders, hearing impairments, learning disabilities, mild mental retardation and attention deficit disorders.

Culton (1999) asked elementary music educators in Iowa to complete a needs assessment regarding instruction of children with special needs who were mainstreamed in their general music classes. Seventeen items were found to be of greatest importance to 75% or more of the educators. The author then completed a content analysis of teachers' editions of the three current elementary music textbook series in reference to these 17 items. Fourteen of these items each received less than 1% of the total coverage of the text material creating a discrepancy between what information teachers need and what is provided through the textbook series.

Using a qualitative approach, Darrow (1999) examined music educators' perceptions regarding the practice of full inclusion by conducting a descriptive analysis of their perceptions and comparing and contrasting choral, instrumental, and general music educators' perceptions. Teachers were asked four questions:

1. What are the critical issues related to the inclusion of students with severe disabilities in music classrooms?
2. How, if at all, has the inclusion of students with disabilities affected your teaching methodology?
3. How, if at all, has inclusion affected your students-those both with and without disabilities?
4. What advice would you offer to beginning music teachers who will be teaching in inclusive music classrooms?

In response to Question 1, teachers listed 13 critical issues among them the need for collaboration/ consultation with those knowledgeable about inclusion, information about specific students in their classroom, and increased time for class preparation. In response to Question 2, seven areas were addressed with use of paraprofessionals and peer partners mentioned most frequently. Teachers felt that the impact of inclusion was essentially positive, yet in response to Question 3, several made more references to benefits for those students without disabilities than for those with disabilities. Encouraging new teachers to ask for help and information and to involve all students in the inclusion process with the two most common areas of response to Question 4. Throughout the interview process, many mentioned music therapy as a possible setting for students with severe disabilities and suggested that music therapists could serve as consultants/ collaborators for music educators involved in inclusion.

A review of the research reveals a particularly critical issue faced by music educators in the mainstreamed music classroom. Researchers have found that music educators' wariness in mainstreaming students with disabilities has often been due to the perceived lack of support from administration regarding the placement of students with disabilities and the lack of planning time to prepare for the mainstreamed classroom (Gfeller et al., 1990). Smith (1989) found that music educators who experienced instructional support also enjoyed positive mainstreaming experiences, while those who had little support had negative mainstreaming experiences.

Mainstreaming Students With Specific Disabilities

One of the problems in mainstreaming survey studies has been the use of the global term *handicapped.* Researchers have found that music educators often feel that students with certain disabilities present significantly more problems than others (Atterbury, 1998; Frisque et al., 1994; Gfeller et al., 1990). The two groups of students with disabilities that have been identified as the most difficult to mainstream are those who have behavior problems or hearing losses (Frisque et al., 1994). Darrow and Gfeller (1991) examined the status of public school music instruction for deaf and hard-of-hearing students and the factors that contributed to the successful mainstreaming of these students in the regular music classroom. Results of their study revealed the following: (a) more than half of all deaf and hard-of-hearing students attend regular music classes; (b) of those students not mainstreamed, more than half receive no music education in the self-contained classroom or otherwise; (c) many music educators lack the specific educational preparation necessary for teaching deaf and hard-of-hearing students; (d) important instructional or administrative support is often not available; (e) several factors, such as lack of communication with other professionals, are obstructions to the successful mainstreaming of deaf and hard-of-hearing students; and (f) few music educators have the same objectives for deaf and hard-of-hearing students as they do for students with normal hearing. Respondents also reported that rhythm-based methodologies such as Orff were the most successful with their deaf and hard-of-hearing students.

In another disability-specific study, Thompson (1986) examined the activities of three general music classes into which students with mental retardation had been mainstreamed. It was found that the predominant activity in these music classes was listening to teachers talk. Singing was the second most frequent activity, followed by listening to recorded music. Additional observations revealed that students with mental retardation were significantly less successful than their peers, although no significant differences were found between the two groups in off-task behaviors.

Jellison and Gainer (1995) examined the behavior of one specific child with mild mental retardation throughout an entire school year in both music education and music therapy settings. The purpose of their study was to describe the child's participation over time, and to provide data to assist in the decision-making process regarding her educational program. Frequency and type of task performance were measured as well as overall time on-task. Results showed that rates for individual correct responses were higher in music therapy than in music education and that her on-task behavior was twice as high in the music therapy setting than in the music education setting. These findings, though seemingly discouraging in regard to mainstreaming, are carefully discussed in regard to the many factors that affect the classroom behaviors of children with mental retardation.

For children who exhibit atypical social behaviors, the music education classroom can serve as a place to learn, not only music skills, but also the socially correct behaviors of their typical peers. In another case study, Kostka (1993) compared selected behaviors (arm flapping, body swaying, and appropriate participation) of a student with autism in special education and regular music classes. Results indicated that all three behaviors were less frequent in regular music classes. When comparisons were made according to activity (singing, playing, moving, listening), he was most attentive during music listening. Results indicate that, for this child, mainstreaming had a positive effect on his appropriate social behaviors. These data corroborate the findings of other studies in general education (Swank et al., 1989).

Additional studies delineating the disability of mainstreamed students would be useful in defining specific problems in mainstreaming practices.

Attitudes Toward Mainstreaming

The degree to which music educators are successful in the mainstreamed classroom depends greatly upon their attitudes toward mainstreaming. Several researchers have examined the attitudes of future music educators and those already teaching in mainstreamed situations. Their data reveal the negative influence of inappropriate mainstreaming practices on the attitudes of teachers and students.

Only one year before the 1978 implementation of PL 94-142, Stuart and Gilbert (1977) reported that college music education majors were less willing to work with mainstream students than were music therapy majors or students majoring in both music education and music therapy. These findings were based on undergraduates' responses to videotaped sequences of disabled individuals. With the mainstreamed music classroom clearly in sight, this study identified an urgent need to improve music education majors' attitudes toward working with mainstreamed students.

Studies have also examined the attitudes of music educators and those of students in mainstreamed situations. White (1981/1982) was interested in possible differences in teacher attitudes toward the integration of mainstreamed students based on various factors, including years of teaching, educational level, previous experience with mainstreamed students, training in the areas of exceptionality, and area of teaching responsibility. None of these variables was found to contribute in any significant way to the positive or negative attitudes expressed by the respondents, a finding that corroborated an earlier study by Shehan (1977) and a later study by Gfeller, Darrow, and Hedden (1990). Although the majority of music teachers reported accepting or positive attitudes toward students with physical and cognitive disabilities, many respondents indicated that there should still be special schools for such students.

General music teachers in the state of Kansas completed the Teacher Integration Attitudes Questionnaire, which was designed to provide knowledge about their attitudes toward availability of funding, materials, and support personnel; willingness to attend workshops; social acceptability of children with disabilities; benefits of integration to children with and without disabilities; and the ability of the teachers to cope with children with disabilities (Sideridis & Chandler, 1995). Teachers felt that they did not have the skills to work with students with emotional and behavior disorders, multiple handicaps, and mental retardation. The questionnaire results indicated that teachers felt that students with emotional, behavior, and mental retardation were not well accepted by their peers but that students without disabilities and those with learning disabilities, orthopedic and multiple handicaps did benefit from integration. They expressed interest in attending workshops designed to help them become more effective teachers in this area and that although financial support (funding, materials) was lacking, support services were considered adequate.

Elliott and Sins (1981/1982) were concerned with the attitudes of music students toward their mainstreamed peers. Middle school students were surveyed regarding their opinions and attitudes toward the presence of mainstreamed peers in the music classroom. The survey was administered to 27 music classes in four Southern and Midwestern states. Students' attitudes were viewed as an indication of their acceptance of mainstreamed students. No differentiation was made among disability conditions. Examples of questions designed to assess respondents' attitudes regarding mainstreamed students were: "Do you think having handicapped students in music class is a good idea?" "Do you think you could learn more in music class if handicapped students were not present?"

Examples of questions designed to assess respondents' opinions (by asking them to state what they believed were their peers' opinions) concerning mainstreamed students were: "Do your classmates think having handicapped students in music class is a good idea?" "Do your classmates sometimes say that they wish that handicapped students would not be in class?"

Results indicated that: (a) only 58.5% of the students answered positively concerning their own attitudes toward integration of mainstreamed students into the music classroom; (b) females tended to be more positive regarding their own attitudes and when projecting the opinions of their classmates; and (c) students in segregated classes were more positive than those in integrated classes, indicating that hypothetical experiences with mainstreamed classmates were viewed more positively than real experiences with mainstreamed peers. An interesting though somewhat contradictory finding was that ninth graders made the largest percentage of positive responses and the sixth graders made the largest number of negative responses, indicating that over time, mainstreaming experiences may have a positive influence on the attitudes of students in the regular classroom.

Darrow and Johnson (1994) found similar results in their study of junior and senior high school music students' attitudes toward individuals with a disability. Junior high school students generally expressed a lower level of sensitivity toward people with disabilities than did the senior high school students. Females also demonstrated a greater acceptance of people with a disability than males in every disability subscale. Further results revealed a rank ordering of disabilities from the most to the least acceptable. The three most accepted disabilities for both gender groups and age groups were visible scars, heart condition, and deafness. The three least acceptable conditions were paralysis, AIDS, and blindness. Possible explanations for these data are that AIDS results in death and both blindness and paralysis have serious implications for personal mobility, which is highly valued, particularly by young people. Using the same attitude measure, Colwell (1998) examined the attitudes of students in four elementary school bands who would be attending the same junior high where an individual with a hearing impairment was to be mainstreamed into the concert band. Results were similar to Darrow and Johnson's study with females demonstrating a more positive attitude than males and with visible scars and heart condition the two most accepted disabilities, yet the elementary students attitudes were lower than both the junior high and senior high students in the previous study. With some contrast to Darrow and Johnson's results, the sixth graders listed visual impairment, amputation, and epilepsy as the three least acceptable conditions.

In an effort to explore whether past experiences in mainstreamed settings had an effect on the attitudes of junior and senior high students, Kostka (1999) examined their responses based on age, specific disabilities with which they had experience, and activities in which they were engaged. Students read scenarios about three students, one with a physical disability, one with an emotional disability, and one with a learning disability, and then answered three questions using a 1 to 7 continuum of agreement that targeted hypothetical situations for interaction. Results indicate that students who had previous experience with mainstreamed peers had more positive attitudes. Most preferred students with a learning disability, followed by physical disability, with emotional disability being least preferred. Students were most comfortable having students with disabilities in their music ensemble, followed by sharing a bus seat and then finally having them come to their homes.

Probably the most important aspect of attitudinal studies is the instrument with which attitude is assessed. In an early study, Stuart and Gilbert (1977) designed a videotape scale to measure attitude toward typical students and their musical behavior. Jellison (1985) developed an Acceptance Within Music Scale (AMS), a questionnaire designed to measure children's attitudes toward mainstreamed peers specific to music activities and to parallel existing items on a general Acceptance Scale (AS) with demonstrated validity for the measurement of children's attitudes toward mainstreamed peers. Both the AMS and the AS were administered to 136 public school children enrolled in Grades 3–6. Of the four dimensions assessed by the AMS, three were found to correspond very well with the Acceptance Scale. With an appropriate measurement device in place, the question arises as to possible interventions to improve the attitudes of teachers and students as well as their social interactions with mainstreamed students.

Experimental Research in Music Mainstreaming

The descriptive studies reviewed above have identified a number of problematic issues related to the mainstreamed music classroom. Very few experimental interventions have been implemented to examine the possibility of remediating these problems. The 1984 study by Jellison, Brooks, and Huck deserves recognition because it is quite possibly the first to address methods of improving attitudes and increasing positive interactions between students with and without disabilities in the music classroom. Jellison et al. examined the effect of three teaching conditions (large group, small cooperative group, and small cooperative group with a music listening contingency for cooperation) on the frequency of positive social interactions between students with and without disabilities in Grades 3–6. Pretest and posttest measures were also taken of students' general acceptance as well as acceptance of mainstreamed peers in the music classroom. Results indicated that the percentages of positive interactions were the highest for all grades under the small-group music contingency condition and the lowest under the large-group condition. Grades with the highest rates of positive interactions indicated a significant positive change for acceptance in music as well as general acceptance. This study provides valuable experimental data for music educators teaching in mainstreamed classrooms.

Humpal (1991) was also interested in the social interactions of young children with disabilities. The purpose of her study was to examine the effects of an integrated early childhood music program on social interactions of children with disabilities and their typical peers. A field test was conducted with 15 students (age 4) from a typical preschool, and 12 students (ages 3 to 5) with moderate levels of mental retardation from a county developmental center. The children came together once weekly at a preschool for integrated music sessions. For 15 sessions following the pretests, the music therapist employed specific strategies to foster interaction. A trend analysis indicated that interaction among the children increased following the music therapy intervention phases. It has often been stated that the mere placement of students with disabilities in the music classroom does not necessarily result in their acceptance by or in positive interactions with their peers (Elliott & Sins, 1981/1982; Sins, 1983). These two studies offer strategies that can be used to foster the social relationships of students with disabilities.

In addition to the descriptive information discussed in the previous section, Colwell (1998), in an effort to alter the initial attitudes of elementary band students toward mainstreaming, implemented four different treatments: (a) normal rehearsal; (b) videotape of individuals with disabilities participating in music activities; (c) videotape with disability label provided; and (d) videotape, label, and attribution of successful music participation. Results of a second administration of the attitude measure found no difference among the four treatments.

One of the common arguments against mainstreaming is that students with special needs demand excessive amounts of teacher time and, as a result, impede the education and progress of other students (Salend, 1994). This argument was examined in a study by Force (1983). She investigated the extent to which learning in a public school music classroom was affected by mainstreamed students. Students in mainstreamed and nonmainstreamed classrooms were pretested and posttested on their knowledge of rhythm instruments, recognition of instrument timbres, and dynamic levels. Pretest scores differed only on the sound identification subtest. Nonmainstreamed students tended to be more proficient at discriminating among instrument timbres. No significant differences were found between the two groups in pretest to posttest gains. Similar studies are needed to refute or substantiate teachers' beliefs regarding the effect of mainstreaming on students' musical achievement.

Another problem associated with mainstreaming, cited often in this review of the research, is music educators' lack of educational preparation. Smith (1987) addressed this problem by examining whether music education majors who had participated in a five-day unit on children with disabilities would demonstrate greater ability than would a control group (music education majors with no concentrated instruction on this topic) in generating adaptive teaching strategies in a mainstream context. Subjects were required to apply their knowledge of educational practices by generating instructional adaptations in response to videotaped teaching segments with four different types of students with disabilities (visual impairment, hearing loss, mental retardation, and emotional impairment). Testing took place three weeks after instruction of the experimental group. Smith found that students receiving classroom instruction on students with disabilities performed significantly better students in the control group on the total number of adaptive strategies generated. When analyzed by specific disabilities, both groups produced the smallest number of adaptations for working with behavior disorders. This is consistent with findings by Gfeller et al. (1990) and Frisque et al. (1994) that teachers find students with behavioral disorders as one of the most difficult groups to mainstream into the music classroom.

Providing information about individuals with disabilities has been shown to have an effect on the attitudes of graduate students in music education. In a one-month unit using discussion, assigned readings, videotapes of successful participation in music, and participation in an inclusive community chorus, Brittin (1995) targeted the topic of mainstreaming in the music classroom. Attitudes changed positively as a result of this unit of study. In a similar study (Brittin, 1997), less change was found with the author suggesting that the omission of participation in the inclusive chorus may have negatively affected the results.

Wilson and McCrary (1996) examined the attitudes of students participating in a graduate summer course in music education for special learners. The course included a legal overview, a survey of disabilities, appropriate resources/strategies, videotape presentations, and simulations. Results of a survey found a decrease in attitudes in willingness to work with students with disabilities and in comfort level in interacting with these students. Researchers felt that perhaps the increased information may have caused course participants to be given a more realistic view which may have caused them to be more idealistic about the situation. Unlike Brittin's 1995 study, no contact with individuals with disabilities was part of the course structure. In a graduate course the following summer, Smith and Wilson (1997) used the same measurement tool and found that students showed an increase in willingness to work with students with disabilities, an increase in comfortableness, and an increase in personal feelings of capability in working with special learners. In this study, the researchers did incorporate the use of a field practicum and concluded, like Brittin (1995), that direct contact may be a major factor in changing attitudes of preservice teachers.

Examining a different type of contact with students with special needs, Kaiser and Johnson (2000) examined the effect of an interactive experience on music majors' perceptions of music for deaf students. Before any discussion arose regarding the interactive concert/presentation, subjects completed a survey that addressed their general perceptions of music for deaf students, and their level of preparedness, comfort, and willingness to work with these students. Results of the initial query indicated that majors were comfortable and willing but did not feel prepared. In preparation for the concert, students participated in a discussion focusing on the performance, what to expect during the interaction, information on adapting instruction and appropriate and effective ways of communicating with deaf students. Results of the second administration of the survey completed immediately after the experience showed a positive increase in all areas with a significant increase found on self-perception of preparedness in working with deaf students.

Although no contact with individuals with special needs was included in a course entitled "Music in Special Education," Colwell (1999) found that the attitudes of graduate education majors toward students with special needs improved after participation in lectures, readings, disability presentations, and inservice preparations supporting the premise that increased information can have an effect on attitudes.

Instructional adaptations were also the focus of a study by Colwell (1995). The purpose of her study was to compare the effect of two music lessons (non-adapted versus adapted) on behaviors of two students, one with cerebral palsy and the other with a traumatic brain injury, in the mainstreamed classroom. Two lesson plans were designed for each class; one was not adapted while the other lesson was adapted specific to each student's special needs. Behaviors for videotape analysis were: on/off task, success rate at music tasks, and social interaction with peers. Overall lesson and activity specific data were obtained for each behavior. Results indicated that both students were more on-task, more successful at music tasks, and more apt to interact with their peers and to self initiate interactions when the lesson had been adapted for their needs. This study is especially important because it highlights the type of information music educators need to successfully integrate students into the mainstreamed classroom. Music educators must receive educational preparation that includes adaptive instructional strategies such as task analysis and shaping.

A review of attitudinal studies indicated that music students often have negative attitudes toward their mainstreamed peers or others with disabilities (Darrow & Johnson, 1994; Elliott & Sins, 1981/1982). These attitudes are often the result of their lack of experience with students who have been successfully mainstreamed. Students, as well as teachers, are often unaware of the strategies can be used to make a mainstreaming situation successful or the music potential of many students with disabilities. The purpose of an experimental study was to examine the effect of five positive models of inclusion on band students' attitudinal statements regarding the integration of students with disabilities in their music program. Elementary, junior high, and senior high school band students from 15 public schools served as subjects for this study ($N = 757$). A Solomon Four-Group design was chosen for this project. Bands were randomly assigned to one of the following four conditions: (a) pretest-treatment-posttest, (b) pretest-posttest, (c) treatment-posttest, or (d) posttest only. The independent variable for this project was a 30-minute videotape containing five segments which documented students with cognitive, physical, behavioral, or sensory disabilities successfully participating in a band in either rehearsal or performance situations. The dependent variable was a questionnaire comprised of attitudinal statements related to the following subscales: (a) inclusion of students with disabilities in band, (b) degree of comfort with inclusion, (c) efficiency of the band with students who have a disability, and (d) procedural issues involving students with a disability in band. Results indicated that treatment group subjects' attitudinal statements were significantly more positive than attitudinal statements of control group subjects on three of the four subscales. In addition, female students were significantly more positive than were male students on the same subscales. No clear trends were found among the different age groups as have been found in other studies (Darrow & Johnson, 1994; Elliott & Sins, 1981/1982).

In a study aimed at altering the attitudes of elementary music students toward children with special needs, Colwell, Berke, and Thompson (2001) used two different presentation formats (information and simulation) to effect change. Prior to treatment, females showed slightly more favorable attitudes than males which corroborates previous research (Colwell, 1998; Darrow & Johnson, 1994) and a rank ordering indicated students were most accepting toward individuals with learning disabilities and least accepting of those with visual impairments. Fourth and fifth grade intact music classes participated in either (a) information-based, (b) simulation-based, or (c) contact-control prior to a second administration of the attitude measure. Results found that although there was no significant difference among groups there was a slight increase noted for those participating in the simulations.

The data reported in this study and the other experimental studies reviewed here support the possibility of effecting positive changes in the learning environment of students in mainstreamed music classrooms. If a research agenda is to be set, it should be to this end. The collaborative research efforts of music therapists and music educators have the potential to make music learning a successful experience for all students.

Conclusions

The studies described in this section reveal little progress in the perceived success of music mainstreaming or in the attitudes of music educators toward mainstreaming. Even recent research reports that music educators are not trained to work with mainstreamed students and often have negative attitudes about teaching them. Since it is doubtful that public education systems will ever go back to self-contained classrooms for students with disabilities, school music therapists need to explore methods of improving teacher attitudes toward mainstreaming as well as methods of increasing positive interactions between music students with and without disabilities.

As is obvious from this review, more experimental studies are needed. Music educators attitudes toward mainstreaming have been adequately described. It is now time to further explore methods of improving attitudes and, more importantly, to examine instructional strategies that will facilitate learning in the mainstreamed music classroom. Mainstreaming studies in general education can give us some direction. By implementing some of the strategies found to be successful in the general classroom and examining their applicability to the music classroom, we should have a research agenda that will take us into the next century and provide us with valuable information. Music therapists, by the nature of their profession, are the likely leaders and researchers to establish this body of literature.

References

Adamek, M. S. (2001). Meeting special needs in music class. *Music Educators Journal, 87*(4), 23–26.

Altman, B. M. (1981). Studies of attitudes toward the handicapped: The need for a new direction. *Social Problems, 28,* 321–337.

Amsel, R., & Fichen, C. S. (1988). Effects of contact on thoughts about interaction with students who have a physical disability. *Journal of Rehabilitation, 54,* 61–65.

Atterbury, B. W. (1986). A survey of present mainstreaming practices in the southern United States. *Journal of Music Therapy, 23,* 202–207.

Atterbury, B. W. (1990). *Mainstreaming exceptional learners in music.* Englewood Cliffs, NJ: Prentice-Hall.

Atterbury, B. W. (1998). Music teacher preparation in special education and the effect of mainstreaming. *Update: Applications of Research in Music Education, 16*(2), 29–32.

Avramidis, E., Bayliss, P., & Burden, R. (2000). Student teachers' attitudes towards the inclusion of children with special educational needs in the ordinary school. *Teaching and Teacher Education, 16,* 277–293.

Bailey, D. B., & Harbin, G. L. (1980). Nondiscriminatory evaluation. *Exceptional Children, 46,* 590–596.

Baker, J., & Gottlieb, J. (1980). Attitudes of teachers toward mainstreaming retarded children. In J. Gottlieb (Ed.), *Educating mentally retarded persons in the mainstream.* Baltimore: University Park Press.

Barnes, E., Berrigan, C., & Biklen, D. (1978). *What's the difference? Teaching positive attitudes toward people with disabilities.* Syracuse, NY: Human Policy.

Bauwens, J., Hourcade, J. J., & Friend, M. (1989). Cooperative teaching: A model for general and special education integration. *Remedial and Special Education Journal, 1,* 4–11.

Bernstorf, E. D. (2001). Paraprofessionals in music settings. *Music Educators Journal, 87*(4), 36–40.

Bradley, D. F., & Calvin, M. B. (1998). Grading modified assignments; Equity or compromise? *Teaching Exceptional Children, 31*(2), 24–29.

Brittin, R. V. (1995, November). *Changing music educators' attitudes toward inclusion of students with disabilities.* Poster session of the annual meeting of the National Association for Music Therapy, Houston, TX.

Brittin, R. V. (1997, November). *Inclusion of students with disabilities: Effects of selected class activities on music educators' attitudes.* Poster session of the annual meeting of the National Association for Music Therapy, Los Angeles, CA.

Brown, M. C. (1981). *Problems in mainstreaming programs in the Los Angeles Unified School District as perceived by junior high school music teachers.* Unpublished doctoral dissertation, University of Southern California, Los Angeles.

Brownell, M. T., & Pajares, F. (1999). Teacher efficacy and perceived success in mainstreaming students with learning and behavior problems. *Teacher Education and Special Education, 22,* 154–164.

Bryan, T., & Bryan, J. H. (1978). Social interactions of learning disabled children. *Learning Disabilities Quarterly, 1,* 33–38.

Budoff, M., & Gottlieb, J. (1976). Special class EMR children mainstreamed: A study of an aptitude (learning potential) × treatment interaction. *American Journal of Mental Deficiency, 81,* 1–11.

Bursuck, W. D., Munk, D. D., & Olson, M. M. (1999). The fairness of report card grading adaptations: What do students with and without learning disabilities think? *Remedial and Special Education, 20,* 84–92.

Calhoun, G., & Elliot, R. (1977). Self-concept and academic achievement of educable retarded and emotionally disturbed pupils. *Exceptional Children, 44,* 379–380.

Carlberg, C., & Kavale, K. (1980). The efficiency of special versus regular placements for exceptional children: A meta-analysis. *Journal of Special Education, 14,* 295–309.

Christiansen, J., & Vogel, J. R. (1998). A decision model for grading students with disabilities. *Teaching Exceptional Children, 31*(2), 30–35.

Clore, G. L., & Jeffrey, K. M. (1972). Emotional role playing, attitude change and attraction toward a disabled person. *Journal of Personality and School Psychology, 23,* 105–111.

Colwell, C. M. (1995). Adapting music instruction for elementary students with special needs: A pilot study. *Music Therapy Perspectives, 13,* 97–103.

Colwell, C. M. (1998). Effect of information (video, label, success) on elementary band students' attitudes toward individuals with special needs. *Journal of Music Therapy, 35,* 19–33.

Colwell, C. M. (1999, January). *Graduate course in music in special education: Can we effect an attitudinal change through knowledge?* Poster session of the annual meeting of the Arizona Music Educators Association, Phoenix, AZ.

Colwell, C. M., Berke, M., & Thompson, L. K. (2001). Disability simulations and information: Techniques for modifying the attitudes of elementary school music students. *Journal of Music Therapy, 38,* 321–341.

Colwell, C. M., & Thompson, L. K. (2000). "Inclusion" of information on mainstreaming in undergraduate music education curricula. *Journal of Music Therapy, 37,* 205–221.

Conway, R. N. F., & Gow, L. (1988). Mainstreaming special students with mild handicaps through group instruction. *Remedial and Special Education, 9,* 34–41.

Cook, B. G. (2001). A comparison of teacher's attitudes toward their included students with mild and severe disabilities. *Journal of Special Education, 34,* 203–213.

Culton, C. L. (1999). The extent to which elementary music education textbooks reflect teachers' needs regarding instruction of students with special needs: A content analysis. (Doctoral dissertation, The University of Iowa, 1999). *Dissertation Abstracts International, 60,* 12A, 4358.

Daane, C. J., Beirne-Smith, M., & Latham, D. (2000). Administrators' and teachers' perceptions of the collaborative efforts of inclusion in the elementary grades. *Education, 121,* 331–338.

Damer, L. K. (1979). *A study of attitudes of selected public school music teachers toward the integration of handicapped students into music classes.* Unpublished doctoral dissertation, University of North Carolina at Greensboro.

Damer, L. K. (2001a). Inclusion and the law. *Music Educators Journal, 87*(4), 19–22.

Damer, L. K. (2001b). Students with special needs. *Music Educators Journal, 87*(4), 17–18.

Darrow, A. A. (1990). Research on mainstreaming in music education. *Update: Applications of Research in Music Education, 9*(1), 35–37.

Darrow, A. A. (1999). Music educators' perceptions regarding the inclusion of students with severe disabilities in music classrooms. *Journal of Music Therapy, 36,* 254–273.

Darrow, A. A., & Gfeller, K. (1991). A study of public school music programs mainstreaming hearing-impaired students. *Journal of Music Therapy, 28,* 23–39.

Darrow, A. A., & Johnson, C. M. (1994). Junior and senior high school music students' attitudes toward individuals with a disability. *Journal of Music Therapy, 31,* 266–279.

Donahue, K., & Zigmond, N. (1990). Academic grades of ninth-grade students. *Exceptionality, 1,* 17–27.

Donaldson, J. (1980). Changing attitudes toward handicapped persons: A review and analysis of research. *Exceptional Children, 46,* 504–512.

Dunn, L. M. (1968). Special education for the mildly retarded—Is much of it justifiable? *Exceptional Children, 35,* 5–22.

Elliott, C., & Sins, N. (1981/1982). Attitudes and opinions of middle school music students toward the presence of handicapped peers in music classes. *Contributions to Music Education, 9*(5), 48–59.

Elliott, S. N., Kratochwill, T. R., & Schulte, A. G. (1998). The assessment accommodation checklist. *Teaching Exceptional Children, 31*(2), 10–14.

Erickson, R., Ysseldyke, J., Thurlow, M., & Elliott, J. (1998). Inclusive assessments and accountability systems: Tools of the trade in educational reform. *Teaching Exceptional Children, 31*(2), 4–9.

Espin, C. A., Deno, S. L., & Albayrak-Kaymak, D. (1998). Individualized education programs in resource and inclusive settings: How "individualized" are they? *Journal of Special Education, 32,* 164–174.

Evans, J. H. (1976, June). Changing attitudes toward disabled persons: An experimental study. *Rehabilitation Counseling Bulletin, 19,* 572–579.

Evertson, C. M., Sanford, J. P., & Emmer, E. T. (1981). Effects of class heterogeneity in junior high school. *American Educational Research Journal, 18,* 219–232.

Ferguson, J. M. (1998). High school students' attitudes toward inclusion of handicapped students in the regular education classroom. *Educational Forum, 63,* 173–179.

Fiedler, C. R., & Simpson, R. L. (1987). Modifying the attitudes of nonhandicapped students toward handicapped peers. *Exceptional Children, 53,* 342–349.

Force, B. (1983). The effects of mainstreaming on the learning of nonretarded children in an elementary music classroom. *Journal of Music Therapy, 20,* 2–13.

Freeman, S. F. N., & Alkin, M. C. (2000). Academic and social attainments of children with mental retardation in general education and special education settings. *Remedial and Special Education, 21,* 3–18.

Frisque, J., Niebur, L., & Humphreys, J. T. (1994). Music mainstreaming: Practices in Arizona. *Journal of Research in Music Education, 42,* 94–104.

Fuchs, L. S., & Fuchs, D. (1986). Effects of systematic formative evaluation: A meta-analysis. *Exceptional Children, 53,* 199–208.

Gavin, A. R. J. (1983). *Music educator practices and attitudes toward mainstreaming.* Unpublished doctoral dissertation, Washington University.

Gearheart, B. R., Weishahn, M. W., & Gearheart, C. J. (1992). *The exceptional student in the regular classroom.* New York: Macmillan.

Gfeller, K., & Darrow, A. A. (1987). Ten years of mainstreaming: Where are we now? *Music Educators Journal, 74*(2), 27–30.

Gfeller, K., Darrow, A. A., & Hedden, S. (1990). The perceived effectiveness of mainstreaming in Iowa and Kansas schools. *Journal of Research in Music Education, 38,* 90–101.

Gibb, S. A., Allred, K., Ingram, C. F., Young, J. R., & Egan, M. W. (1999). Lessons learned from the inclusion of students with emotional and behavioral disorders in one junior high school. *Behavioral Disorders, 24,* 122–136.

Gilbert, J. P., & Asmus, E. P. (1981). Mainstreaming: Music educators' participation and professional needs. *Journal of Research in Music Education, 29,* 283–289.

Gilbert, J. P., & Stuart, M. (1977). A videotaped procedure for assessing attitude toward disabled clientele: Procedural development of initial results. *Journal of Music Therapy, 14,* 116–125.

Goeke, R. E. (1994). *Responses among music teachers and principals in the state of Kansas regarding outcome-based public schools' classroom assessment and related curricular topics.* Unpublished master's thesis. The University of Kansas, Lawrence, KS.

Gottlieb, J. (1980). Improving attitudes toward retarded children by using group discussion. *Exceptional Children, 47*, 106–111.

Gottlieb, J. (1981). Mainstreaming: Fulfilling the promise? *American Journal of Mental Deficiency, 86*, 115–126.

Graham, R., & Beer, A. S. (1980). *Teaching music to the exceptional child.* Englewood Cliffs, NJ: Prentice-Hall.

Greenbaum, J., Varas, M., & Markel, G. (1980). Using books about handicapped children. *The Reading Teacher, 33*, 416–419.

Gresham, F. M. (1982). Misguided mainstreaming: The case for social skills training with handicapped children. *Exceptional Children, 48*, 422–433.

Guerin, G. R., & Szatlocky, K. (1974). Integration programs for the mildly retarded. *Exceptional Children, 41*, 173–179.

Hammel, A. M. (2001). Special learners in elementary music classrooms: A study of essential teacher competencies. *Update: Applications of Research in Music Education, 20*(1), 9–13.

Handlers, A., & Austin, K. (1980). Improving attitudes of high school students toward their handicapped peers. *Exceptional Children, 47*, 228–229.

Haring, N. G., & Krug, D. A. (1975). Placement in regular programs: Procedures and results. *Exceptional Children, 41*, 413–417.

Hawkins, G. D. (1991). *Attitudes toward mainstreaming students with disabilities among regular elementary music physical educators.* Unpublished doctoral dissertation, University of Maryland.

Heller, L. (1995). Undergraduate music teacher preparation for mainstreaming: A survey of music education teacher training institutions in the Great Lakes region of the United States (Doctoral dissertation, Michigan State University, 1994). *Dissertation Abstracts International, 56*, 858A.

Hodge, S. R., & Jansma, P. (2000). Physical education majors' attitudes toward teaching students with disabilities. *Teacher Education and Special Education, 23*, 211–224.

Horne, M. D. (1985). *Attitudes toward handicapped students: Professional, peer and parent reactions.* Hillsdale, NJ: Lawrence Erlbaum.

Humpal, M. (1991). The effects of an integrated early childhood music program on social interaction among children with handicaps and their typical peers. *Journal of Music Therapy, 28*, 161–177.

Hunt, P., & Goetz, L. (1997). Research on inclusive educational programs, practices, and outcomes for students with severe disabilities. *Journal of Special Education, 31*, 3–29.

Idol, L., & West, F. (1991). Educational collaboration: A catalyst for effective schooling. *Intervention in School and Clinic, 27*, 70–78.

Jellison, J. A. (1985). An investigation of the factor structure of a scale for the measurement of children's attitudes toward handicapped peers within regular music environments. *Journal of Research in Music Education, 33*, 167–177.

Jellison, J. A. (1992). Music and students with disabilities: A preliminary study of Texas music educators' experiences, attitudes, and perceptions. *Texas Music Education Research*, 38–46.

Jellison, J. A. (1997). *Principles for the inclusive music classroom: Guidelines for developing, selecting, adapting, implementing, and evaluating lessons and activities.* Paper presented at the 12th National Symposium on Research in Music Behavior, Minneapolis, MN.

Jellison, J. A., Brooks, B. H., & Huck, A. M. (1984). Structuring small groups and music reinforcement to facilitate positive interactions and acceptance of severely handicapped students in regular music classrooms. *Journal of Research in Music Education, 32*, 243–264.

Jellison, J. A., & Gainer, E. W. (1995). Into the mainstream: A case-study of a child's participation in music education and music therapy. *Journal of Music Therapy, 32*, 228–247.

Johnson, A. B. (1987). Attitudes toward mainstreaming: Implications for inservice training and teaching the handicapped. *Education, 107,* 229–233.

Johnson, C. M., & Darrow, A. A. (1997). The effect of positive models on band students' attitudinal statements regarding the inclusion of students with disabilities. *Journal of Research in Music Education, 45,* 173–184.

Jones, T. W., Sowell, V. M., Jones, J. K., & Butler, G. (1981). Changing children's perceptions of handicapped people. *Exceptional Children, 47,* 365–368.

Kaiser, K. A., & Johnson, K. E. (2000). The effect of an interactive experience on music majors' perceptions of music for deaf students. *Journal of Music Therapy, 37,* 222–234.

Kamps, D. M., Dugan, E., Potucek, J., & Collins, A. (1999). Effects of cross-age peer tutoring networks among students with autism and general education students. *Journal of Behavioral Education, 9,* 97–115.

Kearns, J. F., Kleinert, H. L., Clayton, J., Burdge, M., & Williams, R. (1998). Principal supports for inclusive assessment. *Teaching Exceptional Children, 31*(2), 16–23.

Kleinert, H., Kennedy, S., & Kearns, J. (1999). The impact of alternate assessments: A statewide teacher survey. *Journal of Special Education, 33,* 93–102.

Kostka, M. J. (1993). A comparison of selected behaviors of a student with autism in special education and regular music classes. *Music Therapy Perspectives, 11,* 57–60.

Kostka, M. J. (1999). Secondary music students' attitudes toward atypical peers. *Update: Applications of Research in Music Education, 17*(2), 8–12.

Kostland, R., Wilkinson, M. M., & Briggs, L. D. (1997). Inclusion programs for learning disabled students in middle schools. *Education, 117,* 419–425.

Larrivee, G., & Horne, M. D. (1991). Social status: A comparison of mainstreamed students with peers of different ability levels. *Journal of Special Education, 25,* 90–101.

Lazar, A. L., Gensley, J. T., & Orpet, R. E. (1971). Changing attitudes of young mentally gifted children toward handicapped person. *Exceptional Children, 37,* 600–602.

Leinhardt, G. (1980). Transition rooms: Promoting maturation or reducing education? *Journal of Educational Psychology, 72,* 55–61.

Lewis, R. A., & Doorlag, D. H. (1991). *Teaching special students in the mainstream.* New York: Macmillan.

Lindsey, J., Burns, J., & Guthrie, J. D. (1984). Intervention grading and secondary learning disabled students. *The High School Journal, 67,* 150–157.

Litton, F. W., Banbury, M. M., & Harris, K. (1980). Materials for educating handicapped students about their handicapped peers. *Teaching Exceptional Children, 13,* 39–43.

Leung, E. K. (1980). Evaluation of a children's literature program designed to facilitate the social integration of handicapped children into regular elementary classrooms (Doctoral dissertation, The Ohio State University). *Dissertation Abstracts International, 40,* 4528A.

Macy, D. J., & Carter, J. L. (1978). Comparison of a mainstream and self-contained special education program. *Journal of Special Education, 12,* 303–313.

Madden, N., & Slavin, R. (1983). Mainstreaming students with mild handicaps: Academic and social outcomes. *Review of Educational Research, 53,* 519–569.

Madsen, C. K., Smith, D. S., & Feeman, C. C. (1988). The use of music in cross-age tutoring within special education settings. *Journal of Music Therapy, 25,* 135–144.

Maheady, L., Harper, G. F., & Mallette, B. (2001). Peer-mediated instruction and interventions and students with mild disabilities. *Remedial and Special Education, 22,* 4–14.

Maras, P., & Brown, R. (2000). Effects of different forms of school contact on children's attitudes toward disabled and non-disabled peers. *British Journal of Educational Psychology, 70,* 337–351.

Marston, D., & Magnusson, D. (1985). Implementing curriculum-based measurement in special and regular education settings. *Exceptional Children, 52,* 266–276.

McCann, S. K., Semmel, M. I., & Nevin, A. (1985). Reverse mainstreaming: Nonhandicapped students in special education classrooms. *Remedial and Special Education, 6,* 13–19.

McLoughlin, J. A., & Lewis, R. B. (1990). *Assessing special students* (3rd ed.). Columbus, OH: Merrill.

Miller, K. J., Fullmer, S., & Walls, R. T. (1996). A dozen years of mainstreaming literature: A content analysis. *Exceptionality, 6,* 99–109.

Myers, J. K. (1976). *The special day school placement for high IQ and low EMR pupils.* Paper presented at the annual meeting of the Council for Exceptional Children, Chicago. (ERIC Document Reproduction Service No. ED 125 197)

National Association of State Boards of Education. (1992). *Winners all: A call for inclusive schools.* Alexandria, VA: Author.

Nocera, S. D. (1981). *A descriptive analysis of the attainment of selective musical learning by normal children and by educable mentally retarded children mainstreamed in music classes at the second and fifth grade level.* Unpublished doctoral dissertation, University of Wisconsin, Madison.

Peltier, G. L. (1997). The effect of inclusion on non-disabled children: A review of the research. *Contemporary Education, 68,* 234–237.

Perkins, C. K. (1996). Elementary music educators' adaptive teaching strategies for integrated students with disabilities (inclusion) (Doctoral dissertation, University of Illinois at Urbana-Champaign, 1996). *Dissertation Abstracts International, 57,* 11A, 4683.

Ray, B. M. (1986). Measuring the social position of the mainstreamed handicapped child. *Exceptional Children, 52,* 57–62.

Reynolds, M. C., & Birch, J. W. (1988). *Adaptive mainstreaming: A primer for teachers and principals* (3rd ed.). New York: Longman.

Roberts, C., & Zubrick, S. (1993). Factors influencing the social status of children with mild academic disabilities in regular classrooms. *Exceptional Children, 59,* 192–202.

Rodriguez, D., & Tompkins, R. (1994, March). *Inclusive education for all students.* Paper presented at the meeting of the American Council on Rural Special Education (ACRES), Austin, Texas.

Salend, S. J. (1994). *Effective mainstreaming: Creating inclusive classrooms.* New York: Macmillan.

Salend, S. J., & Duhaney, L. M. G. (1999). The impact of inclusion on students with and without disabilities and their educators. *Remedial and Special Education, 20,* 114–126.

Salend, S. J., & Duhaney, L. M. G. (2002). Grading students in inclusive settings. *Teaching Exceptional Children, 34*(3), 8–15.

Salend, S. J., & Knops, B. (1984). Hypothetical examples: A cognitive approach to changing attitudes toward the handicapped. *The Elementary School Journal, 85,* 229–236.

Salend, S. J., & Moe, L. (1983). Modifying nonhandicapped students' attitudes toward their handicapped peers through children's literature. *Journal for Special Educators, 19,* 22–28.

Shehan, P. (1977). A brief study of music education for exceptional children in Ohio. *Contributions to Music Education, 5,* 47–53.

Shepard, L. M. M. (1993). *A survey of music teachers' attitudes toward mainstreaming disabled students in regular music classroom in selected school districts in Georgia.* Unpublished doctoral dissertation, The University of Southern Mississippi.

Sideridis, G. D., & Chandler, J. P. (1995). Attitudes and characteristics of general music teachers toward integrating children with developmental disabilities. *Update: Applications of Research in Music Education, 14,* 11–15.

Simpson, R. L. (1980). Modifying the attitudes of regular class students toward the handicapped. *Focus on Exceptional Children, 13,* 1–11.

Sins, N. (1983). Mainstreaming the music classroom automatically brings about acceptance by the nonhandicapped. Right? (Wrong!). *Update: The Applications of Research in Music Education, 2,* 3–6.

Siperstein, G. N., Bopp, M., & Bak, J. (1978). Social status of learning disabled children. *Journal of Learning Disabilities, 11,* 1–16.

Slavin, R. E. (1987). Grouping for instruction in the elementary school. *Educational Psychologist, 2,* 107–127.

Smaller, A. G. (1989). *The process of mainstreaming special education students in a suburban elementary school: A case study.* Unpublished doctoral dissertation, New York University.

Smith, D. S. (1987). The effect of instruction on ability to adapt teaching situations for exceptional students. *MEH Bulletin, 2,* 3–18.

Smith, D. S. (1989). A content analysis of music educators' attitudes toward mainstreaming in middle school music classes. *Journal of the International Association of Music for the Handicapped, 4,* 3–20.

Smith, D. S., & Wilson, B. L. (1997, November). *Effects of field experience on graduate music educators' attitude toward teaching students with disabilities.* Poster session of the annual meeting of the National Association for Music Therapy, Los Angeles, CA.

Smith, T. E. C., Polloway, E. A., Patton, J. R., & Dowdy, D. A. (1995). *Teaching children with special needs in inclusive settings.* Boston: Allyn and Bacon.

Smith, T. E. C., Price, B. J., & Marsh, G. E. (1986). *Mildly handicapped children and adults.* St. Paul, MN: West.

Soodak, L. C., Podell, D. M., & Lehman, L. R. (1998). Teacher, student, and school attributes as predictors of teachers' responses to inclusion. *Journal of Special Education, 31,* 480–497.

Stainback, W., Stainback, S., Courtnage, L., & Jaben, T. (1985). Facilitating mainstreaming by modifying the mainstream. *Exceptional Children, 52,* 144–152.

Stallings, J. A. (1985). *A study of basic reading skills taught in secondary schools. Report of Phase I findings.* Menlo Park CA: Stanford Research International.

Stevens, R. J., & Slavin, R. E. (1991). When cooperative learning improves the achievement of students with mild disabilities: A response to Tateyama-Sniesek. *Exceptional Children, 57,* 276–280.

Stephens, T. M., & Braun, B. L. (1980). Measures of regular classroom teachers' attitudes toward handicapped children. *Exceptional Children, 46,* 292–294.

Stuart, M., & Gilbert, J. P. (1977). Mainstreaming: Needs assessment through a videotape visual scale. *Journal of Research in Music Education, 25,* 283–289.

Swank, P. R., Taylor, R. D., Brady, M. P., Cooley, R., & Freiberg, H. J. (1989). Outcomes of grouping students in mainstreamed middle school classrooms. *NASSP Bulletin, 73,* 62–66.

Tapasak, R. C., & Walther-Thomas, C. S. (1999). Evaluation of a first-year inclusion program: Student perceptions and classroom performance. *Remedial and Special Education, 20,* 216–225.

Thompson, K. P. (1986). The general music class as experienced by mainstreamed handicapped students. *MEH Bulletin, 1*(3), 16–23.

Treder, D. W., Morse, W. G., & Ferron, J. M. (2000). The relationship between teacher effectiveness and teacher attitudes toward issues related to inclusion. *Teacher Education and Special Education, 23,* 202–210.

Turner, M. D., Baldwin, L., Kleinert, H. L., & Kearns, J. F. (2000). The relation of a statewide alternate assessment for students with severe disabilities to other measures of instructional effectiveness. *Journal of Special Education, 34,* 69–76.

United States Department of Education (1994). *Sixteenth annual report to Congress on the implementation of the Individuals with Disabilities Education Act.* Washington, DC: U.S. Government Printing Office.

Utley, C. A., Mortweet, S. L., & Greenwood, C. R. (1997). Peer-mediated instruction and interventions. *Focus on Exceptional Children, 29*(5), 1–23.

Valdes, K. A., Williamson, C. L., & Wagner, M. M. (1990). *The national longitudinal transition study of special education students.* Menlo Park, CA: SRI International.

VanWeelden, K. (2001). Choral mainstreaming: Tips for success. *Music Educators Journal, 88*(3), 55–60.

Vaughn, S., Hughes, M. T., Moody, S. W., & Elbaum, B. (2001). Instructional grouping for reading for students with LD: Implications for practice. *Intervention in School and Clinic, 36,* 131–137.

Waldron, K. A., & Van Zandt Allen, L. (1999). Successful strategies for inclusion at the middle level. *Middle School Journal, 30*(4), 18–27.

Walker, V. S. (1974). The efficiency of the resource room for educating retarded children. *Exceptional Children, 40,* 288–289.

Wang, M. C., Anderson, K. A., & Bram, P. (1985). *Toward an empirical data base on mainstreaming: A research synthesis of program implementation and effects.* Pittsburgh: Learning Research and Development Center, University of Pittsburgh.

Wang, M. C., & Birch, J. W. (1984). Comparison of a full-time mainstreaming program and a resource room approach. *Exceptional Children, 51,* 33–40.

White, L. D. (1981/1982). A study of attitudes of selected public school music educators toward the integration of handicapped students in music classes. *Contributions to Music Education, 9*(5), 36–47.

White, L. D. (1984). *A follow-up study of the attitudes of selected North Carolina public school music teachers toward the mainstreaming of handicapped students into music class.* Paper presented at XVI ISSME International Conference, Eugene, OR.

Williams, W., Fox, T., Thousand, J., & Fox, W. (1990). Level of acceptance and implementation of best practices in the education of students with severe disabilities in Vermont. *Education and Training in Mental Retardation, 25,* 120–131.

Wilson, B. & McCrary, J. (1996). The effect of instruction on music educators' attitudes towards students with disabilities. *Journal of Research in Music Education, 44,* 26–33.

Zdzinski, S. F. (2001). Instrumental music for special learners. *Music Educators Journal, 87*(4), 27–29, 63.

Zigler, E., & Muenchow, S. (1979). Mainstreaming: The proof is in the implementation. *American Psychologist, 34,* 993–996.

Zigmond, N., Levin, E., & Laurie, T. (1985). Managing the mainstream: An analysis of teacher attitudes and student performance in mainstream high school programs. *Journal of Learning Disabilities, 18,* 535–541.

5

A Special Education
Music Therapy Assessment Process

Betsey King Brunk
Kathleen A. Coleman

Editor's Note: *This chapter is an expansion of an article entitled, "Development of a Special Education Music Therapy Assessment Process" that was published in* Music Therapy Perspectives, 18(1), 2000, pp. 59–68.

In addition to the SEMTAP, several authors in subsequent chapters in this book have described other assessment models and procedures that they use in their clinical practices.

MUSIC therapy eligibility assessment in a public school setting is a comprehensive process that includes much more than the actual administration of a music therapy evaluation. Music therapists who want to work in the public schools need to: (a) understand the federal and state laws governing the provision of related services, (b) be able to articulate the role of music therapy in the public schools and distinguish it from other music-related activities, (c) set and maintain boundaries with parents and school staff, (d) work to build understanding and cooperation when music therapy is unfamiliar or misunderstood, and (e) know how to translate assessment results into reasonable and pragmatic recommendations. Through all of this, the music therapist must focus on the students—on their unique abilities and challenges, and on their individual educational needs.

Although many music therapy articles and presentations address the concern that music therapists need "standardized" assessment instruments, public school music therapists must ask whether such tools would be appropriate for special education evaluations. The special education population is diverse and, even within disability groups, skills and deficits vary widely. Some students require intense assistance with communication issues while being independent in their mobility. Others demonstrate severe physical limitations which can obscure cognitive strengths. Literature on music therapy assessment for children with special needs has focused on evaluating a child's cognitive developmental level through musical tasks (Rider, 1981); on identifying a child's unique skills and adaptive abilities through musical interaction (Grant, 1995); and on using music and music stimuli over several weeks to comprehensively evaluate a child's abilities in the motor, communication, cognitive, affective and social domains (Boxill, 1985). Some assessments are based on a particular therapeutic approach, such as improvisation (Bruscia, 1987). Other approaches suggest the integration of information from standardized assessment tools used by other professionals (Gfeller & Baumann, 1988; Johnson, 1996). These assessment tools and procedures are all valid in certain situations. Assessments often are conducted for the purpose of choosing the best strategies for music therapy sessions, or to determine the level of musical skills in a person with disabilities. A music therapist conducting an eligibility assessment for a student in the public schools, however, must be concerned with only one thing: the impact of specific music therapy interventions on that student's ability to achieve the goals set in his or her Individualized Education Program (IEP).

Assessments and therapies that meet the standards of special education law parallel a student's IEP, addressing specific goals and objectives from that document. The members of an IEP team must demonstrate—first through assessment and then through implementation and documentation—that particular interventions are necessary for the student to achieve his or her IEP goals and objectives. A music therapist need not provide an overall assessment of a student's cognitive, behavioral, social, or physical abilities; other IEP team members (such as the diagnostician and classroom teacher) will have completed these evaluations. Likewise, a music therapist will not want to focus exclusively on a child's musical abilities (i.e., keeping a steady beat, matching pitch), as this does not show the team how music therapy would assist the student in achieving *non*-musical IEP goals, such as color identification, increased attention span, or independence in the community.

In this chapter, we describe the use of an individualized music therapy assessment *process* which allows each therapist to utilize his or her individual therapeutic methodology while providing a clear, convincing rationale for the inclusion of music therapy in a student's IEP. Known as the SEMTAP (Special Education Music Therapy Assessment Process), this process acknowledges each child's distinctive educational profile and highlights the role of the music therapist as a member of a transdisciplinary[1] IEP team. It conforms to current special education law, resulting in recommendations that can be justified to both parents and administrators. It does not depend on a single standardized assessment instrument that may not address the unique needs of each child. Additionally, the SEMTAP can be an educational tool for music therapists working with school districts that are unfamiliar with music therapy.

This chapter will provide an outline and justification for the use of the SEMTAP by music therapists working in the public schools. We will (a) review the federal law that forms the basis of all special education procedure; (b) outline the assessment process (SEMTAP) that was developed in response to the law; (c) present an assessment case study; (d) describe the ways in which a music therapy assessment can be an educational tool for a school district unfamiliar with music therapy; and (e) review the results of 16 independent assessments that we conducted for school districts new to music therapy, reporting on administration and parental responses to our evaluation procedure.

Special Education Law

Music therapists become part of public school special education programs in a variety of ways. Some are hired to provide group music therapy to particular classrooms or programs (such as early intervention). Some assist music educators with the inclusion process for students with disabilities. For this article, we will not focus on these voluntary arrangements between a school district and a music therapist. Instead, we will concentrate on the federally delineated process by which music therapy is included or rejected for a particular student's Individualized Education Program, namely, the music therapy assessment.

Legislation

In 1973, in an amendment to the Rehabilitation Act referred to as Section 504, the United States Congress sought to recognize the civil rights of children with disabilities. Section 504 "prohibited recipients of federal financial assistance from excluding disabled students from participating in, or being denied the benefits of, the school programs offered to others" (Martin, 1991). In 1975, Congress passed additional

---

[1]For an explanation of multidisciplinary, interdisciplinary, and transdisciplinary teams, see Chapter 6.

amendments to existing legislation (The Education of the Handicapped Act—EHA) that came to be known as PL 94-142: the Education for All Handicapped Children Act. This legislation (which provided funding to assist schools with the costs of special education) also came with regulations; as summarized by Martin (1991), it stated that:

> All children would have to be served, regardless of the nature or severity of their handicapping conditions. Parents would be given written notice of their rights and of actions proposed by the schools. Evaluation practices of schools would have to be reformed, and parents would have the right to seek an independent evaluation to contrast with the school's. Parents and school personnel would meet annually to put in writing the Individualized Education Program (IEP) plan that would govern services to the child. Schools would have to make available as needed related services such as physical therapy, occupational therapy, and school nursing services. Students with disabilities would be integrated with nondisabled students to the maximum extent appropriate. Finally, schools would have to agree to let an independent authority, an impartial hearing officer, rule on disputes and order needed changes in the school district's program. (p. 2)

In 1990, after several small amendments to both Section 504 and EHA (made in response to judicial challenges), the EHA became the Individuals with Disabilities Education Act, or IDEA. In 1997, further amendments were made to IDEA. Litigation on Section 504 and IDEA is common, and court rulings sometimes have resulted in changes that are recognized by schools and parents even though they are not part of the statutes.

One section of the 1997 IDEA amendments recognizes that "the implementation of [PL-94-142] has been impeded by low expectations and an insufficient focus on applying replicable research on proven methods of teaching and learning," and adds that "20 years of research and experience has demonstrated that the education of children with disabilities can be made more effective by . . . providing appropriate special education and related services and aids and supports in the regular classroom to such children, whenever appropriate . . ." (*Individuals with Disabilities Education Act Amendments of 1997*, Chapter 2, Section 681, 4–5). This statement, and the definition of related services provided in the law (see below), are the basis for a parent's request for a related service such as music therapy.

Related Services

IDEA states that "the term 'related services' means transportation, and such developmental, corrective, and other supportive services. ..as may be required to assist a child with a disability to benefit from special education" (*IDEA Amendments of 1997*, Part A, Section 602.22). The Senate Report on PL 94-142 states that the list of related services (which includes such diverse interventions as speech-language pathology, social work services, and rehabilitation counseling) is "not exhaustive and may include other developmental, corrective, or supportive services (such as artistic and cultural programs, and art, music, and dance therapy), if they are required to assist a child with a disability to benefit from special education" (cited in Bateman, 1998). Amendments to PL 94-142, including the most current 1997 IDEA amendments, do nothing to change the basic definition of related services or the Senate Report's comments.

The key term in the definition of related services and the attached Senate Report is *required*. In assessing a child's need for music therapy as a related service, the public school music therapist must make his or her recommendation based on this standard. A key United States Supreme Court ruling (*Board of Education v. Rowley*, 1982) stated that a child's IEP "need only be procedurally correct, individualized, and reasonably calculated to allow the student to receive benefit' (cited in Bateman, 1998). Bateman refers to this as "a

Chevrolet, not a Cadillac Standard" (p. 96) and agrees with a Vermont hearing officer[2] who stated that "the IEP is not required to maximize the educational benefit to the child, nor to provide each and every service and accommodation which could conceivably be of some educational benefit" (1993, VT SEA, In re Child with Disabilities, 20 IDELR 314, cited in Bateman, 1998). However, related services, such as music therapy, must be provided by a school district only when they are *required* for a child to benefit from special education.

Assessments

Federal law has set forth specific guidelines for the evaluation of a student being considered for special education programming. These guidelines also are followed for assessments for related services. They are as follows:

1. Evaluation must occur before programming can begin;
2. Parents must be included in the evaluation process;
3. The evaluation must be kept current, to respond to the student's changing needs;
4. The evaluation must be conducted by a recognized specialist;
5. Reevaluation is required at least every 3 years, but must also occur when an IEP team member requests it;
6. Parents may procure an independent evaluation if they disagree with the school's evaluation, and that assessment must be considered in program decisions;
7. If a school refuses to conduct an evaluation, the parents are entitled to a written justification for the refusal (Martin, 1991, pp. 15–16).

When the federal guidelines for assessment are followed, and music therapy is recommended, a district cannot legally refuse to provide services. Therefore, music therapists who wish to introduce or maintain music therapy in a district need to understand the law's related service provisions and be able to articulate them to administrators and other members of an IEP team. They need an assessment process that determines if music therapy is "required" for a student to benefit from his or her education program, and considers the legal concept of "reasonable benefit" in making recommendations.

The Special Education Music Therapy Assessment Process

Background

The Special Education Music Therapy Assessment Process (SEMTAP) is the result of the authors' combined 20 years experience in working with children with special needs, and the school districts that serve them. During this time, we have attended over 300 IEP meetings and provided service to over 600 students. In developing the SEMTAP, we consulted with other music therapists throughout the United States on their special education assessment experiences. Speaking engagements in several states across the country gave us the opportunity to talk with parents about their experiences in obtaining related services for their children. Over a three-year period, we had the opportunity to provide 22 independent assessments for school districts that, in most cases, had little to no experience with music therapy. All this information has led us to develop a comprehensive, *individualized* assessment process that addresses both legal and practical issues in special education music therapy evaluations.

---

[2] A lawyer or judge who presides over a due process hearing (a legal proceeding that may occur when parents and school districts come to an impassse over a student's IEP).

In developing the SEMTAP, we based each step on the guidelines for related service and assessment found in the federal statutes on special education. Many steps were included or adjusted after experiences with parents or school districts who were active in, or considering, legal actions due to disputes over music therapy. We also considered practical safeguards against conflict-of-interest issues over which some school districts expressed concern.

The SEMTAP is an eligibility assessment; its purpose is to determine whether or not music therapy is necessary as part of a student's IEP. The process is designed to have two results. First, the music therapist using the SEMTAP will be able to make a direct comparison of a student's performance on his or her IEP objectives—*with and without* the structure of music therapy strategies. Second, the music therapist will be able to justify a recommendation for or against music therapy in a way that will satisfy both parents and school district personnel. We believe that most confrontations between parents and school districts can be avoided if all parties understand the music therapy assessment process and its legal basis.

The Process

The SEMTAP contains the following steps, each of which is detailed in this section:

1. The formal request for assessment
2. The music therapy assessment process
   a. review of documentation
   b. interviews
   c. observation in a non-musical setting
   d. preparation of the assessment
   e. administration of the assessment
   f. preparation of the assessment report and documentation
3. Presentation of the report and recommendations

The formal request for assessment. A parent, or other member of the IEP team, can ask for a music therapy assessment at an annual IEP meeting or an IEP meeting called specifically to make the request. This is *not* a request for music therapy *services;* it is a request for an *assessment.* It is helpful if the person making the request has some anecdotal or documented evidence in hand (e.g., a student's response to songs sung in the classroom, reports from a private music therapist). Some music therapists provide IEP teams with short checklists or forms that can be used to structure the discussion about an assessment. Supportive informational materials on music therapy and its role as a related service may also be useful to the IEP team considering the request. Most importantly, an outline of the SEMTAP will demonstrate to the IEP team how a decision for or against service will be made.

We recommend that any music therapist who is contacted to conduct an eligibility assessment for an IEP team verify that the members of the team—especially the parents or guardians—are satisfied with the current IEP. Since the SEMTAP is based directly on the goals and objectives in the IEP, parents who feel that the objectives are far above or below their child's actual skills or do not address areas that they are concerned about are unlikely to be satisfied with a music therapy assessment recommendation based on those objectives.

It is our strong recommendation that a student's private music therapist NOT participate directly in the IEP meeting, nor offer his or her services for the assessment. In our experience, the appearance of a private music therapist at an IEP meeting has often resulted in a district's perception that the music therapist is simply seeking additional work. Furthermore, since the private music therapist may have (rightly) evaluated and treated the student under broader, more liberal guidelines than those set forth in special education law, the district, parents or therapist may have difficulty making a distinction between the two. Because the relationship between a music therapist and a client's parents can be a close one, with the parties sharing months or years of struggles and successes, the school district may not feel that the private music therapist has the ability to conduct the assessment impartially. We recommend that the private therapist provide the names of other therapists in the area who can conduct an independent evaluation. If an independent assessor is not available locally, the district will have to bring in a music therapist from outside the area.

The school district may choose to contract with one music therapist to do assessments, and a second therapist to provide recommended therapy. This arrangement helps to ensure that recommendations for service are not based on a therapist's need for work. Some districts have utilized this system for a year or two and then, as personnel felt more comfortable with music therapy, moved to using one therapist for all parts of the process.

If the IEP team denies a parent's request for a music therapy evaluation, the parent has a right to receive a written response, detailing the reasons for the denial.

The music therapy assessment process. If an assessment is ordered by the IEP team, these are the steps we recommend as the SEMTAP:

1. Review the student's current IEP and other records as necessary. Make sure that all confidentiality forms have been signed.

2. Interview members of the IEP team, especially the classroom teacher and a parent. If the IEP focuses on a particular area of need (e.g., language acquisition), interview the related therapist (speech therapist). Ask particularly about areas of the IEP in which the student is not making expected progress. Provide each person interviewed with a transcript of their comments and have them sign it, indicating confirmation of their remarks.

3. Based on the review of the IEP and interviews, target a specific number of IEP objectives on which the assessment will be based. Choose those objectives that can be addressed with music therapy strategies and include, if possible, those objectives mentioned as particular challenges in the interviews. The music therapist will want to look at the IEP objectives and make sure that they are specific and measurable. An objective such as "the student will improve classroom skills" does not provide enough information on which to create a music therapy strategy for the assessment. If some objectives are too vague, the music therapist may wish to have the team clarify its intentions in a *documented* meeting before proceeding. Target only those 4–6 objectives that could be addressed within one or two music therapy assessment sessions. (See Table 1 for considerations in selecting objectives.)

4. Schedule and complete an observation of the student. Make an arrangement with teachers or therapists so that there is an opportunity to observe the student working on the targeted IEP objectives—in a NON-musical setting. Document the observations in real time through notes, audio recording or videotape.

5. Plan a music therapy assessment session that will address each of the targeted objectives. We recommend that the assessment occur in the form of a music therapy session, with opening and closing music, variety in the music strategies, and smooth transitions. The therapist may choose strategies from his or her own practice, from standardized tests, or from other music therapists' assessments. The sole requirement is that each music therapy strategy addresses a specific, targeted objective from the student's IEP—reflecting both the skill itself, and the skill level that the student is being asked to achieve. For example, a target objective from an IEP might state that the student will achieve 80% accuracy in one-to-one correspondence matching of printed numbers 1–5 with pictures of one to five familiar objects. A music therapy song in which the student "fills in the blank" with ordinal numbers as they are displayed on cards would not accurately measure this skill. Neither would a song that asks only for a verbal response to "How many do you see?"

6. When targeted objectives involve a student's ability to participate in a group, the music therapist may choose to conduct part of the assessment by leading the student and his classroom peers in one

Table 1

Considerations in Selecting Objectives From an IEP for the SEMTAP

Objective	Considerations
Student will hop on one foot for ninety seconds.	Is there evidence in the literature that music therapy would be helpful in supporting this objective? Is this one of the more functional objectives on the IEP? Would working on this objective be the best use of time in music therapy?
Student will remain dry for the 2 hour period between supervised bathroom visits.	Is there evidence that music therapy could support this objective?
Student will decrease inappropriate behavior while in the classroom by 50%.	What constitutes inappropriate behavior? Does the IEP committee intend that the student do this independently, or can cues be provided to help the student? Should a concurrent increase in specified appropriate behaviors occur at the same time or will passivity be considered success?
Student will consistently imitate three vocalizations that include initial sounds for "b," "h," and "w."	Can music therapy strategies cue imitation of vocalizations? Is this an objective on which the student has had trouble? Are there other objectives (perhaps related to attention) that will have an impact on the student's ability to achieve this one?
Student will remain seated for the 30 minute "circle time" at the beginning of the school day.	Is there evidence that music therapy could support this objective? Is music used in the circle time? Is it used contingently to cue the students to attend? Can the music therapist participate in a circle time as part of the music therapy assessment?
Student will demonstrate the ability to proceed through the lunch line and into the cafeteria with minimal verbal cues.	Is music therapy effective in teaching sequencing for functional tasks? Is music therapy effective in helping with memorization and impulse control?

    or more group music therapy strategies. We recommend that this take place on the same day as any one-on-one assessment session, so as to observe the student in a similar physical and emotional state.

7. Conduct the music therapy assessment in a quiet, enclosed space at the school that the student attends. Make real time observations through notes, audio recording, or videotape.

8. Before discussing the assessment session with anyone, study the observation and music therapy assessment documentation and make a direct comparison of the student's performance on targeted IEP objectives with and without the structure of the music therapy strategies.

9. Prepare a written report that documents each step of the assessment process, including the following items:

   a. the purpose of the assessment (an educational section that relates the assessment process to the needs of the student, and to the law);

   b. an outline of the assessment procedure;

   c. relevant information from the files reviewed (especially the targeted IEP goals and objectives);

   d. information from the interviews (be sure to indicate who made each statement, and note who has signed the transcripts of their remarks);

   e. summary of the observations of the classroom and/or other "non-musical" settings (specifically citing the student's performance on targeted objectives);

   f. description of the music therapy assessment setting and general student alertness/behavior on the day of the testing;

   g. detailed description of the music therapy assessment session (specifically citing the student's performance on targeted objectives);

   h. results of the music therapy assessment: a direct comparison of the student's performance of IEP skills *with and without* music therapy intervention;

   i. recommendations for or against music therapy service (which result in service provision and are legally binding);

   j. suggestions (which the district may consider voluntarily).

Presentation of the report and recommendations. After the assessment is completed, an IEP meeting will be called to discuss the results and recommendations. The assessing music therapist should attend this meeting; it is not appropriate for the IEP team to review the music therapy assessment without the music therapist present. Since members of the IEP committee (including the parents) may disagree with the findings of the assessment, the music therapist must be prepared to verbally articulate all parts of the process and defend his or her recommendations.

If the assessment process shows that the student receives a significant assist or significant motivation from music therapy strategies to perform IEP skills, then music therapy may be recommended as a related service for that student. When recommending music therapy services, the music therapist may consider the following factors:

1. If the results of the assessment indicate that music is a primary learning modality for the student, then a recommendation for "direct service" is appropriate. "Direct service" means that the music therapist provides all recommended therapy, and usually implies that the music therapist will "pull" the student out of the classroom for individual or group sessions.

2. If the results of the assessment indicate that music therapy assists the student in performing tasks within the classroom (such as participating as part of a group, or completing tasks at a "listening center" or computer), then a recommendation for "consult-to-student" service should be considered. "Consult" service, as part of a student's IEP, means that that therapist will serve the student in the classroom (or as part of another therapy session, such as speech therapy), and provide information, advice, and materials to the classroom teacher (or therapist) that can be used when the music therapist is not present. This model requires strict documentation on the part of the teacher or therapist and that fact should be listed as a condition of the recommendation.

3. In some cases, a combination of direct and consult service may be recommended. In making *any* recommendation, however, the music therapist should take into consideration the legal standard of "reasonable" benefit. A school district is *not* required (under federal statutes) to provide the maximum amount of therapy possible, and a recommendation to that effect will increase the chances of conflict within the IEP team.

If recommending music therapy services, the music therapist must include goals and objectives. Objectives must be written before placement (Bateman, 1998, p. 156)

If music therapy is *not* recommended, the music therapy report should clearly indicate either (a) the *lack* of a significant difference in the student's performance of IEP tasks with and without music therapy structure, or (b) a student's superior performance without music therapy. If the music therapist explains the SEMTAP to the IEP committee (including parents) prior to conducting the assessment, the meeting at which the assessment results are reviewed will be more likely to proceed smoothly. Parents or other members of the team may disagree with the findings, and the parents have the right to ask for another, independent, assessment. Again, the music therapist must be able to articulate the rationale for his or her recommendations verbally, as well as in writing.

Rationale for Single-Session Assessment Sessions

Since the introduction of the SEMTAP in 1997, the most common question posed by therapists who are considering its use is, "How can I see if a student will benefit from music therapy in a single music therapy session?" Although we agree that additional sessions would provide more information on which to make a recommendation, we have designed the SEMTAP for one or two assessment sessions for two reasons. First, it is unlikely that a school district will pay for multiple assessment sessions, especially in the case of a district that does not employ a full-time music therapist. Most other members of the IEP team conduct their assessments in one or two sessions. In certain cases, multiple sessions might be more useful than in others, but a district will be reluctant to authorize, for example, four sessions for a particular assessment because once one student has been assessed this way, a precedent has been set and other parents will insist on the same standard.

Second, there are several indicators of a student's potential to benefit from music therapy that will appear in the very first session. Therapists can look for the following things that, in a student who responds to music therapy, will contrast with behaviors from the non-musical observation:

1. Increased eye contact with the therapist and musical objects.
2. Reaction to the interruption of music; responsiveness to music used contingently.
3. Changes in posture and movement during music therapy
4. Changes in affect
5. Increased vocalization, imitation of sounds and words, or increased use of language (verbal or augmentative communication)
6. Increased initiation
7. Decreased off-task behavior and verbalizations
8. Ability to recall information from newly presented musical material
9. Ability to sequence actions, words, pictures more readily.

Therapists working with a school district must remember the law when deciding on a recommendation. A student's general enjoyment of music without an observable and significant change in his or her ability to work on tasks from the IEP may be enough to recommend that student for private music therapy. It is not enough, however, to meet the IDEA standard for related services.

The SEMTAP as an Educational Tool

The SEMTAP report, which includes an individualized evaluation and a written explanation of its relationship to the student's IEP, can act as an educational tool—emphasizing the legitimate role of music therapy in special education. In 1977, Alley stated that music therapists must show that their services are "unique enough to be viewed as complementary to, but not overlapping with, standard educational disciplines . . . specific to educational . . . and competitive for available funding resources" (p. 50). This advice is still

Assessment Case Study #1

J was a 10-year-old student diagnosed with autism. He was referred for a music therapy assessment by his IEP committee after a request from his parents. The assessing music therapist provided the team with a checklist outline of the SEMTAP and interviewed the student's mother and classroom teacher. The mother stated that she had requested a music therapy assessment because she had read that music therapy was an effective intervention for children with autism. The classroom teacher stated that although she utilized music each day in the classroom, she had not noticed that J responded differently to music than he did to other interventions.

Targeting objectives. Information gained in the interviews, as well as a review of J's IEP, resulted in the therapist's targeting the following objectives for J:

1. Count at least 5 objects with 1:1 correspondence.
2. Match color word to color.
3. Sequence 3 events in pictorial form.
4. Form sentence "I want " with communication system.
5. Follow 2 step directions with 1 verbal cue.

Non-musical observation. Next, the therapist scheduled an observation in the classroom after talking with the classroom teacher about a time when she could observe J working on the objectives listed above. When the therapist arrived at the appointed time, the teacher commented that J might be "sluggish" because he had a headache, and she described how he had used his picture exchange communication system (PECS) to form the sentence "I want medicine." The therapist immediately rescheduled the observation. When she arrived for the second time, a substitute teacher was present and after a few minutes, the therapist determined that the substitute was not a familiar person to J and was not prepared to demonstrate his work on the targeted objectives. A third observation was scheduled and completed the following week.

During the observation period, J demonstrated the ability to count three objects independently (after a verbal cue) and four to five objects with one to two verbal prompts from the teacher. He accurately matched color words to colors for red and blue with moderate cues for attention, and matched "yellow" to yellow objects in 1 of 3 trials. After the teacher demonstrated the sequencing of three pictures, J completed three sequences with moderate cues for the steps ("What picture comes next?") and minimal cues for attention.

Throughout the observation period, the teacher provided opportunities for J to indicate choices using his PECS notebook. He did so twice in four opportunities presented. When instructions came in two steps (i.e., "Take the yellow ball and put it in the tub marked 'yellow'"), J completed them with one verbal cue in 70% of trials.

During the observation, the teacher stated that J had particular trouble following directions when using scissors. The therapist asked her to demonstrate this and observed that once J had the scissors in his hand, he cut indiscriminately without demonstrating any attention to the instructions of the teacher.

Music therapy assessment session. The music therapist planned an assessment session based on the targeted objectives from J's IEP and the observations she had made in the classroom. The strategies she chose were as follows:

1. Greeting song;
2. The Matching Game (a song adapted to cue J to match colored objects to color words);
3. Six Little Fish (a one-to-one correspondence counting song);

4. The Cutting Song (composed specifically for this assessment session, the song provides verbal, melodic, and rhythmic cues to stop and listen while cutting);

5. What Instrument? (a song that cues the student to choose instruments using an "I want" sentence);

6. Take Me Out to the Ballgame (a picture book for the song and cards showing two 3-step sequences from a baseball game); and

7. Closing/Goodbye song.

Results and report. J was cooperative and pleasant throughout the music therapy assessment session; he went with the therapist without protest and did not attempt to leave the assessment area during the session. However, J did not demonstrate any distinctive responses to music therapy strategies or stimuli. This lack of response manifested itself in several ways. First, J did not show any change in his physical posture or movement when the therapist played her guitar and sang in an upbeat, rhythmic fashion; neither did he respond to a quiet, flowing presentation. Second, J did not respond to interruptions in the music as a nonverbal cue for refocusing his attention; if he looked away from the music therapist or music therapy materials, a sudden silence did not provide a cue for him to look back.

Most importantly, J did not demonstrate improved accuracy or consistency on the targeted IEP objectives. He matched one color to the printed word in four trials. He required the same type of verbal cues to count to four, five, and six as he had in the classroom. The musical presentation of counting did not improve his recitation. J used his PECS notebook appropriately during the instrument song, but did not demonstrate any increase in initiation or speed, and he required the same number and type of verbal cues to create his sentence requests. Because the cutting song was new to J, the therapist demonstrated it, showing J how to pause along with the pauses in the music. Once she handed the scissors to J, however, he demonstrated the same unfocused cutting that he had in the classroom. The music therapist changed tempo, volume and pitch of the song, and occasionally stopped suddenly. There were no changes in J's cutting motion. J did not make eye contact with the songbook for "Take Me Out to the Ballgame." He completed one of two sequences correctly, but did not do so when the instructions were sung; he completed the tasks only when the therapist provided verbal cues and physical prompts.

In the summary report for this assessment, the music therapist stated:

> J was cooperative and compliant throughout the music therapy session. He followed verbal instructions and responded to physical prompts with accuracy. He did not, however, demonstrate any significant responses to music as a structure for IEP-related tasks. There were no visible indications that J responded pleasurably to music in his environment, and he did not show any improvement in attention, responsiveness or accuracy when music was the basis for a task.

The therapist presented the report at a meeting of J's IEP team, having delivered copies of the report to several members of the team (including the parents) ahead of time. She did not recommend music therapy services, stating that the assessment indicated that music therapy was not necessary for J to benefit from his special education program. J's mother stated that, although she was disappointed that he would not receive services, she felt J had been "treated with respect," that she understood how the decision was made, and that she would not pursue this related service at the present time.

Assessment Case Study #2

B was a 9-year-old student diagnosed with mental retardation and autism. She was referred for a music therapy assessment by her IEP committee after repeated requests from her parents and threats of legal action. The assessing music therapist provided the team with a checklist outline of the SEMTAP and interviewed the student's mother and classroom teacher. The mother attempted to relate the history of her disagreements with the school district and asked the music therapist to view a 6-month-old videotape of the student playing in her room while listening to music. The music therapist explained that these things could not be considered in the eligibility assessment process.

In her interview, the classroom teacher stated that if she was having difficulty directing B to tasks, music was an effective tool and that B's best participation occurred during the morning "circle" time in which music was used frequently. She stated that it might be difficult to conduct a "non-musical" observation of B because music was used so often in the classroom.

Targeting objectives. Information gained in the interviews, as well as a review of B's IEP, resulted in the therapist's targeting the following objectives for B:

1. Attend to tasks with "good looking" eyes engaged 2 out of 3 times.
2. Respond to two-part verbal request from adult (pair with sign then fade to verbal only).
3. Pair sign with a functional work activity and a Mayer-Johnson picture.
4. Vocalize using single words or approximations to match/replace nonverbal communication while attending.

Non-musical observation. Throughout the 90-minute observation time, B was cued using three methods: spoken instructions, sung instructions, and picture symbols. Overall, B responded to sung instructions more quickly than spoken ones approximately 50% of the time.

After completing her routine for arriving at school, B chose to work at the computer, and was given a program based on the song "If You're Happy and You Know It." She used an adapted keypad with large picture symbols; the keypad activated the computer program that included a digitized voice singing the song. Lyrics changed according to the pictures selected. B demonstrated enjoyment through smiles and clapping, and pushed the keypad without cues; however, she did not demonstrate the ability to follow a specific command related to the pictures (i.e., "Find the picture of the feet").

During the circle time that followed, B responded to moderate verbal cues and minimal physical cues in using her arms to approximate the signs the teacher demonstrated. Circle time activities included working on the calendar, identifying the day's weather, and dressing a large cutout of a bear for the day (appropriate to the season). B required maximal cuing to make choices, and she made good eye contact with the pictures used for the choices 25% of the time—with her better performance coming after sung instructions. During these activities, B frequently scooted her chair backwards, away from the teacher, requiring the teacher to move her back into the circle.

B required maximum spoken and sung cues to make a transition to her work station. The teacher worked 1:1 with her during this time with tasks that included (a) finding small candies under cups, (b) pulling apart plastic beads from one bin and placing them in a second bin, and (c) taking rings off a pole. B required maximum verbal (including sung) cuing for good eye contact with objects and completion of tasks.

Music therapy assessment session. Following is a list of strategies the therapist selected for the music therapy assessment:

1. Greeting song (establishing vocal range; encouraging vocalization);
2. How are you? (choosing a picture symbol; placing appropriately);
3. Goodnight Room (using manipulatives, making choices);
4. Instrument playing (following verbal, visual, and musical cues);
5. "That Bear" (visually attending, using a switch, encouraging vocalization);
6. Fill the Basket and "Ravioli" (making picture choices, following instructions);
7. Body parts song (identifying body parts, following instructions);
8. Work station song (maintaining focus on task).

The music therapy assessment session with B lasted 45 minutes.

B demonstrated significantly different responses during the music therapy session than those seen during the observation. Her eye contact with the therapist and with the manipulatives and instruments used was significantly more consistent than she had demonstrated during the observation period. Her accuracy in making choices was markedly better. She made significantly more vocalizations, and many more of them were accurate approximations of the lyrics. She was immediately responsive to contingent music: for making choices, for following one- and two-part instructions, and for moving between areas of the classroom. Finally, her ability to remain cooperative with a previously unknown person for almost 45 minutes of musical strategies was significant, given that she usually moves between activities in the classroom every 10 to 15 minutes.

The therapist presented the report at a meeting of B's IEP team, having delivered copies of the report to several members of the team (including the parents) ahead of time. She recommended music therapy services, stating that the assessment indicated that music therapy was necessary for B to benefit from her special education program. After the IEP meeting, the special education administrator for the district asked to meet with the therapist. During this meeting, in which the therapist took the administrator step-by-step through the SEMTAP report, the administrator stated, "I never understood the difference between the music the teacher uses in the classroom and music therapy. Now I do." A music therapist was hired by the school district to serve B *and* to provide consultant and assessment services to other classrooms in the district.

relevant today. A report written with this in mind will record in detail the process by which a recommendation for or against service was made, provide background information on music therapy and music therapy strategies, and make a point-by-point comparison of the student's responses with and without music therapy intervention.

As district personnel become more familiar with music therapy, and as music therapy becomes an accepted related service, much of the background information in a report may be eliminated. Streamlined assessment reports are essential for districts where the therapist may be providing direct service to 20 or more students. The basic outline of the SEMTAP, however, can remain the same: documentation review, interviews, observation, music therapy assessment and written report with recommendations.

The Use of the SEMTAP for Independent Assessments

Over the past three years, the authors have had the opportunity to provide independent music therapy assessments for 22 students in 10 districts that, in most cases, had little or no experience with music therapy. The SEMTAP was used for each of these assessments. The students had a variety of disabilities and recommendations were varied. In only one case, however, did a district continue to refuse to provide service after the SEMTAP recommended it; and in only one case did the parents continue to fight for music therapy services after a recommendation against it by the assessing music therapist. In eight of these assessments, statements made by the district or by parents indicated conflict and/or animosity between the two. In some of these same situations, however, district representatives stated that the SEMTAP had educated them about the role of music therapy in special education. In three situations in which music therapy service was denied, parents expressed regret or sadness about the decision but did not pursue it further.

Conclusion

Increased publicity about the power of music and the efficacy of music therapy intervention likely will result in increased requests for music therapy services in public school special education. Music therapists must be prepared to guide parents and school districts in a step-by-step assessment process that respects the individual needs of each student while conforming to federal and state law. Our goal should not be to defend our profession through conflict and legal challenges, but rather to provide the education and professional standards that will make parent/district animosity and court cases rare.

A single, standardized test is not necessary to meet the standards of special education assessment. On the contrary, such an instrument may take the "individual" out of the Individualized Education Program. A standardized *process,* however, such as the SEMTAP can provide consistent, lucid recommendations in a format that educates parents and professionals about the unique role of music therapy as a related service in special education.

References

Alley, J. M. (1977). Education for the severely handicapped: The role of music therapy. *Journal of Music Therapy, 14,* 50–59.

Bateman, B. D. (1998). *Better IEPs: How to develop legally correct and educationally useful programs.* Longmont, CO: Sopris West.

Boxill, E. H. (1985). *Music therapy for the developmentally disabled.* Rockville, MD: Aspen Press.

Bruscia, K. E. (1987). *Improvisational models of music therapy.* Springfield, IL: Charles C. Thomas.

Gfeller, K., & Baumann, A. A. (1988). Assessment procedures for music therapy with hearing impaired children: Language development. *Journal of Music Therapy, 25*(4), 192–205.

Grant, R. E. (1995). Music therapy assessment for developmentally disabled clients. In T. Wigram, B. Saperston, & R. West (Eds.), *The art and science of music therapy: A handbook.* Switzerland: Harwood Academic.

Individuals with Disabilities Education Act Amendments (1997, 20 U.S.C. 1400).

Johnson, F. L. (1996). Models of service delivery. In B. Wilson (Ed.), *Models of music therapy interventions in school settings: From institution to inclusion.* Silver Spring, MD: National Association for Music Therapy.

Martin, R. (1991). *Special education law in America: The rights of the student and the responsibilities of those who serve.* Arlington, TX: Future Horizons.

Rider, M. (1981). The assessment of cognitive functioning level through musical perception. *Journal of Music Therapy, 18,* 110–119.

6

MODELS OF SERVICE DELIVERY
AND THEIR RELATION TO THE IEP

Faith L. Johnson

WHEN Public Law 94-142 was passed into law in 1975, it provided a framework for identifying special education needs, planning and implementing appropriate educational programs to meet those needs, and providing direction for qualified personnel to staff schools with special education programs. As a result of this law, there were significant changes in the way public education designed and delivered services to students with special education needs. School districts identified students with special needs through assessment procedures and provided specialized, and often segregated, services to meet those needs. Music therapy was recognized as a related service that was available for school districts to provide in their special education programs.

In the years that followed this landmark legislation, public school districts focused on providing students with access to educational opportunities. Until the late 1990s, special education continued to evolve according to developments in teacher preparation, advancements in the identification and assessment of student needs, and fluctuations in financial and human resources available to meet those needs. Music therapy, a non-mandated related service, was susceptible to changes in funding and perceived effectiveness.

The Individuals with Disabilities Education Act Amendments of 1997 changed the focus of special education to teaching and learning, so that students with disabilities would have opportunities to achieve real educational results. These outcomes were seen as occurring through meaningful access to the general curriculum. The role of parents in the educational planning and decision making for their children was strengthened. The major issues contained in the IDEA Amendments included: increased involvement of regular education teachers in the education of students with special education needs, coordination of the IEP with the general curriculum, and involvement of students with special education needs in state and district assessments.

Students in special education programs present a variety of needs that may or may not be accommodated in regular education classes, but the focus of IDEA is to make reasonable attempts to meet those needs in a regular classroom. The special education services that are provided for them are regarded as providing support for the student to function within the general curriculum.

These services (i.e., therapies, accommodations and modifications to the learning environment, support services) have been delivered in a variety of models, including self-contained classes, resource services, the "pull out" model (in which students were removed from settings that included their regular education peers), or within the regular classroom setting. While historically it was assumed that special educators could provide the most appropriate programs for students with special needs, the current thinking is that students with special education needs can benefit from exposure to and involvement in the general curriculum. Regular education programs were asked to make reasonable accommodations to meet students' individual needs.

Before the IDEA 1997 Amendments were passed, music therapy was a separate program (a related service), a support program (to existing music education services), or a replacement program (to provide music education services to special education students who may not be receiving them). Music therapists were frequently called upon to provide a different kind of music education (special music education) to students with special needs. In some instances, they were also assigned to provide music therapy services to students with special needs. At times these services were in addition to music education; in other cases music therapy services replaced music education. The typical settings for music therapy, as with other separate special education programs, included self-contained classes, one-on-one therapy, and occasionally a combination program of therapy and education.

In keeping with the changing practices of the changing times, music therapy has had to adapt by being more relevant to the general curriculum and focusing on the child's involvement in regular education. Over the years, special education has decreased the number of separate programs in favor of increasing programs that support regular education. Students with special needs are now more frequently placed in regular education classes, with special educators, therapists, and other personnel providing support to the regular classroom teacher. Special education is no longer viewed as the only way to provide appropriate services to students with special needs, but rather as a partner to regular education, with each component contributing to the education of the students.

Music therapists now provide services using a variety of working models, including direct services in self-contained special education settings, direct services in inclusive settings, and consultant services to staff and community members.

Direct Services Delivery

When music therapy is provided by a music therapist to a student (or case load of students), this is known as *direct services* delivery. The contact between the therapist and student is immediate. The direct services model, which allows for qualified personnel with specific areas of expertise to work with students toward individual goals, is currently the delivery system for most special education services. Students are taught by a teacher, receive speech therapy from a speech pathologist, or attend adaptive physical education classes with an adaptive physical education teacher.

The Music Therapist as a Member of a Multidisciplinary Team

Philosophy of the Multidisciplinary Model

One model of direct service delivery is through a *multidisciplinary team* approach. In this model, professionals with a variety of backgrounds and areas of expertise work with the student toward the IEP goals. In a school setting, the team includes professionals that are affiliated with an educational facility, such as the classroom teacher(s), an adaptive physical education teacher, and a social worker. Other members of the team are representatives of medical or rehabilitative disciplines, such as occupational therapy and speech pathology, plus parents or child advocates. Each member of the team has direct contact with the student, and contributes to the process through assessment, goal-setting, program implementation and evaluation. What separates this model from other team models is the separation of team members from each other. Each member of the team develops a separate plan to meet the needs of the student. In addition, team members implement only their individual sections of the plan.

By working within the parameters of a professional discipline, individual team members contribute to the total educational program, yet each discipline maintains a separate identity. Although communication among team members is assumed, it does not always happen. When team members meet to set goals, write the IEP, or compare student progress in each disciplinary area, the success of this communication is dependent on each member's thorough understanding and knowledge of the other disciplines. The lack of visibility of team members to one another, especially in school settings where meeting time for staff groups is negligible, makes it especially important for the music therapist to educate other team members about the uniqueness and effectiveness of music in meeting student needs.

As a member of a multidisciplinary team, the music therapist should emphasize the interrelationships between music therapy and the features of other disciplines. This includes: setting up meetings with other professionals, offering to demonstrate a success story or technique to another team member, arranging a regular time to discuss students with other team members, inviting other team members to attend part of a therapy session, or distributing printed information regarding student progress in music therapy to other team members.

Program Planning and Implementation

For the multidisciplinary team, assessment is completed in separate areas as each discipline evaluates the student from a different perspective. For example, the physical therapist usually looks at skills that affect the student's motor abilities, the speech therapist examines the student's ability to effectively use language and communicate, and the classroom teacher collects information about academic and/or functional abilities. Assessment practices are implemented separately, and the results are compiled when all the team members meet to make educational plans.

The lack of standardized music therapy assessment tools should not prevent the music therapist from becoming involved in this phase of the multidisciplinary team process. There is an opportunity to introduce assessment results from observation, therapist-made tools, and other informal methods to the team's review of student needs. Since music therapy is a related service, the interpretation of assessment results are both appropriate and essential to the team process.

The role of parents in the multidisciplinary team process is not integral to the team concept. Parents meet with individual team members, each of whom discusses the needs of the student in terms of a specific area of need (e.g., motor, cognitive, language, etc.). It is often difficult to get parents involved in team decisions. At the team meeting, assessment results are discussed by all the disciplines represented on the team, and student goals are written in terms of each individual discipline, based on student needs in that area. The occupational therapist sets the fine motor goals, the classroom teacher addresses academic or classroom goals, and the music therapist establishes goals within the music experience. Musical goals address the musical or music education needs of the students, while non-musical goals can be coordinated with the goals of other disciplines, namely motor, communication, cognitive, and social needs of the student. For example, if a student needs to develop more appropriate group skills (e.g., sitting next to peers during a group activity), the music therapist addresses this goal within a music group experience. The goal is non-musical, but the learning environment is a musical one. In addition, the music therapist can also address a goal that comes from the music education curriculum, such as vocalizing with the group during a singing activity. Working toward musical goals and non-musical goals can occur simultaneously.

It is at the goal-setting level that the student's educational program is coordinated into a single document, the IEP. While goals are written in terms of the discipline itself, there remains a sense of teamwork in working with the student on a daily basis. For example, a physical therapy goal might focus on developing mobility around the school building; the classroom teacher writes goals related to academic ("classroom") development in the areas of reading, math and language development; the music therapist establishes goals so the student can develop in a variety of ways via the medium of musical involvement. While the goals are specific to each professional discipline, they are written in an atmosphere of cooperation among the disciplines.

Following the team's review of assessment results and student goals, implementation of the student's educational program is enacted by professionals who work in relative isolation from each other. Each discipline is part of the educational team, but the program is a sum of many different parts. Among the advantages of the multidisciplinary team approach is the spirit of coordination and cooperation among the specific services in meeting the student's needs. While mutual respect and responsibility among the disciplines is a desirable outcome of the multidisciplinary team process, the resulting fragmented approach to education is also one of its disadvantages. The student seems to receive services in parts, with each discipline addressing a specific area of need. With this method of service delivery, services are often duplicated or overlapped, and it becomes difficult for the student's program to be integrated into a whole.

Staff Development

In the multidisciplinary team model, staff development is independent of the team concept. Each discipline participates in inservice training or continuing education according to that particular discipline's territorial boundaries. For example, a speech pathologist would not necessarily need to be familiar with the work of the music therapist, the influence of music on behavior, or the role of music therapy in the total education of the student. In the multidisciplinary team model, the speech pathologist would be primarily concerned with speech and language development.

The Music Therapist as a Member of an Interdisciplinary Team

Philosophy of the Interdisciplinary Model

In the interdisciplinary approach to education, professionals provide services in a variety of disciplinary areas, just as they do in the multidisciplinary model. However, team members on the interdisciplinary team share their IEP goals and implementation plans with each other. Each member of the team knows how each other member intends to provide services to the student. Since team members implement their own sections of the plan, there is no crossing or blurring of professional boundaries.

Program Planning and Implementation

Assessment takes place in separate disciplines, although the results are shared with the other team members. Parents meet with the team as a group, providing for the possibility of a more coordinated program than in the multidisciplinary approach. The team plan incorporates all the disciplines.

In this model, the music therapist has an opportunity to educate the other team members about music therapy, although this is not an essential element of interdisciplinary teams. Still, there is a greater chance for including music therapy as a legitimate service than in the multidisciplinary approach.

The IEP is developed and implemented by the group, but there is little or no crossover of objectives between professional disciplines. What occurs in the classroom is different from what occurs in physical therapy, which in turn is different from the activities in speech and language. The music therapist can fill a unique role on the interdisciplinary team by demonstrating how boundaries can be changed or eliminated through an all-inclusive pursuit such as music. For example, music therapy goals can reflect classroom goals by working on readiness, academic, or functional skills. Physical therapy goals can be practiced in the music therapy setting through mobility activities, while speech and language goals can be met in an additional setting through opportunities for self expression.

Staff Development

Just as is the case in the multidisciplinary team approach, staff development occurs within each discipline. However, because of the team sharing that takes place at least at the program planning stage, individual professionals often seek additional information or training in other areas.

The Music Therapist as a Member of a Transdisciplinary Team

Philosophy of the Transdisciplinary Model

A *transdisciplinary team* includes members with backgrounds in a variety of fields, but the work of the team surpasses individual professional identities and coordinates all its efforts on behalf of the student. In addition, parents are an integral component of the team. As a result of this approach, all team members are responsible for how the educational plan is implemented. Often, IEP goals are met in a number of settings, with team members truly working together throughout the entire process.

In the transdisciplinary model, the student is not regarded as a set of problem areas or deficient skills, but as a complete person who is capable of functioning within the school setting and society as a whole. Therefore, team members (including parents) plan a coordinated program for the student based on needs, resources, and educational priorities. Rather than working independently of each other, disciplinary lines become blurred or eliminated because the emphasis is for the student to perform functional activities in meaningful contexts. In other words, students learn to complete whole tasks in real school or community settings. For example, instead of learning a fine motor skill in occupational therapy and being expected to transfer that skill in another situation, the student and teacher are instructed by the occupational therapist in how best to complete tasks that use fine motor functions. Rather than doing isolated activities that "drill" hand skills, the teacher uses the knowledge of the skill in daily activities that occur in the classroom to instruct the student in picking up crayons to place them in their appropriate container, or returning a book to its shelf.

In the transdisciplinary model, team members plan, implement, and evaluate the students' educational programs together. Each staff person involved with the student works on instructional tasks that include motor, sensory, communication, cognitive, and social components. Therefore, a group of students with needs in the area of motor development might work with an occupational therapist, an adaptive physical education teacher, and a music therapist since each can design activities that will help meet this goal. In this group, each professional provides the expertise of a disciplinary field, but works cooperatively to provide the most meaningful experiences for the students. The music therapist has an important role in the transdisciplinary approach because music experiences typically provide for the integration of a number of motor, cognitive, communication, sensory and social skills.

For example, if students need experiences that will train the neurological system to adapt to different kinds of movement, the occupational therapists and physical therapists might recommend supervised spinning on a scooter board. With the input of the classroom teacher, who may want to involve as many students in the group as possible, a game is designed in which each individual student is spun on the scooter board inside a circle of students. As the music therapist becomes involved in the design of the activity, music is added to assist in making the activity more fun and more meaningful for the student. The music reflects the character of the activity; it stops when the student stops spinning. The music provides a language base for what is going on in the activity. In addition, the other students remain involved in the activity as they wait for their turns.

For the transdisciplinary approach to be effective, there must be group process among team members, goal identification according to the needs of the student (rather than along traditional disciplinary lines), and established procedures for solving problems. All staff working with the student must assume responsibility for contributing to the complete education of the student, and must be prepared to address the concerns of parents that students receive less direct service. Issues of liability for services provided by "non-designated" disciplines (i.e., physical therapy objectives being addressed in music therapy, or speech and language objectives being met in occupational therapy, etc.) must be resolved. Communication, cooperation, and flexibility among all staff members is essential for the transdisciplinary approach to work.

The transdisciplinary approach has been shown to be effective in meeting the needs of students with multiple disabilities, and in developing an atmosphere in which there is an innovative exchange of ideas among professionals (Anderson, Hawkins, Hamilton, & Hampton, 1999). A music therapist working on such a team has the opportunity to demonstrate first hand how music can meet student needs. Professionals in other disciplines also become familiar with music experiences and are able to recognize the advantages of using music to address a variety of goal areas.

Program Planning and Implementation

In the transdisciplinary team model, students are assessed in terms of whole entities: the student is a person who engages in integrated, functional activities (as opposed to individual skills) which require the interplay of motor, cognitive, sensory, social, communicative, and emotional areas. The purpose of assessment is to gather information that will lead to instructional practices. By focusing on the student holistically, the transdisciplinary assessment often reveals more specific information than do more traditional assessment tools. In addition, time is not wasted assessing skills that are not essential to the educational program. This approach places the needs of the student first, and is not dependent on typical disciplinary approaches. At the assessment level, the transdisciplinary model provides an excellent opportunity for the music therapist to become directly involved with the team at this early stage. Goals for each student are written in terms of prioritized needs, determined by the team, with each disciplinary area regarded as a strategy toward goal attainment, rather than *the* one-and-only way for the student to learn skills. An emphasis is placed on age-appropriate, functional goals, and therapy-related objectives are integrated into everyday classroom situations.

In addition to working together in the assessment and goal-setting parts of the transdisciplinary process, members of the team work cooperatively with students throughout the school day. For example, students with sensorimotor needs might be involved in activities planned and led by an occupational therapist, a music therapist, and a classroom teacher. Likewise, a community-based experience can involve a speech/ communication specialist, a classroom teacher, and an educational assistant working with students whose needs are coordinated into one activity. In the implementation of the program, professionals not only interact with students, but also teach their peers in other disciplines. As professionals work and communicate with each other on a regular basis, information is exchanged, observations are made and validated by other staff, and the students remain at the center of the discussion. This process of crossing professional boundaries is essential to the team building process. Rather than receiving traditional direct services two or three times per week, or during a specific time during the school day, the student's program is coordinated into each instructional area over the course of the entire school week. As a result, the services a student receives are more in the realm of indirect or consultant services, rather than traditional direct services.

In order for the transdisciplinary model to be successful, professionals must meet regularly, and each team member must remain accountable for the student's total program. In the interest of cost-effective educational programs, more than one professional working with even a group of students can be regarded as duplication of energy or an unaffordable ratio of staff to students. Yet, in the long run, students receive a more complete and relevant package of services, since each student's program is integrated at the instructional level. The student's needs remain as the primary focus through all phases of the educational process. Each professional discipline is recognized as an important contributor to the development of the whole student, and, in the case of a lesser known discipline like music therapy, there is the opportunity for promoting the field as a viable and effective way to meet student needs.

Staff Development

Staff development in the transdisciplinary approach is an integral component. Team members learn informally and through formal training about the techniques and strategies that comprise the student's educational program. Team meetings have staff development as a central component, as professionals work across disciplines. The music therapist is an equal partner in the implementation of the plan, and has a prime opportunity to educate other professionals and parents about music therapy.

Traditional Direct Services

A traditional direct services model is often referred to as "pull-out" therapy, since music therapy services are delivered to the student outside the classroom setting. The student is removed from the school activity, taken to another location for therapy, and then returned to the classroom.

The "pull-out" model allows for intense, individualized work toward educational goals. Often, multiple functions are incorporated into the musical experience, as the music therapist works in many goal areas simultaneously. Whatever amount of time is spent in music therapy, the total amount belongs to the music therapist and the student, allowing the musical experience to be focused entirely on the needs of the student.

This model has some potential disadvantages for both the therapist and the student. For example, removing students from the classroom routine reduces the communication among the professionals involved with the student. It is difficult to relay the work that is accomplished in therapy to other members of the educational team when the therapist works in relative isolation. Working in this manner, there is also little opportunity for the music therapist to engage in a professional exchange with other disciplines. In addition, the "pull-out" model sets students apart from their peers, because they are removed from the classroom. Since there is little or no opportunity to learn skills in a real life situation, it is assumed that the transfer of skills from the therapy setting to school, home, and community will occur. Furthermore, the musical experience associated with music therapy in the "pull-out" model appears to the outside observer to be similar to music lessons, music education class, or recreational music. While activities that take place in music therapy resemble typical musical endeavors, the underlying reasons for involving the student in these experiences are quite different. Music lessons are intended to teach a student mastery of the voice or an instrument; in music therapy, the lesson format is often used to help the student achieve non-musical goals, such as increasing vital capacity, facilitating inclusion, or developing skills in appropriate nonverbal expression. The purpose of the music education class is to provide students with fundamental skills in music upon which they can build a lifetime of musical involvement; a music therapist provides music class experiences for a student to develop individually, to increase language, or to practice motor patterns that are used in daily living. Although music therapy may look on the surface like recreational music, it is primarily used to help the student develop leisure time skills, to provide an appropriate outlet for feelings, and to offer an alternative to standard recreational activities.

Working in Self-Contained Classes

In many educational facilities, classrooms for students with special needs continue to be self-contained units, especially when they are established to meet severe and multiple needs of students. Providing music therapy services for students within classroom settings is often difficult since music is an auditory medium that distracts the students who are not working with the therapist. On the other hand, the "spill over" effect may be beneficial for students who receive indirect instruction while the therapist concentrates on the students receiving direct attention.

In self-contained classes of students with severe needs, one approach is to use a "round robin" process, since it can be implemented in a variety of ways. During a class period, the music therapist works with one or two students at a time, while other students are engaged in other activities with other classroom staff. For example, one student might be practicing self care skills, another student is learning a work strategy, and other students are involved in an interactive story. The therapist completes the work with the first small group, and then moves on to the next designated students until all students have received direct services. There are several advantages to using this method. Students receive individual attention from the therapist, and the learning atmosphere for the total time period contains a musical element. For students who need some pre-instruction before receiving direct services, the "round robin" method provides students with a preparatory phase. This model is also effective for half-day classrooms where students have a limited time to complete their instructional activities. Finally, this method can be a non-threatening way to introduce classroom staff to the implementation of music therapy services.

Another in-class model for self-contained classrooms places the music therapist in the role of instructional leader for the entire class. Classroom staff (teachers, educational assistants, aides, parent volunteers) become directly involved in the session through hands-on work with individual students. With this method, each student participates in all activities, group cohesiveness is established, and classroom staff become familiar with the process of music therapy. To get everyone involved in the learning experience, classroom staff can be assigned musical accompaniment parts, such as strumming the autoharp or playing an ostinato on the bass chime bars. This arrangement can serve as an excellent role model because students see familiar people engaged in and deriving pleasure from music experiences. This in-class model also serves to train classroom staff in the implementation of activities to be repeated at times when the music therapist is not present. As the music therapist and staff work together, there is an exchange of ideas for providing effective instruction to students. Using this model, classroom staff witness firsthand the positive responses and the progress of their students to music.

Working in Inclusive Classes

With the realities of inclusion, delivering services such as speech, occupational, and physical therapies to students in the traditional "pull-out" model is being increasingly challenged. Inclusion typically means educating all children with disabilities in regular classrooms regardless of the nature of their disabling conditions (The Association for Persons with Severe Handicaps [TASH}, 1994). Educational services are provided within regular schools, and often within the regular classroom. Friendships between non-disabled and disabled students are encouraged, and the emphasis is on an educational program that is appropriate to students' lifelong needs. In some studies of inclusive settings, improved self-esteem and increased social skills of special learners have been reported (Yasutake & Lerner, 1997), as well as increases in skill development (Fowler & Lewman, 1998). Advocates for inclusion see it as a way to change attitudes about students with disabilities, promote teamwork among teachers and staff, and develop interpersonal skills among diverse groups of students. Many studies have attempted to identify the ingredients and attitudes necessary for successful inclusion practices, including accepting diversity as the norm, performance-based and alternative assessment, and collaborative teaching arrangements (Gerent, 1998; Hobbs & Westing, 1998; Moore, Gilbreath, & Maiuri, 1998).

Students are often placed in inclusive arts and physical education classes before they are included on a regular basis in academic classes. In these cases, the music therapist who provides direct services is in a position to not only affect the student's ability to participate in music education, but also lay the groundwork for successful inclusion practices for the classroom setting as well.

In a model of inclusion, therapists are encouraged to work with students within the classroom and other typical school settings, rather than taking students to isolated therapy rooms for treatment two or three times a week. For example, an occupational therapist might work on fine motor skills with a student in an inclusive home economics class, a physical therapist may assist a student in balance activities during a bowling game in PE class, and the speech therapist can train a student to use a communication device during class discussion. This model of service delivery works toward two main objectives: (a) to diminish the isolation of the student with special needs by providing services in a natural setting, and (b) to provide "spill over" effect in which the work done with the special student also enhances the education of the other students in the group.

Implementing music therapy in the inclusive classroom is often more difficult than in a self-contained class. The sound generated by music and the activity of the students can be distracting for students engaged in other classroom activities. However, there are some options for delivering music therapy in an inclusive setting. For example, the music therapist could involve the entire class in an activity that will serve to benefit all students (IEP goals for the targeted student(s) and other goals for the students receiving indirect instruction). Another way to provide services is through reverse inclusion, in which regular education students are integrated into the classroom activities of students with special needs. A third alternative for providing music therapy in an inclusive setting is to use audio equipment that can accommodate headphones. Electronic instruments (keyboards, guitars, MIDI instruments) involve students in live music experiences, but keep distractions for other students to a minimum.

One of the most effective ways to deliver music therapy services within an inclusive class is to work with the targeted student in music education class. This method not only provides the student with direct instruction, but also supports the music educator with on-site consultation services. In the general music class, the music therapist and the music educator can work as co-teachers. In this situation, it is important for goal-setting, planning, and implementation to be completed by both professionals in the spirit of inclusion. It would be inappropriate for the music therapist to concentrate only on the students with special needs, and the music educator to teach only the students in general education, since this will only serve to divide students into separate groups. The purpose of having the music therapist in the class is to meet the needs of a diverse group of students and to promote cooperation. Therefore, the music therapist needs to be cognizant of the school district's philosophy regarding inclusion and the rationale for including students in regular music classes. Providing music therapy services within the general music class helps reduce the frustration felt by many music educators who assume they must adapt every lesson to a wide variety of individual needs.

Similar strategies are used in inclusive performing groups. During rehearsal of an instrumental or vocal group, the music therapist can provide on-site assistance to the student and teacher by: (a) observing the student's ability to function in the performance group and working with the music educator to set realistic goals, (b) adapting the instructional environment for the student so the rehearsal can proceed, and (c) providing on-site inservice training to the music educator and demonstrating accommodations that can be made. In addition, the student who needs additional practice/lesson opportunities can work with the music therapist in a lesson format. Lessons are structured to work in conjunction with the student's regular music lesson with the music educator and are not meant to replace the inclusive lesson experience.

The Use of Technology in Direct Service Delivery

Music therapists use a variety of tools in their work; the elements of music are manipulated and adapted, and the therapist applies appropriate materials and equipment to the musical experience. If music, instruments, and music activities are the tools of the music therapist's trade, technological devices are additions to this toolbox. Electronic instruments, music applications for the computer, speech synthesizers, and adaptive devices continue to be produced and refined, and many of these are appropriate to music therapy practice. Yet, even with the daily advancements in the variety and range of technological devices available to music therapists, these implements must still be used according to established standards of clinical practice. In other words, technology supports the attainment of IEP goals.

Depending on student needs, equipment availability, and the level of comfort of the music therapist in using technological devices, there is a multitude of applications in clinical practice. For example, the development of the touch-sensitive keyboard has allowed persons with limited hand strength and finger dexterity the opportunity to play a keyboard instrument. Instruments that can be powered by batteries provide students with access to portable leisure time activities. Composition programs for the computer make it possible for students with limited cognitive understanding of the fundamentals of music to have a means for self-expression and a creative outlet. In addition, many of these technological devices can be utilized to facilitate inclusion by providing special education students with disabilities with means to participate in the general curriculum.

Assistive Technology

One segment of the comprehensive field of technology is *assistive technology* (AT), which is defined as the use of devices and services that help people with disabilities of all ages in their daily lives. The definition is broad for a reason, so that programs related to providing assistive technology to people who need it do not restrict themselves to dealing *only* with computers or sophisticated technology. There is much more to AT than computer technology, although this is a significant and very fast-growing part of the field. Devices that fall under the heading of AT may include computers, as well as such things as a remote control to operate a television or CD player, an amplifier for the ear piece of a telephone, and a remote switch that will turn an appliance on and off. Assistive technology services include evaluation of individuals to determine a need for technology, instruction in the use of AT devices, and inservice training for staff to more effectively work with people.

School districts have responded to the growth and widespread use of technology in the classroom by developing staff positions to oversee the technology life of a school. The job descriptions for these coordinators of technology may vary, and they may be known by a variety of titles, but their primary function is to assist staff and students in utilizing computers and software in the educational process. People who coordinate the use of assistive technology may also be identified in specific schools or programs. These people can include speech pathologists with knowledge of language and speech devices, occupational therapists with expertise in adaptive devices and materials, or school staff with experience in using regular and assistive technology in the classroom.

Assistive Technology in Music Therapy

Just as music therapists work in a variety of settings to meet a multitude of individual needs, so are there numerous applications of assistive technology in the field of music therapy. In many cases, the tools themselves may be the same or similar across populations, but the applications vary according to the setting. For example, computer programs (including any music applications) can be adapted so that a student can independently operate the software using a simple switch, an adapted keyboard, or a standard computer keyboard that has been reconfigured to meet the student's specific needs. These adaptations may be used with students with physical disabilities, cognitive or sensory limitations, or learning disabilities. In addition, there are devices that are not related to computers that can be used to provide students in special education programs with access to educational activities. These devices use less complex technology than do computers, but are no less effective and applicable in appropriate situations. One example of such a piece of equipment is the Talkpad, a voice-output speech device developed by Frame Technologies to enable people without speech to express up to four words or phrases. The Talkpad has been used successfully in a musical context by pre-recording a four-phrase song, with each line of the song being associated with each of the four buttons. For students with limited physical or cognitive abilities, but emerging *musical* abilities, the Talkpad, and other devices like it, can be used so students can participate in singing activities. On an even less complicated level than "singing" a four-line stanza, the Talkpad can also be pre-recorded to "sing" a repetitive phrase of a song. The student merely touches any one of the four buttons to produce the repeated line at the appropriate time in the song. The Talkpad can be pre-recorded by a student who has speech. This is best done by a student of the same gender and age as the nonverbal student.

Technology Training

Just as there are daily developments in new technologies that hit the market, so are there an increasing number of opportunities for applied training. As local school districts have placed greater importance on technological literacy, training resources have geared up to meet those needs. Classes, workshops, and seminars provide participants with background information and usually hands-on work with the equipment itself. In the area of music for students with special education needs, staff training has at least two major

---

Case Studies: Direct Service Delivery

"Carrie," a student with cognitive and language disabilities, attended a regular K–5th grade school, and was a member of the school chorus. At the music teacher's request, the music therapist rearranged the choral music so that Carrie could follow the printed page and keep up with the rest of the group. In addition, the therapist worked with Carrie for 30 minutes every week to practice the music individually, and to work on any parts that needed attention. In this setting, Carrie was able to articulate which passages were difficult for her, and she and the music therapist were able to practice strategies for overcoming the musical obstacles she encountered. Carrie was able to rehearse and perform the music with the chorus without any other intervention.

Another student, "Jim," signed up for trombone lessons and band at the high school he attended. Because of his physical limitations, progress was very slow, but steady. Jim had difficulty keeping up with the pace of the band, and no matter how much he practiced at home, the group lessons continued to present a challenge to him. The music therapist was contacted by the band director, who valued Jim's positive attitude and determination, and wanted him to be able to continue in the program. Jim's band music was reconfigured to allow him time within the context of the music to make necessary note changes, and the music therapist also provided one-to-one lessons to help Jim develop new playing strategies. Jim continued to participate in all band and lesson activities, including marching season, a trip to the state basketball tournament, and several concerts throughout the year.

"Mike" was a student in an inclusive general music class in an elementary school. Mike was especially responsive to music, but because of severe behavioral difficulties, was not able to make a satisfactory transition from his class to the music class. The time it took for the teacher to settle the students and get the class started presented an obstacle to Mike's success. The music therapist provided direct services to Mike by assisting him with a transition program. In addition, the therapist worked with the music educator to develop effective strategies for working with a class in which students had very diverse needs. This program helped reduce the number of variables with which the music educator had to cope, and the therapist was able to provide support and on-site assistance to both Mike and the teacher. Mike's success in going from class to music class and back to his regular class carried over into the rest of his educational program.

---

components: teachers and therapists are called upon to become familiar with technological developments in the area of *music* (composition, sequencing, synthesizing, recording, sampling, etc.) as well as the area of *assistive technology* (adaptive devices, adapted software, low tech or high tech uses, etc.).

Music therapists who utilize technology in their daily work can serve as excellent resources for information, training, and product development. Many of those who utilize technology in their practices are self-taught individuals who worked with particular devices until they became skilled in using them. Once familiarity was established, these individuals made the transition from personal use to use in their professional endeavors.

The School Music Therapist: Education or Therapy?

Parents and student advocacy groups have worked diligently for many years so that the educational community will regard students with special needs as a diverse population of *learners*, rather than children with conditions that need to be "fixed" with therapy. Some school districts have moved away from terminology such as *therapist, therapy,* or *treatment* to words that are centered in educational language. In fact, in some states, services can be provided by the local school district only if they are "educationally necessary." Services that have a medical basis (as "therapy" does), must be provided by other agencies. Therefore, if a student receives physical therapy, occupational therapy, nursing services, or music therapy in a school, it should be for educational reasons.

Music therapy in a school setting does not replace music education or recreational music opportunities, but joins these programs as another option for meeting IEP goals. Since music therapy is regarded as an instructional support program, it *is* compatible with the educational model. School music therapists must be prepared to fill the roles of teachers, consultants to teachers, and instructional team members. The result is a blend of education *and* therapy that assists students with special needs in using their strengths to minimize their disabilities and maximize their potential.

The Music Therapist as a Consultant

Music therapists are often assigned to provide consultant support to teachers and additional school personnel. The consultant role is quite different from that of providing direct music therapy services to students. Whereas direct services involve immediate contact with students on a regular basis, consultant services are provided to other individuals who work with the student (namely, teachers, parents, administrators, and other school personnel), and may range from a single meeting to regularly scheduled contacts throughout the school year.

Consulting to Facilitate Inclusion

In some school districts, the music therapist fills the role of consultant in order to facilitate the practice of inclusion. According to The Association for Persons with Severe Handicaps (TASH, 1994), inclusion means "providing necessary services within the regular schools" and "supporting regular teachers . . . by providing time, training, teamwork, resources, and strategies." The support that is provided should not only be for the regular education classroom teachers, but also for music teachers who work with inclusive groups of students. To design and provide appropriate educational activities for students with special needs, a music therapist works with regular education teachers from planning through the implementation stage. The music therapist is qualified by credentials and background to address the unique role music plays in the education of students with disabilities. Dual certification (such as a teaching license in music education) is an additional asset in the area of inclusion and enhances the music therapist's credibility in dealing with special education as well as regular education personnel.

Consulting to Facilitate Music Education

Music educators working with special education classes should have access to trained professionals for the purpose of consultation. Although the similarities between music education and music therapy are numerous, some music teachers regard the music therapist as being concerned only with students with special education needs. If the music therapist remains sensitive to the music educator's complete teaching assignment, consultant work on behalf of students with special needs will be more effective. In addition, the therapist will have to work at making music therapy part of the educational setting and school life. Rather than becoming a threat to the educator's effectiveness as a teacher, the therapist needs to be aware of the complex educational and societal issues facing school staffs. The music therapist filling a consulting role is most effective when maintaining a peer relationship with the educator on behalf of students with special needs. Music therapy services have a different goal emphasis than music education, but should not be portrayed as superior to, or as a replacement for, music education. All students need music education. Some students with disabilities also need music therapy services.

As described in other chapters of this book, music educators typically report having a lack of information regarding the handicapping conditions of students in their classrooms and limited input into the IEP development process. Yet, music educators continue to urge each other to become active participants in the process of inclusion and school policies regarding teaching inclusive groups of students (Thompson, 1999). The same suggestions are made to music educators as to classroom teachers to facilitate inclusion: collaboration with peers (Thompson, 1999), developing peer and cross-age tutoring (Sheldon, 2001), developing competencies (such as having alternative expectations that are suitable to students of diverse abilities), being able to problem-solve and use informal assessment methods, and providing opportunities for daily successes of the students. Music educators who teach hundreds of students per week, including students with special needs, find it difficult to become involved in the planning and implementation process of special education programs for individual students.

With the introduction of National Standards for Music Education (Music Educators National Conference [MENC], 1994), music educators began looking at the components of quality music education programs from a more unified perspective. To be successful, they will need support in order to design appropriate programs that assist students with special education needs in reaching the following standards that have been established:

1. Students will be able to sing, alone and with others, a varied repertoire of music;
2. Students will be able to perform on instruments, alone and with others, a varied repertoire of music;
3. Students will be able to improvise melodies, variations, and accompaniments;
4. Students will be able to compose and arrange music within specified guidelines;
5. Students will be able to read and notate music ;
6. Students will be able to listen to, analyze, and describe music;
7. Students will be able to evaluate music and music performance;
8. Students will be able to understand relationships between music, the other arts, and disciplines outside the arts;
9. Students will be able to understand music in relation to history and culture (MENC, 1994).

School music programs that are able to meet these standards must also address the individual needs of all students. The music therapist who works as a consultant to music educators must become familiar with the MENC National Standards, as well as the state or individual school district's plan for implementing those standards. Students with special education needs can work toward achieving each standard, but the educational opportunities and techniques may be in sharp contrast to what is currently offered. Music education in some districts will have to undergo systemic change in order to accommodate the needs of all the students at all grade levels.

In each area of musical response (i.e., singing, playing, moving, and listening), there is a range of ways students can participate. For example, "singing" is not the only vocalization response there is that relates to a musical experience (see Figure 1). When music is heard, some students will start to produce vocal sounds, including humming, cooing, or "playing" with the voice. This appears to be an attempt to join the musical experience, and is considered to be a "singing" response. Among the additional responses that fall into the singing category are: (a) repeating vocal sounds; (b) imitating the contour of sounds (e.g., moving up or down in pitch relative to what is heard, duplicating the rhythmic feel of the music); (c) joining the music at key vocal phrases (such as a repeated word, the ending of the verse, the chorus); and (d) singing to one's self. Many students who are nonverbal make responses to music within the singing category that should be considered as legitimate "pre-singing" reactions. For example, some students breathe more deeply and smoothly when the music is happening. The music has a physiological effect on them, and since breath control is a necessary component of singing, this physical response falls into the singing category.

Another classification of musical participation is "playing" body rhythms or classroom and performance instruments. Once again, there are many items in the range of playing responses that can be considered to be intentional musical responses on the part of students (see Figure 2). Performing musically on an instrument is one way to play, but other responses include: (a) getting out and putting away an instrument; (b) choosing a preferred instrument; (c) exploring the sounds made on an instrument or with body rhythms;

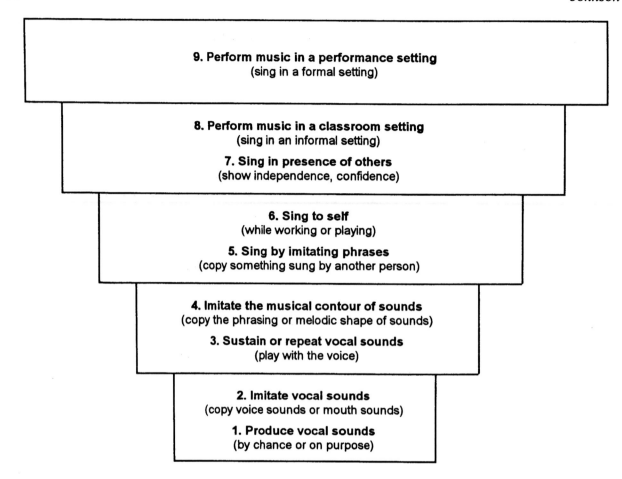

Figure 1. Range of Singing Responses

(d) repeating an action to make a sound; (e) participating in a playing experience for part of the time; (f) being tolerant of a variety of sounds produced by several instruments; (g) changing tempo, style, volume, or rhythm; and (h) practicing. There are also physiological "pre-playing" responses to be included. For example, some students' muscle tone is improved when music is heard. The music positively affects their posture and strength, which are components of the ability to play. Therefore, these very basic responses also are included in the playing category.

Similarly, "moving" and "listening" to music include a wide range of responses which are acceptable for considering how a student is participating in music experiences (see Figures 3 and 4). For example, moving to music refers to rhythmic and stylistic action, but can also include (a) turning or moving toward the music source, (b) imitating the movements of others in relation to the music, and (c) coordinating purposeful movements in response to music. In addition, physiological responses of changes in muscle tone and posture are "pre-moving" reactions that are within the realm of movement to music. In the category of "listening," a student responds by (a) regarding sounds/music, (b) acting to repeat the sounds, (c) developing simple discrimination skills and preferences, (d) selecting music as a free time option, (e) and practicing appropriate audience skills.

The frustrations, concerns, and questions of music educators who teach students with special needs are often beyond the scope of the music therapist's consultant role to address. When this happens, the music therapist acts as a resource person, who can steer the educator toward appropriate services that can help. Sometimes educators seek further training, and the music therapist is in a position to either provide inservice

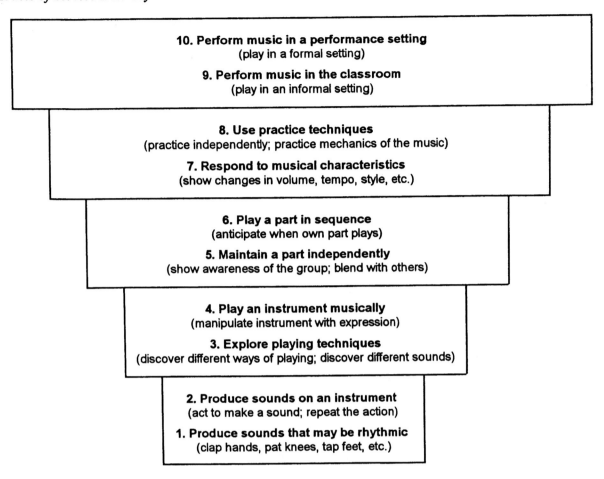

Figure 2. Range of Playing Responses

training in specific areas, or to recommend workshops or college courses that will be beneficial to music educators.

Consulting to Facilitate Musical Performance

When working in a consultant role with performance group teachers, the role of the music therapist is more specifically designed than in general music classes, where a variety of music experiences is available to the music educator. In the general music class, the learning process can be seen as more comprehensive, appearing to make it easier for the music educator to design appropriate activities that will meet the needs of all students in the class. But in performance groups, the ability of the student to contribute to the expectations of the class will be the main concern of music educators. Some performance group teachers will question how or why a student came to be in the band, orchestra, or choir. The role of the music therapist consultant is to help identify and interpret district policy for placement of students in performance groups. District policy should reflect federal and state guidelines for special education services.

One of the most difficult aspects of consulting with performance groups, especially in school districts that have long histories of musical performance, is to keep the focus on process over product. The award-winning band that suddenly includes a student with a physical disability in the percussion section, or the madrigal group into which several students who are nonverbal are scheduled are not uncommon occurrences in these times of inclusivity. Yet these scenarios, and others like them, create challenges and questions for music educators, who often begin to doubt their abilities to accommodate the needs of students with disabilities.

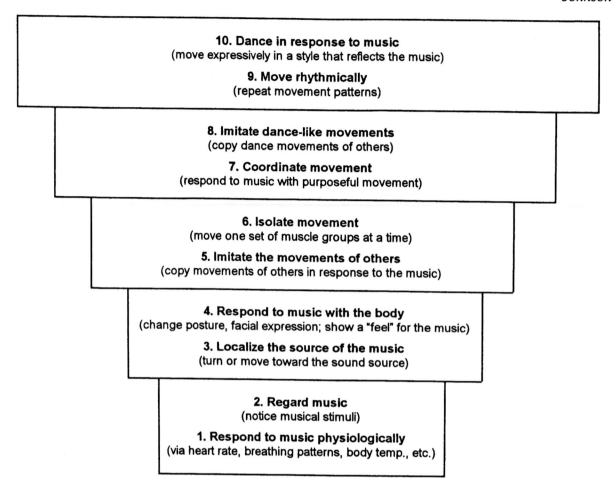

Figure 3. Range of Movement Responses

Music educators, however, are well aware of the influence that music has on young lives, and are interested in providing music experiences that will benefit all students for a lifetime.

In performance classes, the music therapist assumes the position of helping the student function within the parameters of the performance group. The main focus for the therapist is the student, although it is also necessary to work with the music educator to expand the mission of the band, orchestra, or choir to a more inclusive one. As the music therapist explores options with the music educator, it is necessary to remain aware of and sensitive to the role that the music educator plays in the educational program.

The music therapist must be prepared to provide real support. Rather than just *talking* about options, the therapist should be ready to assist in *implementing* as many options as it takes to help accommodate the student. Since physical presence is a major component of good consultation services, the music therapist should attend rehearsals on a regular basis, observing the entire group, as well as the student with special education needs. If the written music is a major obstacle to the student's participation, the music can be enlarged or rearranged so it is easier to follow (keeping in mind the copyright laws!). Another option is to make rehearsal tapes so the student can work on the music at home or in the classroom. Or a combination program can be developed in which the student participates in the performance group, but also receives direct services in the form of specialized lessons or extra help.

When typical performance groups do not meet the needs of all the students who would like to be involved in musical performance, nontraditional groups can be developed. These include, but are not limited to percussion ensembles, Orff groups, guitar classes, bell choirs, or singing groups that perform pops literature

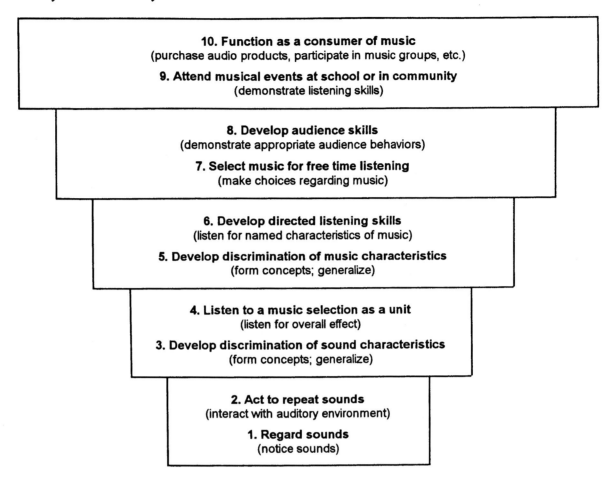

Figure 4. Range of Listening Responses

as a community service. The role of the consultant music therapist in these groups is much the same as it is in the traditional school musical groups. However, the music therapist is able to offer valuable assistance in getting nontraditional performance groups started and in training the music educator in techniques, methods, and identifying appropriate performance goals and objectives.

Consulting With Nonmusic Education Staff

In some districts, the music therapist provides consultation services to staff besides music educators. Classroom teachers (both regular education and special education), teaching assistants, and other school personnel are recipients of such services. In these cases, the music therapist provides support in the following areas: (a) designing appropriate music activities to meet IEP goals, especially in the areas of leisure skill and social skill development; (b) training classroom personnel to implement basic music activities; (c) teaching classroom staff simple accompaniment techniques or other skills that will assist in implementing appropriate music activities; (d) collecting and providing appropriate music resources in the form of song sheets, song books, recordings, and instruments; (e) providing in-class demonstration of appropriate music activities and appropriate expectations for the students; (f) providing other assistance that supports classroom instruction.

Consulting Guidelines

The following guidelines have been used to provide beneficial consultation services to music educators and classroom teachers at the elementary, middle, and high school levels:

1. Keep a schedule that is flexible and allows the music therapist to be available when the students and teachers need assistance;

2. If teachers are reluctant to ask for assistance, seek out their input with surveys, phone calls, and other communication techniques;

3. To efficiently determine what the teacher needs/wants, use a simple checklist or flow chart to help the teacher better utilize resources that are already available in the school;

4. Instead of providing quick solutions to every problem, work through the problem-solving process with the teacher to identify some reasonable options and strategies;

5. Develop options that fit the situation, including the teacher's current comfort level and background, the profile of the class, time constraints, district goals, etc.;

6. Encourage the teacher to keep trying a chosen strategy; demonstrate the strategy and show that sometimes a solution needs to be tried over and over again before it is successful;

7. Remain visible and accessible; attend meetings, send memos or mailings, make phone calls, provide inservice offerings, etc.; sometimes teachers will know that a support person is available, but will only let the therapist know there is a concern if the therapist makes the contact;

8. Let administrators know what consultant services have been provided for the students and teachers in a particular school;

9. When developing strategies to address a concern, give teachers examples of other teachers that have been in similar situations, and the options that were tried in those instances (i.e., team teaching, sample lessons, resource equipment, networking assistance);

10. Target the teachers new to the district for extra attention throughout their first year, even if they seem to be working effectively with the students;

11. When providing inservice training, make topics specific; teachers want specific information about behavior management, students with severe multiple disabilities, how to play the guitar, etc.;

12. Give teachers an opportunity to vent frustrations, concerns and problems without responding with a judgment call or an easy answer;

13. Know the limitations of the consultant position, which is that of an outsider.

Resource and Equipment Distribution

In some districts, there is a central supply of music materials and equipment that teachers can borrow. Usually these materials are for music educators, but more and more districts are making them available to classroom teachers as well. As a consultant, the music therapist is responsible for recommending appropriate equipment to be ordered, either at the district or the school level. To accomplish this task effectively, it is often possible for the music therapist to get equipment on a trial basis. Once equipment has been procured, the therapist can ask for teacher input regarding the usefulness of specific items. Regular communication with school staff is necessary, in order to let them know what materials are available, as well as what materials have been added to the supply. By dividing equipment into areas of application, such as materials appropriate for early childhood, accompaniment instruments, technological equipment, or multicultural instruments, the therapist is able to keep materials easily organized for functional use.

In addition to keeping track of equipment that is available, ordering appropriate materials to have in the resource library, and evaluating quality of materials used, the music therapist is also responsible for demonstrating how the materials can be used most effectively. One way is to demonstrate the materials with actual students in the classroom or music setting. In addition to showing the students how to use the equipment, the therapist should also familiarize staff with the appropriate way to use, play, store, and care for the equipment.

Music Therapy and the IEP

According to legislation related to students with special education needs (Individuals with Disabilities Education Act–IDEA Amendments of 1997), all students should have access to educational opportunities in the general curriculum. The 1997 amendments to IDEA changed the focus from merely providing students with access to an education to emphasizing the process of teaching and learning, and improving results for all students. School districts are charged with determining classroom placement, providing related services, and meeting IEP goals as much as possible within the general curriculum framework. As a related service, music therapy must support the achievement of real educational results for students with special education needs. IDEA 1997 calls for the promotion of meaningful access to the general curriculum, so when music therapy provides services within a school district's music education program, there must be appropriate involvement of music educators in the development of IEP goals.

For some school districts, the provision of appropriate music education experiences involves support services for music educators in the form of inservice training and consultation by music therapists or special education personnel. In other districts, designing music education services that meet individual needs of all students, including those with disabilities, will require systemic change and a re-examination of the music education program for all students.

The IEP Process

The Individualized Education Program (IEP) is a process, a working document. The IEP is developed by a group of individuals who have contact with the student, including staff and family members. It is reviewed and revised at least yearly, and serves to determine appropriate goals, objectives, and educational services based on ongoing observation, assessment, and appraisal of program effectiveness. The IEP is not the plan itself, but the dialogue that occurs on behalf of the needs of the student. The IEP identifies services that are necessary to address the needs of the student, and includes the following components: (a) the current abilities and needs of the student; (b) a statement of how the student's disability affects the student's involvement and progress in the general curriculum; (c) a statement of measurable annual goals that enable the student to be involved and make progress in the general curriculum; (d) a statement of special education services, related services, and supplementary aids needed for the student to achieve the goals; and (e) program modifications or supports for school personnel that are necessary. IDEA 1997 also requires that students with disabilities be included in state and district-wide assessment programs. If a student participates in general assessment, any accommodations or modifications are described in the IEP. Similarly, if a student participates in alternate assessment, this is also outlined in the IEP. Since IDEA 1997 increased the involvement of regular education in the education of students with disabilities, a regular education teacher must be part of the IEP team.

Most special education programs rely on some version of a team approach for providing services. For an integrated program to be effective, teamwork among staff and parents is critical. The implementation of the IEP is dependent on cooperation and communication among teachers, support personnel, parents, and peers of the student. The following is a brief explanation of how IEPs are integrated with the most common team models:

1. *Multidisciplinary*—in which communication between team members is unidirectional and limited. In this model, the focus of service delivery is discipline-centered; assessment of students is done in isolation from other disciplines. IEPs are developed with minimal group input from team members; service delivery is isolated within each discipline;

2. *Interdisciplinary*—in which communication among team members occurs at the IEP planning stage. In this model, the teacher works with each individual discipline to reach decisions. Assessment of students is done in isolation, but results are shared with other team members. IEPs contain portions contributed by each discipline; and

3. *Transdisciplinary*—in which communication among team members is multidirectional and frequent. Parents are an integral part of the team, and decisions regarding the student are reached by consensus. The focus of service delivery is child-centered. Assessment, IEP planning and service delivery are integrated and holistic.

Professional identities and territories often become entangled in the course of setting priorities for the student. However, if IEP development is viewed as an on-going process, the team will be able to provide appropriate services according to what the student really needs. Professionals who remain committed to making the IEP student-centered can design an integrated educational program for the student. Strategic development of an integrated IEP includes the following steps in the process: (a) examine the student's current abilities to identify strengths and needs; (b) determine priority areas; (c) to the maximum extent possible, integrate the student into regular class environments *first* ; (d) revise and implement IEP priorities as needed, including providing special services.

Music Therapy in the IEP

The inclusion of music therapy in the IEP process is sometimes a controversial practice. If music therapy is named specifically as *the* way to achieve goals, school districts are obligated to provide music therapy services. On the other hand, if music therapy is listed as *a* way for achieving goals, it is regarded as one of many possible services that could assist the student. For example, a goal that focuses on motor development of a student, specifically mobility over a variety of floor surfaces, can be addressed in physical education class, in physical therapy, in the classroom, and in music therapy. In this scenario, music therapy is a strategy for achieving a goal that is also being met in other locations under the direction of other professionals.

If the general curriculum is adapted to meet the special education needs of the student, this information must be included in the IEP. When a music education program requires adaptation, it does not automatically imply that music therapy services, or the expertise of a music therapist are needed. These adaptations can be implemented by music educators who have a history of teaching students with diverse needs. Adaptations to the music education program can be curricular in nature, or designed to provide the student with physical access to materials and equipment used in class. For example, to help a student develop an understanding of musical form, picture representations are matched with the aural material, or examples are used that involve touch or movement. This is an example of a lesson modification. On a curricular scale, a student might be involved in activities that promote appropriate audience behavior at musical events. An example of a physical modification might be an adaptive mallet for playing the drum or placing a mallet instrument to the side of a student in a wheelchair for easy access. Modifications to the music education program are often referred to as *special music education* or *adapted music education*.

When it is determined through assessment that a student does require music therapy services, specific information about the nature and delivery of these services is included in the IEP. Depending on the level of involvement of the music therapist working with special education programs, assessment is completed at the intake level (if the music therapist is a member of the standing assessment team), the programming stage (if there is a determination to be made between music education or music therapy), or at the IEP development phase, in which programming is determined. Many music therapists utilize standardized assessment tools to determine the appropriateness of music therapy services for individual students. In addition, many music therapists have developed effective assessment tools that are specifically designed to meet their assessment needs. The way in which music therapy is included in the IEP depends on how the IEP itself is constructed, which, in turn, depends on the type of educational team that is assembled to provide a coordinated program.

For example, if the music therapist is working within a model in which all phases of the student's educational program—assessment, planning, and implementation—are done together with the other members of the team, music therapy is more likely to be an integral element in the IEP. This is because, in an integrated program, the other members of the team are more likely to gain a better understanding of the value of music therapy services in achieving IEP goals. Furthermore, an integrated IEP deals with the student holistically, and team members are more inclined to disregard strict disciplinary definitions in favor of what is the most effective program for the student. On the other hand, if the music therapist is part of a team in which all phases of the student's program are implemented separately, according to specific disciplinary boundaries, then music therapy is more likely to be isolated from the progress that is made in other areas.

Developmental vs. Functional Music Activities

Many educational assessment tools measure a student's abilities, such as motor, cognitive, and social skills, in terms of developmental age. Developmental skills are those milestones that are reached at typical ages for most infants and children. They are norms of development, or ways of measuring the developmental process for the average person.

Since, in developmental tools, assessment results are stated in developmental terms (age equivalents), the special education programs that result are designed to increase the student's age equivalent in each area where a discrepancy exists. For example, a 5-year-old student who uses a grasp typical for a 2-year-old receives educational support services to develop this fine motor skill to a level that is more commensurate with the student's age. In the area of music education, a student in a similar early stage of the primary level works on the skill of determining whether, in a recorded or live example, the voice is that of a woman or a man. A child who has not yet acquired this discrimination ability presumably receives additional attention in this area to make the responses to music more in keeping with the chronological age.

Programs based solely on developmental ages present a major drawback for students with severe disabilities as well as for students with special education needs who are older than the primary years. The problem with such programs is that, as the student gets older, the discrepancy between the actual chronological age and the age equivalent of skill development becomes greater. It is difficult to provide age-appropriate educational programming for students when only their developmental skills are considered.

Special education programs often use a functional skill approach to educational planning and service delivery. Functional skills are needed for those tasks that relate to everyday living, including being able to participate in the general curriculum. Examples of functional skills include taking care of general personal needs (eating, dressing, toileting) as well as more specific needs in a classroom setting (such as blowing one's nose), performing work-related tasks (cooperating with others, completing a job, being on time for a job) as well as classroom related tasks (paying attention to an activity, acquiring and using materials in an activity), getting along in the community (shopping for needs, using transportation) as well as getting along in a classroom setting (interacting with other students, following along with an activity), and using free time productively (pursuing special interests, developing hobbies).

Among the functional skills specifically associated with the music education class are selecting/obtaining an instrument from among a group of choices, participating in singing by vocalizing during a portion of the song, and starting/stopping a motor response according to musical cues. While these activities involve skill development that is typical at certain ages, each activity is regarded as a unit of effort that requires a combination of skills in different areas to be meaningful. The activity takes place in the context of a real setting under real circumstances.

In a music education setting the developmental age of a student with special needs is often quite different from the chronological age. For example, if the student is 7 years old, but the developmental assessment provides a functional age of 9 months, it is considered best practice to provide music activities appropriate for a 7-year-old student. Developmental ages are considered only as a frame of reference, rather than to determine the curriculum content for the student. It is not unusual for a discrepancy of 2 years or more between the developmental age and the chronological age to remain as a discrepancy throughout the student's life. Rather than becoming "stuck" in the area of developmental skills (which fall strictly into the social, motor, cognitive, communication, and sensory areas), the student would be better served working toward goals in functional areas (life experience areas).

Therefore, a recommended practice is for the music educator/music therapist to work on developmental objectives during the chronological years when childhood development occurs (through approximately age 7). After this age, the student's program should be centered around goals and objectives that will help the student function more effectively within the school environment, the home setting, and throughout the community.

All people progress through several stages of growth in music experiences (see Figure 5). The first stage, *exploration*, is the stage in which individuals get to know the materials, try things out, and gain some preliminary experience in the medium. In the *control* stage, the person has enough early experience with the materials or activity to gain some basic-to-advanced control over the activity or materials. This enables the person to participate more fully in the group experience and have access to additional activities and materials through prior knowledge. The next stage is the development of *independence*. The person is able to be a musician and carry a part within a group, or use fundamental skills to create music. In the final stage, the *functional* stage, the individual uses the medium of music vocationally, avocationally, for further study or refinement.

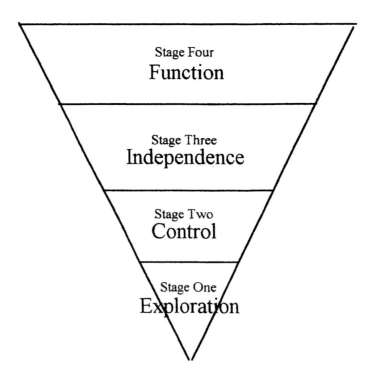

Figure 5. Stages of Growth in Musical Experiences

An example of a student operating within the *exploration* stage is in the area of playing classroom instruments, such as the autoharp, tambourine, or drum. A student in this stage of development would look at, touch, pick up, and explore the instrument by experimenting with ways to make a sound, ways to hold the instrument, and how the student acts upon the instrument. Many students proceed through this stage very quickly, but some students spend a longer period of time investigating what makes the instrument "tick."

In the *control* stage, the student is able to have some command over the instrument. By this point, the instrument is familiar to the student, and the exploration that took place before is incorporated into the playing of the instrument. The student is able to consistently start or stop playing, change tempo, volume, or style of playing, and achieve a level of mastery over the instrument. Many students spend a long time in this stage, depending on the inherent difficulty of the instrument itself.

The *independence* stage occurs once a student has achieved a certain level of musicianship. In this stage the student is able to participate with a minimum of outside intervention, and can follow the guidance of a leader or members of the group. Because of the independence that is developed, a student is able to proceed to the next stage, that of *functional* use of the instrument in recreational or vocational experiences. The student is able to play in a school group, perform for an audience, practice independently, maintain a part within an ensemble or on a solo basis, and be involved in music for personal pleasure or as a service to others.

Music Therapy in Various IEP Team Models

The Multidisciplinary IEP

Because of the separateness of individual members of the *multidisciplinary team*, this model often isolates the work of the music therapist from the work of other professionals. In some cases, goals are generated that (a) are not related to other IEP goals, or (b) do not reflect a specific *need* for music therapy. For example, if the IEP team has determined that finger strength is less of a priority than other issues for the student, a music therapy goal of "increasing finger strength by playing a keyboard" is clearly not related to the IEP process. In addition, the goal of playing the keyboard does not show a need for music therapy services unless prior assessment has indicated that music therapy could capitalize on the student's motivation and abilities, provide appropriate adaptations for the student, and offer an efficient and effective way to meet the student's goal. The responsibility lies with the music therapist to demonstrate to the rest of the team that music therapy is a unique and legitimate related service. For example, in addressing the aforementioned goal regarding finger dexterity, the needs of the student can be better served if the music therapist works with the occupational therapist to determine what functional hand skills need attention. Then the music therapist can design an appropriate program that will work on those hand skills, such as reaching all parts of the keyboard, isolating finger movement, and developing finger strength that in turn can be used in feeding, dressing, and other functional hand activities.

The Interdisciplinary IEP

In the *interdisciplinary team* model, individual members share their evaluations, goals, and implementation plans with each other. Therefore, the music therapist encounters more opportunities to educate other professionals about the benefits of music therapy. Because team members share assessment results and program plans with each other, there is increased opportunity for communication. One disadvantage similar to the multidisciplinary model is that the need for music therapy services is often determined without the benefit of standardized assessment tools. Therefore, input by the music therapist can be regarded by other team members as self-serving.

Music therapy in the interdisciplinary IEP can be included as a separate disciplinary area, with goals and objectives that are particular to the music setting. Another way of including music therapy is as a strategy for achieving goals that have been determined by other members of the team. For example, the music therapist can incorporate into music therapy the motor goals articulated by the adaptive physical education teacher, the fine motor goals identified by the occupational therapist, and the speech and language goals listed by the speech pathologist.

The Transdisciplinary IEP

The *transdisciplinary* model, like the other models, is used for planning the IEP. The team identifies student needs, prioritizes goals and objectives, and determines how the services of each education professional will be coordinated into a team concept. Team members cooperate to plan instructional experiences that require the expertise of all staff involved. This model of IEP development is also known as "integrated IEP" construction. In this model, music therapy is regarded as "a way," but not necessarily "the way" to accomplish goals. To diminish this negative side effect, it is imperative that music therapists working in the transdisciplinary model contribute to the goal-writing process with a knowledge of specific student responses to music and the ability to see music as an *integral* part of instruction.

In some transdisciplinary or integrated IEPs, goals are "domain-based," developed from the educational perspective that people function in a variety of locations, territories, or domains. For example, when people are at home or involved in home-related situations, they perform domestic tasks. In the vocational domain they work at a job or train to work at a job. When they are anyplace but home and work, they function in a community domain, and during their leisure time, they participate in leisure activities. For goals that relate to the domestic domain, the music therapist teaches the student to get materials to be used in the music activity and then return them to their appropriate containers. The community domain includes activities that expose the student to community music activities and train the student in the exercise of appropriate audience skills. For vocational skill development, the music therapist addresses the areas of task completion or the acquisition of computer skills that assist the student in the creative process. Leisure skill development includes those activities that occupy the individual's free time: chosen activities that are pleasurable and rewarding to the student.

Since the *transdisciplinary* model is based on crossing disciplinary boundaries, it is recognized that students function in different domains or settings, and perform a variety of tasks that go together to form complete activities. This is different from the other models because students are involved in real settings with real activities, rather than in isolation (e.g., the occupational therapy room as an occupational therapy client, or as a student on the speech/language caseload).

Music therapy most often relates to domain-based goals in the area of "leisure skills." For example, listening to music for pleasure, learning to play an instrument as a hobby, or attending concerts in the community are activities that people choose to do in their spare time. However, when music therapy services are delivered, the goals in the other domain areas are also addressed, providing an integrated instructional setting. Music therapy that addresses the domestic domain involves any self-help skills, such as getting equipment out and putting it away, taking care of materials, and operating home-based music equipment. In the vocational domain, music therapy addresses goals in the area that relate to the world of work: namely, work habits, attitudes, and the completion of a variety of tasks. The community domain includes such music therapy goals as independence during community events, becoming aware of opportunities in the community, and practicing appropriate behaviors.

Other Team Models

In some cases, the music therapist works with students whose instructional program is not determined by the IEP, such as students in general education classes who have been determined to be At-Risk and students who qualify for services under Section 504. Typically, these students do not meet the criteria needed to receive special education services, but are in need of support services that include music therapy. In these cases, the music therapist functions as a member of student services team (or Sec. 504 team) which meets on a regular basis to insure that appropriate services and resources are provided for each student.

Music therapists are assigned to provide services according to a number of different models, depending on who employs them. For example, music therapists (a) may work out of centralized county, state, or multi-district systems; (b) are employed by local private or public school districts; or (c) receive contracts through a service provider structure. In any of these employer models, music therapists are assigned on a departmental, school-assignment, or district-wide basis. Each of these models has an internal team structure to which the music therapist contributes.

One school operation model that is currently being explored in school districts nationwide is Site-Based (or School-Based) Management (also known as Shared Decision-Making), in which the local school staff has control of the budget, staff allocation, hiring practices, program direction, and provision of necessary services for the students attending that school. A music therapist working in a Site-Based Management school faces both an opportunity and a challenge. The opportunity is to participate as a member of a Site-Based Management team and to demonstrate the effectiveness of music therapy for students with special needs, regardless of whether the school district provides music therapy services. Under Site-Based Management, the opportunities for employment of music therapists in school settings are increased. However, Site-Based Management demands greater accountability at the local school staff level, and music therapists who are members of SBM teams need to provide documentation that their services are necessary to the student population.

References

Anderson, N. B., Hawkins, J., Hamilton, R., & Hampton, J. D. (1999). Effects of transdisciplinary teaming for students with motor disabilities. *Education and Training in Mental Retardation and Developmental Disabilities, 34*(3), 330–341.

The Association for Persons with Severe Handicaps. (1994). *Inclusion in education: A choice for your child* [Brochure].

Fowler, S. A., & Lewman, B. (1998). *SPARK: Skills promoted through arts, reading, knowledge.* Project Head Start Demonstration Project, Final Report.

Gerent, M. (1998). *Successful inclusion of students with disabilities: Modifying content delivery and materials in inclusive classrooms.* Paper presented at the Annual China–U.S. Conference on Education, July 14–18, 1998.

Hobbs, T., & Westing, D. L. (1998). Promoting successful inclusion through collaborative problem-solving. *Teaching Exceptional Children, 31*(2), 12–19.

Moore, C., Gilbreath, D., & Maiuri, F. (1998). *Educating students with disabilities in general education classrooms: A summary of the research.* University of Oregon.

Music Educators National Conference. (1994). *National standards for music education.*

Sheldon, D. A. (2001). Peer and cross-age tutoring in music. *Music Educators Journal, 87*(6), 33–39.

Thompson, K. P. (1999). Challenges of inclusion for the general music teacher. *General Music Today, 12*(3), 7–9.

Yasutake, D., & Lerner, J. (1997). Parents' perceptions of inclusion: A survey of special education and non-special education students. *Learning Disabilities: A Multidisciplinary Journal, 8*(2), 117–120.

7

INSERVICE TRAINING: A MAJOR KEY TO SUCCESSFUL INTEGRATION OF SPECIAL NEEDS CHILDREN INTO MUSIC EDUCATION CLASSES

Carol L. Culton

CONTAINED within this book are many activities, suggestions and approaches for the use of music in mainstreamed (integrated) music education settings. These ideas and methodologies will assist both music educators and music therapists to plan effective educational and instructional strategies for mainstreamed students. But are these enough? In addition to helpful hints and strategies for musical activities, what do music educators and music therapists need to meet the creative challenges that mainstreamed music classes present? A number of studies and surveys indicate that music teachers who work in mainstreamed music settings need: (a) a positive attitude toward mainstreaming (Darrow, 1990b; Thompson, 1986; White, 1981/1982); (b) inservice training beyond the preservice, college curriculum (Frisque, Niebur, & Humphreys, 1994; Gfeller, Darrow, & Hedden, 1990; Gilbert & Asmus, 1981; Stein, 1983); (c) inservice providers who recognize the importance of the teacher–participant; and, therefore, (d) inservices with content and format based on the needs and the strengths of the teacher–participants (Hutson, 1981; Powers, 1983).

The Music Teacher is the Key

Special needs students are routinely placed in elementary general music classes (Atterbury, 1986a, 1990; Damer, 1979/1980; Gavin, 1983/1984; Gilbert & Asmus, 1981; Graham, 1988; Nocera, 1981; Sideridis & Chandler, 1995); and as such it is the music teacher who is responsible for providing opportunities for children to learn, participate, and create enjoyable, reinforcing, and meaningful musical experiences. It is the music teacher who, with a realistic, but positive attitude, will determine each day's success (Schultz & Turnbull, 1984) and will stimulate and promote positive attitudes and interactions among all children (disabled and non-disabled) in the mainstreamed music education setting.

In addition to a positive attitude, it is imperative that music educators have proper training, skills and support to accomplish the tasks and meet challenges of the mainstreamed setting willingly and with confidence and security. It cannot be denied that the process of mainstreaming requires music educators to develop new and more specific knowledge and skills not generally acquired in preservice college curricula (Atterbury, 1990; Gfeller & Hedden, 1987; Gilbert & Asmus, 1981; Stuart & Gilbert, 1977). However, many music educators continue to report having received limited or no extensive or formal training to enable them to work with special needs children in either integrated or self-contained classes (Frisque et al., 1994;

Gfeller et al., 1990; Goldsmith, 1984/1985; Smith & Wilson, 1999; Stein, 1983; Stuart & Gilbert, 1977). This means that "Most music educators are attempting to meet the educational needs of handicapped students with little or no educational preparation" (Gfeller et al., 1990, p. 99). As a result, many music teachers feel unprepared to teach students with special needs within their integrated classes and continue to indicate a desire to have additional training that addresses their special and specific needs (Atterbury, 1990; Frisque et al., 1994; Gfeller et al., 1990; Pratt, 1986; Thompson, 1990).

The availability of useful resources, materials, and elementary music textbook series that focus on instructional guidelines and adaptive techniques for music teachers is also problematic. Resource materials are hard to find and many are out of print. In addition, after thoroughly analyzing the content of the three major music education textbook series, Culton (1999/2000) found them woefully lacking in the amount of content devoted to instructional guidance and adaptive techniques useful for teachers with special children in their music classes.

For many teachers, this lack of preparation and useful information may contribute to feelings of inadequacy, frustration, and negativism (Hawkins, 1991/1992), and, undoubtedly, affect teachers' attitudes towards mainstreaming and special needs children. Clearly, this indicates a great need for effective inservice for music educators teaching in mainstreamed situations.

Inservice

Definition

Inservice is a developmental activity provided to teachers who engage in professional practice. Inservice provides: (a) training to improve present levels of skill and knowledge, (b) opportunities to learn new teaching methods and strategies (Joyce & Showers, 1980), and (c) self-renewal for teachers and schools within a supportive and positive climate (Dillon-Peterson, 1981). According to Fresko and Ben-Chaim (1986, p. 205), "Inservice education has become the main vehicle to meet the needs of teachers currently working within the school," and, in fact, according to some experts, inservice is a critical factor in successful mainstreaming (Tymitz-Wolf, 1982; Williams, 1988).

What Is Good Inservice?

There are several criteria that make up what can be labeled as "best practices" in inservice training. A list of best practices for inservice in music and mainstreaming appears at the end of this chapter. However, three essential issues critical to effective inservice must be addressed as they relate to inservice for music educators: (a) teacher attitude, (b) needs-based inservice content, and (c) evaluation. The following sections of this chapter focus on these three essential components of successful inservice.

Attitude

The first critical component of effective inservice is attention to participant attitude. Teacher attitude is an important factor in the successful integration and learning success of students with disabilities in music classes (Damer, 1979/1980; Darrow, 1990b; Elliott & Sins, 1981/1982; Sideridis & Chandler, 1995; Smith, 1989; Thompson, 1986; White, 1981/1982). Student productivity, student responses, and successful implementation of instructional strategies are influenced and often dictated by teacher expectations and attitudes (Darrow, 1990a; Gavin, 1983/1984). Positive teacher attitude helps to encourage positive responses, enthusiastic involvement, motivation, enjoyment and participation among special needs children in music classes as well as other children.

Attitude is recognized as an especially important issue in facilitating successful integration of students with disabilities into music classes. Some studies suggest that educators support the principle of mainstreaming and feel positive toward mainstreaming of special needs children into music classes (Hock, Hasazi, & Patten, 1990; Jellison, 1992; Sideridis & Chandler, 1995; Sins, 1983), while other research reveals that this support is only moderately favorable (Gfeller et al., 1990; Gfeller & Hedden, 1987; Hawkins, 1991/1992). Smith and Wilson (1999, p. 34) note that while there is "abundant evidence of the existence of negative teacher attitudes toward mainstreaming, less is known as to the most effective methods to remedy the situation." Perhaps ambivalent or negative attitudes among music educators toward mainstreaming stem in part from several factors including: (a) lack of input into the placement decision; (b) lack of information about the unique characteristics and needs of the student; (c) lack of teacher preparation and training; (d) lack of current, up-dated materials and resources; and (e) limited amount of content within the covers of elementary music basal series devoted to information, instructional guidance, and adaptive techniques for teachers with special needs students in music classes.

Lack of Input Into Placement Decisions

While PL 94-142 does not specifically mandate mainstreaming into music classes, music educators have traditionally been among the first to provide classroom settings for special needs students (Hock et al., 1990). Unfortunately, many education personnel view the "least restrictive environment" clause as blanket permission to include all children with disabilities in music classes (Atterbury, 1986a), and placement in music classes is often perceived as one means of meeting the intent of PL 94-142 (Goldsmith, 1984/1985). Thus, students with disabilities may be placed in music classes, especially in elementary school (Atterbury, 1986a; Gilbert & Asmus, 1981; Sins, 1983), out of expediency rather than because the music class is the best educational setting for mainstreaming. In addition to inappropriate placement (Goldsmith, 1984/1985), music educators often report limited participation in the placement process (Frisque et al., 1994; Gfeller et al., 1990) or exclusion from curricular and placement planning meetings regarding the special needs students mainstreamed into their music classes (Wilson & McCrary, 1996).

It is clear that music educators face unique problems concerning the placement of special needs children into music classes. The fact that general music educators may see as many as 700 to 1,000 regular students in class each week (Atterbury, 1986b) is quite an instructional challenge in and of itself. Now, as a result of PL 94-142, many music teachers are faced with the addition of significant numbers of special needs students who bring unique instructional demands to the music classroom.

Lack of Information About Individual Students

In addition to placement issues, there are other factors that may influence the attitudes of music educators working in mainstreamed settings. Because music teachers may have less contact with children with disabilities, they have less opportunity to become aware of specific problems (Goldsmith, 1984/1985). Often they are not given any information regarding the specific disabilities of the children mainstreamed into their classes (Wilson & McCrary, 1996), and they experience a lack of educational and instructional support and resources, e.g., lack of preparation time, aides and consultation (Gfeller et al., 1990).

Lack of Teacher Preparation and Training

Another problem that interferes with teacher attitude toward integrating children with disabilities into mainstreamed music settings is the lack of teacher preparation and training. This lack of preparation exists not only at the undergraduate, or preservice level, but also at the professional, or inservice level.

In terms of preservice preparation, music educators may not have much previous educational preparation for dealing with the challenges of mainstreaming. This lack of preparation may lead to feelings of uneasiness. Stuart and Gilbert (1977) found that preservice music education students were less comfortable and less willing than preservice music therapy students in working and interacting with persons with disabilities. With mainstreamed music classes a reality of the not too distant future, this 1977 study heralded the importance of concerns and attitudes of music educators. In light of these concerns Stuart and Gilbert (1977) recommended more attention to inservice training.

However, little change has apparently occurred since the Stuart and Gilbert report was published. In a national survey, Gilbert and Asmus (1981) found that 63% of music educators were involved in mainstreaming, but few felt adequately prepared to work with students with disabilities. In another survey to investigate, among other things, music educators' opinions about working with students with mental and learning disabilities (Stein, 1983) music teachers reported that they lacked foundation, understanding, or skills to undertake appropriate planning or adaptations necessary for successful education in mainstreamed music settings. Indeed, of the music teachers surveyed by Stein, over 56% of the respondents had not taken any post-baccalaureate educational courses, and only 19% had taken a course on mainstreaming in college. Sixteen percent had participated in workshops, 3% had taken a workshop in special education, and 12% had ever had any inservice training.

Similar findings were reported in other published studies (Frisque et al., 1994; Gfeller et al., 1990; Hock et al., 1990; Jellison, 1992). Gfeller et al. examined the perceived status of mainstreaming among music educators in two Midwestern states. Responding to an author-developed questionnaire, music educators reported a low level of pre-service educational preparation focusing on teaching in mainstreamed music settings. Results of the survey indicate that teachers continue to receive little preparation in terms of course work pertinent to working with mainstreamed students. In fact, only 25% of the survey respondents had taken even one college course related to teaching students with disabilities. Hock et al. surveyed a cross section, albeit small sample ($N = 27$), of music teachers in Vermont. Consistent with other surveys, they found that although 92% of the respondents taught in mainstreamed music settings, only 37% reported any special training, which typically consisted of one or two inservice workshops.

Similar results were reported by Jellison (1992) and Frisque et al. (1994). Jellison conducted an investigation of the experiences, attitudes and perceptions of 149 Texas music educators. Using an author-designed questionnaire, she chose certain items from the Gfeller, Darrow, and Hedden questionnaire addressing demographic information and educational preparation. She found, as did Gfeller and her colleagues (1990), that the majority of respondents reported little (only a few hours of workshops or inservice) or no formal education or inservice training. Frisque et al. obtained information from a random sample of elementary music teachers ($N = 107$) in Arizona. Their data (p. 98) reveal that while 84% of the respondents were currently responsible for teaching in mainstreamed settings, more than 40% had no formal training and another 20% reported limited inservice and workshops. In addition, opportunity for inservice was rare, with 34% of the responding teachers receiving inservice training only upon request and 44% receiving none at all.

In addition to these four surveys, three more recent studies substantiate the lack of appropriate educational preparation in the area of special education, disabilities and mainstreaming (Wilson & McCrary, 1993, 1996; Smith & Wilson, 1999). Using Stuart and Gilbert's 1977 study as a benchmark, the Wilson and McCrary study (1993) found that little had changed in terms of preparing teachers for mainstreamed music settings. Their study revealed that, among other things, preservice music education students continued to report minimal college course work in special education and experience with special needs students. Of the 31 music education and music therapy preservice students who responded to this survey, 11 (35%) reported having no special education preparation, 10 (32%) had taken one special education course, 13 (42%) reported having only minimal experience with special needs children, and 8 (26%) reported extensive experience.

The other study by Wilson and McCrary (1996) reported a similar lack of training and preparation for special education or mainstreaming. The participants ($N = 18$) were music educators enrolled in a graduate course focusing on music for the special learner. Thirteen (72%) of the participants reported having no previous special education training, 3 (17%) had taken either one workshop or college-level course, and 2 (11%) had taken more than one college-level special education course.

In addition to the Wilson & McCrary studies (1993, 1996), a later study by Smith and Wilson (1999) reported similar trends in teacher preparation. This study, like the Wilson and McCrary study (1996), focused on the effects of a summer graduate course on the attitudes of music educators toward integration of special learners into music classes. Of the 18 participants, 10 reported having had no formal training concerning special education, 5 reported having had a college course, and 3 had attended workshops (p. 36).

It is important to note that music educators have indicated a more willing attitude to participate in mainstreaming if provided additional training and support (Damer, 1979/1980; Sideridis & Chandler, 1995; Smith & Wilson, 1999; Stein, 1983). Damer found that teachers expressed more willingness to teach a wider spectrum of children with disabilities if they had additional support and inservice training. When she surveyed the same sample of teachers five years later she found that: (a) there was an increase in the number of special needs students in mainstreamed music settings, and (b) attitude toward mainstreaming had deteriorated significantly (White, cited in Atterbury, 1990). She believed that the primary reason for this decline in teacher attitude was related to a lack of continuing support and training.

In her descriptive survey to study the efficacy of curriculum in meeting the needs of special area teachers (music, art, and physical education), Stein (1983) found that teacher attitude was a key factor in willingness to teach in mainstreamed music settings. Sixty percent of the music teachers surveyed ($N = 62$) stated that they would be willing to attend workshops, and over 60% said they would welcome opportunities to interact and talk with other music educators who faced similar challenges. Similar results were obtained by Sideridis and Chandler (1995) who surveyed 55 music teachers in Kansas. According to Sideridis and Chandler, the music teachers who participated in this study were "willing to attend workshops that pertain to the teaching of children with disabilities in an effort to become more effective teachers" (p. 14). Similarly, Smith and Wilson (1999) found that, after attending a four-week summer graduate course on music and special learners, teacher–participants reported that they were not only more willing to work with special need students in their classes, but also felt, for the most part, more capable as well.

Conclusions

Concerns regarding lack of preparation for music educators in the area of mainstreaming special needs students have been reiterated through the 1980s and the 1990s, and the need for additional college and on-the-job inservice training has been identified (Frisque et al., 1994; Gfeller et al., 1990; Gilbert & Asmus, 1981; Stuart & Gilbert, 1977; Wilson & McCrary, 1993, 1996). Unfortunately, while many music educators continue their efforts to meet the challenges in the mainstreamed music classroom, there seems to be little opportunity to receive on-the-job training (Gfeller at al., 1990). In addition, Goldsmith (1984/1985) suggests that because music educators may teach in more than one school, they may not have opportunities to participate in available inservice. Needless to say, without continued support and opportunities for additional training, Goldsmith fears that the attitudes of these teachers will continue to suffer. He recommends that, because of the frequent placement of special needs children in art, music and physical education classes, meeting the needs of these teachers through inservice training should be a priority (1984/1985, p. 114). It seems reasonable to conclude that, as we move into the 21st century, music educators require educational and inservice opportunities that provide knowledge and skills necessary for integrating the special student into the general music classroom.

Inservice Content

The second component of quality inservice training is needs-based content. In fact, for inservice to be useful to music teachers, the content must address the needs and concerns of the teachers (Broadwell, 1986; Hayden, 1989/1990; Hutson, 1981; Powers, 1983). We cannot assume we know what music teachers need or want, because, as all adult learners, music educators bring to the learning environment many different experiences and levels of knowledge and skills. When planning inservice training and educational opportunities for music teachers, the approach should not be a deficit-oriented one, but rather one in which the strengths and needs of the teachers are seen as guideposts for determining inservice content and format.

Inservices must provide teachers with specific information (Spanier, 1987) that, in turn, may help them acquire new teaching methods and strategies to "improve the conditions for learning and teaching" (Miller & Wolf, 1978, p. 141). In short, effective, well-planned inservice programs provide music educators with the knowledge and skills necessary to work effectively and positively within mainstreamed settings, thereby enabling these teachers to become a positive and effective force in the education of children with disabilities.

In addition to offering topics deemed important by the educators themselves, the literature on "best practices" (Hutson, 1981; Powers, 1983) recommends that inservice content incorporate an approach and format practical and useful to the participating teachers. In addition, content should be practical, be directly applicable, emphasize instructional activities, focus on specific difficulties in the classroom, and reflect teacher needs. In short, it should translate theory into practice and be reality-based.

This is especially true of music education inservice. In a survey of music educators, Gilbert and Asmus (1981) found that teachers desired practical information about methods and techniques, and lacked information about or access to new and adaptive materials and pedagogical strategies. Similarly, the teachers surveyed by Sideridis and Chandler (1995) reported having inadequate instructional materials and funds.

In summary, it is important to determine the needs of music teachers prior to providing an inservice program. It should provide content that: (a) is based upon perceived needs of the participants; (b) brings to music educators current research and trends in methodology and pedagogy; (c) provides music teachers with pragmatic, applicable materials; and (d) is presented in a sensible and enjoyable manner, providing opportunities that encourage and enhance participation and group discussion.

Needs Assessment

The most important factor in determining inservice content and, indeed, the success of inservice training, is assessment of participant needs. In fact, in music education, several researchers have indicated that a needs assessment is essential to successful and effective inservice (Brown, 1985; Stuart & Gilbert, 1977). According to Hutson (1981) and Powers (1983), a needs assessment must focus on three specific areas: knowledge, skills, and attitudes. In terms of developing better attitudes and successful classroom experiences for both music teachers and their mainstreamed students, it is essential to employ a needs assessment that can be used for the following: (a) identification of teacher needs; (b) identification of inservice content and format that are perceived by music educators as necessary and relevant to their instructional settings; (c) measurement of pre-to-post inservice changes in attitude and knowledge as it relates to perceived need for inservice; (d) evaluation of changes in felt needs, attitude, and knowledge gain; and (e) determination, if desired, of the long-term effectiveness of the training.

Needs assessments help identify content relevant to music teachers. Music teachers, as all adult learners, have varying levels of knowledge, attitudes, competencies, concerns, experiences, and backgrounds, and as such, their training needs are both numerous and diverse. Listening to the needs of music educators can lead to the creation of specific inservice programs designed and modified to meet the needs of each group. Therefore, to be relevant, inservice content must focus upon topics considered important to the teachers themselves, providing insight into teacher perceptions regarding their abilities to adapt curriculum and use support services (Hesse, 1977/1978), as well as a relatively accurate view of current competency levels and needs for additional training (Nevin, 1979).

A needs assessment instrument, The Music Education in Mainstreaming Needs Assessment, has been developed by Heine as part of the "Music in Mainstreaming Survey"(see Appendix) to assist inservice trainers in determining music educators' needs for specific topics and skills perceived as necessary to enhance their teaching in mainstreamed music settings. In 1999, Heine's needs assessment instrument was used in a study by Smith and Wilson. The purpose of this study was to examine the effects of classroom and practicum instruction on the attitudes of music educators toward special needs students. Eighteen graduate music education students participated in a four-week summer course dealing with music and special learners.

The Music Education in Mainstreaming Needs Assessment was administered at the beginning of the course to assess teacher needs for the course, and during the final class of the course to measure whether or not their needs had been met. When examining needs assessment posttest responses, Smith and Wilson found significant differences between pre- and postranked means for each question on the needs assessment. It is clear that utilizing a needs assessment helped to shape the course content and to meet the needs of the participants. Heine's complete "Music in Mainstreaming Survey" (MMS) is discussed in more detail later in this chapter.

Needs assessments can help evaluate inservice effectiveness. A needs assessment can be used to examine pre-to-post changes in felt needs, attitudes, skill levels, and knowledge base of teachers as a result of inservice training (Haire, 1976; Waggoner, 1976/1977). Parker (1990/1991) used a needs assessment as pre- and posttreatment evidence of improved attitude and knowledge of disabilities, instructional strategies, and behavioral management techniques. Parker used several pretest assessments of knowledge, skills, and attitudes, as well as topics and skill-areas identified in the general education literature to help to determine the instructional content of her inservice program. Inservice effectiveness was determined not only through participant evaluations, but also by statistical evaluation of pre-to-post knowledge gains and attitude changes. Parker (1990/1991) was able to demonstrate positive changes in attitude, as well as significant ($p < .05$) pre-to-post gains in knowledge.

Needs assessments may influence long term inservice benefits. A study by Rappa, Genova, and Walberg (1983) suggests that using inservice content based on a needs assessment has important implications for the long-term effectiveness of inservice training. This two-and-one-half year research study involved pre- and postworkshop questionnaires completed by 235 regular classroom teachers who participated in 36 inservice projects. They found that teachers who cited content and skill inadequacies as a need for inservice were usually those who reported predicted, continued and future use of the knowledge and skills gained. They reported statistically significant correlation ($p < .001$) between predicted use and continued use (.44), as well as with the amount of new knowledge acquired from the inservice (.60), knowledge used either during or immediately after an inservice (.55), and with indications of future use (.53). They concluded that "continued use of knowledge appears to hinge on two factors: early success in using the knowledge as well as current need and relevancy" (p. 23).

Evaluation of Inservice Effectiveness

The third essential component of effective inservice is evaluation. Evaluation is the process of determining whether or not inservice is meaningful, meets the needs of the participants, and has been successful. It provides a measure of accountability, and helps to judge the effectiveness of inservice (Pochowski, 1988). However, inservices often lack systematic evaluation of their effectiveness (Knowlton, 1980, p. 59). Rather than knowledge and/or skills gained or attitudes changed, inservice evaluations typically use a variety of "ill-conceived questionnaires and feedback forms" that attempt to assess how participants feel about the inservice program, whether or not the coffee was hot, if the seats were comfortable, the personal appearance of presenter, or the convenience of the lunch hour (Brinkerhoff, 1980, p. 27; Knowlton, 1980, p. 59; Wieck, 1979).

Nevertheless, guidelines for an efficient, functional workshop evaluation are available (Knowlton, 1980; Skrtic, Knowlton, & Clark, 1979). First of all, effective evaluation must permeate all program components, including the planning phases (Knowlton, 1980). Second, evaluation must be needs-based (Brinkerhoff, 1980). That is, it must discover and clarify the needed knowledge of inservice participants that can then be used to help design and implement strategies that address those needs. If these evaluative aspects were added, evaluation could become formative, that is, it could help inservice providers improve future endeavors

(Brinkerhoff, 1980). Finally, evaluation should address whether or not the needed knowledge and/or strategies have been acquired. The rationale and guidelines provided by Knowlton (1980) and Brinkerhoff (1980) can be used to develop and implement inservice delivery, and can serve to guide the methodology to evaluate an inservice.

Evaluation of Inservice in Music Education

In the music education literature, several studies report outcomes of inservice based on evaluative measures. Lehr (1977/1978) reported inservice outcomes using a survey completed by participants in a one-term course, Music for Slow Learners. After surveying former course members, Lehr utilized primarily qualitative data to draw positive conclusions regarding: (a) competencies needed by those who teach students with disabilities, and (b) types of music experiences most beneficial and most enjoyed by special needs students. A study by Gilles (1978/1979) involved inservice training via a special education music methods course. She was able to demonstrate significant results regarding knowledge gain ($p < .001$) and frequency of music usage ($p < .05$) during the course. She also reported a significant, positive increase ($p < .002$) in attitude toward teaching music to special needs students. Donley (1985) focused on outcomes of a summer workshop on music methods for mainstreaming settings. Evaluating teacher attitude before and after the workshop, Donley was able to demonstrate significant positive changes ($p < .01$) in attitude. Providing a workshop to preservice participants, Smith (1987) was able to demonstrate statistically significant evidence that this training can influence improvements in knowledge and skills considered important to music educators working with special needs children.

Wilson and McCrary (1996) studied the pre- and postresponses to a questionnaire given to students before and after completing a graduate course about music and special students. Unlike other studies, the participants in this study indicated an increase in their capabilities to work with special needs children, but a decrease in their willingness to work with special needs students. Wilson and McCrary (1996) conclude that the lack of positive change in attitude "may be reflective of participants' having developed a more realistic understanding of both the rewards and the challenges in providing music education services for students with disabilities" (p. 30).

Music in Mainstreaming Survey

A valid and reliable measuring instrument that can provide information useful to inservice providers has been developed by Heine (see Appendix). The "Music in Mainstreaming Survey" (MMS) includes three main sections: a Background Survey, a Needs Assessment, and an Attitude Survey. The Background Survey contains items asking for information about the respondent's age, gender, educational background, years of teaching experience, including those with children who have disabilities, and availability of administrative and educational support services. The second section of the MMS, the Needs Assessment, can be used to identify the perceived needs for inservice information as identified by general elementary music teachers working with mainstreamed students. This information can be used to: (a) ascertain what areas of knowledge and skills are considered important to music educators participating in inservice, and (b) develop the content of inservice programs. The third section of the MMS is an Attitude Survey and is designed to be used both as a pre- and posttest. Its purpose is to identify any changes in attitude attributable to inservice training.

All sections of the MMS were developed in a step-by-step procedure to ensure that the final instrument was inclusive, reliable, and valid. With the establishment of both content validity and reliability, the "Music in Mainstreaming Survey," including the Needs Assessment, is believed to be an inclusive instrument that not only can assist inservice providers determine content based upon the assessed needs of music teachers working with special needs children, but also is designed to help inservice providers collect important pre-and posttreatment data regarding the effectiveness of the inservice training. The final form of the MMS appears at the end of this chapter in the Appendix.

Inservice Delivery Models

Selecting inservice content that is recognized as necessary and applicable is an essential first step toward effective inservice (Hutson, 1981; Leyser & Cole, 1987; Powers, 1983; Spanier, 1987), but how such information is delivered to music teachers may be as important as the information itself. Prior research indicates that the mode of delivery, as well as content, is critical to inservice effectiveness (Blietz & Courtnage, 1980; Edelfelt, 1981; Hutson, 1981; Jamison, 1983; Korinek, Schmid, & McAdams, 1985; Leyser & Cole, 1987; Pochowski, 1988; Powers, 1983; Silver & Moyle, 1984). Yet, it is safe to say that even the best inservice programs fail unless there is a realistic and effective mode of delivery. In other words, inservice programs must be reasonable in terms of scheduling, location, and financial demands, and may differ from area to area.

The choice of inservice model may also be important. This is especially so when considering inservice in music education. For example, music educators have had access for many years to textbooks that give information about music education for special learners. However, textbook information requires teachers individually to derive applicability from this type of information delivery. Research studies in general education have indicated that interaction, collaboration and, by implication, opportunity for discussion among teachers, appear to make inservice more effective. In fact, deficit-oriented prescriptive models, in which teachers are viewed as "passive pawns to be remediated" (Hunt, 1978, p. 239), are generally not viewed as effective. Therefore, it appears that providing information alone, such as written material, may be ineffective in preparing teachers to work with students with disabilities. This seems especially true for a content area such as music education that includes many active and experiential types of learning experiences.

Inservice models come in all shapes and sizes. Some of these include short- and long-term workshops, statewide inservices, extension courses, graduate courses, or year-long, school-based inservice training programs. These inservice programs may also incorporate consultation, training booklets, field observations and practice, and may utilize didactic, audiovisual, and experiential components.

In music education, research studies about the delivery of inservice training in music and mainstreaming are limited. Moreover, only descriptive information and limited empirical data exist to substantiate the relative benefits of delivery for music education inservice. However, several modes of inservice delivery have been attempted in providing inservice training for music educators. These include a variety of workshops, statewide inservices, and college-based or extension courses.

Inservice Workshops

The most typical and widely used mode of inservice delivery in education is the workshop format (Griffin, 1982; Stein, 1983). There are several positive aspects of a traditional inservice workshop. First of all, teachers seem to prefer workshop models to other types of inservice programming. For example, Blietz and Courtnage (1980) surveyed teachers and administrators ($N = 278$) in a Midwestern state to determine attitudes and perceptions regarding mainstreaming. They found, among other things, that the majority of the respondents preferred inservices that were for shorter periods of time, that is, one-day and/or half-day sessions. Similarly, Beard (1989/1990) surveyed a random sample of 1,250 teachers across the United States regarding their preferences for 12 inservice delivery models and eight methods used to deliver inservice content. Comparing ratings percentages she found that one of the most frequently and highly rated delivery models was the short-term inservice planned to meet individual needs.

In addition, workshops offer qualities of flexibility, cost efficiency, and group dynamics. An inservice workshop model provides flexibility in terms of length of time, site, format, and target populations (Leyser & Cole, 1987). The length of workshops can vary from a one-hour after school lecture; a two-day, weekend workshop; or a workshop during the summer lasting for one or more weeks. In addition to varied lengths, workshop sites may also vary from on-site, school-based programs to inservices offered on college campuses or a program offered at a centrally located facility within the school district. Workshops provide a format that offers experiential opportunities, as well as theoretically based lectures. In addition, the focus of a workshop may be on one or more topics that are based on specific needs, concerns, and interests of the teachers (Carberry, Waxman, & McKain, 1981; Healy, 1983). Furthermore, workshops, when content-specific, can provide meaningful training that may help to increase knowledge and skills, improve attitude, and in turn, be cost effective (Jacobson, 1984).

In addition to the ability to meet specific needs of the participants, the workshop format also may provide a group dynamic believed to be important. In a study comparing differences between group workshops and individual consultation with instructional materials, Bernard (1988/1989) found that group workshops were the only ones in which collaborative planning and patterns of collegiality were observed and enhanced.

Not all studies support the workshop format as most effective. For example, Bass (1981) surveyed 243 teachers from 21 schools with diverse geographical locales. She found that teachers preferred impromptu help from school resource personnel in addition to one-day workshops. Zigarmi, Betz, and Jensen (1977) surveyed a random sample of 1,239 teachers in South Dakota. In response to one part of their questionnaire, teachers were asked to identify and rate usefulness of various inservice models and activities. They found that summer workshops at local schools and "current trends" workshops were the preferred modes of delivery. They also found that, while short-term workshops were the most widely used, they were considered the least useful to teachers when compared to other types of inservice, and workshops held on college campuses were considered moderately to very useful.

In summary, there is considerable, though not conclusive evidence, that inservice workshops enhance teacher attitude and knowledge. They promote the exchange of ideas and offer opportunities to learn from other teachers by providing a venue that enables teachers to talk freely and discuss concerns (Carberry et al., 1981; Zigarmi et al., 1977). These key factors suggest that well planned, on-site inservice workshops can be especially helpful in providing a participant-friendly atmosphere for music educators.

Inservice Workshops and Short Courses in Music Education

Three studies by Smith (1987), Smith (1989), and Donley (1985) describe the use of short-term inservice workshops or instructional units with preservice or inservice music teachers as participants. Smith (1987) offered a five-day workshop focusing on knowledge and skill adaptation in the education of children with disabilities. Results of this project revealed significant gains ($p < .01$) in instructional skills, and indicated that a short-term workshop can be an effective mode of inservice delivery. In another study utilizing a short-term workshop delivery model, Smith (1989) was able to examine teachers' perceptions and attitudes toward mainstreaming. Results from his analysis supported current research findings regarding teacher needs, and demonstrated the ability of a short-term workshop model to better prepare music educators to teach students with disabilities. Similarly, Donley (1985) reported that a short-term summer workshop focusing on teachers' attitude toward mainstreaming resulted in significant positive changes in attitude ($p < .01$).

Two studies focused on statewide inservice projects for special education teachers (Kearns, 1986/1987; Sheridan, 1979/1980). Sheridan provided a series of statewide workshops for music educators to introduce her curriculum guide for music in mainstreaming. Her workshops also provided special packets for each inservice participant containing ideas for mainstreaming. While she reported that, after participating in the workshops, teachers expressed increased confidence about teaching children with disabilities, Sheridan offered no detailed analysis of program effectiveness.

In Kearns' 1986/1987 post hoc evaluation of a statewide integrated arts inservice project, 96% of the survey respondents ($N = 254$) reported that the inservice program (workshop format) had been valuable to them and 89% reported positive effects on teaching practices. The only problem cited by some of the respondents was that the inservice had not been as beneficial to them because: (a) they were already familiar with the information and materials covered in the inservice content, or (b) the inservice did not meet their specific needs (p. 77). Once again, these outcomes indicate that, to have truly effective inservice training, it is important to provide needs-based inservice programs.

Graduate and Extension Courses

As in the workshop inservice model, college graduate and extension courses for teachers can be successful in changing teachers' perceptions and increasing knowledge about disabilities and mainstreaming (Hudson, Reisberg, & Wolf, 1983). Similar and often significant results have been reported in research studies that compare college-sponsored, on-site delivery models to other types of delivery models for general classroom teachers (Berrigan, 1979/1980; Brown, 1985; Hudson et al., 1983; Wang, Vaughan, & Dytman, 1985). This mode of inservice delivery may include university-sponsored inservice programs offered at a centrally located school within the school district (Cavallaro, Stowitschek, George, & Stowitschek, 1980; Hall, Benninga, & Clark, 1983; Waggoner, 1976/1977), as well as summer and extension courses.

College-Sponsored Courses in Music Education

Several studies in the music education literature demonstrate successful use of college-sponsored courses to help music educators working with special needs children (Gilles, 1978/1979; Lehr, 1977/1978; Smith & Wilson, 1999; Wilson & McCrary, 1996). The primary emphasis of Lehr's course was on the musical development of regular classroom teachers to help them utilize music with special needs students in their classes. Gilles offered a college course on the topic of music in special education to inservice teachers. Using a pre-post questionnaire, Gilles was able to show significant changes in knowledge gain ($p < .001$), music usage ($p < .05$), and teacher attitude ($p < .002$). Wilson and McCrary offered a graduate course, Music for Special Learners. To determine participants' attitudes toward children with and without disabilities before and after the course, participants were given a questionnaire with responses based upon their comfort level and willingness to work with individuals with disabilities. While results indicated an increase in participants' perception of their capability to work with individuals with disabilities, pre-to-post scores revealed a decline in subjects' comfort level and a significant decrease ($p < .05$) in their willingness to work professionally with these individuals. For future replication of this study, the authors recommended the addition of a practicum component to the course content.

In 1999, Smith and Wilson conducted a study which replicated the research questions originally proposed by Wilson and McCrary (1996). Smith and Wilson offered a four-week summer graduate course in music education for special learners. The participants ($N = 18$) were music educators representing a variety of teaching levels (K–12) and areas of emphasis (i.e., choral, instrumental).

Like the Wilson and McCrary study (1996), Smith and Wilson were interested in how a graduate course would influence the attitudes of music educators toward the integration of special learners into music classes. Would music educators feel more capable, willing, and comfortable working in an integrated music setting after taking this course? Unlike the 1996 Wilson and McCrary study, a practicum component was added to the graduate course requirements. In addition, a pre and post needs assessment was administered to identify participant needs, to help shape and adjust course content, and to assess on a posttest level whether or not the needs of the teacher–participants had been met. In league with the Heine needs assessment, Smith and Wilson administered an attitude survey developed by Wilson and McCrary (1996) to examine teacher perception of comfortableness, willingness, and capability in working with special needs students. Responses to the posttest needs assessment indicated that the teachers' needs were met. In addition, results of their study indicated a significant increase in teachers' feelings of capability. Teachers were "more comfortable and more willing to interact with special learners after the completion of the course" (p. 43). The authors attribute this to the addition of the practicum experience.

Inservice Using a Self-Guided Study Format

Direct instruction using workshop, graduate, or extension course formats are commonly reported models of inservice delivery. Another model for disseminating information relevant to teachers is through self-guided inservice packets, manuals, or books with topics reflecting general needs and concerns based upon current research, pedagogical practice, or needs assessments. Wade (1984/1985) suggests that independent study and self-instruction are viable alternatives to the traditional workshop format. Similarly, Griffin (1982, p. 19) asserts that self-study programs can play an important role because teachers have hands-on materials presented in a manual that is reality-based, situation specific, and is written in a clear, concise manner.

According to some researchers, a self-guided delivery model may be preferred by some teachers (Bass, 1981; Beard, 1989/1990). Bass (1981), for example, found that, unlike their urban counterparts, rural teachers were willing to consider college courses, correspondence courses, and formalized self-study, but may have less access to conferences and may lack opportunities for formal university courses. As such, these teachers might welcome well-organized self-study programs for which little or no travel is required. In a study mentioned previously, Beard (1989/1990) surveyed a random sample of 1,250 teachers to find out their preferences regarding inservice models and method of delivering inservice content. She found that the two most highly rated, that is, preferred methods of content delivery were: (a) varied formats and take-home packets, and (b) independent study.

While Beard (1989/1990) did not offer reasons for these preferences, one can predict several advantages to this mode of inservice delivery. Certain texts, books, and self-guided inservice manuals are self-contained and usually well organized. As such, they can be at-hand for class use (Griffin, Hughes, & Martin, 1982). In addition, they can be distributed easily and inexpensively to a large number of teachers. This may be important not only in large metropolitan areas, but also in sparsely populated, rural areas where access to a more formal or on-site inservice training workshop or extension course is not readily available. In addition, contrary to the workshop model, self-guided books and manuals provide flexibility and ease time constraints. They can address specific topics, and can be practically oriented, theoretically based, or based on needs assessment. However, it is important to determine whether or not a self-study program, though it may be inexpensive and convenient, is actually an effective inservice mode, especially for a specialty area such as music education.

Music Education Inservice Through Self-Directed Study

To date, no studies in music education were found that parallel those in general education regarding self-directed inservice formats. A number of "how-to" books recommend techniques and instructional materials for use with special needs children, e.g., *Music for the Special Learner,* by Sona Nocera (1979), *Music for Special Education,* by Kay Hardesty (1979), *Music in Developmental Therapy,* by Shelly Purvis and Jennie Samet (1976), or MENC's *In Tune with PL 94-142* (1980). While most of the books listed here are popular among music educators and music therapists, most are out of print. In addition, while most elementary music basal series do include some mention of music with special needs students, success of incorporating ideas and suggestions for instructional adaptations has yet to be investigated. In fact, no data or content analysis seems to exist regarding how effective any of these books, instructional materials or basal series are in preparing music educators to work with students who have disabilities.

Combination of Delivery Models

The literature in general education reports that a combination of delivery models, including both workshops and well-designed, self-guided inservice manuals, may contribute to successful inservice outcomes (Beard, 1989/1990; Bernard, 1988/1989; Fenton, 1974; Griffin, 1982; Stainback, Stainback, Strathe, & Dedrick, 1983). For example, Emmer, Sanford, Evertson, Clements, and Martin (1981) demonstrated that teachers who had access to a three-hour workshop, plus a well-designed instructional manual, were more effective ($p < .05$) in demonstrating desired changes in classroom management behaviors than control group teachers who did not participate in the formal training program. While it was not clear whether the successful outcomes were a result of the short-term workshop alone or the combination of workshop and instructional manual, Griffin (1982, p. 19) asserts that the manual played an important role in this experiment because it was well written, was varied in format and addressed teacher needs and concerns. On the other hand, the researchers (Emmer et al., 1981, p. 65) suggest that perhaps the workshop was also important because it helped focus teachers' attention on content of the manual, and may have enhanced treatment participants' sense of accountability for following the manual.

There are very few studies that contrast the use of workshops and instructional books or manuals in terms of overall inservice outcome effectiveness; however, Fenton (1974) found that a variety of delivery systems, including the use of self-guided manuals, may be effective. Using the Rutgers-Gable Scale as a pre-post measure, he compared the effectiveness of four inservice programs on changing attitudes toward children with disabilities and knowledge of special education placement procedures. Each of four school districts took part in four different, state-funded inservice projects. The four models included: (a) a series of eight short-term workshops with a practicum after each workshop, consultation, and access to a demonstration center; (b) eight workshops plus a series of videos and access to a professional library; (c) 30 hours of instruction with self-guided training packets, observation of master teachers, access to 30 hours of support personnel services and optional college course offerings, and (d) 30 hours of instruction including workshop, class visits, and a materials fair. Teachers in each of the four school districts volunteered to participate in the project. Fenton (1974) found that, in all but the third model (30 hours of instruction with training packet), posttreatment scores for teacher attitudes were significantly lower ($p < .05$). Although the participants in the third project showed no changes in attitude after inservice training, they were the only group to show any significant pre-to-post increase ($p < .05$) in knowledge gain. Interestingly enough, this is the only model of the four used in his study that combined the use of group interaction (workshop) with training packets.

A research project that is especially important to the discussion of modes of inservice delivery is a study by Kelly and Vanvactor (1983). Conducted with general classroom teachers, it is one of few that compared the effectiveness and cost efficiency of several modes of inservice delivery provided to regular classroom teachers in a sparsely populated state. The purpose of this study was to compare four inservice delivery models on the following dependent variables: knowledge gain, cost effectiveness, long-term knowledge retention, and the teacher's classroom effectiveness. The four types include: (a) on-site, school-based workshops provided by a master teacher who presented 40 hours of on-site instruction; similar content, follow-up activities and evaluations were provided to all workshop participants, with posttest on knowledge acquisition occurring at conclusion of the inservice week; (b) on-site, school-based workshop provided by university personnel who presented forty hours of on-site instruction with similar content, follow-up, and evaluation; (c) on-campus workshop offered by university personnel on the college campus with similar content, follow-up, and evaluation; and (d) a self-guided, instructional packet, which was given to participants who received no formal instruction or assistance. The instructional packet, based on a needs assessment, included information about definitions and characteristics of various disabilities, mainstreaming materials, teaching strategies, and behavior management techniques. Assessment of knowledge gain and attitude change was conducted before and after the subjects' independent study of the instructional packet.

Results of the Kelly and Vanvactor study (1983) indicated that, compared to leader-directed workshop formats for inservice delivery, the least expensive delivery type was the instructional manual. However, while instructional manuals were less costly, they were not, in terms of long-term knowledge gain and overall effectiveness, the most cost effective. In fact, compared to the other models, the packet was the least beneficial.

According to Kelly and Vanvactor (1983), the most cost effective and beneficial model in terms of learner outcomes was the university personnel on-site model, followed by the master teacher on-site model, and then the university personnel on-campus model. The least beneficial and cost effective model was the instructional packet-alone format. In other words, the instructional packets were less costly, but in terms of cost effectiveness (knowledge gain and learner outcomes) both on-site delivery models were the more cost effective.

Combined Inservice Models in Music Education

A training package for music educators working with special needs children has been published by Silver Burdett Ginn. "Music for All Children" (Dark, Graham, Hughes, McCoy, & McKinney, 1996) offers an inservice training package including a facilitator manual, a participant handbook and a video. A review of the materials revealed no descriptions of field testing or other evaluative efforts. Although the authors urge inservice facilitators to gather background information on participants, no needs assessment or evaluation instruments are provided.

Summary

In summary, if the transmission of information is the only goal for inservice, self-directed, instructional packets or manuals may be sufficient (Korinek et al., 1985). However, when a self-guided instructional manual is the sole delivery format, group interaction is diminished, and it is precisely this group dynamic that, according to some, is essential for improvement of skill acquisition and behavioral change (Bernard, 1988/1989; Korinek et al., 1985). While Zigarmi et al. (1977) found that, in general, teachers do not like self-study formats, provision of such self-contained instructional materials may be a viable alternative for teachers in locations where distance and cost may interfere with the availability of on-site training.

Past research in general education indicates that the traditional workshop format is effective in helping teachers improve attitudes and knowledge about mainstreaming. The workshop has the advantage of being flexible (it can be geared to specific content) and facilitating group interaction and participant involvement. In addition, on-site delivery makes it relatively convenient to teachers.

The workshop is not the only viable inservice format, however. Other research has noted the benefits of summer graduate and extension courses, statewide inservice training programs, self-guided, individualized study, and combinations of different inservice formats. The majority of evidence to date, however, is related to general education. Little data are available regarding the relative merits of inservice delivery in music education. Those extant studies reflect workshops that are as short as a few hours to as long as a multi-week extension or college course. The studies that include some evaluation suggest that such inservice models are effective in improving knowledge and attitude.

Music Educators Have Special Inservice Needs

It is possible that, for several reasons, music educators may differ in terms of their inservice needs and preferences for specific inservice delivery formats. Perhaps these differences have to do with the nature of the music education curriculum itself. Music education tends to include a substantial amount of experiential group activity such as playing instruments, singing, and movement. For instance, then, can we assume that the opportunity for group participation and discussion is essential to inservice in music education? In her study about music educators and their concerns and inservice needs regarding mainstreamed music settings, Stein (1983) found, among other things, that music teachers preferred workshops in which they could discuss problems and situations with other music educators. However, some music educators may work in small, remote school districts where regular inservice programming is unavailable. Is the self-guided information packet a viable alternative for improving knowledge and attitudes toward mainstreaming? Perhaps a combination of inservice formats would be beneficial. Would an inservice utilizing a workshop format that included a well-organized manual or packet of information better meet the needs of music educators? Since no extant studies address these concerns, we can only speculate.

What is clear, however, is that whatever mode of delivery is used, we must examine and devise ways in which to provide meaningful and effective inservice training to music educators. We also know that research indicates that successful and meaningful inservice training must offer teachers information on current trends or ideas presented in a new way and designed in response to teacher needs (Zigarmi et al., 1977).

Best Practices for Inservice in Music Education

Positive teacher attitude is the key to successful integration of special needs children into the elementary music class, and is influenced by training. Teacher attitude is also an important key to successful inservice. The goal of inservice training is to help music teachers gain knowledge and positive attitudes about their jobs. In order to feel prepared and positive about mainstreamed music settings, teachers need adequate training and preparation. Inservice is a practical and positive way to achieve this goal. The following ideas will help inservice providers as they prepare inservices to meet the needs of their colleagues facing the challenges of music in the mainstream.

1. Inservice requires good planning, demanding attention to the rest of the "best practice" statements.
2. Inservice should be teacher-oriented, focusing on the development of additional skills rather than attempting to ameliorate teacher-deficits. It is important to recognize teachers as adult learners who bring to the inservice a host of ideas, experiences, needs and strengths.
3. Inservice should focus on the development of knowledge, skills and positive attitudes.
4. Inservice providers must be enthusiastic, interesting, well prepared, interested in meeting the needs of the participants, and willing to utilize a variety of inservice delivery models and formats.
5. Inservices must be needs-based. A well-planned inservice program will incorporate a needs assessment because: (a) it provides specific background information about inservice participants, (b) it provides information regarding the needs of inservice participants, and (c) it helps the inservice provider select meaningful content and a variety of formats to meet the needs of inservice participants. Needs assessments should provide a broad survey of possible information to identify specific needs of each inservice audience. A needs assessment may include questions about special needs children in mainstreamed music classroom settings, the components of IDEA (formerly PL 94-142), Individualized Education Program (IEP), Least Restrictive Environment (LRE), full inclusion, instructional needs and skills, classroom management, methods and materials, teaching strategies, resources, and teacher attitude. Not every inservice audience will need information on all these topics. Providing information that participants do not need is contrary to best practices in inservice. Teacher–participants prefer inservices that provide them with useful information.
6. Inservice delivery and content must be practical and directly applicable. They should translate theory into practice, focus on specific needs or differences in classroom as identified by inservice participants, and emphasize instructional activities. Inservice content should be interesting and varied in format. Varying content delivery may add to learner interest and comprehension. Inservice providers may want to employ both didactic and experiential approaches and incorporate some of the following: lectures, demonstrations, simulations, group discussions, feedback sessions, audio/visual components, and field experiences.
7. Inservices should incorporate an evaluation component. Evaluation is based on a needs assessment, is content-based, and must be not only a critique of the inservice presentation, but also must be used to measure pre-to-post changes in participant behaviors such as: (a) positive (realistic) changes in teacher attitude, (b) increase in knowledge base, (c) increase in motivation to try newly learned skills and ideas (long-term, post check), and (d) improvement in skill level (long-term, post check).
8. Other factors that may influence the perceived success and usefulness of inservice programs are: (a) scheduling: where, when, and what time of day is the inservice program being offered; (b) financial demands: cost of inservice; (c) incentives: free materials, CEUs, and college credits, certificates; and (d) location: participants tend to prefer inservices that are on-site, centrally-located, or as near to the work place as possible.

Chapter Conclusions

1. The music teacher is the key to success in the mainstreamed (integrated) music setting.
2. Music educators need adequate educational preparation to meet the challenges and opportunities of mainstreaming.
3. Many music educators are willing to teach in mainstreamed settings despite lack of input into placement decisions, lack of information about special needs students, and lack of preparation and training.
4. Most research indicates that in the past 20 years, little has changed in terms of preparing teachers for mainstreamed music settings.
5. The need for inservice training has been identified as crucial to success of music in the mainstream.
6. For inservice to be successful, it must focus on content and formats designed to address the needs, concerns, strengths, and attitudes of the music teacher.
7. A needs assessment will provide inservice providers with ideas for content.
8. Inservice content that is practical and applicable to the music classroom will more readily engage the interests of the teacher–participants.
9. Music teachers are adult learners, and as such, they bring a wealth of ideas and insights to the inservice experiences.
10. Inservices should include evaluation of training outcomes such as changes in attitudes, knowledge gain, skill development, and long-term effectiveness.
11. Inservice delivery models come in all shapes and sizes, including short-and long-term workshops, summer and extension courses, school-based, on-site programs, statewide inservices, and self-guided instruction.
12. Inservice in music education should include opportunities for group participation and discussion, experiential activities, and practical classroom strategies.
13. It is essential to provide well-organized, needs-based inservices to promote positive and successful music experiences for everyone (teacher and students alike) involved in the mainstreamed music setting.

Inclusion of special needs students in music education classes is a reality. However, in an article on mainstreaming, Graham (1988) warns that, "Music educators see themselves as unprepared to teach disabled students and are often reluctant to make curricular and program modifications for mainstreamed students" (p. 33). This statement is supported by research (Frisque et al., 1994; Gfeller & Hedden, 1987; Gfeller et al., 1990; Gilbert & Asmus, 1981; Stein, 1983) that suggests many music educators feel inadequately trained and unprepared to work with special needs children in their classes. This concern is probably related to limited preparation for instructing students with disabilities. In fact, several surveys suggest that if administrative support and opportunities for training are provided to music teachers, their attitudes toward mainstreaming improve (Gfeller & Hedden, 1987; Gfeller et al., 1990; Gilbert & Asmus, 1981).

While most teachers acknowledge the lack of preparation and opportunities for inservice training, there is some evidence to suggest that music teachers have positive attitudes toward mainstreaming (Jellison, 1992). In addition, some teachers have indicated a willingness to attend workshops that focus on teaching special needs students (Sideridis & Chandler, 1995). Nevertheless, it is clear that music teachers need and want training to meet the challenges and opportunities of the mainstreamed music class. Inservice education is an important key to the success of mainstreamed music education. Inservice programs provide opportunities for teachers to acquire additional knowledge, skills, and training essential to the successful integration of special needs students into the mainstreamed music class. Inservice experiences can uplift teacher attitude and provide the professional help needed to improve teachers' feelings of confidence as they plan musical experiences for the special needs children in their music classes.

For those who are called upon to provide inservice training to music educators so that they may work more effectively with students who have disabilities, the following components are deemed necessary for inservice to be effective. First, the content should be based on the needs identified by the music teachers themselves. Second, the most effective mode of delivery for music education content should be utilized. Third, the inservice training should include a systematic evaluation of inservice outcomes. Unless this occurs, we will, as in the past, be obliged to theorize on inservice effectiveness. Unless we provide well-planned, needs-based inservices to music educators, we will, as many current studies have concluded, continue to promote a cycle of inadequate teacher preparation and professional development that does nothing to serve the needs of the music educator nor change the status of music with special needs children within the general music classroom.

Frequently Asked Questions (FAQs)

What do music teachers who work in mainstreamed music settings need?

Music educators who teach special needs children in elementary music classes need to have: (a) a positive attitude toward mainstreaming, (b) inservice training beyond the preservice, college curriculum, (c) inservice providers who recognize the importance of the teacher–participant as an adult learner with a variety of talents and experiences, and (d) inservices with content and format based on the needs and the strengths of the teacher–participants.

What is an inservice and what does it provide?

Inservice is a developmental activity designed to provide teachers with opportunities to: improve skills, increase knowledge, learn new teaching methods and strategies, and experience self-renewal within a supportive and positive climate (Dillon-Peterson, 1981).

What are the critical components of a good inservice?

The three critical components of a good inservice are: (a) attention to teacher–participant attitude, (b) inservice content based on teacher–participant needs, and (c) evaluation.

What are some possible causes for ambivalent and/or negative attitudes among music teachers toward the integration of special needs students into music classes?

Negative attitudes may be a direct result of: (a) lack of teacher preparation and training, (b) lack of input regarding placement decisions, (c) lack of information about the needs and characteristics of students, (d) lack of current, up-dated materials and resources, and (e) limited amount of content within the covers of elementary music basal series devoted to information, instructional guidance, and adaptive techniques for teachers with special needs students in music classes.

What do we need to keep in mind when planning and providing inservices for music educators?

When planning inservice training and educational opportunities for music teachers, the approach should not be a deficit-oriented one, but rather a developmental approach in which the strengths and needs of the teachers are seen as guideposts for determining inservice content and format.

How can inservice content meet the needs of the music educator?

Inservice content can meet the needs of music educators if it is based on the needs of the teacher–participants, is based on current trends in methods and teaching practices, provides pragmatic and realistic instructional suggestions and materials, and is designed in a sensible, enjoyable, and supportive way that encourages participation and discussion.

What information should be included in an inservice regarding music with special needs children?

Information and topics included in an inservice should be determined by assessing the needs of the participants. As such, inservice content might include any number of topics such as: components of IDEA (formerly PL 94-142), Individualized Education Program (IEP), Least Restrictive Environment (LRE), full inclusion, instructional needs and skills, classroom management, methods and materials, teaching strategies and adaptive approaches, educational resources and support personnel, and teacher attitude.

What information can be eliminated from an inservice?

Not every inservice audience will need information on all topics. Providing information that participants do not need is contrary to best practices in inservice. Teacher–participants prefer inservices that provide them with useful information. When planning and delivering an inservice, how can a needs assessment be utilized to enhance and increase a teacher's knowledge, skills, and attitude?

We need to do more than ask questions about coffee breaks, the luncheon menu, and seating arrangements. While these may be important questions, a needs assessment should focus on the following: (a) identification of teacher–participant needs, (b) identification of content and format that are considered useful and relevant to teacher–participants, (c) measurement of pre-to-post inservice changes, and, when possible, (d) long-term effectiveness of the training.

What does the "Music in Mainstreaming Survey" offer to inservice providers?

The MMS has: (a) a background survey (demographics, teaching experience, support services, etc.); (b) a needs assessment (areas of knowledge and skills considered important to music educators participating in inservice); and (c) an attitude survey (pre-post opportunities to assess changes attributable to inservice training.

What are the various types of inservice delivery models, and which one is best?

There are many types of inservice delivery models, and the type of inservice one chooses can depend on a number of variables including: participant needs, setting and environment, budget, etc. Some inservice models include short-term or long-term workshops, graduate and extension courses, statewide curriculum projects, school-based projects, and self-guided instructional programs. These inservice programs may also incorporate consultation, training booklets, field observations and practice, and may utilize didactic, audiovisual, and experiential components.

Is it possible that music educators have special needs and preferences for inservice training and formats that may differ from other inservice participants?

Whether they differ or not from other inservice participants in general education is not especially clear. What is clear, however, is that music educators require and desire inservices that offer experiential group activities, incorporate opportunities for a meaningful exchange of ideas, and provide realistic, useful, and specific information, instructional methods, and materials that are directly applicable to the mainstream music setting.

What are the "best practices" for inservice in music education?

Good inservice provides the following: (a) evidence of good planning; (b) developmental approach to needs-based content focusing on knowledge, skills, and attitudes; (c) enthusiastic and well-prepared inservice providers; (d) needs-based approach that incorporates background information about inservice participants, information regarding the needs of inservice participants, and information to help determine meaningful content and inservice formats; (e) practical, interesting, varied, and applicable inservice delivery, format, and content; (f) inservice evaluation that is content-based, and which can be used to measure pre-to-post changes in participant behaviors such as positive (realistic) changes in teacher attitude, increase in knowledge base, increase in motivation to try newly learned skills and ideas (long-term, post check), and improvement in skill level (long-term, post check).

Other factors that may influence the perceived success and usefulness of inservice programs are: (g) scheduling: where, when, and what time of day is the inservice program being offered; (h) financial demands: cost of inservice; (i) incentives: free materials, CEUs and college credits, certificates, and (j) location: participants tend to prefer inservices that are on-site, centrally-located, or as near to the work place as possible.

References

Atterbury, B. W. (1986a). A survey of present mainstreaming practices in the Southern United States. *Journal of Music Therapy, 23*(4), 202–207.

Atterbury, B. W. (1986b). Success in the mainstream of general music. *Music Educators Journal, 72*(7), 34–36.

Atterbury, B. W. (1990). *Mainstreaming exceptional learners in music.* Englewood Cliffs, NJ: Prentice-Hall.

Bass, M. B. (1981). *Special education inservice priorities for regular educators* (Report No. EC 152 607). (ERIC Document Reproduction Service No. ED 231 162)

Beard, N. V. (1989/1990). Education reform time: Teacher preferences for inservice content types and methods (Doctoral dissertation, University of South Carolina, 1989). *Dissertation Abstracts International, 51*(02), 351A.

Bernard, T. A. (1988/1989). Special education staff development and curriculum innovation (Doctoral dissertation, Columbia University Teachers College, 1988). *Dissertation Abstracts International, 50*(01), 117A.

Berrigan, C. R. (1979/1980). Effects of an inservice education workshop on the attitudes of regular classroom teachers toward disabled students (Doctoral dissertation, Syracuse University, 1979). *Dissertation Abstracts International, 40*(09), 5009A.

Blietz, J., & Courtnage, L. (1980). Inservice training for regular educators. *Teacher Education and Special Education, 3*(4), 10–18.

Brinkerhoff, R. O. (1980). Evaluation of inservice programs. *Teacher Education and Special Education, 3*(3), 27–38.

Broadwell, M. M. (1986). Five ways to keep supervisory training alive and well. *Training, 23*(9), 45–47.

Brown, K. R. (1985). Regular education teachers' attitudes and knowledge concerning the mainstreaming of handicapped students (Doctoral dissertation, Texas Southern University, 1985). *Dissertation Abstracts International, 47*(O3), 871A.

Carberry, H., Waxman, B., & McKain, D. (1981). An inservice workshop model for regular class teachers concerning mainstreaming of the learning disabled child. *Journal of Learning Disabilities, 14*(1), 26–28.

Cavallaro, C. C., Stowitschek, C. E., George, M., & Stowitschek, J. J. (1980). Intensive inservice education and concomitant changes in handicapped learners. *Teacher Education and Special Education, 3*(3), 49–58.

Culton, C. L. (1999/2000). The extent to which elementary music education textbooks reflect teachers' needs regarding instruction of students with special needs: A content analysis (Doctoral dissertation, University of Iowa, 1999). *Dissertation Abstracts International, 60*(12), 4358A.

Damer, L. K. (1979/1980). A student of the attitudes of selected public school teachers toward the integration of handicapped students into music classes (Doctoral dissertation, University of North Carolina, 1979). *Dissertation Abstracts International, 40*(07), 3862A.

Dark, I. D., Graham, R. M., Hughes, J., McCoy, M., & McKinney, D. D. (1996). *Music for all children*. Parsippany, NJ: Silver Burdett Ginn.

Darrow, A. A. (1990a). Beyond mainstreaming: Dealing with diversity. *Music Educators Journal, 76*(8), 36–39.

Darrow, A. A. (1990b). Research on mainstreaming in music education. *Update, 9*(1), 35–37.

Dillon-Peterson, B. (1981). Staff development—Overview. In B. Dillon-Peterson (Ed.), *Staff Development/ Organization Development* (pp. 1–10). Alexandria, VA: Association for Supervision and Curriculum Development.

Donley, C. R. (1985). The effects of an inservice workshop for music teachers on teachers' attitudes toward teaching music to handicapped children. In R. R. Pratt (Ed.), *The third international symposium on music in medicine, education, and therapy for the handicapped* (pp. 101–111). New York: University Press of America.

Edelfelt, R. A. (1981). Six years of progress in inservice education. *Journal of Research and Development in Education, 14*(2), 112–119.

Elliott, C., & Sins, N. (1981/1982). Attitudes and opinions of middle school music students toward the presence of handicapped peers in music classes. *Contributions to Music Education, 9*(5), 48–59.

Emmer, E. T., Sanford, J. P., Evertson, C. M., Clements, B. S., & Martin, J. (1981). Classroom management improvement student: An experiment in elementary school classrooms (Research Report No. 6050). Austin, TX: Research and Development Center for Teacher Education, University of Texas at Austin.

Fenton, T. R. (1974). The effects of inservice training on elementary classroom teachers' attitudes toward and knowledge about handicapped children (Doctoral dissertation, University of Northern Colorado, 1974). *Dissertation Abstracts International, 34*(09), 5966A.

Fishbein, M., & Ajzen, I. (1975). *Belief, attitude, intention, and behavior: An introduction to theory and research*. Reading, MA: Addison-Wesley.

Fresko, B., & Ben-Chaim, D. (1986). Assessing teacher needs and satisfaction of needs in inservice activities. *Studies in Educational Evaluation, 12*, 205–212.

Frisque, J., Niebur, L., & Humphreys, J. T. (1994). Music mainstreaming: Practices in Arizona. *Journal of Research in Music Education, 42*(2), 94–104.

Gavin, A. R. J. (1983/1984). Music educator practices and attitudes toward mainstreaming (Doctoral dissertation, Washington University, 1983). *Dissertation Abstracts International, 45*(02), 446A.

Gfeller, K., Darrow, A. A., & Hedden, S. K. (1990). Perceived effectiveness of mainstreaming in Iowa and Kansas schools. *Journal of Research in Music Education, 58*(2), 90–101.

Gfeller, K., & Hedden, S. K. (1987). Mainstreaming in music education: The state of the state. *Iowa Music Educator, 40*(3), 24–27.

Gilbert, J. P., & Asmus, E. P. (1981). Mainstreaming: Music educators' participation and professional needs. *Journal of Research in Music Education, 29*(1), 31–37.

Gilles, D. K. C. (1978/1979). The development and evaluation of a special education music methods course for preservice and inservice teachers (Doctoral dissertation, St. Louis University, 1978). *Dissertation Abstracts International, 40*(05), 2602A.

Goldsmith, G. K. (1984/1985). The effects of a university inservice program on the knowledge and attitudes of elementary school principals and teachers on the mainstreaming of handicapped children (Doctoral dissertation, George Washington University, 1984). *Dissertation Abstracts International, 45*(11), 3327A.

Graham, R. M. (1988). Barrier-free music education: Methods to make mainstreaming work. *Music Educators' Journal, 74*(5), 29–33.

Griffin, G. A. (1982). *Staff development*. Washington, DC: National Institute of Education. (ERIC Document Reproduction Service No. ED 221 537)

Griffin, G. A., Hughes, R., & Martin, J. (1982). *Knowledge, training and classroom management* (Report No. 6054). Austin, TX: Research and Development Center for Teacher Education, University of Texas at Austin. (ERIC Document Reproduction Service No. ED 251 445)

Haire, C. D. (1976). Effects of an inservice education model for supportive personnel on factors regarding exceptional children (Doctoral dissertation, Texas Tech University, 1976). *Dissertation Abstracts International, 37*(05), 2796A.

Hall, J., Benninga, J., & Clark, C. (1983). A three-part model: A comprehensive approach to the inservice training of teachers. *NASSP Bulletin, 67*(61), 17–21.

Hardesty, K. W. (1979). *Music for special education.* Morristown, NJ: Silver Burdett.

Hawkins, G. D. (1991/1992). Attitudes toward mainstreaming students with disabilities among regular elementary music and physical educators (Doctoral dissertation, University of Maryland, 1991). *Dissertation Abstracts International, 52*(09), 3245A.

Hayden, H. A. (1989/1990). A study of Maryland public school principals' perception of their special education inservice training needs (Doctoral dissertation, University of Maryland, 1989). *Dissertation Abstracts International, 51*(03), 727A.

Healy, S. (1983). Planning inservice programs. *The Pointer, 28*(1), 12–15.

Hesse, R. M. (1977/1978). A procedure for determining needs for inservice training of classroom teachers in a mainstreaming approach to the education of the mildly handicapped (Doctoral dissertation, University of Oregon, 1977). *Dissertation Abstracts International, 38*(10), 6055A.

Hock, M., Hasazi, S. B., & Patten, A. (1990). Collaboration for learning: Strategies for program success. *Music Educators Journal, 76*(8), 44–48.

Hudson, F., Reisberg, L. E., & Wolf, R. (1983). Changing teachers' perceptions of mainstreaming. *Teacher Education and Special Education, 6*, 18–24.

Hunt, D. E. (1978). Inservice training as persons-in relation. *Theory into Practice, 17*(3), 239–244.

Hutson, H. M. (1981). Inservice best practices: The learnings of general education. *Journal of Research and Development in Education, 14*(2), 1–10.

Jacobson, W. H. (1984). Teacher attitude toward mainstreamed blind children: The short term and long term effects of inservice training (Doctoral dissertation, University of Arkansas, 1984). *Dissertation Abstracts International, 45*(08), 2483A.

Jamison, P. J. (1983). Systematic development and evaluation of quality practices for inservice education. *Teacher Education and Special Education, 6*(2), 151–158.

Jellison, J. A. (1992). *Music and students with disabilities: A preliminary study of Texas music educators' experiences, attitudes, and perceptions.* Austin, TX: Texas Music Education Association. Paper presented at the annual meeting of the Texas Music Education Association, San Antonio, Texas.

Joyce, B., & Showers, B. (1980). Improving inservice training: The messages of research. *Educational Leadership, 37*(5), 379–385.

Kearns, L. H. (1986/1987). Outcomes of inservice programs on the arts in special education: The arts in special education project of Pennsylvania (Doctoral dissertation, Pennsylvania State University, 1986). *Dissertation Abstracts International, 47*(11), 3950A.

Kelly, E. J., & Vanvactor, J. C. (1983). The relative cost effectiveness of inservice approaches in remote, sparsely populated schools. *Exceptional Children, 50*(2), 140–148.

Knowlton, H. E. (1980). A framework for evaluating inservice workshops. *Teacher Education and Special Education, 3*(3), 58–70.

Korinek, L., Schmid, R., & McAdams, M. (1985). Inservice types and best practices. *Journal of Research and Development in Education, 18*(2), 33–38.

Lehr, J. K. (1977/1978). An investigation of music in the education of mentally and physically handicapped children in the United Kingdom, with particular reference to the course, Music for Slow Learners, at Dartington College of Arts (Doctoral dissertation, Ohio State University, Columbus, Ohio, 1977). *Dissertation Abstracts International, 38*(11), 6594A.

Leyser, Y., & Cole, K. B. (1987). The reconceptualization and delivery of quality inservice education under Public Law 94-142. In J. Gottlieb & B. W. Gottlieb (Eds.), *Advances in special education* (Vol. 6, pp. 87–117). Greenwich, CT: JAI Press.

Miller, L., & Wolf, T. E. (1978). Staff development for school change: Theory and practice. *Teachers College Record, 80*(1),140–156.

Music Educators National Conference. (1980). *In tune with PL 94-142: Guide for training teachers responsible for music education of handicapped learners.* Reston, VA: MENC.

Nevin, A. (1979). Special education administration competencies required of the general education administrator. *Exceptional Children, 45*(5), 363–365.

Nocera, S. D. (1979). *Reaching the special learner through music.* Morristown, NJ: Silver Burdett.

Nocera, S. D. (1981). A descriptive analysis of the attainment of selected musical learnings by normal children and by educable mentally retarded children mainstreamed in music classes at the second and fifth grade levels (Doctoral dissertation, University of Wisconsin-Madison, 1981). *Dissertation Abstracts International, 42*(10), 4347A.

Parker, D. O. (1990/1991). Preparing vocational teachers to effectively serve special needs students: An inservice education model (Doctoral dissertation. University North Carolina, 1990). *Dissertation Abstracts International, 51*(09), 3002A.

Pochowski, A. E. (1988). Compliance with educational legislation for handicapped children in relationship to the status of staff development in special education (Doctoral dissertation, University of Wisconsin, 1988*). Dissertation Abstracts International, 49*(05), 1117A.

Powers, D. A. (1983). Mainstreaming and the inservice education of teachers. *Exceptional Children, 49*(5), 432–439.

Pratt, R. R. (1986). Music education of the handicapped: Some insights gained during the last decade. *MEH Bulletin, 1*(3), 24–34.

Purvis, S., & Samet, J. (1976). *Music in developmental therapy.* Baltimore: University Park.

Rappa, J. B., Genova, W. J., & Walberg, H. J. (1983). *Staff, school and workshop characteristics affecting continued use and adaptation of knowledge: A follow-up study* (Report No. SP 024 323). Boston: Massachusetts State Department of Education. (ERIC Document Reproduction Service No. ED 243 872)

Schultz, J. B., & Turnbull, A. P. (1984*). Mainstreaming handicapped students: A guide for classroom teachers* (2nd ed.). Boston: Allyn & Bacon.

Sheridan, W. F. (1979/1980). Public Law 94-142 and the development of the Oregon plan of mainstreaming in music (Doctoral dissertation, University of Oregon, 1979). *Dissertation Abstracts International, 40*(09), 4878A.

Sideridis, G. D., & Chandler, J. P. (1995). Attitude and characteristics of general music teachers toward integrating children with developmental disabilities. *Update, 14*(1), 11–15

Silver, P. F., & Moyle, C. R. J. (1984). The impact of intensive inservice programs on educational leaders and their organization. *Planning and Changing, 13*(1), 18–33.

Sins, N. J. (1983). Mainstreaming the music class automatically brings about acceptance by the nonhandicapped. Right? (Wrong). *Update, 2*(1), 3–6.

Skrtic, T. M., Knowlton, H. E., & Clark, F. L. (1979). Action vs. reaction: A curriculum development approach to inservice education. *Focus on Exceptional Children, 2*(1), 1–16.

Smith, D. S. (1987). The effect of instruction on ability to adapt teaching situations for exceptional students. *MEH Bulletin, 2*(4), 3–18.

Smith, D. S. (1989). A content analysis of music educators' attitudes toward mainstreaming in middle school music classes. *Journal of the International Association for Music and the Handicapped, 4*(3), 3–20.

Smith, D. S., & Wilson, B. L. (1999). Effects of field experience on graduate music educators' attitude toward teaching students with disabilities. *Contributions to Music Education, 26*(1), 33–49.

Spanier, L. D. (1987). Intensive in-school/inservice training of secondary special educators: An efficacy study (Doctoral dissertation, George Washington University, 1987). *Dissertation Abstracts International, 48*(02), 264A.

Stainback, S., Stainback, W., Strathe, M., & Dedrick, C. (1983). Preparing regular classroom teachers for the integration of severely handicapped students: An experimental study. *Education and Training of the Mentally Retarded, 18*, 205–209.

Stein, A. R. (1983). The efficacy of the curriculum of special area teachers for servicing the needs of handicapped students and its implications for curriculum planning (Doctoral dissertation, State University of New York-Buffalo, 1983). *Dissertation Abstracts International, 44*(09), 2672A.

Stuart, M., & Gilbert, J. P. (1977). Mainstreaming: Needs assessment through a videotape visual scale. *Journal of Research in Music Education, 25*, 283–289.

Thompson, K. P. (1986). The general music class as experienced by mainstreamed handicapped students. *MEH Bulletin, 1*(1), 16–23.

Thompson, K. P. (1990). Working toward solutions in mainstreaming. *Music Educators Journal, 76*, 30–35.

Thurstone, L. L. (1970). Attitudes can be measured. In G. F. Summers (Ed.), *Attitude measurements.* Chicago: Rand McNally.

Tymitz-Wolf, B. L. (1982). Extending the scope of inservice training for mainstreaming effectiveness. *Teacher Education and Special Education, 5*(2), 17–23.

Wade, R. K. (1984/1985). What makes a difference in inservice teacher education? A meta-analysis of research. *Educational Leadership, 42*(4), 48–54.

Waggoner, L. G. (1976/1977). Effects of an inservice training model for mainstream teachers on factors regarding exceptional children (Doctoral dissertation, Texas Tech University, 1976). *Dissertation Abstracts International, 38*(02), 714A.

Wang, M. C., Vaughan, E. D., & Dytman, J. A. (1985). Staff development: A key ingredient of effective mainstreaming. *Teaching Exceptional Children, 17*(2), 112–121.

White, L. D. (1981/1982). Study of the attitudes of selected public school music educators toward the integration of handicapped students into music class. *Contributions to Music Education, 9*, 36–47.

Wieck, C. (1979). Training and development of staff: Lessons from business and industry. *Education Unlimited, 1*(3), 6–13.

Williams, D. W. (1988). Regular classroom teachers' perceptions of their preparedness to work with mainstreamed students as a result of preservice course work (Doctoral dissertation, Indiana University, 1988). *Dissertation Abstracts International, 49*(09), 2622A.

Wilson, B., & McCrary, J. (1993). *A comparison of music education and music therapy students' attitude toward learners with disabilities.* Unpublished manuscript, Western Michigan University, Kalamazoo.

Wilson, B., & McCrary, J. (1996). The effect of training on inservice music educators' attitudes towards students with disabilities. *Journal of Research in Music Education, 44*(1), 26–33.

Zigarmi, P., Betz, L., & Jensen, D. (1977). Teachers preferences in and perceptions of inservice education. *Educational Leadership, 34*(7), 545, 547–551.

Appendix

MUSIC IN MAINSTREAMING SURVEY

Please fill out the following background information: ____Female   ____ Male
Please check age category: ___20-29 ___30-39 ___40-49 ___50-59 ___60 and above

Number of years you have taught elementary music   _____
Number of years you have taught children with disabilities in music   _____
Total number of students seen in music each week   _____

Number of children with disabilities seen each week in **self-contained** music classes _____
(classes comprised of children with disabilities only)
Number of children with disabilities seen each week in **mainstreamed** music classes _____
(integrated classes containing both children with and without disabilities)

Highest level of academic preparation:

Bachelor's _____   Master's _____   Educational Specialist _____   Doctorate _____
Music Therapy Registration _____   Other _____

Number of college courses taken in music for special-needs children in last 15 years _____
Number of college courses taken in special education in the last 15 years   _____

Number of workshops/inservices taken in music for special-needs children
in last 15 years   _____
Approximately how many total hours of workshop/inservice does this represent?   _____

Number of workshops/inservices taken in special education?   _____
Approximately how many total hours of workshop/inservice does this represent?   _____

I have had students in my **self-contained** music classes with the following disabilities. Please
check (√) all that apply:

       ___Mentally Disabled-Educable   ___Visually Impaired
       ___Mentally Disabled-Trainable   ___Hearing Impaired
       ___Mentally Disabled-Severe/Profound ___Deaf-Blind
       ___Emotionally Disabled   ___Other Health Impaired
       ___Orthopedically Disabled   ___Multiply Handicapped
       ___Learning Disabled   ___Speech Impaired
       ___Behavior Disabled   ___Other (specify)_____

I have had students in my **mainstreamed** music classes with the following disabilities. Please
check (√) all that apply:

       ___Mentally Disabled-Educable   ___Visually Impaired
       ___Mentally Disabled-Trainable   ___Hearing Impaired
       ___Mentally Disabled-Severe/Profound ___Deaf-Blind
       ___Emotionally Disabled   ___Other Health Impaired
       ___Orthopedically Disabled   ___Multiply Handicapped
       ___Learning Disabled   ___Speech Impaired
       ___Behavior Disabled   ___Other (specify)_____

Which of these special education support services are available to you? Check (√) all that apply.

_____ School Psychologist   _____ Special Education Teacher _____ Music Therapist
_____ Special Education Consultant _____ Speech Therapist   _____ Physical Therapist
_____ Behavior Specialist   _____ Occupational Therapist   _____ Social Worker
_____ Other _____

From which of the following have you received services? Check (√) all that apply.

_____ School Psychologist   _____ Special Education Teacher _____ Music Therapist
_____ Special Education Consultant _____ Speech Therapist   _____ Physical Therapist
_____ Behavior Specialist   _____ Occupational Therapist   _____ Social Worker
_____ Other _____

My administration supports the concept of mainstreaming.   _____ Strongly Agree
    _____ Agree
    _____ Disagree
    _____ Strongly Disagree

If you agree or strongly agree, please check (√) ways in which you feel your administration provides meaningful support of mainstreaming in music classes.

_____budgetary support   _____adaptive and supplementary equipment/materials
_____time for professional development _____additional preparatory time/instructional time
_____teacher aides   _____personal encouragement
_____other (specify)_____

Special education teachers in my school support mainstreaming   _____ Strongly Agree
in music.   _____ Agree
    _____ Disagree
    _____ Strongly Disagree

If you agree or strongly agree, please check (√) ways in which you feel special educators in your school provide meaningful support of mainstreaming in music classes.

_____ offers information regarding instruction   _____ offers assistance in class
_____ asks questions about music program   _____ encourages student musical involvement
_____ other (specify)_____

MUSIC EDUCATION IN MAINSTREAMING NEEDS ASSESSMENT

<u>Directions to Inservice Participants</u>:

Please indicate the extent to which you have a need for inservice education by drawing a circle around the appropriate letters (**SA A D SD**) in the column at the right. Please be as honest as possible. Your answers will be confidential, and your answers will provide valuable and meaningful information.

LEGEND:	**Strongly Agree**	=	**SA**
	Agree	=	**A**
	Disagree	=	**D**
	Strongly Disagree	=	**SD**

<u>I need information about</u>:

1. Handicapping conditions defined in PL 94-142.   **SA A D SD**

2. Federal, state, and local guidelines for implementation of PL 94-142.   **SA A D SD**

3. Special education terminology and definitions (e.g., "least restrictive environment").   **SA A D SD**

4. Requirements for Individualized Education Plan (IEP) development and implementation.   **SA A D SD**

5. Legal requirements regarding child referral, evaluation, staffing, and annual review process.   **SA A D SD**

<u>I need information about the basic characteristics and learning needs of students who are</u>:

6. Mentally Disabled-Educable.   **SA A D SD**

7. Mentally Disabled-Trainable.   **SA A D SD**

8. Mentally Disabled-Severe/profound.   **SA A D SD**

9. Hearing Impaired.   **SA A D SD**

10. Visually Impaired.   **SA A D SD**

11. Deaf-Blind.   **SA A D SD**

12. Emotionally Disabled.   **SA A D SD**

13. Orthopedically Disabled.   **SA A D SD**

14. Multiply Handicapped.   **SA A D SD**

15. Other Health Impaired.   **SA A D SD**

Code #_____ Page 4

16. Learning Disabled.   SA A D SD

17. Speech Impaired.   SA A D SD

18. Behaviorally Disabled.   SA A D SD

I need information about:

19. Preparation of the music classroom and students for the entry   SA A D SD
    of special students.

20. Developing lesson plans which include options for students with   SA A D SD
    disabilities.

21. Selecting and adapting songs and instruments appropriate for use by   SA A D SD
    students with disabilities.

22. Adapting teaching methods to meet each student's level of functioning. SA A D SD

23. Structuring music activities that will facilitate interaction between   SA A D SD
    and among regular and special education students.

24. Identifying optimum level of achievement of various disabling conditions. SA A D SD

I need information about:

25. Establishing a realistic evaluation system for the school and the   SA A D SD
    students with disabilities.

26. Methods to assess the present level of functioning on musical tasks   SA A D SD
    for each student with disabilities.

27. Formulating appropriate instructional objectives for various levels   SA A D SD
    of functioning.

28. Organizing a system to collect and record data by which to evaluate   SA A D SD
    student progress toward goal achievement.

29. Understanding educational disabilities (i.e., physical or cognitive   SA A D SD
    conditions) which will impact on music learning.

30. Evaluating non-musical correlates (i.e., behavior and socialization)   SA A D SD
    which are desirable goals for mainstreamed students.

<u>I need information about</u>:

31. Principles of reinforcement (i.e., selection, presentation, timing, type.)   SA   A   D   SD

32. Steps in behavioral management (target behavior, implementation, intervention).   SA   A   D   SD

33. Methods to increase desirable and decrease undesirable behaviors (i.e., prompting, token economy, time-out).   SA   A   D   SD

34. Surface management techniques (i.e., planned ignoring, signal interference, proximity control).   SA   A   D   SD

35. Role of structured lesson plans in behavior management.   SA   A   D   SD

36. Generalizing behavioral management programs from the special education classroom to the music classroom.   SA   A   D   SD

MUSIC IN MAINSTREAMING ATTITUDE SURVEY

Directions to Inservice Participants:

Please indicate the extent to which you agree with the following statements by drawing a circle around the appropriate letter (**SA A D SD**) in the column at the right. Please be as honest as possible. Your answers will be confidential, and your answers will provide valuable and meaningful information.

LEGEND:	Strongly Agree	=	**SA**
	Agree	=	**A**
	Disagree	=	**D**
	Strongly Disagree	=	**SD**

1. Those who favor integration of students with disabilities into regular music classes are not concerned with quality music education.　　**SA　A　D　SD**

2. Attendance of students with disabilities in integrated music classes is similar to that of non-disabled students.　　**SA　A　D　SD**

3. Musical enjoyment is generally more difficult for students with disabilities than for non-disabled students.　　**SA　A　D　SD**

4. Students with disabilities are as compliant in music classes as are non-disabled students.　　**SA　A　D　SD**

5. Non-disabled students often resent having to work with students who are disabled.　　**SA　A　D　SD**

6. Students with disabilities participate in music education as successfully as non-disabled students.　　**SA　A　D　SD**

7. Mainstreaming regulations provide little real help to music teachers.　　**SA　A　D　SD**

8. Because students with disabilities tend to interact inappropriately with non-disabled peers, placement in self-contained music classes seems more appropriate.　　**SA　A　D　SD**

9. Students with disabilities participate in music education as easily as non-disabled students.　　**SA　A　D　SD**

10. Placement of students with disabilities in regular music class is often inappropriate.　　**SA　A　D　SD**

11. Students with disabilities usually interact appropriately in class with non-disabled peers.　　**SA　A　D　SD**

12. Musical creativity is a realistic educational goal for students with disabilities in mainstream music classes.   SA   A   D   SD

13. Students with disabilities have a hard time adjusting in regular music classes.   SA   A   D   SD

14. Having students with disabilities in a classroom tends to hamper the musical progress of non-disabled students.   SA   A   D   SD

15. Students are placed in music class in order to provide an appropriate and complete education.   SA   A   D   SD

16. Attendance of disabled students in music class tends to be erratic and irregular.   SA   A   D   SD

17. In general students with disabilities can be easily accommodated in mainstream music classes.   SA   A   D   SD

18. School participation in music class is more difficult for students with disabilities than for non-disabled students.   SA   A   D   SD

19. Students with disabilities in self-contained classes have little opportunity to interact with their non-disabled peers.   SA   A   D   SD

20. Students with disabilities generally have lower achievement levels in music than do their non-disabled peers.   SA   A   D   SD

21. Students with disabilities generally are accepted socially by their peers in music classes.   SA   A   D   SD

22. The special needs of students with disabilities are adequately met in mainstreamed music classes.   SA   A   D   SD

23. The musical progress of non-disabled students in mainstream classes is not affected by the presence of students with disabilities.   SA   A   D   SD

24. A self-contained class allows teachers to provide more adequate instruction for students with disabilities.   SA   A   D   SD

25. Students with disabilities in self-contained classes are seldom accepted socially by non-disabled peers.   SA   A   D   SD

26. Students with disabilities can be participants in most music activities.   SA   A   D   SD

27. Students with disabilities generally are less creative than non-disabled students.   SA   A   D   SD

28. Music classes often contain too many mainstreamed students.   SA   A   D   SD

Code #_____ Page 8

29. Music teachers are usually asked for their input concerning   **SA** **A** **D** **SD**
    individual placement of students with disabilities into music classes.

30. Mainstreaming students with disabilities generally results in   **SA** **A** **D** **SD**
    discipline problems in music classes.

31. Students with disabilities enjoy music as much as non-disabled.   **SA** **A** **D** **SD**
    students.

32. Having children with disabilities in regular music classes does not   **SA** **A** **D** **SD**
    inhibit the quality of instruction provided for non-disabled students.

33. I am satisfied with current mainstreaming processes.   **SA** **A** **D** **SD**

34. Students with disabilities can be best served in self-contained   **SA** **A** **D** **SD**
    music classes.

8

GETTING MUSIC THERAPY INTO THE PUBLIC SCHOOLS: THREE DIFFERENT APPROACHES

Mike D. Brownell
Amber Weldon-Stephens
Michelle T. Lazar

Editor's Note: *This chapter contains contributions from three music therapists who describe their own unique journey in introducing, developing, and/or maintaining music therapy for children in public school systems. Mike Brownell has a private practice in the Ann Arbor, Michigan area where he provides subcontracted services for both individuals and groups of children with varying disabilities. Amber Weldon-Stephens was the first music therapist hired by the Fulton County School System in Atlanta, Georgia in 1990. Since that time, music therapy services have been greatly expanded and are now provided district-wide by several staff music therapists. Through individual IEPs, Michelle Lazar has been successful in developing short and long-term contracts with multiple school districts in the San Diego, California area that did not previously have music therapy as a related service. These examples will hopefully serve as models for other music therapists who are attempting to respond to the growing demand for music therapy assessment, direct, or consultant services in public school settings.*

OPENING INITIAL LINES OF COMMUNICATION

Mike D. Brownell

Phase I: Information Gathering

BEFORE any initial contact is made, a sizeable amount of information should be obtained. The hours taken to acquire this information will be time well spent. When the time comes to actually speak with district personnel, teachers, other professionals, or parents, it is vital that you be able to answer their questions in a reliable and fact-based fashion. Possession of this knowledge will reflect investment in the process of contract development and service implementation, and will further others' perception of your professionalism. A cursory list of the information with which you should be familiar includes:

1. *The history (if there is one) of music therapy in your district.* If you are new to the area, speak with other music therapists who have been around longer. Establish if music therapy is now currently or

has ever been offered as a related service. If music therapy was available previously, knowing the reasons why that program was discontinued will be essential if you are attempting to restart it.

2. *The hierarchical make-up of your district's special education program.* In public schools, this information is part of the public domain. Obtaining this information will ensure that you are contacting the person or persons who are directly responsible for deciding whether or not music therapy should be implemented.

3. *The types of special education services currently being offered in your district.* Ascertaining the service delivery model used by other professionals (e.g., speech/language pathologists, occupational therapists, physical therapists, and teacher consultants) will be useful when deciding what type of service to market for yourself. You will also be better able to articulate how music therapy can complement services already offered by other professionals.

4. *Pertinent financial information about your district.* This, again, is information that is in the public domain. Financial information will give some insight on the district's ability to implement new programs, and what average salaries are for other professionals.

5. *The make-up of the special education student population, and the service delivery model used.* In what grade levels are the highest concentrations of students receiving special services? What labels are most common? Learn the terminology used in your district; this may vary widely among districts. What percentage of the student body receives special services? What service delivery model (e.g., multidisciplinary, interdisciplinary, or transdisciplinary) does the district adopt, and how would music therapy services fit into that model?

6. *Parent involvement.* How are the parents of special education students involved in your district? Locate parent committees and local chapters of organizations such as the Autism Society of America, the Council for Exceptional Children, etc.

7. *The federal laws as they pertain to the provision of music therapy services in the public schools.*

8. *The state and local laws as they pertain to the provision of music therapy services in the public schools.*

Phase IIa: Making Initial Contact—From the Top

After gathering all of the necessary information from Phase I, locate the highest-ranking individual who has direct influence and decision-making power over the implementation of new services. In many cases, this will be the director of special services or special education, but these titles vary widely between districts. Initial communications should be simple: a brochure or introductory letter mentioning your presence in the area and a brief description of what music therapy is. The goal here is not to immediately begin marketing or selling the concept of music therapy services in the district. Rather, name and concept recognition are of paramount concern.

Subsequent communiqués should gradually increase the amount of information regarding music therapy. Still, the goal is only sharing information. Be sure contact information is available on all correspondence so that follow-up questions can be answered should any arise.

Eventually, request a short, informal meeting. If you are confident that the recipient of your previous mailings is likely to follow-up, this request can be made in writing. Otherwise, call their secretary and establish the best way to set up a short meeting. The sole purpose of this engagement is information sharing, not marketing. Discuss the benefits of music therapy with the population(s) you are targeting within the district. The examples should relate directly to educationally relevant goals; public schools will not fund programs that address non-educational issues. Leave illustrations of music therapy research literature that document the efficacy of music therapy treatments with educationally significant goals with your target population(s). Describe specifically how music therapy can work in concert with existing services offered, but also how it is unique from other programs currently in place. It is essential that music therapy be recognized as a unique service that can only be provided by a credentialed (viz., board-certified) music therapist.

Be prepared to answer any questions that might arise. If all of the information from Phase I has been obtained, this should go relatively smoothly. If questions surface that you are not prepared to answer, offer to get accurate information as soon as possible. Recall that the primary objective of this meeting is information sharing. Hold off on attempting to market yourself or your program unless specific questions are asked. Offer to leave all of the written information that you have brought, and request a follow-up meeting after the director has had a chance to review everything.

At the follow-up meeting, the primary objective will begin to shift from information sharing to marketing. Have a clear goal in mind. After reviewing information from Phase I, you should be equipped to identify perceived needs in the district's current special education program. What type of service are you looking to provide? District-wide services? Consultations? Direct service to a specific population or age group? All of these options are of course acceptable, but it is essential to have a focus. General marketing to an institution as broad as a school district will likely prove fruitless. Be flexible if the administrator's vision differs from your own.

If possible, bring examples of your service delivery plan, either from your own experience or from the experience of other music therapists. Discuss how music therapy is a cost-effective service that need not benefit only those students in special education. Stress that music therapy can only be provided by a credentialed music therapist, and discuss the relevance of that credential.

Phase IIb: Making Initial Contact—At the Bottom

Parents typically wield a great deal of influence when it comes to the implementation of programs or services for their children. While simultaneously speaking with district administrators, avail yourself of any opportunity to speak with parents of children with disabilities in your district. Frequently, organizations such as local chapters of the Council for Exceptional Children and the Autism Society of America are happy to have guest speakers at their meetings. Oftentimes parent advisory committees or support/information groups are very active within the district. Here again, information sharing is of primary concern. Speak to these groups about what music therapy is in general, and also what specifically music therapy might address with their particular child. Demonstrate what you're talking about in any way possible. Do sample interventions that involve the parents in the meetings. Show videos (with appropriate confidentiality releases) of your specific work with a child in the corresponding population. Make yourself very accessible for follow-up questions that the parents may have.

Phase III: Bringing the Top and the Bottom Together

After speaking to both administrators and parents, do whatever is possible to facilitate a dialogue between the two. Encourage parents to ask teachers, administrators, and other professionals about the role music therapy could play with their children. Make your administrative contact(s) aware that you have spoken to parents, and let them know about the positive reactions you have had. If parents become passionate about implementing a music therapy program for their children, they can act as exemplary and powerful advocates.

Phase IV: An Alternate or Supplemental Route

In some cases, it may be necessary to provide the district with more specific and relevant examples of the efficacy of music therapy. One possible way to provide this method is to show the benefits that music therapy has had with children in their own district. Although generally more time-consumptive, supplying documented results of children under their own supervision can be persuasive to some administrators.

To obtain these results, the students must obviously be receiving music therapy services. After speaking with parents, it is possible that some will become so excited about having music therapy services for their child that they may pursue services privately. After having received private music therapy services for a substantial amount of time, parents can take the written or taped results and documentation from their child's sessions to the district as an additional advocacy tool for a district-supported program. Word-of-mouth spread between parents will also garner further support for the implementation of a music therapy program.

In Sum

1. Gather information in advance. Having done research ahead of time will prove invaluable when fielding questions from various sources.
2. Share information with appropriate district administration.
3. Share information with parents of students with disabilities in your district.
4. Foster communication between administrators and parents.

A DISTRICT-WIDE MUSIC THERAPY PROGRAM: CONTACT, DEVELOPMENT, AND IMPLEMENTATION

Amber Weldon-Stephens

Phase I: Information Gathering

AT the end of a great internship, every new music therapist hopes to find that perfect job with long-term stability, wonderful clients, good benefits and attractive work hours. Through a yearlong process and a great deal of determination, I was able to find that job. After completing my internship with the Clayton County School System near Atlanta, Georgia in the spring of 1990, I was asked to interview with the Fulton County School System in the hopes that they were ready to create their first music therapy position beginning that fall. Within just a few days after the interview, I received a call from the Coordinator of Music Education for the Fulton County Schools offering me the first music therapy position. I was thrilled and terrified but ready for the challenge. I signed my contract in June; however, during the first week of August I was told that the funds had been cut for the position and that the only available job was teaching general music at an elementary school over 75 miles from my home. I was extremely disappointed but needed a job so I said yes and my journey in Fulton County began.

From the beginning interview in Fulton, I knew I would have to complete the requirements for a teaching certificate in the state of Georgia. Prior to my internship in a school setting, I was able to go back to the University of Georgia where I had received my Bachelor's Degree in Music Therapy and work on an additional Bachelor's Degree in Music Education. I had already completed over half of the course work before my internship began. Once I had taken and passed the Teacher Certification Test (which is now a national exam known as the PRAXIS), I was able to apply for a temporary teaching certificate. This provisional certificate was good for three years upon completion of the course work and student teaching. In 1990, the state of Georgia did not recognize a 6-month internship in a school setting as equal to a 10-week student teaching experience. This was a battle I fought during my entire first year working in Fulton County. Due to the size and need of the Fulton County School System, the Staff Development Department in the county offered a year-long class to all the provisional certificate teachers to fill the requirement of student teaching. Therefore, we were all able to student teach while on the job and had to attend a class twice a month for the entire first year. On a positive note, I finally won the battle with the state department two years later.

Now, in the state of Georgia, a music therapist who interns in a school setting and who wishes to go back and receive an additional degree in music education and/or teacher certification can use the internship experience to fill the requirement of student teaching.

During my first year in Fulton County, I truly received my teaching legs. Many music therapists do not like to be called a teacher, but I have always felt that what I do with my students whether with or without disabilities is very therapeutic. I taught 782 low-income students from preschool to 5th grade on a once-a-week basis. I even had an 80-member chorus that really brought me out of my comfort zone since I am a saxophone player and not a chorus girl. At the school were three special needs classes that were absolutely my favorites. I could use all those therapy techniques from my internship and feel like I was doing what I had been called to do. Six months into the school year I was given the Teacher of the Year Award from my school. This shocked no one more than me since I had yet to see myself as a teacher. A first-year teacher had never been given such an award in the Fulton County Schools, and I believe that my skills as a music therapist helped me to receive this award. Nevertheless, at the end of that school year, I asked to have a full-time music therapy position rather than a general music job. I informed my supervisor that if Fulton County could not create the position for the following school year I would have to resign and look elsewhere. Within one hour of my discussion with my supervisor, the superintendent had approved a music therapy position to begin the following fall. I was told that there would be no start-up budget and I would have to travel between many schools, but they could afford to pay for mileage between schools. Most people might not have been so happy, but I was thrilled. The following school year I started with 13 elementary schools all over Fulton County and the mission had begun.

During the spring of 1991 after the superintendent had approved the therapy position, my supervisor and I and one of the heads of special education met in a small room to explain music therapy and its benefits. I had drafted a preliminary list of which disabilities I felt would benefit from music therapy and at what level we would begin services. Much of the initial scheduling was based on the music therapy model in the Clayton County Schools where I had interned. In Clayton County, the music therapy department is funded through the special education department. In Fulton County the music therapy department is funded through the music education department. During the meeting, it was decided that music therapy would serve students with disabilities by disability. For example, all students with a diagnosis of Moderate, Severe, or Profound Intellectual Disability would receive music therapy initially once a week for 45 minutes. This has now gone to twice a week for 30 minutes at the elementary level, and once at week for 45 minutes at the middle and high school level. The 13 elementary schools were decided upon due to the disabilities at those schools. Music therapy served Moderate, Severe, and Profound Intellectual Disabilities, Special Needs Kindergarten, Children with Autism, Hearing Impairments, Severely Emotionally Behaviorally Disturbed, and Orthopedically Impaired/Other Health Impairment.

Since music therapy was replacing the regular music time, every class received music therapy once a week for 45 minutes. Music education is a weekly part of every student's schedule in Fulton County. My supervisor was able to fund my position by slotting me into a music specialist position. For example, if one general music specialist at the elementary level teaches 30 classes a week that teacher is considered 100% at her school. If her school has an excess of 30 classes and some of those are special education, then the music therapist comes in for the special education percentage at that school. The music therapist could have 10% at one school, 40% at another, 20% at another and 30% at another to equal 100% and, in layman's terms, a full-time position.

For the next four years, I was delivering music therapy services throughout the Fulton County School System. Each year as the budget was being discussed, I was gradually given funds to purchase equipment and music needed for therapy. It was not until five years into the program that music therapy had its own line item on the budget submitted to the school board. During my third and fourth year in the county, I submitted a proposal to hire an additional music therapist to split the music therapy caseload. During the spring of 1994 the school board approved the hire of an additional music therapy position to begin the following fall. As an additional music therapist was hired, the student caseload increased by disability. The Special Needs

Preschool students were added, and the amount of delivery time per week was increased for certain disabilities.

As music therapy services increased throughout the county, the need for additional therapists was recognized. Fulton County now has seven music therapists and an additional five in other music positions. Music therapy services span preschool through high school with delivery methods and scheduling a continual challenge. Some of our therapists teach general music at the elementary and middle school level while others are teaching orchestra and high school chorus. The music coordinator has realized the quality of teacher/therapist in music therapist and has sought out these individuals to work throughout the county.

Early in the development of the music therapy department, the role of the student's Individualized Education Program (IEP) was discussed. I initially wanted to have music therapy as an active part in the development of the IEP for each student served in music therapy. I was quickly brought to my senses when I realized the number of students served weekly in music therapy. During those early years I was serving over 400 students with disabilities a week and could not have effectively been able to assess, write, and document treatment plans needed to be a vital part of the IEP. Twelve years later, music therapy is still not documented on the IEP. Since the parents are told that their child will be receiving music therapy services, we are considered a related service but are only mentioned in the minutes of the IEP meeting and not in a separate section. This is an area in Fulton County that I feel still needs to be addressed and improved upon. I have seen several students move from our county into other counties. After serving that student up to as many as 10 years in music therapy, no official documentation of service is mentioned in the IEP. In time I would like to see music therapy mentioned and checked off on the IEP as an official service offered and required for each student who receives music therapy services.

During the 1998 school year, the Fulton County Music Therapy Department started training their first interns as an approved internship site under the American Music Therapy Association. We feel we have developed a well-rounded internship experience that can give each intern an array of students to learn from as they complete the transition from student to committed professional. The therapists in our county have continued to go above and beyond the call of their daily jobs to promote music therapy in our state, region, and nation. From serving as presidents in our state organization, to officers in our regional association, to presenting at the national level at our AMTA conferences, our therapists have continued to give back to the profession and our interns as a professional role model. I believe that this dedication has been an integral part in the success of the music therapy program in Fulton County. From the beginning much of our vision has been shared and supported by the Coordinator of Music Education. He has inspired and believed in the healing power of music and its role in the educational process in Fulton County. I hope that every young and aspiring music therapist has someone in a decision-making role believe in them and their abilities to bring the power of music to children.

INITIATING AND MAINTAINING CONTRACTS IN THE PUBLIC SCHOOL SETTING USING AN IEP-BASED MODEL

Michelle T. Lazar

Overview

THE most difficult part of a music therapist's job in the public school setting is often the art of initiating a contract. Due to budget concerns and misinformation or lack of awareness about music therapy, school district personnel are not typically seeking out music therapy to add to various programs and therapies already in place. Therefore, when initiating and maintaining contracts in the public school setting, it is of key importance to have a good understanding of what the administration's potential concerns may be, and how to effectively alleviate these concerns in a concise and professional manner. The following model has proven to be highly successful when developing short- and long-term contracts for music therapy as a related service through the Individualized Education Programs (IEPs) of qualifying students.

Agency Background

Coast Music Therapy and Consulting (CMTC) is a contractual agency servicing individuals with special needs throughout San Diego County, California, with a main focus on IEP-based service in the public schools. Within the seven school districts serviced by CMTC, parents played an integral role in the push to make music therapy available to students. After these initial contracts were developed, close to 100 evaluations were funded by the school districts over the course of two years. Approximately 60% of those students evaluated were recommended for some form of limited or ongoing service through the IEP. Although the number of students who qualify for music therapy through the IEP is significantly less than through other models of service, it is felt that this approach gives students the unique opportunity to have an individualized music therapy program tailored specifically to their educational needs.

Step 1: "Getting Your Foot in the Door": The Role of Parents When Pursuing Music Therapy Through the IEP

While it is ideal to first approach school district administration when promoting music therapy in the school setting, it is often parents who are most successful in these efforts, as was the case in San Diego County. Several music therapists in the area reported that presentations to various school districts had been well received but had not resulted in a contract or further pursuance of music therapy in these districts. Therefore, it was not surprising that requests for music therapy were often initiated through the IEP by parents who felt their child might benefit from the service.

Many of these cases were students receiving private music therapy in the home setting who were showing significant gains in areas related to educational need. Parents who were successful in getting an evaluation and/ or service were typically those willing to go to mediation or take legal action if their request (within reason) was challenged by the district. The following is a description of the first two students approved for music therapy services in one of San Diego County's larger school districts:

- "Donald" was a 7-year-old student with autism who had been receiving private music therapy in the home setting. His parents paid for a private music therapy evaluation, administered in the home setting, which also targeted his responses to educational goals. Within the evaluation, it was determined that he did show significant gains in areas of educational need when music was used (compared to IEP baselines and school progress reports). The results of this evaluation were presented at a mediation meeting and the district agreed to provide weekly music therapy services.

- "Tiffany" was a 14-year-old student with developmental delays and mild hearing loss who had been receiving adapted music lessons in the home setting. Her parents were successful when requesting a music therapy evaluation to take place in the school setting paid for by the district. This was due in part to her mother being proactive in contacting the supervisor of the deaf program to facilitate this process. Direct and consult services were recommended.

This initial transition from private music therapy to IEP-based therapy can be somewhat challenging due to the varying philosophies of each approach. While private music therapy may address educational goals, it may also focus on teaching musical skills, exposing the student to various instruments and styles of music, and providing overall enrichment through music. Similar to private music lessons for the typically developing child, there is no formal criteria for students with special needs to be accepted into private music therapy. In comparison, music therapy as a related service must follow specific guidelines of the Individuals with Disabilities Education Act (IDEA), which states that related services must be found "necessary" for the student to benefit from his or her educational program.

Based on these differences, it would not be expected for the private music therapist to make recommendations directly related to the student's school program. However, if parents are not able to obtain an evaluation through the school by following the appropriate protocol, it may be necessary to present a private assessment as the first step in negotiating a school evaluation for the student.

Practical Tips

1. If the student appears to be an appropriate candidate, have parents who are seeking a private music therapy evaluation first make a request through the IEP team. This request should be documented in writing in the IEP notes. Remind parents that when approaching the school district they should always request an evaluation as opposed to requesting ongoing music therapy services.

2. If the school district is not familiar with music therapy, the music therapist should give the parents and/ or district staff materials including an overview of music therapy, a sample of the eligibility criteria, and a description of the evaluation to be used. The team can then review the material and have a better idea if the student is a good candidate.

Step 2: Presentation to District Administration

After parents receive approval for a music therapy evaluation, the school district will need to initiate a contract with a music therapist of their choice. Assuming that you would like to pursue the contract yourself, this is an appropriate time to take the initiative and formally approach the administration. Scheduling an inservice for relevant staff members is an effective way to discuss how music therapy can be implemented as an IEP-based service.

CMTC supports a scientific model of music therapy when presenting to various school districts, giving specific examples of how research supports music in the areas of intellectual development and academic learning, communication, social/emotional functioning, and motor performance. Thaut (2000) and Taylor (1997) outline scientific paradigms for music therapy that are valuable resources for the music therapist using this approach. Adequate time during your presentation should also be devoted to the assessment methods to be used, and the various models of service delivery. Video clips of a typical music therapy session can also be helpful if the student's parent is willing to grant permission for its use.

Provide a packet of written materials (with copies made for those attending), including general information about music therapy, the credentials of a music therapist, how music therapy is provided as a related service, and reference materials relevant to educational areas of need (see Appendices A through D).

As school district staff may be unaware of the differences between an adapted music education or enrichment model of music therapy and an IEP-based approach, a focus should be placed on the typical eligibility criteria. Examples of students who would be good candidates for music therapy through the IEP could include:

- Students who respond well to music, but are not progressing as expected with current non-music methods being used (due to poor attention, behavioral concerns, processing deficits, etc.)

- Students who may only respond to a limited number of teaching techniques, such as students with visual impairments or severe handicaps.
- Other specific populations that may be "predisposed" to strengths in music such as students with autism, Retts syndrome, and Williams syndrome.

Even within these populations, it is still stressed that music therapy is only recommended if it is found through evaluation to be necessary for the student to benefit from his or her educational program.

Step 3: Negotiating a Written Contract for IEP-Based Service

When scheduling an inservice for district staff, secure a separate meeting time to discuss details of the proposed contract. The following information has been included in contract negotiations between CMTC and the various school districts in San Diego County. In some cases, this information was discussed over the phone, and the contract was delivered through the mail.

- Certificate of credentials, documentation of liability insurance, and an agency policies and fees sheet are presented to the district.
- Hourly rates are based on current rates of contractual therapists working in special education (e.g., speech pathologists, occupational therapists). A separate fee schedule applies for documentation time, assessment service, and staff workshops.
- Mileage can often be negotiated as part of the total contract allotment, or under "administrative fees."
- Find out if there are any other legal requirements such as fingerprinting or TB testing that the music therapist must complete before commencing service.

Sample criteria stated in the contract:

"Applicant Agency (CMTC) will provide music therapy services to identified students in compliance with state and federal law. The Individuals with Disabilities Education Act (IDEA) specifically mandates related services; music therapy may be a related service for individual students."

"Applicant Agency will provide appropriate number of support personnel, contingent on student enrollment, who will provide music therapy services, direct to implement the activities identified in the targeted students' IEP. In addition, Applicant Agency will provide a designated supervisor who will work with the student's teacher/ case manager in the development, implementation and quality review of the IEP."

Practical Tips

1. The district usually delineates an estimated dollar allotment for the fiscal year. However, as the number of referrals increase, you may soon exceed this amount. Designate the amount remaining in the contract on each monthly invoice and notify the district well in advance if you think they will need to amend the contract.
2. It is ideal to register a "fictitious business name" for your music therapy agency before negotiating a school district contract, especially if you anticipate having to hire or subcontract to other music therapists in order to accommodate a growing number of students.

Step 4: Addressing School District Concerns and Maintaining Your Contract

In the experience of CMTC, similar concerns have been raised by school district administrators when first introducing music therapy as a related service. Being prepared to answer each of these questions can make a significant difference in your presentation to a school district.

1. How will parents be informed that music therapy as a related service has different criteria than private music therapy?
2. What is the validity of a music therapy assessment tool?
3. What procedures and forms will be used for screening students and determining eligibility?
4. Why do we need to contract with a music therapist, when staff are already implementing music strategies in the classrooms and music education classes are available?
4. Will the student generalize the skills learned in music therapy to the general curriculum?
6. How will the music therapist be held accountable for student progress?

School District Concern 1: *How will parents be informed that music therapy as a related service has different criteria than private music therapy?*

After the first few students are approved for music therapy services in a particular school district, the question arises of how to make music therapy available to other appropriate candidates. This can be challenging for the music therapist, especially if the school district does not choose to notify district staff that music therapy is a potential related service. Marketing music therapy as an IEP-related service in this context needs to be handled very delicately in order to promote the benefits of music therapy while at the same time upholding the support of the school district.

Presenting to parent groups is one way to get the word out. However, even after specifying the differences between private music therapy and an IEP-based approach, you may still find the result to be an overwhelming number of requests for music therapy from parents in these groups and other networking circles. This can create some concern from school districts who were not anticipating this "snowball" effect of parent requests. Reinforce to school district administrators that parents are being informed of the specific criteria for IEP-based music therapy, and screening procedures will still be upheld once the request is made to the district.

Practical Tips

1. Let the parents of your private clients know that participation in private music therapy does not guarantee eligibility for music therapy in the school district.
2. Give the school district the option to include specific criteria for music therapy in procedural manuals distributed to staff, and offer to provide additional inservices to assist staff in making appropriate referrals.

School District Concern 2: *What is the validity of a music therapy assessment tool?*

Since there are currently no standardized music therapy assessment tools specific to an IEP-based approach, it is understandable that districts would have questions regarding the validity of the evaluation used. Because this issue has been one of the most common concerns presented by school district administrators to CMTC, it is imperative that you are well prepared when presenting and discussing the components of the assessment tool you will be using. When choosing your evaluation tool for IEP-based service, it is most important to consider if it will assist you in determining whether music therapy is a "necessary" service in order for the student to benefit in his or her educational program.

The SEMTAP (Special Education Music Therapy Assessment Process), created by Kathleen Coleman and Betsey Brunk (1999) is an excellent assessment tool to consider as it was specifically developed for determining the necessity of music therapy as a related service. This model has been used for all evaluations administered by CMTC in the school setting. The SEMTAP determines eligibility for music therapy by comparing the student's performance on IEP-related tasks with and without musical presentation. If the student performs significantly better when music is used, it is considered that music therapy in the form of consult or direct service would be "necessary" for the student to benefit in his or her educational program.

Using this approach, you are able to reinforce to the school district that the music therapist is not determining musical ability or re-assessing areas already evaluated by other IEP team members, but rather determining whether music offers a significant and necessary assist to the student's current program.

Practical Tip

Give examples of other assessment models already used in the district that may be similar to music therapy evaluation procedures. For example, an "assistive technology" evaluation is used to determine if a student is eligible for devices (ranging from pencil grips to voice output devices) that increase, maintain, or improve functional capabilities. This is similar to music therapy in that it acts as a support to the entire program, with eligibility determined through staff and parent input, student observation and a trial of various supports that may be of benefit.

School District Concern 3: *What procedures will be used for screening students and determining eligibility?*

Determining Eligibility for Assessments

Other related services in San Diego County school districts have screening and referral processes to help identify appropriate candidates for each service. Most screenings include a teacher checklist giving insight into the student's functioning, which is then reviewed by the designated therapist who will administer the evaluation. Often based on a score derived from the checklist, a determination is then made if the student qualifies for an evaluation. Using this model and the sample forms from the SEMTAP, new forms were created to better fit the philosophy of CMTC and the school districts serviced. The following protocol was developed.

After inquiring about a music therapy evaluation, the teacher and/ or parent is given a packet of materials to include:

1. Music Therapy Referral Procedures
2. Determining Appropriateness of a Music Therapy Evaluation (see Appendix A)
3. Description of the Music Therapy Evaluation (see Appendix B)
4. Music Therapy Referral/ Screening Form Given to Teacher (see Appendix C)
5. Music Therapy Parent Questionnaire Given to Parents (see Appendix D)

If an assessment plan has not already been signed, a screening sheet ("Music Therapy Referral Form") is completed by the classroom teacher with additional input from parents and other relevant staff members as needed. The music therapist assists the IEP team in determining whether the evaluation appears appropriate based on several factors: (a) Are there designated needs in the student's program for which additional support would be warranted? (b) Is the student showing enhanced responses to music when performing IEP-related tasks? (c) Does the student show significant concerns in the areas of behavior, attention, or motivation that impede school performance with significant improvement in these areas when music is used?

After reviewing the referral sheet the music therapist contacts the case manager to discuss whether the student appears appropriate for an evaluation. If the student is recommended for an evaluation, an assessment plan is signed by the parents and the music therapist has 50 days to complete the evaluation and discuss the results at an IEP addendum meeting. If the student does not seem to be an appropriate candidate for an evaluation, this information is given to the IEP team. In rare cases, the parents or other IEP team members may disagree with the music therapist's recommendation, in which case an evaluation is typically provided.

Administering an Evaluation

Main Components of the SEMTAP:

1. Complete a records review.
2. Interview members of the IEP team. (CMTC does not typically conduct formal interviews with staff, but rather collects this information through the referral form, parent questionnaire, and during observations.)
3. Target a specific number of IEP objectives on which the assessment will be based.
4. Schedule and complete an observation of the student. (CMTC often observes in the classroom music setting as well to determine what strategies are already being used.)
5. Plan a music therapy assessment session.
6. Prepare a written report. (It is helpful to submit this to the parents and case manager for review prior to the IEP meeting.)

[A SEMTAP handbook can be ordered through Prelude Music Therapy @ (817) 481-2323.]

Practical Tips

1. Expect an evaluation to take 4-6 hours of time, not including attendance at the IEP meeting.
2. CMTC bills for assessments using either a "lump" sum (not including IEP attendance), or case by case depending on the number of hours needed for the evaluation.
3. If a student is recommended for service, you may also be required to present proposed IEP goals at the meeting.

After an Evaluation Is Completed

After a student is evaluated, an IEP addendum meeting is held to review the results. This agenda can also be presented at an annual IEP review if it does not compromise the 50-day timeline given for assessments. Service recommendation can include: no service, consultation only, combination of consultation and direct service, or direct service only (it is rare that direct service is recommended without consultation).

A typical recommendation for ongoing service is 30 minutes per week direct service with an additional 30 minutes to 1 hour per month consultation. The maximum level of service typically recommended is 60 minutes per week delivered as a combination of direct and consult service. This is consistent with other related services in the district. A trial period of 12 sessions is often recommended for students who show less consistent responses during the evaluation. A trial period goal is monitored and another addendum meeting is held after the trial period to discuss continuation or termination of service.

Practical Tips

1. If you have only one student at a particular site, and the session duration is less than 1 hour, it is typical to still charge for 1 hour of service due to the travel time involved.
2. When presenting a "no service" recommendation to the team, stress that the student may still benefit from music education in the school environment or private music therapy/ adapted music lessons in the home setting. Emphasize effective music strategies already implemented by staff in the school setting, and give additional resource material such as recommended reading/ tapes/ CDS or activity suggestions.

School District Concern 4: *Why do we need to contract with a music therapist, when staff are already implementing music strategies in the classrooms and music education classes are available?*

Based on the diverse needs of students in special education, it is highly appropriate for classroom staff to educate students using a variety of methods including musical, verbal, kinesthetic, and visual presentation. However, many students require additional assistance from various specialists such as speech pathologists, occupational therapists, and physical therapists who design, implement and adapt interventions specific to the student's goal areas. The music therapist fulfills a similar role in that music strategies are designed using specific styles of music, types of musical instruments, song lyrics, and song structure specific to the student's unique needs and IEP goal areas. Whenever possible, the music therapist, along with other service providers, attempts to integrate these activities throughout the student's day to eliminate unnecessary pull-out. However, in many cases, ongoing consultation and/ or direct service is needed until it is determined that specialized strategies are no longer necessary.

When addressing this issue with district administrators, you may wish to include a statement such as: "Within the evaluation process, it is first considered whether current music strategies used by staff are already adequate to meet the student's needs, or if the student would benefit from more individualized music strategies designed to target IEP goals." In addition, it is important to stress to the school district the differences between music therapy and music education, and to review the eligibility requirements for music therapy as a related service.

School District Concern 5: *How will the music therapist be held accountable for student progress?*

Once a student is receiving music therapy services, the following forms of documentation are used in the school districts serviced by CMTC:

- Specific goals are written by the music therapist, or the music therapist initials goals proposed by other IEP team members. (see next section for sample)
- Data are recorded during each session to monitor progress on designated IEP goals.
- Quarterly or tri-annual progress reports are submitted in the form of a summary report or annotation of IEP goal pages (i.e., the level of progress is stated briefly under "progress review" for each designated goal).
- Whenever possible, the music therapist attends each student's IEP meetings.

- At the annual IEP, the music therapist states the student's status on each designated goal and reviews "Present Levels of Performance" which summarizes the student's current strengths and needs.
- Every three years, the student is re-assessed for music therapy (a comprehensive renewal of all assessments is completed at this time).
- Service is modified or terminated when appropriate.

School District Concern 6: *Will the student generalize the skills learned in music therapy to the general curriculum?*

This is an interesting topic for consideration as "functional educational outcome" seems to be a common phrase used by administrators when determining new IEP goals for a particular student. Teachers have often given examples of individuals who learned their phone number through a song, but could not restate it in any other setting. Other accounts were given of students who could sing the letters of the alphabet but could not identify any of them in isolation. Due to the limitations of various disabilities, many students in special education already have difficulty applying information they learn from one setting to another. Therefore, it is important for the music therapist to address this concern by facilitating the generalization of skills presented through music when appropriate. Note that in some cases, such as students with more severe cognitive impairments, the IEP team may agree that generalization is not a key concern.

Developing Goals That Facilitate Generalization

At IEP meetings, CMTC presents music therapy as an "overlap" service to support goals determined necessary by the IEP team. Goals to be addressed by the music therapist are written in a format such that music is used as the initial cue to teach the skill, followed by fading of the music and generalization to the non-music setting. For example:

Communication Goal

By 5/02 (annual review), Grace will address 4 areas of communication ("Wh" questions, attributes, prepositions, social language) from songs in the non-music setting with 80% accuracy. [overlap with goals #3, 5, 6, 7 proposed by SLP]

Baseline: Grace can sing songs from memory using long phrases and appropriate grammatical structure, but often needs multiple prompts when speaking similar phrases.

Benchmark A: By 9/01, Grace will sing designated phrases in songs related to above areas of communication with minimal prompts, with 80% accuracy as measured by therapist records.

Benchmark B: By 1/02, Grace will sing/speak phrases related to above areas when music is partially faded (i.e., chanting, stopping music and asking question in spoken language, etc.), with 80% accuracy as measured by therapist records.

Although in many cases almost all of the student's goals can be in some way supported through music therapy, it is helpful to prioritize which tasks could be best presented through music and still lead to functional educational outcomes. Ask yourself the following question for each goal you wish to target: If musical cueing (i.e., singing, chanting, musical instruments) is removed from the activity, is the student still performing a functional educational task? Some tasks are intrinsically difficult to cue using music strategies with functional results such as: requesting to use the restroom, learning complex math problems that do not involve rote memory, writing a sentence, or completing a school job (taking attendance to the office). Once goals are selected based on their relevance to the music therapy setting, interventions should also be carefully designed to facilitate generalization.

Sample of interventions less likely to facilitate generalization:

1. Addressing literacy skills by teaching the student to read music.
2. Addressing a student's ability to sequence events by playing rhythm instruments in a sequential order.

Sample of interventions most likely to facilitate generalization:

1. Addressing literacy skills by having the student sing a story set to a song.
2. Addressing a student's ability to sequence events by singing a song in which the student has to recall events of the day and put corresponding pictures in order.

Facilitating the Generalization of Skills During Service Provision

There are also many ways to facilitate the transfer of skills from the music to the non-music setting when working directly with the student or staff. The following methods used by CMTC have been quite effective:

- Use the same visual aids from the classroom setting when presenting songs in the music therapy session.
- When designing songs to promote communication skills use the exact language and length of phrase the student would be expected to use in other environments. For example, a student would be more likely to say "bye" than "so long" or "farewell."
- After a song, present a "quiz" of the material in spoken language (you may need to use another form of reward such as stickers or praise to complete this portion).
- For higher functioning students, have them complete a worksheet after a song to review what was learned.
- Demonstrate the above techniques to the classroom teacher and other support staff. For example, demonstrate asking the students to identify alphabet letters in isolation after singing the alphabet.
- For students who are seen individually, add a peer to the session occasionally to reinforce skills learned in the social setting.

Summary

Music therapists willing to take on the challenge of an IEP-based model of service will find many benefits in this approach, including the ability to invest more time into programming for each individual, in addition to being an integral part of the IEP team. It is also an opportunity to help set standards for future legislation regarding music therapy, which has faced setbacks such as the removal of music therapy from the stated list of related services in the March 1999 revisions of IDEA. Although this has still allowed music therapy to be included as a related service, it has led to many misinterpretations by school district administrators. Therefore, demonstrating the success of an IEP-based approach will help to open doors for other music therapists working in special education, especially as the public school setting continues to push for more measurable outcomes in student achievement.

References

Coleman, K. A., & Brunk, B. K. (1999). *SEMTAP—Special education music therapy assessment process handbook.* Grapevine, TX: Prelude Music Therapy.

Taylor, D. B. (1997). *Biomedical foundations of music as therapy.* St. Louis, MO: MMB Music.

Thaut, M. H. (2000). *A scientific model of music therapy and medicine.* San Antonio, TX: IMR Press.

Sample of Reference List Provided to School Districts

Addison, R. (1991). Music with special needs children: A powerful aid. *Child Language Teaching and Therapy, 7*(3), 286–298.

Braithwaite, B., & Sigafoos, J. (1998). Effects of social versus musical antecedents on communication responsiveness in five children with developmental disabilities. *Journal of Music Therapy, 35*(2), 88–104.

Buday, E. M. (1995). The effects of signed and spoken words taught with music on sign and speech imitation by children with autism. *Journal of Music Therapy, 32*(3), 189–202.

Chen-Hafteck, L. (1997). Music and language development in early childhood: Integrating past research in the two domains. *Early Child Development and Care, 130,* 85–97.

Gfeller, K. (1983). Musical mnemonics as an aid to retention with normal and learning disabled students. *Journal of Music Therapy, 20*(4), 179–189.

Gunsberg, A. (1988). Improvised musical play: a strategy for fostering social play between developmentally delayed and nondelayed preschool children. *Journal of Music Therapy, 25*(4), 178–191.

Hoskins, C. (1988). Use of music to increase verbal response and improve expressive language abilities of preschool language delayed children. *Journal of Music Therapy, 25*(2), 73–84.

Humpal, M. (1991). The effects of an integrated early childhood music program on social interaction among children with handicaps and their typical peers. *Journal of Music Therapy, 28*(3), 161–177.

James, M., Weaver, A., Clemens, P., & Plaster, G. (1985). Influence of paired auditory and vestibular stimulation on levels of motor skill development in a mentally retarded population. *Journal of Music Therapy, 22,* 129–145.

Levitin, D. J., & Bellugi, U. (1998). Musical abilities in individuals with Williams syndrome. *Music Perception, 15*(4), 357–389.

Morton, L. L. (1990). The potential for therapeutic applications of music on problems related to memory and attention. *Journal of Music Therapy, 27*(4), 195–208.

Nelson, D., Anderson, V., & Gonzales, A. (1984). Music activities as therapy for children with autism and other pervasive developmental disorders. *Journal of Music Therapy, 21*(3), 100–116.

Overy, K. (2000). Dyslexia, temporal processing and music: the potential of music as an early learning aid for dyslexic children. *Psychology of Music, 28,* 218–229.

Pellitteri, J. (2000). Music therapy in special education. *Journal of Educational and Psychological Consultation, 11*(3–4), 379–391.

Spencer, S. (1988). The efficiency of instrumental and movement activities in developing mentally retarded adolescents' ability to follow directions. *Journal of Music Therapy, 25,* 44–50.

Standley, J., & Hughes, J. (1997). Evaluation of an early intervention music curriculum for enhancing pre-reading/writing skills. *Music Therapy Perspectives, 15,* 79–86.

Thaut, M. (1985). The use of auditory rhythm and rhythmic speech to aid temporal muscular control in children with gross motor dysfunction. *Journal of Music Therapy, 22*(3), 108–128.

Toolan, P., & Coleman, S. (1994). Music therapy, a description of process: Engagement in five people with learning disabilities. *Journal of Intellectual Disability Research, 38*(4), 433–444.

Ulfarsdottir, L., & Erwin, P. (1999). The influence of music on social cognitive skills. *The Arts in Psychotherapy, 26*(2), 81–84.

Wallace, W. (1994). Memory for music: effect of melody on recall of text. *Learning, Memory, and Cognition, 20*(6), 1471–1485. [underlying rationale for music to cue memory]

Wolfe, D., & Hom, C. (1993). Use of melodies as structural prompts for learning and retention of sequential verbal information by preschool students. *Journal of Music Therapy, 30*(2), 100–118.

Wylie, M. (1983). Eliciting vocal responses in severely and profoundly mentally handicapped subjects. *Journal of Music Therapy, 20*(4), 190–200.

Appendix A

Determining the Appropriateness of a Music Therapy Evaluation

> **The IEP team should consider and discuss the following indicators before referring a student for an evaluation. Students who demonstrate some or most of these characteristics are more likely to be appropriate for an evaluation.**

✓ Music appears to provide a *unique assist* to the student's learning abilities; student learns skills *first or quickest* through songs and/or has marked memory deficits but has excellent recall for song lyrics.

✓ *Music is one of the key motivators for this student;* for example, he/she consistently requests music or sings to self, gravitates towards music resources in the classroom, or demonstrates levels of engagement during music activities that are not typically seen at other times during the day.

✓ Student demonstrates very poor attention and it is difficult to gain his/her focus during tasks; *attention is best or significantly improved during music involvement.*

✓ Student has limited spoken language abilities and *initiates singing more than speaking* and/or easily transfers language from songs to everyday use; speech intelligibility and/or phrase length is considerably improved during singing activities.

✓ Music is one of the *most successful tools* used in the student's program to address major behavioral concerns.

✓ Student exhibits marked difficulty when completing basic motor tasks due to severe coordination deficits or physical limitations, but *will readily attempt and perform actions in songs or when musical instruments are used.*

For further questions, contact Michelle Lazar, MT-BC @ (555) 555-5555

Appendix B

Music Therapy Eligibility Assessment
For Use in the Special Education Setting

1. Overview

Upon referral, a music therapy evaluation can be conducted to determine whether music therapy is a *necessary service* for the individual to benefit from his or her educational program. Prior to an evaluation, the IEP team should identify if the student demonstrates a need for this type of assistance due to insufficient progress, severity of need, or specific nature of the disability. It should also be discussed whether the student has shown significant responses to music that would indicate musical cueing as a key component when addressing IEP goal areas.

2. Components of the Evaluation

This evaluation follows the protocol of the SEMTAP (Special Education Music Therapy Assessment Process), a nationally used and field-tested tool to determine eligibility for music therapy as a related service. The SEMTAP is administered in the student's educational setting, and consists of records review, staff/ parent interviews, observation, and direct interaction with the student. When assessing the student's responses to music, the music therapist utilizes individualized songs and rhythmic techniques specifically designed to target skills that are indicated as need areas on the most recent IEP. Goals are only addressed if there is research to support that music can be of benefit to improve functioning in the designated area of need.

3. Service Recommendation

In order to receive a recommendation for service, it must be clearly shown that the student's performance is significantly enhanced on *IEP-related tasks* when musical cueing is used. *Because music therapy is an "overlap" service, it is not considered necessary if the student can achieve similar levels of success through services already being offered.* If the student does qualify, services are provided by a credentialed music therapist on a direct or consult basis. Students who do not qualify for services through the IEP process may still benefit from music enrichment programs, music education classes, or private music therapy.

Any questions pertaining to the use of this assessment tool can be forwarded to Michelle Lazar, MT-BC, Director of Coast Music Therapy and Consulting at (555) 555-5555.

Underlying rationale for provision of music therapy relates to the use of musical cueing as a therapeutic tool to facilitate non-musical functioning. Research and scientific theory support parallels between speech/singing, rhythm/motor behavior, memory for song/ memory for academic material, and overall ability of preferred music to enhance mood, attention, and behavior to optimize the student's ability to learn and interact. Focus of sessions is on presenting skills initially using melodic and rhythmic strategies, and then fading musical cues to aid in generalization.

Appendix C

Music Therapy Evaluation: Referral Form

Student Name: _____ ID:_____
School: _____ Teacher:_____
Contact Phone #: _____ Date: _____

Compare the student's responses in the music and non-music settings, using the rating scale below. Please write "N/A" if the need area is not applicable to the student's program.

> 1 = consistently best in non-music setting
> 2 = somewhat better in non-music setting
> 3 = same/ similar performance in music and non-music setting
> 4 = somewhat better in music setting
> 5 = consistently best *in* music setting

	Non-Music	Same		Music
1. Length of On-task Participation/Attention	1	2	3	4 5
2. Level of Independence/ Initiation (reduced prompts needed)	1	2	3	4 5
3. Compliance/General Behavior	1	2	3	4 5
4. Memory/Recall/Ability to Learn New Concepts	1	2	3	4 5
5. Initiation of Language	1	2	3	4 5
6. Phrase Length When Communicating (or singing)	1	2	3	4 5
7. Speech Intelligibility	1	2	3	4 5
8. Initiation/Completion of Motor Tasks	1	2	3	4 5
9. Level of Social Interaction/Emotional Engagement	1	2	3	4 5

List areas of need music therapy is being requested to address:

_____
_____
_____

Has the student shown insufficient progress or interfering behaviors in the current program that indicate a need for additional assistance such as music therapy to support the IEP?

_____
_____
_____

Describe any of the student's specific responses to music that support the need for this service:

_____
_____
_____

> This portion will be completed by the music therapist; please phone or fax Michelle Lazar, MT-BC at (555) 555-5555 when form is completed.
>
> _____ Assessment plan has already been signed; parent request. (an evaluation must be completed)
> _____ Student is *not* recommended for an evaluation; current programming is meeting his/ her needs adequately. (only applicable if pre-screened)
> _____ Student *is* recommended for an evaluation. (only applicable if pre-screened)

Appendix D

Music Therapy Student Profile: Parent Copy

This profile is used to gather background information regarding your child's responses to music in the home environment. Please complete all questions that are applicable and return the profile as soon as possible (see page 2 for details).

Student's Name _____ D.O.B._____ Date Completed _____

Form Completed By_____ Contact Phone # _____

On average, how often are you able to observe your child's responses to music?

Times per day _____   Typical duration of _____ each time

In which settings and what types of music activities are used (live, recorded, instruments, dancing, etc.)

_____

_____

1. Are there any significant changes in your child's *attention, motivation, ability to follow directions, or compliance* during music activities that are unique to this setting, or that you do not typically observe during non-music activities?

_____

_____

_____

2. Has your child shown ability to *quickly learn and memorize new information* or concepts through song lyrics that he/ she otherwise would have difficulty with if not presented musically?

_____

_____

_____

3. Are there any major changes in you child's *communicative responses* when he/ she is singing, such as increased phrase length, spontaneity (initiates singing more than speaking), or improved intelligibility when compared with his/ her spoken language?

_____

_____

_____

4. Are there other areas where you notice significant and unique differences in your child's abilities (such as motor functioning, emotional engagement, etc.) that indicate music is a primary learning modality or method of interaction?

_____

_____

_____

5. Please list student's preferences in types of music/ favorite recordings/ musical instruments:

_____

_____

6. Please list several songs the student is able to sing most or all of the words to (if applicable):

_____

7. Main Reason(s) for Referral:

_____

_____

_____

Completed form can be returned to Michelle Lazar, MT-BC
Coast Music Therapy and Consulting
Fax: (555) 555-5555   Mail: P.O. Box 0000, Anytown, USA 00000

Section Two:
Models of Music Therapy Interventions in School/ Educational Environments

9

MUSIC THERAPY FOR LEARNERS WITH PROFOUND DISABILITIES IN A RESIDENTIAL SETTING

Laurie A. Farnan

Overview

RESIDENTIAL placement and education of children with mental retardation has a long history. This history, like that of many long-standing traditions and institutions in our society, reflects the beliefs of the society at the time. For example, the *primary role* of a residential treatment setting in the 1850s and early 1860s was *to provide educational programs* for mentally retarded youngsters and adolescents chronological age (CA) 6–16 or 18 (Scheerenberger, 1983). Facilities were reported to be small (5–10 students) and began as experiments in private homes or wings of existing facilities such as the Perkins School for the Blind in 1848 in South Boston (Crissey & Rosen, 1986). Between 1848 and 1898, the number of residential schools increased to 24 and the resident census to approximately 8,000 (Crissey & Rosen, 1986). Until the turn of the century, public schools had little role in educating students with mental retardation. Formal education was available only in residential settings and few public school programs were available before 1940 (Crissey & Rosen, 1986). There were some authorities who believed that after an appropriate education in a residential facility, a student would be able to return to their home and community (Sequin, as cited in Scheerenberger, 1983). It appears that the notion of least restrictive educational environment is deeply rooted.

As the years evolved, so did the role of residential care and placement. Facilities grew larger; some would suggest too large. By 1950, 125,375 people with mental retardation resided in residential facilities across the United States. The height of population was reached between 1967 and 1970 with a resident census peaking at 194,650 to 189,549 (Lakin, Prouty, & Bruininks, 2000; Scheerenberger, 1983). Various models of treatment and education developed ranging from Edouard Seguin's physiological method, to behavior modification, to developmental models, on to normalization, mainstreaming, and deinstitutionalization philosophies. Historically, these models effected both residential education and public school education programs. But it was with the passage of PL 94-142 in 1975 that the most sweeping changes in education for persons with mental retardation occurred. Public schools began to assume a much more active role in development of individualized education programs for students with special needs. Subsequently, the role of education in residential settings changed as well.

Many of those involved in providing education in the early institutions (circa mid to late 1800s) believed that "music" should be part of the training experience. Scheerenberger (1983) cited five references from that era that mentioned music as a scheduled part of the educational day. Along with standard curriculum areas (i.e., arithmetic, reading, writing, and gymnastics), these early programs viewed child development and sensory stimulation/development as important components of an appropriate education for students with mental retardation. We can see that there is a historical precedent for involvement in music activities as part of a developmentally based education program.

It is within current residential educational programs that the medical and education models converge. In the residential setting, a physician and/or nurse is available 24 hours every day since the medical needs of the residents can be quite complex. Students are sustained by tube feedings, dependent on others for all aspects of care (e.g., feeding, dressing, personal hygiene, positioning), and may experience seizures, often severe, and in some cases, life threatening. Yet, these same residents do attend school as their health status allows. The music therapist practicing in this type of setting must have knowledge of models of infection control practices, emergency procedures, child development, education, and rehabilitation. The purpose of this chapter is to describe the role of music therapy service delivery within the educational program of a residential setting for persons with developmental disabilities who have pervasive and intense needs.

Population

Central Wisconsin Center (CWC) for the Developmentally Disabled in Madison, Wisconsin, is one of three Intermediate Care Facilities for the Mentally Retarded (ICF/MR) residential treatment centers in the State of Wisconsin maintained by the Division of Care and Treatment Facilities in the Department of Health and Family Services. It is designated to provide long- and short-term services for adults and children with developmental disabilities. Central Center provides 24-hour daily care including access to medical, dental, nursing, psychological, religious, and social services plus music, occupational, physical, recreation, respiratory, and speech therapies. Adult education programs and vocational services are also available for the residents over age 21. In addition, there is an on-grounds education program (Cardinal School), which serves school age students (ages 3–21), plus an early childhood program for very young children (ages birth–3). For the 2000–2001 school year, only 13% (49) of the 370 residents at Central Center were school age. Four percent (17) of the Central Center school age population were served by Madison Metropolitan School District (MMSD), while 9% (32) attended CWC's Cardinal School program. It is projected for the 2001–2002 school year that those numbers will drop to 9% of the total population living at Central Center being school age, with 3% (11) attending MMSD and 6% (22) attending Cardinal School. These declining statistics are important as indicators of trends in residential facilities. With the onset of the philosophy of deinstitutionalization (circa 1970), the population of residential treatment centers has been steadily decreasing (Lakin et al., 2000; see Figure 1).

Central Center's population has followed this national trend in population reduction (CWC, 2001; see Figure 2). It is projected that long-term admissions will cease and short-term admissions will increase in the years to come. While long-term admissions have almost stopped, short-term admissions are increasing (CWC, 2001; see Figure 3). Ten students were served in the 2000–2001 school year at Central Center in the Short-Term Care Unit.

Decreasing the population in residential centers was and is an important element of deinstitutionalization. Additional elements include preventing initial admission, increasing the independence of persons residing in facilities, preparing them for community placement, and developing community services necessary to maintain placement (Scheerenberger, 1983, 1987). Not only were individuals being placed elsewhere thus decreasing residential populations, but long-term admissions have also been decreasing. Where in the past, a person with mild cerebral palsy, spina bifida, mild to moderate retardation, ambulation abilities, and no severe medical problems may have been admitted to a residential facility, only the person with the most profoundly medically fragile conditions (nonambulatory, profound retardation, failure to thrive, severe osteoporosis, and severe respiratory conditions including tracheotomies, etc) will now be admitted for short-term services. Subsequently, the demographics of the school age population have changed as well. Figure 4 shows the changes in enrollment statistics over years 1984–2000 for Cardinal School and MMSD (CWC Annual Reports, 1984–2000).

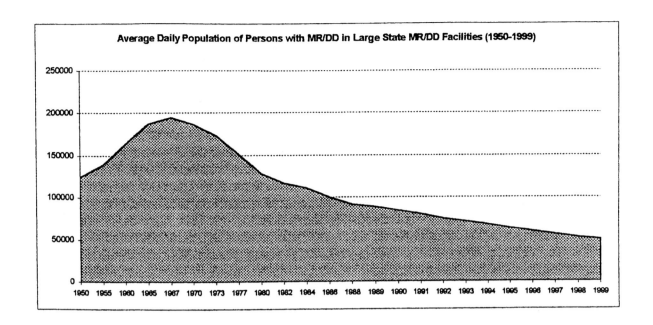

Figure 1. Total Average Daily Population Trend in State MR/DD Facilities

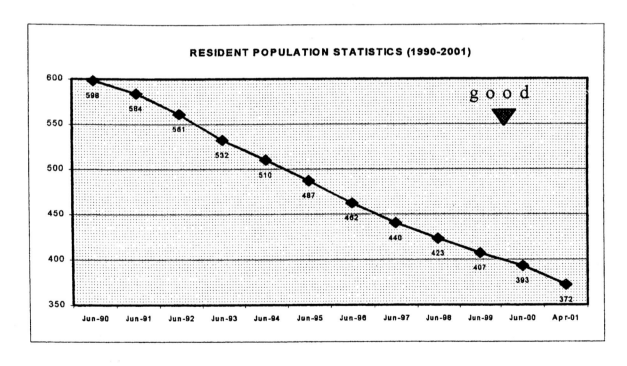

Figure 2. Central Wisconsin Center Resident Population Statistics

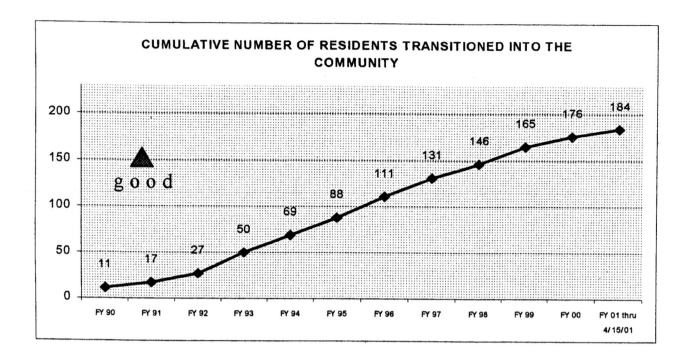

Figure 3. Central Wisconsin Center Resident-to-Community Transition Statistics

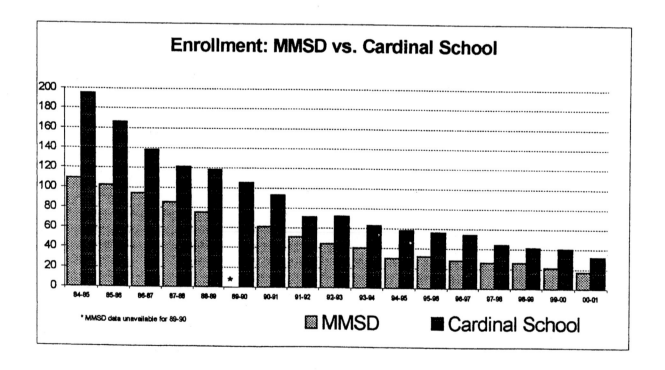

Figure 4. School Enrollment Comparison of MMSD and Cardinal School

It is important to note that though an educational program may be physically located within a residential treatment setting, the laws and regulations which govern delivery of services to students in the public schools also apply to students who live in a residential setting. Students with identified exceptional educational needs receive educational services as outlined and identified on their Individualized Education Program (IEP). These services include but are not limited to classroom instruction, adaptive physical education, occupational, physical, and speech therapy, community outings, all school programs, and in some situations, music therapy.

Although those individuals under the age of 22 years are *residents* of the facility, when they go to school they are *students* of Cardinal School. They attend school Monday through Friday and follow the same school calendar year as the local school district. Each of these students has a diagnosis of profound mental retardation. Based on the 1992 terminology of the American Association for Mental Retardation (AAMR), these students would be described as persons with mental retardation with pervasive support needed in the areas of at least two adaptive skill areas. The 1992 AAMR definition states:

> Mental retardation refers to substantial limitation in present functioning. It is characterized by significantly sub-average intellectual functioning (IQ 70–75 and below), existing concurrently with related limitations in two or more of the following applicable adaptive skill areas: communication, self-care, home living, social skills, community use, self-direction, health and safety, functional academics, leisure, and work. Mental retardation manifests before age 18. (p. 5)

Note that changing terminology has been an ongoing process. AAMR has published six revised definitions of mental retardation since the first definition issued in 1877. Gone are the 1877 terms such as *imbecile, idiot,* and *moron.* Also, the four classifications of *mildly, moderately, severely,* and *profoundly retarded* are no longer used by AAMR (although these classifications are mentioned in PL 94-142.). The new (1992) definition, classification, and system of supports seeks to describe a person as either having or not having mental retardation and then identifies the types of supports in adaptive skill areas necessary for this person to function as independently as possible in free society.

From individual to individual the identified adaptive skill area of need varies, as well as the intensity and type of support needed. The four possible intensities of needed support are defined as *intermittent, limited, extensive,* and *pervasive* (AAMR, 1992, p. 26). Using the current AAMR diagnosis criteria, a typical student at Cardinal School "is a person with mental retardation with pervasive support needed in the areas of self-care, social skills, community use, health and safety, self-direction, leisure, communication, and functional academics." AAMR suggests this terminology to be "more functional, relevant, and oriented to service delivery..." (1992, p. 34). All of the Cardinal School students are nonambulatory and use assistive devices for mobility. They are also nonverbal although they may use assistive devices or technology for communication. Table 1 illustrates the chronological age, functional behavioral age as assessed by the Wisconsin Behavior Rating Scale (WBRS), and the diagnosis of six students. The composite picture of these six students reveals chronological ages ranging from 9 to 17, with functional behavioral ages assessed at 2.7 to 5.7 months.

Service Delivery Model

All Cardinal School students are served by the music therapy department at Central Center. The students attend music therapy sessions once or twice a week with their special education teacher and teacher assistant. Students attend with their class (class size is generally 3 or 4 students) and in some situations two classes are combined for group music therapy. Students must get out of their wheelchairs every two hours while they are in school to relieve any possible pressure points and maintain skin integrity. Classrooms include mat tables to provide the students with out-of-chair accommodations. Music therapy sessions must either be planned for in-chair or out-of-chair times. When their out-of-chair time coincides with their scheduled music therapy session, the emphasis in music therapy is out-of-chair sensory stimulation activities, range of

Table 1

Student Profiles: Chronological Age/Assessment of Functional Age/Diagnosis

CA	WBRS Score	Diagnosis
17	5.2 months	Profound MR due to microcephaly, CP spastic quadriplegia, cortical blindness and seizure disorder.
15	2.8 months	Profound MR due to hydrocephalus spastic quadriplegia and an uncontrolled seizure disorder.
15	5.7 months	Profound MR due to unknown prenatal influence, seizure disorder of unknown etiology.
12	2.7 months	Profound MR due to other endocrine disorder, visually impaired.
9	4.7 months	Profound MR—microcephaly, impaired vision.
19	3.5 months	Profound MR due to unknown prenatal influence, perceptual blindness.

motion, gross motor activities, and activities that can be performed while in supine, prone, sidelying, or supported sitting positions. Sessions are held in the school classroom or students are transported to one of the three treatment rooms used for group music therapy. Changing location allows the students opportunities to socialize with others and to move freely within their environment. Two larger music therapy rooms allow for in chair motor and music activities. In a smaller room designed for out-of-chair activities, students are lifted from their wheelchairs and positioned following physical therapy recommendations on a specially designed wooden sound floor used to provide students an opportunity to feel tactile vibrations of live music. The music therapist provides vibrations through the use of subcontra bass tone bars, guitar, electronic instruments, drums, or piano.

IEP or IPP or Both?

Interesting situations can occur when multiple regulations coexist simultaneously in a person's life. PL 94-142 mandates a free and appropriate education is provided through implementation of the Individualized Education Program (IEP). (Refer to previous chapters for specific regulations.) The 1971 amendments to the Federal Title XIX (Medicaid) of the Social Security Act mandate that certain standards be followed in providing care and treatment to persons in ICF/MR facilities. The following two standards directly influence the music therapist working in such a setting.

STANDARD: Each client must have an individual program plan developed by an interdisciplinary team that represents the professions, disciplines or service areas that are relevant to: (i) identifying the client's needs, as described by the comprehensive functional assessments required in paragraph (c)(3) of this section; (ii) designing programs that meet the client's needs; (iii) identifying the client's need for services without regard to the actual availability of the services needed; and (iv) including physical development and health, nutritional status, sensorimotor development, affective development, speech and language development and auditory functioning, cognitive development, social development, adaptive behaviors or independent living skills necessary for the client to be able to function in the community, and as applicable, vocational skills. These objectives must be stated separately, in terms of a single behavioral outcome; be assigned projected completion dates; be expressed in behavioral terms that provide measurable indices of performance; be organized to reflect a developmental progression appropriate to the individual; and be assigned priorities.

(a) STANDARD: Active Treatment

Active treatment: (1) Each client must receive a continuous active treatment program, which includes aggressive, consistent implementation of a program of specialized and generic training, treatment, health services and related services described in this subpart, that is directed toward: (i) the acquisition of the behaviors necessary for the client to function with as much self determination and independence as possible; and (ii) the prevention or deceleration of regression or loss of current optimal functional status. (State of Wisconsin, 1989)

(It should be noted that at the time of this writing revisions to the Active Treatment Standards were being considered by the Health Care Financing Administration [HCFA].)

The Individual Program Plan (IPP) dictates the overall plan of care through the delivery of the concept of active treatment. It is, therefore, possible for one person to have two major individual plans (IPP *and* IEP) guiding the delivery of care, treatment, and education. The system of checks and balances is vast.

To illustrate this situation consider the example of two individual students, "Sarah" and "Kellie" (both age 6), who are residing at Central Center. Both youngsters have been diagnosed as profoundly mentally retarded and assessed to be functioning at the 3.6 month level of development. Both girls receive a full gamut of services (see above) including attending special education classes in Cardinal School. They each receive music therapy five times a week. Two of those music therapy sessions occur during school time, while the other three times occur after school, on the living unit in coordination with the girls' therapeutic recreation program. Does their music therapist follow the goals and objectives on the IEP or the IPP or both?

The answer is both. According to the Standards of Clinical Practice for Music Therapists (AMTA, 1999), the music therapist is to deliver an integrated individualized plan of care and treatment once assessment procedures are completed. Therefore, if a music therapist is working with a client in more than one setting, and under more than one set of regulations, it is the responsibility of the music therapist to integrate *all* plans of care. Such integration might include designing music therapy goals and objectives that reflect the emphasis of both the IEP and IPP for school age children and adolescents. In that way the music therapist can report relevant data back to both systems: reporting progress to the special educator for IEP reviews and M-team meetings, *and* writing Quarterly and Annual Review Progress Reports for the transdisciplinary team and the Qualified Mental Retardation Professional (QMRP). In other words, the music therapist reports on the IEP to the teacher and on the IPP to the QMRP! More importantly, the music therapist must be able to report progress on integrated objectives for the individual person. This is not an impossible situation. The music therapist can, through careful analysis of goals and objectives, implement specifically designed music based interventions which address either the educational objectives and/or the adaptive skill areas of need.

In the case of Sarah, the *IPP* developed by her transdisciplinary team includes a long-term goal area (LTG) to use her tactile senses as a priority need, and the short-term objective (STO) for Sarah is to maintain contact with a textured object using an open hand for 10 seconds, 60% of all trials by the stated ending date. Her *IEP* suggests an annual goal area of working toward increasing her appropriate head and arm movements in response to sensory materials. One of her short-term objectives is to move one or both arms with a relaxed, controlled pattern to initiate contact with toys near her, six times per classroom period, 80% of all trials (see Table 2).

The music therapist would then combine approaches and focus on development of an objective that would provide opportunities for Sarah to develop these skills in all of her music therapy sessions (see Table 3). Two sample objectives for Sarah in music therapy may read:

Sarah will reach to touch an instrument presented to her in midline once per session, 60% of all trials by a specified ending date. Further, using an open hand, Sarah will maintain contact with the vibrating surface of an instrument as it is played with her, once per session, for 10 seconds, 60% of all trials by a specified ending date.

Table 2
Sample IEP and IPP Objectives

	IEP		IPP
LTG:	S will increase her appropriate head and arm movements in response to sensory materials.	LTG:	S will use her tactile senses.
STO 1:	S will raise her head up in a variety of positions for one minute, 60% of recorded trials.	STO: .	Following relaxation procedures, S will maintain contact with textured objects using an open hand for 10 seconds, 60% of all trials, by 5/21/03.
STO2:	S will move one or both arms with a relaxed, controlled pattern to initiate contact with toys near her, 6 times per class period, 80% of recorded trials.		
STO 3:	S will purposefully grasp a small object placed in either hand for 30 seconds, 80% of recorded trials.		

Table 3
Sample Music Therapy Objectives

Music Therapy Integrated Objectives	
LTG:	S will use her tactile senses.
STO:	S will reach to touch an instrument (drums, maracas, bells, tambourines, guitar, etc.) presented to her in midline, once per session 60% of recorded trials, by 5/21/03.
STO:	S will maintain contact with the vibrating surface of an instrument (drums, maracas, bells, tambourines, guitar, etc.) As it is played with her once per session for 10 seconds, 60% of recorded trials, by 5/21/03.

For Kellie, the transdisciplinary team identified responding to auditory stimuli as a priority need area. Her *IPP* short-term objective suggests localizing a sound source by turning her head toward the sound 80% of all trials by a specific end date. Her *IEP* suggests a short-term objective of after localization of a sensory target demonstrated by a head turn, Kellie will reach out to touch the object (see Table 4). The music therapist can integrate both systems in service delivery through implementation of objectives which will use musical sounds and instruments as motivation for Kellie to develop these life skills and responses (see Table 5).

Table 4
Sample IEP and IPP Objectives

IEP	IPP
LTG: K will reach out to touch objects or people.	LTG: K will respond to auditory stimuli.
STO: Following a head turn towards a sensory target, K will reach out to touch the object two times per class period, 75% of recorded trials, by 6/6/03.	STO: K will localize a sound source to either side (turning head towards auditory presentation) 80% of recorded trials, by 5/21/03.

Table 5
Sample Music Therapy Objectives

Music Therapy Integrated Objectives
LTG: K will respond to auditory and tactile stimulation.
STO: When presented with a musical sound source (drums, maracas, bells, tambourines, guitar, etc.), K will localize the sound source by turning her head toward the sound, twice per session, 80% of recorded trials by 5/21/03.
STO: After localizing a musical sound source (drums, maracas, bells, tambourines, guitar, etc.), K will reach to touch the sound source, once per session, 75% of recorded trials by 5/21/03.

Assessment

All students are assessed annually, in the fall using the CWC music therapy assessment form (see Appendix A). The music therapy assessment includes the following developmental areas: sensory/cognitive, communication, psycho-social, and motor skill development, plus the music skill areas of vocal, instrumental, and specific music preferences. The assessment concludes with identifying developmental and behavioral needs for the student. IEP objectives are reviewed with teachers and IPP goals and objectives are reviewed using the CWC IPP Goal Summary form (see Appendix B). Specific objectives are adapted from both the IEP and the IPP to provide for a coordination of both systems. Data are taken each time the student (client) is seen, whatever the setting—during school time or during other programs.

Task Analysis

What are the "best practice" music interventions and activities for this population? How does a music therapist design appropriate interventions for use in this setting? The answer is no different than in any other setting. The therapist looks to the needs and abilities of the student (client) and manipulates the materials of music—rhythm, melody, and harmony—to enhance the student's achievement of a particular experience, task, or understanding. Figure 5 illustrates an intervention/activity development loop based on assessment and objectives. Once an objective has been identified, the music therapist can design an appropriate intervention to meet the client needs based upon the components of the objective. For example, if a student is to look toward sound, the intervention design would include the particular cueing phrase paired with an instrument sound within a song specifically composed for the task. Data from the client's responses would help the therapist decide whether to rewrite the objective or redesign the intervention to provide the greatest success for the client.

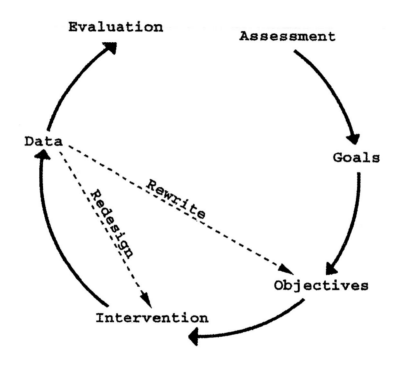

Figure 5. Objective-based Activity Development

Refer back to Sarah and Kellie. Their assessments included phrases such as looks toward sound source, reaches to touch objects, smiles when name is heard, takes deep inhalations when relaxed, notices the presence of others, etc. The music therapist can develop specific objectives based upon such information and other existing documentation to create or adapt appropriate music materials, interventions, and activities (Farnan, 1987). If intervention/activity development begins with student assessment, then the data back from the intervention/activity will tell us whether the objective needs to be rewritten or the intervention/activity has to be redesigned. It is a student/client-engendered model of activity development (Farnan, 1989).

Role of Music Therapy

The mission of the music therapy department at Central Wisconsin Center is "to provide professional program planning and implement goal oriented, quality, music therapy services specifically designed to develop and enhance functional life skills for individuals with developmental disabilities." (Farnan, 1993). The three music therapists at Central Center are responsible primarily for delivery of active treatment through music therapy services. Sixty percent of the music therapist position description calls for direct service. As such, the IPP is of utmost importance in program design. At present, the school age population represents only 9% of the total population at Central Center, with 6% served at Cardinal School. The school age population, therefore, is only 9% of the caseload served by CWC music therapists. The remaining 91% of the population are adults served in conjunction with other programs (vocational services, occupational therapy, speech therapy, therapeutic recreation, adult education), not with school. As students age and graduate, the school age population will continue to decrease.

In addition, the music therapists are expected to function within the *transdisciplinary team* format. In this format, all staff are expected to *learn, teach*, and *work* together (Schmiedlin, 1982; see Figure 6). Traditional professional boundaries are to be transcended and authoritative disciplines are expected to role release when possible. For the music therapist, this may mean setting the tempo for a particular activity, but the special education teacher would be playing the two-note pattern on the tone bar while the music therapist works directly with the students. The music therapists may offer introductory piano or guitar lessons to education staff so they can better use classroom instruments with the students. Providing suggestions and guidance on the use of electronic instruments in the classroom is also important. In that regard, the music therapist in this setting also provides consultation regarding music materials and equipment. Farnan (1989) identified the role of a music therapist in the transdisciplinary setting as that of composer, consultant, and session leader (see Figure 7). The MT as composer must *learn* about the needs and abilities of the student in order to write appropriate music for sessions. The MT as consultant must *teach* other staff about the role of music and music materials in achieving goals and objectives. The MT as session leader *works* side by side other staff in modeling delivery of direct service using the medium of music in a therapeutic way.

The Future

Fewer people are living their entire lives in residential settings. Intermediate care is not considered a life-long living arrangement. As the role of residential facilities continues to evolve, the need for specialized intermediate residential care, treatment, and education for people with profound mental retardation and intense needs still exists. Nevertheless, a music therapist in such a setting must design services with future transitions and placements in mind. Programming must assist the client in acquiring the functional skills necessary to lead a more independent life. Expression of choices, development of preferences, acquiring life experiences, and personal interests all contribute to building an independent quality of life. If transitions are in the future, music may provide a familiar link to bridge one situation to another. For example, if school-age children participate in music therapy in a self-contained classroom in a residential setting, care must be taken

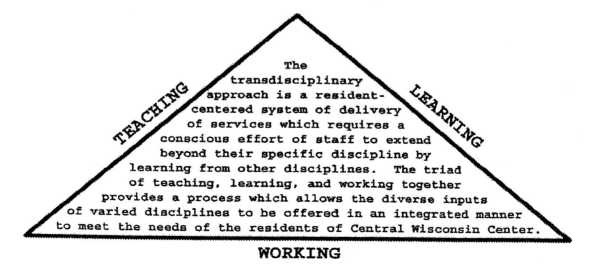

Figure 6. Transdisciplinary Team Approach

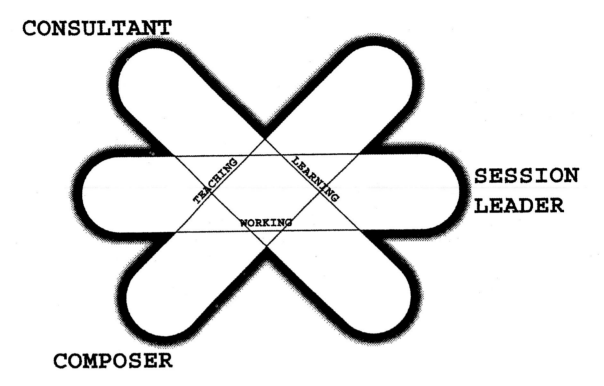

CONSULTANT

SESSION
LEADER

COMPOSER

TEACHING   LEARNING

WORKING

Figure 7. Music Therapist Roles in the Transdisciplinary Setting

to provide those children with music activities commensurate with their school-age peers. Besides offering a variety of specifically composed and goal-oriented programmatic songs, a diverse musical diet of culturally based children's songs should also be provided. Checking local curriculums and adapting commonly used songs may build a familiar repertoire for a child. If such children are to be eventually included in the public school setting, these songs may provide a familiar link in transition to that new setting. For the children who may not be appropriately accommodated in public school but rather will make their transition to adult programming within the facility, the familiar program activities may provide a link to their transition.

Strategies

The delivery of music therapy in a self-contained classroom in a residential setting can at first glance appear complicated. The children and adolescents have profound mental retardation and may have complex medical needs. Despite the fact that there are two systems of documentation, and the convergence of the medical and educational models, the center of the delivery of service must always be the student. Such a student deserves quality music and effective therapy designed to assist him or her to attain educational goals and functional life skills by fully participating in musical activities. Sensory stimulation and usage are important developmental activities for such students and have been so documented since 1843. Practitioners should remember to use more than one sensory channel for stimulation and to allow sufficient time for the student to process the information and make a response. Such multisensorial stimulation is critical with students whose sensory systems can be so profoundly impaired. Response time may be longer and responses more subtle than with other populations. Responses to live musical stimuli through auditory and tactile stimulation can be achieved by assisting students to touch the vibrating sound surface of instruments. Such assistance may include facilitation to touch the vibrating front surface of a guitar during an opening or closing song, or placing an open hand on a tone bar or tambourine as it is played with a steady predictable rhythm, creating both auditory and tactile stimulation. Responses may be as subtle as a change in facial expression, a change in pupil dilation, a change in respiration rate, a vocalization, or reaching or turning toward the sound source. These responses indicate an awareness and basic processing of stimuli—a necessary life skill.

Conclusion

What will the picture of education in a residential setting be in the future? The beliefs of current society embrace inclusion, downsizing, and deinstitutionalization. Progressive and sophisticated medical interventions have given life and sustained life with children who previously would probably not have survived birth (L. Leggett, MSW, Admission Social Worker, personal communication, May 17, 1995). Community-based services are in place for many children with identified special needs but may not be readily available for the children who are the most medically complex, fragile, and profoundly impaired with intense needs. These students may be served on a short-term basis in residential settings. Residential interventions and programs will continue to be provided to these students, including music therapy as long as such interventions are deemed appropriate and necessary. Recommendations for successful community-based service delivery are becoming an important component of treatment. History illustrates that the populations served in residential settings change as the values and politics of a society change.

Inclusion in music-based programs as a component of the education of persons with mental retardation has been documented since 1843. We now must shift with societal changes to develop techniques and procedures for the future of these students, however and wherever that future may continue to grow. Residential facilities are downsizing and their populations are decreasing. Students are being served elsewhere. The direct service model of music therapy intervention may evolve to be increasingly more consultative to public schools in order to provide resource models and effective techniques for direct service delivery.

References

American Association for Mental Retardation. (1992). *Mental retardation 9th edition: Definition, classification, and systems of support*. Washington, DC: Author.

American Music Therapy Association. (1999) *Standards of clinical practice*. Silver Spring, MD: Author.

Crissey, M. S., & Rosen, M. (1986*). Institutions for the mentally retarded: A changing role in changing times*. Austin, TX: PRO-ED.

Central Wisconsin Center Annual Reports. (1984–2000). *Education/Cardinal School report*. Madison, WI: Author.

Central Wisconsin Center. (2001). *Wisconsin Forward Award health care criteria application*. Madison, WI: Author.

Farnan, L. A. (1993). *Strategic information technology planning statement*. Madison, WI: Music Therapy Department, Central Wisconsin Center for the Developmentally Disabled.

Farnan, L. A. (1989). Music therapy service delivery within a transdisciplinary model. *Journal of Practical Approaches to Developmental Handicap, 13*(2), 14–17.

Farnan, L. A. (1987). Composing music for use in therapy. *Music Therapy Perspectives, 4*, 8–12.

Lakin, K. C., Prouty, R. W., & Bruininks, R. H. (2000). Longitudinal trends in large state operated residential facilities, 1950–1999. In *Residential services for persons with developmental disabilities: Status and trends through 1999, Report #54*. Minneapolis, MN: Research and Training Center on Community Living, Institute on Community Integration/UAP; the College of Education and Human Development, University of Minnesota.

Scheerenberger, R. C. (1983). *A history of mental retardation*. Baltimore: Brooks.

Scheerenberger, R. C. (1987). *A history of mental retardation: A quarter century of promise*. Baltimore: Brooks.

Schmiedlin, J. (1982). *Transdisciplinary concepts* [Staff training handout]. Madison, WI: Central Wisconsin Center for the Developmentally Disabled.

State of Wisconsin Department of Health and Social Services, Division of Health, Bureau of Quality Compliance. (1989). *Federal regulations document: Interpretive guidelines—Intermediate care facilities for the mentally retarded.* Madison, WI: Author.

Appendix A

Central Wisconsin Center
Music Therapy Assessment

Name of individual:_____

Music Therapist/Intern:_____

KEY: + = response observed,
       completes task independently
       0 = no response observed
       S = sometimes observed
       NA = not applicable

Sensory/Cognitive Development Date:							
A. Awareness/Response to live music							
1. Startle reflex							
2. Increase in muscle tone							
3. Decrease in muscle tone							
4. Increase in eye movement							
5. Decrease in eye movement							
6. Increase in rate of respiration							
7. Decrease in rate of respiration							
8. Turns head to locate source of music							
9. Looks to locate source of music							
10. Reaches for instrument/object							
11. Changes facial expression							
12. Other responses up presentation of music							
B. Attention Span / Eye Contact							
1. Localizes sound source							
2. Attends to sound source							
3. Attends to therapist/staff							
4. Attends to peer							
5. Tracks sound source							
C. Imitation Skills							
1. Imitates movements							
2. Imitates vocalizations							

Communication Development

System of communication used:							
A. Receptive Language Repertoire							
1. Name							
2. Peer's name							
3. Follows 1-step requests (stand/sit...)							
4. Follow 2-step requests							

B. Expressive Language Repertoire							
1. Audible response to musical stimuli							
2. Indicates yes							
3. Indicates no							
4. Vocalizes to music							
C. Discussion Skills							
1. Understands questions							
2. Answers questions more than yes / no							
3. Communicates preferences / choices							

Psycho-Social Development   Date:

A. Interactive Skills							
1. Interacts as directed							
2. Initiates interaction with others							
3. Withdraws from interaction							
B. Social Reward System							
1. Shows pleasure for personal accomplishments							
2. Responds to verbal praise							
3. Responds to physical praise							

Motor Skills Development

A. Fine Motor Skills							
Instrument Adaptation Used:							
Hand preference: R L							
Grasp							
1. Hypotonic grasp							
2. Hypertonic grasp							
3. Ulner deviation of hand							
4. Cortical thumb							
5. Demonstrates finger extension							
6. Uses cylindrical grasp							
7. Uses palmar grasp							
8. Uses pincer grasp							
Release							
1. Demonstrates voluntary release							
2. Does not release instruments/objects							
Hand Usage							
1. Brings hands to midline							
2. Reaches for instruments/objects							
3. Touches vibrating surface							
4. Maintains touch on vibrating surface							
5. Plays instruments in midline							
6. Plays one-handed instrument							

7. Plays two-handed instrument						
8. Crosses midline						
9. Transfers instruments / objects from hand-hand						

Music Skills

A. Vocal Skills						
1. Vocalizes to music						
2. Vocally matches pitches						
3. Sings words to songs						
4. Sings recognizable melodies						
B. Instrumental Skills						
1. Imitates rhythmic patterns						
2. Visually discriminates instruments						
3. Auditorially discriminates instruments						

Music Preferences:

Instrument Preferences:

Favorite Types of Music:

Favorite Songs:

Developmental & Behavioral Needs:

Appendix B

Central Wisconsin Center for the Developmentally Disabled
Individual Program Plan Goal Summary – Music Therapy

Individual: _____ CWC # 5-_____

Birthdate:_____ Apartment:_____ WBRS/FV Assessed Level of functioning: _____

Name of Therapist/Intern: _____ Date:_____

Medical Diagnosis:_____

_____

_____

Means of Ambulation: WC/semi-am/orthocart/walks/WC for transit:_____

Communication system: _____

Sensory functioning: _____

_____

LTG:

STO:

Baseline data/date:

Performance/Summary of procedure and criteria:

Implement in Music Therapy? ____yes ____no _____

LTG:

STO:

Baseline/date:

Performance/Summary of procedure and criteria:

Implement in Music Therapy? ____yes ____no

10

MUSIC THERAPY FOR JUVENILE OFFENDERS IN A RESIDENTIAL TREATMENT SETTING

Susan C. Gardstrom

Introduction

SOME researchers indicate that the rate of serious and violent juvenile crime in this country is escalating (National Coalition of State Juvenile Justice Advisory Groups, 1993). Other organizations report a decline in violent offenses by youngsters, citing statistics of the Federal Bureau of Investigation (FBI) as one source which may exaggerate the problem of youth violence (Jones & Krisberg, 1994). Despite conflicting data and resulting confusion, one thing is for certain: More than ever, this country is keenly aware of the issue of violent crime among juveniles. Increasingly, youths are being committed for rehabilitation and education in secure, residential settings. Music therapists are joining the ranks of professionals who share the challenging task of facilitating the academic, physical, social, and emotional growth of the young offender in residential treatment. In 1993, the National Association for Music Therapy (NAMT) reported that 14 of its members worked in adult and juvenile correctional facilities (National Association for Music Therapy, 1993). As of 2000, the number of clinicians working with the forensic population had increased to 46 (American Music Therapy Association, 2001). It is this author's belief that many more music therapists are servicing an "unidentified" delinquent population, that is, adolescents found in public schools, psychiatric treatment facilities, and community centers, who exhibit delinquent behaviors but who have not yet been formally involved in the juvenile adjudication process.

Offender Defined

Various terms are used to describe young people who have been in trouble with the law. "Juvenile offender," "youthful offender," and "delinquent" are used interchangeably to denote a child or adolescent who has committed a status, misdemeanor, or felony offense. *Status* offenses (such as curfew violations, incorrigibility, and truancy from home and school) are behaviors that, if committed by adults, would not be considered a crime. The terms "misdemeanor" and "felony" are borrowed from the adult correctional system. *Misdemeanor* offenses include such behaviors as simple traffic violations and trespassing. *Felonies* are the most severe offenses and include both nonviolent crimes such as manufacture of a controlled substance and car theft, and violent crimes like rape, armed robbery, and murder.

Juvenile Court

Before a child has contact with the juvenile justice system, he or she has typically established a pattern of antisocial behavior, often manifested first in the classroom. Teachers are quick to recognize "problem kids," those youths who constantly miss assignments, cheat, act in a hostile or withdrawn manner, or behave disrespectfully toward adults. Trips to the principal's office and discussions with parents may or may not be effective in modifying such behaviors. More severe acts of delinquency (e.g., fighting, stealing, carrying a weapon, and substance use) are most often met with detention, suspension, or expulsion. Depending upon the frequency, intensity, and duration of his or her delinquent behaviors, the child may be referred to the courts for legal action.

The juvenile justice process differs from state to state and a youth who is charged with having committed an offense is subject to that individualized process. In general, an alleged offender is required to participate in a preliminary hearing during which the facts of the case are reviewed by a judge or appointed court representative. A teen who is charged with a serious felony offense may be transferred to adult criminal court for trial by means of a legislative, prosecutorial, or judicial waiver; lesser offenses are usually tried in juvenile or family court. (Public opinion polls indicate that the majority of all voting age adults want juveniles who commit felonies tried in the adult criminal courts rather than in juvenile courts [Schwartz, 1992] even though the evidence suggests that such transfers do not result in harsher penalties [Jones & Krisberg, 1994].) Before a formal court appearance, a child is often removed from the home and school and placed in a county youth home or detention center. These centers are not designed for long-term treatment of adjudicated delinquents, but, rather, for the short-term, pretrial holding of alleged offenders who are deemed a high risk to commit additional offenses or flee before their trial (Barton, 1994). However, in this author's experience, some youths may spend up to 12 months in crowded, chaotic youth homes awaiting trial or placement in a treatment/education facility.

If found guilty, the child is sentenced. This process is also affected by statutory schemes, as well as by individual factors like age, record of prior offenses, severity of the current offense, and resources and attitudes of the youth and his or her family. Eisenman (1991) found that the severity of sentences for juvenile felons seemed to depend on jurisdiction with some judges routinely sentencing while others almost never exercising this right. Sentencing may result in relatively lenient solutions such as probation, community service, or acts of restitution. In these cases, the child would continue to attend his or her regular school. More restrictive sanctions include mandated therapy, placement in day treatment, or incarceration in a public or private residential institution. In 1989, it was estimated that approximately 80,000 youths occupied beds in adult and juvenile correctional facilities in this country (United States Department of Justice, 1991).

Demographics

Delinquent behavior is not restricted to youths of a particular race, socioeconomic status, gender, or intelligence; it appears in all groups of youths. However, it surfaces three times more frequently in males than females (Schwartz, 1992) and more often in youths exhibiting the following characteristics: (a) a delinquency adjudication prior to age 13, (b) low family income, (c) being rated troublesome by teachers and peers between the ages of 8 and 10, (d) poor school performance by age 10, (e) psychomotor clumsiness, (f) poor nonverbal IQ, and (g) having a sibling convicted of a crime (Blumstein, Farrington, & Moitra, 1985; Greenwood, 1986; Mahoney, 1991). Further, studies of serious juvenile offenders typically show disproportionate rates of mental health problems, including chemical dependency (Baird, 1987; Elliot, Huizinga, & Morse, 1988; Krisberg, 1987). A history of physical or sexual abuse and an unusually high incidence of head injuries has been linked to violent offenders as well (Lewis et al., 1985; Lewis et al., 1988).

Needs

Emotional/Social Needs

By definition, a delinquent youth manifests a constellation of antisocial behaviors, of which aggression is perhaps the most problematic. Aggressive behaviors in youths have been linked to genetics, acquired biological factors, such as birth trauma or head injury, and psychosocial factors. Antisocial behavior among parents and punitive or inconsistent disciplinary parenting styles seem to contribute to a child's aggressive patterns. Exposure to violence in the media is also correlated with increased violent behavior (American Psychological Association, 1993).

Interpersonal problems are common among those who demonstrate delinquent behaviors. Brendtro and Ness (1983) write, "It is assumed that many problems of children, both those that are situational and those that are chronic, exist because children lack the skills to build relationships, handle interpersonal conflicts, and manage their own emotions in constructive ways" (p. 163). With lifelong histories of turbulent family relationships, these children generalize deep-seated fear and mistrust to relationships outside the family system. At first meeting, they may appear hostile, indifferent, resistive, aloof, guarded, or superficial. They may do everything in their power to project themselves as "tough" so as not to risk ridicule, rejection, or harm from what they perceive to be yet one more intervening adult or aggravating peer.

In both rural and urban areas, opportunities for safe, legal, and productive socialization may be limited. "Cruising" or "hanging out" on the streets may be the most attractive recreational options for adolescents who come from overcrowded or poverty-stricken communities in which leadership is scarce and few positive role models exist. All too often, the unmet need for bonding among males from single-parent, female-headed households is met through socialization into a gang, with its "attendant delinquent/criminal system" (Schwartz, 1992, p. 21).

Physical Needs

Physical needs within this population are varied. Medical and dental care may have been neglected due to financial strain and a lack of health insurance. The importance of proper nutrition and personal hygiene may not have been emphasized in the home and the use and abuse of alcohol and other drugs may have caused or contributed to specific illnesses. Some youths may have chemical imbalances that contribute to emotional problems. Many females designated as delinquent have experienced one or more pregnancies which were unplanned and problematic.

The physical symptoms of stress may be tempered by the stability and structure of a residential treatment program in that a consistent, predictable schedule may reduce anxiety. While sleeping in a locked room may be unnerving for some teens, others could find relief in the physical security it provides, taking comfort in the knowledge that no one will physically or sexually abuse them during the night.

The importance of providing these youths with basic physical needs of food, clothing, and shelter cannot be overstated. The three nutritious meals received each day in residential care may be one or two more than they have ever known.

Academic Needs/Educational Services

Many of the youths classified as juvenile offenders are believed to have learning disabilities, mental or emotional impairments, or substance abuse problems that interfere with learning. Others may have experienced repeated failure in a school system which is ill-equipped to deal with the student's needs and the family's resources. Still others come from families in which education is not valued or, if valued, falls by the wayside in the face of more pressing emotional or economic concerns. Some students have lagged behind academically while in detention awaiting placement in a treatment facility. Still others have little consistency in their lives. Attendance in school may be interrupted when the family uproots and relocates.

The scope and delivery of educational services in juvenile corrections are influenced by federal and state policies as well as related issues such as institutional security, students' prior school experiences, and fiscal constraints. Unfortunately, the juvenile justice system is ". . . largely segregated from other systems such as medical care, mental health services, and schools that serve children and families" (Jones & Krisberg, 1994, p. 7). Residential facilities for juvenile offenders frequently offer on-campus remedial reading, spelling, writing, and mathematics instruction as well as core academics such as history, social studies, health education, science, and English. Depending upon its financial and human resources, a facility may also offer vocational training or specialty classes, e.g., home economics, computer literacy, parenting skills, art, music, etc. Incarcerated students are educated most often in small, self-contained classrooms for several reasons. First, these individuals' behaviors can be unpredictable and unmanageable, even violent, posing a threat to the community and an undue challenge to the regular education system. Second, due to resistance to treatment and education, some students are a truancy risk. Finally, because these students' needs are so complex and disparate, individualized instruction in a highly monitored setting is often crucial to academic success.

Educational programs do exist within public school systems for students whose delinquent behaviors are manageable in these settings. *Alternative education* programs, for example, may serve at-risk or mildly delinquent students for some or all of the school day. These programs, usually staffed by special educators, are tailored to nontraditional styles of learning and tend to embrace experiential teaching techniques and emphasize the development of social and interpersonal skills. In rare cases, incarcerated students are mainstreamed into regular education programs.

Special Education Services

The provisions of the Individuals with Disabilities Education Act (IDEA) apply to all states receiving federal financial assistance. However, states may be slow to extend these rights to eligible *incarcerated* students (Leone, 1994). Ideally, within 30 days of arrival at a residential facility, a student must undergo academic and psychological testing to determine strengths, deficits, and educational needs. Based on this information, a committee will develop the student's Individualized Education Program (IEP). Committee members usually include a teacher or educational consultant from the facility, the student's case worker, and parents or legal guardians. Leone (1994) cites that, although the IEP is required under federal law, IEP committees are typically slow to convene, parents or legal guardians rarely attend planning meetings, and educational programs may not be implemented when the student is sent to disciplinary segregation. In this writer's experience, music therapy is very rarely included as a required service on the IEP of incarcerated youths.

Students who do not carry a special education label when they arrive may be reassessed for special education services. It is crucial to complete accurate and timely educational assessments on each student so that designated funds can be accessed for those needing specialized services. When a student leaves residential treatment, the receiving school may accept the recommendations of the treatment facility with respect to that student's specific educational needs.

Music Therapy Services

Introduction

Where, with whom, how frequently, how long, and in what way music therapists work with juvenile offenders is impacted by a variety of factors including work setting, state law, regulation and policy, internal organizational structure and treatment philosophy, and financial resources, all of which are constantly changing. Youth homes, typically overcrowded and understaffed, do not usually have the financial resources to employ nonmandated professionals. Some music therapy services, however, may be funded by governmental, community, or private foundation grants. Most music therapists in juvenile corrections work in long-term public or private rehabilitation/education facilities.

The Work Setting

Despite extensive reform spawned in the 1970s by growing public dissatisfaction with governmental programs, large state-run institutions (a.k.a. training schools) still operate in many states. In 1991, the Office of Juvenile Justice and Delinquency Prevention estimated that 28,535 youths resided in public training schools (as cited in Barton, 1994). A music therapist in this type of school is usually a state employee with the civil service administration, bearing one of a number of professional titles such as Music Therapist,

Activity Therapist, or Recreation Specialist. Typically, in this setting, caseloads are large, money is limited and tedious to access, and working conditions are less than ideal; yet jobs are relatively secure. The complexion of music therapy services varies depending upon the agency's overall philosophy and specific treatment program.

Private programs service a significant proportion of total delinquent admissions in the United States. The number of youths confined to private juvenile facilities increased from 100 per 100,000 in 1979 to 150 per 100,000 in 1991 (Jones & Krisberg, 1994). Programs in the private sector enjoy freedoms and benefits not possible in state institutions. Private agencies: (a) can easily circumvent the burdensome bureaucracy of the state system, (b) are more receptive to innovative treatment philosophies and "cutting edge" techniques, (c) tend to be housed in newer and well maintained facilities, and (d) acquire instruments and equipment of higher quality. The music therapist in this setting is more likely to gain access to "state of the art" training and education opportunities.

The number of adjudicated youths educated in public schools is on the rise in this country (Jones & Krisberg, 1994). Music therapists may be hired by the public schools or the residential facilities from which the students are referred. One state training school for young felony offenders in Michigan places many of its students in their regular junior high or high school, depending upon the youths' safety within the community, the level of risk they pose to the community, and their educational needs. In this particular situation, music therapy is provided after school, in the evenings, and on weekends at the residential facility and is viewed as a rehabilitative/supportive service, along with therapeutic recreation, individual counseling, and academic tutoring.

Despite blatant differences between most public and private facilities, a successful music therapy program can be launched and maintained in either setting. In this writer's opinion, more important than the environment is the therapist's competence, dedication to the students, enthusiasm for the work, resourcefulness, and creativity.

Music Therapy and the Interdisciplinary Treatment Team

The complex nature of delinquency requires treatment that is highly coordinated. Ideally, this coordination is overseen by an interdisciplinary treatment team comprised of professionals who represent all facets of the therapeutic program. Teachers, educational aides, youth workers, group leaders/counselors, family therapists, psychologists, social workers, and adjunct staff (i.e., music, art, recreational, and occupational therapists; healthcare workers; volunteers; religious/spiritual counselors; and community liaisons) all have a role in assessing and treating the young people to whom they have been assigned. Unlike some professionals who serve on only one treatment team representing a finite group of youth, the music therapist in juvenile corrections may serve the entire student population of a residential facility. In this case, he or she is an active member of several interdisciplinary teams. This position can be an awesome responsibility, for it requires not only becoming acquainted with all staff but also understanding and respecting the unique personality of each team. Rules and "norms" may differ from team to team even though each operates as part of the same facility. Likewise, each team may respond differently toward the music therapist. Ideally, the music therapist's input is welcomed and his or her services are solicited. In the worst case scenario, however, the music therapist is viewed as an outsider who competes for time with other "more necessary" educational or therapeutic services. Therefore, in-service training on the foundations and benefits of music therapy in this field is often needed.

Referrals

Since music therapy is not ordinarily mandated by the IEP committee, referrals for treatment may come from a variety of sources, especially if a facility espouses *team primacy* (i.e., each member of the interdisciplinary team has equal power and equal responsibility in the adolescents' treatment). Referrals may be informal (e.g., a phone call from the group leader requesting treatment), or formal (e.g., a written referral form specific to the facility and signed by all members of the team). It is the music therapist's task to educate his or her colleagues as to which students might be indicated for involvement in therapy. General referral criteria are specific to each facility, but may include: treatment needs/goals (e.g., develop interpersonal relationships, express feelings related to criminal behavior, boost sense of individuality, etc.), interest in music, musical talent, and prior involvement in music activities or music therapy.

Assessment

As with other populations, the music therapist who works with young offenders gathers crucial information through a multifaceted process of assessment. This process may begin with an informal conversation with the referring agent. Each student entering a treatment facility is preceded by a file folder containing comprehensive and helpful information about the student's history and resulting needs. A dialogal interview or written survey enables the clinician to identify the student's preferences and interests, as well as prior musical training. Through engaging students in both receptive (e.g., song discussion, life music collage) and active music experiences (e.g., improvisation, singing/playing), the therapist is able to determine individual strengths and deficits as well as peer group dynamics that may not be revealed through conventional verbal assessment techniques. Ongoing appraisal allows for changes in treatment aims, scope, configuration, or methodology related to the student's progress. Standardized music therapy assessments for this population are not readily available; rather, they must be created for unique settings and circumstances with each agency's treatment philosophy as a guide.

Goals and Interventions

The goals of music therapy treatment for young offenders can be classified within four behavioral domains: emotional, social, physical, and cognitive (academic). Table 1 outlines long-term goals and short-term objectives in each of these domains and provides music therapy interventions that can be used to accomplish these aims.

Emotional Domain

Music experiences can assist teenagers in exploring and expressing their feelings, values, ideas, opinions—even secrets. For example, music with powerful lyrics can be used therapeutically to stimulate group discussion about themes such as drug use, crime, sexuality, interpersonal relationships, current social events, or family dynamics. Group songwriting encourages the expression of thoughts and feelings. Freed (1987) reports that writing songs can provide opportunities for validation of feelings, self-awareness, socialization, listening, establishing rapport, building empathy, and solving problems within a group. Self-esteem can also be positively altered through the use of music. Successful singing and playing experiences can lead to increased confidence and a sense of mastery and control of one's world.

Social Domain

Music therapy programs in residential care can address adolescents' valid needs for peer interaction, appropriate competition, relaxation, and leisure. Brooks (1989) suggests that, ". . . music therapy is the preferred treatment method in helping adolescents improve their interaction skills with peers" (p. 38). A performance group, such as a band or handbell choir, assists in the development of many social skills. Besides learning care, maintenance, and basic playing technique on a particular instrument, a sense of responsibility and cooperation is fostered. Youths learn to give and accept constructive feedback about their playing from their peers. A successful performance in the community may help the young offender and the citizens of that community feel more positively toward one another. Finally, music is a viable leisure pursuit for students who have few nondelinquent interests.

Physical Domain

Regular exercise is a vital component of a rehabilitation program for any age group, particularly adolescents. This may be offered through traditional physical education and recreation programs as well as through creative arts such as music, dance, and drama. Motor activity can not only help to increase strength, endurance, and flexibility, but can also provide an outlet for excess energy, anger, or frustration. Exercise to music may promote muscle toning and weight loss, thereby improving self-image. Body image is particularly negative among youthful offenders, a high percentage of whom have been physically and/or sexually abused (Lewis et al., 1988).

Educating youths about their bodies is also essential. Using music activities to generate open talk about topics such as anatomy, sexuality, and pregnancy, for example, can help alleviate some of the anxiety teens commonly feel about their rapidly changing bodies and labile emotions. Through music and movement techniques, adolescents can learn to appreciate their bodies, their space, and the space of others (Brooks, 1989).

Cognitive (Academic) Domain

Music can serve as a reinforcer for the development of academic skills. It may be used as a contingency (e.g., the students who have completed their mathematics assignments are allowed to sing with the chorus which meets immediately after school). Music therapy interventions can also teach academic concepts. Songwriting, lyric analysis and musical games can promote spelling, reading, and writing skills. Learning about current and historical events can be fun when music is interjected into the learning process. Students who have difficulty learning via traditional methods may especially benefit from the multisensory nature of the musical experience.

Goals typically associated with music education may be addressed, depending upon the needs and interests of the students, the educational requirements of the state, and the educational philosophy of the facility in which the therapist works. Often, basic rhythmic and melodic concepts are taught as a prerequisite to other activities (e.g., songwriting and performance ensembles).

Music Therapy Service Delivery

Documentation

In both public and private residential settings, documentation is of utmost importance. Students' behaviors are closely monitored and recorded. As with other aspects of service in this setting, documentation requirements will vary from site to site. Once a student has been referred for treatment, a written *assessment* form may be required before a *program plan* (i.e., treatment plan outlining educational and therapeutic goals) is developed. Both of these records may be placed in the student's permanent file. Ongoing *progress notes* inform other members of the interdisciplinary treatment team as to the student's progress toward goals and objectives. Finally, an *after-care plan* detailing future goals and interventions may be required.

Direct Service

Music therapists in residential settings for juvenile offenders are most often hired to provide direct client service to both groups and individuals. Recognizing that young offenders are typically resistant to adult authority, many rehabilitation programs embrace a group-oriented treatment modality such as Positive Peer Culture (PPC), in which the peer group is viewed as the principal agent of change (Brendtro & Ness, 1983). In this environment, the music therapist may be limited to group experiences. In many instances, a student may attend a music therapy session because it has been mandated by his group's professional treatment team, not because he wants to be involved. Some students may feel afraid, apprehensive, or resentful about participating. Thus, initial music therapy experiences should be low risk, requiring minimal musical skill

Table 1
Goals/Objectives/Interventions

DOMAIN: EMOTIONAL

    Goal: To enhance the identification and healthy expression of feelings

        Objective: To stimulate feeling responses
        Interventions: Guided music listening*, creative movement

        Objective: To increase the verbal and nonverbal expression of feelings
        Interventions: Instrumental improvisation, song-writing, singing, creative movement, singing and sign language

    Goal: To build self-esteem

        Objective: To improve body image
        Interventions: Creative movement, dance, music and exercise

        Objective: To reduce shame for past behaviors and experiences
        Interventions: Guided music listening, song-writing

        Objective: To build confidence through skill mastery
        Interventions: Performance ensembles, vocal and instrumental instruction

DOMAIN: SOCIAL

    Goal: To promote the development of positive relationships

        Objective: To decrease isolation
        Interventions: Performance ensembles, dance, recreational music

        Objective: To increase verbal interaction
        Interventions: Singing, musical games, guided music listening

        Objective: To increase self-disclosure
        Interventions: Song-writing, guided music listening

        Objective: To develop leadership skills
        Interventions: Musical games, performance ensembles

        Objective: To provide opportunities for healthy competition
        Interventions: Musical games

DOMAIN: PHYSICAL

    Goal: To improve physical health (i.e., strength, mobility, endurance, coordination, and balance)

        Objective: To develop gross motor skills
        Interventions: Creative movement, dance, singing and sign language, music and exercise

        Objective: To develop fine motor skills
        Interventions: Creative movement, singing and sign language, instrumental instruction

        Objective: To reduce physical stress
        Interventions: Guided music listening, dance, creative movement

DOMAIN: COGNITIVE (ACADEMIC)

> **Goal**: To increase ability to receive, process, and express information
>> *Objective*:   To increase attending and following directions
>> *Interventions*: Performance ensembles, musical games, instrumental instruction
>>
>> *Objective*:   To improve short- and long-term memory
>> *Interventions*: Performance ensembles, singing, instrumental instruction, dance, musical games
>>
>> *Objective*:   To support specific educational goals (e.g., reading, history, etc.)
>> *Interventions*: Guided music listening, song-writing, musical games

---

Adapted by this writer with permission from M. Thaut (Ed.). (2002). *Music Therapy in the Treatment of Adults With Mental Disorders*, MMB Music.

* "Guided Music Listening" is defined as music and relaxation, Guided Imagery and Music (GIM), and music listening and discussion activities.

level and little individual self-disclosure from the youths in the group. The therapist's goal is to equalize the group so that each individual member feels he or she has made a competent contribution to the musical experience (Gardstrom, 1987). Group drumming, chanting, and singing are interventions suitable for a "fledgling" group in which participation, trust, and cohesiveness are minimal. As a group matures, "riskier" interventions such as improvisation and songwriting are indicated.

Several therapeutic aims can be accomplished through individual music therapy. Individual sessions can provide students the opportunity to: (a) develop a positive relationship with an adult/authority figure, (b) express thoughts and feelings in a personal way, (c) develop an interest or skill needing concentrated attention, (d) gain confidence and learn how to maintain it within the context of the peer group, and (e) experience unconditional care and concern from an adult/parent figure. Consider the following case example:

> "Paula," age 15, was sent to the state training school after having assaulted two peers at her junior high school with a baseball bat. Although the assault was Paula's first felony offense, she had exhibited problem behaviors at home and in the classroom since age 10.
>
> Paula had a moderate hearing loss in one ear and a mild loss in the other due to physical abuse by her father when she was a toddler. Although she had an IQ within normal range (95), Paula was labeled a "slow learner" by teachers in elementary school and "isolative" by the school social worker. Her slight speech impairment was thought to be the result of her problematic home life. In fourth grade, her hearing was tested and the impairment discovered. She was fitted for hearing aids which she wore sporadically prior to her arrival at the school.
>
> Paula was transported to the training school in hand and foot restraints due to her assaultive behavior. She spit and cursed at the other students and attempted to bite anyone who touched her. Paula was separated from her peer group until she no longer proved a physical threat to herself and others, about 1 week. When she rejoined the group, she was withdrawn and sullen. She rarely spoke, although she appeared to listen and occasionally wept when the other students talked in group meeting about problems in their families.
>
> When Paula was first introduced to the music therapist at the school, she was shy but polite. She told the music therapist that she had taken 1 year of piano lessons when she was 8 or 9 years

old and had "really liked it." The therapist informed her that students could "earn" individual music therapy sessions and then referred her to her peer group for more information.

During group music therapy, Paula vacillated between isolating herself and acting in a belligerent manner. Several times during the first 3 months of treatment, Paula was physically restrained during music therapy after threatening to hurt her peers.

One day in the fourth month, the music therapist asked Paula's group to participate in a special activity involving a musical timeline. Students were allowed to browse through a collection of tapes and CDS and were directed to choose four musical selections which represented significant years or periods in their lives. Paula refused to participate in the activity and sat quietly while the others shared their findings. As one group member played "Luca" and spoke about the sexual abuse she had endured from both her father and her uncle, Paula began to sob. The group supported her efforts to talk about her own secret—that she, too, had been sexually abused as a child. This admission was a turning point in Paula's treatment. She became gentler, less hostile, and more cooperative. She also began taking responsibility for her own behavior.

After Paula had been at the school for 6 months, she requested individual music therapy sessions. This first request was denied by her treatment team because she had been refusing to wear her hearing aids to school on campus and had fallen behind in her work. Three weeks later, Paula asked for music therapy again. The request was approved as she had worn her hearing aids every day without fail and had completed all homework assignments.

Paula came to her first Tuesday session without either of her hearing aids. The therapist explained that it was imperative Paula wear the aids so that teaching and learning could be successful. Paula was then escorted back to her living unit to retrieve the aids but she refused to put them on. She sat in the corner of the room, seemingly embarrassed. The therapist noted Paula's behavior in the staff log book and restated the expectation that Paula wear her hearing aids to each and every session. On the following Tuesday and every Tuesday henceforth, Paula met the expectation.

Based on observations of Paula in her group, discussions with the interdisciplinary treatment team, and a brief interview with Paula, the music therapist determined the following objectives for treatment: To increase the verbal and nonverbal expression of feelings, to build confidence through skill mastery, to decrease isolation, and to develop fine motor skills. Initially, Paula's reason for wanting the sessions was to "learn to play the piano again." During the first three sessions, the music therapist reviewed rhythmic and melodic concepts. Musical notation was introduced and homework was assigned.

The course of treatment changed as the therapeutic relationship blossomed and Paula's skills improved. She began to disclose information about her physical and sexual abuse and her resulting feelings. The focus of the sessions turned to listening and discussion and songwriting activities. One original song, which Paula entitled, "Devil in My Dreams," talked about the intense fear she felt each evening and her rage toward her mother for "letting the devil come in." At the music therapist's suggestion, Paula played a tape of the song in her family meeting in order to help her convey these feelings to her mother.

After 11 months at the training school, Paula earned her release from the treatment program. A few weeks before Paula left, the music therapist conducted an "exit interview" during which Paula had a chance to communicate her impressions of the therapy sessions and to set some musical goals for her return to regular public education. Before she left, Paula indicated a desire to play percussion in the marching band at her school. The therapist gave Paula a "crash course" in marching band instrumentation and mallet techniques. She then placed a phone call to the band director and offered support for Paula's future involvement.

A follow-up call 6 months after her release indicated that Paula was living with her mother and had not been re-arrested. She was enrolled in school and was maintaining average to above-average grades. She was working in a supermarket and was described by her boss as a "friendly, hardworking girl." Although the band teacher at Paula's school determined that her musical skill level did not allow her to play in the marching band, he invited her to serve as the band librarian, assist in fundraising events, and travel with the band to all social and athletic activities.

Consultation/Collaboration

Music therapists who provide direct service may also serve as consultants. For example, in one detention facility in Ohio, the music therapist provided treatment for the youth as well as communicated on a regular basis with the program school, social service and probation division, and the staff psychologist. In addition, the therapist collaborated with community-based organizations, helping students become involved in positive music experiences upon discharge (Steele & Smith, 1996).

The Future of Juvenile Justice

Juvenile justice experts are voicing concern about the increase in juvenile admissions to detention centers and the overcrowding and fiscal strain which results. Research suggests that the numbers of youths confined in these facilities can be substantially reduced without unduly jeopardizing the community (Schwartz, Barton, & Orlando, 1991). Small, intensive programs for serious and violent offenders can succeed with most youths when coupled with integrated community-based systems (Jones & Krisberg, 1994). Such alternatives to long-term residential treatment have been successfully implemented in Massachusetts, Utah, and Missouri (Barton, 1994). One can only speculate as to the impact this type of reform may have on the profession of music therapy. Will jobs be lost with the downsizing and closing of large residential institutions? Or will jobs be gained in community programs? Jones and Krisberg (1994) write:

> Existing research strongly supports the need for a comprehensive violence reduction strategy. This strategy should include prevention programs, intermediate sanctions, well-structured community based programs, small secure facilities for the most serious offenders and sound re-entry and aftercare services. (p. 7)

They continue:

> . . . prevention programs must emphasize opportunities for healthy social, physical, and mental development. Such programs must involve all components of the community, including schools, healthcare professionals, families, neighborhood groups, law enforcement, and community-based organizations. (p. 41)

Will more prevention-based programs be established thereby opening the door to a whole new form of preventative school music therapy?

Privatization of state correctional systems may also affect the status of music therapy with the delinquent population. Barton (1994) writes:

> Maryland and Colorado have already turned over their training schools to private providers, and other states may follow suit. The merits of private institutions have not yet been determined. Proponents claim that private programs offer greater administrative flexibility, more treatment

integrity, and greater cost-effectiveness. Critics note the lack of standards and monitoring and the potential for cost cutting at the expense of the youths in care. (p. 1572)

Will private music therapy practitioners find their niche in this new system?

Summary

Youths are being confined in detention centers, state training schools and private correctional facilities at an alarming rate. Many of these youths respond to and benefit from the unique power of music. With the support and guidance of an interdisciplinary treatment team, the music therapist uses prescribed interventions to promote the emotional, social, physical, and cognitive (academic) growth of young offenders.

References

American Music Therapy Association. (2001). *Member sourcebook*. Silver Spring, MD: Author.

American Psychological Association. (1993). *Violence and youth: Psychology's response*. Washington, DC: Author.

Baird, S. C. (1987). *The development of risk prediction scales for the California Youthful Offender Parole Board*. San Francisco: National Council on Crime and Delinquency.

Barton, W. H. (1994). Juvenile corrections. In National Association of Social Workers (Ed.), *Encyclopedia of Social Work* (19th ed.). Washington, DC: NASW Press.

Blumstein, A., Farrington, D. P., & Moitra, S. (1985). Delinquency careers: Innocents, desisters, and persisters. In M. Tonry & N. Morris (Eds.), *Crime and Justice, 6*, 187.

Brendtro, L., & Ness, A. (1983). *Re-educating troubled youth*. New York: Aldine.

Brooks, D. M. (1989). Music therapy enhances treatment with adolescents. *Music Therapy Perspectives, 6*, 37–39.

Eisenman, R. (1991). Is justice equal: A look at restitution, probation or incarceration in six states. *Louisiana Journal of Counseling and Development, 11*(2), 47–50.

Elliot, D., Huizinga, D., & Morse, B. (1988). A career analysis of serious violent offenders. In *Violent juvenile crime: What do we know about it and what can we do about it?* Ann Arbor: University of Michigan Press.

Freed, B. (1987). Songwriting with the chemically dependent. *Music Therapy Perspectives, 4*, 13–18.

Gardstrom, S. (1987). Positive peer culture: A working definition for the music therapist. *Music Therapy Perspectives, 4*, 19–23.

Greenwood, P. (1986). Differences in criminal behavior and court responses among juvenile and young adult defendants. In M. Tonry & N. Morris (Eds.), *Crime and Justice, 7*, 151.

Jones, M. A., & Krisberg, B. (1994). *Images and reality: Juvenile crime, youth violence, and public policy*. San Francisco: National Council on Crime and Delinquency.

Krisberg, B. (1987). Preventing and controlling violent street crime: The state of the art. In *Violent juvenile crime: What do we know about it and what can we do about it?* Minneapolis: Center for the Study of Youth Policy.

Leone, P. E. (1994). Education services for youth with disabilities in a state-operated juvenile correctional system: Case study and analysis. *Journal of Special Education, 28*, 43–58.

Lewis, D. O., Moy, E., Jackson, L. D., Aaronson, R., Restifo, N., Serra, S., & Simos, A. (1985). Biopsychosocial characteristics of children who later murder: A prospective study. *American Journal of Psychiatry, 142*, 1161.

Lewis, D. O., Pincus, J. H., Bard, B., Richardson, E., Prichep, L. S., Feldman, M., & Yeager, C. (1988). Neuropsychiatric, psychoeducational, and family characteristics of 14 juveniles condemned to death in the United States. *American Journal of Psychiatry, 145*, 584.

Mahoney, A. R. (1991). Man, I'm already dead: Serious juvenile offenders in context. *Notre Dame Journal of Law, Ethics & Public Policy, 5*, 443.

National Association for Music Therapy. (1993). *Sourcebook*. Silver Spring, MD: Author.

National Coalition of State Juvenile Justice Advisory Groups. (1993). Myths and realities: Meeting the challenge of serious, violent, and chronic juvenile offenders. *1992 Annual Report*. Washington, DC: Author.

Schwartz, I. M. (1992). *Juvenile justice and public policy: Toward a national agenda*. New York: Lexington Press.

Schwartz, I. M., Barton, W. H., & Orlando, F. (1991). Keeping kids out of secure detention. *Public Welfare, Spring 20–26*, 46.

Steele, A., & Smith, L. (1996). *Music therapy in a center for juvenile offenders: A program development model*. Cleveland, OH: The Cleveland Music School Settlement.

Thaut, M. (Ed.). (2002). *Music therapy in the treatment of adults with mental disorders* (2nd ed.) St. Louis, MO: MMB Music.

United States Department of Justice. (1991). *Juveniles taken into custody: Fiscal year 1990 report*. Washington, DC: Office of Juvenile Justice and Delinquency Prevention.

11

MUSIC THERAPY FOR LEARNERS WITH SEVERE DISABILITIES IN A PUBLIC SCHOOL SETTING

Kathleen A. Coleman

IN the public school setting, students with the label "severely/profoundly handicapped" or "SPH" or "MH" are generally the most impaired and lowest functioning students served by the district. Typically, their functioning tends to be under a two-year developmental level and may reflect a diagnosis of mental retardation, autism, cerebral palsy, and/or sensory impairments. It is also common in this setting to find students who have more than one handicapping condition.

Despite the diversity of their disabilities, these students often have some similar educational needs. Since academic goals in the traditional areas of reading, writing, and mathematics have little relevance for this population, educational programming for these students primarily focuses on the acquisition of the most functional life skills in the areas of communication, socialization, and self-help (activities of daily living). The music therapist who works with this group of students will need to focus his or her energies on developing strategies that reinforce these very basic skills.

According to IDEA, the educational placement for each student with special needs is to be made on an individual basis; thus, placements even for students with similar disabilities can vary widely. For example, students in Texas with severe/profound disabilities may be found in segregated special schools, self-contained special education classrooms on age appropriate campuses, or in fully inclusive placements in their home schools. Placements for students with severe disabilities can also vary within the same school district, as a result of different opinions among families as to the educational needs of their child. The music therapist will need creativity and flexibility in order to provide meaningful services to students within their particular type of educational placement.

Service Delivery Models and Choices

With the help of the special education administrator, the first step for the music therapist is to determine the types of service delivery models that can potentially be utilized when a student is designated as requiring music therapy to benefit from his or her education. The final choice of service delivery for a student, though, can only be made once the assessment is completed. It is illegal to predetermine (without parental input) exactly the services or type of service delivery a student will receive. The potential choices of models that can be utilized are shown in Table 1.

Table 1
Music Therapy Service Delivery Model

Direct: Student	Consult: Student	Consult: Teacher & Program
Must be referred by IEP committee for assessment	Must be referred by IEP committee for assessment	No official IEP committee referral
Formal assessment required	Formal assessment required	No formal assessment required
Observation/Record review required	Observation/Record review required	Observation/Record review required
Teacher interview required	Teacher interview required	Teacher interview required
Parent input required	Parent input required	Parent input may be solicited
Separate music therapy goals and objectives OR initialing of IEP goals and objectives required.	Separate music therapy goals OR initialing of IEP goals and objectives required	No separate music therapy goals and objectives
Therapist designs and implements hands-on music therapy program for student as designated in his/her IEP	Therapist designs, demonstrates and monitors carry through of music therapy program for a special education student as designated in his/her IEP	Therapist designs and demonstrates music therapy program appropriate for the whole classroom and/or designated students
Therapist sees students individually OR in small groups (size of group depends on the student's disability)	Therapy is carried out individually or in small groups initially by the therapist, then continued by designated special education personnel AND monitored by the therapist.	Therapy is carried out with the class as a whole or with designated students by the therapist, with teacher providing reinforcement of the techniques throughout the week

Direct Service

In this model, the student receives weekly or biweekly individual or group sessions directly from the music therapist. The related service of music therapy is identified on the student's IEP as a required service that will assist the student in benefiting from his or her special education program. An individual music therapy assessment is required under this model of service. For students who qualify for music therapy, the therapist will either write a separate page of goals and objectives, or, in the case of an integrated IEP, will initial specific objectives on the master IEP that can be addressed through music therapy. With students who have severe/profound disabilities, the "integrated IEP" approach is often the most effective route to take, since the skills being addressed by the teacher and other therapists will be very similar in nature, due to the low functioning level of the students. Writing separate goals and objectives in these types of situations is generally seen as repetitious. Delivery of service through this model can be effective whether the student is in a self-contained setting or an inclusive setting.

Consult Service

In this model, the student initially receives weekly or bi-weekly individual or group sessions directly from the music therapist for a set period of time—perhaps 6 to 10 weeks. During this period, the teacher is observing the sessions and being trained by the music therapist to carry out a specifically designed program for a student or group of students. Once the teacher begins implementing the program, the music therapist then monitors the program on a consistent basis, usually a minimum of once or twice a month. This ongoing monitoring of the music therapy program is necessary for the model of service to be considered an actual "consult to student." Without the regular monitoring from the music therapist, the service cannot meet the educational needs of the student. When a student receives consult service, the related service of music therapy continues to be identified on the student's IEP as a required related service that will assist the student in benefiting from his or her special education program. An individual music therapy assessment is also required under this model of service. Goals and objectives are developed in the same manner as described above for the direct service model. Consult service to the student can be effective, provided the teacher is willing to carry out the program designed by the music therapist and is also responsive to ongoing supervision and consultation. Delivery of service through this model can be effective with students in the self-contained setting. If the student is in an inclusive setting, consult service to the student will be successful only if there is personnel available to regularly implement the program designed by the music therapist.

Consult Service—Program Based

In this model, the services of the music therapist are designed to support the overall programming for self-contained classrooms such as early childhood, autism classes, and life skill classes. The music therapist works with the teacher in designing a group-based music therapy program that can be implemented with the entire class. Under this service delivery model, each student's IEP states that a music therapist will be serving as a consultant to the specific program (e.g., early childhood). An individual music therapy assessment is not required under this model. However, each student's IEP is reviewed by the music therapist in order to extract a list of skills that will then be a part of the group program designed by the therapist. In this model of service delivery, the music therapist provides weekly demonstration sessions with mandatory teacher and aide participation. The focus is on familiarizing the teacher and aide with the session materials, so that the music therapy session can be repeated throughout the week. This model is often the most effective with severe/profound disabilities. The weekly presence of the therapist combined with the consistent follow-through by the teacher tends to generate the greatest results. Paperwork is minimized under this model, allowing the music therapist more time to design strategies and materials for use in the sessions.

Assessment

The music therapist cannot begin an actual music therapy assessment until a student has been referred for such an assessment by the Individualized Education Program (IEP) committee. The assessment of a student with severe/profound disabilities should be done utilizing both a formal and informal approach. Since these students are very low functioning, it is critical to observe them in several settings, in addition to conducting the actual music therapy assessment. Students can respond very differently, depending on the personnel with whom they are interacting, their current state of health, effects of medications, as well as many other factors. In order to make an accurate decision as to whether or nor music therapy is a required related service, the music therapist has to determine whether, in fact, music therapy interventions provide the student with significant motivation and/or significant assists in meeting IEP goals and objectives.

One method of assessment that has been effective with students with severe/profound disabilities is the "SEMTAP: Special Education Music Therapy Assessment Process" (Brunk & Coleman, 2000). This method consists of a study of each student's unique problems and needs. It compares the student's performance of skills *with* and *without* music therapy strategies. (See Chapter 5 for additional information about the SEMTAP.)

Since the IEP committee members will most likely not have observed the assessment process and assessment session, the only input they will consider at the meeting is the written report. Therefore, regardless of the assessment procedure that is used, it is critical that the report be professional and thorough and include the following information:

- the purpose of the assessment
- an outline of the assessment procedure
- relevant information from the files reviewed by the therapist
- information from the interviews (be sure to indicate who made each statement)
- summary of the classroom observation
- description of the setting and general student behavior on the day of testing
- results of the assessment
- recommendations
- suggestions

It is important to remember that the standard for therapeutic intervention in a school district is different from one that would be used in a residential facility, private practice, or medical facility (see Table 2). In order to recommend music therapy, the music therapist must describe how the music therapy intervention would significantly assist the student in benefiting from his or her educational program. The therapist may see potential or abilities that could be nurtured, but the special education administration only wants to know whether music therapy will provide a necessary and effective way for the student to meet IEP goals and objectives. If the music therapist is new to working in the school system, it is important to talk with other experienced therapists to make the language in the report consistent with that used by other education professionals.

Comparing the student's demonstrated abilities with and without music therapy intervention is a primary objective of the assessment process. If the student performs as well or better in the classroom without music, then music therapy is not an educationally necessary service. With an individual who has severe/profound disabilities, the response to music is usually very definite—he or she may be much more alert and responsive, or may not react al all.

When writing a report for the IEP committee, it is necessary to make a *clear* distinction between recommendations and suggestions. Recommendations indicate your professional opinion regarding the school district's responsibility to the student. Because these recommendations can be used as future evidence in legal proceedings, statements made in this section need to be substantiated. Another section entitled "Suggestions" is appropriate for your comments on the role music could play in the home, or the availability of

Table 2
Music Therapy Models

School Based Model	Medical Model	Private Therapy
Goal: To assist a student with disabilities in attaining educational goals. To train educational staff in the use of music therapy strategies to assist students in attaining educational goals.	*Goal:* To treat the client's continuum of needs (from acute through rehabilitated status).	*Goal:* To assist the client with disabilities in attaining educational goals. To provide more intensive help towards meeting educational goals than is possible in the school setting. To provide enrichment and quality of life.
Frequency of Sessions: Based on educational need as specified in the Individualized Education Program (IEP) for a student.	*Frequency of Sessions:* As prescribed.	*Frequency of Sessions:* As decided upon by the parent and the therapist. May also be prescribed.
Caseload of Therapist: Larger, students usually seen in small groups ranging from two to eight students.	*Caseload of Therapist:* Smaller, clients usually seen individually.	*Caseload of Therapist:* Smaller, clients usually seen individually or in very small groups.
Implementer of Services: Therapist, school personnel, parent.	*Implementer of Services:* Therapist, parent.	*Implementer of Services:* Therapist, parent.
Duration of Therapy: Ranges from one time consult to weekly or bi-weekly services for one or more years.	*Duration of Therapy:* Determined by medical needs of client. May be short or long term.	*Duration of Therapy:* Weekly or bi-weekly services for as long as client indicates need.
Decisions on Therapy: Made by the IEP committee.	*Decisions on Therapy:* Made by doctor, therapist, and parent.	*Decisions on Therapy:* Made by the parent and therapist.
Service Delivery: Direct therapy, and/or with the following: consult with student and/or teacher, program equipment consultation, individual and classroom modifications, inservice training.	*Service Delivery:* Direct service with some parent consultation; recommendations and suggestions for equipment.	*Service Delivery:* Direct service with some parent consultation; recommendations and suggestions for equipment.

programming in agencies outside the school district. This is helpful information for families, but does not designate services the school district is obligated to provide.

The IEP Process

Once the assessment has been completed, including the recommendation as to whether or not service should be provided, a meeting of the IEP committee is scheduled. Several days prior to the meeting, the parents and all others on the IEP team should be provided a copy of the music therapy assessment report to review. It is inappropriate to ask people to make meaningful educational decisions based on a lengthy report that is read for the first time at the meeting. Prior preparation, in the form of reading the music therapy assessment report, by all team members ensures that a thoughtful, meaningful discussion of that student's educational needs will occur.

During the IEP meeting, the music therapy assessment, along with any other assessments of the student will be reviewed. The results of the reports will be discussed, and the committee will attempt to arrive at a consensus of opinion as to which recommendations will be implemented. Remember that the recommendation could be for or against the provision of music therapy. The therapist may be called upon to defend the recommendation and answer questions but will not (because music therapy is a related service) be part of the group (administration representative, teacher, and parents) that arrives at the final consensus.

If it is determined that music therapy service will be provided, a discussion and development of IEP objectives will follow. While the music therapist may bring a draft of suggested objectives to the meeting, it must be *only* a draft. Developing an IEP is a group process completed at the meeting and must include the presence and full participation of the parents of the student. As discussed earlier in the chapter, the music therapist may develop a separate page of objectives for the IEP or initial objectives on the main IEP draft that would be appropriate for music therapy intervention. Choosing which approach to use is determined by the school district.

A music therapist can be a helpful part of the IEP process, particularly in assisting the committee to write clearly worded, functional objectives for the student. The acronym "SMART" is a valuable tool when writing objectives:

S   specific
M   measurable
A   attainable
R   realistic
T   time frame

With students who have severe/profound disabilities, it is important to look at the long term value of a skill. Because the learning process will be very slow with these students, it is critical that the skills chosen by the IEP committee reflect functional, age appropriate skills that will have potential for assisting the student later in life. When an IEP has been drafted and approved by the core committee members (parent, teacher, administration), the document can be signed and the meeting is over.

If the music therapist is unable to attend the IEP meeting where the music therapy assessment is to be reviewed, he or she should review the report with a committee member and with the parents prior to the meeting. Otherwise, the parents may exercise their right to request the re-scheduling of the IEP meeting to a time when the music therapist can be present to discuss the assessment.

Session Planning and Task Analysis

Music therapy sessions for students with severe/profound disabilities will tend to focus on very basic skills. Some of the most commonly addressed skills in music therapy sessions for this type of student include:

- holding and grasping objects
- manipulating objects
- eye contact
- focus of attention
- indicating by gesture or movement these words: finished, hello, goodbye, more, yes/no
- following simple one step directions
- accessing and operating a pressure switch
- utilizing simple augmentative communication devices (Big Mack, etc.)
- imitating gestures
- reaching and touching objects
- recognizing voices and faces
- showing awareness of self
- localizing sound
- making choices between several items
- matching
- sorting

For students with severe/profound disabilities, skills need to be task analyzed into the smallest and simplest of steps. Conferring with the special education teacher and other therapists can be an enormously helpful way to ensure that all tasks have been broken down sufficiently. Progress is often measured in tiny increments with these students.

Sessions need to balance frequent repetition with some variety. A significant advantage of music therapy for this population is that students can work on the same learning task for a long time since music therapy strategies can be varied in order to maintain their interest. A group session for students with severe/profound disabilities is typically more like a series of one-to-one interactions since each student frequently lacks the requisite skills to respond as a collective group. For example, rather than give a group direction such as "everybody clap your hands" and then expect everyone to respond appropriately, the therapist would most likely need to provide individual attention to each student to accomplish this task. Even though the students are not able to respond as a group, they can still benefit from watching their peers respond. In some cases, the students will learn important concepts such as waiting and taking turns simply by watching others.

Age appropriateness is also an issue to carefully consider when providing music therapy interventions for these students. Even though they will learn very slowly and function at a low developmental level, it is important whenever possible to use music and materials that are consistent with chronological age. This definitely demands creativity on the part of the therapist!

One way to plan effective sessions for students with severe/profound disabilities is to work from a general session outline—choosing songs and strategies using the materials listed below and matching the materials and strategies to an overall list of skills from each student's IEP. The following outlines suggest a plan for elementary school students and a plan for middle school/high school students.

Elementary School Outline

- **Hello song:** Select a song that will be consistently used to open the session. It is helpful if the song offers opportunities for the group members to attempt to perform simple actions such as shaking hands, making eye contact, patting knees or clapping hands.

  Possible Objectives: Eye contact, name recognition, hand shaking

- **Puppets:** Select a song or two that feature puppets that are colorful and that have interesting fabric textures. Songs that feature the puppets making silly sounds or performing silly actions may provoke responses from the students.

Possible Objectives: Vocalizing, holding and grasping items, focus of attention, reaching and touching objects

- **Percussion instruments:** Select percussion instruments that have an unusual sound or appearance, such as the rainstick, cabasa, or clatterpillar. These types of instruments are often more motivating to low functioning students and encourage increased attention and interaction. Choose songs that match the sound quality of the instrument. Adapt mallets (see end of this chapter) for students who can not hold them in typical ways.

  Possible Objectives: Focus of attention, cause and effect, localizing sound, making a choice between several items, manipulating objects

- **Vocal imitation using voice activated device:** Select a song with a reoccurring line (e.g., "Train Is A Coming," which has "oh, yes" as a reoccurring line). Record this line on a voice-activated device such as a "Big Mack" (made by Ablenet). Prompt the students to depress the device at the correct time; thus allowing them to "sing" along.

  Possible Objectives: Vocal imitation, utilizing a voice activated device, following simple one step directions

- **Motor imitation:** Select a song with one or two actions. Prompt the students (hand over hand, if necessary) to complete the actions. Selected songs will need to be repeated many, many times with these students before responses are consistent.

  Possible Objectives: Imitating gestures or actions, following one step directions

- **Tagboard books:** Make a simple illustrated version of a familiar song into a book with tagboard pages. Pictures from magazines or coloring books can be used to develop patterns if the music therapist is not skilled at drawing. Commercially developed songbook patterns can be utilized to develop materials (see resource section). Attach small pieces of sponge between the pages to make the pages thicker and easier to turn. Prompt students to turn the pages as the song is sung.

  Possible Objectives: Holding and grasping objects, manipulating objects, focus of attention

- **Song file folders:** Make or locate pictures to illustrate key words in a song. It is best to choose a song with basic, concrete vocabulary words. Attach black and white pictures illustrating these words to the file folder and have students match the colored version of the picture to the folder as the song is sung. Severely physically involved students may indicate the correct picture for matching via eye gaze, or other alternate communication method.

  Possible Objectives: Matching, following simple one step directions

- **Large tone bars:** High quality wooden tone bars (such as those made by Sonor—see resource section) produce vibrations and sounds which can be appealing to low functioning students. Use the tone bars to play ostinato patterns to simple, familiar songs. Place the students between the tone bars or have them sit on the tone bars for additional stimulation.

  Possible Objectives: Localizing sound, showing awareness of self, eye contact, focus of attention

- **Manipulatives:** Use items such as bean bags, plastic hoops or yarn balls and encourage the students to pick up and manipulate these items according to directions in a song.

Possible Objectives: Localizing sound, showing awareness of self, eye contact, focus of attention

- **Good-bye song:** For closing the session, select a song that encourages eye contact, name recognition and waving good-bye.

Possible Objectives: Imitating gestures, eye contact, focus of attention, hand shaking

Middle School/High School Outline

- **Hello song:** Select a song to regularly begin the session. Aim to be age appropriate by using adapted versions of popular songs, or songs that stylistically approach popular or folk types of music. (e.g., "Hello, How Are You" recording by The Doors).

Possible Objectives: Eye contact, handshaking, self-awareness, name recognition

- **Q-Chord:** Have available a selection of song choice cards which contain a picture illustrating the song on the front and words and chords printed on the back. Allow the student to choose a song from a choice of two cards. Program the Q-Chord with the chords to the selected songs and prompt the student to depress the "one touch play" button at the correct time.

Possible Objectives: Making choices between several items, following one step directions, finger isolation

- **Percussion instruments:** Use a variety of percussion instruments, including those with unusual sound or appearance. Encourage the students to play the instrument for the duration of a song. Utilize popular music when possible. Older rock and roll songs from the 50's and 60's are good choices (e.g., "La Bamba," recorded by Richie Valens). Adapt mallets (see end of chapter) for students who can not hold them.

Possible Objectives: Holding and grasping objects, manipulating objects, making choices between several items

- **Singing using a voice output device:** Select a song with a reoccurring line or a frequently repeated word (such as "I Get By With A Little Help From My Friends," recorded by the Beatles, which frequently repeats the word "friends"). Record this word on the voice output device (e.g., "Big Mack" by Ablenet). Prompt the students to depress the device at the correct time and "sing" along.

Possible Objectives: Vocalizing, operating a voice output device, responding to verbal cues in a song

- **Motor imitation:** Select an age appropriate song with one or two actions. Folk or camp songs are good song sources for older students. Prompt the students (hand over hand, if necessary) to complete the actions. Selected songs will need to be repeated numerous times with these students before any independent imitation starts to take place.

Possible Objectives: Imitating gestures, following one step directions

- **Tagboard books:** Make a simple illustrated version of a familiar song into a book made out of tagboard (heavier weight) paper. Pictures from magazines or coloring books can be used to develop patterns by the therapist or teacher who does not possess drawing skills. Commercially developed songbook patterns also can be utilized to develop materials (see equipment resource list at the end of the book). Attach small pieces of sponge between the pages to make the pages easier to turn. Prompt students to turn pages as the song is sung.

Possible Objectives: Holding and grasping objects, manipulating objects, following simple one step directions

- **Song file folders:** Make or locate pictures to illustrate key words in a song. It is best to choose a song that uses simple, concrete vocabulary words. Attach black and white pictures to the file folder and have students match the colored version of the picture to the folder as the song is sung. Severely physically involved students may indicate the correct picture for matching via eye gaze, or other alternative communication method.

  Possible Objectives: Matching, manipulating objects

- **Choir Chimes:** Use choir chimes to have students (if they can grasp) play a simple repeated ostinato to accompany a song (e.g., ring "C" and "G" over and over to "Row, Row, Row Your Boat"). For students who cannot grasp, the therapist can play the ostinato and encourage them to focus and turn towards the sound.

  Possible Objectives: Localizing sound, recognizing voices and faces, object manipulation

- **Good-bye Song:** Select a song to close the session that encourages eye contact, name recognition and waving good-bye. In consideration of age appropriateness, try to select a song that is an adaptation of a popular or folk song.

  Possible Objectives: Imitating gestures, focusing attention, eye contact, hand shaking

Consulting With Special Educators and Other Therapists

Regardless of which service delivery model is utilized (direct, consult, or consult to program), the music therapist's ability to consult and communicate effectively with the special educator and other therapists is the key to positive outcomes for the students. It is a rare school district that provides music therapy more than twice a week; therefore, follow through by the teacher (or other therapists) on the days between music therapy sessions is essential to the student's ability to benefit fully from music therapy.

Consulting with school district personnel is not just a matter of issuing orders and commands for others to follow. Skilled communication, demonstration of techniques and preparation of quality materials and tapes is essential. If the teacher feels that he or she is being treated in a demeaning manner by the music therapist, there will be no follow through. Since teachers and other personnel often may be apprehensive about their ability to sing or perform musical tasks, it is the job of the music therapist to task analyze this situation so that the teacher can easily carry through with the prescribed programming.

One helpful method is to create a notebook for the teacher that contains the following:

- general information about music therapy
- a schedule, showing where and how the music therapist can be contacted
- charts or data forms showing the relationship of learning objectives to the musical tasks
- copies of songs to be utilized in the sessions (only original songs, those in the public domain or those for which you have written permission to use)
- a cassette tape containing a completely recorded session—or a series of "ten minute" tapes containing one or two strategies each
- a section where the teacher can jot down questions, data, and other student responses for discussion with the music therapist during the next scheduled consultation

A notebook system, such as that described above, clearly shows the teacher what to do and how to do it. Since special educators are busy, with many demands on their time, developing a clearly organized program increases the likelihood of regular, weekly follow-through with the students.

Inclusion in Music Education Classes

Students with severe/profound disabilities may or may not be included in a regular music education class. This is an individually based decision that should be made at the student's IEP meeting. It is helpful at the meeting to consider the following questions before a decision is made to send a student to a regular music education class.

- Does the student have any hypersensitivity to sound that would make attending the regular music education class a problem for him or her?

- Can the student remain seated for the duration of the class?
    Independently?
    With a few verbal reminders from teacher or peers?
    With the presence of an adult support staff member?

- Can the student remain quiet at appropriate times during the class?
    Independently?
    With a few verbal reminders from teacher or peers?
    With the presence of an adult support staff member?

- Can the student keep his/her hands to himself and avoid hitting, pinching, or otherwise distracting the other students from learning?
    Independently?
    With a few verbal reminders from teacher or peers?
    With the presence of an adult support staff member

- Can the student use materials in the classroom in a reasonably appropriate manner? (i.e., refrain from tearing up textbooks, or mouthing or throwing instruments?)
    Independently?
    With a few verbal reminders from teacher or peers?
    With the presence of an adult support staff member?

- Would attending the class have a particular value or meaning for the student?

- Can the student participate in at least one of the activities presented in the lesson plan with or without modifications?

- If an adult support staff member is required, will there be an available person to attend the class with the student at the scheduled time?

When discussing this issue, there may be some confusion among school personnel as to why the student would be considered for a music education class if he/she is already receiving music therapy. It is important at that time to review with the school personnel the difference between a public school class (music education) and a related service (music therapy). Typically, music education classes teach music literacy and aesthetic appreciation to the students as a group, while music therapy focuses on individual learning skills selected from the IEP and presented to the student through the medium of music.

Although there is no easy answer as to whether a student with severe/profound disabilities should be included in regular music education classes, careful discussion of the above questions can enhance the chances for a successful experience for the student.

Basic Instrument Adaptations

Many students with severe/profound disabilities have physical or cognitive problems that require adaptation of materials. It is important to have quick and easy methods to adapt common materials used by the music therapist, particularly adaptations for use with simple percussion instruments. The following adaptations are inexpensive and easy to use.

One Wrap Velcro Straps: One wrap Velcro is Velcro that comes in one long strip with the rough texture on one side and the fuzzy texture on the other side. To assist a student in keeping grasp on an instrument (such as bells or a shaker), try the following:
- Cut two pieces of one wrap Velcro long enough to wrap around the student's hand.
- Place the instrument in the student's hand and wrap the two pieces of one wrap Velcro snugly around the student's hand, with the FUZZY side against the student's hand.

Mini Mallet: This adaptation will give you a "handle" in which to place the mallet securely. It will then attach to the student's hand with one wrap Velcro. This adaptation is best for students with small hands. The "mini mallet" is made as follows:

- Materials:
  — One piece of built up foam for spoon handles, cut to equal slightly more than the width of the student's palm
  — Two pieces of one wrap Velcro cut so that the pieces will wrap easily around the student's hand
  — One mallet, appropriate for use with that particular student
- Put the mallet inside the built up foam. Place the mallet and foam combination in the student's hand so that the end of the mallet sticks out between the index and middle fingers. Wrap the two pieces of one wrap Velcro snugly against the student's hand with the fuzzy side against the hand.

Super Mallet: This adaptation will give you a "handle" in which to place the mallet securely. It will attach to the student's hand with one wrap Velcro. This adaptation is best for students with larger hands. The "super mallet" is made as follows:

- Materials:
  —Eight inch piece of one wrap Velcro
  —One large rubber triangle pencil grip
  —One bicycle handlebar grip
  —One mallet
- Thread the piece of Velcro through the pencil grip, keeping the ends unattached.
- Thread the Velcro and the pencil grip through one end of the bicycle handlebar grip. Sometimes one end of the bicycle handlebar is larger than the other. In that case, thread it through the larger end.
- Pull the Velcro through the hold at the other end of the bicycle grip. You may need tweezers to do this if the grip has a smaller hole at the other end.
- Place a mallet in the pencil grip that is now inside of the bicycle grip. It will hold the mallet securely. The adapted mallet can now be placed in the student's hand and attached snugly with the ends of the Velcro.

Tips for Working with Students with Severe/Profound Disabilities

- Be patient, and remember that creative repetition is the key with this population.
- Be as age appropriate as possible!
- Think long term and functional; these students take a long time to learn skills; spend time on what is truly valuable.
- Use voice output devices to give students a voice to "talk" and "sing."
- Encourage teachers and parents by pointing out the positive improvements; people who are with the student every day may not notice these small increments of progress.
- Purchase and utilize quality, durable, and drool-proof equipment!

Tips for Working Collaboratively with Parents, Staff, and Administrators

- Use "active listening" approaches when conflicts arise, e.g., "What I hear you saying is . . . . . . and yet what I think is . . . ."
- Work at seeing a situation from the other person's perspective.
- Consistently show how music therapy dovetails with the school's approaches.
- Provide articles and handouts on music therapy for parents and staff to read.
- Be a "team player"; work cooperatively with parents and school personnel.
- Avoid communicating via "triangle." If you have a concern with a person, talk directly to that person and resolve your concern. Don't complain to third parties about the issue.
- There is no substitute for quality work when it comes to music therapy. See that the agencies and students with whom you work receive top quality service from you.

References

Brunk, B., & Coleman, K. (2000). Development of a special education music therapy assessment process. *Music Therapy Perspectives, 18*(1), 59–68.

12

MUSIC THERAPY FOR LEARNERS WITH AUTISM IN A PUBLIC SCHOOL SETTING

Angela M. Snell

> People treating autistic children should avoid falling into the trap of using just one type of treatment. A variety of methods used together would probably be the most successful. . . . A good program should also have flexible non-aversive behavior modification, sensory treatment, speech therapy, exercise, and music therapy.
>
> (Grandin & Scariano, 1986)

> The following are just some of the noises that still upset me enough to cover up my ears to avoid them; shouting, noisy crowded places, polystyrene being touched, balloons and aeroplanes, noisy vehicles on building sites, hammering and banging, electric tools being used, the sound of the sea, the sound of felt-tip or marker pens being used to colour in and fireworks. In fact when I am feeling angry and despairing of everything, music is the only way of making me feel calmer inside.
>
> (Jolliffe et al. as quoted by Attwood, 1998)

WHEN reviewing the literature related to autism, one finds there is an abundance of references to remarkable and/or unusual responses to music by persons with autism spectrum disorders, often with inconsistent responses to environmental sounds (Applebaum, Egel, Koegel, & Imhoff, 1979; Attwood, 1998; Berard, 1993; Edgerton, 1994; Grandin & Scariano, 1986; Kaufman, 1994; Kolko, Anderson, & Campbell, 1980; Rimland, 1964; Sherwin, 1953; Thaut, 1984; Toigo, 1992). Persons with autism may use music to block out their surroundings in order to cope with overwhelming stimuli. Is this an acceptable way to calm down after a stressful incident or could it be a perseverative action blocking cognitive and social development? Those trained in treatments for autism spectrum disorders know to look for ritualistic or perseverative behaviors which impede cognitive, motor, and/or social development. It is at this point that treatment techniques designed to interrupt the unproductive behavior are applied to reconnect the person with reality.

There are many types and combinations of treatment techniques ranging from physically adversive to noninvasive guidance. A music therapist would consider and support the treatment team's approach, but would first and foremost, use music to affect and support the individual. Therapeutic music applications allow the therapist to set firm or loose rules according to immediate needs effectively in a noninvasive manner. How does one decide if the person with autism who retreats to listen and rock stereotypically to music in a solitary world is productively "calming down" or is unproductively perseverating? The answer will depend upon the unique way autism affects the person and the individual's immediate and long-term needs. If the individual responds and conforms with live changes in the music (i.e., tempo, rhythm, or accompaniments added by a person in the room rather than a recording), this indicates a relationship to reality. If the person continues to rock or self-stimulate without regard to the live musical changes, chances are this individual is stuck in ritualistic or perseverative behavior and/or is trying to avoid participating in a task which is difficult or not to his or her liking. The music therapist carefully considers the events surrounding the behavior in combination with the music-related-behavior displayed.

What components of music help a person with autism find comfort? A music therapist would observe what musical components the individual responds to and note the physical reactions (i.e., breathing, eye gaze, body rocking, vocalizations). The therapist notices if the responses occur in relation to a specific key, an interesting melody pattern, instrumentation, tempo, or rhythmic accents, among others. With the prescribed use of music therapy interventions the person with autism can develop a larger repertoire of responses to music, thereby learning more ways to couple thoughts with actions. As additional responses to music develop, the person is learning more ways to relate to people and objects in a socially acceptable fashion. Even better, the therapist can support development of the responses and guide the person to use musical strategies to develop and apply functional use of nonmusical skills (e.g., cooperative use of math skills, give-and-take interaction, sequencing and sustaining work tasks, etc.).

When a child with uneven skills and poor communication abilities is able to respond to subtleties such as harmonic progressions, phrasing, tempo, and melody, it seems wasteful to ignore vital learning pathways. Moreover, responses to the aforementioned musical subtleties require social skills needed to engage in joint attention, skills which are often severely impaired in persons with autism outside of the music medium. Music therapy techniques can help the child with music sensitivity venture much farther into learning than solitary self-stimulation or even "hit-or-miss musical luck." *The cornerstone of music therapy's success is musical assessment of physical, cognitive and emotional needs, followed by prescriptive music interventions based on the disciplined study of music's relationship to human functioning.* Through immediate assessment of physical and emotional needs, the music therapist uses music to guide the person with autism to practice sustained use of skills and interaction by supporting him or her with the proper volume, tempo, strategically placed accents, and instrumentation. Although the untrained onlooker is often unaware of the prescribed changes in the supporting music and rhythmic gestures (or non-gestures), the result is an apparently effortless coordination of thoughts and actions by the student, synchronized with another person. The student is practicing sustained, uninterrupted cooperative use of his or her skills, so that eventually the prescribed music therapy support will no longer be needed. A glance between child and therapist on the final chord of the experience holds instant mutual joy and understanding of accomplishment, without the use of verbal comments or physical gestures. Success is noninvasively reinforced musically and understood by the child. Abstract concepts regarding trust and social timing are instantly reinforced with the perfectly timed strum of the guitar, strategic rhythmic placement and/or use of harmony. These are only a few of the many ways a music therapist begins to build a therapeutic foundation to support development and discovery of important life skills and experiences.

Monroe County Intermediate School District

Music therapy is included in the continuum of programs and services for Monroe County, Michigan students. The Monroe County Intermediate School District (MCISD) is a regional educational services agency including 9 constituent public school districts, 1 charter school, and 15 nonpublic schools. It serves as a link between the local school districts of Monroe County and the Michigan Department of Education. Their mission statement reads as follows:

The Monroe County Intermediate School District promotes educational excellence by serving in a visionary leadership role to collaborate and facilitate improvement of school programs and services. These efforts will be driven by pertinent research, continual assessment of needs, and coordination of community resources. As a result, county students will be prepared to live, learn, and work in an ever-changing world. (MCISD Board of Education, 2001)

MCISD's efforts toward this mission continue today. In 1998 MCISD gained successful passage of the first countywide educational technology millage in the state and a renewal in June 2001. With new equipment, Internet access, and distance learning offered to all county public schools, area teachers and students now have access to an unlimited number of resources. The impact has been felt in both the regular education and special education spheres.

The district provides programs and support for all Monroe County students covering the full range of needs from giftedness to severe and multiple disabilities. In recognizing the unique needs of students, a continuum of services and educational settings are coordinated with the families, local school districts and the community in order to provide the best opportunity for full realization of each student's educational potential. Important components of MCISD's services include specially trained personnel, professional development training, parent education, technological support, and links to the community. This chapter will give a brief overview of the district's special education structure and detail how music therapy is effectively used to meet the diverse needs of students with autism spectrum conditions in Monroe County, Michigan. While the information focuses on autism, it should be noted that the music therapy services outlined are available to any Monroe County student whose Individualized Education Program (IEP) deems it necessary for the student to realize their educational goals. The MCISD's music therapy program creatively uses both an Integrated Service Delivery Model and a Caseload Service Delivery Model to maximize quality treatment and the number of students served. See Table 1 for a description of the pros and cons associated with each model.

Background

History

Monroe County residents approved a ½ mill for nonmandated special education in 1956. A county board of education administered programs until 1963 when Michigan legislation required formation of Intermediate School Districts (ISDs) in each county. Throughout the 1960s, students who were considered slow learners or educable mentally impaired were placed in self-contained classrooms in local schools that served special education students of varying ages and functioning levels. In addition, there were separate classrooms for students with hearing impairment and for students who were physically or otherwise health impaired (POHI). Although they had been receiving some services through the mental health agency, in 1971 the state mandated that ISDs run programs for students diagnosed as trainable or severely mentally impaired. That same year, Monroe County passed a bond issue to build the Monroe County Educational Center (MCEC). The MCEC was officially opened in 1973 to house center-based categorical programs for students, age 26 and younger, who were labeled as severely mentally impaired (SMI), severely multiply impaired (SXI), and trainable mentally impaired (TMI).

With the passage of PL 94-142 and subsequent changes in the state special education code regarding autism, the MCISD opened its first autistically impaired (AI) categorical classroom in the early 1980s. The classroom was located in the center based program at the MCEC and included newly labeled county students, most of whom were already attending the school. Initial available services included speech and physical therapy, but by 1985 had grown to include occupational therapy, adaptive physical education, and music therapy. As more children were identified with the disorder, another AI categorical classroom was added in

Table 1
Pros and Cons of the Caseload Music Therapy Service Model vs. the Integrated Music Therapy Service Model

Caseload MT Service Model	Integrated MT Service Model
Brief definition: Serves a limited number of students according to defined parameters and usually documents via the IEP	**Brief definition:** Serves all or most students in a program and documents via the IEP as deemed appropriate
Pro (+) / Con (−)	**Pro (+) / Con (−)**
+ Opportunity to design individual specific treatment plans	+ Can design normalized situations expanding treatment options
+ More thorough assessment procedures	− *Less time for individual assessment procedures
+ *Opportunities for more involvement on the education team	− *Involvement on education team depends on program design
+ *Opportunity to document more clearly	− *Documentation time depends on program design
+ *More individualized teacher support via direct consultation, involvement with curriculum	+ *Teacher and staff attending MT groups learn valuable info regarding students
+/− See far fewer students (15 to 60)	+/− *One MT could cover hundreds of students
+/− *Staff/parents wouldn't expect to automatically get MT for child	+/− *May be forced to appear like music education
− *Could create adversarial situations between parents and employer	+ One set of equipment needed
− *Could be difficult for needy students to access service	− *Difficult to serve in decentralized program if time is limited
− Time and equipment needs would be similar to Integrated Model	+ Can impact many students and the emotional fabric of the school environment
− *Quality of impact depends upon many variables	+/− Parents feel their child is being adequately serviced
− *Treatment options in normalized situations could be limited	+ MT present for program-wide activities
− *Less direct service time/more intensive paperwork	+ Staff more likely to hear important information regarding students' emotional/physical states affecting session plans
	+/− *Less intensive documentation

* Depends on program design

1987. Those identified with autism in the 1980s tended to be children who today would fall at the low end of the autism spectrum.

The passage of the Individuals with Disabilities Education Act (IDEA) in 1990 and the Reauthorization of IDEA (PL 101-476, formerly PL 94-142) in 1996 broadened and changed many program requirements for persons with disabilities influencing the options available to students with autism in Monroe County. The current Michigan Revised Administrative Rules for Special Education requires a classroom program for those with autism to have a ratio of no more than 5 students to 1 teacher and 1 aide (Michigan State Board of Education, 1997). If a program has more than one AI classroom the student number can exceed five as long as the average student-to-teacher-and-aide ratio does not exceed 5 students to 1 teacher and 1 aide. The AI program must include (a) language and communication development, (b) personal adjustment training, and (c) prevocational education (Michigan State Board of Education, 1997).

The law also requires that students with special needs receive services in the least restrictive environment (LRE) (IDEA, Michigan State Board of Education 1997). This has moved the focus away from categorical placements and programming to an emphasis on services according to individual educational needs. Consequently, today MCISD offers an array of options for all students with disabilities. Specific to autism, the district currently has three categorical AI classrooms in a center based program and special programming and services for those placed in preschools, self contained classrooms, vocational settings and regular education classrooms in various school locations throughout the county.

MCISD's Continuum of Special Education Programs and Services

The MCISD provides a wide range of special services to the nine local public districts and the one public school academy including diagnostic services, teacher consultants for disability areas, and categorical classroom programs. Some programs are run by the local districts, such as elementary and secondary resource programs, as well as large portions of the speech and language services. Ida Public Schools, one of the local districts, operates the county hearing impaired program. MCISD provides a variety of related services including physical therapy (PT), occupational therapy (OT), speech therapy, music therapy (MT), school psychologist, social work, adaptive physical education, and orientation and mobility trainers. Additionally, there are vision consultants, transition facilitators, and work study coordinators.

With the Reauthorization of IDEA (PL 101-476, formerly PL 94-142) and the push for inclusion and the Least Restrictive Environment (LRE), the Individualized Education Program Team (IEPT) advocates that the students be placed according to their educational needs rather than their special education label. Placement in the regular education setting with age-appropriate peers must be considered each time the IEPT convenes. If it has been determined that the inclusion setting would not be least restrictive, an alternative setting can be recommended from a continuum of placement options (see Figure 1). Each one of these placements can be supported by law if it is deemed "least restrictive" for the student by the IEPT. The combination of services and placement as related to one's educational needs are interdependent when considering LRE.

Note that the MCISD Continuum of Placements chart is simply a flow chart of placements and that the full range of services are generally available in any setting as outlined by the IEP. The *placement settings* are indicated on the top row of the chart. Placement in a setting located to the left of the chart (such as "Homebound/Residential") is considered "most dependent," reflecting the belief that the severity of the student's disability, typically medical in nature, requires that the educational programming be done in a residential setting. As one moves across the diagram to the right, the settings are considered more independent. Inclusion (i.e., full-time placement in the special education student's home district regular education system with chronological age grade placement) would then be considered "most independent" for the special education student. In some cases, however, inclusion may not be considered as either "most independent" or "least restrictive." Since the methods necessary for each student to attain his or her educational goals are uniquely individual, there are cases in which the inclusion setting may be viewed as

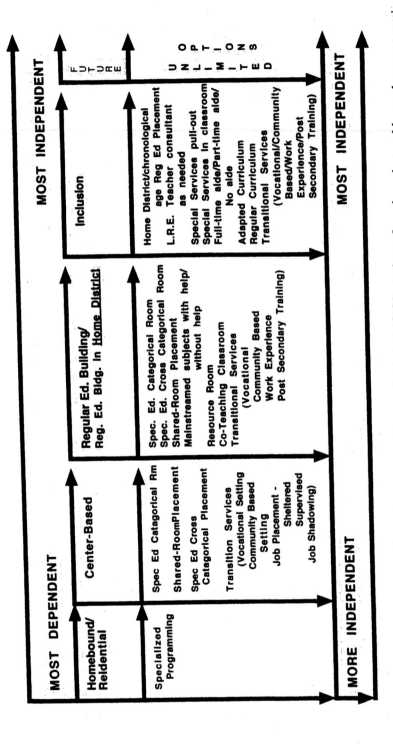

MONROE COUNTY INTERMEDIATE SCHOOL DISTRICT
Special Education Continuum of Placements

Figure 1. Monroe County Intermediate School District Continuum of Placements

The Continuum of Placements chart briefly outlines placement settings available to MCISD students. It seeks only to address placement settings and does not outline specific program designs. The settings listed are not exhaustive but placed in an approximate sequential order from "most dependent" to "most independent." Recognize that each student's needs and conditions are uniquely varied, so placement in the "most independent" setting may not be age-appropriate or "least restrictive," thus the need for a continuum. Movements down and to the right are considered progress toward increased independence. Conversely, if a student is placed too far ahead on the continuum, there is a safety net of options the individual can access by reconvening the IEPC.

inadequate by the IEPC. For example, support systems necessary for inclusion (i.e., a full-time aide, an adapted curriculum, and a battery of special services) of a particular student may foster dependency rather than function as a stepping stone to increased independence in the achievement of educational goals (academic and/or social). Having the availability for a continuum of placements then becomes very important since some individuals may realize more success in a center-based program like the Monroe County Educational Center (MCEC).

Placement options within each placement setting are listed in approximate sequential order with items shown at the top of the chart being "more dependent" and the bottom being "more independent." For instance, in the center-based school, the most dependent setting for a student with autism would be the special education AI categorical room, and the most independent setting would be a cross-categorical placement (i.e., student with autism placed in a TMI classroom) with community based, work experience, and transitional services.

The AI categorical room is designed to help the student more severely afflicted with autism develop skills and strategies to interact effectively with people and objects. But as time passes, the self-contained classroom could become restrictive and exclusionary if the educational team does not guide the student toward more independence in other settings. For example, consider that the AI categorical room is located close to the "most dependent" corner of the chart. On the one hand, a self-contained classroom with a 5 (students) to 2 (adults) ratio could be viewed as a positive teaching situation. On the other hand, there may not be peer role models who can demonstrate normal social interaction. Or the student with autism may become too dependent upon the classroom adults and room environment, preventing him or her from learning to generalize skills outside of those controlled dynamics. This is especially problematic when the student must move to a new classroom, teacher, and/or building due to age requirements. It could be argued that the student was *taught* to be more dependent. To prevent this, the MCEC multidisciplinary team designs experiences demanding generalization of skills and interaction with peers from other classrooms. As the student becomes successful in these situations, the IEPT may consider a shared-room (i.e., placement divided between an AI classroom and a TMI classroom) or a cross-categorical placement for the student.

The student is not restricted to the center-based program if the IEPT determines an even more independent setting is needed. For example, programming for the MCEC teenaged students who are trainable mentally impaired involves work experiences and activities of daily living such as cooking. The 8-year-old MCEC student with autism whose functional skills match those of the teenagers would not be placed in an older TMI classroom because the activities and peers would not be age-appropriate. Instead, this student could be placed in a more independent setting, like a regular education building cross-categorical room (a self-contained special education classroom with a maximum of 15 students of various ages and disabilities) or fully included in regular classes. The student with autism, or any other disabling condition, can be placed in any setting along the continuum despite the label or diagnosis if the IEPT determines it to be the "least restrictive environment." Generally speaking, the education team strives to support the student to move toward the right and/or, at the very least, down the chart shown in Figure 1.

Autism Defined

The initial description of children with early infantile autism (Kanner, 1943) has been debated and modified over the past 50 years (Center for Quality Special Education [CQSE], 1993). Kanner's definition and the various definitions existing today include a predominant amount of problems associated with communication development (American Psychiatric Association, 1994; Attwood, 1998; Autism Society of America, 2001). The behavioral criteria, rather than medical tests, used to diagnose autism continue to be modified. Grandin (1995) reports that the criteria listed in an earlier version of the American Psychiatric Association's *Diagnostic and Statistical Manual* (3rd ed., revised) (*DSM-III-R*) (1987) would result in 91% of children displaying autistic symptoms being labeled as autistic. Based on criteria published in the latest edition of this manual (*DSM-IV*) (American Psychiatric Association, 1994), only 59% of the same children would be labeled as having autism. In addition to autism, *DSM-IV* lists several autism-related disorders under the general heading "Pervasive Developmental Disorder" (PDD) that includes Autistic Disorder, Rett's Disorder, Childhood Disintegrative Disorder, Asperger's Disorder, and Pervasive Developmental Disorder Not Otherwise Specified (PDD-NOS). While some believe that these categories reflect distinctly separate conditions, others feel they lie on a continuum of autism, from mild to severe. This "Autistic Continuum" (Grandin, p. 52) places children with Kanner's or Asperger's Disorder at the highest functioning level with a wide range of combinations throughout the middle. Grandin also describes this as a "sensory processing continuum"; those with high-functioning autism have mild sensory oversensitivity problems and the low-functioning person receives severely distorted information visually and aurally (p. 52).

The evolving definition and diagnostic procedures surrounding autism spectrum disorders requires parents, professionals, schools and other service agencies to frequently monitor the literature. Currently, diagnosis relies on observations, behavior checklists, and rating scales, as there are no known medical tests to conclusively diagnose the condition. The Autism Society of America (ASA) describes autism as a complex developmental disability appearing in the first three years of life with neurological etiology affecting the functioning of the brain (2001). Manifestations appear as difficulties in verbal and nonverbal communication, social interaction, and leisure or play activities. Other behaviors include repeated body movements, unusual responses to people or objects, and resistance to changes in routine. The ASA reports that in 1997 the Centers for Disease Control and Prevention estimated occurrence at 1 in 500 with autism being four times more prevalent in boys than girls. The ASA also states that there are more than one half million people with autism spectrum disorders, making it one of the most common developmental disabilities. Questions remain associated with the numbers due to the diagnosis debate. The numbers stated by the ASA appear to be based on the autism spectrum, rather than the specific autism definition in *DSM-IV.*

The *Diagnostic and Statistical Manual* (4th ed.) (*DSM-IV*), published by the American Psychiatric Association (1994), identifies autism as one of the "pervasive developmental disorders" and lists the following conditions as indicative of the specific "Autistic Disorder":

1. Qualitative impairment in social interaction, such as the inability to decode nonverbal behaviors (i.e., facial expression, gestures), develop interpersonal relationships, and/or respond to other people socially or emotionally.

2. Qualitative impairments in verbal and nonverbal communication, such as a lack of or delay in verbal language, impaired ability to initiate or sustain a conversation with others (when speech is present), repetitive use of unrelated phrases, abnormal voice quality (i.e., monotone or question-like), inability to understand questions or directions, and/or the absence of imaginative play.

3. Limited, repetitive, and stereotypical patterns of behavior, interests, and activities, such as stereotyped body movements (i.e., clapping, finger flicking, rocking), odd body postures, preoccupation with parts of objects, restricted range of interests (i.e., electricity, traffic signs), unusual play rituals, insistence on sameness (i.e., even minor details like the layout of the dinner table), fascination with moving objects (i.e., spinning blades of a fan) and/or attachment to an inanimate object (i.e., a piece of string or a chain).

4. Associated characteristics emerge as unusual responses to sensory stimuli, abnormal posture and motor behavior, uneven development of cognitive skills, self-injurious behavior, peculiar eating and sleeping habits, or abnormal mood swings. (p. 66)

Based on each professional's training, jargon, and experience with autism, there can be a multitude of labels used to describe a person with autistic traits. The applied labels include autistic-like, learning disabled with autistic tendencies, high functioning or low functioning autism, classic autism, severe, moderate or mild autism, Asperger's Disorder, atypical autism, and autism spectrum disorder. Professionals working with individuals with autism, and/or persons with a range of developmental delays, should review the literature and become familiar with the extensive list of behavioral traits associated with autism and related disorders.

Most of the literature reviewed for this chapter tended to use the terms *autism* and *autistic spectrum* to refer to those conditions falling under the *DSM-IV* category heading of Pervasive Developmental Disorder or PDD. The term *classic autism* tended to refer to the middle and lower end of functioning on the autism continuum, with little to no functional verbal skills and pragmatic skills. Asperger's Disorder, High-Functioning Autism, Atypical Autism, or Pervasive Developmental Disorder-Not Otherwise Specified (PDD-NOS) referred to those at the high end of the autism continuum, with verbal skills present and pragmatic skills low or absent. Professionals or caregivers who use the term *PDD* to describe a student on the high end of the autism spectrum most likely really mean PDD-NOS. PDD is the general heading for autism spectrum disorders and PDD-NOS is one of the specific diagnoses listed under PDD.

Simplification

DSM-IV differentiates the Pervasive Developmental Disorders by comparing them to a different group of disorders titled Specific Developmental Disorders (SDD) (i.e., Developmental Language Disorder or Developmental Reading Disorder). The comparison is as follows:

PDD	vs.	SDD
1. Multiple functions are affected.		1. Only one specific function affected.
2. Severe qualitative abnormalities not normal for any stage of development (Distortion in development)		2. Follows a developmental sequence (Delay in development)
		(p. 77)

The Autism Society of America (ASA, 2001) points out that a specific diagnosis under the category of PDD requires a specific number of characteristics listed in *DSM-IV* be present. They outline the major points of the specific diagnoses as follows:

Autistic Disorder: Impairments in social interaction, communication, and imaginative play prior to age 3 years. Stereotyped behaviors, interests and activities.

Asperger's Disorder: Characterized by impairments in social interactions and the presence of restricted interests and activities, with no clinically significant general delay in language, and testing in the range of average to above average intelligence.

Pervasive Developmental Disorder—Not Otherwise Specified: (commonly referred to as atypical autism)—A diagnosis of PDD-NOS may be made when a child does not meet the criteria for a specific diagnosis, but there is a severe and pervasive impairment in specified behaviors.

Rett's Disorder: A progressive disorder which, to date, has occurred only in girls. Period of normal development and then loss of previously acquired skills, loss of purposeful use of the hands replaced with repetitive hand movements beginning at the age of 1–4 years.

Childhood Disintegrative Disorder: Characterized by normal development for at least the first 2 years, significant loss of previously acquired skills.

(American Psychiatric Association, 1994, as summarized by ASA, 2001)

For the purposes of this chapter, the terms *autism* and *autism spectrum* will refer generally to the various conditions on the autism continuum. Persons with autism each have their own unique combination of behaviors and conditions. A skilled therapist will be able to observe and assess the uneven, inconsistent abilities in communication, motor skills, sensory functioning, and functional, pragmatic use of skills. Regardless of the classified label or lack thereof, the treatment or educational plan would be based on demonstrated need. A label or label change does not necessarily change the plan, but can serve as another piece of information for the educational team.

Unique Educational Needs

Since there is a wide range of ability levels manifested in individuals with autism, individualized programming is essential (Schopler & Mesibov, 1988). For example, although approximately 75% of the people diagnosed with autism have functional abilities in a mentally retarded range, many have uneven cognitive abilities, such as an advanced reading level (i.e., hyperlexia) or mathematical knowledge simultaneously present with the inability to engage in meaningful verbal conversations (American Psychiatric Association, 1994). In addition to severe deficiencies in communication and social skills, unusual behaviors, such as stereotyped body movements (i.e., flapping, clapping, rocking), odd responses to sensory stimuli (i.e., over- or under-sensitivity to tactile, visual, and auditory stimuli) (Ayres, 1979; Grandin, 1988, 1995; Ornitz as cited in Thaut, 1984), self-stimulation, and resistance to change present challenges when implementing the Individualized Education Program in the recommended social setting (CQSE, 1993).

Highly structured treatment models using various combinations of therapies, including music therapy, are recommended for individuals with autism (Clarizio & McCoy, 1983; Grandin, 1995; Olley, 1987). Early interventions designed to address the development of functional language and communication skills are crucial when one considers that the degree of language development in the child with autism by age 5 is directly related to the child's degree of success later in life (Bagley & McGeein, 1989; Kurita, 1985; Schopler & Mesibov, 1985). Special education programming should also include opportunities to expand functional skills (Alper, 1981), learn social and interpersonal skills (i.e., imitation, interactive play, sensitivity toward others) (Schopler & Mesibov, 1983), and develop control over stereotypical behaviors (CQSE, 1993). The educational team should plan lessons that teach the student how to decode nondirect verbal or nonverbal communication (Hermelin, 1978; Volkman, 1987). Special emphasis should be placed on helping the student generalize learned behaviors in as many situations as possible (Paul, 1987; Schopler & Mesibov, 1988).

In her review of the literature, Edgerton (1994) found that structured intervention approaches were predominantly recommended. However, her research findings, related to the communicative behaviors of children with autism, suggest that gains in communication can be made using low-structured intervention, specifically, therapeutically applied improvisational music. Nordoff and Robbins (1964, 1968, 1971, 1977) and Alvin and Warwick (1992) have documented the efficacy of using improvisational music in programming for students with autism. The literature relating to autism is filled with references to the unusual attraction and responses of children with autism to musical stimuli (Applebaum et al., 1979; Grandin & Scariano, 1986; Kolko et al., 1980; Rimland, 1964; Sherwin, 1953; Toigo, 1992; Wigram, 2000). Edgerton's review of studies relating to autism lists the following areas as favorably affected by music therapy: "Prosocial behaviors, attention span, self-expression, mental age, spontaneous speech, vocal imitation skills, interpersonal relationships, task accuracy, and shopping skills" (p. 34).

The attempts of individuals with autism to interact appropriately with people and objects are sometimes awkward and difficult. Despite impairments in the ability to understand social situations (Volkman, 1987), decode meaning from nondirect verbal or nonverbal communications (Hermelin, 1978), and sensory perception abnormalities, the person with autism continues to look for ways to have human contact. Music therapy interventions often can facilitate the individual with autism in establishing appropriate contact with people and objects.

Framework of MCISD Music Therapy Services

Background

The formation of categorical AI programs in the early 1980s played an important role in MCISD's decision to pursue music therapy services. The students identified under the new AI classification had diverse educational barriers and music as therapy held promise. In 1985 a part-time music therapy position was created to serve center based programs for students with autism (AI) and preprimary impairment (PPI). The students in the AI classroom received 1:1 and small group music therapy, while the students in the PPI classrooms received group music therapy by classroom. As music therapy became increasingly valued to both the AI and PPI programs, the MCISD administrators looked for ways to provide those services to other students with special needs. In 1987, a full-time music therapy position was established to serve the PPI Program and the Monroe County Educational Center Program (which included the trainable, severely/ multiply impaired, and autistic programs). Additionally, the new position served the center based Day Treatment Program for students with emotional impairment (EI) and one self-contained categorical classroom for those who were physically or otherwise health impaired (POHI).

By the following year, the music therapy program evolved to include written goals on the IEPs for all the MCEC students. The therapist attended the IEPT meetings for each of the students from the AI classrooms and participated in their Three-Year Multidisciplinary Evaluation Team (MET) assessments. The classroom teachers for the other MCEC students submitted the recommended music therapy goals to the IEPT, as time restraints prevented the music therapist's attendance. Eventually, a music therapy curriculum (Snell, 1990) was developed and included in the Curriculum Guide for Trainable Mentally Impaired Students: A Sequence of Annual Goals, Short-term Instructional Objectives, and Performance Objectives (Monroe County Intermediate School District, 1990) (see Appendix A). This music therapy curriculum was subsequently used for the students in the AI and SMI/SXI programs as well.

The decentralization trend of the late 1980s and early 1990s resulted in the restructuring of categorical programs. A number of students and categorical classrooms from self-contained programs shifted to regular education buildings. Eventually the Day Treatment Program was closed, the POHI classroom was eliminated, and the MCEC and PPI programs were restructured. Students formerly in categorical programs were absorbed into regular education classrooms or other special education programs. Some positions were eliminated, while others were created. Educational approaches were re-evaluated and the music therapy program changed accordingly.

The music therapy program provided (a) direct music therapy, (b) music therapy consultation, and (c) music therapy workshops to meet the changing needs of students. Students in the AI categorical program received 1:1, small group, and gained access to larger group music therapy with age-appropriate peers in the TMI and SMI programs. The PPI program began to re-locate rooms into local school buildings making it necessary for support services to travel to the students. Music therapy served the PPI classrooms in the local districts on a rotating 6-week schedule and provided parent workshops to preschool parents. Three classrooms located in local school buildings became extensions of the MCEC, accepting students with various special needs labels. The music therapist provided consultation to these cross-categorical classrooms and became involved in other least restrictive environment (LRE) projects linking students with special needs to local regular education and community members. Music therapy services to the former Day Treatment students and those with POHI faded away.

Related service personnel were increasingly assigned caseloads according to individual needs rather than special education label. The music therapist picked up a small caseload of individual students located in inclusion settings based on referrals and assessments. Most of the music therapy caseload was documented through the IEP process except for the PPI services, where all received group music therapy not documented on the IEP. The music therapist continued to be a full participant on the IEPT at various levels in the rest of the caseload. Music therapy participation in the 3- year MET evaluations continued for the 1:1 caseload and assessments were conducted for referrals from local special programs. Following suit with the trends in the county, state, and nation, the interdependence of direct service combined with consultation and workshops became central to the music therapy program. In the mid 1990s Transition Planning became a part of the IEP for students who were 16 years and older. Where appropriate, the music therapist (like other team members) participated in helping the team plan for the student's transition out of school and into the community. This new part of the IEP was intended to remind the education team of the students lifetime goals to ensure annual goals would relate to the student's life expectations.

Today

Monroe County Intermediate School District continues to recognize the unique role music therapy plays in the education of exceptional children. By using creative program designs the district is able to make music therapy services available to students with defined needs across the entire Continuum of Placements (see Figure 1) for county students and families, despite decentralization and continual changes in special education law.

As a member of the multidisciplinary team, the music therapist participates in all team meetings, the IEPT meeting (including Transition Planning) and Three-Year MET evaluations for each of the students who receive individual music therapy, including all those serviced in the Caseload Music Therapy Service Model. It is optional for the music therapist to attend these meetings for the remaining students unless music therapy observations/assessments could impact IEPT/MET decisions. The teachers for those students propose the music therapy goals to the IEPT meeting as directed by the music therapist.

MCISD Music Therapy Program Description

Generally the district's current music therapy program is described as follows:

The MCISD music therapy program is designed to help students develop learning readiness skills, develop social skills, prepare for transitions into least restrictive environments and develop functional use of isolated skills in multiple settings with the highest level of independence possible. This is achieved by using music to address nonmusical skills in communication, academics, motor, emotional and social areas. An equal emphasis is placed on staff consultation, parent and community involvement, and education.

By assessing music-related behaviors and recognizing their relationship to nonmusical abilities, music therapy interventions can assist students with developmental delays in bridging the gap between isolated skills and their functional social applications. Music therapy is noninvasive and allows students to experience abstract concepts in a concrete fashion.

The music therapy program at the MCISD is carried out by a board-certified music therapist who is able to assess music-related behavior, interpret the relationship to nonmusical skills and recommend specific music interventions which can be eventually supported by teachers and parents. Music therapy activities take place in the least restrictive environment possible, from one-to-one sessions to all types of classroom and community settings. The music therapist is an education team member, participating in planning and on-going evaluation.

The philosophy behind the music therapy program design is that:

- direct music therapy—1:1, small and large group therapy
- music therapy consultation—parents, teachers, support personnel, community, and
- workshops and presentations—parents, staff and community

are interdependent and must happen with

- meaningful connections to the community (see Figure 2).

Additionally, the program is assessment driven and supports growth towards independence by striving to fade away services when the child can be successful without music therapy interventions.

By using a combination of both the Integrated Music Therapy Service Model and the Caseload Music Therapy Service Model, a maximum number of people are served while maintaining a level of quality service. The Integrated Model assigns service to most or all of the students in a program. The therapist documents progress through the IEP process for each student with graduated levels of involvement according to students' needs. The Caseload Model provides service to a limited number of students, usually with initial

MCISD'S MUSIC THERAPY PROGRAM DESIGN

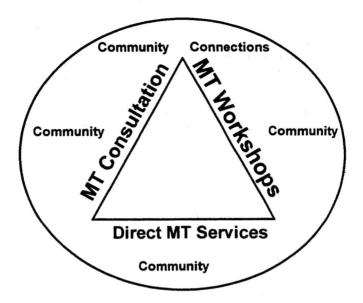

Figure 2. MCISD's Music Therapy Service Model

defined criteria. Full participation on the education team by attending meetings, reporting assessment results, and IEPT involvement is necessary.

For example, the MCEC is a center based school with approximately 140 students with TMI, SMI/SXI, and AI, ages 2½ to 26. A significantly larger number of these students qualify for music therapy services due to the high needs nature of their disabilities. In this case serving only a caseload would take 2½ to 5 days a week to serve, depending upon the 1:1 and grouping needs. Creating normalized school situations necessary in helping the student realize goals would require the involvement of students not on the music therapy caseload. This potentially creates a higher probability of adversarial situations, as teachers and parents naturally advocate for nonqualified students who respond and like music to participate in MT groups. The required referral system would likely be burdened. However, the MCEC uses the Integrated Model approach which results in the school receiving music therapy for 2½ days a week. Each classroom, with a ratio of 5–15 students to 1 teacher and at least 1 aide, receives group music therapy. There are approximately 18–20 students who receive 1:1 and small group therapy. Fewer students end up on the 1:1 caseload, as needs often can be met in the group settings. For the older students there are music therapy designed school music groups, i.e., chimes choir, vocal choir, rhythm band, and creative movement/dance group. The school has music therapy designed assemblies and music performances that are appropriate to students' needs and dignity, as the music therapist is trained to follow standards of practice and codes of ethics regarding client performance (AMTA, 2001). The specialized performing groups and school music programs receive frequent public attention. The annual school music program draws audiences of up to 500 people year after year. The MCEC music therapy component is woven into the emotional fabric of the school and provides a vehicle for school unity and pride.

Most MCEC students have one annual goal with objectives supported by music therapy. Progress is reported to parents quarterly using a simple marking system on a copy of the IEP goal sheet. Progress is summarized and goals are updated a fifth time at the IEPT. This procedure is followed by the entire education team and assures the school's compliance with IDEA provisions for progress report frequency (IDEA). Note that attendance to the IEPT by the therapist is optional, so the therapist can send information and recommendations for updated goals and objectives with the teacher. MCEC students on the 1:1 service list (most of which have autism spectrum conditions) require more active involvement in the team meetings, IEP, and Three-Year MET evaluations by the music therapist. There is a priority in the schedule for the music therapist to attend meetings for these students. The students with autism attending this school have ample opportunities for music therapist assisted involvement in normalized activities where development of social interaction and functional use of skills take place. The MCEC's creative use of the Integrated Model also assures music therapy practices to be in line with the profession's standards of practice, codes of ethics, and best practice models.

The MCISD's Preprimary Impaired Program (PPI) has used the Integrated Music Therapy Service Model, serving anywhere from 110 to 150 students within the span of a year. While every student received group music therapy, only students with dramatically demonstrated needs had music therapy assisted IEP goals. There was not very much time allowed for 1:1 and smaller group therapy for students with high communication and sensory needs. However, the weekly groups served the students, allowed for music therapy consultations with the teachers, and parent workshops. The groups provided for music therapist assisted language, motor, sensory, and social/emotional experiences. The teachers expressed value in the discovery of hidden skills not found through other tests and observed significant student gains in language, self control, and social/emotional skills. Often students demonstrated educational, physical, and emotional "firsts" during music therapy assisted experiences.

Over the past 10 years, the PPI Program has undergone a gradual decentralization of its placements and services. As travel distances increased between the 14–16 half-day classrooms (7–8 teachers), the music therapy services were creatively adjusted. Music therapy was restricted to 1 to 1½ days for direct service, so a rotating schedule ensued. Service focused on significantly less direct student work, but continued to provide parent workshops and some teacher consultation. This posed some difficulties in meeting service time for the few students with music therapy assisted IEP goals and the loss of direct student work limited the discovery of hidden skills.

For the 2000–2001 school year, the PPI Program changed to a Caseload Music Therapy Service Delivery Model and developed a conservative referral system to address evolving program needs. This coincided with the integration of higher needs students into the PPI program and a significant enrollment increase in young children with autism spectrum symptoms. After an initial music therapy caseload of 5–7 children in four locations, 10 more assessment referrals were ordered. The PPI caseload grew to 12 students in six locations. Twelve new PPI assessments were requested for the 2001–2002 school year, in addition to three assessments for older students from inclusion and cross-categorical settings. The new assessments requests submitted by teachers and parents, went through a pre-referral screening and were not deemed to be frivolous. Again, a majority of these referrals involved young children who presented behaviors that lie on the autism continuum, i.e., poor communication, uneven use of skills, sensory modulation problems, and marked social skills deficits. In Monroe County, it appears there is a combination of improved identification of children with autism and an unexplainable (but debated) increase in children with these types of conditions. At this writing, MCISD has decided to add another music therapist (a total of two) and restructure the program delivery systems to allow time for direct service, consultation, workshops, and new community initiatives. In addition, MCISD offers a MT internship program to help in the training of undergraduate music therapy students interested in school music therapy.

Monroe County students placed in special education programming in regular education buildings in cross-categorical rooms and inclusion settings receive music therapy under the Caseload Music Therapy Service Model. The classroom teacher, parent, or other team members are encouraged to look at the Guide for Music Therapy Consideration form (see Appendix B) as they consider a formal request for a music therapy assessment. The music therapist can look at the items circled on the form and give informal feedback as the team considers a request. Important statements relating to qualification include: (a) if the student is not making expected progress as related to ability level; (b) the student has difficulty generalizing or applying skills at ability level; (c) other interventions are not resulting in significant progress; and (d) music-related behaviors, as interpreted by a board-certified music therapist, indicate music interventions can have significant positive impacts on school goals and objectives.

Once a formal request is made, the music therapist conducts a music therapy assessment which compares how the student is impacted by current interventions (speech, OT, behavior modification, etc.) with the impacts influenced by music therapy interventions. If music therapy interventions can significantly help the student to access education, music therapy is recommended and deemed appropriate. The students who qualify typically are having significant communication difficulties, behavior problems, and/or are unable to functionally apply skills. But there are also students who simply have unique learning disabilities and can improve learning with prescribed music strategies or whose program can benefit by music therapy teacher/ student consultation.

Usually the music therapist provides service in the classroom with the peers. When 1:1 therapy is required, the music therapist works to gradually prepare the student for sessions back in the classroom. Since the charge of special services is to enable the student access to education in typical learning atmospheres, the music therapist will set goals which support group learning and cooperation. This is the goal in all settings across the MCISD Continuum of Placements from the center-based program to full inclusion. In the Caseload Model, the music therapist networks to create normalized school situations involving peers, whereas in the Integrated Model, there are multiple situations for group learning that naturally occur.

Case Example: Jerry

As a sixth grade inclusion student with high functioning autism and significant impairments in social skills and pragmatics, "Jerry" had no trouble remembering the material presented in class but needed to learn how to relate to peers cooperatively. The music therapist conducted sessions during various subjects throughout the school year (i.e., science, social studies). The regular education teacher provided the music therapist with her curriculum goals and lesson plans for the particular class. The music therapist then designed music therapy experiences to specifically meet the needs of the student with autism which incorporated the curriculum. This normalized the session and did not take away valuable instructional time from the rest of the class. The class tested significantly better on the content supported by the music therapy experiences. The teacher was especially pleased with improvements exhibited by her struggling students. The student with autism needed to learn how to observe social clues and to cooperate with group agendas. One social studies session involved music significant to the Canadian fishing industry. Jerry had to synchronize the pulse of his accompaniment with groups of peers. A Canadian circle dance required him to hold hands with various classmates to help him overcome his fear of standing next to or touching a particular classmate. Other lessons on the Revolutionary War involved British marching drills in the gymnasium, saying no to drugs, and cooperative science songs. "John Jacob Jingleheimer Schmidt" was adapted to incorporate the names of skeletal bones. Each session involved consultations to Jerry, the teacher, and classmates on how the musical exercises were important for Jerry and why. The students received information and strategies on which portions of the musical exercises would help them with their lessons and overall well being. The teacher received enough support through consultation and materials that she replicated the exercises during the rest of the week. The classmates' attitudes and compassion for Jerry dramatically improved, helping the general atmosphere of the room. Some of the teachers continued to use the music therapy designed experiences to benefit other students in subsequent school years. Important to the success of the music therapy techniques in the classroom setting was not only the music therapist's prescriptive music, but the music therapist's direct contact in applying the interventions. Real time music therapy assessed adjustments needed to occur to establish the proper behavioral responses from Jerry before the experiences could be successfully led by the teacher.

The Unique Role of Music Therapy

Whether students with special needs are placed in an AI categorical classroom or in a regular education setting, they are provided with supports to help them access learning. Each person on the education team brings expertise and/or unique information regarding the student's development and education plan. Ideally the teacher's training and expertise pertains to the type of room he or she is assigned, such as a categorical special education classroom (i.e., autistic, educable mentally impaired, etc.) or regular education classroom (i.e., K–12 education, physical education, music education, etc.). Due to the LRE initiatives regarding placement, a student with autism spectrum disorder could be placed in a classroom with a teacher who has little or no training in autism, but has the expertise in the type of academic curriculum the student needs. If this is true the IEPT considers the proper supports needed in the classroom for the student and teacher. The support personnel (i.e., speech pathologist, music therapist, occupational therapist, social worker, etc.) have the training to assess and implement services for persons with exceptionalities and are usually assigned to consultative and/or direct service. The parents and the student also have vital roles on the team by defining the student's needs, outlining immediate and long-range student expectations, sharing information, and sharing responsibility in program outcomes. The administrator oversees the student's program by managing and approving necessary supports. The team's unified goal is to help the student achieve his or her educational potential with a maximum amount of independence.

The music therapist collaborates and consults with the other team members to help facilitate development and generalization of skills in different settings. Music therapy techniques can support and direct cooperative generalized use of skills without the cumbersome use of verbal explanations which disrupt the flow of normalized situations. Because students with autism spectrum disorders often need to learn skills in isolation and then have difficulty generalizing independent use of those skills in group settings, the noninvasive music supports can be a vital and necessary component in the educational program. It is for this reason that the music therapist must be familiar with the student's communication system, sensory program, and isolated academic and motor abilities. Collaborative, interdependent work with the other team members is absolutely necessary to implementing music therapy supports in the school setting. The teacher and classroom aide, who spend most of the school day with the student and function as a clearinghouse of information among team members, are the central players in the student's program. The team relies heavily on the classroom staff, but the music therapist should still seek to make direct contact with the speech pathologist, occupational therapist, social worker, and other team members. It is important that the music therapist make sure these individuals also know and understand the reason music therapy is included in the educational plan and how the techniques work to compliment and support their goals for the student. The therapist must especially explain how the music process relates to the individual's nonmusical skills and where applications outside the music therapy session are appropriate. For instance, given a student whose music-related behaviors include abilities to match *and* anticipate changes in tempo and dynamics, the music therapist can prescribe and implement musical tempo and dynamic interventions to support a myriad of nonmusical skills. The list may include attention span, give-and-take interactions, self control, toleration for change, behavior during transitions, cooperative applications of academic knowledge, sequencing, coordination of thoughts with actions, turn taking, and so on. When abilities emerge within a musical context, the music therapist first helps support and strengthen the musical skills which exposes the abilities. Then the therapist can guide the student in connecting the skills in a broader realm outside of the music medium. Refer to the case examples throughout this chapter for a sample of specific examples.

Music therapy plays a unique role on the education team by providing:
1. Valuable alternative assessment information.
   a. Interpretation of music-related-behavior (MRB) and its significance to nonmusical functioning.

2. Effective techniques in uncovering and developing hidden skills.
    a. Therapist ability to create opportunities for exposure of hidden abilities and the trained ability to know why and how to use the music medium to support emergence of the possible skill.
3. Specific noninvasive real-time supports to bridge the gap between isolated skills and their functional applications.
    a. Prescribed therapeutic applications of musical tempo, rhythm, dynamics, and style to specifically support independent, functional use of isolated skills. Reinforcement feedback to the student is instantaneous, noninvasive and given in a normal, dignified fashion.

Alternative Assessment Information

The music therapist is the only one on the treatment team trained to assess music-related behaviors (MRB) and skills to determine significant applications to nonmusical functioning. This trained assessment ability allows the music therapist to bring unique information about the student to the team for comparison with potentially narrow standardized test results. IDEA stipulates that school districts must seek alternative assessments so the true picture of the child is not masked behind quotients and developmental age scores. Musical expression can reveal personality traits, abilities and nonabilities (Bruscia, 1987; Wigram, 2000). Music therapy information is able to assist the team in finding an approach angle in difficult treatment situations. The music therapy assessment pieces are also used for support or nonsupport of other test results. Other times the music therapist uncovers a skill that otherwise may not have been discovered and developed. It is in knowing music's relationship to human functioning that allows the music therapist to assess "on-the-spot" needs and instantly make live musical adjustments to support the child. These type of "on-the-spot" musical adjustments, coupled with the child's responses, help the MT determine long-term treatment or nontreatment recommendations.

Typically when there are exceptional needs present the teachers "have tried everything," including music. They are often limited to recorded or live music that the teacher does not know how or why to adjust. Even when "hit-or-miss" luck reveals a glimpse at a skill, the untrained person often does not know what to do next. Teachers, administrators, and parents most likely are not aware of the studied practices and applications of music therapy. Therefore, it is up to the music therapist to define and frame MT's unique role in helping children access education through music interventions in the least restrictive environment.

The music therapist applies techniques that are based on study, experience, and research. This is why the teacher may see "so much more" happening in group music therapy rather than in classroom music. When a student with special needs has difficulty in the regular music education setting, for example, the special education teacher sometimes erroneously concludes that the "music teacher is terrible" or "he doesn't like 'our' kids," when actually the child may have been overstimulated, unable to handle fast complex rhythms or unpredictable percussive sounds. The powerful element in the music therapy process is the ability to emotionally and physiologically support the person without having to use physical or verbal interaction.

Whether the assessment is for diagnostic, eligibility, or programming purposes, the music therapist still needs to use musical response indications to form concluding recommendations. The MRB music therapy interpretation can also give support or nonsupport of information reported by other team members. Remember, other team members have many types of unique testing procedures that bring bits and pieces of information to the education team so an appropriate education plan can be outlined. The music therapist, of course, participates in the team process in the same fashion. However, the music therapist frequently needs to effectively explain his or her unique assessment procedures, because both the music medium and music therapy processes are misunderstood and oversimplified by others. Using the MRBs enables the therapist to refer to the importance of the specific musical elements, establish their importance to nonmusical functioning, and explain the rational for the prescriptive use of music by a trained therapist for a given student. Additionally, while other team members may involve the student in music activities to support educational objectives, they may not be able to interpret musical emotional and physical responses accurately.

Therefore, it is important for the music therapist to observe first-hand the reported musical behavior before the information is accepted conclusively.

Wigram (2000) lists the following factors to include in a music therapy assessment:

1. Exploring the child's range of responses.
2. Exploring the child's lack of responses.
3. Looking at both the difficulties and potential of the child.
4. Evaluating the child's response to the novelty of the situation.
5. Testing diagnostic hypotheses proposed for the assessment.
6. Evaluating the child's response in terms of their potential for responding to other forms of therapy or intervention.
7. Considering the child's behavior and response in music therapy assessment in relation to the wider picture of the child's response to other media. (pp. 15–16)

Wigram also stresses the importance of *comparing the child's music investigations to normal musical exploration.* For example, when "Stan," an 11-year-old MCISD student with autism, was presented with a drum set, he immediately went to the suspended cymbal, looked underneath it, and began to spin the cymbal. He did not tap, hit, or pound the instrument or foot pedal like a typical 11-year-old. When he did hit the drum, he held his ear close to the drum head, hit it once sharply, then made a loud abrupt vocal sound as he hit his chest. Stan also did not automatically sing, clap, or stomp along with exciting group music activities. He would sit passively and let an adult move him through the actions. Wigram offers a possible explanation:

> Children on the autistic continuum reveal significant difficulties in social interaction and communication in music making, and often demonstrate a lack of skill or intuitive ability in turn-taking, sharing, anticipating, copying, reflecting or empathic play. Because of their apparent lack of interest and awareness of others for normal or typical social interaction, they can also show a lack of interest in, and ability for, responding to or sharing changes in tempo, rhythm, timbre, intensity, and many other elements of a shared musical engagement.
>
> Not all children with autism reveal these difficulties during assessment, and they may develop abilities and motivation for social interaction through interpersonal engagement in music. What needs to be understood is that an analysis of musical events (and the interpretation of meaning in the child's music) must be considered in terms of communicative intentionality and meaning in either individual expression, initiating connection to the therapist, or responding to music initiated by the therapist. (p. 16)

Uncovering and Developing Hidden Skills

Music therapists may uncover abilities and deficits any time they engage their client in the musical process. Music therapists' training and education in music and affect, influence of music on behavior, physiological responses to music, perception and cognition of music, psychomotor components of music behavior, and so on, are critical in the process of musical behavioral observations. A person not trained in music's intimate ties to emotional and physical functioning may sense a significance when a child with a disability can sing or rock to the beat. What is the significance, if there is one? The music therapist looks at the quality of the singing. Does the child keep singing when another joins in her song? Are the notes sung in pitch or at least related to the presented key? Will the child rock to the beat in different tempi? Are there changes to the rocking pattern during changes in the music? Answers to these questions will impact the assessment, findings, and recommendations. Furthermore, music therapy interpretation for two different children who can each sing the same song most likely will result in two different conclusions according to the quality of each individual's participation. Note that uncovering a hidden skill can lead to its functional use if one knows what to do with the discovery.

Case Example: Aaron

The PPI teacher informed the music therapist about a new student who had evidence of autism. "Aaron" was very afraid of sounds and the teacher warned the music therapist not to involve loud sounds in her classroom's music therapy session. Apparently the fear responses to noise were disruptive and frequent enough as to limit places he could go and family routines like vacuuming. Time would not allow an initial 1:1 evaluation of Aaron, so the music therapist planned a group session which would allow assessment of the child's sound sensitivity. Aaron had difficulty entering the music therapy room. He was fearful and clung to the teacher. He was persuaded to sit in a chair next to the teacher. As the opening gentle songs were presented, the therapist did not put performance demands on Aaron and simply watched his responses. His eye glances and subtle attempts at hand clapping were timed with interesting spots in the melody. His body relaxed at the end of predictable harmonic progressions. At this point the therapist had begun to form a hypothesis and tested it by adding a gentle "start and stop" surprise in the live accompaniment. He looked at the therapist and tried to resist a half smile. Aaron's fear of sound may partially be related to issues of trust and predictability. Maybe sudden sounds had scared him in the past, or perhaps his ability to modulate sound was inconsistent and he never knew when a sound would induce pain to his sensory system.

The therapist did a few more experiences to build his trust by incorporating predictable chord progressions, which allowed Aaron to experience the satisfaction of predictable beginnings and endings. Within 15 minutes the therapist felt confident in having the student enjoy a "big" sound. When the gong and a drum were silently presented to the group, the teacher became very alarmed and assertively suggested she take Aaron out of the room. She obviously was unable to observe the musical indicators and wanted to protect her student. The teacher was assured that the therapist would proceed carefully with Aaron's best interest. Using melody, harmonic progressions, rhythm, and tempo tailored to Aaron's needs for safety and predictability, the music therapist played the gong with medium intensity timed with the music. Aaron sat up, leaned forward, and flashed a smile at his teacher. By the end of the experience, he had listened to each classmate play the gong and had volunteered to play it himself.

The music therapist's assessment was that Aaron could indeed tolerate and even enjoy sound. His teacher and family needed to work on effective ways to communicate the order of events and explain why and how specific sounds are produced. The therapist cautioned the possibility that Aaron may have inconsistent gross distortions of sound. Care should be taken to not overstimulate him. After further assessment of Aaron, the music therapist recommended that he receive group music therapy focusing on expanded interactions with sound, communication, and functional use of skills. Today Aaron very rarely indicates trouble with sound and is working on functional use of skills and social interaction.

Case Example: Wesly

"Wesly" was a 13-year-old student with developmental delays. He did not have autism, but is a good example of how music therapy assessment can impact changes in education approaches. Wesly transferred to the MCEC's self-contained school from a cross-categorical room in a local junior high school. He presented himself as a good conversationalist with street wisdom. On the surface his unpredictable noncompliant behavior pointed toward learning disabilities and possible emotional impairment. He had handwriting in cursive. His manipulation of other students indicated that he understood his classmates had mental limitations. His behavior was very disruptive and dominated class time. Despite the fact that Wesly could play complex rhythm patterns on the drum set and sing with self-initiated creativity and embellishment, he was very uncooperative and demanding. The education team thought he was grossly "under" placed, but Wesly was very fearful about going back to the regular school. The team searched for reasons for his behavior and feelings. Wesly's music making was beautiful, but he was not flexible to the therapist's changing tempo. He played with one volume—loud. He would not play rhythms directed by the therapist, but had to play his rhythms even if they didn't match the musical style. These musical responses recorded on paper could appear to have autistic relationships, but his social interactions and functional use of skills definitely did not indicate this type of disability. Upon further assessment, the music therapist found Wesly was very successful at reproducing complex rhythm patterns modeled by the therapist when verbal explanations were replaced with musical examples. He could not grasp number or time concepts unless they were in a musical context absent of verbal references. The music therapist alerted the team and suggested a speech and language evaluation, even though speech services were not indicated via prior reports or Wesly's presented behavior. The speech pathologist tested him and found language processing deficits. Speech therapy services were recommended. The rest of the team changed their interventions to fit Wesly's unique needs, and today his behavior rarely becomes disruptive.

Case Example: Sal

Sometimes hidden skills or sensitivities are very small and hard to find. "Sal" was a preschool student in the PPI program and displayed severe low functioning autism. He frequently was very distressed and self-injurious. He appeared to be experiencing sensory overload. He was placed in a classroom with eleven other children, but he did not tolerate group circle times. The OT helped to prescribe strategies to address his sensory difficulties. The only way the speech therapist could get beginning levels of cooperation was to provide her services to Sal while he was in a swing hanging from the ceiling. The music therapist also had significant problems working with him. But the constant fretting and crying could consistently be interrupted with the following music elements: (a) sudden contrasting loud/soft sounds, (b) dramatic changes in tempo, and (c) sounds of a homemade rainstick which was relatively large and heavy. Upon suggestions from the music therapist, the teacher used these elements in her classroom. She commented that the loud/soft contrasts was often the "only thing she could do to snap him out of his crying fits." The team recommended he move to the AI classroom where sensory issues could be better addressed. He received OT, speech, adaptive physical education, and music therapy (both 1:1 and small group). The three musical elements continued to work and he eventually began to learn to anticipate his turn within certain music experiences. His teacher was able to guide him to sit in small school work groups. He began to show more affect and some expressions of likes and dislikes. He showed little response to picture cues, but he would respond to some concrete items, like food. However, today inconsistencies still remain and progress has slowed with some regression. Sal is obviously enduring very difficult physical conditions. The team continues to search for medical and psychological assessments for clues to treatment strategies. Through improvisational techniques, the music therapist has discovered that Sal responds with eye contact, body posture, and vocal play when she musically matches a repetitive melodic sound he makes. His responses come with general consistency when the music therapist matches the sounds in the key he produces them (key of "C"). He coos "EE — UO, EE — UO" on C – G, C – G. The therapist has composed "Sal's Song" based on his vocal motif. This approach elicits eye contact, vocal play and sustained drum beating for 12 to 18 measures. Using sound and tempo contrasts, musical tactile experiences and "Sal's Song," the therapist will search for strategies to expand communicativeness and possibly find other clues to assist in Sal's educational plan.

Bridge From Isolated Skills to Functional Applications

Perhaps music therapy's more important role to the team is bringing specific interventions to support *functional use of skills*. When striving for generalization of a skill, one approach would be to concretely define the skill (using a picture representation coupled with other communication formats), design opportunities for application of the skill, explain or prepare the student for what may happen, and provide motivators and reinforcements. Following music therapy standards, the therapist seeks pertinent information regarding the student, studies current methods and techniques, and works cooperatively with the education team to determine if music therapy interventions can help. Using information from the student's MRBs, the music therapist then designs experiences to support the music therapy goals and the team's approach. Interventions would include the use of musical elements assessed by the music therapist which elicit responses from the student. The elements could include a specific key or mode, a tempo, musical quotes which create expectations, and/or a specific instrument. The prescription is at least initially carried out by the therapist so that "on-the-spot" needs are supported musically to ensure that musical reinforcements are properly timed. Proper timing is important in assisting the student to develop an automatic response to the music stimuli.

Case Example: Stan

Eleven-year-old "Stan," referred to earlier, is a wonderful example of how specific elements of music can be applied to bring isolated skills to functional applications. He had severe autism with uneven skills. Tests showed communication and socialization skills were between 10 months and 1 year of age. But reading, writing, and math skills fell between 6 and 7 years of age. He had significant delays in communication, social interaction, and functional use of skills. Important parts of his programming included routine and Total Functional Communication (TFC), i.e., a combination of picture cues, gestures, and verbal communication techniques. The rates at which he displayed his skills were inconsistent and unpredictable. When musical skills emerged he showed ability to match pitches and tempo. He inconsistently giggled at interesting musical games and patterns. In the past he displayed delayed responses by singing songs from music therapy sessions hours, sometimes days, after their presentation. Due to this type of delayed response, musical synchronization was assessed as the skill Stan should develop in order for him to be able to generalize his skills. Music therapy approaches included repetition and the establishment of routine connecting songs. Incorporation of picture cues was important to link the skills learned in the classroom and speech therapy to generalized use in other settings.

The therapist designed musical experiences to increase the probability of real-time responses associated with current events within the session. Stan responded to tempo changes, musical surprises, and the connecting songs established by the music therapist. Once he consistently had at least one self-initiated, related response *per session* more was expected. Adapted music using quotes from the songs Stan consistently responded to were incorporated into new experiences. He soon was expressing at least one real-time action or verbal/vocal response during *each song in the session.* At this point, the music therapist began to support sustained responses and tracked the number of measures he sustained musical interaction. In his 1999 Three-Year MET evaluation, the other team members reported imitation skills to still be sporadic and inconsistent. But the music therapist was able to report that Stan would consistently imitate actions from a specific song in any setting with and without the music therapist. Stan was even able to imitate changing and unpredictable actions within the structure of his MT connecting song when led by the music therapist, teacher, or a peer.

The use of *timed* picture cues was also incorporated into music therapy. Even though Stan used picture cards to make choices and could understand visual sequences for classroom duties, he did so according to his own rate. Music therapy interventions were designed to support timed actions requiring visual tracking of words and picture cues synchronized with another person's timing. If Stan could be successful with this type of musical activity, he would be strengthening abilities to (a) couple thoughts with actions, and (b) cooperatively apply skills cooperatively in a social context. Following are the sequenced approaches used in music therapy to support these objectives:

1. Copied computer pictures of an alphabet book from a CD-ROM program Stan ritualistically viewed every day during free-time.

2. Composed music to the written verse on a specific page which could be supported by a one-note drone on a contra bass bar, placed the picture of the book page on the instrument, presented another copy of the picture in time with the musical cue; Stan eventually played unassisted;

3. Repeated the previous process with other pages using different music and different contra bass pitch bars;

4. Composed related two-chord music which required Stan to play instruments labeled with two different book pages precisely when presented with the matching page as it was coupled with the timing of the musical cue;

5. Faded away the visual cues from the book pages by replacing them with correct representations of the musical notes;

6. Eliminated the visual printed cues and demanded Stan's musical accompaniment to match the therapist's subtle hesitations and tempo changes;

7. Arranged different music with different cues and increased social and cooperative demands placed on Stan.

It is important to note that the success of this approach was not in simply presenting the picture cues or physically helping Stan through the steps. The prescribed music interventions encouraged, supported, and sustained Stan in coordinated use of his skills. By using tempo, dynamics, instrumentation, melody, and musical anticipation tailor-made to meet Stan's immediate physical and emotional needs, he was able to self-organize and use interactive nonverbal communication skills. Everyone else on the team was using techniques to engage Stan in cooperative use of skills, but results still lacked consistency and skill generalization. Additionally, the most important element missing in Stan's interactions was joint attention. He was unable to have effortless cooperative interaction involving mutual attention to another person and a joint activity. However, he was able to consistently engage in joint attention for a few specific songs in multiple settings, like the "Clapping Hello" song (Snell, 1987).

Learning skills in isolation is important for person's with autism, as sensory overstimulation often occurs in larger group settings. But when learned in isolation, the skills must then be socially applied in a group as soon as possible. Persons with autism often compartmentalize skills and must be re-taught specific skills in each new situations. Prescribed music support carried over from the 1:1 situation to the group setting supports skill generalization by developing associations related to the music rather than the physical surroundings.

Today Stan is able to engage in more complex cooperative use of his skills. His latest music therapy accomplishment was following a two-page chart with five different shapes placed under words to a favorite folk tune. Copies of the shapes are placed on different parts of the drum set to indicate which instrument to play. He can play independently, following a fluctuating tempo. Stan is also able to adjust to placements of the shapes on different instruments. Each time these types of musical interactions emerge in a student, the music therapist notes that functional skills in other areas begin to emerge. Results for Stan are no exception. Now Stan has more real-time responses in his classroom and his mother reports a significant increase in reality-based verbalizations at home. The education team is now working to help Stan apply these skills with peers in larger social settings and in prevocational and recreational activities.

Case Example: Rolly

Each time the group went down the hall, 10-year-old "Rolly" dropped to the floor and would spit, hit, or kick. His behavior frequently dominated the classroom events. The teacher tried several techniques including negotiating, picture schedules, increasing adult attention, and decreasing adult attention. The classroom became so frenzied that the school hired an extra aide for the room, but to no avail. After several meetings and exhausted approaches, the team studied the behavior and brainstormed possible approaches. The team decided that Rolly truly didn't know how to wait and thought he needed to learn how to transition to different activities. He possibly was experiencing hormonal changes and needed adjustments in medication. The teacher was desperate to find a respectful, safe way to deal with the behavior until he stabilized. Music therapy was one of the few positive times for his behavior during the week. The music therapist knew several of his reliable responses to music. After observing him during the problematic transitions a therapy approach was designed. A "waiting song" was composed using the proper tempo, accents, and silences spaced to match Rolly's needs. Strategically placed accents were placed in the music and arm motions to address his short attention span and gross motor/sensory needs. Use of tempo changes, and a chord progression which elicited anticipatory responses in Rolly were used. The music therapist wanted the song to effect a slower heart and breathing rate, as he usually increased breathing and movement when his behavior escalated. It needed to be something Rolly would be motivated to sing on his own, with a picture representation of the song, and accompanying hand gestures. Picture cues and gestures were a part of the student's communication system designed by the speech pathologist. The following song resulted:

PLEASE WAIT
by A. Snell

>
PLEASE   WAIT.............................1.......2...........
hand rubs chest palm out like "stop"   1 finger, 2 fingers
(accent this motion each time)

>
PLEASE   WAIT.............................1.......2...........
hand rubs chest palm out like "stop"   1 finger, 2 fingers

>   >   >
PLEASE   WAIT   WAIT   WAIT
hand rubs chest palm out like"stop" bounce "stop" 1x bounce "stop" 1x

1.....................2...........................
1 finger,   2 fingers

>
PLEASE   WAIT.............................1...........2...........
hand rubs chest palm out like "stop"   1 finger, 2 fingers

>
PLEASE   WAIT.............................1...........2...........
hand rubs chest palm out like "stop"   1 finger, 2 fingers

                                  >   >   >
PLEASE (sudden rapid tempo)   WAIT   WAIT   WAIT
hand rubs chest   bounce "stop" 1x bounce "stop" 1x bounce "stop" 1x

            >   >
        WAIT   WAIT   (deep breath) WHEW!
     bounce "stop"1x bounce "stop" 1x   hands on hips

The above song was first implemented by the music therapist. The classroom teacher and aide were asked not to use it until the music therapist felt firm responses associated with the music were developed and locked into memory. Rolly was used to the staff using the word "later" or "stop" during times of noncompliance. The therapist purposely replaced those cues with the word "wait." Rolly could develop trust and understanding of the word "wait" if caregivers only used the word when they were prepared to follow through with giving him attention after the very brief "wait" time. The music therapist wanted to present timed use of the picture cue to coincide with the word and gesture "wait." The picture cue and gesture could serve as future tools for the teacher to cue Rolly without singing. The therapist also wanted Rolly to experience using the song while waiting to play an instrument (highly motivating for him) and other positive situations first. This intervention was very successful as a behavioral support. While Rolly and the classroom continued to endure medication changes and the continued search for the root of the behavior, the classroom staff said "the only thing getting us through the day is 'Please Wait.'" The song was so useful that his peers were taught to use it, too. Soon the entire school used "Please Wait." Today you will see "Please Wait" pictures in every room and hear the phrase/gestures being actively used at the MCEC. The song enabled Rolly and others to concretely experience and label the time concept of "wait." Later "waiting" times were changed to the count of 3 or more to adapt to other immediate needs.

Case Example: Jerry

"Jerry" was a 9-year-old student at MCEC with autism whose emerging verbal skills were rapidly developing. He had severely impaired social skills, was resistant to change, and was preoccupied with subjects such as electricity, traffic signs, and cartoon characters. Jerry was able to sing, imitate simple rhythm patterns, match music dynamics, move creatively to music, and identify tonal/mood changes in recorded music. His previously slow physical reactions to musical subtleties were beginning to improve as related to rhythm. With his developed ability to respond to rhythmic patterns and accents the music therapist felt Jerry had the potential to learn better social skills. His teacher and speech therapist were helping him improve reading, math, and communication, while the music therapist supported generalization of these skills in cooperative peer situations. Using rhythm and subject matters that interested Jerry, the music therapist created experiences supported in larger group settings. The student's skill needs began to surpass the age-appropriate peers with trainable mental impairment at the school, so he began to visit therapy groups with older students. Jerry needed to move to a less restrictive school environment. He gradually moved to his local school's cross-categorical classroom. Due to his improving rhythm responses and interest in music, the music therapist felt he could handle more challenging social demands. So the MT service followed him to his new school placement where music therapy consultation and interventions enabled Jerry to transition into regular classrooms. He became a full inclusion student in third grade with special education teacher consultant, classroom aide, and music therapy supports following him into junior high school. Music therapy services were credited by the regular education teachers with exposing hidden skills and providing important modeling and consultation on strategies to help the student apply curriculum content (functional use of skills). Music therapy addressed concepts of gradiation (i.e., a little, maybe, sometimes), interaction and friendship, and social timing (i.e., when to talk out loud, ask questions, take turns, etc.). Today he is a junior in high school and no longer requires direct music therapy service. He has maintained A's and B's since junior high school. He continues to struggle with pragmatics and social skills, but Jerry is constantly learning and applying adaptive strategies to attain accomplishments.

Obtaining Music Therapy Service at MCISD

Referral

When a parent, teacher, therapist or other team member feels that a Monroe County student may benefit from music therapy services, he or she can fill out the Guide for Music Therapy Consideration (see Appendix B). Circling one or more of the items on the form does not qualify or disqualify service. It helps to organize one's reasons for seeking music therapy in the school setting. The interpretation of IDEA is that the school must provide services which are necessary for the child to access Free and Appropriate Public Education (FAPE). The Michigan special education rules go further by stating children have the right to opportunities to achieve their "maximum potential." However, "maximum potential" is not clearly defined and many state due process rulings appear closer to supporting the FAPE standard, which does not require every available service. Nevertheless, children with special needs must be making appropriate progress in their education; therefore, more than one service frequently is needed.

The Guide for Music Therapy Consideration attempts to highlight telltale areas of program needs and notable responses to music. When a child is functionally performing below assessment scores, has trouble with effective communication, and/or behavior creates barriers to learning, there is evidence that something in the educational approach or plan should be reviewed. Subsequently, when other interventions are not resulting in significant improvements and there are marked responses to music, music therapy services may be appropriate. Note that negative responses to music count as significant, too, as was illustrated in Aaron's case example earlier in this chapter.

The form can be forwarded to the music therapist, which will result in a phone conversation or visit to discuss the appropriateness of a formal music therapy referral. The form can also be used to justify music therapy consideration to educational supervisors or other team members. Regardless of whether or not the music therapist feels there is justification for a referral, anyone on the team has the right to request an assessment. Voluntary use of the guide helps to significantly cut down on the number of unnecessary assessments required of the music therapy department.

Any person on the education team can use the pre-referral guide and/or skip directly to formal referral by filling out the required form (see Figure 3) or by ordering it directly on the IEP. Once the formal request is articulated and permission from the parent is obtained in writing, the assessment is completed within the outlined timeframe. In a few instances, the IEP team recommends music therapy services and includes provisions for the service on the IEP before an assessment has taken place. Usually, if the team feels that strongly about the need for music therapy services, the music therapist may have been invited to the IEP. This way the therapist can help determine music therapist assisted goals and objectives. Whether or not the music therapist is present, an assessment will still take place in keeping with music therapy standards of practice (AMTA, 2001). If the music therapist assesses a need to change goals, objectives, or service time, he or she will approach the IEPT to request another IEP.

Assessment

Assessments in the school setting contain:

1. Background Summary
2. Present Level of Performance
3. Results from Evaluator's Unique Form of Assessment
4. Professional Interpretation
5. Conclusions and Recommendations
   a. Recommendations are submitted for consideration by the education team and are not acted upon unless the team so directs.
   b. Recommendations can include suggested areas of need to be addressed by the IEP, even if the need areas are not outlined on the current IEP, i.e., strategies, services, other tests. This does not mean the recommendations will automatically be addressed on the IEP, as the team must make that decision.

The initial or Three-Year MET evaluation is conducted to not only identify a disability defined by IDEA, but also to report present levels of educational performance and determine recommendations for the content of the IEP. According to Bateman and Linden's review (1998) of the law:

> The purposes of the evaluation and identification provisions of the law are to gather functional and developmental information necessary to determine whether a child has one of the disabilities defined in the IDEA, whether the child needs special education and related services, and the child's present levels of performance and individual educational needs (20 U.S.C. *1414).
>
> Evaluations must cover all areas related to a child's suspected disability, including, if appropriate, health, vision, hearing, social and emotional status, general intelligence, academic performance, communications needs, and motor abilities. (p. 5)

The assessment methods may not focus solely on IQ and must include other information from objective tests, subjective reports, and observations (IDEA, Bateman & Linden, 1998; Siegel, 2001). In his review of the legal requirements for assessments Siegel advises parents:

Monroe County Intermediate School District

SE 1013
Rev. 02-01
Referral and Request for Consent to Conduct an Educational Evaluation

Student Information

Student: *Ned Smith*   Parent/Guardian/Surrogate: *Rick and Anna Smith*

Address: *222 Anywhere Street, Somewhere, MI*   Phone: *711-1111*

Resident District: *Monroe*   Building: *Young Elementary*   Grade: *PPI*

Non-English language spoken by the student: _____   Birthdate: *3-3-97*

Reason for Referral

Your child is being referred for an educational evaluation for the reason stated below. The accompanying **PARENT HANDBOOK** contains important information about the evaluation process in addition to a full explanation of the procedural safeguards available to you under State and Federal law. Please contact me if you have any questions and thank you for considering this request for your consent.

Music therapy evaluation to determine how Ned's musical behavior relates to nonmusical functioning and if music therapy services are necessary to his educational plan.

Carrie T. Ice   *1-15-00*

Signature   Date

Type of Evaluation Proposed

_____ 1) To determine if the student is **ELIGIBLE FOR SPECIAL EDUCATION.** Results of this initial evaluation

will be presented at an Individualized Educational Planning Team (IEPT) meeting within thirty (30) school days.

_____ 2) To conduct an **AUXILLARY SERVICES** evaluation of a student attending a Non-Public School.

___✓___ 3) To determine the need for **ADDITIONAL** special education services.

The following persons **may** be involved in the evaluation specified above:

__ School Psychologist   __ School Social Worker   __ Teacher Consultant   __ Speech/Language

__ Special Education Teacher   __ General Education Teacher   __ Occupational Therapist   __ Physical Therapist

__ Physician   __ Audiologist   _✓_ Other *Music Therapist*

A medical and/or personality (circle selection) assessment will be conducted as part of this evaluation   __ Yes   __ No

Parent Consent

Please check the statements that apply to your decision and sign below.

_✓_ I have received and reviewed the accompanying Parent Handbook.

_✓_ I understand the content of this notice.

_✓_ I give my consent for the above evaluation.

__ I have not received a Parent handbook.

__ I do not understand the content of this notice.

__ I do not give my consent for the above evaluation.

Anna Jr. Smith   *1-22-00*

Signature of Parent/Guardian/Surrogate   Date

Referral Tracking

Date Referral/Consent given to Parent _____

Date Consent Received from Parent _____

Projected Date for IEP _____

DISTRIBUTION: White - School File   Green - Evaluation   Canary -ISD   Goldenrod - Resident District   Pink - Parent

Figure 3. MCISD Referral and Request for Consent to Conduct an Educational Evaluation

Under IDEA (20 U.S.C. *1414(a)(6)(B); 34 C.F.R. *300.532), initial or subsequent assessment material must:

- include a variety of assessment tests or tools and strategies to gather information about your child;
- not be racially or culturally discriminatory;
- be given in your child's native language or communication mode (such as sign language if your child is deaf or hard of hearing);
- be valid in determining your child's status—that is, the right test, given your child's suspected areas of disability;
- be given by trained and knowledgeable personnel in accordance with the instructions provided by the producer of the tests;
- not be used to only determine intelligence;
- if your child has impaired speaking or sensory skills, accurately reflect your child's aptitude or achievement level and not your child's specific impairment;
- assess your child in "all areas of suspected disability" including health, vision, hearing, social and emotional status, general intelligence, academic performance, communicative status, motor abilities, behavior and cognitive, physical and developmental abilities; and
- provide relevant information that will help determine your child's educational needs.

In addition, IDEA requires that the assessment process include a review of other material on the child, such as information parents provide (a doctor's letter or statement of their observations), current classroom assessments and observations (objective tests or subjective teacher reports), and observations by other professionals. (20 U.S.C. *1414(c)(1,2,4); 34 C.F.R. *300.533) (p. 64)

Special Considerations When Assessing a Student With Autism Spectrum Disorders

The unique conditions associated with autism (e.g., complex sensory problems, severe communication deficits, inability to understand social cues, limited ability to generalize skills, and unusual behavior patterns that limit interaction) should be considered when conducting an assessment in the school setting. Prescribed use of the music medium can effectively address the diverse barriers caused by autism to expose hidden abilities. While the purpose of the music therapist's evaluation may not be to actually term a classification label, the information contained in the report will be important to the team as they consider special education classification at the time of the report or in the future (the report becomes a permanent part of the student's file). Rather than basing a special education classification on a doctor's diagnosis, the team considers the disability definitions in IDEA to make a determination (Bateman & Linden, 1998). Music-related behavior and nonmusical behavior observed by the music therapist that support or refute other evaluations are documented and reported. Again, it is especially important to effectively interpret and communicate the music-related behavior's nonmusical indications. Individuals with autism can interact with music in ways markedly different from normal development, and those behaviors can provide support or nonsupport for autism spectrum diagnoses (Wigram, 2000). And in further investigations, research indicates persons with autism spectrum disorders who exhibit sensitivity to the music medium can learn strategies for functional use of skills with music intervention support (Edgerton, 1994). In addition to documenting observations that support a special education classification, the IEPT also needs to justify the need for supports and related services (Siegel, 2001).

The music therapist seeks information on the types of tests and rating scales the school uses for autism screening, in addition to general information about other testing instruments and curriculum. For example, the Gilliam Asperger's Disorder Scale and the Asperger Syndrome Diagnostic Scale may be used by the school psychologist with students who present autistic behaviors lying at the higher side of the continuum. The Gilliam Autism Rating Scale and the Childhood Autism Rating Scale (CARS) may be used for students with skills at the lower end of the continuum. The psychologist will also choose nonverbal tests of intelligence, such as the Leiter International Performance Scale-Revised or the Wexler International Scale for Children–3rd Edition. Each testing instrument has drawbacks, so results are interpreted and put into context by the psychologist as related to the individual student. And because autism disorders present different combinations of behaviors unique to each person, the psychologist will also strongly consider observations and interviews to determine support or nonsupport for an autism classification. For the purposes of this chapter, the Autism Checklist (Autism Society of America, 2001), a short observational guide, is described below to help illustrate the point. Persons with autism usually exhibit at least half of the following characteristics from this checklist:

- Difficulty in mixing with other children
- Insistence on sameness; resists changes in routine
- Inappropriate laughing and giggling
- No real fear of dangers
- Little or no eye contact
- Unresponsive to normal teaching methods
- Sustained odd play
- Apparent insensitivity to pain
- Echolalia
- Prefers to be alone; aloof manner
- May not want cuddling or act cuddly
- Spins objects
- Noticeable physical overactivity or extreme underactivity
- Tantrums—displays extreme distress for no apparent reason
- Not responsive to verbal cues; acts as if deaf
- Inappropriate attachment to objects
- Uneven gross/fine motor skills (may not want to kick ball but can stack blocks)
- Difficulty in expressing needs; uses gestures or pointing instead of words

Individuals who display several of the aforementioned behaviors should be referred for a more thorough assessment in order to confirm the diagnosis of autism.

In order for persons with autism spectrum disorders to access education they must overcome significant barriers such as uneven cognitive abilities, sensory processing abnormalities, and poor communication and social skills. Recommendations for school supported interventions should clearly be for educational purposes. Educational purposes would include academics, communication, motor, emotional, and social skills. The list also includes functional skills in the least restrictive environment, group learning skills, and skills needed for transitioning out of school to the community. These types of functional skills are critical to successful adult living and are uniquely supported using music therapy interventions via the time-related, noninvasive qualities in the music medium. Often goals specifically targeting independent functional, group skills are unintentionally left out of IEPs simply because other treatments and support services use techniques to build a repertoire of skills rather than to support sustained interactive use of the skills. Building a repertoire of skills can work sufficiently for those who are able to generalize abilities across settings and situations. But one of the predominant conditions in individuals with autism spectrum disorders is the inability to generalize skills, sustain use of skills, and decode social cues. The music therapist would, of course, note these need areas in the body of the assessment report, and then list recommendations for appropriate music therapy interventions (if evident) even if there are not current IEP goals addressing the issue.

Consider how the IEPT uses an occupational therapy assessment conducted to evaluate needs and/or the need for OT services. If the evaluation reveals areas of need not addressed on the current IEP, the team: (a) considers the information; and (b) adds goals and/or services as needed, even if it means convening a new IEP. In this case, the OT does not mandate a service or intervention in the report, but gives credible information and recommendations for the team to seriously consider. Similarly, music therapy conclusions and recommendations would include areas of strength and need newly discovered in the assessment, just as other team members or independent evaluators do in their reports. The IEPT can then discuss and consider appropriate adjustments to the IEP at the next meeting or simply use the information to adjust behavioral or academic approaches, as necessary. Recommendations outside of the scope of the school setting also can still be given, as long as that fact is made clear. Additionally, this type of information may support participation in normalized programs, which may be important to the IEPT when considering transition services. Note that it is important to attend meetings discussing and considering music therapy assessment results. Those untrained in music therapy practice are unable to interpret music-related assessment results and their relevancy to nonmusical functioning (Brunk & Coleman, 2000; Wigram, 2000). A person with knowledge or expertise relevant to the student may attend the IEP; this includes persons who can interpret the assessment and its impact on instructional strategies (Bateman & Linden, 1998; Siegel, 2001). Therefore, it would be inappropriate to exclude the music therapist from the IEP meeting or other team meeting where the content of the report is being considered.

Music Therapy's Unique Role in Student Assessment

1. Alternative assessment information via the music medium
2. Can uncover hidden skills and deficits undetected by other tests
3. Provides support or nonsupport for other evaluation results and interventions
4. Provides support or nonsupport for music therapy services

Music Therapy's Unique Form of Assessment

1. Music-Related Behavior (MRB) Assessment
2. MRB Interpretation
3. Recommendations for:
   a. Student and Family
   b. School Education Team
      1) Information and recommendations for the IEPT regarding MRB's relevance to nonmusical functioning, including any indications for other approaches, tests, or services;
      2) Provides specific music and therapy information pertaining to music therapy service delivery or nondelivery.

Music therapy assessment procedures follow the AMTA Standards of Clinical Practice and special education rules and regulations. Music therapy standards of practice are very much in line with what the law would accept or require. The assessment:

- Is conducted by a trained music therapist.
- Will include psychological, cognitive, communicative, social, and physiological needs and strengths, as well as responses to music, music skills, and preferences.
- Will use methods appropriate to the student's age and functioning. Information from observations in and out of music situations, interviews, and other information from other treatment specialists may be included.

- Will note background information which could have or had an impact on functioning, including medications, adaptive devices, positioning, other therapies, health status, psychosocial conditions, and family support systems.
- Will interpret results based on appropriate norms or criterion referenced data.
- Results will be reported to others involved with client services (including the client where appropriate) and include recommendations for other services, if needed (AMTA, 2001).

MCISD Music Therapy Assessment

The MCISD music therapy assessment follows the above procedure. Its format and process have been influenced by the following: (a) research specific to disability, physiology, normal development (both musical and nonmusical development), and music therapy; (b) school curriculum and student needs; (c) other assessments including the MCISD Music Therapy Curriculum (Snell, 1990); Boxhill Music Therapy Assessment (1985); the Scale I: Child-Therapists Relationship in Musical Activity, and Scale II: Musical Communicativeness (Nordoff & Robbins, 1977); Diagnostic Assessment of Music Related Expression and Behavior (DAMREB) (Boone, 1980); the Checklist of Communicative Responses/Acts Score Sheet (CRASS) (Edgerton, 1994); the Special Education Music Therapy Assessment Process (SEMTAP) (Coleman & Brunk, 1999); and the Music Therapy Music Related Behavior Assessment (MT-MRB) (Snell, 2001); (d) state, federal, and local requirements; and (e) formats of other MCISD professional reports.

The music therapy assessment needs the following main content areas in order to provide conclusions and recommendations: (a) summarized student background, (b) current functioning levels and educational approaches, and (c) music therapy's unique form of evaluation (MRB assessment). Currently the music therapy assessments at MCISD follow the format and steps outlined in The Music Therapy Music-Related Behavior Assessment (see Appendix C). The MT-MRB includes a format to note music-related behavior and to sort observations into categories for comparisons between musical expressions and nonmusical functioning. The music therapist is then able to professionally interpret how the music-related behavior correlates to nonmusical functioning and go on to formulate conclusions and recommendations.

The MCISD music therapy assessment report is submitted through the initial referral procedure or as a part of the Three-Year MET evaluation. In either case, the report has the same format. Generally the report lists information under headings that correspond with the MT-MRB Assessment tool, adding or deleting topics appropriate to the individual student. The headings include:

A. Personal Information—name, parents, school, classification, date, etc.
B. Statement—general description of the student, history—including medical past, medications, developmental milestones, school placements, and current related services
C. Psychological and Other Test Scores—most recent test scores, including name of examiner, and sometimes a comparison to past test scores if significant
D. Reason for Evaluation—lists person(s) initiating the evaluation and outlines the purpose of the assessment
E. Present Levels of Performance—includes any information from the Guide for MT Consideration, current IEP performance status and goals, education team interviews, observations in nonmusic therapy school settings and others as appropriate, and notes current educational approaches
F. MT-MRB Assessment Results—further examination of present levels of performance as exposed through the music medium, sorts information, notes music therapy interventions used and their effects upon the student, makes comparisons and correlations to nonmusic functioning outlined by the IEPT and other relevant people
G. Conclusions and Recommendations—brief restatement of student description, including most marked deficit(s) and skill(s); brief statement of significant music-related behavior; addresses "reason for evaluation" statement; lists recommendations for need, or lack thereof, for music therapy, including

conditions, frequency, and recommended target goals and approaches; and lists recommendations for team strategies and/or other service needs for the IEPT to consider.

MCISD offers the Guide for Music Therapy Consideration (see Appendix B) as an option for team members who are not sure if a music therapy assessment is appropriate. The parent(s) or other team members (with parental permission) can fill out the form, send it to the music therapist, and then discuss the appropriateness of music therapy consideration. Evidence pertaining to a lack of functional performance in defined ability levels coupled with a lack of results from current program interventions (statement numbers 1, 11, and 12) support possible need for adding a related service. The other statements refer to barriers which music therapy interventions could have success in treating. Affirming one or more of the statements neither indicate or negate the need for service, but provides the team members unfamiliar with music therapy a way to ask appropriate questions when deciding whether to have music behavior evaluated.

Whether the consideration form is used or not, the MCISD Referral and Request for Consent to Conduct an Educational Evaluation (see Figure 3) is filled out or articulated directly on the IEP so the assessment process can begin.

PRELIMINARY ASSESSMENT INFORMATION: AN EXAMPLE

The beginning of the report may look as follows:

Monroe County Intermediate School District
Music Therapy Assessment

Name:	Stan Student
D.O.B.:	3-11-90
Classification:	Autistic Impairment
Placement:	Mrs. Good, MCEC AI Classroom
Date of Report:	10-4-99

Statement

"Stan" is a 9½-year-old Caucasian boy who presents mental retardation associated with autistic impairment (AI). Reports indicate birth was normal and uncomplicated. He is in good health except for occasional ear infections. Vision and hearing tests are normal. Developmental milestones were within normal limits until age 15 months when verbal expressions disappeared. Stan is unable to use functional verbal communication. He presents self-stimulating behaviors, such as, hand flapping, covering of his ears, and vocal sounds or unrelated utterances. Sleeping patterns are abnormal in that he remains awake until late into the night or morning hours.

He was first seen by the MCISD Early Intervention program in 1991 and classified as speech and language delayed. In 1992 he attended a TMI preschool program classified as trainable mentally impaired, with some time spent in the AI classroom. In 1993 his certification changed to AI and he attended a TMI/AI split placement school program. In 1997 Stan was placed full time in the AI program where he remains to this date. He is in general good health and is not on any medication. He receives speech, OT, music therapy, and adaptive physical education.

Reason for Evaluation

Stan has been referred for a music therapy assessment as a part of his Three-Year MET. This assessment is provided to evaluate how Stan's music-related behavior indicate nonmusical needs and abilities, how this relates to learning, and to determine if music therapy interventions are necessary to his Individualized Education Program. He currently receives music therapy (MT) weekly on an individual and group basis. The MT targeted IEP goal is to improve generalization of skills in a social context. Objectives supporting the goal include applying academic subjects to cooperative music making with peers, expression of timed responses relating to group experiences, and generalization of skills in multiple social settings. This report will summarize the above and give recommendations for future school programming.

Or a "Reason for Evaluation" for an initial assessment for a 1st grade child placed in a regular classroom as an inclusion student may read:

Reason for Evaluation

Due to significant positive responses to music, "Suzy" was referred for a music therapy (MT) assessment by the education team for her Three-Year MET. The purpose of this assessment is to evaluate how Suzy's music-related behavior indicate nonmusical needs and abilities, how this relates to learning, and to determine if music therapy interventions are necessary to her Individualized Education Program. Of particular interest to the team is whether music therapy interventions are needed to address developmental delays, difficulty with social skills and emotional outbursts in the school setting. This report will summarize the above and give recommendations for future school programming.

In yet another example from a 3-year-old boy's initial assessment, the reason for referral can specifically outline qualification criteria:

Reason for Evaluation

This evaluation was requested by "Kevin's" mother to determine if music therapy services are relevant to his educational program. This assessment will evaluate Kevin's music-related behavior to determine if music therapy interventions are necessary to his Individualized Education Program. Qualification protocol considers the following: (1) Student is not making expected progress as related to established ability level; (2) Has difficulty generalizing or applying skills at ability level; (3) Other interventions are not resulting in significant progress; and (4) Music-related behaviors, as interpreted by a board-certified music therapist, indicate music interventions can have significant positive impacts on school goals and objectives.

Psychological tests and any other results can be summarized, as below, or outlined in more detail if the information pertains to considerations for the evaluation.

Psychological and Other Test Results

Stan's most recent psychological test results, as reported by Mildred C. Examiner, school psychologist, and Mrs. Good, AI teacher, are as follows: Vineland Adaptive Behavior Scales— Communication Domain Age Equiv. 1-1; Daily Living Skills Age Equiv. 2-0; Socialization Age Equiv. 10 months; Motor Skills Age Equiv. 4-1; Adaptive Behavior Composite Age Equiv. 1-4; Draw a Person Age Equiv. less than 5 yrs.; Gen. Knowledge 2.6 to 5.6 yrs.; Soc. Emotional 4 to 6 yrs.; Basic Reading Skills 7 yrs.; Manuscript Writing 6.6 yrs.; Basic Math Skills 6.3 to 7 yrs.

Notice in the example above how psychological test scores expose uneven abilities in Stan, a 9-year-old boy (at the time of the test) with autism. For instance, his socialization age equivalency was 10 months and his basic math skills age equivalency was between 6 and 7 years of age. In reviewing the specifics of the test, one finds further evidence of Stan's uneven skills. For example, the motor skills age equivalency may be low because Stan was unable to apply motor skills upon command.

Current IEP Information

A summary of Stan's current IEP (1-26-99) information pertaining to deficit performances and IEP goals is as follows:

Deficit performances listed include:
a) Significant difficulty communicating and applying skills cooperatively with peers
b) Frequent cues required to attend, follow directions and participate in learning
c) Inconsistently makes choices with intent
d) Difficulty processing a variety of sensory input
e) Delayed gross motor development
f) Below age level in functional academics
g) Poor communication skills

IEP goals are as follows:
a) Improve generalization of skills in a social context
b) Develop early communication/interaction skills
c) Will express wants/needs/feelings using adapted communication modes
d) Improve sensory processing
e) Attain age-appropriate gross motor skills
f) Improve functional academic skills
g) Improve basic learning skills

The next section of the report will summarize information from interviews and observations outside of the music therapy setting. This information is helpful in examining "present level of educational performance" (PLEP or PLOP) reported on the IEP. Samples follow:

Interview Information

September 20, 1999, Stan's teacher reported that he is very comfortable with the classroom routine. He participates in opening circle by putting the numbers on the calendar. He needs prompts to participate in 1:1 and group activities. He often needs hand-over-hand guidance. He does not indicate wants and needs. She states that he has trouble following new directions and becomes distressed when the routine is interrupted. Stan can make choices using picture cues, but success is inconsistent. He has his "own ideas" of how to do the worksheets presented by the teacher or aide. He does not interact with peers. He has apparent favorite songs during their class music activities in group or at the computer, as he will smile, laugh, or chuckle. Stan will sing songs heard in music therapy hours or days after experiencing them. He interacts with specific computer programs daily in a ritualistic, perseverative fashion. At home he continues to have unusual sleep patterns and is not yet toilet trained. He is a picky eater and prefers dry cereal to eat.

Below is another sample from the "Interview Information" section in an initial assessment for a 3-year-old boy with autism.

Interview Information

January 5, 2001, Mrs. Nice, "Ned's" preschool teacher, reported that Ned is functionally nonverbal, will parrot words, memorizes songs, names numbers to 20, and needs adult help to remain seated. The teacher also reports that Ned likes computers and is able to start, stop, take out discs, and independently navigate simple preschool children's computer programs. He likes play dough. He does not interact with the other children in the class. He is distressed by changes in routine. While Ned needs help to be seated in the group activities, he now independently will come to circle time if the teacher sings the gathering song. She notes that Ned also responds well to picture cues rather than verbal directions.

Ned's responses to music especially stand out at home, according to his father, Rick, on January 9, 2001. The parents feel he does not have hearing impairment because he instantly runs to the television from upstairs when music occurs in a show or movie. Rick feels that Ned's motivation to attend to a movie is the music rather than the story. Ned also shows interest in the computer at home. He is generally independent on the computer and is especially drawn to programs with songs built into them. He is beginning to read words embedded into these programs, but evidence of pragmatic understanding is unclear. He can identify the word "play" on any computer program and currently enjoys the Arthur reading game program. Ned enjoys running and singing when his 5-year-old sister plays Disney sing-along music tapes. Ned will initiate interaction with his parents by crawling up onto their lap and imitating the crying hand motions to "Wheels on the Bus" so they will sing it to him. His mother, Anna, has meaningful interaction when singing "Row Your Boat" with a fast tempo. Ned also initiates echo vocal play with his parents. Ned expresses a negative response to "scary music" embedded in movies and television shows. He does not appear to be attentive to the program, but when the dramatic music presents, Ned covers his ears and then his eyes. His dad feels music is an understandable cue for Ned. He labels animals with their corresponding sound rather than their name. And in like fashion, Ned labels the alphabet letters with the corresponding sound rather than the letter name. He is also functionally nonverbal at home, but will imitate words.

Observations in nonmusic therapy settings are helpful in clarifying descriptions of student behavior from team member interviews. Below is a portion of the observation section from "Stan's" MET.

Observations in Nonmusic Therapy Settings

The following observations were made in the week prior to 9-29-99. During the classroom observation, Stan was participating in the classroom's regular "Opening Circle Time" involving calendar activities and group "table work." The teacher indicated it was a typical day for Stan. He sat passively and waited for the teacher to direct him during the opening calendar activities, displaying no affect. He did not present eye contact that was connected to the teacher or peers. Stan was unable to locate a picture of himself even though this activity has been presented daily, both this school year and last school year. Stan required gentle physical facilitation to complete most tasks. However, he was able to independently place randomly presented numbers properly on the calendar. Even though placing the numbers on the calendar had relevance to the group task, it was not the activity required by the group (i.e., placing the number of today's date on the calendar). Stan did not fill out the worksheet presented according to directions, despite 1:1 attention from his teacher. He chose to color in sections of the picture that were to remain unaltered. His teacher said Stan "follows his own agenda when doing worksheets." Stan's actions and responses were inconsistent as related to timing. For example, when asked to stand up via a verbal and gestural cue, he did so at the time of request, but when asked in similar fashion to find his picture, get the crayons, and other specific tasks, Stan displayed inaction and appeared to stare through or beyond the teacher. He did not display self-initiated peer interaction during or between activities.

When observed during occupational therapy, Stan displayed similar behavior as observed in the classroom. However, Stan did demonstrate appropriate affect and eye contact when on the giant pillow as the OT rocked him forward and backward. During fine motor tasks he attempted to follow his own agenda, but accepted most of the OT's redirection. He did not imitate the OT during gross motor movement activity or during fine motor simple writing tasks (i.e., drawing a circle, line, and a cross). The OT said imitations skills are presented "in a sporadic and inconsistent fashion." With the OT's permission, the music therapist initiated the "Clapping Hello" song during the imitation portion of the OT session. Stan instantly imitated the motions simultaneously with the music therapist, including changing and unpredictable improvised movements.

Stan was not observed in speech therapy, but an interview with the therapist indicates similar behavior observed in the classroom and OT. The speech therapist stated that Stan's time-ordered responses are sporadic and inconsistent. She said he is able to make choices using total functional communication, such as pointing to pictures. He is successful in following established routines.

Music-Related Behavior Assessment

After gathering the necessary preliminary information, conducting interviews and observations, the music therapist prepares for the music-related behavior assessment portion of the evaluation. The therapist designs experiences which will have a high chance of encouraging musical expressions and interactions by considering all of the preliminary information. The music therapist knows musical expression is highly personal and depends upon a person's comfort level with the people and the environment in the immediate surroundings. New situations can be especially stressful to persons with autism who have difficulty dealing with change, sensory input, and social interaction. Observers must keep in mind that an over- or under-response to music by a person with autism can be due to normal personal comfort and/or the conditions associated with autism. In understanding the normal range of responses and those associated with exceptional conditions, the music therapist is trained to apply live music supports to increase the probability of musical responses and emotional comfort. The therapist's training in observation of nonmusical behavior and musical behavior is equally important as his or her training in music's affect on emotional and physical functioning. These trained skills enable the therapist to (a) prescribe and apply the necessary music interventions according to immediate changing needs; (b) interpret resulting music behaviors; and (c) recommend, design, and implement research-based music therapy applications to support long-term and short-term goals related to productive living.

Whether the tool is a published assessment or a therapist's tailor-made evaluation, the music therapist follows the assessment criteria established in the Standards of Practice (AMTA, 2001) referred to earlier. The client's immediate needs take precedence over long-term established protocol and written session plans. The ability to manipulate the music medium to affect well-being and to make on-the-spot assessments ensures client safety, as relates to both emotional and physical states. The Music Therapy Music-Related Assessment (see Appendix C) currently used at MCISD allows for flexibility regarding individual needs and provides a vehicle to obtain useful assessment information in both over- and under-reactionary situations. The assessment procedures can be used in totality, in portions, or in combination with other assessments.

The Music Therapy Music-Related Behavior Assessment

The MT-MRB Assessment authorizes only therapists certified by the Certification Board for Music Therapists or those with a qualified recognition by the National Music Therapy Registry to administer the evaluation due to the necessary skills needed to plan, implement, and interpret the assessment. The assessment portion of the MT-MRB is conducted after the preliminary information is gathered. Both nonmusical and musical background information provide the basis for an initial evaluation session plan. If the assessment is a re-evaluation of a student in an already established music therapy program, a description of the program and the student's musical behavior relevant to the initial evaluation session plan is summarized.

Objectives and materials are outlined for each music therapy experience based on the preliminary information. Further "back-up" plans are made regarding alternative materials, instruments, and music to have on hand in case the student's immediate needs do not match the predetermined initial plan. The session is conducted in a one-to-one or group situation in the school setting according to the goals and objectives of the plan. Frequently the therapist will design evaluation sessions for both 1:1 and group situations to make behavioral comparisons. Each session is implemented according to music therapy practices. Observations of physical and emotional responses are noted along with their musical correlations. Notes are taken on the specific music therapy interventions needed in each experience as well as the resulting behavior. If the session plans were altered from the original outline the therapist notes the reason for the change. A second or third session is planned only if necessary. Typically a 1:1 and a group session can take place within the course of an hour. Interaction with the student in a group setting can be important, as normalized school work frequently happens in group learning situations. Sometimes a second session is needed in either or both one-to-one and group situations. Only rarely has a third session been required.

Important immediate observations are noted for each experience, including pertinent musical information. Observations involving the student's use of voice, body, interactions with instruments, and communicative intent associated with rhythm, melody, tempo, and harmony among other musical interventions are especially noted. The purpose of the music therapy evaluation session is to engage the student in the process of music to expose music-related behavior which indicates communication, cognitive, motor, emotional and social needs and abilities. The music therapist is noting observable behavior expressed physically. Later, further analysis of the behaviors will require interpretation based upon relevant research, including music therapy-based research and best practices. The session is designed for success via a noninvasive, flexible musical atmosphere which can be altered to meet the immediate physical and emotional needs of the student. Again, the goal of the evaluation session is to engage the student in music making to expose needs and abilities. The emphasis is placed upon the immediate needs of the student, as assessed by a trained therapist. Within this process it is important to note the prescribed music therapy interventions and the effect they have on the student. These observations help provide rationale involving the need for direct music interventions administered by a trained therapist.

Below is an example of a particularly difficult initial evaluation, which becomes more easily navigated by using the MT-MRB assessment.

Caryn: Case Example

"Caryn" was a 3-year-old girl newly enrolled in the MCISD Preprimary Impaired (PPI) Preschool Program, who presented uneven social, communication, and cognitive skills. Her mother, "Vicki," was unable to verbally communicate with Caryn and stated that her daughter had never referred to her as "Mom." Vicki had two older daughters, ages 6 and almost 5. Caryn was very sensitive to noises and fearful of people outside the family circle. She had a vocabulary of less than 50 words and only used one-word utterances. Her mother stated that Caryn would eat inappropriate items, such as sand, and would hurt others and laugh inappropriately about it. Caryn seemed to have a high tolerance for pain. She was referred for a music therapy evaluation to assess possible need for services, as Vicki said Caryn was very interested in and seemed to enjoy music. Vicki played the piano and was hopeful that the music therapist could help her try to connect meaningful communication with her daughter through music. In the preschool classroom, Caryn ran around the room during group circle time and other structured activities. She received speech therapy two times a week through the school.

The student file indicated formal test results were unattainable due to "Caryn either not understanding what she was to do and/or her lack of cooperation." She was classified as Preprimary Impaired (PPI) for the following reasons:

1. Impairment could not be differentiated through existing criteria for other impairments.
2. Impairment manifestations occurred in one or more developmental areas which were at least one-half of expected development for chronological age as measured by more than one developmental scale.
3. Information was based on parent input and two or more qualified evaluators.
4. Impairment could not be resolved with medical or nutritional intervention.
5. Evaluation was not based solely on behaviors relating to environmental, cultural, or economic differences.
6. Established existing need for special education or related services related to the impairment.

The IEP ordered further testing, including a music therapy evaluation, to investigate concerns related to language and cognitive delays. The document merely listed present level of performance as: "Communication skills are significantly delayed in all areas." One annual goal was selected, which asked for increased "efficiency of receptive/expressive language function." The resulting four objectives read as follows:

1. Increase vocabulary used and understood using pictures or other modes.
2. Lengthen task attention tolerance.
3. Improve appropriate use of therapy items.
4. Develop physical/verbal imitation at earliest emergence level.

Observations and interviews gave clearer evidence of Caryn's present levels of functioning. For example, emerging progress during speech therapy consisted of cooperation during repetitive tasks involving puzzle pieces when seated one-to-one with the therapist at a table barricaded on all sides. And Caryn was beginning to parrot some words used in therapy. While her behavior was rote and "robot-like," she was at least cooperative and readily attended speech therapy sessions. These skills were not, however, carrying over to the classroom as expected and she was still not conforming to group activities.

The timing of the music therapy evaluation allowed preliminary information, including observations, to be collected before the end of the school year. However, the music therapy evaluation sessions took place in the summer after the end of the school year. Vicki reported Caryn's sudden fixation with balls since school ended. Caryn would not let her two sisters or anyone else touch any type of ball, as she would hoard and hide every ball within view. Her fixation had recently expanded to include any sports equipment. Her behavior was so extreme that Vicki stayed home with Caryn when the rest of the family attended a family reunion picnic, fearing Caryn would disrupt the family event.

The first music therapy evaluation session produced very minimal music-related behavior, as Caryn did not separate well from Vicki. After walking down the hall to find her mother, Caryn was able to stop crying, but clung to Vicki as if her life depended on it. The rest of the session was spent in the gross motor room, which was the nearest empty room, since Caryn refused to re-enter the music therapy room. The therapist had only her guitar and a container of bubble blow liquid, as the preliminary information indicated Caryn's affinity to popping bubbles. The rest of the session was simply spent by rocking gently in her mother's arms to children's songs. At one point, Vicki blew bubbles to a familiar song adapted to include "bubbles." The music therapist noted the musical times Caryn peeked out from her mother's chest, which later proved helpful in planning the next evaluation session. For example, Caryn "peeked out" during musical verses when little or no physical activity was required. She hid her face when the therapist smiled during direct eye contact. Caryn also hid her face during musical surprises, such as sudden stops, rapid tempo changes, and sudden dynamic contrasts, but while doing so, the therapist could see a smile on Caryn's face. Caryn could anticipate the musical surprises in repeated phrases.

The second session plan again included music Caryn was exposed to in her preschool classroom and items usually popular with preschool children. This time, however, the main goal was to associate positive events with the music therapy room and the music therapist. The therapist used the previous information to plan tempi, sound colors, and dynamics tailored to Caryn's emotional needs. The therapist planned structured experiences which allowed Caryn to "hide within the music" or choose not to participate. And the music therapist would take special care to display an even, low emotional reaction to Caryn's behaviors. The therapist asked Vicki and Caryn's two sisters to participate in the session, among other details, to help Caryn feel safe in the therapy room by eliminating separation from her support base. Both large and small instruments were placed in plain view and positioned for easy access. Electronic sound devices, colorful instruments typically enjoyed by preschool children, and, of course, bubble liquid was readily available as "back-up" items. The resulting notes from the first three song experiences are shown in Figure 4.

MT-MRB Assessment Portion, pg. 2

ACTUAL SESSION

SESSION NUMBER __2__   DATE/TIME: __7-2-01__
                                                                              10:00 a.m.

__Vicki C. (Mother)__ reports __Caryn C.__ is:
(Name & relationship to student)   (Student's name)

✓ having a typical day

_____ having an abnormal day (comment):
C. didn't want to walk down "music hallway" but followed
sisters reluctantly - reported by Vicki.

Circle/Fill-in: 1:1   (Group) — Describe (number, type of participants/surroundings) _w/ mother +_
2 sisters (Shari 6 yrs. + Kathy 5 yrs.) as pre-arranged to decrease separation
anxiety. Held in MT room w/ materials arranged as pre-determined. Door
was open + favorite music was playing as family entered. Session
began immediately.

Experience No. & Title

1. __The More We Get__   Objective(s)   Materials

_____ Same
✓ Altered, explain: – rapport   – chairs set in
Planned song had no   – eye contact   semi-circle
accompaniment. C.   – responses   – guitar
need familiar   to tempo
3/4 rocking w/   predictable
live accompaniment.   melody +
                             phrasing

MT Interventions

guitar = non-threatening
andante → fast-slow

w/ surprise

– Tempo, accent, +
dynamics required
prescription to
immediate needs

Observations:
C. clung to mom + buried head into mom's shoulders
S. + K. followed directions at age levels
Mom rocked C. to accented downbeats
C. quieted by 4th measure
Eye contact w/ MT during safe, undemanding phrases
Giggled repeatedly each in "sleep/wake-up" but did not imitate.
Indications:
– understands re-occurring musical phrases, likes tempo contrasts
+ musical surprises; will likely respond more as trust increases.
– Rocking calms
– Responds to prescribed accents, predictable harmonic progressions.
– Interested in musical aspects = to chron. age (tempo changes, predictability, musical surprises)

Quality & conditions of transition to next experience: __ Compliant ✓ Non-compliant __ Other
Explain: _Still clinging to mom. Refused to sit in chair. MT allowed_
C. to stay on mom's lap.
Interventions used:
Improvised "Bubble Song" using tempo, accents + melody line
See notes for #2 below.

MT-MRB Assessment Portion, pg. 2a - ACTUAL SESSION

<u>Experience No. & Title</u>   Student Name *Caryn C.* Session Number _2_

2. *Popping Bubbles*   Objective(s)   Materials
___Same   - rapport/trust   - Bubble liquid
_✓_Altered, explain: - to match C's   wands &
C. still clinging to mom   actions w/   bubble machine
Previous info said C.   music reinforces   - Guitar
likes bubbles. Improvised
song to support immediate needs.

MT Intertentions

's turn to pop the bubbles

Pop Pop ..... pop
> > >> >

Observations:
- C. watched sisters by 4th measure, ran around
room + yelled "yeah"
- Complied w/ "stay in seat" during verse
- Did not want to blow bubbles, but swatted and
stomped on bubbles saying "pop, pop" at proper time.
- Looked at MT when music matched her actions.

- Prescribed tempo
changes to match
C's actions. Accents
used to match "popping"

Indications:
- Understood "sit" in verse + "run" or "pop" during
chorus - employed a level of self-organization
- Needed music interventions to make social
connection to MT. Music needed to match C's needs.

- Use of accents +
musical anticipation
to support engagement.
I V I / I IV V I

Quality & conditions of transition to next experience:___Compliant ___Non-compliant _✓_Other
Explain: Did not stop w/ music - Ran to mom when understood song
was done.
Interventions used: V - I
"all done" - Chanted improvised song "Get ready for the next song"
incorporating 1-2-3!

3. *Give Me One Beat*   Objective(s)   Materials
_✓_Same   - Observe musical   Floor tom
___Altered, explain: timing, anticipation   Sus. cymbal
- Could comply w/   + self control   gong, mallet
"sit to take a turn"   - motor planning   guitar
- Ready for more   - turn taking
structured demands.   - Response to changing music

MT Intertentions

Observations: (did not use gong)
- S. + K's role modeling observed by C. C. Ran around
room during S's turn. Complied to sit during K's turn.
- Difficulty keeping body at the drum + cymbol.
- Waited during anticipatory notes, but played
repeated notes on drum despite sib's example of 1 beat.
- Played stronger when MT matched her accented drumming

- anticipatory
notes supported
"waiting" + "anticipating."
+ eye contact
- sudden stops + V-I cadence
at end of phrase
to help C. stop
- matched C's

Indications:
- Potential to comply w/ more group rules if she
understands expectations
- Continuous beating may be related to Developmental
age or having own agenda rather than non-compliance

accented playing "> > >..."
- MT could direct
tempo by end
of song.

Quality & conditions of transition to next experience:___Compliant ___Non-compliant _✓_Other
Explain: Hugged mom, then sat on her lap
Interventions used: MT accepted behavior w/o interventions.

Figure 4. MT-MRB Assessment Example

Three more music therapy experiences followed the song exercises described above. They were brief and not demanding, as the therapist felt further requirements would have had a negative effect on the developing rapport between herself and Caryn. By sorting the emotional and physical responses observed into subcategories related to musical expression, the therapist could decide to proceed directly to writing a report with recommendations, rather than ordering another evaluation session.

The music therapist could tell Caryn had a general understanding of musical structure commensurate to her chronological age. She was interested in musical contrasts and could self-organize as she anticipated predictable musical occurrences. Additionally, Caryn responded quickly to prescribed music therapy interventions tailored to her needs, such as tempo and strategically placed accents. In a very short time, the therapist was able to convey to Caryn the concept of "people who are seated get a turn" without touching or scolding her. Caryn's responses in the music therapy session indicated verbal language processing difficulties resulting in fear and confusion, all of which could be lessened with prescribed music therapy supports. Caryn could be calmed and encouraged using live music via the guitar (stringed sounds were nonthreatening), strategically placed accents, and prescribed melodic, rhythmic, and harmonic applications. She did not yet display compliance and interaction skills with recorded music. It was significant to note that Caryn was able to learn some general group rules, appropriate interaction with the musical equipment, and begin to build a trusting relationship with a relatively new person (the therapist) all within the first 10 minutes of the session. With support from music therapy interventions, she was able to time responses to coincide with specific musical cues and even begin to engage in beginning levels of give-and-take interaction.

The music therapist concluded that noncompliance issues in the classroom were initially resulting from a genuine lack of understanding directions and were beginning to turn into avoidance behaviors. Caryn's ability to understand musical structure revealed she was able to self-organize and engage in some level of interaction when using a communication medium she could decipher. While interacting within a predictable musical context, Caryn displayed normal eye-gaze and joint attention, anticipating the succession of events. While she needed prescribed music therapy interventions to engage in more organized meaningful interaction, the therapist felt this indicated clear potential for Caryn to be able to conform to group rules, like sitting in a chair and waiting for a turn.

The therapist felt music therapy was needed to (a) support an increase in understood and used vocabulary in a functional setting, (b) lengthen task attention span, (c) improve appropriate use of objects, and (d) develop imitation skills. Additionally, the therapist felt Caryn was capable of learning in and conforming to basic group learning situations. Music interventions could provide strategies for adaptive means to decode verbal and social cues. Music therapy was recommended to take place 30 minutes a week within a group of preschool peers to support language and functional social skills. Individual sessions were initially recommended to build rapport and basic understanding of musical cues relating to interactive cooperation.

Music therapy enabled observation of Caryn's interaction skills in an environment where she did not have to decode verbal language so the team could decide if behaviors resulted from an autism spectrum condition or from only a language processing deficit. Today she is participating in classroom group lessons, conforming to higher expectations, and using more words to communicate. At age 4 she continues to need support in decoding social cues, functional use of skills, and interacting with others via group music therapy and other special education supports. Her diagnosis and classification is still under consideration with at least one doctor and some team members suggesting an autism spectrum condition.

Analysis of Music-Related Behavior

After the music therapy evaluation session and observations are noted, the information is sorted into categories to help the therapist draw conclusions and provide clear explanations for recommendations. The two main analysis sections are the MRB Areas of Expression and the MT-MRB Functional Expression/ Response Wheel. The evaluator can opt to use either or both sections depending upon needs pertaining to the student. The MRB Areas of Expression section is fast and easy for the trained therapist to fill out. Observations are sorted into areas of musical expression, specifically, vocal expression, instrumental expression, and motor expression. Each category notes behavior quality pertaining to rhythm and other musical components. Imitative expressions and social/emotional expressive qualities are noted, too. There is a section in each category requiring the specified music therapy interventions used in each experience along with any resulting behaviors. After the information is summarized, the therapist can write conclusions and recommendations or proceed to the MT-MRB Functional Expression/Response Wheel.

Musical Expression Summary Examples

Summary subsections of musical expression can either be brief or very detailed depending upon the responses the child exhibited during the assessment. Information gathered in the preliminary stages of the assessment can be included in the musical expression summaries if it pertains to the subject area. See the following brief examples:

Caryn, Age 3, Possible Autism Classification—Vocal Expression Summary Example

Caryn has significant limits in the use of words to communicate. She could be heard stating words like "wow!" or "yeah" at both appropriate and inappropriate times. She could be heard to say "no," cry, or scream to express displeasure. During the evaluation sessions Caryn used crying and screaming to indicate distress. Rocking in her mother's arms to prescribed tempo and accents which match immediate needs resulted in a quiet voice and calmer body. She giggled at musical jokes and surprises. Caryn took quick, audible deep breaths during sudden musical stops. She imitated "pop, pop" during the improvised "Popping Bubbles" song when supported with tempo and accents produced to conform to Caryn's actions. Breathing and sounds made during the music indicated an ability to anticipate musical phrases and endings. Responses indicate more vocal responses may result within the music medium after a more trusting rapport is established with the therapist.

Todd, Age 10, Autism Classification—Instrumental Expression Summary Example

Todd will shake shaker-type rhythm instruments, beat a drum with or without a mallet, tap a cymbal, play tambourine, xylophone/glockenspiel with mallet, sticks and ethnic rhythm instruments. He may flick, engage in perseverative actions, kick, or push away instruments. Motor planning and sensory issues, as well as, noncompliance impede proper use of instruments. He is unable to interact with the objects in a sustained musical fashion independently. However, with highly structured music therapy support, Todd can sustain approximate engagement for up to 36 measures.

Todd shows interests in exploring the guitar, rainstick, drums and ethnic rhythm instruments by choosing them during free time and/or touching them when it is not his turn. Despite his interest level he is unable to hold the instrument or mallet for long without fidgeting, flicking, or throwing.

He shows ability to hold and play the instruments, but cannot maintain it for functional use independently. With live music therapy interventions he can maintain acceptable use for 24–36 measures with instruments that require gross motor movement (i.e., rainstick, large drum, maraca). Todd indicates an understanding of reoccurring patterns in the music. However, it is difficult for him to perform a pattern rhythmically, even at a slow tempo. He prefers to go straight through the pattern as fast as possible without regard for tempo or note values. His difficulties indicate motor planning deficits and a significant lack of ability to decode social cues. However, with prescribed "suspense - resolution" type chord progressions, accents, and tempo, Todd is able to follow words and letters to musically play a pattern for 12–36 measures with the proper rhythmic speed.

Cal, Age 10, Severely Mentally Impaired (Primary Classification) and Autistically Impaired (Secondary Classification)—Motor Expression Summary Example

Observed expressive movements related to music have been rocking forward and back, deep breathing, instrument manipulation, and sporadic out of seat behavior. He will move or "dance" around the room to live music independently for an average of four measures. He will "dance" longer when physically assisted. The teacher reported Cal has been running out of the classroom. While initially Cal needed physical assistance to remain seated during music therapy, today he is able to remain seated unassisted during both 1:1 and group therapy sessions.

Cal is able to imitate tempo and dynamics for up to six measures, but is unable to imitate other motor movements during structured activities. Approximate imitations occurs during improvisational music making when Cal matches the therapist's tempo or dynamics.

Additional summary subsections include "Rhythmic and Other Musical Expressions," "Imitative Expressions," and "Social/Emotional Expressions." Sample "Social/Emotional Expressions" subsections follow:

Todd, Age 10, Autism Classification—Social/Emotional Expressions Summary Example

Todd has a limited repertoire for emotional expressions. He is able to express happiness and discomfort with cries, humming, repeating words, flapping his arms, stomping his feet, hitting his legs, giggling, noncompliance, rocking, and clapping. Todd does not initiate interaction with peers. However, he has begun to share the alphabet board with a classmate during free time. Using picture communication he was able to choose a student from another classroom to attend a music therapy session with him. Todd repeatedly chanted his chosen friend's name ("Josh"), clapped, and smiled. But during the session he repeatedly grabbed Josh's eye glasses and threw them. Engagement in familiar musical experiences helped to calm Todd, but he was not able to participate at his ability level. Investigating physical, sensory means for self-expression and self-control through drumming and improvisational music has supported Todd in learning the concepts of "change," "surprise," "be quiet," and "please wait." Music therapy reinforcements used to support learning these concepts included dynamic accents and predictable chord progressions timed during the anticipatory portion of the lesson. Musical cadences unique to each concept were then timed with the moment the above "concepts" occurred. For instance, C7–G7 played to coincide with the presentation of a "change" within a familiar musical experience resulted in smiles and clapping from Todd to celebrate the "change."

Dylan, Age 12, Trainable Mentally Impaired (Primary Classification) and
Autistic Impairment (Secondary Classification)—Social/Emotional Expressions
Summary Example

Dylan becomes upset when his is not first. Use of live music interventions, such as rhythm, three-step patterns, harmonic progressions, and/or melody can easily help Dylan accept not being first. His actions (walking, eating, and doing his work) are increased in tempo when he is agitated or excited. The above mentioned music interventions are also effective in helping Dylan to move at the appropriate speed for as long as 65 measures of music. He does not seek out peer interaction, but he imitates negative behaviors (i.e., screaming, unusual hand flapping, or body positioning) of peers in his presence. Despite Dylan's abilities in music making he has significant difficulty applying and generalizing these skills in a group without live music therapy interventions. For example, he can be flexible within the music medium, but remains rigid in his demands for being first and following routines. This discrepancy may imply that Dylan's autistic impairment is the primary barrier to functional use of skills and trainable mental impairment may be secondary. Proper use of music helps Dylan to regain self-control, remain focused, interact with others and functionally apply his skills. Harmonic progressions and the process of music making help to reassure Dylan and organize his thoughts with his actions. He will accept change within a musical structure. He is also able to problem solve for the sake of the time limit in a song, i.e., if the instrument or mallet falls, he will skip a head to catch-up to the proper place in the music after retrieving the instrument.

The MT-MRB Functional Expression/Response Wheel

The MT-MRB Functional Expression/Response Wheel uses a multi-dimensional continuum wheel to analyze functional abilities and potentials. It investigates music therapy interventions which support increased or decreased success in some 20 or more musical expression/response areas. The areas used depend upon the student's needs and the MRBs displayed during any of the evaluation sessions. Each area has ties to nonmusical functioning abilities or potentials and can help to pinpoint areas of need which may be positively influenced by music therapy interventions. Evaluators using this system find that the therapist must be current with normal and exceptional musical and nonmusical development in order to interpret useful information. Data from the evaluation session(s) must include observations pertaining to timing, quality, emotional and interactive actions related to the music and, even more specifically, observations related to the prescribed music therapy interventions used during the actual session(s).

Each expression/response area has a continuum of displayed behavior ranging from low functional results to high functional results. Information interpreted by the music therapist is plotted on two opposing "pie pieces" with lowest ratings falling to the left and below the horizontal line (see Figure 5). The higher ratings fall to the right and above the horizontal line. The pie pieces are then combined to form a wheel. Again, interpretation by the trained professional is necessary, as each set of results require consideration of subtleties, like musical intent of the behavior and the effect a prescribed harmonic progression had on motor planning, among many others. The shaded results provide a visual model of strengths and weaknesses illustrated through the music medium and can be compared to an Expression/Response Wheel plotting information from nonmusical settings and interventions. In addition to helping the therapist find useful assessment comparisons, it attempts to further assist in articulating the differences in music therapy treatment interventions from teacher, speech pathologist, occupational therapy, or physical therapy interventions.

For instance, Caryn's scoring for the following two areas might look as detailed in Figure 5. Once the pie pieces are combined to form a wheel, the resulting visual picture can provide a means to quickly summarize evaluation results and conclusions to the education team without having to explain minute details of specific music therapy interventions used. The musical references are important in establishing rationale for music therapy services, but an overly detailed explanation can confuse team members and blur music therapy's relevance to nonmusical outcomes outlined in the educational plan. For example, the following MT-MRB Functional Expression/Response Wheel shows how live music therapy interventions were responsible for all but one of the shaded results in "positive" expression/response top portion of the wheel (see Figure 6).

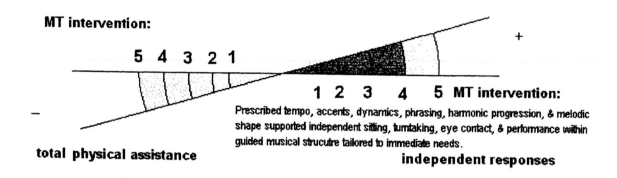

MT intervention:

5 4 3 2 1

1 2 3 4 5 MT intervention:

Prescribed tempo, accents, dynamics, phrasing, harmonic progression, & melodic shape supported independent sitting, turntaking, eye contact, & performance within guided musical strucutre tailored to immediate needs.

total physical assistance

independent responses

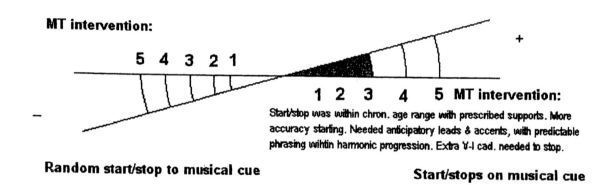

MT intervention:

5 4 3 2 1

1 2 3 4 5 MT intervention:

Start/stop was within chron. age range with prescribed supports. More accuracy starting. Needed anticipatory leads & accents, with predictable phrasing wihtin harmonic progression. Extra V-I cad. needed to stop.

Random start/stop to musical cue

Start/stops on musical cue

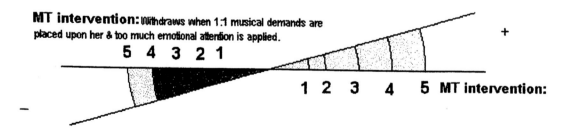

MT intervention: Withdraws when 1:1 musical demands are placed upon her & too much emotional attention is applied.

5 4 3 2 1

1 2 3 4 5 MT intervention:

Little or no imitation

Imitation synchronized at age level or above

Figure 5. Continuum of Displayed Behavior

In Figure 6, positive functional expression/responses are shaded in the top half of the wheel. Shading in the outermost sections of the pie pieces indicates music therapy intervention supports were needed to obtain the positive results in all but one section. In this particular example, music therapy interventions were not associated with any of the negative expressions/responses results in the bottom portion of the wheel. The narrative report outlined the numerous music therapy interventions used. This illustration helped the music therapist quickly explain her rationale in recommending direct music therapy services, rather than merely suggesting music activities administered by the teacher.

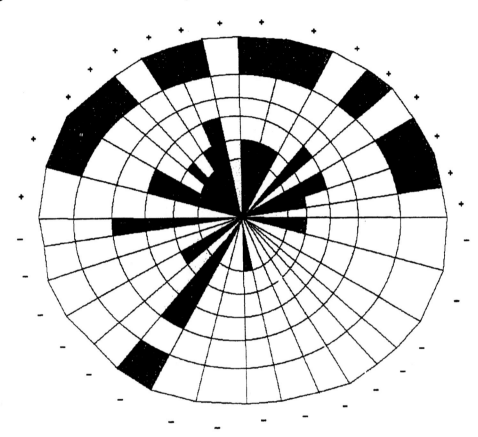

Figure 6. Sample MT-MRB Functional Expression/Response Wheel
for an MCISD Preschool Student With Autism

Conclusions and Recommendations

The MT-MRB Assessment Analysis helps the music therapist form responsible conclusions. When a music therapist is applying the information toward public school special education programs, the present level of educational performance absent of music therapy interventions can be considered when recommending service levels. If the assessment is a re-evaluation to determine if current music therapy services need to continue, then the report should document progress levels and music therapy interventions being used to establish continuation or termination. In remembering the intent of IDEA (see section below), the therapist should outline how her recommendations support movement toward independent, functional use of skills in the community with age-appropriate peers. By referring to music-related behaviors and explaining their relevance to nonmusical, functional skills, the therapist is able to clarify the unique, *necessary* rationale for music therapy support in the educational program. The MRB analysis also provides clarity in situations of nonservice recommendations. When music therapy is not the result, the therapist maintains professional integrity by not suggesting frivolous service and can use the analysis to provide useful information to the family and IEPT, i.e., musical tips for learning in the nonmusical classroom, insight into undefined abilities, suggestions for appropriate regular education inclusion (both musical and nonmusical), and private music lessons or private music therapy service options, among others. Below are examples of Conclusion and Recommendation sections from evaluations involving students mentioned in earlier examples.

Dylan, Age 12, Trainable Mental Impairment (Primary Classification) and Autism (Secondary Classification)—Conclusions and Recommendations

Dylan is a 12-year-old boy who presents developmental delays and autistic impairment. He shows a discrepancy in the functional use of skills in a social context at his skill level. The autistic disability may be the primary barrier to functional applications of his skills. He tolerates and performs better in smaller group settings. Dylan shows definite strengths in music abilities. He has marked positive responses to music therapy interventions, which especially help him to self-organize, relate to others, emotionally stabilize himself, and functionally use skills cooperatively. It is recommended that he continue to receive music therapy services by a professionally trained music therapist who is able to assess the appropriate use of tempo, melody, harmony, and rhythm as related to Dylan's specific long-term and immediate needs. Therapy goals and objectives should serve to challenge social interaction skills, functional use of academics, explore abstract concepts, and explore strategies to assist with emotional upset. He should receive group, small group and consider a level of 1:1 music therapy services within the structure of his school program.

Todd, Age 10, Autism Classification—Conclusions and Recommendations

Todd has significant difficulty in decoding social cues and functionally applying his skills in a group setting. He continues to experience impairments in communication, adaptive skills and tolerance for sensory stimuli. These impairments are effecting delays in learning, social development, motor abilities, relating to people and objects, as well as the functional application of knowledge and skills. Todd's behavior, interactions and functional use of skills are positively influenced with specific music therapy interventions that are assessed and applied by a board-certified music therapist. These interventions include changes in tempo, use of live music and adapted recorded music with live elements, dynamic contrasts, strategically placed accents and cadences, use of style, texture and harmonic progressions, and the rhythmic timed use of visual cues. He is developing abilities in coordinated use of cognitive and motor functioning in a social context with music therapy support.

It is recommended that Todd continue to receive music therapy services in both a small and larger group setting. One-to-one music therapy opportunities should be available on an as needed basis since there are some skills he may need to initially learn outside of the group setting. The following suggestions should be considered within the treatment design:

1. Begin a concrete list of motivators.
2. Use music therapy techniques to develop concrete experiences and labels for abstract concepts dealing with feelings, transitions, time concepts, and social skills.

3. Continue to demand time-ordered cooperative use of skills, working to expand duration. Develop anticipation skills and flexibility with unpredictable cues. Give ample time and defined space to perform sequenced motor movements. Teach and string together 1–3 step patterns.
4. Demand use of skills with peers.
5. Integrate and expand upon subjects Todd is preoccupied with to engage him in functional use of skills.
6. Develop appropriate outlets for built up emotions.
7. Remain mindful of chronological age and develop age appropriate experiences.

Kevin, Age 3, Autism Classification—MRB Summaries, Conclusions, and Recommendations Direct Music Therapy Not Recommended

Music-Related Behavior Summaries

Music therapy evaluation sessions were conducted in the classroom in a group, circle-time-type of situation, as it was seen as the most natural and nonthreatening atmosphere for Kevin.

Vocal Expression

Kevin easily engaged in music experiences after the therapist was able to build a beginning rapport with him. Use of his voice as an initial response to musical elements was not his first choice. However, when musical surprises or interesting rhythmic patterns were interjected, Kevin laughed and smiled in relationship to musical happenings. Re-occurring melodic phrases prompted Kevin to blurt out the ending word, i.e., Hello, hello, HELLO, and STOP or Be QUIET, Be QUIET, Say SHH. Voice quality had a plain intonation, but volume and consonant accents were clearly being used. Kevin was more likely to utter a given word if there was cadence (rhythmic or melodic) coupled with a simultaneous motor action, such as hands patch knees right when singing the word "stop" or moves finger to mouth timed with "shh."

Rhythmic Expression

Kevin is able to match simple changing tempi or pulse speed of the music. He is able to effortlessly watch the therapist's model, glance away, then bring his visual focus back to the therapist without loosing synchronization. Arms, legs, head, and body begin to move as soon as a beat is presented. Kevin is able to move isolated parts of his body in rhythm (an arm or leg) while the rest of his body remains still, all while remaining visually engaged. Kevin physically responded to rhythmic changes in the music whether he was visually looking or not. Kevin was successful in rhythmic expression with both live and recorded music.

Instrumental Expression

Kevin held, touched, and interacted with musical percussion items in a typical fashion and in some instances in a more advanced fashion. For example, Kevin was able to synchronize to therapist directed musical changes while playing the tonic notes of a two chord song (Skip to My Lou) on large contra bass xylophone bars. His musical breathing and gross motor weight shifting happened unconsciously as he produced music to match the accompaniment. He interacted successfully with maracas, drums, cabasa, rainstick, and sticks. Rhythmic accents especially help Kevin to engage in group music experiences. He was successful in both live and recorded musical applications.

Imitation

As can be seen in the previous two sections, Kevin is very successful at imitating modeled movements and is able to remain rhythmically accurate according to beat or pulse. Vocal imitation needs more concentration, and he has not been observed to express a sustained musical use of his voice. Because he responds vocally to repetition, reoccurring phrases, and rhythmic cadences with relative immediacy, his behavior indicates that productive, sustained use of his voice is about to blossom.

Social/Emotional

Kevin cried and looked fearful during the initial session with the music therapist. The therapist was surprised to observe this behavior as Kevin had portrayed a definite comfort level in his classroom during other observations. The teacher gently sat with him to demand that he at least stay in the group. Music interventions coupled with the teacher's support were successful in re-directing Kevin into the music experiences. Music interventions used were familiar chord progression sequences, gentle beat accents, musical rocking, and strategically placed musical surprises (sudden stops, starts, changes in tempo or dynamics). Soon into the session he was smiling and joining in. Note that at the beginning of the next session he stared to act fearful again. The therapist ignored this behavior and immediately presented his favorite song from the previous week and his mood instantly modulated to a positive one. The third session only elicited a positive response. Due to the quick change in Kevin's demeanor related to the newness of the initial music therapy session, coupled with the types of interventions (musical surprises, etc.), the therapist feels the issue of fear was related to trust. Once musical trust was established, Kevin did not have problems with people, things, or sounds during the sessions. Kevin was comfortable participating in the group with peers and adults, accepting the structure of the 30 minute sessions.

Kevin displayed a high level of musical interaction in that he responded to all elements of the music presented physically and emotionally. He smiled at appropriate times in the music and glanced at everyone else as if to see if they were smiling, too. He physically displayed the ability to anticipate beginnings, endings, phrases, dynamics, reoccurring surprises, etc. And, as noted earlier, he is able to display musical breathing, movement, and timing. Kevin also responded to the mood of the music presented and could have his mood positively changed with the presence of musical elements.

Conclusions and Recommendations

Kevin is a delightful 3-year-old classified with autistic impairment. Concerns include communication deficits and inconsistencies, difficulty interacting with peers and staff (though improving), transitions, new situations, and behavior such as tantrums or head banging. During the music therapy observations and evaluation sessions Kevin displayed low-level use of his voice and verbal language, but musical behavior indicates potential for use of voice to blossom and advance in it's development. Both home and school environments are providing effective stimuli to foster his use of verbal/vocal language. Kevin presented behavior consistent with verbal language processing difficulties, as when there is visual modeling he understands whole concepts and even applies single words appropriate to the situation. His sensitivity and understanding of numerous musical concepts (i.e., harmonic progressions, phrasing, rhythm, changes and surprises) indicate that he can cognitively understand, respond to, and apply abstract concepts via sound and musical movement. Kevin even laughs at the higher meaning of musical concepts such as "jokes" or "tricks." Musical aptitude is not dependent upon verbal language processing.

Some of the same concepts used in the music presented are not understood by Kevin when presented to him verbally without a visual model. Kevin did not display physical difficulty interacting with others in structured situations; however, his lack of verbal skills limited his ability to interact via use of his voice. Kevin displayed difficulty with a new situation regarding the first music therapy evaluation session; however, he did not have difficulty with the therapist being in the room during nontherapist directed times. His responses to the music interventions applied to help him acclimate to the situation indicate that he may be distressed during transitions or new situations due to lack of understanding "what's going to happen to him next." Yet Kevin was able to tolerate and even enjoy unpredictable musical surprises and changes. This is probably because he understands harmonic progressions and resolutions, regardless of changing nuances. A lack of understanding the sequence of events can negatively impact trust issues causing a child to become fretful and resistive in new situations.

Kevin does not meet the criteria for (1) lack of expected progress as relates to ability level, (2) difficulty generalizing or functionally applying skills at ability level, or (3) other interventions are not resulting in significant improvements to qualify for direct music therapy in the school setting. However, due to his marked responses to music and his emerging use of his voice, the education team may consider group music therapy consultation to the teacher. Group consultation would require some weeks of music therapy directed classroom groups with the teacher present. These groups should be conducted in a way that does not make Kevin dependent upon the music therapist. Lack of this group consultation will not adversely affect Kevin's program, but can support his language program. Kevin's mother may want to some day pursue regular music lessons when a regular music teacher deems him old enough.

Stan, Age 9, Autism Classification—MRB Summaries, Conclusions and Recommendations
Direct Music Therapy Recommended to Continue

Evaluation sessions were conducted in Stan's usual music therapy 1:1 and group settings. The information includes on-going observations from his current music therapy service program.

Vocal Expression

Stan can be heard making vocalizations and verbalizations as if he is chatting to himself. Often there are times when words or phrases can be clearly recognized during this chattering. The content may or may not pertain to the current situation. Sometimes Stan is heard making loud sudden vocalizations as if to stimulate himself. Stan will cry when he is distressed and cling to the adult with him. This is especially true when there is a change in his routine. He is now able to tolerate more changes in his environment and when traveling to other parts of the school than reported in his previous MET. Stan can be heard saying short phrases such as, "stop that," or "go sit down." He can be heard frequently imitating dialogue or jingles from TV videos in a perseverative fashion.

Stan has been observed to laugh inappropriately and sometimes appropriately, especially when tickled or during a song with anticipated surprises. He is unable to communicate verbally in a functional manner. He has significant difficulties making sounds or saying words upon request. However, he has made marked gains in spontaneous vocal and verbal responses that are time-related to songs. This is true during music therapy experiences that are specifically designed to support Stan in vocal expressions. He will exhibit an appropriate verbal or melodic expression one to three times during 95% of his music therapy sessions for the past year.

Rhythmic Expression

Stan is not able to consistently exhibit his rhythmic abilities cooperatively in a time-ordered fashion. When his abilities do emerge, Stan demonstrates the ability to synchronize with the pulse of the music in different meters. He consistently responds to changes in tempo and volume. Stan specifically attends to the auditory presentation of live music and appears to be able to relate to the harmonic progressions within phrases and cadences. He can anticipate beginnings, endings, phrase patterns, and predictable musical surprises. He has difficulty tracing abstract symbols (letters, numbers) to play a pattern, but he is beginning to respond to familiar pages in a book when it is presented in conjunction with a music therapy experience.

Instrumental Expression

Stan continues to be able to accept redirection when playing musical instruments. Typically he will hold them in unusual fashions and investigate the mechanics of the instrument. He has increased demonstration of continuous playing of drums or other percussive instruments as related to the music. Previously he would need physical support to complete a short passage. Now he will independently complete an entire 24 to 36 measure song without help in three out of five therapy sessions.

Motor Expression

Stan is very coordinated and can manipulate small and large objects. He is often observed to be using or playing with objects in unusual ways. Despite his abilities in motor movement he is unable to apply them cooperatively or upon command. Routine and musical support increase Stan's functional use of these skills.

Imitative Expression

Imitation of motor and vocal models from the therapist are not consistent. However, Stan is showing a significant increase in this area as related to routine and familiar music. It is important to note that he will consistently imitate the "Clapping Hello" song motor movements and occasionally he simultaneously sings the words in various settings. He will also imitate changing and unpredictable motor movements as long as they are within the structure of the "Clapping Hello" song. Additionally, during this song he exhibits appropriate eye contact and social flexibility. Stan has also exhibited appropriate use of song association. For example, he sang the "Yucky" song when presented with a new music therapy experience that talked about mud.

Social/Emotional Expression

Stan expresses distress by crying and/or clinging to his teacher or care giver. He has not been observed to beat or play a musical instrument in anger or with aggression. He has not been observed to interact with or seek attention from peers. He will engage in cooperative musical interaction with others in a limited fashion with structured music therapy support.

Conclusions and Recommendations

Stan continues to have significant delays in communication, social interaction, and functional use of skills due to conditions associated with autism. His increased emergence of time-ordered use of skills and expressions during music therapy experiences indicate he is making gains in his current program. He also is demonstrating the ability to apply these skills in various settings and with changing expectations (as in the "Clapping Hello" song) with music therapy support. It is recommended that he continue to receive individual and group music therapy. The music therapy program should emphasize functional applications of skills in a time-ordered fashion in a social context. Music therapy interventions should be applied across settings and with groups of peers outside of his classroom. Particular attention should be applied to use of routine, familiarity, and the interjection of change within the structure of the routine and familiar experiences.

IEP Information

The student's present level of functioning is documented within the IEP and supported by standardized tests, assessments, observations, and IEPT interviews. However, sometimes primary areas of concern voiced by the team are not clearly noted on the IEP document. Additionally, problems not identified in the documentation may be contributing factors to the noted deficit performance(s). In referring to Caryn's case example earlier, one can see that the deficit performance only referred to communication deficits, even though there also was evidence of sensory issues, marked behavioral problems, and impaired social skills. Each IEPT member conducting an assessment, including those independently contracted (Michigan Department of Education, November 7, 2001), is uncovering strengths, weaknesses, and abnormalities which may be at the root of the presented learning delays. The evaluators are looking for both support and nonsupport of the classification and program strategies so comparisons with skill levels noted in the IEP and various tests can be made. Subsequently, the collective results and conclusions of the assessments, along with the progress status of the expiring IEP, are considered by the IEPT to formulate a new IEP.

IEPT

The Individualized Education Program Team (IEPT) coordinates the student's individualized education program (IEP). The team must make sure the IEP is in compliance with federal and state rules and regulations as stipulated in IDEA-97 and the Michigan Department of Education. Understanding the *intent* of the law helps explain the resulting rules and regulations that influence curriculum, services, and placements. Current law places heavy emphasis on education in the least restrictive environment, access to regular education curriculum, and transition from school to adult living. Furthermore, in attempts to strengthen parental rights, accountability and evaluation are more clearly outlined in IDEA-97. In addition to various evaluations, this includes regular progress reports and formal testing comparing special education students' progress with state and national data on similar students' progress. Other provisions supporting the parental role include: parent input during evaluation, parent participation in the eligibility decision, parent participation in the placement decision, parent consent for reevaluation, parent participation in meetings, and parent receipt of progress reports. IDEA also stipulates a student may not be expelled from school if the offending behavior is due to a disability.

The rules and regulations are developed on the state level to comply with IDEA and dictate how local schools conduct programs. Since the rules and regulations clarify when, where and how all levels of programs and services occur in the school setting, familiarity with them is important. Each school district will have their own forms, which may resemble state recommended formats. The local forms and procedures have a direct impact upon a school district's compliance with the law. Note that the forms should not prohibit or impede individualization of the IEP, an especially important aspect for those with autism spectrum disorders. The federal government holds the states accountable for compliance and the states, in turn, monitor the local districts for the same. Consequently, the forms are updated and changed frequently, so one must be diligent to remain current with the procedures. Parents and citizens can request the school district's parent handbook containing rules, definitions, and parental rights. Referring to the state and federal websites for special education via the Department of Education sites will usually provide copies of the law, rules and regulations, and other pertinent information.

Special Education Components

There are three important components in special education procedures to especially understand. There is, of course, *the IEP,* which establishes present levels of educational performance, outlines goals and objectives, and determines necessary services and adaptive supports to access curriculum in the least restrictive environment. *Assessment components,* such as the Initial Evaluation, the Three-Year Meeting of the Education Team (MET) evaluation, and progress reports, report functional and developmental information to help determine classification, levels of performance, and program needs in the IEP. *Transition services* are a coordinated set of activities which prepares a student to move from school to post-school activities and is reflected in the IEP (Bateman & Linden, 1998; Siegel 2001). The plan must be based upon student needs, interests, and preferences. Transition planning and services are gaining more importance as there have been court rulings which found district transition planning practices to be minimal and noncompliant with IDEA-97 (Bateman & Linden). It appears that noncompliant rulings resulted from poorly defined plans and a lack of appropriate actions by IEP teams.

When practicing music therapy in school settings, careful examination of the special education components is necessary and in keeping with music therapy standards of practice (AMTA, 2001). Merely studying disabling conditions will not prepare the assessor to delineate between recommendations necessary to the IEP and those outside the school jurisdiction. For example, transition action plans include instruction, related services, community experiences, employment goals, other adult living objectives, and daily living skills and functional vocational evaluation. Knowing that related services are assigned to support community involvement, daily living, and functional skills is important when interpreting assessment results and determining school services, curriculum, and timelines for objectives. Related service personnel know that, in addition to academics, it is appropriate to recommend interventions which support functional use of skills needed in both work and leisure settings. Having a skill in isolation is different than having the ability to apply the skill in various situations. It is necessary for persons with autism who have difficulty generalizing isolated skills, social interactions, and tolerating environmental changes to begin early in their school career to develop functional adaptive skills enabling a life in as normal of a setting as possible.

The rules and procedures for assessment and for transition planning help service providers pinpoint and prioritize goals and objectives. Take, for instance, the below information pertaining to transition.

Transition Planning

1. Transition planning formally begins by age 14, or younger if appropriate, by including a statement of transition service needs, such as advanced-placement courses or vocational education programming, in the IEP (Bateman & Linden, 1998).
2. Transition services and a statement of inter-agency alliances, if appropriate, are included in the IEP by age 16. IDEA defines transition services as a coordinated set of activities that:
    a. Is designed within an outcome-oriented process, that promotes movement from school to post-school activities, including post-secondary education, vocational training, integrated employment (including supported employment), continuing and adult education, adult services, independent living, or community participation;
    b. Is based on the individual student's needs, taking into account the student's preferences and interests; and
    c. Includes
        (1) Instruction;

(2) Related services;

(3) Community experiences;

(4) The development of employment and other post-school adult living objectives; and

(5) If appropriate, acquisition of daily living skills and functional vocational evaluation (34 CFR 300.27).

Commenting on the research pertaining to the inclusion of students' perspectives in transition plans Severson (2001) states:

We are now required to provide a statement of transition services in each student's IEP by age 14 (PL 105-17). It is through the assessment of needs that we identify if there is a discrepancy between current performance and the skills needed to achieve aspirations for adult life. Transitional planning addresses how student "needs, preferences, and interests" (US Congress, 1990) must evolve from comprehensive assessment that generates answers to the following three questions:

- What are the student's future goals?
- What skills must the student possess and acquire to achieve his/her goals?
- What planning issues need to be addressed to allow the student to experience success in vocational, residential, and community environments?" (December 2001, pg. 8)

Severson goes on to point out that (a) early assessment of preferences is necessary when planning educational experiences focusing on the student's future goals; (b) important skills essential to adult functioning should take precedence over remedial or tutorial approaches; and (c) the assessment process should pinpoint needs, timelines to address needs, and identify those responsible for action plans.

State-wide Assessments

One can find further evidence of the emphasis on critical thinking, functional skills, and social skills in school settings by examining state-wide assessments. The intention of state-wide tests is to provide another vehicle to report progress or lack-thereof, of school curriculums and programs to parents. IDEA requirement (34 CFR 300.347 (a)(5)) stipulates that the IEPT determine whether and how students with special needs participate in regular education state- or district-wide assessments. The Michigan Educational Assessment System (MEAS) is responsible for testing *all* students in the state. At various grade levels, Michigan students are given the Michigan Educational Assessment Program (MEAP). MEAS also includes the English Language Learners Alternate Assessment (ELL-Access) and Michigan's Alternate Assessment Program, the MI-Access. Michigan students with special needs are administered the MI-Access assessment if the IEPT determines that the MEAP or other alternate assessments are not appropriate for the individual. The team chooses the specific MI-Access test instrument based on student performance and the level of independence the IEPT feels the student will achieve by the end of their school career.

The level of independence for each student is based upon the following five questions which relate directly to a student's transition plan:

1. Where will this student live and with what supports?
2. In what type of daily activities will this student be involved and with what supports?
3. In what type of community experiences will this student be involved and with what supports?
4. In what type of post-secondary opportunities will this student be involved and with what supports?
5. In what type of environment will this student be employed and with what supports?

The transition and assessment procedures conducted to guide the IEPT in constructing an appropriate, outcomes based IEP clearly stress independence, age-appropriateness, functional skill, and the least restrictive environment, as per the intent of IDEA. Persons conducting assessments and designing action plans must be focused on this intent as they engage in IEPT decision making.

MCISD IEP Process

In honoring the new requirements to increase parental involvement, MCISD has found more continuity to hold the initial evaluation or the MET at the IEP meeting, unless circumstances call for another arrangement. Transition planning for students who are 14 years and older also takes place at the IEP. The transition plan is actually a subsection of the IEP and forms are included with the IEP planning packet. Storms, O'Leary, and Williams (2000) recommend the IEP process for transition to flow in this order, regardless of the format dictated by preprinted forms:

1. Post-school Goals (Vision)
2. Present Levels of Educational Performance
3. Statement of Transition Service Needs
4. Statement of Needed Transition Services
5. Annual Goals
6. Short-term Objectives/Benchmarks

When considering the student's life or "exit" goals for transition at the IEP, the IEPT has the opportunity to gain a unified view of where the student hopes to be upon completion of school. Annual goals should be addressing the skill areas the student will need to fulfill his or her life goals. This affords the music therapist the opportunity to explain the relevance of music therapy goals to nonmusical gains. For example, if the teenage student diagnosed with autism has "supported living in a group home" as a part of his or her transition plan, it will be important for him or her to have effective means for expression, communication, functional use of skills, as many independent daily living and leisure skills as possible, social skills, tolerance for change and sensory input, and effective strategies to deal with stress. Functional, cooperative use of skills in a variety of settings will provide a means for effective access of community living and should be a focal point of an IEP for a student with autism.

Music Therapy Interventions

Autism spectrum disorders afflicts each person in unique and unusual ways, resulting in uneven skills ranging from areas of giftedness to areas of severe dysfunction. Because human beings respond to music in both conscious and unconscious ways music interventions can have powerful effects. Treatment approaches are individually designed according to immediate and long-term goals. The therapist must be aware of the educational team's philosophies, methodologies, behavioral approaches, and especially the communication system being designed by the speech pathologist. Even those students who have verbal skills will likely be using some type of written or picture system. In both high and low functioning individuals with autism there are common interaction issues which are likely to be present. These include insistence on sameness, compliance or control issues, behaviors which isolate, perseverations and rituals, poor mood modulation, delayed or hyper reaction time, poor use of objects, and inability to decode social cues or understand abstract concepts. Note where these traits manifest within the music medium. Design elements of reciprocity and change into every musical interaction. Begin by documenting every observable musical expression. Consider the quality displayed of any of the following list of music behaviors by the student:

- vocal direction
- approximate melodic pitch
- matches isolated pitches
- hums
- matches tempo
- matches tempo changes
- instrument exploration

- imitates simple rhythm patterns
- self-corrects

Are their musical qualities approximate, imitative, interactive, or inconsistent? Are their musical responses equal to chronological age or developmental age? What are their physical responses regarding posture and eye gaze? What are their reactions to the following musical elements?

- tempo changes
- volume changes
- phrasing
- harmonic progression
- anticipated musical resolutions
- musical surprises
- tailored accompaniments
- dynamic changes
- accented sounds and movements

The child's music sensitivities provides the basis for treatment approaches. If the student has very few music expressions, like in Sal's case earlier in the chapter, the therapist designs interventions which will broaden their response repertoire. He had positive responses to contrasts of loud and soft, enjoyed the rainstick, and quieted when his vocalizations were echoed on the piano. The "Loud and Soft" song was first done as a finger play and later, after it was established as a positive connecting song, changed to a loud and soft drum play experience. The therapy sessions were very brief so only quick positive events would be associated with the music. Sal now has several songs and sound colors he enjoys.

At the other end of the spectrum are seemingly very capable individuals who are unable to sustain musical interaction or are trying to control musical, physical and instrumental portions of the music therapy experiences. "Taylor's" constant verbal interruptions were clearly associated with the autism disorder. He constantly suggested new story lines to the songs, different rules to our instrument play, and became extremely distressed if he felt the class was not listening to his thoughts. The therapist developed a picture card on the computer to represent an "idea." She made several cards with magnets on the back side. As soon as Taylor had an "idea," the therapist instantly played a major chord low in his singing range and sang "I-DE-A." She handed Taylor the picture as she sang "I-DE-A" prompting Taylor to sing too, slowing his heart rate and interrupting his interruption. The expanded version of the "Idea" song required deep breaths and allowed reminders of the rule. New ideas were to be shared only during "idea time" on the schedule. The first day this occurred, Taylor needed constant music support to remain in control. Tears rolled down his face and his body shook, but he did not blurt out his idea. Today he will grab the "idea" picture and politely wait until the appropriate time in the session to share without the need for musical support.

By applying music therapy interventions unique to the individual with autism, the therapist works to (a) build a trusting relationship focused on the music and (b) create physical and emotional associations with songs, sounds, musical patterns, and themes which require timed actions or inaction based in reality. The individual music therapy session strengthens the student–therapist rapport and allows for skill building in a controlled environment. Individual sessions should be coupled with group sessions so the student will have immediate opportunities to generalize skills learned in isolation in a normalized setting. The musical stimuli provides the child with sameness and helps to eliminate his or her dependency on associating the safety with the environment. Establish beginning, ending, and "time-to-change" songs to support successful transitions. Engage the student in guided exploration and not discovered preferences. Design musical interventions which produce a calming response or other emotion appropriate to the student's needs. Incorporate picture and gestural cues simultaneously with the musical cues to prepare for the moment when the musical stimuli will be faded away. Model and encourage the proper use of instruments and various musical movements. To prepare the student for group experiences establish the concepts of "my turn" and "your turn." Use music to reinforce and illustrate each concept, even for ideas like "stay in your seat," and moving or playing the instruments only in the designated area during a "moving song." To help with transitions between experiences, an ending or "time to change" song/musical phrase can be established (i.e., "We're all done" sung on a V-I cadence).

As basic skills are reinforced and expanded upon, the music therapist encourages their use in the group setting as soon as possible. At first, this can be done by using the same greeting and ending songs, even the same 1:1 session experiences adapted for a group setting. Acceptance of and participation in a group setting might be a significant accomplishment for the student who has a severe inability to adapt to change and a low tolerance for sensory input.

Change within the familiar music experience is introduced at a level the student can handle. The change may be as subtle as a tempo, accompaniment, or key change. Changes in the words or directions are gradually introduced while increasing the demand for social interaction. As the student is guided through these or other changes, the connecting song and "time to change" passages are used. The music therapist then begins to expand the student's repertoire to include multiple connecting/calming/changing songs. Gestures are coupled with these "transitional" music cues as stated earlier, so as to support elimination of the musical cue. When the student is able to handle more significant differences, such as a total change in session structure, he or she is perhaps ready to participate in group music therapy with different peers independent of the classroom staff.

When a student is not progressively tolerating more change over a long span of time, he or she can still be exposed to new peers and situations. For instance, the therapist can bring visiting peers into the structured music therapy session. A staff member can accompany the student to observe other music therapy groups. The music therapist strategically inserts the familiar music experiences into the "new" group's session plans.

Suggested Techniques

The student with autism often needs to develop attention span, in-seat behavior, purposeful use of objects, self-control, tolerance for sensory input, and acceptance of change. Beginning communication and interaction skills also need to be developed. By providing structured and low-structured (i.e., improvisation) music therapy interventions, the student with autism can be supported to experience periods of satisfying concentrated use of abilities in a social atmosphere. This can be done by involving the student in experiences in which each action or interaction has a meaningful relationship to the musical stimuli. Consider the following suggestions:

- Establish transition songs, i.e., beginning, ending, calming, and "time to change" songs.
- Couple gestures with the transition songs so that future elimination of the musical cue might be possible.
- Use familiar music and transition songs/cues in new situations to calm and encourage generalization of skills.
- Expand repertoire of transition songs.
- Establish "my turn" and "your turn" to help encourage manageable group skills and awareness of others.
- Develop and expand basic music interaction skills and encourage their application in a social context.
- Support and encourage rhythmic and/or vocal synchronization (exact or approximate) with others.
- Use AGE APPROPRIATE music.
- Use a variety of music and instruments, as tolerated.
- Use both structured and improvisational music interventions.
- Encourage the use of two or more skills simultaneously if the student is able to tolerate it (i.e., reading and melodic singing; social skills and music/motor skills).

- Help student indicate likes/dislikes of self and others, provide some form of "choices" in each session to provide another way for student to have control of life situations.
- Use gentle physical support if needed (i.e., touch shoulder, support elbow), then fade out physical support when possible.
- Use visual representations of music, commands, feelings, places, people, etc.
- Support generalization of goals/objectives established by other professionals.
- Communicate and consult with staff/others regarding the student's responses to music and how these responses relate to nonmusical skills and indicate hidden potential
- Breakdown and teach/define gestural social skills and rules
- Be aware of the continuum of placements/services available and help support movement toward increased independence and socialization
- Define music therapy's relationship to annual and long-term goals outlined in the IEP and Transition Plan.

Coda

Autism presents great obstacles in effective social interaction and sensory processing, which often causes a lack of functional use of skills and isolation from society. Music therapy approaches can take a critical step farther than developing isolated skills. Music therapy interventions can be specifically tailored to provide real-time support for the purposeful, sustained use of abilities in cooperation with others. The Monroe County Intermediate School District offers creative educational options for individuals with autism and related disorders. Music therapy is one component of the district's collaborative efforts to assist Monroe County students with autism successfully prepare for adult life. By assessing music related behaviors and recognizing their relationship to nonmusical abilities in communication, academic, motor, emotional, and social areas, music therapy interventions can assist the student with autism in bridging the gap between isolated skills and their functional social applications. In cooperation with other related services and a variety of approaches, music therapy techniques can ease the individual's movement into settings which provide the greatest opportunity for independence and realization of life goals.

References

Alper, S. (1981). Utilizing community jobs in developing vocational curriculums for severely handicapped youth. *Education and Training of the Mentally Retarded, 16*(3), 217–224.

Alvin, J., & Warwick, A. (1992). *Music therapy for the autistic child* (Rev. ed.). London: Oxford Press.

American Music Therapy Association. (2001). *Standards of clinical practice/Code of ethics*. Silver Spring, MD: Author.

American Psychiatric Association. (1987). *Diagnostic and statistical manual of mental disorders* (3rd ed., rev.). Washington, DC: Author.

American Psychiatric Association. (1994). *Diagnostic and statistical manual of mental disorders* (4th ed.). Washington, DC: Author.

Applebaum, E., Egel, A. L., Koegel, R. L., & Imhoff, B. (1979). Measuring musical abilities of autistic children. *Journal of Autism and Developmental Disorders, 9*, 279–285.

Attwood, T. (1998). *Asperger's syndrome: A guide for parents and professionals*. Great Britain: Athenaeum Press, Gateshead, Tyne and Wear.

Autism Society of America. (2001). *What is autism?* [Brochure]. Bethesda, MD: Author.

Ayres, A. J. (1979). *Sensory integration and the child*. Los Angeles: Western Psychological Services.

Bagley, C., & McGeein, V. (1989). The taxonomy and course of childhood autism. *Perceptual and Motor Skills, 69*, 1264–1266.

Bateman, B. D., & Linden, M. A. (1998). *Better IEPs: How to develop legally correct and educationally useful programs* (3rd ed.). Longmont, CO: Sopris West.

Berard, G. (1993). *Hearing equals behaviour.* New Canaan, CT: Keats.

Boone, P. (1980). *The diagnostic assessment of music related expression and behavior.* Pottstown, PA: Author.

Boxhill, E. H. (1985). *Music therapy for the developmentally disabled.* Austin, TX: PRO-ED.

Brunk, B., & Coleman, K. (2000). Development of a Special Education Music Therapy Assessment Process (SEMTAP). *Music Therapy Perspectives, 18*(1), 59–68.

Bruscia, K. E. (1987). *Improvisational models of music therapy.* Phoenixville, PA: Barcelona

Center for Quality Special Education [CQSE]. (1993). *Special education program outcomes guide: Autism.* Lansing, MI: Disability Research Systems, Inc., & Michigan Department of Education.

Clarizio, H., & McCoy, G. F. (1983). *Behavior disorders in children.* New York: Harper Row.

Coleman, K., & Brunk, B. (1999). *Special Education Music Therapy Assessment Process (SEMTAP) handbook.* Grapevine, TX: Prelude Music Therapy.

Edgerton, C. (1994). The effect of improvisational music therapy on the communicative behaviors of autistic children. *Journal of Music Therapy, 31*(1), 31–62.

Grandin, T. (1988). My experiences as an autistic child and review of selected literature. *Journal of Orthomolecular Psychiatry, 13,* 144–174.

Grandin, T. (1995). *Thinking in pictures.* New York, NY: Doubleday.

Grandin, T., & Scariano, M. M. (1986). *Emergence: Labeled autistic.* Novato, CA: Arena Press.

Hermelin, B. (1978). Images and language. In M. Rutter & E. Schopler (Eds.), *Autism: A reappraisal of concepts and treatment* (pp.141–154). New York: Plenum Press.

Kanner, L. (1943). Autistic disturbances of affective contact. *Nervous Child, 2,* 217–250.

Kaufman, B. N. (1994). *Son rise: The miracle continues.* Tiburon, CA: H. J. Kramer.

Kolko, D. J., Anderson, L., & Campbell, M. (1980). Sensory preference and overselective responding in autistic children. *Journal of Autism and Developmental Disorders, 10,* 259–271.

Kurita, H. (1985), Infantile autism with speech loss before the age of thirty months. *Journal of the American Academy of Child Psychiatry, 24,* 191–196.

Michigan Department of Education & Michigan Jobs Commission. (1995). *Fundamentals of transition.* Lansing, MI: Author.

Michigan State Board of Education. (1997). *Revised administrative rules for special education* (Rev. ed.). Lansing, MI: Author.

Monroe County Intermediate School District. (1990). *Curriculum guide for trainable mentally impaired students: A sequence of annual goals, short term instructional objectives, and performance objectives.* Monroe, MI: Author.

Monroe County Intermediate School District Board of Education. (2001). *Mission statement.* Monroe, MI: Author.

Nordoff, P., & Robbins, C. (1964). Music therapy and personality change in autistic children. *Journal of the American Institute of Homeopathy, 57,* 305–310.

Nordoff, P., & Robbins, C. (1968). Improvised music as therapy for autistic children. In E. T. Gaston (Ed.), *Music in therapy* (pp. 191–193). New York: Macmillian.

Nordoff, P., & Robbins, C. (1971). *Therapy in music for handicapped children.* New York: St. Martin's Press.

Nordoff, P., & Robbins, C. (1977). *Creative music therapy.* New York: John Day.

Olley, J. G. (1987). Classroom structure and autism. In D. Cohen & A. Donnellan (Eds.), *Handbook of autism and pervasive developmental disorders* (pp. 411–417). Silver Spring, MD: V. H. Winston and Sons.

Paul, R. (1987). Communication. In D. Cohen & A. Donnellan (Eds.), *Handbook of autism and pervasive developmental disorders* (pp. 61–84). Silver Spring, MD: V. H. Winston and Sons.

Rimland, B. (1964). *Infantile autism*. New York: Appleton-Century.

Schopler, E., & Mesibov, G. B. (1983). *Autism in adolescents and adults*. New York: Plenum Press.

Schopler, E., & Mesibov, G. B. (1985). *Communication problems in autism*. New York: Plenum Press.

Schopler, E., & Mesibov, G. B. (Eds.). (1988). *Diagnosis and assessment of autism*. New York: Plenum Press.

Schopler, E., Reichler, R. J., & Renner, B. R. (1986). *The childhood autism rating scale*. Los Angeles, CA: Western Psychological Services.

Severson, S. (2001, December). Transitional assessment should include students' needs, interest, and preferences: empowerment and self-determination lead to student involvement in the assessment process. *Newsline* (p. 8). Michigan Department of Education.

Sherwin, A. C. (1953). Reactions to music of autistic (schizophrenic) children. *American Journal of Psychiatry, 109*, 823–831.

Siegel, L. M. (2001). *The complete IEP guide: How to advocate for your special ed child*. (2nd ed.). Berkeley, CA: Nolo.

Snell, A.M. (1987). "Clapping hello." Unpublished song.

Snell, A. M. (1990). Music therapy curriculum. *Curriculum guide for trainable mentally impaired students: A sequence of annual goals, short term instructional objectives, and performance objectives* (pp. 48–59). Monroe, MI: Monroe County Intermediate School District.

Snell, A. M. (1991). "Shake their hand." Unpublished song.

Snell, A. M. (2001). *The Music Therapy Music-Related Behavior Assessment*. Monroe, MI: Author.

Storms, J., O'Leary, E., & Williams, J. (2000). *Transition requirements: A guide for states, districts, schools, universities and families* [Monograph]. Ideas that Work, U.S. Department of Education, Office of Special Education Programs.

Thaut, M. (1984). A music therapy treatment model for autistic children. *Music Therapy Perspectives, 1*, 7–13.

Toigo, D. (1992). Autism: Integrating a personal perspective with music therapy practice. *Music Therapy Perspectives, 10*, 13–20.

U.S. Congress. (1990). *Individuals with Disabilities Education Act*. Public Law 101–476.

Volkman, F. R. (1987). Social development. In D. Cohen & A. Donnellan (Eds.), *Handbook of autism and developmental disorders* (pp. 41–60). Silver Spring, MD: V. H. Winston and Sons.

Wigram, T. (2000). A method of music therapy assessment for the diagnosis of autism and communication disorders in children. *Music Therapy Perspectives, 18*, 13–22.

Appendix A

MONROE COUNTY INTERMEDIATE SCHOOL DISTRICT
ANNUAL GOALS AND SHORT-TERM INSTRUCTIONAL OBJECTIVES
APPLIED IN MUSIC THERAPY
STUDENT_____PLACEMENT_____DATE_____
MUSIC THERAPIST_____
ANNUAL GOAL: *THE STUDENT WILL DEVELOP/IMPROVE EXPRESSION IN THE MUSIC SETTING*

A. EVALUATION PROCEDURES
1. Observation
2. Standardized Test
3. Teacher Made Test
4. Developmental Profile
5. Skill Inventory
6. Curriculum
7. Other_____

B. SUCCESS CRITERIA
1. With 100% Accuracy
2. With 75% Accuracy
3. With 50% Accuracy
4. With 25% Accuracy
5. With____% Accuracy
6. Maintain present level of functioning
7. Standard Score of_____

C. ASSISTANCE LEVEL
1. Passively cooperating
2. With physical assistance
3. With physical prompts
4. With imitation
5. With verbal and/or gestural prompt
6. With repeated requests, no prompts
7. Independently w/wo adaptive device
8. Maintain Skill

A) INCREASE RESPONSES TO MUSIC

1. Quiets when music stimuli is present
2. Exhibits movements related to music stimuli (i.e., startle, eye contact, etc.)
3. Moves rhythmically in response to pulse of music (i.e., tap, rock, clap, etc.)
4. Exhibits spontaneous singing or humming
5. Accepts sound of various instruments representative of each instrumental family
6. Touches/holds instruments from each Instrumental family
7. Accepts by touch sound vibrations from musical/nonmusical sources (i.e., drum head, strings, amplifier, wood, etc.)
8. Locates hidden sound
9. Matches individual rhythm instruments by sound: a. drum b. sticks c. bell d. maraca e. other

10. Start and stops a musical response
11. Matches/anticipates changes duration, tempo, or dynamics of music (i.e., stop/go, loud/soft)
12. Indicates likes/dislikes of musical stimuli (i.e., smile, frown, verbalize opinion)
13. Names/indicates 3 or more favorite songs
14. Identifies at least 3 musical styles (i.e., Pop/Rock, Country, Classical)
15. Identifies tonal/mood changes in live or recorded music
16. Labels at least 2 musical passages with a feeling (i.e., happy, sad, etc.)
17. Expresses feelings musically by engaging in improvisation, dance, creative movement, song writing, or by choosing a song.

Appendix B

GUIDE FOR MUSIC THERAPY CONSIDERATION
MT-MRB Consideration Form

Student name:_____ Age_____

Placement_____ Classification_____
    (Include teacher's name)

Submitted by_____ Date_____
Contact information (include phone, email, & times available)_____
_____

CIRCLE THOSE THAT APPLY:

1. Student is not making <u>expected progress</u>, as <u>related to ability level</u>, in areas significant to success in school.
    (communication, academics, motor, social, emotional)

2. There are significant limits in expressive language.

3. Has difficulty imitating others and/or sustaining engagement in group activities.

4. Imitates negative behaviors dramatically more than positive models.

5. Becomes over-stimulated easily / is under-responsive to stimuli / has multiple sensory problems.

6. Has significant difficulty engaging in group learning.

7. Emotional/behavioral disturbances create barriers to cooperative learning.

8. Consistently responds positively when music is present.

9. Has an extreme negative response to music and/or other sounds.

10. Has difficulty relating to people and/or objects.

11. Has difficulty generalizing or functionally applying skills at ability level.

12. Other interventions (OT, PT, speech, behavior modification, etc.) are not resulting in significant improvements.

Other comments (use back if needed):

NOTE: One or more circled item does not necessarily indicate or negate need for service.

Appendix C

MT-MRB Assessment Portion, pg. 2

ACTUAL SESSION

SESSION NUMBER_____   DATE/TIME:_____

_____reports _____is:
(Name & relationship to student)   (Student's name)

                                                                    _____having a typical day

                                                                    _____having an abnormal day (comment):
_____
_____
_____
_____

Circle/Fill-in: 1:1   Group - Describe (number, type of participants/surroundings)_____
_____
_____
_____

Experience No. & Title

1. _____   Objective(s)   Materials

___Same
___Altered, explain:

MT Intertentions

Observations:

Indications:

Quality & conditions of transition to next experience:___Compliant ___Non-compliant ___Other
Explain:

Interventions used:

MT-MRB Assessment Portion, pg. 2a - ACTUAL SESSION

<u>Experience No. & Title</u>   Student Name_____ Session Number_____

___._____ Objective(s)   Materials

___Same
___Altered, explain:

MT Intertentions
_____
_____
_____

_____
_____
_____

Observations:

Indications:

Quality & conditions of transition to next experience:___Compliant ___Non-compliant ___Other
Explain:

Interventions used:

___._____ Objective(s)   Materials

___Same
___Altered, explain:

MT Intertentions
_____
_____
_____

_____
_____
_____

Observations:

Indications:

Quality & conditions of transition to next experience:___Compliant ___Non-compliant ___Other
Explain:

Interventions used:

13

MUSIC THERAPY FOR LEARNERS WITH LEARNING DISABILITIES IN A PRIVATE DAY SCHOOL

Ned D. Gladfelter

Description of the Population

THOSE who work with children categorized as learning disabled realize that no two children with this diagnosis are identical. Because of this, there are a variety of definitions used to describe this population. Internet sites such as www.ldonline.org and www.ld.org provide many definitions from sources such as the U.S. Office of Education, the Learning Disabilities Association of America, and The National Joint Committee on Learning Disabilities, in addition to a wealth of information about learning disabilities.

Public Law 101-476, the Individuals with Disabilities Education Act (IDEA), defines a *learning disability* as a "disorder in one or more of the basic psychological processes involved in understanding or in using spoken or written language, which may manifest itself in an imperfect ability to listen, think, speak, read, write, spell, or to do mathematical calculations" (National Information Center for Children and Youth with Disabilities, 2000). The term includes such conditions as perceptual handicaps, brain injury, attention-deficit hyperactivity disorders, dyslexia, and developmental aphasia. In accordance with the law, learning disabilities do not include learning problems that are "primarily the result of visual, hearing, or motor disabilities; mental retardation; or environmental, cultural, or economic disadvantage" (National Information Center for Children and Youth with Disabilities, 2000). Although persons with a learning disability generally have normal or above average intelligence, the manner in which the individual selects, retains, and expresses information is negatively affected. Each child with a learning disability is unique, and can display a different combination and severity of problems. Some of the most frequently displayed problems include: short attention span; difficulty following directions; poor memory; difficulties with sequencing; inadequate ability to discriminate between and among letters, numerals, or sounds; poor reading ability; coordination problems; disorganization; and numerous other problems which may affect the sensory systems (Learning Disabilities Association of America, 1994).

There are many children with learning disabilities in schools across the nation. Given the proper attention and assistance, they can be successful in their school environment. If a learning disability is not diagnosed and proper corrective measures taken, the child will often perform poorly in school, become angry and frustrated, and be faced with continued failure. Some of these children may need more specialized, individual attention that is not available in many school settings. They are likely to benefit from the one-on-one attention that is only available in a school with small class sizes and a variety of support staff trained to teach children with learning disabilities. This is where a special school setting, such as the Pilot School, can be helpful.

The Pilot School

At the Pilot School Incorporated in Wilmington, Delaware, approximately 160 students, ranging in age from 5–14 years, receive individual attention to assist them in dealing with their learning problems. This independent day school attracts students from Delaware and bordering counties in Pennsylvania, New Jersey, and Maryland. Students are referred largely by parents, as well as by professionals and private and parochial schools in the surrounding area.

Once admitted to the Pilot School, the children are assigned to one of three divisions. Children from 5 to 8 years of age are in the lower division, children ages 9 to 11 make up the middle division, and children ages 12 to 14 are in the upper division. In the lower division, students are placed within homerooms by age. However, they are also grouped within the division by instructional levels in phonics and are grouped for basic reading and math skill levels. In the middle division, the students receive instruction within their classroom group much of the school day, receiving the majority of their instruction from their homeroom teacher. In the upper division, the students move from one classroom to another to attend classes with teachers who specialize in each academic area. In order to prevent the academic lapses that can occur over a long summer holiday, the Pilot School year for students begins in September and continues until the end of June. Students generally attend the school for an average of 3–5 years. Approximately 80% of the students return to a regular school. A smaller percentage of the population continues in a special education school setting after leaving Pilot.

The Pilot School specializes in identifying each child's strengths and weaknesses and assists him or her to grow into a successful and independent learner. Since each child who attends the Pilot School has unique needs, the school focuses on meeting the needs of the child, rather than on following any one particular teaching method or educational approach. To better focus on each individual student, the class sizes are small (approximately 6–8 students per class) and ungraded. Children work at their own pace, with their own material, and on their own programs and goals. Emphasis is placed on building self-esteem and confidence, and providing the child with adequate problem solving and coping skills, in order to facilitate the return to a regular classroom as soon as possible.

The Pilot School has a language-based curriculum that focuses on developing the reading, writing, spelling, speaking, and listening skills of each student. Children also receive instruction in the same subject areas they would study in a regular school including language arts, mathematics, science, social studies, art, music, computer, health, and physical education. In addition, training in basic skills such as gross and fine motor skills, visual and auditory perception, memory skills, and speech and language therapy, occupational therapy, and physical therapy is provided for children who have deficits in those areas.

Music Therapy Program

Every student attending the Pilot School participates in the music therapy program under the direction of a board-certified music therapist who also holds a degree in music education. The amount of contact each student has with the music therapy program depends on the needs and interest of each child.

Group Music Therapy—All students take part in a group music therapy session with their homeroom class on a weekly basis. Sessions, which run for the entire school year, are 45 minutes in length. During these weekly group sessions, the students take part in activities which include playing instruments, singing, listening to music, creating music, improvising, lyric writing, producing music videos, and drama exercises. Through participation in these activities, the following group program goals are addressed:

- Building self-esteem through successful experiences
- Developing and refining auditory processing skills
- Encouraging attention to task
- Enhancing speech and language skills

- Improving fine and gross motor skills
- Promoting academic concepts
- Developing appropriate social skills
- Expanding leisure-time activities
- Encouraging self-expression

Individual Music Therapy— In addition to attending weekly sessions with their class, some students are selected to participate in individual music therapy sessions with the therapist so they can receive additional attention in their deficit areas. These students are referred to the music therapist by their classroom teachers and division chairpersons. Those referred often have more severe disabilities than the traditional Pilot School student. By attending individual music therapy, children are provided with an additional resource to strengthen below-average skills. Individuals referred attend a weekly 30-minute session throughout the school year. Activities in these sessions are specifically tailored to meet the needs of each individual student. Goals for the individual music sessions, as well as more specific areas that are often addressed during the individual sessions, might include:

- Improving visual perception—Correctly identifying symbols used in academic areas (letters, numbers, music notation)
- Improving auditory memory—Developing ability to sequence information in a specified order, following verbal directions, and understanding lyrics
- Enhancing expressive and receptive language skills—Articulating vowel and consonant sounds, speaking fluently while speaking and singing
- Reinforcing basic concepts—Understanding directional words such as left, right, forward backward, beside, behind, high, and low
- Enhancing self-esteem—Successfully participating in a variety of music activities
- Strengthening specific academic information—Monetary values, multiplication tables, colors, shapes
- Developing fine or gross motor skills needed for specific tasks—Holding a pencil, holding mallets and striking an instrument

Due to the large number of students seen by the music therapist each week, it is not possible to create specific student goals for each child in the group sessions. Specific goals are only developed for the students receiving individual music therapy services.

Special Music Groups—Students at the Pilot School also have the opportunity to take part in special music groups throughout the course of the year. These special music groups provide the children with necessary skills to become involved in similar groups at other schools after leaving the Pilot School. For example, through participation in large choral groups, the students learn to focus their visual and auditory attention on a director so they can participate successfully during rehearsals. They also learn when to communicate with their peers so as not to be disruptive in the rehearsals. Participation in these music groups offers students a variety of opportunities for exposure and involvement in activities designed to help them discover their strengths and instill the confidence needed to succeed in school.

Two of the special music groups involve singing. Singing is considered to be a very valuable experience at the Pilot School because it assists in the sequencing of verbal ideas, reinforces sight vocabulary, enhances pronunciation, modifies speech behaviors, improves auditory awareness, and involves memory training.

Middle Division Glee Club—The glee club is a mandatory vocal group for all students in the middle division. This group rehearses once a week and performs for their peers and parents at school functions. The objectives of the glee club are to: (a) promote positive self-esteem through successful experiences, (b) learn to function as part of a large group, (c) develop poise and self-confidence, and (d) develop interest in singing through exposure to appropriate vocal techniques.

Upper Division Chorus—The upper division chorus is a voluntary activity for all students in the upper division. Rehearsals are scheduled once each week and the chorus performs at school functions several times each year. The objectives of the chorus are to: (a) develop social skills through participation in group activities, (b) promote positive self-esteem through successful experiences, (c) develop poise and self-confidence, and (d) enhance singing ability through exposure to appropriate vocal techniques.

Instrumental Ensemble "Early Morning Jammers"—The instrumental ensemble meets once a week before the start of the school day, hence the name, "Early Morning Jammers." The ensemble consists of students who show interest in developing skill on a particular instrument. This rock/pop ensemble includes keyboards, drum set, bass and electric guitars, wind instruments, and vocalists. The group performs at school functions and in the community. As part of the ensemble, the band members are able to: (a) develop skill on a particular instrument, providing an appropriate leisure-time activity that can be used throughout life; (b) develop the social skills and cooperative efforts needed to play with other instrumentalists; (c) gain confidence and a more positive sense of self-esteem through successful experiences; and (d) gain exposure to a variety of musical styles.

Music Therapy Sessions—All group, individual, and special music ensembles are held in a fully-equipped music room designed specifically for music sessions. The room, which is carpeted and climate-controlled, has ample natural and electric lighting that can be manipulated with blinds to reduce external distractions. The room is set up in different sections, so that the students and therapist can focus on particular activities with ease while being surrounded by a minimal amount of distractions in any one area.

At the entrance of the room are chairs, which comfortably seat up to eight students, located by a chalkboard and bulletin board. This is the area in which the students first gather and it is where the students are encouraged to focus their energy on the music session about to occur. The remainder of the room consists of a percussion area, a keyboard lab, an Orff ensemble, a guitar center, and a recording studio area. There is also storage for recordings of music, a wide variety of books and sheet music, and autoharps and tone chimes.

Percussion Area—The percussion area is one of the most popular areas with this student population. Instruments used in the percussion area are a drum set, conga drums, bongo drums, djembes, Native American drums, and a wide assortment of smaller percussion instruments. By participating in rhythm activities, the students can develop fine and gross motor skills, improve coordination, and develop auditory memory. In addition, playing percussion instruments can enhance the understanding of concepts such as left and right, and allows the students to express themselves through improvisation. Students are also encouraged to combine speaking with their drumming to assist in expressive language development. Many of the activities done in this area are ensemble activities where everyone is encouraged to work cooperatively as a group. In this way, many social skills can be reinforced among the group members.

Keyboard Lab—The keyboard lab is equipped with electronic keyboards, each with a wide variety of stimulating tones and rhythms and a headphone so that the students can work individually. Having each student work independently while wearing headphones helps the student to focus their attention on their own playing rather than being distracted by their peers or other musical stimuli. The therapist can also move among the students, providing individual attention in a group setting. At the keyboard the students can play melodies and rhythms, improving fine motor and auditory processing skills. Students can improvise for self-expression, imitate rhythms for quick success and improved self-esteem, or they can read some type of music notation across a page, reinforcing visual perception and eye-hand coordination. For an added dimension, the headphones can also be unplugged, so the entire group can play as an ensemble if so desired.

Orff Ensemble—The Orff ensemble consists of xylophones and metallophones that are used both in individual and group music sessions. Since the Orff philosophy utilizes repeated patterns known as ostinati, the students participating in these ensembles can find security in playing the repetitive parts. As students play these instruments their coordination is developed, they learn to sequence patterns, they develop auditory awareness, and they can be encouraged to express themselves through improvisation.

Guitar Center—Since most school-aged students relate to some type of guitar playing, folk, classical, electric and bass guitars are often utilized in the music sessions. Although playing the guitar is generally more challenging than playing percussion, keyboard, or Orff instruments, the guitar has wide appeal due to influences from many of today's recording artists. Visual, auditory, and motor skills are all integrated as the students create music on the guitar.

Recording Studio—With the advent of many new technologies in recent years, the recording studio portion of the music therapy program has been playing a more prominent role in many of the music sessions. Digital audio and video technologies are used to record the student's verbal, motor, and musical expression. Once recorded, the students can receive instant feedback on their form of expression and the recordings can be saved to chart progress or the recordings can be shared with others if appropriate. All students regularly take part in creating original music videos. They first analyze current music that they are listening to through lyric discussions and song analysis. They then write and record their own lyrics, create and record their own instrumental accompaniment, and then act out scenes to go with the lyrics and music they created. This entire process addresses a majority of the goals designed for the group music therapy sessions.

Although many of the music therapy activities are centered around playing instruments in the music room, the therapist in this setting also has the opportunity to interact with the classroom teachers on a regular basis. This enables both the music therapist and the classroom teachers to utilize each other as consultants in order to integrate music activities into the regular classroom and academic material into the music sessions. When the classroom teachers and music therapist use such an integrated approach, it allows the children to experience important concepts and information in an exciting way, with a variety of repetition so more effective learning can occur.

Assessment

Students in this setting are assessed in a variety of ways. The school psychologist, speech therapist, and educational diagnostician assess each student upon admission to the school. Once they are assigned to a classroom group, their first contact with the music therapist is usually in a group setting.

Group Music Therapy Assessment—During the first few group music sessions, a variety of activities are presented to each group of peers so the therapist can gain insight into their academic, social, sensory perception, and musical abilities. These activities often involve playing instruments since most of the students are quite motivated when involved in playing an instrument. Students in the group music therapy session complete a musical skills assessment, which enables them to keep track of their musical abilities on a variety of instruments throughout their stay at the Pilot School (see Figure 1). The date that the skill level has been achieved is written on the line next to the appropriate level. This allows the students to see their musical progress over time and helps to keep them focused on the specific tasks. As they are charting their musical skills and participating in the activities, the therapist gathers information about their social/behavioral abilities and becomes aware of their auditory, visual and motor difficulties or strengths as well. Musical interests are also noted, helping the therapist to plan group music therapy sessions that will be interesting and beneficial to the students in the group.

Individual Music Therapy Assessment—When assessing individual students in this setting, information is gathered in the following areas; sensory perception, social/behavioral abilities, and musical skill level. The sensory assessment involves gathering information about the student's auditory skills (memory and perception), motor skills (fine/gross motor and coordination), and visual skills (identifying written notation and tracking ability). The social/behavioral assessment identifies the student's ability to follow directions, focus, express ideas, accept challenges, work cooperatively with others or work independently, and show respect to others/themselves. The musical skills assessment reveals the student's ability level on instruments such as the drum set, keyboard, or guitar.

Musical Skills Assessment

Drum Skills

____Level 1 - Steady Beat with Bass and Snare (Bass on 1 & 3, Snare on 2 & 4)
____Level 2 · - Add Cymbal with Bass Drum (Beats 1 & 3)
____Level 3 - Add Cymbal with Bass Drum and Snare Drum (Beats 1, 2, 3, 4)
____Level 4 - Add Hi-Hat (left foot) on beats 2 & 4
____Level 5 - Add a 4-beat fill beginning on beat 1 using quarter notes
____Level 6 - Play 8th notes on the Cymbal (1 & 2 & 3 & 4 &)
____Level 7 - Add a 4-beat fill beginning on beat 1 using 8th notes

Keyboard Skills

____Level 1 – Play Chopsticks with 2 <u>fingers</u>
____Level 2 - Play a 3-note melody with 3 fingers ("Hot Cross Buns")
____Level 3 - Play a 5-note melody with 5 fingers ("Beethoven's 9th Symphony")
____Level 4 - Play a 5-note melody which skips notes ("Skip To My Lou")
____Level 5 - Play a melody with sharps and flats ("The Adams Family")
____Level 6 - Play a melody with sharps and flats that skips notes ("Mission Impossible")
____Level 7 - Play a 3-chord song with C, F, G Chords ("Wild Thing")
____Level 8 - Play a 5-chord song with C, Dm, Em, F, G7 Chords ("Lean on Me")
____Level 9 - Play a 3-chord song with G, C, D Chords ("Twist and Shout")
____Level 10 - Play the Level 2, 3, and 4 songs with two hands:
       (Right hand plays the melody and the left hand plays the chords)
       ____"Hot Cross Buns"
       ____"Beethoven's 9th Symphony"
       ____"Skip To My Lou"
____Level 11 - Play the Level 7, 8 and 9 songs with two hands:
       (Right hand plays the chords and the left hand plays a bass note)
       ____"Wild Thing"
       ____"Lean On Me"
       ____"Twist and Shout"
____Level 12 – Play a duet with a partner
       ____"Chopsticks"
       ____"Mission Impossible"
       ____"Heart and Soul"

Vocal Skills

____Level 1 - Can listen to a pitch and echo it back with their voice (pitch matching)
____Level 2 - Can echo a 3-pitch pattern with syllables (do-re-mi)
____Level 3 - Can echo a 5-pitch pattern with syllables (do-re-mi-fa-so)
____Level 4 - Can sing an entire scale (1 octave) with all 7 syllables
____Level 5 - Can sing a melody with words on key (solo)

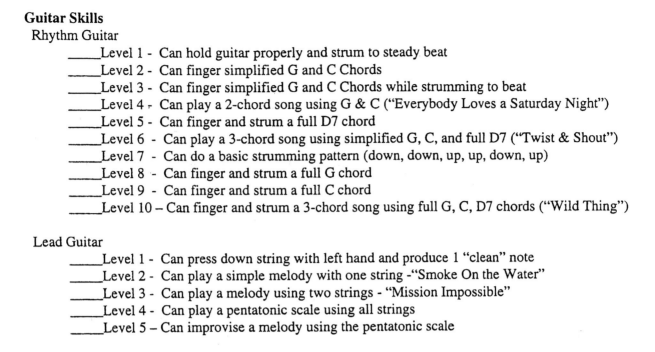

Figure 1. Musical Skills Assessment

Individual music therapy assessments are only done for those students who participate in individual music therapy sessions. Students who participate in individual music therapy sessions are assessed during their first few music sessions. Since many of the students are particularly interested in the drum set, an assessment form was created to gather information about the students as they complete a series of tasks while sitting at the drum set (see Figure 2). After completing the task, the appropriate column is checked that corresponds with the student's ability to complete the task.

In addition to the information collected by the music therapist in the individual music session, the classroom teacher and speech therapist provide the music therapist with details regarding the student's language and academic skills. These are noted in the comments section of the assessment form and are also used to help develop goals and objectives for the individual music therapy sessions.

Relationship to the IEP

To ensure that each student receives proper attention in his/her deficit area, an Individualized Education Program (IEP) is developed at the beginning of each school year. The IEP is based upon evaluative date and input from the classroom teacher, division chairperson, school psychologist, educational diagnostician, and family members. It is updated at least three times a year by the classroom teacher. The student's progress in his or her IEP is discussed with the parent/guardian of the child in three separate conferences throughout the school year. The division chairperson, classroom teacher, and any other staff members who have direct contact with the child may attend these conferences. Since the music therapist works with every child in the school, it is not possible to attend each one of these conferences. Instead, information about each student's progress in music therapy is written on a progress report for the students in the group sessions or on a music IEP for the students taking part in individual music therapy. Information on these reports may be shared in the conferences. Each classroom teacher also routinely gathers information about each student's progress in the music sessions directly from the therapist before the conferences occur. On occasion the music therapist will attend a conference to share specific issues about a student.

Individual Music Therapy Assessment
Using the Drum Set

Skill Area	Task	0%	50%	100%
Social Skills	Follows directions			
Focus	Maintains interest in the activities			
Respect	Shows respect for the drum set			
Esteem	Accepts challenges			
Expression	Organizes musical ideas into rhythmic patterns			
	Verbally contributes ideas			
	Musically contributes ideas through improvisations			
	Seems to enjoy playing the drum set			
Auditory Skills	Imitates 2-beat rhythm patterns			
Memory	Imitates 4-beat rhythm patterns			
	Imitates rhythm patterns spoken with words			
	Recalls words spoken with rhythm patterns			
Perception	Differentiates between low, middle, and high (toms)			
	Remembers sequence of rhythm patterns (drum fills)			
	Differentiates between loud and soft			
	Plays in tempo while accompanying the piano/guitar			
	Prefers to play "by ear"			
Motor Skills	Differentiates between left and right hands			
	Differentiates between left and right feet			
	Demonstrates adequate finger strength to hold sticks			
	Demonstrates adequate hand strength to strike drums			
	Plays softly (controls fine motor movement)			
	Plays loudly (controls gross motor movement)			
	Comprehends directional words (above, below, etc.)			
	Coordinates hands and feet to play rhythm patterns			
Visual Skills	Moves hands to designated drums with success			
	Moves feet to pedals with success			
	Verbally reads notation (music symbols) across page			
	Plays appropriate drums while reading notation			
	Makes eye contact with others while playing			
	Prefers to play while reading written notation			
	Shows interest in learning to read drum notation			
Drum Set Level	Level 1: Plays steady beat with bass and snare			
	Level 2: Adds cymbal with bass drum			
	Level 3: Adds cymbal with bass and snare drum			
	Level 4: Adds hi-hat using left foot			
	Level 5: Inserts a 4-beat fill using quarter notes			
	Level 6: Plays 8th notes on the cymbal			
	Level 7: Inserts a 4-beat fill using 8th notes			

Comments:

Musical Experiences

Figure 2. Individual Music Therapy Assessment Using the Drum Set

In addition to the academic IEP, a music therapy IEP is created for the students who attend individual music therapy sessions. Using information gathered in the assessment process, the music therapy IEP states specific goals and objectives with corresponding music activities. The music therapy IEP is updated three times throughout the school year to provide staff and family members with specific feedback on the student's progress in the music therapy sessions. It is included in the student's file, along with the academic IEP and other information about the student. Figure 3 shows a music therapy IEP for a hypothetical child with learning disabilities. The child in this example is an 8-year-old boy with attention-deficit/hyperactivity disorder and dyslexia. He has been enrolled in the Pilot School since age 7 and reads at the first grade level. Visual symbols are challenging, and he experiences frustration when writing and reading. He enjoys physical activities and has very advanced motor coordination skills, but his expressive language skills are quite weak. He shows much interest in percussion activities, particularly the drum set, and his auditory memory skills are excellent.

Progress Report

Each student's progress in the group music therapy sessions is reported on a mid-year and end-of-year progress report. This report is included in the student's file and provides feedback to the classroom teachers on each student's progress in the group music sessions. A sample progress report can be seen in Figure 4. The progress report includes a checklist that identifies attitudes and behaviors of the child. Written comments about progress on the music therapy goals are reported by the therapist, along with comments on progress and behavior in any special music groups in which they may be involved.

The hypothetical student mentioned in Figure 4 is a female, 11 years of age, who has been attending the Pilot School since age 9. Next year she will be returning to a Catholic school as a sixth grader. When she arrived at Pilot three years ago, she had difficulty interacting with her peers and her lack of social skills was creating behavior problems with her classmates. Because of previous failure in school, she had a low sense of self-esteem and put little effort into school work. During her years at Pilot, she experienced success in school, which helped her to begin to realize that it was possible to enjoy school. She also gained the organizational and study skills necessary to keep her school work organized, which helped in all of her academic areas. In addition, she had the opportunity to take part in many small group situations with her peers, which helped her to develop the social skills to interact positively with others. Figure 4 reveals her progress in the group music therapy sessions during her final year at the Pilot School.

Unique Role of Music Therapy

The music therapy program at the Pilot School offers every student, regardless of ability level, the chance to participate in some form of musical expression with success. The music therapy program complements the other academic areas and programs in the school while providing the students with another arena in which they can feel good about their participation in school.

Music is one area in which almost every child seems to want to get involved. In addition to the group and individual music therapy sessions, the special music groups are popular with practically every Pilot student. These groups not only give the students a chance to develop some of their musical abilities, but also provide them an opportunity to share their musical talent with others in the school and community. The children in these groups learn that they must each work together so they can progress toward a common performance goal. Through these performances, which involve public speaking, singing, and playing instruments, they can begin to gain more confidence and a sense of accomplishment.

The music therapy program complements the other academic areas in a variety of ways. Each fall, many of the activities presented in the music sessions coincide with topics and issues that are being explored by the students and teachers in the classroom groups. These activities are then turned into a musical production that is presented as part of a holiday show each December. Every student in the school takes part in this

Goals	Objectives	Specific Educational Services	Evaluation Procedures	Dec.	March	June
To promote expressive language skills	1. The student will create original lyrics in a song about his life. He will verbalize the ideas, and then write them down with the assistance of the therapist. 2. The student will read and sing the lyrics of his song into a microphone for a musical recording.	Individual music therapy once a week for 1/2 hour	Completed Lyric Sheet of Original Song Audio Recording of the Original Song			
To improve visual perception	1. The student will extinguish letter reversals by correctly identifying the letters of the alphabet, and place cardboard figures of each letter in the appropriate direction and order during music activities. 2. The student will enhance visual tracking skills used in reading by following the printed notes of a melody across a page while playing the melody on a xylophone.	Individual music therapy once a week for 1/2 hour	Letters placed with 100% accuracy during the "ABC Song" and "Bingo" Successful Performance of "Lean on Me" on Xylophone			
To encourage attention to task	1. The student will gradually remain focused when playing drum set levels, for longer periods of time as the school year progresses.	Individual music therapy once a week for 1/2 hour	By December - 10 minutes of focused playing on levels 1-3 By March - 15 minutes of focused playing on levels 3-5 By June - 20 minutes of focused playing on levels 5-7			
Comments:						

Figure 3. Music Therapy IEP for Hypothetical Child With Learning Disabilities

Group Music Therapy Progress Report

Goals for the Group Music Therapy Sessions include:

Building self-esteem through successful experiences
Developing & refining auditory processing skills
Improving fine and gross motor skills
Enhancing speech and language development

Encouraging attention to task
Developing appropriate social skills
Promoting academic concepts
Expanding leisure time activities

Activities include:

Instrument playing
Music listening

Singing
Writing music & lyrics

Movement activities
Drama activities

Class Attitudes and Behaviors:	Mid-year	End-of-year
Follows Directions	S	G
Uses good Listening Skills	S	G
Participates in Activities	S	E
Interacts Appropriately with Peers	S	E
Works Independently	N	S
Accepts Praise and Encouragement	E	E
Respects Musical Equipment	E	E

E=Excellent   G=Good   S=Satisfactory   N=Needs Improvement

Comments:

Mid-year: This student willingly participates in each music therapy session. She does not hesitate to get involved, and she seems to enjoy the activities, particularly when she is interacting with the group members. On occasion, she gets distracted and acts immaturely with her peers and she then needs to be refocused. When working independently at an instrument, she has much difficulty remaining focused on the given task for more than a minute. She seems to give up quite easily, and she needs to be encouraged to put forth effort. When the therapist provides her with success-oriented, one-step tasks, interspersed with much positive verbal reinforcement, she seems to stay more motivated and on task for longer periods of time. It should also be noted that she sings on key quite well, and she shows an interest in singing.

End-of-year: As the year progressed, this student seemed to feel better about her abilities in the music sessions. She began to show more effort and determination on her own, and she depended less on the therapist's prompts to stay on task. She also acted more appropriately with her peers, engaging in appropriate, mature dialogue that contributed to the activities. The development of her singing voice gave her the confidence to successfully sing a solo with the Glee Club this year. The positive attention she received from her family, friends, and teachers from this performance seemed to increase her self-esteem. She even mentioned that she will audition for the choir at her new school next year.

This student has also participated in the Middle Division Glee Club this entire year.

Figure 4. Group Music Therapy Progress Report

production, and the students and staff work together cooperatively to create the show. This helps to create a feeling of unity among all of the students and staff in the school.

In the spring, all of the students are encouraged to write poetry by their homeroom teachers. The poetry that is created is then brought to the music therapy sessions and combined with music to create original songs. These songs are then performed by each homeroom group and are recorded by the students so they can use them for the music track in an original music video. The completed music videos are then shown to everyone in a large assembly. This extremely popular project involves every Pilot student and aids in the self-expression and language development of each child.

The music therapy program at the Pilot School has been developed by a music therapist with a dual degree in music education. Because of this background, and because of the fact that some of the children attending Pilot for many years have no other exposure to a music program, the therapist does incorporate some music education into the therapy sessions when appropriate. The overall focus of the program uses musical activities to accomplish the nonmusical goals stated earlier in this chapter. However, there are situations (such as the special music groups) where a performance-oriented musical goal is desired. In some of these group situations, the therapist will encourage students who are functioning at a high cognitive level, or who have previous musical experience, to use appropriate music notation rather than adapted music. Students are also encouraged to sing correctly and accurately on key, with the aid of Kodaly hand signals. By being exposed to some of the techniques typically used by music educators, it is believed that the children will be able to more likely make a successful transition back into a regular music education setting.

It is believed that through exposure to the music therapy program at the Pilot School, the child with learning disabilities will have another avenue to explore which will assist them in their quest to become a successful and independent learner.

References

Learning Disabilities Association of America. (1994). *When learning is a problem,* Pittsburgh, PA: Author.
National Information Center for Children and Youth with Disabilities. (2000). *Fact sheet number 7.* Washington, DC: Author.

Tips

Below are some suggestions which may be of use when working with students with learning disabilities in a music environment:

- Try to limit the size of your music group so that it will be easier to address the variety of learning problems and learning styles that you will encounter. Individualize your sessions as much as possible, offering several levels of participation within a session.

- When working with large groups of students, strategically seat certain students in locations which reduce distractions. Keep the distance between yourself and a highly distractible student to a minimum.

- Since some students will be challenged to stay focused on an activity, set up the room where the therapy session is to occur with a minimum amount of distractions (close blinds, cover materials not being used, position instruments out of sight until they are needed).

- Keep structure in the sessions to help the students be more successful. For example, have a predictable schedule of activities, allow students to move about the room one at a time during activities, define the space for their activity with tape or carpet mats.

- Because many students have difficulty understanding sequences of events, keep verbal directions simple, specific, and to the point.

- Be sure that you have the students' attention before giving directions. Use the music, rather than talking, to grab their attention. Students can easily learn that a short chord progression played on the piano means to stop talking and focus on the therapist.

- Present concepts and new material using more than one of the senses (visual, auditory, and kinesthetic) to enhance the students' ability to understand the information. For example, when introducing singing activities, use Kodaly hand signs that correspond to the syllables being sung. This gives the students both auditory and visual cues which may assist them to better sing on key. Also, try starting with the music (auditory stimulus) first, and then introduce the visual concepts that coincide with what they are hearing.

- Since some students may need the freedom to move around more than usual during the music sessions, devise a plan for those students so they can have this freedom without disrupting the other group members. For example, allow them to stand while others are doing work in their seats.

- Live music seems to be quite effective with this population since the students can visually see the music being produced in addition to just hearing it. Through live performance, the therapist can also modify a variety of musical elements (tempo, pitch, rhythm, and dynamics) so the students can be more successful in the music activities.

- Present small pieces of new information one at a time. Repetition with some variety can help ensure success and interest in the activities.

- Set verbal time limits for some activities to assist the students in managing their time appropriately ("You have 3 minutes to . . . You have 1 more minute". . .).

- Have many large, clearly identifiable cards with symbols (such as letters, numbers, music notation, words, etc.) available to use in the sessions. Providing the students with visual reinforcement of these symbols may help the children to understand them more fully.

- Use an overhead projector to focus an entire group on song lyrics or visual symbols. With the projector, you can enlarge visual symbols, reduce the field of vision, and point to words to help them better focus on specific areas.

- On some occasions, you may want the students to get involved quickly when they play "by ear" in a musical situation (without the use of written symbols). However, on other occasions adapted music can be helpful by providing the students with an opportunity to practice visual tracking, an important skill used in reading. Guitar tablature, chord charts, lyric sheets with chord symbols, colors or numbers which correspond to certain pitches, and pictures of the piano keyboard with dots on the intended keys are all useful visual devices.

- Use laminated charts so you and the students can create spontaneous visual symbols of any size and color during the music sessions.

- Have the students rotate through all of the instruments presented so every student has the opportunity to explore each instrument being used.

- When creating original song lyrics, reduce the amount of handwriting by having the students fill in blanks with individual words rather than having them write entire sentences. For those with more advanced writing ability, try using poetry forms such as haiku or 3-lines of blues for the basis of song lyrics.

- Some students have difficulty filtering out other sounds in a group music situation, creating additional stress for these children. Provide them with headphones to help keep them focused on a specific auditory sound.

- Get advice and suggestions from the other professional staff in your setting. What do they find effective? What assessments do they use? How can you adapt their ideas to conform to your music situation? Can you work together to reinforce some specific skills?

- Work with the classroom teachers to integrate information from a topic the students are studying into the music sessions. Give the teachers suggestions for music activities that they can use to enhance the lessons in their classroom.

- Recognize the children's strengths by providing a brief time at the end of a session for the students with extra musical talent to perform for their peers.

- Keep the music sessions enjoyable. Reinforce positive behaviors and provide opportunities for success to help build the students' self-esteem. Use music to help them have more success in an academic area that they find challenging so the student can gain more confidence in that academic area.

14

MUSIC THERAPY FOR LEARNERS
WHO ARE DEAF OR HARD-OF-HEARING

Alice-Ann Darrow
Heather Schunk Grohe

A Note to the Reader: *Throughout this chapter, we will use the abbreviation "D/HH" to denote the term "deaf and/or hard-of-hearing." We choose to use "deaf or hard-of-hearing" rather than "hearing impaired" because it is the terminology most often used by deaf adults. Many deaf adults view "hearing impaired" as a negative term denoting "broken or defective"; however, many professionals and parents of deaf children, particularly those who are hearing, frequently use the term "hearing impaired." Further, because those who are deaf or hard-of-hearing do not view their degree of hearing as a disability, it is not seen as pejorative in the Deaf culture to use the descriptors "deaf" or "hard-of-hearing" before references to the individuals. Music therapists should be sensitive to the terminology used by their students, their students' parents, as well as teachers and other professionals working in the school.*

Introduction

THE role of the music therapist in school programs for students who are deaf and hard-of-hearing is often multidimensional. Music therapists working in deaf education programs must be flexible and sensitive to the overall goals and objectives of the program. The nature of therapeutic goals and objectives is heavily dependent upon the school's philosophy regarding deaf education. There are two diverse philosophical approaches to educating students who are deaf or hard-of-hearing. The proponents of each approach have been at odds for many years. The primary controversy exists between those who support oral approaches and those who support manual communication approaches. Further controversies exist over specific methodologies utilized within each of these two major approaches. Music therapists must take into account the overall goals of the deaf education program and design their music therapy program objectives accordingly.

Given the educational environment, the music therapist should also include program objectives which address not only therapeutic goals, but also the musical education of D/HH students, particularly if they are not mainstreamed into regular music classes. Fortunately, many music therapy and music educational goals overlap. Both types of goals can often be met through similar classroom activities. Music therapy goals center around the communication needs of D/HH students, particularly in relation to language development. Music education goals center around D/HH students' need for avenues of self expression as well as their educational and personal development in relation to the larger hearing world (Darrow, 1995).

The frequent communication problems that D/HH children experience are a result of their status as a linguistic minority within the society of hearing persons who use spoken language as their primary means of communication. Left to socialize within their own subculture, D/HH children communicate freely and with all the expressiveness of any person using spoken language. Communication problems arise when D/HH children must interact with hearing individuals. These problems center around differences in their development of language and in their styles of communication.

Children who are born deaf or hard-of-hearing are neglected in language input, which must necessarily precede language output. Most young children receive language passively, soaking up the spoken word of their parents, older siblings, the television media, and even the conversations of strangers they encounter in public (Gfeller, 1999). In a similar way, a small percentage (about 10%) of infants who are deaf or hard-of-hearing are born to deaf parents, and they may develop a strong foundation for language development if they are exposed to the native, visual and manual language of deaf people in the United States: ASL (American Sign Language). Still, they are apt to struggle with the spoken and written forms of English, the language of America's majority culture. Deaf or hard-of-hearing children of hearing parents, however, are usually completely shut off from language in those early stages. As a result, they can encounter more pronounced communication barriers and exhibit an even greater delay in language development. For most deaf and hard-of-hearing children, the primary challenge is developing language in an often deprived language environment. Beyond that, for those who intend to and are able to learn spoken English, additional challenges include speech perception and production (Gfeller, 1999).

In the educational environment, the function of music in teaching language deserves attention. Good communication habits that maintain clear interaction and enhance incidental exposure to language can help the child to experience fewer delays (Gfeller & Schum, 1994). Music is communication. Music participation not only serves to mediate communication by organizing people into interactive behavior, but it also provides structure for both spoken and visual languages. "Music activity and active listening to music can produce functions supporting the acquisition of language, of attention and perception, the transfer of movement to sound and of sound to movement, such as an experience of the unity of language, music and movement" (Bang, 1986, p. 25). Darrow (1985) identifies some elements of music that parallel inherent qualities of spoken language, such as rhythm, intensity, duration, accents, pitch, and intonation. Rhythm, intensity, duration, accents, and inflection are also characteristic of signed language.

Beyond the facilitative aspects of music, there is the inherent value of music as a motivator which further supports the use of music therapy with deaf and hard-of-hearing children. Music therapy provides a creative, expressive, self-esteem-building, group-oriented, and reinforcing medium in which D/HH children can learn. Thus, music is significant in establishing a positive learning and therapeutic environment for children who often are presented with exceptional challenges in their educational experiences.

The ability to adapt music therapy procedures to the learning characteristics and communication styles of deaf and hard-of-hearing children requires specialized preparation. Along with some prerequisite skills, there is considerable background information that the music therapist must have in order to work successfully with these students. Background information in the following areas should be particularly helpful to the music therapist: speech and hearing science, audiology, aural habitation, manual and oral communication methods, and the impact of hearing loss on language development. An additional important area of background study is Deaf culture. Sensitivity to, and respect for, the culture of the Deaf community is essential to working successfully with children who are deaf and hard-of-hearing.

Deaf Culture

Culture embodies the beliefs, experiences and practices of an integrated group of people. These commonalities unify and strengthen the individual members who find understanding from and belonging with others like themselves. Cultural affiliation gives purpose for and insight into the collective values, needs and ways of achieving group goals (Kaplan, 1996; Padden, 1996). Through their endeavors, sub-groups develop distinct behaviors which are functional for survival within a larger world community. For people who do not hear to be able to survive in a sound-reliant world, they draw together to engage in a silent society. According to Rutherford (1988, pp. 134–135), some clear evidence of the Deaf as a distinct community include a high "endogamous marriage rate," "the existence of a formal societal structure," and "material artifacts." Beyond these characteristics, however, the key feature which defines and maintains virtually all cultures is language. It is through language that people are able to socialize, and thereby they transmit group customs, mores and expectations. Deaf people thus emerge as a unique group with strong solidarity and identity.

> Indeed, what makes Deaf people a cultural group instead of simply a loose organization of people with a similar sensory loss is the fact that their adaptation includes language. An environment created solely by a sensory deprivation does not make a culture. Blind people find themselves in a visual void. This similarity in circumstance certainly provides for a strong group bonding of individuals of similar experience; it does not, however, form a culture. Blind people are vision-impaired members of the variety of Americas' linguistic communities. What does form a culture for Deaf people is the fact that the adaptation to a visual world has by human necessity included a visual language. In the United States this is American Sign Language. (Rutherford, 1988, p. 132)

American Sign Language (ASL) is the native language of Deaf people (Armstrong, 1999). It originated in the early nineteenth century through the efforts of Laurent Clerc, a Deaf French educator, and the Reverend Thomas Gallaudet, an American, who saw the need for Deaf education in the United States. It has not been until recently, however, that ASL has gained recognition as an independent, manual/visual language with its own grammar, syntax and rules. Through the research of William Stokoe in the late 60's and early 70's, the myths of ASL being broken English and impeding the development of any language for its users were finally dispelled.

The development of the body of linguistic research related to American Sign Language resulted in an attitudinal shift which moved from viewing deafness as a pathological inability to identifying it as a cultural difference. Increasingly, Deaf people are seen as a linguistic minority within the hearing world (Padden, 1996). They are not defective or impaired people who are intellectually or cognitively inferior to those who do hear. They can be equally brilliant, witty, or expressive.

Past misconceptions about the language and the abilities of those who are Deaf built many barriers and obstacles to mutual understanding and interaction between Deaf and hearing communities. This has had an impact on the educational and political experiences of the Deaf. They feel that traditionally hearing educators and leaders have made decisions about the teaching practices and social position of those who are Deaf without consideration for the special needs and views of the group itself. As a result, Deaf people are compelled to advance their group's acceptance within the hearing world to gain respect and rights. They have made great strides in exerting their issues by educating the public about their language, social and political organizations, and rich legacy of Deaf folklore, art, and literature. For further readings on deaf culture, see Appendix A.

Music and Deaf Culture

Music in Deaf culture has a long and varied history (Darrow & Heller, 1985; Sheldon, 1997). In respect for the Deaf community, it is important to discuss the role of music in a cultural context (Darrow & Loomis, 1999). This respect means expanding the conventional constructs through which music involvement is traditionally defined. The adaptability of music makes it accessible to D/HH people. It is important to note that very few individuals actually have no hearing. Usually, deaf and hard-of-hearing people have some degree of residual, or existing, hearing. Therefore, there are certain frequencies, timbres, and intensities of music which can be auditorily detected. Further, music becomes visual and tactile. Aspects of music participation among Deaf people include vibrations, rhythm, movement, and expression. There are Deaf instrumentalists, rock bands, concert fans, country dancers, and more. Research, however, indicates that it is erroneous to assume that all Deaf people value music (Darrow, 1993). Some individuals reject music as a hearing value and find no use for it in their lives. This caution is noted in discussing the implications of music therapy with Deaf and hard-of-hearing children. Music therapists must recognize and understand their students' place within or outside of Deaf culture.

Those who uphold the values of Deaf culture and use ASL take pride in their cultural identity and they describe themselves as "Deaf" with a capital "D." There are others, however, who do not share the language or social ties and thus function more in the hearing world. These individuals are more apt to describe themselves as "deaf" with a lower case "d" or with the term "hard-of-hearing" (Padden & Humphries, 1988). For the purposes of this chapter, we will attempt to address music therapy implications as they apply to these combined groups of individuals. They will be referred to in the encompassing category of Deaf and hard-of-hearing persons.

Terminology Related to Deafness

There are numerous terms used in the field of deaf education. We have included selected terms below. Knowledge of these terms is essential to working effectively with D/HH students and interacting credibly with other professionals.

Types of Hearing Loss

There are four types of hearing loss, each of which can result in different possibilities for remediation:

Conductive Hearing Losses are caused by diseases or obstructions in the outer or middle ear (the conduction pathways for sound to reach the inner ear). Conductive hearing losses usually affect all frequencies of hearing and do not result in severe losses. Because of this, a person with a conductive hearing loss usually is able to use a hearing aid with success.

Sensorineural Hearing Losses result from damage to the delicate sensory hair cells of the inner ear or the nerves which supply it. These hearing losses can range from mild to profound deafness. They often affect certain frequencies more than others, and this results in distorted perception even when the sound level is increased. The distortion accompanying some forms of sensorineural hearing loss is so severe that successful use of a hearing aid is impossible.

Mixed Hearing Losses are those in which there is a problem in the outer or middle ear and in the inner ear.

Central Hearing Losses result from damage or impairment to the nerves or nuclei of the central nervous system, either in the pathway to the brain or in the brain itself.

Onset of Deafness

The onset of deafness varies from person to person, and it holds implications for an individual's language development.

Congenital Deafness: When a person is born deaf.

Adventitious Deafness: When deafness occurs sometime after birth, usually as a result of an accident or illness.

Prelingual Deafness: When deafness occurs before the acquisition of language (usually before three years of age). Such a person will have no language frame of reference when learning to speak, write, or speechread.

Postlingual Deafness: When deafness occurs after the acquisition of language (usually after 3 years of age). In most cases, persons who have lost their hearing after this age have a relatively strong language base.

Classifications of Hearing Loss

Hearing Level Effect on the Clinical Environment

An individual's hearing loss is generally described in terms of slight, mild, moderate, severe, and profound, based on their average hearing level, in decibels, throughout the frequencies most important for understanding speech (500 to 2,000 Hz). Each level of hearing loss will have a differential effect on the client's interaction with the clinical environment. Table 1 outlines the effects each level of hearing loss will have on the clinical environment.

Table 1
Effect of Hearing Loss on the Environment

Degree of Loss	Effect on Environment
Slight loss (27 to 40 dB)	May have difficulty hearing faint or distant speech. May experience some difficulty with language arts.
Mild loss (41 to 55 dB)	Understands conversational speech at a distance of 3 to 5 feet. May miss as much as 50% of conversation if not face-to-face. May have limited vocabulary and speech irregularities.
Moderate loss (56 to 70 dB)	Can understand loud conversation only. Will have difficulty in group discussions. Is likely to have impaired speech, limited vocabulary, and difficulty in language use and comprehension.
Severe loss (71 to 90 dB)	May hear loud voices about 1 foot from ear. May be able to identify environmental sounds. May be able to discriminate vowels, but not consonants. Speech and language likely to be impaired or to deteriorate.
Profound loss (91 dB or more)	More aware of vibrations than tonal patterns. Relies on vision rather than hearing as primary means of communication. Speech and language likely to be impaired or to deteriorate. Speech and language unlikely to develop spontaneously if loss is prelingual.

(Hardman, 1999, pp. 398–401; Heward & Orlansky, 1988, pp. 259–260)

Descriptive Terms

<u>D</u>eaf (with a capital "D"): People who share a language— American Sign Language—and a culture.
<u>d</u>eaf (with a lower case "d"): Individuals who are oral, or often those who lose their hearing adventitiously through illness, accidents, or old age. This group does not have access to the language, heritage, beliefs, and practices of Deaf people.
Hard-of-hearing: A condition in which one's residual hearing is functional for processing speech—usually with the help of a hearing aid (Padden & Humphries, 1988).

Terms Related to the Measurement of Hearing

Since music therapists are concerned with the response of the human ear to music stimuli, it is helpful to know those terms that relate to the measurement of hearing. Sound consists of vibrations that travel in waves, generally through the air. Sound waves can vibrate at different speeds as they travel through the air. The faster the wave vibrates, the higher the pitch. Frequency is the number of vibrations produced per second and is measured in Hertz. One vibration per second equals one Hertz. The frequency of a sound is a physical reality while pitch is our subjective judgment of its frequency. Table 2 gives familiar frequency ranges.

Table 2
Frequency Ranges in Hertz

Frequency Range	Hertz
normal hearing:	20 – 20,000 Hz
normal speech:	500 – 2000 Hz
the piano:	27.5 – 4186 Hz

The duration of sound has to do with its continuance in time. The aural discrimination of varying lengths of sound is the basis of rhythm perception. Intensity is the amount of energy in a sound wave. Intensity is a quantitative measurement of sound. Loudness is our subjective judgment of this measurement. The intensity of sound is measured in decibels. Zero decibels (0 dB) is the quietest audible sound while sounds above 120-140 dB can actually cause pain to the ears. Table 3 gives some common decibel ranges:

Table 3
Decibel Ranges of Common Sound Sources

Decibel Levels	Sound Source	Musical Levels
0 dB	just audible sound	
20 dB	soft rustle of leaves	
30 dB	quiet whisper	background music
40 dB	soft speech	p
50 dB	normal conversation	mp
60 dB	loud conversation	mf
80 dB	shouting	f
90 dB	heavy traffic	marching band
100 dB	riveter 35 feet away	
120 dB	jet engine	

Audiology, the science of hearing, has made great strides in the development of instruments which assist in the detection and assessment of hearing loss. Audiologists measure the degree of hearing loss by generating sounds at specific frequencies and intensities on an audiometer, and then measuring an individual's response to these sounds. By viewing these responses displayed graphically on an audiogram, the music therapist can determine the aural accessibility of music stimuli and the degree of amplification required in the clinic setting.

Fortunately for us as music therapists, our medium, music, is usually more aurally accessible to D/HH individuals than speech. Music is generally more intense than conversational speech, employs many more frequencies than normal speech, and is composed of notes which are greater in duration than speech sounds. This is why even individuals with severe hearing losses will still be able to listen to and enjoy music, yet they may have difficulty in aurally processing speech.

Communication Methods

In the United States, D/HH persons use a variety of methods and symbol systems for communication. These communication styles represent differing philosophies, and supporters of the controversial theories are sometimes at odds. These methods and philosophies include American Sign Language, Fingerspelling, Manual Communication, Oral Communication, Cued Speech, Simultaneous Communication, and Total Communication.

American Sign Language

ASL is a natural language with its own grammar and syntax. It is a beautiful and graceful visual-gestural language which developed naturally among deaf people and is used widely in the United States and several other countries. The signs in ASL are word-like units which have both concrete and abstract meanings. Signs are made by either one or both hands assuming distinctive shapes in particular locations and executing specified movements. The use of spatial relations, direction, orientation, and movement of the hands, as well as facial expression and body shift make up the grammar of ASL.

Fingerspelling

A manual alphabet is merely an alternative form of a written alphabet with hand shapes and positions corresponding to the letters of the written alphabet. In a very real sense, fingerspelling is "writing in the air." In a fingerspelling conversation, one person spells the message letter by letter to a second person who reads it and responds by spelling a reply. The use of fingerspelling as the primary mode of communication in combination with spoken English is known as the Rochester Method.

Manual Communication

The term *manual communication* includes a combination of sign language and fingerspelling used for both expressive and receptive communication. A number of manual communication systems combine sign language and fingerspelling with the grammar and syntax of standard English. There are four major systems in this group: (1) Seeing Essential English (SEE), (2) Signing Exact English (SEE II), (3) Linguistics of Visual English (LOVE), and (4) Signed English.

Oral Communication

This term denotes the use of speech and speech-reading as the primary means for the transmission of thoughts and ideas with deaf persons. Educators who believe in the Oral Communication philosophy, in their work with deaf children, emphasize, exclusively, the teaching of speech and speech-reading together with amplification and the use of whatever residual hearing individuals have.

Cued Speech

Cued speech is a system of communication in which eight hand movements supplement the information being spoken. This is not a form of sign language. The hand "cue" is used to indicate, visually, the exact pronunciation of every syllable spoken. With Cued Speech, a person with hearing loss can see all the words a hearing person hears. It is a speech-based method of communication aimed at taking guesswork out of speech-reading.

Simultaneous Communication

This term is used to denote the combined use of speech, signs, and fingerspelling. An individual receives the message both by speech-reading what is being said and by reading the signs and fingerspelling simultaneously.

Total Communication

Total Communication is a philosophy of communication which implies acceptance, understanding, and use of all methods of communication to assist the deaf child in acquiring language.

Historically, proponents of the various systems have been at odds. There is increasing consensus that whatever system or method works most successfully for the individual should be used to allow the person who has a hearing loss access to clear and understandable communication.

Additional Information

Inclusive background information regarding children who are deaf and hard-of-hearing cannot, of course, be included within this chapter. Music therapists working with D/HH children should request inservice as needed. Suggested topics for inservice might include the following:

1. Sign language instruction.
2. Deaf culture.
3. Current literature in deaf issues.
4. D/HH musicians.
5. Psychosocial aspects of deafness.
6. Seminar offerings in basic hearing science.
7. Parts and functions of the ear.
8. Introduction to hearing aids and other assistive listening devices.
9. Methods of nonverbal communication.
10. Speechreading concepts.
11. Causes and prevention of deafness.

Adaptations in the Music Therapy Setting

There are two primary aspects of the music therapy setting for which adaptations should be made in order to meet the needs of children who are deaf or hard-of-hearing. The purpose of these adaptations is to facilitate communication. Aspects of the music therapy setting which require adaptations are the physical environment and interpersonal communication.

Adaptations to the Physical Environment

1. Unnecessary noise, such as air conditioners or outdoor traffic, should be eliminated or minimized.

2. The clinical setting should have good lighting.
3. Clinic room fixtures such as draperies, carpeting, and upholstery should be used to absorb unnecessary noise.
4. Seating should be in a circle for group activities.
5. If the D/HH children wear hearing aids, they should be positioned with their hearing aids toward the group.
6. The speaker's face must be clearly seen.
7. Optimal speechreading distance should be kept at 6 feet.
8. If necessary, additional assistive communication devices such as microphones, visual aides, tactile aides, sign language interpreters, and appropriate technological aides should be added to the physical environment.

Adaptations in Interpersonal Communication

One-to-One Communication

1. Get the deaf person's attention before speaking. A tap on the shoulder, a wave, or other visual sign of soliciting attention.
2. Speak slowly and clearly; but exaggeration and over-emphasis of words distorts lip movements, making speechreading more difficult. Speechreading is a skill not all deaf persons are able to acquire. Only about 1/3 to 1/4 of all speech is visible on the lips, and even the best speechreaders can't read everything although they can pick up contextual clues to fill in some of the gaps.
3. Look directly at the person when you speak. Even a slight turn of the head can obscure the deaf person's view. Other distracting factors affecting communication include mustaches obscuring the lips, smoking, chewing gum, and putting your hand in front of your face.
4. Don't be embarrassed about communicating via paper and pencil. Getting the message across is more important than the medium used.
5. Try to maintain eye contact with the deaf person. Eye contact helps convey the feeling of direct communication. If an interpreter is present, continue to talk directly to the deaf person who can turn to the interpreter if the need arises.
6. If you are having some difficulty getting an idea across, try to rephrase a thought or restate a sentence, rather than repeating exactly the same words. Sometimes a particular group of lip movements is difficult to speechread.
7. Use pantomime, body language, and facial expression to help communicate.

Group Situations and Meetings

1. Seat the deaf person near the speaker where he or she can see the speaker's face.
2. Try to avoid standing in front of a light source, such as window. The bright background and shadows created on the face make it almost impossible to speechread.
3. Aid the deaf person in following a lecture, movie, or filmstrip by providing a brief outline or script printout. This can be provided in advance or accompanied by lighting for the deaf person.
4. In a training situation, try to provide new vocabulary in advance. It is almost impossible to speechread unfamiliar words.
5. Use visual aids. They can be a tremendous help to deaf persons. Vision is a deaf person's primary channel for receiving information. Make full use of overhead projectors. chalkboards, films, diagrams, charts, and other visual media where appropriate.
6. Try to avoid unnecessary pacing and speaking while writing on the chalkboard or lecturing. It is difficult to speechread a person in motion and impossible from the side or from the back.

7. Slow down the pace of communication slightly. This often helps to facilitate understanding. Many speakers tend to talk too fast. Try to allow a little extra time for the deaf person to assimilate the information and respond.

8. Make sure the deaf person is not left out when vital information is presented. Write out any changes in meeting times, special arrangements, additional instructions. Allow extra time when pointing out the location of materials, referring to manuals and other media, because the deaf person must look, then return attention for further instruction.

9. Repeat questions of statements from the back of the room. Deaf persons are cut off from whatever is not in their visual field. Since it is often necessary to know the question in order to fully understand the answer, questions or statements should be repeated.

(Handout from the National Technical Institute for the Deaf at the Rochester Institute of Technology.)

Music Therapy Objectives

The term *therapy* usually implies the remedial treatment of a disease or other physical or mental disorder. The deaf community has made great strides in recent years to depathologize their disability. Deafness is no longer viewed as a medical condition, a deficit in need of treatment. The only true handicap related to deafness is being cut off from the usual means of acquiring and transmitting language. As a result, most deaf individuals communicate manually rather than orally. They regard this alternative form of communication as their only "difference." The loss of hearing, however, has many implications for the development of communication skills. Consequently, music therapy remains a viable educational intervention for children who are D/HH. The range of goals which are targeted for this population comprise the following categories of therapeutic objectives: *linguistic, behavioral, academic, motor skills, social interaction skills, and self concept.*

Linguistic

[T]he main focus of educational programs for deaf children is the acquisition of English. Whereas some educators have recently argued that this rigid focus on English is unhealthy and that more attention should be given to learning history, science, math, etc.--through any available means of communication—it is still generally true that the majority of a deaf child's time and energy in school is spent on developing skills in English. (Baker-Shenk & Cokely, 1991, p. 63)

With the focused training of English literacy being the critical chore in deaf education, music therapy serves as a motivating and engaging method of successfully achieving linguistic objectives. Through music therapy, other academic goals can be incorporated into activities relating to language development to enhance the educational foundation of deaf children. The design of these applications can be further influenced by the needs and priorities of the individual student, as discussed in the section on Deaf culture. Therefore, the linguistic objectives for Deaf children fit into two distinct categories: developing aural-oral English literacy and learning English as a second language through American Sign Language.

Aural-Oral English

The spoken language objectives for music therapy with clients who have a significant hearing loss, are related to communication: (1) auditory training, (2) speech production, and (3) language development of children who have a hearing loss.

Auditory Training. The goal of auditory training is to teach the complex task of listening. The ability of individuals to use their hearing for the purpose of listening varies. Good hearing does not necessarily ensure skilled listening; conversely, poor hearing does not necessarily indicate an inability to listen. Listening is a mental process; hearing is a physical process. It is the function of the ear to collect auditory stimuli and deliver them to the brain; at which time the brain takes over and hearing becomes listening (Darrow, 1990). The development of good listening skills allows the D/HH individual to use their residual hearing to the maximum extent possible. When D/HH individuals learn to interpret the sounds around them, they also increase the rate and quality of their social and communicative development.

Training the ear to listen requires: (1) analysis of the desired auditory task, (2) the structuring of successive approximations to the desired goal, and (3) regular and systematic evaluation of the client's auditory skill level. Auditory training should consist of sequential listening exercises. Nearly all auditory tasks can be broken down into four very basic levels of aural processing (Erber & Hirsh, 1978). These levels of aural processing follow as well as ways of integrating music to determine a client's present level.

1. Detection: The listener determines the presence or absence, initiation or termination of music stimuli;
2. Discrimination: The listener perceives differences in music stimuli (such as fast and slow, high and low);
3. Identification: The listener appropriately applies labels (such as forte or piano, woodwind or brass) to music stimuli;
4. Comprehension: The listener makes critical judgments regarding music stimuli (such as judgments concerning form, harmony, or texture).

Most D/HH individuals develop detection and discrimination skills through normal interaction with the environment. It is the third and fourth levels of auditory processing, discrimination and comprehension, that require the attention of the music therapist.

There are a number of other listening behaviors that are subsumed within these four basic levels of auditory processing. These additional listening behaviors are prerequisites to auditory comprehension. Derek Saunders (1977) developed a hierarchy of auditory processing which should assist the music therapist in developing sequential listening objectives for a wide range of clients. The hierarchy was developed with the processing of the speech signal in mind; however, music applications can be made and are given in each of the hierarchical steps. Speech and music contain many common properties, though perhaps identified by different names. In music, reference is made to intonation, tempo, accent, and rhythm. Speech counterparts are speech inflection, rate, stress, and speech rhythm. Once again, proficiency at the first four levels of the hierarchy is usually acquired naturally. The remaining six levels of auditory processing should provide a guide for music listening experiences.

1. *Awareness of acoustic stimuli*
   Is the client aware that music is in the environment ?

2. *Localization*
   Can the client identify the location of the musical sound source ?

3. *Attention*
   Can the client attend to the music over time ?

4. *Discrimination between speech and nonspeech*
   Can the client discriminate between music and nonmusic sounds ?

5. *Auditory discrimination*
   Can the client discriminate between the timbre of different instruments or the entrance and exit of specific instruments within the total music context (figure/ground discrimination) ?

6. *Suprasegmental discrimination*
    Can the client make discriminations about the expressive qualities of the music (dynamics, tempo, phrasing) ?

7. *Segmental discrimination*
    Can the client make discriminations about changes in pitch ?

8. *Auditory memory*
    Can the client remember what instruments were heard ?

9. *Auditory sequential memory*
    Can the client remember in what order the instruments were heard ?

10. *Auditory synthesis*
    Can the client make critical judgments regarding form, texture, harmony ?

There are controversial views regarding the transfer of music listening skills to linguistic use; however, teaching a client to develop focused and analytical attention to sound will undoubtedly transfer to the development of good listening habits, regardless of the source of sound stimuli. Although we can do little to improve D/HH individuals' ability to hear, we can do much to improve their ability to listen. Our goal is to increase the amount of information they receive through the sense of hearing. We do this by teaching them to interpret the sounds they hear. Listening, like any other skill, must be practiced through regular, sequential listening exercises. The ear is a valuable listening device; and music, a powerful medium through which listening skills can be taught, practiced, . . . and rewarded.

Language Acquisition and Development. Language is the means by which people communicate. Native languages are generally learned auditorily, with ease, and over a relatively short period of time. Aural exposure to language is the most important ingredient in the development of communication skills. Without adequate aural exposure to language, D/HH children essentially learn a "foreign" language with only the assistance of nonverbal cues such as facial expression, body language, and small movements of the lips — on which approximately only one third of all speech is visible. It is understandable that, without alternative forms of communication such as sign language, D/HH children are at a tremendous disadvantage during the process of language development. Even children with mild hearing impairments experience difficulty with the fine discriminations that must be made in comprehending language (Luetke, 1998; Weisel, 1998).

Other more subtle forms of language, such as sarcasm and play-on-words, are dependent on the aural processing of speech. Many verbal behaviors are also learned auditorily; some of these include social customs such as "please" and "thank you," use of compliments, and avoidance of inappropriate questions. Young children are generally able to comprehend various words or phrases long before they are able to use them appropriately; demonstrating the importance of exposure as an antecedent to expression. Every professional involved in the habilitation of young D/HH children, including music therapists, should have among their objectives, the acquisition and development of language (Luetke, 1998; Srinivasan, 1996).

The two fundamental components of language with which the music therapist is most likely to work are vocabulary knowledge and word-class usage (Gfeller & Darrow, 1987). Receptive and expressive skills, as well as reading and writing skills, should be employed as a part of instructional strategies. In order to foster language development to the fullest extent possible, methods of achieving these goals should not be confined solely to lesson objectives, but to every procedure employed in the music therapy setting. The music therapist can make most interactions an opportunity for learning language (Rickard, Robbins, & Robbins, 1990).

For young D/HH clients, the most important language objective will be the increased and appropriate use of vocabulary (Weisel, 1998). Developing vocabulary skills is not as simple as defining words. Word meaning in a single context measures only one component of vocabulary knowledge. Words often have multiple meanings and serve separate language functions. D/HH children tend to know fewer words and to use them in a singular context (Davis & Hardick, 1981). A D/HH child may know the word "kid" in its noun form, a child or young goat, but not in its verb, adverb, or adjective form. It is the therapist's task to introduce vocabulary words, their multiple meanings, and their proper use in as many circumstances as possible: in song texts, song writing, informal conversation, and contrived situations. The therapist's choice of target words should be made in consultation with the child's classroom teacher or professionals who specialize in the language development of D/HH children.

D/HH children may also experience difficulty with word-class usage. D/HH children with a moderate degree of residual hearing tend to use most word classes adequately with the exception of adverbs, pronouns, and auxiliaries; D/HH children with minimal residual hearing use fewer words in all classes than children with no hearing loss. A characteristic of most D/HH children's language is a tendency to overuse nouns and articles; thus, the speculation that impaired hearing interferes with the function of words as well as understanding of their meaning (Davis & Hardick, 1981). The music therapist must attempt to provide good models of word usage, opportunities for variety of word use, and corrective feedback. Again, this can be accomplished through the study of song texts, informal conversation, or contrived situations. Additional approaches are activities such as song writing, song signing, and small group ensembles where communication is essential (Gfeller, 1987; Gfeller, 1990). Gfeller and Baumann (1988) give suggestions for the assessment of language skills in music therapy.

Speech Production and Reception. Speech production is acquired and controlled through the auditory system. Children learn to speak by imitating the sounds of others. The degree to which these sounds are available to the D/HH child will directly influence the quality of speech production and the ability to receive the speech signal. The aspects of speech which are most severely affected by impaired hearing are phonation, rhythm, and articulation. D/HH children often do not associate breath control with the power source needed for fluid speech; consequently, they may breathe in the middle of words or phrases. Errors of rhythm constitute one of the most deviate aspects of D/HH individuals' speech. The speech is generally slower, the syllables prolonged, and stress placed on inappropriate syllables. Speech intelligibility varies widely among D/HH individuals, however, even individuals with very little hearing are capable of developing intelligible speech.

Hearing one's own voice allows the speaker the aural feedback necessary to self correct pronunciation of words, adjust vocal inflection and imitate speech rhythm. D/HH children are dependent on corrective feedback and instruction in remedial strategies from others. The music therapist can provide assistance in both of these areas. Music therapy objectives may include, though not be limited to, the following: vocal intonation, vocal quality, speech fluency, and speech intelligibility. In speech, the melodic elements such as rhythm, intonation, rate, and stress are referred to as the prosodic features of speech. These prosodic features convey important contextual information. Music activities such as singing can aid in the recognition and development of these melodic aspects of speech (Darrow & Starmer, 1986; Shurman, 1999). Appropriate procedures include free vocalization, vocal imitation, rhythmic vocalization, and work on vocal phrasing and dynamics. Traditional music activities such as pitch matching practice, singing songs and vocal exercises, and following notated melodic contours are also helpful (Bang, 1986).

The remediation of poor vocal quality can also be enhanced through traditional music activities. A breathy quality can be alleviated by vocalise that exercise the diaphragm; a nasal quality can be minimized by incorporating vocal exercises that utilize the head voice. The volume of a client's voice can be monitored during music therapy by teaching and practicing the use of expressive terms such as *piano* and *forte, decrescendo* and *crescendo.*

Speech fluency and articulation are not as easily influenced by the use of music therapy techniques. Speech fluency can be improved by the rhythmic chanting and singing of syllables, syllable combinations, words, word combinations, phrases, and, finally, complete sentences. Articulatory problems constitute the greatest challenge for speech and music therapists. Problems with articulation usually involve sound omissions, such as final consonants; substitutions, such as "thoup" instead of "soup;" interjections, such as "boyee" instead of "boy;" and mispronunciation of sounds, such as "sh," "th," or "s." The music therapist can carefully select song literature which focuses on specific speech sounds or words. The therapist should also maintain a record of the number of intelligible words in a given song (Darrow, 1989). Consultation with the client's speech therapist can be extremely helpful in selecting appropriate and realistic objectives. In addition to directed music activities, feedback regarding a client's speech intelligibility should be given by the music therapist during everyday interactions in the clinical setting. Traditional assessments used in speech therapy can also be of use to the music therapist (Darrow, Gfeller, Gorsuch, & Thomas, 2000).

English as a Second Language

For children who affiliate with the Deaf community, the approach to language instruction should adhere to the group's philosophy regarding the learning of English. Because ASL is the central facet of Deaf culture, they strongly support it as their native language. Subsequently, they consider English a second language. Educators have attempted to teach English in combination with signing, but typically they ignore the role of ASL and employ English sign systems. These systems have been artificially created and are not generally accepted by members of the Deaf community (Baker-Shenk & Cokely, 1991).

In learning ASL, deaf children follow rules of grammar and syntax when communicating thoughts and ideas. Therefore, they have an established language base which provides an understanding of the building blocks of language and through which they can learn English. Given this premise, the traditional curriculum in aural-oral language remediation for some of these students may not be viable. It is critical to accept the use of their native language, ASL, for English instruction. Through their complete and independent language, complex concepts are successfully communicated; and thereby, they can learn fundamentals of English and achieve bi-lingual literacy. In addition to incorporating ASL into practice, the music therapist should seek direction from members of the Deaf community in designing and implementing therapeutic interventions. The best experts on the subject can be found among the cultural members.

The goal of instruction in English as a second language is to develop "communicative competence" (Diaz-Rico & Weed, 1995, p. 13). This refers to a point when the learner can effectively and idiomatically-- that is, as a native would--use the language. For children who are Deaf, this process aims at somewhat different outcomes from those of hearing students learning English as a second language. Training in verbal and auditory skills to comprehend and speak English is necessary for children whose first language is Spanish, Russian, Urdu, or another spoken language. When the first language is ASL, however, the required cognitive skills are transmitted manually and visually.

Diaz-Rico and Weed (1995) suggest four areas of desired competence when teaching English as a second language that could apply to spoken and non-spoken English: grammatical, sociolinguistic, discourse, and strategic competence. There are verbal components of the following explanations, however, that would be non-applicable; they are marked with an asterisk (*). *Grammatical competence* "involves knowing the language code: vocabulary, word formation and meaning, sentence formation, *pronunciation, and spelling" (Diaz-Rico & Weed, p. 14). *Sociolinguistic competence* refers to comprehending the language in the context of various factors, such as "the status of participants, the purposes of the interaction, and the norms or conventions of interaction" (Diaz-Rico & Weed, p. 14). Both form and meaning of the discourse should be appropriate. *Discourse competence* "involves the ability to combine and connect *utterances (spoken) and sentences (written) into a meaningful whole" (Diaz-Rico & Weed, p. 14). *Strategic competence* involves behaviors and techniques which manipulate the language "to compensate for breakdowns in communication" and "to enhance the effectiveness of communication" (Diaz-Rico & Weed, p. 14).

These complex goals of language remediation warrant clever ways of structuring the educational experience to reinforce comprehension and functional usage. Music has been documented as a key tool for such achievement (Little, 1983; "Teaching and learning aids: Musical ESL," 1983). Curriculum for teaching English as a second language (ESL) is complex, and the music therapist is not expected to have all the necessary training to implement such a program. In cooperation with a qualified professional, however, the music therapist has an unlimited resource for supplementing and developing ESL applications. Little (1983) explains that "music cuts across cultural and linguistic boundaries so easily" (p. 41). Although his research involved hearing children, the adaptability of music makes the same statement true in working with deaf children.

Properties of music, such as rhythm, accents, tempo, and repetition, organize and direct behavior toward educational objectives. These same features support the structure of language, and teaching Deaf children English songs to sign can be useful for practicing syntax, vocabulary, and idioms. Songs also facilitate some of the strategies Diaz-Rico and Weed (1995) emphasize that ESL teachers should employ in order to help students build communicative competence: repetition, memorization, formulaic expressions, elaboration, monitoring one's own errors, appealing for assistance, requesting clarification, and role playing.

Beyond signing English songs, there are other uses of music therapy for teaching ESL to children who are Deaf. Some other applications of music therapy include playing instruments, dancing, song writing, and performing. Each of these activities can be designed to correspond to specific principles of language. Further, the musical involvements can be organized into skits, games, and storytelling. Numerous books describe the use of skits and games to teach ESL, such as *101 Word Games: For Students of English as a Second or Foreign Language* (McCallum, 1980), *Once Upon a Time: Using Stories in the Language Classroom* (Morgan & Rinvolucri, 1983), and *Skits in English as a Second Language* (Hines, 1973). Unfortunately, there is a dearth of such writings which also incorporate music, and there is virtually none that pertains to teaching ESL to children who are Deaf.

The creative role of the music therapist working with Deaf children not only demands originality in designing goal-directed applications, but it also challenges him or her to draw on a multitude of instructional resources, not limited to musical equipment. Instruments are used, but additional visual and tactile aids must be incorporated, such as picture files, charts and posters, slides, printed material, and costumes (Diaz-Rico & Weed, 1995). These materials can compliment the musical structure of the session and serve to facilitate comprehension and to reinforce participation.

As the students' knowledge of English improves, they will have more expertise in conveying English concepts through music. Evidence of their literacy can take the form of written songs or it can be displayed by role playing the literal and the intended meanings of English idioms through dance. For example, the phrase "let the cat out of the bag" can be performed first in a literal scene with one dancer opening an imaginary bag and letting out another character who dances like a cat. In a second scene, other dancers can convey the concept when one person tells another a secret. Then, the second character dances around anxious to tell someone the news until a third dancer enters and the second "lets the cat out of the bag."

The use of music to teach English as a second language is not only positively indicated for this population, but importantly, it includes culture-specific adaptations which fosters acceptance from the Deaf community and invites insightful input from its members.

Other Objectives

Clearly, the emphasis of music therapy interventions with D/HH children is on the linguistic objectives. It is important to note, however, the various other therapeutic goals supported by D/HH students' participation in music applications.

Behavioral

1. To increase motivation for learning
2. To improve compliance
3. To increase on-task behavior
4. To improve turn taking
5. To improve sharing

Academic
  1. To learn fundamentals of music
  2. To improve reading skills
  3. To improve writing skills
  4. To rehearse and develop additional academic concepts

Motor Skills
  1. To develop gross motor skills
  2. To improve coordination
  3. To improve balance
  4. To develop fine motor skills

Social Interaction Skills
  1. To increase personal expression
  2. To improve interpersonal communication
  3. To develop group cooperation

Self Concept
  1. To improve self esteem
  2. To increase opportunities for individual success
  3. To develop a sense of group achievement

Music Education Objectives

Some people believe that to be musical, one must have good hearing; however, many D/HH individuals are indeed musical. The degree of interest in music among D/HH individuals varies as it does among those with normal hearing (Darrow, 1993; Gfeller, Witt, Spencer, Stordahl, &Tomblin, 2000). Many D/HH students enjoy participating in musical activities, and their education in the arts should not be forfeited for entirely nonmusical goals (Birkenshaw-Fleming, 1990). Music educators often find that they enjoy teaching D/HH students, and that it can be quite rewarding (Burgess, 1997; Johns, 2001; Kaiser & Johnson, 2000; Vassall, 1997). Their objectives for D/HH students can follow those that are often outlined for normal hearing students. Objectives should include various forms of music participation:

  1. Listening to music
  2. Singing
  3. Playing instruments
  4. Moving to music
  5. Creating music
  6. Reading music

Music education objectives might also include knowledge about masterpieces of music and the elements of music: rhythm, melody, harmony, form, and expression. Traditional approaches to teaching music concepts can be employed with D/HH students (Ford, 1990; Robbins & Robbins, 1980; Robbins & Robbins, 1990; Schatz, 1990). Because of their visual and movement components, music educators of D/HH students have indicated that Orff and Kodaly approaches are particularly useful (Darrow & Gfeller, 1991). D/HH students are at a distinct disadvantage if they are taught music solely through listening. Most D/HH students learn best through active participation in music making. Learning music through performing, reading, and writing music is essential for the students with a hearing loss. Additional adaptive strategies include the use of visual and tactile aides. Almost any aural concept can be represented in some visual way. Using kinesthetic movement, such as having students outline the movement of a melody with their hands, is also helpful for the D/HH student.

Special attention should also be given to amplification of music stimuli (Dalgarno, 1990; Geers, Hojan, & Hojan-Jezierska, 1997), the quality of recording equipment and instruments, as well as the suggestions given earlier for adaptation of the physical and communication environment. Every individual, regardless of hearing status, deserves the right to participate in the musical arts and, as a result, experience a part of our culture. Some D/HH individuals do not consider music a part of deaf culture and consequently, look upon musical study as a "hearing value." Many members of the deaf community, however, do find music to be an important part of their lives (Darrow, 1993).

Adaptive Instructional Strategies

In teaching music, the music therapist must be aware of the use of music with this population as it relates to their strengths and preferences (Darrow, 1991; Gfeller, Knutson, Woodworth, Witt, & Debus, 1998; Gfeller, Woodworth, Robin, Witt, & Knutson, 1997). There are some generalizations that can be made regarding the musical characteristics of D/HH individuals based upon research in music perception and performance. Be reading the research and reviewing these characteristics, the music therapist can make the appropriate adaptations in teaching music to students who are D/HH. A list of selected research related to the D/HH is given in Appendix B. Following are some of the implications for teaching derived from this body of research.

1. Rhythmic abilities tend to be stronger than pitch related abilities.
2. Discrimination of or production of rhythmic patterns are more difficult than beat reproduction.
3. Music stimuli must be presented at appropriate level of amplification.
4. Tactile perception can, in part, compensate for auditory deficits.
5. Visual cues, such as tapping the beat, are particularly helpful.
6. Music skills may be delayed rather than deviant.
7. Pitch discriminations can be made more easily in lower frequency ranges.
8. Pitch discrimination skills can be developed with training.
9. Discrimination skills may be misjudged because of language problems in individuals who are D/HH which interfere with their ability to describe what is heard.
10. The vocal range of D/HH individuals is often lower and more limited in range.
11. Individuals who are D/HH can benefit both musically and academically from participation in music activities.
12. These individuals are more responsive to the rhythmic aspects of music than the tonal aspects.
13. They may require greater exposure, both in duration and intensity, to music stimuli than do normal hearing individuals in order to meet therapeutic objectives.
14. Sustaining instruments may provide more useful aural feedback than do percussive instruments.
15. Use of moderate tempi assist in greater rhythm performance accuracy.
16. D/HH individuals may perform more accurately by reading standard music notation than by relying on the ear to imitate or learn by rote.
17. D/HH individuals can improve their vocal intonation, both in singing and in speaking by participating in vocal activity.
18. The vocal range of song literature should be taken into consideration with D/HH singers.
19. D/HH individuals are capable of improvements in ear training as are hearing individuals.
20. Vibrotactile stimuli are a useful supplemental tool in the music instruction of D/HH individuals.
21. As with hearing individuals, D/HH individuals can develop an ear more sensitive to sound over time.
22. D/HH individuals could benefit from instruction in the use of musical vocabulary.
23. D/HH individuals exhibit certain musical preferences in regard to sound, source, intensity, and listening conditions.
24. Amplification and sound quality of the musical media should be given particular attention when instructing D/HH individuals.

25. Music instruction can assist in the development of a number of nonmusical behaviors such as speech production, listening, language, social, and academic skills.

Interpreting Songs Into Sign

Interpreting songs into sign is a popular activity for D/HH as well as hearing students. Darrow and Gfeller (1991) surveyed public school music educators teaching D/HH students and found that signing songs is a frequent activity in the music classroom. With increasing adoption of the total communication philosophy, students in deaf education programs are finding song signing to be a useful means of sharing cultural values and performing popular music. Signing songs, however, should not be simply "finger play." Many of the elements of music and expressive aspects of music can be illustrated through the signing of music: rhythm, tempo, changes in tempo, style, texture, tone color (male signers for male voices, etc.), form, and dynamics. Careful attention should also be given to the art of interpreting songs into sign. The signing should be as meticulously executed as the singing of the songs. The following guidelines will assist in interpreting songs into sign (Darrow, 1987):

1. Signs used for song interpretation can reflect volume, pitch (though rarely used), rhythm, and mood, as well as the lexical content by a variety of uses of body language, facial expression, space, and manner of execution.
2. Incorporating rhythm into signs is the most important factor distinguishing musical from nonmusical signing. Signing is paced to match the rhythm of the words.
3. Signs are drawn out or accelerated depending on the duration of the sung word.
4. Fingerspelling is rarely used.
5. Instrumental sections or humming require the creative uses of mime. The viewer should be aware of what is happening in the music at all times.
6. Figurative language or symbolism require creativity on the part of the signer.
7. Many times a single sign can reflect an entire phrase in a song.
8. Musical signing should transmit emotion as vividly as the audible song.
9. Some interpreters suggest that signs move upward as the melody moves upward, and as the melody moves downward, so should the signs. This adds very little to the performance for the deaf audience.
10. For sections marked *forte,* signs should be larger and executed with more force than sections marked *piano*.
11. *Crescendos* can also be expressed by gradually making signs larger and more intense. *Decrescendos* likewise should be expressed by gradually making signs smaller and more gently.
12. Sign should also follow the phrasing of the song, flowing one into the next with a slight pause at the end of the phrase.
13. The song style, whether it be classical, folk, rock, country, or pop, can be interpreted through the rhythm of signs, facial expression, body language, and, though unrelated to the signs, the dress of the signer.
14. When groups are performing in sign, special attention should be given to ensemble work. Signs should be synchronized: all hands moving in unison, all signs executed the same way, all signs made in the same amount of space.
15. Signs like voices, should also, blend. No individual signer should stand out among the group. Practice with a mirror or videotape.
16. Use a deaf individual as your "sign master." Acknowledge him/her in the program.
17. Sign performers should wear solid colors.

Conclusion

The sensory and cultural differences of many D/HH children provide unique challenges for the music therapist. For D/HH children, music may not always be an auditory experience; though music can, most assuredly, be a tactual, visual, social, and aesthetic experience for these children. By adapting music so that it can be experienced through other senses, the music therapist utilizes alternative pathways to further the academic and musical growth of D/HH children. Many music therapists find that such pathways lead to truly enjoyable and enriching experiences for themselves as well as for D/HH children.

References

Armstrong, D. F. (1999). *Original signs: Gesture, sign, and the sources of language.* Washington, DC: Gallaudet University Press.

Baker-Shenk, C., & Cokely, D. (1991). *American Sign Language: A teacher's resource text on grammar and culture.* Washington, DC: Gallaudet University Press.

Bang, C. (1986). A world of sound and music. In E. Ruud (Ed.), *Music and health* (pp. 19–36). Oslo, Norway: Norsk Musikforlag.

Birkenshaw-Fleming, L. (1990). Music can make a difference. In A. A. Darrow (Ed.), *Proceedings from the Second National Conference on Music and the Hearing Impaired at Gallaudet University* (pp. 14–20). Lawrence, KS: The University of Kansas.

Burgess, S. F. (1997). But I don't know anything about music for the hearing impaired. *Early Childhood Connections, 3,* 35–37.

Dalgarno, G. (1990). Technology to obtain the best musical sound for hearing impaired listeners. In A. A. Darrow (Ed.), *Proceedings from the Second National Conference on Music and the Hearing Impaired at Gallaudet University* (pp. 43–59). Lawrence, KS: The University of Kansas.

Darrow, A. A. (1985). Music for the deaf. *Music Educator's Journal, 71*(6), 33–35.

Darrow, A. A. (1987). Exploring the art of sign and song. *Music Educators Journal, 74*(1), 32–35.

Darrow, A. A. (1989). Music therapy with the hearing impaired. *Music Therapy Perspectives, 6,* 61–70.

Darrow, A. A. (1990). The role of hearing in understanding music. *Music Educators Journal, 77*(4), 24–27.

Darrow, A. A. (1991). An assessment and comparison of hearing impaired children's preference for timbre and musical instruments. *Journal of Music Therapy, 28,* 48–59.

Darrow, A. A. (1993). The role of music in Deaf culture: Implications for music educators. *Journal of Research in Music Education, 41*(2), 93–110.

Darrow, A. A. (1995). Music therapy for hearing impaired clients. In T. Wigram, R. West, & B. Saperston (Eds.), *The art and science of music therapy: A handbook.* Chur, Switzerland: Harwood Academic Publishers.

Darrow, A. A., & Gfeller, K. (1991). A study of public school music programs mainstreaming hearing impaired students. *Journal of Music Therapy, 28,* 23–39.

Darrow, A. A., Gfeller, K., Gorsuch, A., & Thomas, K. (2000). Music therapy with children who are deaf and hard of hearing. In *Effectiveness of music therapy procedures: Documentation of research and clinical practice* (pp. 135–157). Silver Spring, MD: American Music Therapy Association.

Darrow, A. A., & Heller, G. N. (1985). William Wolcott Turner and David Ely Bartlett: Early advocates of music education for the hearing impaired. *Journal of Research in Music Education, 33,* 269–279.

Darrow, A. A., & Loomis, D. (1999). Music and deaf culture: Images from the media and their interpretation by deaf and hearing students. *Journal of Music Therapy, 36,* 88–109.

Darrow, A. A., & Starmer, G. J. (1986). The effect of vocal training on the intonation and rate of hearing impaired children's speech: A pilot study. *Journal of Music Therapy, 23,* 194–201.

Davis, J., & Hardick, E. (1981). *Rehabilitative audiology for children and adults.* New York: John Wiley & Sons.

Diaz-Rico, L. T., & Weed, K. Z. (1995). *The crosscultural, language, and academic development handbook: A complete K–12 reference guide.* Needham Heights, MA: Allyn & Bacon.

Erber, N. P., & Hirsh, I. J. (1978). Auditory training. In H. Davis & S. R. Silverman (Eds.), *Hearing and deafness*, Chicago, IL: Holt, Rinehart and Winston.

Ford, T. A. (1990). Development of rhythmic concepts and skills. In A. A. Darrow (Ed.), *Proceedings from the Second National Conference on Music and the Hearing Impaired at Gallaudet University* (pp. 21–30). Lawrence, KS: The University of Kansas.

Geers, W., Hojan, E., Hojan-Jezierska, D. (1997). Fitting of hearing aids with loudness scaling of music and environmental sounds. *Applied Acoustics, 51,* 199–201.

Gfeller, K. (1987). Songwriting as a tool for reading and language remediation. *Music Therapy, 6*(2), 28–38.

Gfeller, K. (1990). A cognitive-linguistic approach to language development for preschool children with hearing impairments. *Music Therapy Perspectives, 8,* 47–51.

Gfeller, K. (1999). Music therapy in the treatment of sensory disorders. In W. B. Davis, K. E. Gfeller, & M. H. Thaut (Eds.), *An introduction to music therapy theory and practice* (pp. 179–194). Dubuque, IA: McGraw-Hill College.

Gfeller, K., & Baumann, A. (1988). Assessment procedures for music therapy with hearing impaired children: Language development. *Journal of Music Therapy, 25,* 192–205.

Gfeller, K., & Darrow, A. A. (1987). Music as a remedial tool in the language education of hearing impaired children. *The Arts in Psychotherapy, 14,* 229–23.

Gfeller, K., Knutson, J. F., Woodworth, G., Witt, S., & Debus, B. (1998). Timbral recognition and apprisal by adult cochlear implant users. *Journal of the American Academy of Audiology 9,* 1–19.

Gfeller, K., & Schum, R. (1994). Requisites for conversation: Engendering social skills. In N. Tye-Murray (Ed.), *Let's converse: A "how-to" guide to develop and expand conversational skills of children and teenagers who are hearing impaired.* Washington, DC: Alexander Graham Bell Association.

Gfeller, K., Witt, S., Spencer, L., Stordahl, J., & Tomblin, B. (2000). Musical involvement and enjoyment of children who use cochlear imolants. *The Volta Review, 100,* 213–233.

Gfeller, K., Woodworth, G., Robin, D. A., Witt, S., & Knutson, J. F. (1997). Perceptions of rhythmic and sequential pitch patterns by normally hearing adults and adult cochlear implant users. *Ear and Hearing, 18,* 252–260.

Hardman, M. L. (1999). People with hearing loss. In M. L. Hardman, C. J. Drew, & M. W. Egan (Eds.), *Human exceptionality: Society, school, and family* (6th ed., pp. 398–401). MA: Allyn and Bacon.

Heward, W. L., & Orlansky, M. D. (1992). *Exceptional children.* New York: Macmillan.

Hines, M. E. (1973). *Skits in English as a second language.* New York: Regents Publishing Company, Inc.

Johns, E. (2001). Introducing music to the hearing-impaired. *Teaching Music, 8*(6), 36–40.

Kaiser, K., & Johnson, K. (2000). The effect of an interactive experience on music majors' perceptions of music for deaf students. *Journal of Music Therapy, 37,* 222–234.

Kaplan, H. (1996). The nature of deaf culture: Implications for speech and hearing professionals. *Journal of Academy of Rehabilitative Audiology, 29,* 71–83.

Little, J. (1983). Pop and rock music in the ESL classroom. *TESL TALK, 14*(4), 40–44.

Luetke, B. S. (1998). *Language issues in deaf education.* Hillsboro: Butte Publications.

McCallum, G. P. (1980). *101 word games: For students of English as a second or foreign language.* New York: Oxford University Press.

Morgan, J., & Rinvolucri, M. (1983). *Once upon a time: Using stories in the language classroom.* Cambridge, Great Britain: Cambridge University Press.

National Technical Institute for the Deaf. (no date). *Communicating with the deaf.* Rochester, NY: Author.

Padden, C. (1996). *From the cultural to the bicultural: The modern deaf community.* New York: Cambridge University Press.

Padden, C., & Humphries, T. (1988). *Deaf in America: Voices from a culture.* Cambridge, MA: Harvard University Press.

Rickard, P., Robbins, C., & Robbins, C. (1990). Experiences in developing a creative language arts program. In A. A. Darrow (Ed.), *Proceedings from the Second National Conference on Music and the Hearing Impaired at Gallaudet University* (pp. 11–13). Lawrence, KS: The University of Kansas.

Robbins, C., & Robbins, C. (1980). *Music for the hearing impaired: A resource manual and curriculum guide.* St. Louis, MO: Magnamusic-Baton.

Robbins, C., & Robbins, C. (1990). Musical activities with young deaf children. In A. A. Darrow (Ed.), *Proceedings from the Second National Conference on Music and the Hearing Impaired at Gallaudet University* (pp. 8–10). Lawrence, KS: The University of Kansas.

Rutherford, S. D. (1988). The culture of American Deaf people. *Sign Language Studies, 59,* 109–147.

Sanders, D. A. (1977). *Auditory perception of speech.* Englewood Cliffs, NJ: Prentice-Hall, Inc.

Schatz, V. (1990). Using percussion to teach music concepts and enhance music and movement experiences. In A. A. Darrow (Ed.), *Proceedings from the Second National Conference on Music and the Hearing Impaired at Gallaudet University* (pp. 85–92). Lawrence, KS: The University of Kansas.

Sheldon, D. A. (1997). The Illinois School for the Deaf: A historical perspective. *Journal of Research in Music Education, 45,* 580–600.

Shurman, D. (1999). Antonio Provoio: Hero or villain? *Journal of Deaf Studies and Deaf Education, 4*(1), 69–72.

Srinivasan, P. (1996). *Practical aural habilitation: For speech-language pathologists, and educators of hearing impaired children.* Springfield: Charles C. Thomas.

Teaching and learning aids: Musical ESL. (1983). *TESL TALK, 14*(1–2), 180–185.

Vassall, L. (1997). The creative arts: Tool to deaf pride—and hearing friends. *Perspectives in Education and Deafness, 15*(3), 12–14.

Weisel, A. (1998). *Issues unresolved: New perspectives in language and deaf education.* Washington DC: Gallaudet University Press.

Appendix A

Readings in Deaf Culture

Benderly, B. L. (1980). *Dancing without music: Deafness in America.* Garden City, NY: Anchor Press/Doubleday.

Gannon, J. R. (1981). *Deaf heritage: A narrative history of Deaf America.* Silver Spring, MD: National Association of the Deaf.

Garretson, M. (1990). *Communication issues among Deaf people.* Silver Spring, MD: National Association of the Deaf.

Garretson, M. (1991). *Perspectives on deafness.* Silver Spring, MD: National Association of the Deaf.

Kannapel, B. (1980). Personal awareness and advocacy in the deaf community. In W. C. Stokoe (Ed.), *Sign language and the Deaf community.* Silver Spring MD: National Association of the Deaf.

Lane, H. (1984). *When the mind hears: A history of the Deaf.* New York: Random House.

Neisser, A. (1983). *The other side of silence.* Washington, DC: Gallaudet University.

Padden, C. (1980). The deaf community and the culture of the deaf people. In W. C. Stokoe (Ed.), *Sign language and the Deaf community.* Silver Spring, MD: National Association of the Deaf.

Padden, C., & Humphries, T. (1988). *Deaf in America: Voices from a culture.* Cambridge, MA: Harvard University Press.

Sacks, O. (1989). *Seeing voices.* Berkeley, CA: University of California Press.

Stokoe, W. C. (1980). *Sign and culture.* Washington, DC: Linstock Press.

Appendix B

Selected Bibliography of Articles and Research
on Music and the Deaf

Amir, D., & Schuchman, G. (1985). Auditory training through music with hearing impaired preschool children. *Volta Review, 87*, 333–343.

Atkins, W., & Donovan, M. (1984). A workable music education program for the hearing impaired. *Volta Review, 86*(1), 41–44.

Baird, S. (1979). A technique to asses the preference for intensity of musical stimuli in young hard-of-hearing children. *Journal of Music Therapy, 6*, 6–11.

Bang, C. (1977). *A music event.* Hicksville, NY: M. Hohner.

Buechler, J. (1982). *Music for handicapped children: Hearing impaired.* Washington, DC: National Association for Music Therapy.

Byrnes, S., Darrow, A. A., & Fredrickson, W. (1999). Sign language and choral performance: An exploratory study of performer and audience attitude. *Missouri Journal of Research in Music Education, 36*, 35–43.

Coffman, D., Gfeller, K., Coffman, S., & Darrow, A. A. (1992). Computer-assisted comparison of melodic and rhythmic discrimination skills in hearing impaired and normally hearing children. *The Arts in Psychotherapy, 18*, 449–454.

Dalgarno, G. (1990a). A computer-based music system for the hearing impaired. In A. A. Darrow (Ed.), *Proceedings from the Second National Conference on Music and the Hearing Impaired at Gallaudet University* (pp. 31–42). Lawrence, KS: The University of Kansas.

Dalgarno, G. (1990b). Technology to obtain the best musical sound for hearing impaired listeners. In A. A. Darrow (Ed.), *Proceedings from the Second National Conference on Music and the Hearing Impaired at Gallaudet University* (pp. 43–59). Lawrence, KS: The University of Kansas.

Darrow, A. A. (1979). The beat reproduction response of subjects with normal and impaired hearing: An empirical comparison. *Journal of Music Therapy, 16*, 6–11.

Darrow, A. A. (1984). A comparison of the rhythmic responsiveness in normal hearing and hearing impaired children and an investigation of the relationship of the rhythmic responsiveness to the suprasegmental aspects of speech perception. *Journal of Music Therapy, 21*, 48–66.

Darrow, A. A. (1985). Music for the deaf. *Music Educators Journal, 71*(6), 33–35.

Darrow, A. A. (1987a). *A comparison of vocal ranges of hearing impaired and normal hearing children.* Unpublished manuscript, The University of Kansas, Lawrence.

Darrow, A. A. (1987b). Exploring the art of sign and song. *Music Educators Journal, 74*(1), 32–35.

Darrow, A. A. (1987c). An investigative study: The effect of hearing impairment on music aptitude. *Journal of Music Therapy, 24*, 88–96.

Darrow, A. A. (1989a). Music and the hearing impaired: A review of the research with implication for music educators. *Update: Applications of Research in Music Education, 7*(2), 10–12.

Darrow, A. A. (1989b). Music therapy in the treatment of the hearing impaired. *Music Therapy Perspectives, 6*, 61–70.

Darrow, A. A. (1990a). The effect of frequency adjustment on the vocal reproduction accuracy of hearing impaired singers. *Journal of Music Therapy, 27*, 24–33.

Darrow, A. A. (Ed.) (1990b). *Proceedings from the Second National Conference on Music and the Hearing Impaired at Gallaudet University.* Lawrence, KS: The University of Kansas.

Darrow, A. A. (1990c). The role of hearing in understanding music. *Music Educators Journal, 77*(4), 24–27.

Darrow, A. A. (1991). An assessment and comparison of hearing impaired children's preference for timbre and musical instruments. *Journal of Music Therapy, 28*, 48–59.

Darrow, A. A. (1992) The effect of vibrotactile stimuli on the identification of pitch change by hearing impaired children. *Journal of Music Therapy, 29*, 103–112.

Darrow, A. A. (1993). The role of music in deaf culture: Implications for music educators. *Journal of Research in Music Education, 41*, 93–110.

Darrow, A. A., & Bolton, B. (1988, April). *A comparison of rhythmic performances by hearing and mainstreamed hearing impaired children.* Paper presented at the Music Educators National Conference, Indianapolis, Indiana.

Darrow, A. A., & Cohen, N. (1991). The effect of programmed pitch practice and private instruction on the vocal reproduction accuracy of hearing impaired children: Two case studies. *Music Therapy Perspectives, 9*, 61–65.

Darrow, A. A., & Gfeller, K. (1987, November). *Verbal identification of music concepts by hearing impaired children.* Paper presented at the National Association for Music Therapy Annual Conference, San Francisco, CA.

Darrow, A. A., & Gfeller, K. (1988). Music therapy with hearing impaired children. In C. A. Furman (Ed.), *Effectiveness of music therapy procedures: Documentation of research and clinical practice* (pp. 137–174). Washington, DC: National Association for Music Therapy.

Darrow, A. A., & Gfeller, K. (1991). A study of public school music programs mainstreaming hearing impaired students. *Journal of Music Therapy, 28*, 23–39.

Darrow, A. A., Gfeller, K., Gorsuch, A., & Thomas, K. (2000). Music therapy with children who are deaf and hard of hearing. In *Effectiveness of music therapy procedures: Documentation of research and clinical practice* (pp. 135–157). Silver Spring, MD: American Music Therapy Association.

Darrow, A. A., & Goll, H. (1989). The effect of vibrotactile stimuli via the SOMOTRON™ on the recognition of rhythmic concepts by hearing impaired children. *Journal of Music Therapy, 26*, 115–124.

Darrow, A. A., & Heller, G. N. (1985). William Wolcott Turner and David Ely Bartlett: Early advocates of music education for the hearing impaired. *Journal of Research in Music Education, 33*, 269–279.

Darrow, A. A., & Loomis, D. (1999). Music and deaf culture: Images from the media and their interpretation by deaf and hearing students. *Journal of Music Therapy, 36*, 88–109.

Darrow, A. A, & Schunk, H. (1996). Music therapy for learners who are deaf/hard-of-hearing. In B. Wilson (Ed.), *Models of music therapy intervention in school settings: From institutions to inclusion* (pp. 200–223). Silver Spring, MD: National Association for Music Therapy.

Darrow, A. A., & Starmer, G. J. (1986). The effect of vocal training on the intonation and rate of hearing impaired children's speech: A pilot study. *Journal of Music Therapy, 23*, 194–201.

Edmonds, K. (1984). Is there a valid place for music in the education of deaf children? *ACEHI Journal, 10*(3), 164–169.

Edwards, E. (1974). *Music education for the deaf.* South Waterford, ME: Merriam Eddy.

Eisenson, J., Kastein, S., & Schneiderman, N. (1958). An investigation into the ability of voice defectives to discriminate among differences in pitch and loudness. *Journal of Speech and Hearing Disorders, 23*(5), 577–582.

Fahey, J., & Birkenshaw, L. (1972). Bypassing the ear: The perception of music by feeling and touch. *Music Educators Journal, 58*(8), 44–49.

Fisher, J., Baker, B., & Darrow, A. A. (1989, November). *The effect of two selected variables on the tonal perception of hearing impaired children.* Paper presented at the National Association for Music Therapy Annual Conference, Kansas City, MO.

Ford, T. A. (1985). *The effect of musical experiences and age on the ability of deaf children to discriminate pitch of complex tones.* Unpublished doctoral dissertation, University of North Carolina, Greensboro.

Ford, T. A. (1988). The effect of musical experience and age on the ability of deaf children to discriminate pitch. *Journal of Music Therapy, 25*(1), 2–16.

Ford, T. A. (1990). Development of rhythmic concepts and skills. In A. A. Darrow (Ed.), *Proceedings from the Second National Conference on Music and the Hearing Impaired at Gallaudet University* (pp. 21–30). Lawrence, KS: The University of Kansas.

Ford, T. A., & Shroyer, E. H. (1987). Survey of music teachers in residential and day programs for hearing impaired students. *Journal of the International Association of Music for the Handicapped, 3,* 16–25.

Galloway, H. F., & Bean, M. F. (1974). The effects of action songs on the development of body-image and body-part identification in hearing impaired preschool children. *Journal of Music Therapy, 11,* 125–134.

Gengel (1969). Practice effects in frequency discrimination by hearing impaired children. *Journal of Speech and Hearing Research, 12,* 847–855.

Gfeller, K. (1986). Music as a remedial tool for improving speech rhythm in the hearing impaired: Clinical and research considerations. *Music Education for the Handicapped Bulletin, 2,* 3–19.

Gfeller, K. (1987). Songwriting as a tool for reading and language remediation. *Music Therapy, 6*(2), 28–38.

Gfeller, K. (1988, April). *A comparison of hearing aids and tactile aids in facilitating accuracy of profoundly deaf children on rhythm subtest of the PMMA.* Paper presented at the Music Educators National Conference, Indianapolis, Indiana.

Gfeller, K. (1990). A cognitive-linguistic approach to language development for the preschool children with hearing impairments. *Music Therapy Perspectives, 8,* 47–51.

Gfeller, K. (2000a). Accommodating children who use cochlear implants in the music therapy or educational setting. *Music Therapy Perspectives, 18*(2), 122–130.

Gfeller, K. (2000b). Musical perception and aesthetic enjoyment of adult cochlear implant recipients: Interdisciplinary perspectives. *Proceedings of Multidisciplinary Perspectives on Musicality: The Seashore Symposium. Bulletin of the Council for Research in Music Education.*

Gfeller, K. (2001). Aural rehabilitation of music listening for adult cochlear implant recipients: Addressing learner characteristics. *Music Therapy Perspectives, 19,* 88–95.

Gfeller, K., & Baumann, A. (1988). Assessment procedures for music therapy with hearing impaired children: Language development. *Journal of Music Therapy, 25,* 192–205.

Gfeller, K., Christ, A., Knutson, J., Witt, S., & Murray, K., & Tyler, R.S. (2000). The musical backgrounds, listening habits, and aesthetic enjoyment of adult cochlear implant recipients. *Journal of the American Academy of Audiology, 11,* 390–406.

Gfeller, K., & Darrow, A. A. (1987). Music as a remedial tool in the language education of hearing impaired children. *The Arts in Psychotherapy, 14,* 229–235.

Gfeller, K., Knutson, J. F., Woodworth, G., Witt, S., & Debus, B. (1998). Timbral recognition and apprisal by adult cochlear implant users. *Journal of the American Academy of Audiology, 9,* 1–19.

Gfeller, K., & Lansing, C. R. (in press). Melodic, rhythmic, and timbral perception of adult cochlear implant users. *Journal of Speech and Hearing Disorders.*

Gfeller, K., Lansing, C., Fryauf-Bertschy, H., & Hurtig, R. (1990, November). *Rhythmic perception by hearing impaired children using assistive devices.* Paper presented at American Speech and Hearing Association national conference, Seattle, WA.

Gfeller, K., & Lansing, C. R. (1992). Musical perception of cochlear implant users as measured by the Primary Measures of Music Audiation: An item analysis. *Journal of Music Therapy, 29*(1), 18–39.

Gfeller, K., & Schum, R. (1994). Requisites for conversation: Engendering social skills. In N. Tye-Murray (Ed.), *Let's converse: A "how-to" guide to develop and expand conversational skills of children and teenagers who are hearing impaired.* Washington, DC: Alexander Graham Bell Association.

Gfeller, K., Witt, S. A., Kim, K.-H., Adamek, M., & Coffman, D. (1999). A computerized music training program for adult cochlear implant recipients. *Journal of the Academy of Rehabilitative Audiology, 32,* 11–27.

Gfeller, K., Witt, S., Spencer, L., Stordahl, J., & Tomblin, B. (2000). Musical involvement and enjoyment of children who use cochlear imolants. *The Volta Review, 100,* 213–233.

Gfeller, K., Witt, S., Stordahl, J., Mehr, M., & Woodworth, G. (2001). The effects of training on melody recognition and appraisal by adult cochlear implant recipients. *Journal of the Academy of Rehabilitative Audiology, 33,* 115–138.

Gfeller, K., Woodworth, G., Robin, D. A., Witt, S., & Knutson, J. F. (1997). Perceptions of rhythmic and sequential pitch patterns by normally hearing adults and adult cochlear implant users. *Ear and Hearing, 18*, 252–260.

Gray-Thompson, H. (1985). *The use of picture song books on the vocabulary development of hearing impaired children.* Unpublished master's thesis, The University of Kansas, Lawrence.

Hagedorn, V. S. (1992). Musical learning for hearing impaired children. *Research Perspectives in Music Education, 46*(3), 13–17.

Hummel, C. J. (1971). The value of music in teaching deaf students. *Volta Review, 73*(4), 243–249.

Klajman, S., Koldej, E., & Kowalska, A. (1982). Investigation of musical abilities in hearing-impaired and normal-hearing children. *Folia Phoniatrica, 34*, 229–233.

Korduba, O. M. (1975). Duplicated rhythmic patterns between deaf and normal hearing children. *Journal of Music Therapy, 12*, 136–146.

Kracke, I. (1975). Perception of rhythmic sequences by receptive aphasic and deaf children. *British Journal of Disorders of Communication, 10*, 43–51.

Leach, K. (1982). *Discrimination of musical elements made by hearing impaired residential school children.* Unpublished master's thesis, University of Kansas, Lawrence.

Madsen, C. K., & Mears, W. G. (1965). The effect of sound upon the tactile threshold of deaf subjects. *Journal of Music Therapy, 2*, 64–68.

McConnell, L. (1990). There's music in the air: Deaf and hard of hearing people are exploring the language of music. *Gallaudet Today, 20*(2), 8–15.

Rickard, P., Robbins, C., & Robbins, C. (1990). Experiences in developing a creative language arts program. In A. A. Darrow (Ed.), *Proceedings from the Second National Conference on Music and the Hearing Impaired at Gallaudet University* (pp. 11–13). Lawrence, KS. The University of Kansas.

Rileigh, K. K., & Odom, P. B. (1972). Perception of rhythm by subjects with normal and deficient hearing. *Developmental Psychology, 7*, 54–61.

Robbins, C., & Robbins, C. (1980). *Music for the hearing impaired: A resource manual and curriculum guide.* St. Louis, MO: Magnamusic-Baton.

Robbins, C., & Robbins, C. (1990). Musical activities with young deaf children. In A. A. Darrow (Ed.), *Proceedings from the Second National Conference on Music and the Hearing Impaired at Gallaudet University* (pp. 8–10). Lawrence, KS: The University of Kansas.

Schatz, V. (1990). Using percussion to teach music concepts and enhance music and movement experiences. In A. A. Darrow (Ed.), *Proceedings from the Second National Conference on Music and the Hearing Impaired at Gallaudet University* (pp. 85–92). Lawrence, KS: The University of Kansas.

Schulz, E., & Kerber, M. (1994). Music perception with the MED-EL implants. In I. J. Hochmair-Desoyer & E. S. Hochmair (Eds.), *Advances in cochlear implants.* Manz, Wien. 326–332.

Shroyer, E. H., & Ford, T. A. (1986). Survey of music instruction and activities in residential and day schools for hearing impaired students. *Music Education for the Handicapped Bulletin, 2*, 28–45.

Solomon, A. L. (1980). Music in special education before 1930: Hearing and speech development. *Journal of Research in Music Education, 28*, 236–242.

Sposato, M. (1983). *Implications of maximal exploitation of residual hearing on curriculum planning in music education for hearing impaired children.* Unpublished doctoral dissertation, State University of New York, Buffalo.

Spitzer, M. (1984). A survey of the use of music in schools for the hearing impaired. *The Volta Review, 86*, 362–363.

Squires, V. L. (1982). *The beat maintenance and beat reproduction response of hearing-impaired and normal hearing children on sustained and percussive temporal intervals.* Unpublished master's thesis, University of Kansas, Lawrence.

Staum, M. J. (1987). Music notation to improve the speech prosody of hearing impaired children. *Journal of Music Therapy, 24*, 146–159.

Sterritt, G. M., Camp, B. W., & Lipman, B. S. (1966). Effects of early auditory deprivation upon auditory and visual information processing. *Perceptual and Motor Skills, 23,* 123–130.

Tyler, R. S., Gfeller, K., & Mehr, M. A. (2000). Preliminary investigation comparing one and eight channels at fast and slow rates on music appraisal in adults with cochlear implants. *Cochlear Implant International, 1*(2), 82–87.

Van Deventer, E. L. (1991). *Music therapy with hearing impaired children* (Afrikaans text). Unpublished doctoral dissertation, University of Pretoria, South Africa.

Vassallo, L. (1997). The creative arts: Tool to deaf pride and hearing friends. *Perspectives in Education and Deafness, 15*(3), 12–14.

Weibe, J. (1989). *The effect of adjusted frequency on the tonal perception of older hearing-impaired adults.* Unpublished master's thesis, The University of Kansas, Lawrence.

Weinstein, D. (1991). Music on deaf ears: Musical meaning, ideology, and education. *Theory, Culture and Society, 8*(4), 97–109.

Williams, H. (1989). The value of music to the deaf. *British Journal of Music Education, 6*(1), 81–98.

Woike, D. O. (1987). *Preferred audio response equalization in the hearing impaired.* Unpublished manuscript, Ohio State University, Columbus.

15

MUSIC THERAPY FOR LEARNERS IN COMPREHENSIVE PUBLIC SCHOOL SYSTEMS: THREE DISTRICT-WIDE MODELS

Jane E. Hughes and Brenda J. Rice (contributing author Janet Ter Louw)
Jennifer K. DeBedout
Lalah M. Hightower

Three district-wide public school models are exemplified in this chapter and are described separately. This is followed by descriptions of different intervention models with programmatic examples drawn from all three districts.

Leon County School System

THE music therapy program is within the Leon County School System's Exceptional Student Education program. Located in Tallahassee, Florida, the Leon County Schools serve approximately 38,000 students. Of this number, over 8,500 students (including gifted and pre-kindergarten) receive some type of special services through Exceptional Student Education (ESE). ESE is an integral part of the total school program with schools, special services, related state and local agencies, and the community being utilized to provide quality programs for students. The school district's philosophy is to educate exceptional students to their maximum potential in the least restrictive environment. Music therapy has been a comprehensive special service offered through ESE since 1978. Over 1,000 students from infancy through high school and beyond and 100 teachers annually receive some type of service from music therapists and their interns. The primary purpose of the music therapy program is to assist students to benefit from their educational experience.

The term *mainstreaming* describes the placing of students with disabilities into general education settings. Other terms sometimes used by state and local school systems are *inclusion, continuum of services,* and *regular education initiative.* The legal mandate is found in the Individuals with Disabilities Education Act (IDEA). While terms such as *mainstreaming* and *inclusion* are in common usage, the legal terminology references *least restrictive environment.* Under this mandate no exceptional student is taught apart from other students without evidence that segregation is for the exceptional student's benefit or is necessary due to difficulties involved in providing a program for the student in a regular class. Such difficulties might include items that may have a harmful effect such as injury to others or self, excessive disruptive behavior, student safety, health status, or lack of progress. Whenever possible, students are educated in the school they would normally attend, and every effort is made to educate them with their regular education peers. Most ESE students, no matter what their degree of disability, attend the district's regular elementary, middle, and high schools with others of the same age. In addition to the regular schools, the district maintains several alternative schools. Though attending self-contained schools, students still have interaction with their regular education peers and the community through special programs provided by the schools. Placement decisions are based on individual instructional needs as outlined in Individualized Education Programs (IEPs).

Since music therapy is provided within the scope of the IEP, mainstreaming is a major focus of the program. In addition to addressing learning needs in traditional curriculum subject areas such as language arts, social studies, and music, the district's music therapists often work within mainstreaming initiatives such as community based instruction (CBI), cooperative collaboration, team teaching, transition, career preparation, employment training, and pro-social skills development and skillstreaming (McGinnis & Goldstein, 1990, 1997a, 1997b). Music therapists use music to address needs in any curriculum area considered important to student growth (Alley, 1979).

Music therapists consult with classroom teachers and other professionals in the development of music therapy interventions based on the assessed needs of individuals as specified by their IEPs. Psychologists and other evaluation specialists and classroom teachers perform the assessments for the IEPs. Several types of evaluative measures are used in the development of IEPs, including psychological, medical, and curriculum based assessments. Music therapists collaborate with educators to develop, implement, and report the results of interventions, but they are not directly involved in primary assessment for IEPs. They can, however, recommend IEP modifications based on music therapy program data. Typical goal areas chosen for music therapy intervention include the following: integration with nonhandicapped peers, developmental language and school readiness in young children, auditory training and communication in students with speech and hearing impairments, affective education and pro-social skills development in students with emotional or behavior disorders, dexterity and mobility training in students with physical challenges, and community-based skills in students requiring a functional curriculum.

The Leon County Schools' ESE music therapy program is planned and implemented by two board-certified music therapists (MT-BCs) who are also state certified in music education. Although each state establishes its own certification rules, music therapists in Florida must hold state professional educator certification in order to work in professional (as opposed to paraprofessional) public school positions. Most music therapists working in Florida public schools are teacher certified in music education. However, some are certified in other areas such as special education or early childhood. Music therapy provides additional staff for the district by participation in the American Music Therapy Association's internship program. As many as four music therapy interns work district-wide at any given time during the year, serving hundreds of students who would not otherwise receive music therapy (see Figure 1). Music therapists and interns serve students from the following Florida exceptionalities categories: autistic; deaf or hard of hearing; developmentally delayed (birth to age 5); dual-sensory impaired (deaf-blind); emotionally handicapped (emotionally handicapped, severely emotionally disturbed); homebound or hospitalized; mentally handicapped (educable, trainable, profound); physically impaired (orthopedically impaired, other health impaired, traumatic brain injured); specific learning disabilities; speech and language impaired; visually impaired (blind and partially sighted); and gifted. Music therapists also may serve students in the areas of school readiness (pre-K), academic delayed, and juvenile justice. Age groups range from infancy through adult. Direct services to students occur in large groups, small groups, or individually, in inclusive or self-contained groupings, and in many different physical settings. The settings might be classrooms and other space in regular schools, special center/alternative schools, private preschools, juvenile detention centers, or the community at large.

Each music therapist spends approximately one-half time providing music therapy services directly to students. The other one-half time is spent supervising interns in locations throughout the district, providing consultation and training for educational staff and parents, advising secondary IEP committees on music course electives, conducting research, pursuing grants and collaborative projects with community arts providers, coordinating experiences for university music students, and serving on school committees teams and advisory councils (see Figure 2). Needs-based requests for music therapy services may come from

MUSIC THERAPY INTERN SCHEDULE

TIME	MONDAY	TUESDAY	WEDNESDAY	THURSDAY	FRIDAY
9:00-9:30	8:45-9:15 PreK (Hearing Impairments)	9:00-9:15 (Toddlers)	8:45-9:15 PreK (Hearing Impairments)	Primary- K-1 (Inclusive Class)	8:45-9:15 Primary- K-2 (Speech and Language)
9:30-10:00		9:30- 9:50 (3 year olds)		9:40-10:10 - PreK Early Intervention	
10:00-10:30	9:45-10:05 Primary-K-2 (Speech and Language)		10:15-10:45 Primary –Grades 1-3 (Varying Exceptionalities)	10:20-10:50- PreK (Early Intervention)	10:10-10:40 PreK (Early Intervention) Team with MT-BC
10:30-11:00		Adult Day Care (intergenerational)			
11:00-11:30					
11:30-12:00	High School -individual (Developmental Disabilities)			High School- class (Developmental Disabilities)	
12:00-12:30			Primary –Grades 3-5 (Varying Exceptionalities)		
12:30-1:00					
1:00-1:30	Primary –Grades 1-3 (Varying Exceptionalities)		1:26-2:10 H.S./M.S. Chorus (Developmental Disabilities)		1:20-2:10 H.S./M.S. Chorus (Developmental Disabilities)
1:30-2:00			Team with MT-BC		Team with MT-BC
2:00-2:30	Primary –Grades 3-5 (Varying Exceptionalities)	Middle School (Severe Emotional Handicaps)		Middle School (Severe Emotional Handicaps)	
2:30-4:00					MT Staff Meeting

Figure 1. Music Therapy Intern Schedule

MUSIC THERAPY SCHEDULE

Music Therapist: MT-BC 1

	ESE School	District	ESE School	District	ESE School
TIME	**MONDAY**	**TUESDAY**	**WEDNESDAY**	**THURSDAY**	**FRIDAY**
8:10- 9:00	Set-up	observations and/or consultations	Set-up	observations and/or consultations	Set-up
9:00-9:30	Primary 4 *(Grades 2-3)*		Primary 4 *(Grades 2-3)*		Primary 8 *(Grades 5-6)*
9:35-10:05	Toddlers *(2 year olds)*		Toddlers *(1 year olds)*		PreK- *(Early Intervention)*
10:10-10:40	Primary 7 *(Grades 4-6)*	10-30-11:00 Adult Day Care *(intergenerational)*	Primary 2 *(K-1)*	10:30- 11:00 Residence for Seniors *(intergenerational)*	Primary 7 *(Grades 4-6)*
10:45-11:15	Primary 8 *(Grades 5-6)*		Primary 6 *(Grades 4-5)*		Primary 6 *(Grades 4-5)*
11:15-11:55	Lunch/ set-up	observations and/or consultations	Lunch/ set-up	observations and/or consultations	Lunch/ set-up
11:55-12:30	Middle School Elective		Middle School Elective		Middle School Elective
12:40-1:10	High School 1		High School 3		High School 2
1:25-2:10	H.S./M.S. Chorus		H.S./M.S. Chorus		H.S./M.S. Chorus
2:10- 4:00	Meetings		Meetings		MT Staff Meeting

MUSIC THERAPY SCHEDULE

Music Therapist: MT-BC 2

	District	ESE School	District	ESE School	District
TIME	**MONDAY**	**TUESDAY**	**WEDNESDAY**	**THURSDAY**	**FRIDAY**
8:10- 9:00	observations and/or consultations	Set-up		Set-up	
9:00-9:30		Primary 1 *(Grades K-2)*	PreK- HI *(Ages 3-5)*	Primary 1 *(Grades 1-2)*	PreK- HI *(Ages 3-5)*
9:35-10:05		3 year olds	observations and/or consultations	PreK *(Early Intervention)*	observations and/or consultations
10:10-10:40		Primary 9 *(Grades 5-7)*		Primary 5 *(Grades 3-4)*	
10:45-11:15		Primary 3 *(Grades 1-2)*		Primary 3 *(Grades K-2)*	
11:15-11:55		Lunch/set-up		Lunch/set-up	
11:55-12:30		Middle School Elective		Middle School Elective	
12:40-1:10		High School 4		High School 4	
1:25-2:10		High School Chorus		High School Chorus	H.S./M.S Chorus
2:10-4:00		Meetings		Meetings	MT Staff Meeting

Figure 2. Music Therapy Schedules

administrators; special, regular, and music educators; occupational, physical, and speech therapists; psychologists; guidance counselors; and parents. Music therapists accept or deny requests based on the availability of staff time and other considerations such as number of students to benefit, administrative requests, potential effectiveness of music intervention, music therapy services received in the past, importance to interns' training program, and opportunities for investigating cutting-edge educational situations such as Early Intervention (the effect of music intervention on pre-reading and writing development), and total inclusion schools (the role of music therapy). Upon acceptance, therapists consult with classroom teachers and others and review the music and education research literature as they plan music therapy interventions based on goals already established in the IEP. Music therapy objectives are then developed as indicated for specific skills. A sample of typical student objectives includes:

- stand and sit on cue with the rest of the chorus,
- improve spatial awareness,
- demonstrate an awareness of sound and silence,
- improve fine motor skills (grasping and manipulating musical instruments/other objects),
- work cooperatively with peers in inclusive/community settings, and
- increase their ability to recognize letters and numbers.

Funding for music therapy comes from the school district. Costs to the district include salaries plus appropriate supplement for the MT-BCs; vicinity travel mileage for MT-BCs and interns; funds for office, storage, and program space; equipment; materials and supplies; transportation to community events; and staff development costs, including professional conferences for MT-BCs and sometimes for interns. The majority of funds are from IDEA and General State Revenue. Budgeting for the program comes from ESE's district-wide and individual school budgets. A small amount of additional funding is generated through local and state arts and special activity grants.

The school district benefits from the music therapy program in numerous ways. The needs of students, teachers, and parents are addressed; positive attitudes are promoted within the schools and community; and school district goals are implemented. Making others aware of these benefits is considered very important, especially during times of funding cuts in public education. The district's music therapists consistently use a positive, active, collaborative, and student-centered approach that promotes music therapy as a service to be valued among faculty, staff, parents, and administrative decision-makers. They also disseminate various types of evaluative data including periodic whole-program data as well as student data. An example of whole-program evaluation data resulted from a survey of perception and attitudes of exceptional student educators toward district-wide music therapy services (Hughes, Robbins, & King, 1988). Survey data demonstrated the high esteem in which music therapy was held by those teachers most directly involved, and documented the overall perception of effectiveness as related to specific music therapy objectives. These data have been periodically updated and widely used as a public awareness tool.

Clayton County School System

The Clayton County Public Schools (CCPS) in south metro Atlanta, Georgia serve over 47,000 children, more than 5,000 of which receive services from the Special Education Department. In partnership with regular education services, the mission of the Special Education Department is to provide services for students with disabilities that facilitate an educational progression. Music therapy is a respected model of service delivery in Clayton County that furthers this mission by using music as its primary teaching and therapeutic tool. The department currently provides services throughout the school year to approximately 700 children in more than 85 classrooms. The music therapy department consists of a team of four board-certified music therapists and as many as four music therapy interns per school year.

The CCPS operating budget comes from four sources: federal funds, state funds, local taxes, other local funds. The music therapy department is funded through local taxes and receives monies for salaries, travel stipends, equipment needs and storage, continuing education opportunities, and department-sponsored trips for the students served. In addition to the county's requirement for music therapy board certification for its staff, each music therapist is required to hold Georgia's professional educator certification in music or a field related to special education in accordance with state rules.

Because Clayton County is experiencing a population explosion bringing an average of 1,200 new students into the system each year, the number of children served by Special Education is expected to grow rapidly. As more students move into the county and are included in music therapy service delivery, new therapists are hired and more school special needs populations are targeted for inclusion in the program. Service priority is given to those students for whom early service has the most impact. The music therapy team offers services to the following special education programs: intellectual disabilities in the moderate, severe and profound ranges (pre-kindergarten through high school); orthopedic impairments (pre-kindergarten through middle school); hearing impairments (pre-kindergarten through elementary school); emotional and behavioral disorders and severe emotional and behavioral disorders (kindergarten through elementary school); and autism (pre-kindergarten through high school).

Students receive music therapy either once or twice weekly for 30–45 minutes per session, depending on the program being served. Service delivery occurs primarily in groups that may range in size from 3 to 30 students. Efforts are made for inclusion where possible in weekly sessions, and special events throughout the year also structure the participation of regular education peers with their special education counterparts.

In CCPS, students qualify for music therapy services based on their enrollment in specific special education programs. It is assumed by the county that a student receiving educational services in a classroom for students with moderate intellectual disabilities will benefit from group music therapy services. They will receive such services until they leave the program or the department ceases to serve that program as a whole. Although students do not enter the program through an assessment process, they are tested individually if music therapy has been included on their IEP. Goals and objectives are developed by the music therapist and are then embedded by the classroom teacher into the IEP according to the county's curriculum model (see Figures 3 and 4). This model focuses on functional skills for survival in the community and transfer of skills across all domains of functioning (Ford et al., 1989). Consequently, each professional with access to the child is responsible for working on the total IEP. For example, the music therapist may have submitted a goal for a student to increase attending from 1 to 2 minutes, but will also be responsible for addressing the pre-academic skills listed elsewhere on the IEP.

Because the majority of children are seen in a group setting, documentation of individual progress is difficult for the music therapist to accomplish alone. However, updates about student progress are recorded six times during the school year and sent home to parents in the form of report cards. The teacher or classroom paraprofessional sitting outside of the music therapy session may take data on specific observable behaviors for this purpose, as may music therapists supervising sessions conducted by music therapy interns. Where data are not taken, progress is marked through collaboration between the music therapist and the classroom teacher. Music therapists and interns also take anecdotal notes on student progress when new behaviors surface.

As each student enters a program served by a music therapist, the Special Education Department prepares a file with relevant information (age, type and severity of disability, other support services received, nonmusic goals) from the evaluation process and the IEP for the music therapist serving that student. In February, music therapy services to most classes are discontinued for two or more weeks while the serving music therapist formally assesses specific student populations on an individual basis. These populations include students in the pre-kindergarten and special need kindergarten (SNK) classes (who will be graduating into classes served by music therapy) and students in the intellectual disability, orthopedic impairment, hearing impairment, and autism classrooms through elementary school. Students in the behavioral disabilities, pre-kindergarten, SNK, middle, and high school classrooms do not have music therapy on the IEP (though they continue to receive services) and are therefore not formally assessed on an annual basis.

Student name:_____

Classroom teacher/school:_____

Date given: _____

Music Therapy Assessment
Clayton County Board of Education

Social skills
Moderate

0 – does not perform task, even with assistance and/or prompts

1 – performs task with physical assistance

2 – performs task with model (2 or fewer)

3 – performs task with verbal assistance (2 or fewer)

4 – independent

N.A. – non-applicable
N.V. – non-verbal
N.C. – non-compliant
H.I. – hearing impaired
V.I. – visually impaired
P.L. – physically limited
A.T. – autistic-like tendencies
* – see notes

Therapist should offer no more than 3 trials per task.

Student:

___ Will remain in MT group for ____ (secs or mins)

___ Participates in ___ of out five musical activities

___ Spontaneously participates in ____ out of 5 musical activities

___ Follows verbal directions ____ out of 5 times.

___ Identifies an array of 2 or more peers

         Verbal

         Communication device

         Pictures

         Other

___ Remains quiet during others' turns ____% of the time

         verbal noises

         other noises

___ Attends to others' turns for up to a ____ sec/min interval

___ Plays musical instrument/equipment appropriately

___ Responds appropriately to social interactions initiated

___ Refrains from touching others inappropriately (clinging, sexually suggestive or provocative behavior, hitting)

___ Accepts and adheres to music rules including not getting upset or acting out when unhappy.

___ Refrains from initiating conflict between others in the group.

Figure 3. Music Therapy Assessment

Music Therapy Goal Sheet

Student name:_____Date:_____Therapist:_____

The student will be able to:

Pre-cognition
1. _____ Attend toward source of auditory stimulus by body responses or by looking.
2. _____ Attend to MT activities for ___ s/mins with two or fewer verbal cues
3. _____ Make eye contact with the therapist for ___ seconds
4. _____ Reach for items offered within field of vision.
5. _____

Cognition
1. _____ Follow oral directions during music for 3/5 activities
2. _____ Recognize ___ rhythm instruments
3. _____ Identify ___ rhythm instruments
4. _____ Identify an array of rhythm instruments (by pointing to a picture or verbally) when heard but
   not seen
5. _____ Actively sign or sing familiar songs used in Music Therapy
6. _____

Social
1. _____ Remain in MT group for ___ (sec/min)
2. _____ Wait quietly during turn taking activities
3. _____ Attend to others' turns for ___ (sec/min)
4. _____ Spontaneously participate in 3/5 activities
5. _____ Actively participate in 3/5 activities
6. _____ Tolerate physical assistance for participation
7. _____ Initiate appropriate social interactions with peers
8. _____ Initiate appropriate social interactions with adults
9. _____ Respond appropriately to social interactions initiated by another student
10. _____ Respond appropriately to social interactions initiated by an adult
11. _____ Lead peers in group activities
12. _____ Give and take manipulatives appropriately
13. _____

Motor
1. _____ Imitate fine/gross motor movement
2. _____ Originate fine/gross motor movement
3. _____ Coordinate a sequence of ___ moves involving ___ body parts
4. _____ Perform a sequence of ____ moves
5. _____

Communication
1. _____ Imitate vocal sounds
2. _____ Offer 2-5 meaningful utterances
3. _____ Express a need or want by an affect, word, gesture, or alternative communication device
4. _____ Express a need or want through complete sentences
5. _____

Figure 4. Music Therapy Goal Sheet

Notes about progress and general target goals are shared with the teachers of these programs on an informal basis, however.

The assessment process used is one developed by the CCPS music therapy team and is revised and refined on an annual basis. The domains specifically assessed with this instrument include cognitive functioning, social skills, musical skills, auditory processing, and physical (fine and gross motor) skills. Although much of the assessment is completed during a 20–30 minute period, the social skills section relies on knowledge of the student's interactions during music therapy group. Results are shared with the classroom teacher and are then used by the music therapist to develop goals for each student (see Figure 4). Three or four appropriate goals are given to the teacher for each student so that these might be embedded in the student's IEP.

In preparation for writing goals and objectives for the upcoming school year, a statement is developed for each student that summarizes student progress and current level of functioning in each domain during music therapy. This document is included in the yearly IEP meeting. By convention, music therapists do not attend IEP meetings because one music therapist might have 170 students on his or her caseload. Therefore, attending a meeting for each student would effectively eliminate music therapy services to all students for the last 2 months of the school year. Exceptions are made when necessary. Since music therapy is a standard part of the elementary, middle, and high school curricula for many special education populations, IEP meetings in CCPS rarely reach the place where parents or advocates must fight for music therapy service provision.

As mentioned previously, the CCPS music therapy department participates in the American Music Therapy Association's internship program involving as many as four interns each school year. Interns work primarily with one supervisor, taking over much of the supervisor's caseload, and are scheduled to provide services to groups with a second therapist as well. Though both have input into intern evaluation, the primary supervisor bears the significant responsibility for meeting observation time and feedback guidelines. Following an observation period, interns' responsibilities increase on a weekly basis from leading a single segment within each co-led session on their caseload to full responsibility for all of the classes on their caseload (typically up to 18 classes, approximately 30 sessions per week). By design, the classes for which they are responsible cover a variety of special needs populations.

Each week interns also observe other student support services staff. They observe sessions led by occupational therapists, physical therapists, adaptive physical educators, speech therapists, art therapists, assistive technology specialists, music educators with inclusive classrooms, audiologists, teachers on community-based instruction trips, ESOL teachers, and any other programs or professionals about which the interns express interest. These time slots can also be used for continuing to observe music therapists in various populations.

In addition to therapy responsibilities, interns play large parts in other special projects and programs throughout the year. They participate in planning and leadership of the Annual Special Education Holiday Play, caroling with classes of children with orthopedic impairments or intellectual disabilities, the Very Special Arts Festival, and Scouting Outing. They are responsible for using the music therapy assessment tool to develop appropriate goals for a few children on their caseload. In order to address the significant stress and changing worldview of interns during this high-pressure time, interns are offered the option of meeting with a school system counselor several times during the internship.

The music therapy program benefits the county through the provision of an effective, efficient, and positive intervention strategy to numerous groups of students with diverse special needs. The individuals on the music therapy team provide leadership to some 40 schools around the county on current and research-based best-practice guidelines for working with children of all ages and abilities. Inservices are provided to special education teachers and classroom staff as well as to music education teachers regarding the roles that music therapists are able and willing to play in their classrooms. The CCPS music therapists are also active in presenting at conferences and special education departments outside of Clayton County. The music therapy department actively promotes student ability over disability in numerous community settings in Clayton County as a whole.

Fulton County School System

Fulton County Schools, located in the metro Atlanta area and spanning north and south of the city, serves over 70,000 students. Within the county there are 45 elementary schools, 13 middle schools, and 11 high schools. Of the many unique programs Fulton County schools offers, music therapy is recognized and respected as an integral special service within the county. Music therapy serves approximately 800 students with special needs in a total of 26 schools throughout the district.

The music therapy program in Fulton County Schools is funded and supported through the music education department. Initially, music therapy was sought out by the music education administration of Fulton County in an effort to better address the needs of special learners attending general music classes. This was due to concerns raised by Fulton County music educators who were, at that time, responsible for teaching all students served by the Fulton County Services for Exceptional Children (SEC) program. The difficulties associated with meeting varying needs of Fulton County special learners in the general music setting correlated with research findings that many music educators do not feel adequately prepared to teach students in the mainstreamed classroom (Frisque, Niebur, & Humphreys, 1994; Gfeller, Darrow, & Hedden, 1990; Graham, 1972).

Fulton County Schools promotes the inclusion of all students into regular school programming when deemed appropriate. In addition, the school system believes in providing remedial and rehabilitative services to SEC students when indicated. Philosophical approaches include behavior modification, sensory integration, group counseling, and education support and remediation. Fulton County recognized the specialized training of music therapists to fit into this philosophical framework. The music therapy program established by the county functions to assess student needs and be an integral part of the interdisciplinary team in order to benefit student success through the targeted use of music.

In Fulton County schools, SEC students attend the district's regular elementary, middle, and high schools based on where their designated programs are located. Music therapists travel within the county to schools with classes involved in those programs. During the 2000–2001 school year, there were five full-time music therapists providing services within the county to approximately 130 classes total. Music therapists working in the county are required to hold Georgia's professional educator certification in music in accordance with state guidelines. Music therapists are board certified or pending board certification. The music therapy department receives funding through the county budget that in turn is funded by federal funds, local funds, local taxes, and state funds. The county allots funds to the music therapy department for salaries, travel stipends, equipment requests, and continuing education opportunities.

The music therapy department has worked closely with both the music education department and the SEC administration to decide on the program's service delivery and components of the program. Music therapy program meetings occur annually with music therapy team members and county administrators. Through these meetings, populations are identified that are believed to benefit most from music therapy services. Decisions are made based on current research correlating music with specific populations, input from team members including parents, and a review of previous music therapy practice. Once a population is designated for music therapy services, all students in that special education program throughout the county qualify to be seen by a music therapist.

Populations receiving direct music therapy services in Fulton County, under Georgia categories, are moderate, severe and profound intellectual disability, special needs preschool, special needs kindergarten, orthopedically impaired/other health impairment, hearing impaired, autism, speech and language disorder, and severe emotional behavior disorder. All populations listed receive music therapy at the elementary level. In the middle school level, music therapists see students with moderate, severe, and profound intellectual disabilities, orthopedically/other health impairments, and autism. The Fulton County music therapists work with only moderate, severe, and profound intellectual disabilities at the high school level.

As Johnson (1996) suggests, Fulton County music therapists have increased their capacity in consultant roles with growth of the program. Specifically, this involves providing input to staff and parents about students who will best succeed in the mainstreamed music setting. This collaboration and increased communication, via the trained input of music therapists, has alleviated some of the general frustration of the Fulton County music educators. For students deemed lacking the skills needed to succeed in the general music setting, music education concepts are incorporated into their music therapy treatment where appropriate.

Music therapists in Fulton County discuss student needs and responses frequently with classroom teachers and related professionals to provide the highest quality service throughout the county. Music therapy sessions are held primarily in groups with sessions being held twice a week for children with intellectual disabilities and once a week for all other populations. Occasionally, one-on-one therapy is delivered when deemed most appropriate for the individual by the music therapist and other interdisciplinary team members.

Individual needs of SEC students are outlined on their Individualized Education Programs (IEPs). While the IEP of each student served is carefully reviewed by the music therapists as part of the treatment plan development process, music therapy is not a direct component of student IEPs in Fulton County. Music therapists are often consulted for input on the development of goals and objectives but do not document specific information in this capacity. The numbers of students seen by each therapist is the primary reason that music therapy is not on student IEPs. As music therapy was adopted as a countywide program from the beginning, the documentation necessary for all students receiving services would be overwhelming and would detract from the quality of music therapy delivered.

Fulton County music therapists provide reports of student achievement and intervention results via team meetings and system requirements for continued service. System requirements vary with the population receiving treatment and the schools receiving services. Music therapy treatment plans are developed for all sessions. Primary goals for most music therapy sessions include the use of music activities to promote academic learning, practice social skills, provide sensory experiences, and enhance mobility training. Objectives are outlined under these goals to target specific needs. Typical objectives might include the following: establishing eye contact with students with severe intellectual disabilities, strengthening balance and coordination in students with orthopedic impairments, or increasing expressive communication in students with speech and language disorders.

Additional avenues are taken to promote the use and success of the Fulton County music therapy program. County music therapists perform special projects each year. As part of the music therapy programming, student groups perform at their schools and within the community. Often these performances are structured to provide a rewarding opportunity for SEC students to work together with age appropriate regular education peers. Recognition has also been gained with county sponsored grant writing projects. Projects entitled "Karoake for Kids," "Rhythm and Reason," and "Sing Me a Story" were funded and helped to raise awareness about the therapeutic nature of the program. Lastly, the music therapy department members have provided information about service delivery at various international, national, state, and local presentations.

Delivery of service was expanded with the addition of the American Music Therapy Association's internship program that was initiated during the 1998–1999 school year and has hosted up to five interns at one time. Fulton County provides a challenging and well-rounded internship experience. Interns begin their program with a period of observation of the music therapists in the county and in outside facilities, related professionals and classroom environments. This is followed by co-leading experiences with music therapy team members. Interns then gain thorough experience with a variety of populations as they assume responsibility for an entire caseload starting mid-point of their training and continuing to the end of their internship. Through a required "Create-a-Class" project, the intern implements a program from scratch with a population of their personal interest that does not currently receive music therapy services. The success of interns with this particular project has highlighted potential areas of growth for the music therapy program.

In addition to the full-time music therapists and music therapy interns, there are also several music therapists who have been hired to work as "music specialists" in the general music setting. This is a result of county administrators recognizing the high level of expertise and training exhibited by music therapists. The addition of music therapists working as music specialists within the county has helped achieve the overall goal of enhancing SEC student services. Input from the music therapy perspective is given for populations who are not receiving formal music therapy services and on issues regarding curriculum development and teaching practice for the special learners in the general music setting. This partnership integrates the element of consultation and collaboration with specialists suggested by Darrow (1999) in order to enhance successful inclusion of students by music educators.

Music therapy has been embraced by Fulton County Schools. The increase of music therapy staff and services indicates the school district's recognition of music therapy as an effective program, which promotes the system wide mission of educating students to be responsible, productive citizens. The positive and engaging medium of music used by the music therapy team contributes to the Fulton County vision of providing educational experiences where all children learn to their full potential in a safe, nurturing environment. That environment is supported by involved and committed staff, family, and community who use proactive collaboration to achieve the county vision. The success of music therapy has inspired Fulton County to create an adaptive art program modeled after its program, and music therapists are often invited to participate in overall curriculum design and integration within Fulton County Schools. With continued support and expansion of services, the Fulton County music therapy department looks forward to developing innovative techniques and research for the music therapy profession while looking at many different aspects of program design and service delivery.

Intervention Models

Music therapists provide services throughout the three school districts in many different ways. Some of the music therapy programs are planned for district-wide impact while others are specific to particular settings (Hughes & Robbins, 1992). Examples of both types of services are exemplified in the brief program descriptions found later in this section.

District-wide Services

Consultant Services

Consultant services are provided by music therapists as requested by teachers, parents, or administrators. These services may be rendered in a variety of ways. Sometimes music therapists make one-time recommendations to the teachers requesting assistance. This is done after the music therapist observes and assesses the problem in the classroom setting and meets with the requesting teacher. At other times, after observation and assessment, the music therapist and classroom teacher decide that support in the classroom is required. Support may then be provided on a short- or long-term basis by music therapists or designated others. Designated others may be university music practicum students or volunteers, trained paraprofessionals, music volunteers from the community, and ESE resource personnel. Music therapists may also assist IEP teams in music placements. The following examples are typical of these various types of consultant services.

EXAMPLE 1

Service Provider: Music therapist
Course: First grade inclusive classroom
Students Enrolled: 23

Problem: The teacher complained about her entire class's behavior while making transitions. The class was observed by the music therapist during transition to other locations, and in homeroom and music class activities. Students seemed unclear about procedures and often exhibited unruly behavior. The teacher gave verbal instructions to the students but rarely captured their attention. In addition, the paraprofessional constantly talked aloud to individual students.

Strategies: 1. Condition the children and the paraprofessional to respond with silence to a specific musical signal.
2. Give spoken directions only if necessary.
3. Use engaging action songs to direct the class from one place to another and to change pace or mood.
4. Reward appropriate behavior.
5. Communicate regularly with the music teacher in order to learn new action songs.

Outcomes: Music strategies were recommended because the children displayed appropriate and enthusiastic participation during music and movement activities. The music therapist taught the teacher a few short music activities that had been proven effective in similar circumstances. She also helped the teacher to establish a process for obtaining similar activities from the school's music teacher. A month after music intervention was initiated, the classroom teacher reported much smoother transitions and a happier classroom atmosphere.

EXAMPLE 2

Service Providers: Music therapist and university music therapy practicum student
Course: Sixth grade band
Students Enrolled: 42
Targeted Student: 1 (vision impaired)

Problem: Learning new music was a problem for the sixth grade band student. While her clarinet playing skills were more than adequate, due to her vision impairment she was unable to read music notation at the tempo required by the band director.

Strategies: 1. Provide tutoring sessions once a week to practice new music before it is presented in class.
2. Enlarge clarinet music scores.
3. Suggest collaborative procedures between the band teacher and vision resource teacher.

Outcomes: The music therapist observed in band class and met with the student for individual practice. She found that the student could read enlarged music notation at a very slow tempo and was able to learn her part quickly once she heard it a few times. A university music therapy practicum student was assigned to tutor her over a period of months and to work with her vision resource teacher to develop procedures of support. The band student gradually gained confidence as she herself discovered ways to learn new music with a minimum of assistance. She continued in the band program and eventually went on to play in her high school band.

EXAMPLE 3

Service Provider: Music therapists
Course Descriptions: High school music electives
Recipients: District ESE staff, school-based ESE staff, parents

Problems: High school music electives in the Leon County Schools are limited in number and variety of offerings. The main music courses offered at all high schools are band, chorus, piano, and guitar. Individual schools also have specialized courses such as steel drum band, world music, introduction to music performance, and music technology unique to that particular school. The district publishes a guidebook containing two-line course descriptions given to students in the spring of each year to help them select their courses for the coming year. These descriptions do not always contain enough information on course content and requirements to allow ESE students, their parents and advisors to make informed selections. This has been especially true in music performance classes. In the past some ESE students elected courses where they were not successful due to the requirements of that class. Sometimes parents and/or ESE advisors discouraged students from enrolling in music at all because of their disability. These problems arose despite the fact that there were elective music courses available in most high schools to suit the diverse needs of students wishing to elect music.

Strategies: 1.   Selected music teachers at each high school described their school's elective course offerings.
2.   A school-by-school handout with descriptions of music courses contents and requirements was compiled.
3.   Course descriptions were distributed to district and school ESE staff and parents prior to IEP conferences and course selections for the next year.
4.   Information was updated and the process was evaluated annually.

Outcomes: District and school ESE staff and parents reported that the handout made them more aware of the course requirements, their responsibilities, and the concerns of the music teachers. Music teachers found that more ESE students elected music courses and were making wiser selections. Positive attitudes, especially on the part of music teachers, became an important outcome of this service. Music teachers often expressed appreciation for the opportunity to describe their courses, have input into student placement, and state the need to have enough support when needed. Four sample course descriptions (see Figure 5) reflect the expectations of music teachers for a variety of high school electives.

Inservice Training

Inservice training for teachers is provided by music therapists on a "needs" basis. Training sessions are offered on topics such as pre-kindergarten music, mainstreaming in music, use of music in behavior management, therapies and services in inclusive settings, arts in the classroom, activities for learning academics through music, and use of music by parents at home. District needs are identified through teacher and parental requests, surveys and observation. As one example, the results of music teacher surveys conducted over a 3-year span led to a grant to fund teacher training (see Figure 6). A series of workshops on cooperative collaboration in mainstreaming was conducted for music teachers and ESE teachers together. The development of guidelines for ESE paraprofessionals in the music classroom was another outcome.

High School Music Course Descriptions

Music Teacher Interview Questions

Teacher_____ School_____

Gospel Choir
Inclusive course recommended for a wide range of abilities.

1. **Prerequisite courses or music skills needed:**
   None, but it would be helpful if the student sings in tune.

2. **Class size**   *55-60*
   Room size   *Large Choral Room*
   Type of students usually enrolled
   Choir includes a variety of students with multicultural backgrounds and an extremely wide range of abilities.

3. **Individual Skills Required:**

   (1) Physical
       Music is taught by rote, therefore good listening skills are required

   (2) Social
       Requires a person who interacts appropriately with peers. Must have self discipline and restraint—no display of anger

   (3) Academic
       Reading the text (words) of the music

4. **Homework?** *Yes, at times—occasional quizzes on theory/fundamentals*

   After-school rehearsals/performances? *Yes—Several performances outside of school are required. (more than other choirs) Students need to arrange their own transportation. Some after-school rehearsals. (grade penalty policy for after-school absences)*

5. **Type and amount of ESE assistance needed? (specify)**
   Paraprofessional to help students study the music and administer tests and quizzes. (computer bubble sheets are used)

6. **Comments: (include recommended ESE : non-ESE ratio)**
   Has a talented, "cool" FSU Graduate Assistant who is trying to build commitment and responsibility to the group. Students with special needs are welcome if they meet the above requirements.

High School Music Course Descriptions

Music Teacher Interview Questions

Teacher_____   School_____

Introduction to Music
Inclusive course recommended for a wide range of abilities.

1. **Prerequisite courses or music skills needed:**
   None

2. **Class size:** *30 students*
   Room size: *Large choral room with permanent risers for chairs*
   Type of students usually enrolled: *10th-12th grade students with a
   wide variety of abilities and past music experiences.*

3. **Individual Skills Required:**

   (1) Physical
      Will play a variety of percussion instruments, move/dance
      Will play guitar for three weeks

   (2) Social
      *Requires participation in group music performance activities—individual
      concentration—good audience behavior for visiting community and university guest
      artists/instructors*

   (3) Academic
      Reading: words and some music notation—written tests
      Note taking

4. **Homework?** *Yes (bringing in articles on community arts current events and other
   classwork- related assignments)*

   After-school rehearsals/performances?
   None

5. **Type and amount of ESE assistance needed? (specify)**
   *Would welcome observation and collaboration of ESE personnel as needed for students'
   success (especially to follow through on class assignments)*

6. **Comments: (include recommended ESE : non-ESE ratio)**
   About five: twenty-five

High School Music Course Descriptions

<u>Music Teacher Interview Questions</u>

Teacher_____   School_____

<u>Beginning Band</u>
Inclusive course recommended for a wide range of abilities.

1. **Prerequisite courses or music skills needed:**
   None—Small instruments (clarinets, flutes, most trombones, etc.) are provided

2. **Class size:**   *30 students*
   Room size: *Large band room*
   Type of students usually enrolled: *Variety of grades and abilities*

3. **Typical Skills Required:**

   (1) Physical
   Good eye-hand coordination
   For woodwinds—ability to coordinate fingers (9 out of 10 fingers)

   (2) Social
   Requires working together as a group. Must be able to sit and wait while another section works

   (3) Academic
   Can read language
   Understands math (small fractions and counting for rhythmic notation)

4. **Homework?** *No, unless extra study is needed for occasional quizzes and tests—not required to play at home*

   After-school rehearsals/performances?
   None (except in school)

5. **Type and amount of ESE assistance needed? (specify)**
   Would welcome observation and assistance of ESE personnel in and after class as needed for students' success

6. **Comments: (include recommended ESE : non-ESE ratio)**
   10% - 15% of total students

High School Music Course Descriptions

Music Teacher Interview Questions

Teacher_____   School_____

Keyboard I
Inclusive course recommended for a wide range of abilities.

1. **Prerequisite courses or music skills needed:**
   None required

2. **Class size:**   *20 maximum*
   Room size: *Moderate classroom size—individual keyboard instruments*
   Located in the new building
   Type of students usually enrolled: *Students in grades 9-12*
   Many take the course to satisfy the Performing Fine Arts graduation requirement—wide variety of abilities

3. **Typical Individual Skills Required:**

   (1) Physical
   Motor skills (basic finger dexterity) needed to manipulate keys

   (2) Social
   Requires a person who is self-disciplined and works independently—avoids socializing in class. Most interaction is teacher : student

   (3) Academic
   Ability to read simple directions, follow instructions, and concentrate on the tasks given

4. **Homework?** *None*

   After-school rehearsals/performances? *Recitals are scheduled periodically during class. Students need to be present in class on those previously scheduled days. There are two evening recitals each year.*

5. **Type and amount of ESE assistance needed? (specify)**
   An aide in the piano class every day is essential. The amount of assistance depends on the abilities of the students

6. **Comments: (include recommended ESE : non-ESE ratio)**
   1) Would like to have a written description of each ESE student's special needs. 2) Would appreciate the courtesy of being informed about field trips. 3) Biggest Concern: so many CBI students in one section. Would like no more than two ESE students per class

Figure 5. High School Music Course Descriptions

Questionnaire Items

❏ **Which ESE areas are represented in your class load?**

Emotionally Handicapped (EH) _____
Severely Emotionally Disturbed (SED) _____
Special Class _____
Community Based Instruction (CBI) _____
Profoundly Mentally Handicapped (PMH) _____
Profoundly Handicapped (PH) _____
Physically Impaired (PI) _____

Vision Impaired (VI) _____
Hearing Impaired (HI) _____
Gifted _____
Speech/Language Impaired (S/L) _____
Deaf/Blind (D/B) _____
PreKindergarten (PreK) _____

❏ **How are they scheduled for music?**

Mainstreamed with chronological age peers _____
In self-contained music classes _____
Other _____

❏ **Were you consulted before ESE students were scheduled into music classes this year?**
❏ **Do you have any contact/communication with ESE teachers concerning your mainstreamed students?**
❏ **Would you like to have more regular contact or a different type of contact?**
❏ **Do any paraprofessionals ever attend music classes with ESE students? Are they helpful?**
   Ideally, how would you like them to assist you in your classes?

❏ **Please number, in priority order, the areas of concern to you based on your present and past students.**
   ("1" = greatest concern)

Motivation/Self-Esteem _____
Remembering _____
Following Directions _____
Working in Groups _____
Motor Skills _____
Reading Music _____
Oral Expression _____
Taking Tests _____

Paying Attention _____
Generalizing _____
Completing Assignments _____
Learning from Lectures _____
Singing _____
Organization _____
Starting Tasks _____
Understanding _____

Seeing Relationships _____
Behavior Problems _____
Class Discussion _____
Listening _____
Staying on Task _____
Reading Words _____
Learning from Tape Recordings _____
Writing _____

❏ **Check areas of concern as relating to you, the music teacher.**

Prior knowledge about individual students _____
Communication with ESE teachers _____
Assistance in the music class _____
Assistance in choosing and/or adapting materials/equipment for a wide range of abilities _____
Time to give individual attention to special needs in a large class _____
Educational training in teaching students with special needs _____
Other (please specify) _____

❏ **If you were offered assistance in teaching mainstreamed music students, which of the following would**
   you choose?   (Check all applicable)

____ **Inservice Training** for music and ESE teachers together in the Cooperative Consultation Model (a time-efficient method of on-going communication between teachers which includes necessary background information on students, their learning needs, social skills, performance in the music class, etc.)
Please comment _____

____ **Consultation services** to music and ESE teachers by qualified music specialists (such as regularly scheduled on-site assistance in the development of strategies to deal with identified behavior problems, adaptive music materials/techniques, assessment of music skill levels, etc.)
Please comment _____

____ **Support in the classroom** (by trained paraprofessionals, university music students, volunteers). For example, someone to attend the music class and then assist students to practice needed music and other skills in the ESE setting for transfer back to the music class.
Please comment _____

Figure 6. Leon County Music Teacher Survey

The following examples illustrate types of music therapists' training programs for school personnel.

EXAMPLE 4

Service Providers: Music therapists and selected teachers
Inservice Course: Music mainstreaming
Personnel Trained: ESE, regular education and elementary music

Problems: Surveys of music teachers have identified problems relating to mainstream music classes in many different locales (Atterbury, 1986; Gfeller, Darrow, & Hedden, 1990; Robbins, 1989). Likewise, mainstreaming has not always resulted in positive social or music learning experiences for students. Music teachers reported that they were rarely consulted on placement decisions and some students were inappropriately placed in their music classes. Concern was also voiced over a personal lack of knowledge and skills for working with certain populations. Little communication existed between music and ESE teachers and there was even less effective support available for mainstream music classes. The music teachers thought that few available curriculum resources were applicable to their needs.

Strategies: 1. Survey mainstream music teachers to determine concerns.
2. Organize a team of ESE and music teachers to plan a series of inservice workshops.
3. Present three workshops for ESE teachers and music teachers together.

The workshop agendas seen in Figure 7 contain the inservice objectives and activities.

Outcomes: Responses by teachers indicated that inservice objectives were met. According to the ESE teachers' evaluation sheets, their participation in grade level music activities led them to a greater understanding of the response requirements in music performance. Music teachers unanimously agreed that, with input from the ESE teachers, they had new ideas concerning ways to "make a place for everyone" without lessening the quality of the musical experiences. Teachers collaborated during the workshops on issues of concern, and then initiated on-going communication procedures back at their local school sites.

EXAMPLE 5

Service Providers: Music therapists and ESE teachers
Inservice: Paraprofessionals in the music class
Personnel Trained: ESE paraprofessionals district-wide

Problem: Many ESE paraprofessionals attending music class with their students were not working effectively due to a lack of understanding their role in music's unique setting. It has been found that a list of guidelines can be helpful in clarifying music teachers' expectations to both paraprofessionals and their supervising ESE teachers.

Strategies: 1. Request that music teachers fill out a form listing their expectations of the role of paraprofessionals who accompany ESE students to mainstream music classes.
2. Compile and categorize the results.
3. Distribute the guidelines to ESE teachers for their use in training their own paraprofessionals.

The guidelines in Figure 8 were developed by music therapists and music teachers based on the top "do's" and "don'ts" of more than 100 music teachers from many different school districts.

Outcomes: The guidelines are now being used by ESE teachers to train their paraprofessionals at the beginning of each year, and by music teachers as reminders throughout the year. ESE

INSERVICE FOR MUSIC MAINSTREAMING

Inservice Objectives
1. Teachers will increase awareness of (a) music education (values/subject content/techniques/desired outcomes), and (b) special needs of mainstreamed music students.
2. Teachers will increase knowledge and skills related to the use of Cooperative Consultation for mainstreaming in music.
3. Teachers will enjoy participating together.

AGENDA
November 6, 3:30–5:30 p.m., Sealey Music Room
- Sign-in and refreshments beginning at 3:15
- **Music Education: Values and Outcomes**—Address by June Hinckley, Music Consultant, Florida Department of Education
- **Objectives of the Program**—Jane Hughes
- **Awareness of Students' Special Needs**—Activities led by Diane Johnson, Director, FDLRS/Miccosukee
- **Introduction to the Cooperative Consultation Model**—N. Stokely, ESE; P. Kargel, Sabal Palm; M. A. Sauers, Chaires
- First Steps (Work in School Teams)
- Questions

**Music Teachers: Bring your new FEMEA Curriculum Outline on 11/13/92!

AGENDA
November 13, 3:30–5:30 p.m., Sealey Music Room
- Sign-in and refreshments beginning at 3:15
- "Wonderful World" attention-getter, singing .... Patti Shay & Brenda Robbins
- "Names" Grade 5 opener, motor coordination, rhythm, speech .... Julie Fredrickson
- **Music Education: Student Experiences**
  Session Overview/FEMEA Curriculum .... Jane Hughes
  Grade K–1: Creative Movement/instruments/drama .... Carla Houck
  Grade 2–3: Listening .... Ginny Densmore
  Grade 3–4: Singing/Orff process/instrumental ostinato .... Shirley Kirwin
  Grade 4–5: Kodaly process/singing/reading .... Blair Clawson
  Reinforcing strengths/social interaction in music/paraprofessionals .... Brenda Robbins
  Evaluation/grading/student information .... Jane Floyd
  Cooperative Consultation: School teams plan together .... Nancy Stokely

AGENDA
March 31, 3:45–5:45 p.m., Sealey Music Room
- Sign-in and refreshments beginning at 3:30
Opening Activities .... **Leader**
(1) Singing for Fun and Beauty
  - Scotland's Burning (Action Song) .... Rebecca Ream
  - Music Is Everywhere (German Folk Round) .... Jane Hughes
(2) Announcements
  - Paperwork Deadlines
  - Evaluations
Learning Non-Musical Skills Through Music (Development and Transfer)
(1) Discussion and Experiential Activities .... Blair Clawson
(2) Folk Dancing .... Brenda Robbins
(3) Creating/Cooperating .... Julie Fredrickson
Questions/Comments from Participants
Tips for Using Music in the ESE Classroom (for Satisfying and Music Results)
- Choosing Songs & Recorded Selections
- Children's Singing Ranges
- Using Music in Musical Ways
- Attending
- Auditory Stimuli (avoiding distracting sounds, stimulus overload, etc.)
- Academic Skills (counting, rhymes, language, speech, coordination, etc.)

Figure 7. Inservice for Music Mainstreaming

Guidelines for Paraprofessionals in the Music Classroom

Things Paraprofessionals Do That Music Teachers Love

- Model desired behaviors by participating in the singing, dancing, playing instruments, etc., as the children are expected to do.
- Sit or move about the room as the activity directs, in order to assist all students, not only those in ESE.
- Actively and enthusiastically participate in all activities.
- Allow students enough time to perform expected task or behavior before assisting. First give them the freedom to try.
- Redirect inappropriate behavior.
- Correct students "up close and personal."
- Assist the music teacher in any way possible by being another pair of hands and eyes.
- Help the music teacher with discipline, while not usurping the music teacher's authority.
- Communicate with the music teacher about any unusual problems before class begins.
- Ask questions in order to clarify instructions or procedures.
- Give suggestions on how materials or parts may be adapted for individual students.
- Serve as a communication link between ESE teacher and music teacher.
- Sign everything in the class for students with hearing impairments.
- Physically help students experience an activity by assisting them when needed.
- Outside of music class, make/adapt materials so all children can fully participate.
- Teach prompting/assisting skills to peers. Model the interaction, then allow classmates to interact within personal time frames.

Things Paraprofessionals Do That Drive Music Teachers "Out of Tune"

- Are not on task (reading the paper, grading papers, eating lunch, etc.).
- Look bored, disinterested, irritated, or sleepy.
- Talk to others or the music teacher during class.
- Discuss a student in front of the student.
- Shout instructions or corrections to students during class.
- Use discipline which conflicts with that of the music teacher's.
- Expect "more or better" behavior from the student who is mainstreamed.
- Use rude, condescending, or irritated voices when addressing students.

Figure 8. Guidelines for Paraprofessionals in the Music Classroom

teachers have also referred to the guidelines in training paraprofessionals for other mainstreamed subject area classes. Music teachers reported a marked improvement in paraprofessional effectiveness when the guidelines were read and discussed.

Training in the use of music at home is provided to parents individually through formal and informal communication. Examples are: scheduled parent conferences, informal meetings at school functions, written feedback on student progress, lists of repertoire/resources experienced by their children in music therapy sent to parents at report card time (see Figure 9), and invitations to visit sessions and student performances. Workshops occur at school advisory committee meetings for parents, teachers, and administrators and at district-wide workshop sessions. Music therapy interns gain experience by developing and presenting sessions at district-wide workshops for parents and others.

Preservice Experiences

Preservice experiences for university music students are coordinated by music therapists who assist in placing the music education and music therapy practicum students with mainstream music teachers. University students fulfill their practicum requirements while gaining valuable first-hand experience with music teachers in mainstream classes. Music teachers identify students who would benefit from tutoring sessions in individual or small group settings. The duration of each practicum is from six weeks to one semester.

EXAMPLE 6

Service Providers:	Music therapists and university music professors
Course:	Music practicum with ESE students
Students Enrolled:	University music education and music therapy students
Students Served:	Selected mainstream music students
Teachers Served:	Music teachers

Problem: Because of their unique learning needs, some students require extra assistance in order to perform successfully in music classes with others of their own age. People not trained in music are often unable to effectively teach skills related to music learning, and it is difficult to find enough trained musicians who are available to serve as volunteers. Local university undergraduate music education students usually have few opportunities to work closely with exceptional students, and music therapy students rarely have a chance to work with music teachers. Music therapists developed a way to bring extra support for students and teachers in mainstream music classes, and to provide valuable practicum experiences for music education and therapy students.

Strategies: The practicum cover sheet provides information about program objectives and procedures (see Figure 10).

Outcomes: Preservice music education and music therapy students have served numerous students and teachers in many different schools. ESE students have increased skills related to successful participation in music classes with their peers. Music progress reports in general have documented the improvement of skills in individual ESE student performance. The practicum students have been highly praised by music teachers, ESE teachers, and parents for the benefits they brought to the students. University students expressed their appreciation for the opportunity to experience diverse learning styles and relate to individual students in meaningful and joyful ways.

Music Therapy Report

Student	Dates	Teacher
John Doe	8/14/00- 10/12/00	MT-BC

This middle school elective music class is designed to address student IEP goals in the areas of arts performance, social , academic, sensory and motor skills. The course incorporates the Sunshine State Standards goals for the Arts, students experience music repertoire through singing, listening, playing, moving, creating and reading. For the months of August, September and October students studied many composers and performers, learned a variety of musical styles, and explored exciting musical events in history. The music class meets every Tuesday and Thursday from 11:55pm-12:30pm. You are invited to visit and join in the fun.

Music selections for this grading period include:

Consider Yourself *from Oliver*
Hail, Hail the Gang's All Here
This Little Light of Mine
Stop, Look, Listen
Semper Fedelis *by John Philip Sousa*
Josephine
Michael Row
Introduction to precorders
Goodbye my Friends
A Good Old Happy Song
America the Beautiful *performed by Whitney Houston*
Gettin' Ready Rag *from Ragtime*
Golliwogs Cakewalk *by Claude Debussy*
I've Got Rhythm *performed by Charlie Parker*
One O'clock Jump *performed by Count Basie*
Morning Has Broken
Precorder playing techniques
One Moment in Time
America *from West Side Story by Leonard Bernstein*
A Round of Goodbyes
What'd I Say *performed by Ray Charles*
Oh What a Beautiful Morning *from Okalahoma*
Precorder Music: All Alone
Positive Thinking Rap
The Olympic Theme
Australian National Anthem
Star Spangled Banner

Many Ways to Say Hello
Canon in D *by Johann Pachelbel*
I'm in the Mood
Waltzing Matilda
Land Down Under *by Men at Work*
Amazing Grace *performed by Jessye Norman*
Hush Little Baby *performed by Yo Yo Ma and Bobby McFerrin*
My Favorite Things *from The Sound of Music performed by Julie Andrews*
The Toreador Song *from Carmen*
Don't Sit Under the Apple Tree
Apple Picking
Farmer Brown
October
Rosamunda (German Polka)

Comments
John is becoming a leader in the music elective class. His vocal skills both in singing and speaking are developing well. His breath control and articulation have shown significant improvement. John has become more focused and remains attentive for longer periods of time. Within the next two weeks, John will begin to study keyboard with a music therapy intern.

Figure 9. Music Therapy Report

MUSIC PRACTICUM WITH EXCEPTIONAL STUDENTS

Cover Sheet

_____
University Student

_____
School Telephone

_____   _____
Music Class Time   Indiv./Sm. Group Time
(Once Weekly)   (Once Weekly)
                    _____
                    Beginning/Ending Dates

Exceptional Student Education Objective
Exceptional Students will be effectively mainstreamed in age-appropriate music classes.

Objectives of the Practicum
1) To provide experiences for university music education/therapy students in working with mainstreamed music students.
2) To facilitate transfer of skills targeted by the music teacher to both the ESE student and ESE teacher.
3) To document "alternative strategies" for students in music, and provide consultative services through the Cooperative Consultation Model.

Supervisors
University Professor   _____
Music Teacher   _____
ESE Teacher/Classroom Teacher   _____

Coordinators
ESE Music Specialists   Jane Hughes and Brenda Robbins

Tips for Practicum Students
Be Responsible

1) Arrive at assigned school in time to park, report to the main office sign-in, and be at the Music or ESE room at appointed time.
2) If you are ill and <u>must</u> be absent (hopefully not), call the school as soon as you can to notify the teacher involved. **This is very important.** Review excused absence policy with your professor.
3) Be prepared with a plan and materials for your sessions with individuals and your teaching assignments in the music classroom. Remember to document results each time.
4) Show both the Music and ESE teachers your **Monitor Form** and **Practice Session Planning Form** as soon as the top portion is completed during the second week of the practicum, and periodically discuss your individual/small group activity plans with the ESE teacher to let her know what you are doing (see objective #2 above).
5) Fill in the log completely on your Monitor Form immediately following each music class, individual session or teacher contact. Show your log to the music teacher and ESE teacher as often as possible. Ask for their comments on the "outcomes, comments" portions (see objective #3 above).
6) Share your mainstreaming experiences with your professor.

Figure 10. Music Practicum With Exceptional Students

Community Experiences

Music therapists help to provide community experiences for students on an academic curriculum and also for those enrolled in community-based instruction (CBI). Music therapists teach social and musical skills for transfer into the community, relay information about community arts events to students, parents, and teachers, make contacts with potential volunteers from the local arts community, and develop community arts performance programs for students.

CBI teaches students with disabilities the practical skills they need through direct application in real life settings and should not be confused with "field trips." Students are selected for CBI based on factors including:

- nonreader or low academic performance
- needs a functional approach to instruction
- long history of poor school performance
- socially immature

CBI is in place at all age levels. Priority is placed on skills that will help students become as independent as possible. Skills are identified in four areas:

- self-management/home living
- community functioning
- vocational
- recreational/leisure

Following are descriptions of six community arts experiences for secondary school students under the direction of music therapists.

EXAMPLE 7

"Studying the Environment Through the Arts" was designed and implemented through the collaborative efforts of music therapists, classroom teachers, the director of a university dance repertory company, school administrators, the education director of a local natural history museum, a university composer, and school media specialist. The program has provided students with a multi-arts experience in which they can learn about the environment of their local region. The program includes high school students with physical and mental disabilities and university undergraduate dance performance majors of approximately the same age. The focus of the program has been the creation and performance of a multi-site and multi-movement work called "Earthworks." In creating the first movement, university students worked with the high school students at their ESE center school, at a university dance studio, and at the outdoor museum. The movement was a choreographed dance piece with original music, costumes, sets, and narration. It was performed for a large audience at the museum. Sites for additional movements included a local lakeside, a bird sanctuary, and an art museum.

EXAMPLE 8

Middle and high schoolers in a school for students with severe developmental disabilities have the opportunity to participate in a choral music education program. The students attend 50-minute choral classes three times each week to learn vocal technique and repertoire. Choral classes are conducted by district music therapists and interns working at the school on alternating days. The high quality performance of standard choral literature is a major goal of the class. Another goal is to maintain a program in which the center school students benefit from performance in the community. The chorus members from the center school are sometimes joined by students from nearby high schools and universities for rehearsals and public performances in the local community and out of town. Students in the program develop self-discipline, musicianship, social skills, leadership qualities, and many other attributes contributing to their increased ability to function productively in the community (Hughes, 1991; Hughes, Robbins, Smith, & Kincaid, 1987). Being able to share the gift of music with others enriches their lives in school and beyond. Graduates of the choral program have taken a love of singing into their adult lives. As working members of the community, many graduates participate in scheduled alumni rehearsals and join the students in concerts.

EXAMPLE 9

Middle school students from CBI classes participate in weekly intergenerational music therapy in the community. The facilities include both residential health care and adult day care programs. The intergenerational program is designed to create a stimulating music environment for students and give residents/clients the opportunity to actively experience music together. The primary purpose of the program for students is to increase prevocational skills emphasized in their CBI curriculum: socially interacting, paying attention, participating, leading/following, taking responsibility, and appropriately expressing feelings. The 30-minute sessions are planned and implemented by school music therapists and/or interns in collaboration with classroom and facility staff. Music repertoire is carefully selected for appeal to both populations. Students and residents/clients assume leadership roles and offer assistance to each other when needed. The development of positive relationships and other benefits is widely acknowledged among both populations. Music therapy interns benefit from meeting the challenge of planning and implementing successful music experiences each week. One valuable lesson for them involves their own musicianship. They learn quickly that the quality of the response depends on the quality of their musical presentation. As Groene (2001) suggests, it is for the benefit of the clients that music therapists work to increase their own music skills and repertoire as "musical therapists."

EXAMPLE 10

The Annual Special Education Holiday Play is a long-standing district-wide tradition. Whereas students in regular education have ample and frequent opportunities for participating in choral, theater and dance productions throughout the school year and particularly in the winter holiday season, no similar opportunities for students in special education existed when this event was started in 1975. The original production takes place on a performing arts center stage with props, sets, routines and lighting. It involves over 20 classes of children with moderate, severe, and profound intellectual disabilities at the elementary school level. The students participate in four performances for over 3,000 people, including school aged typical peers, students from other special education programs, school staff, parents, and many members of the local community. Each year the music therapy department writes a new play with musically based scenes. They collaborate with classroom teachers and other resource providers to develop routines which (a) incorporate gross motor skill acquisition as found in the IEP, (b) incorporate use of assistive communication technology with students with severe and profound disabilities, and (c) can be performed as independently as possible, but which also use and value the strengths of regular education peers as helpers on stage. Routines are taught to students, peer helpers and teachers during twice weekly music therapy sessions. Teachers are provided with audio tapes for practicing the skills with students between sessions. Then the more than 20 elementary school classes come together on stage for a week of practicing prior to the three daytime and one evening performances. The students with special needs are able to demonstrate skills they are acquiring and to participate successfully in a program that receives tremendous public affirmation. They have the opportunity to demonstrate following directions, an increasing attention span, cooperation in a group activity, appropriate on-task behavior, and independent performance of a routine. Students in regular education, parents, and the general community who attend the play are able to see and help celebrate student abilities rather than disabilities. Peer helpers on stage develop awareness of diversity within the school population and continue their developing relationships with the students in special education. Parents have the opportunity to see their children perform at a time and in ways similar to their children's typically developing peers. By providing this service to children, the music therapy department benefits from public exposure as parental support for the music therapy program is strengthened.

EXAMPLE 11

Students with intellectual disabilities often participate in fewer summer activities than is typical of children in regular education. The Special Education Department developed a program called Scouting Outing, designed as a way to give children in the intellectual disabilities program some feel for scouting and outdoor camping. The music therapy department was called upon to provide a typical music experience for the program. Typical camp and outdoor songs were targeted for teaching prior to the event. The songs were presented and taught in a variety of ways (listening, singing, body and percussion instruments, marching, structured and free dancing) in the music therapy session environment in preparation for Scouting Outing. These songs were performed and other not previously introduced songs were learned around a campfire at the event. Teachers reported hearing students sing the songs at various times during the school day. Many students were able to participate fully at the campfire/song circle because they had learned the songs in advance. Songs typical to the camp environment were chosen so that students who did participate in a camp over the summer would already be familiar with the repertoire.

EXAMPLE 12

Middle and high school female students in an at-risk alternative education setting participate in a vocal ensemble. It is led by a music therapist at the school and often includes a district music therapy intern and university music therapy students. The group consists of 10–15 students who meet two times a week during the school day. The ensemble is voluntary and is considered a privilege for students who must meet behavior criteria for community involvement and also make up academic work that is missed. The goals established include focus and attention building, team work, communication skills, responsibility and commitment, leadership, peer interaction, and enhancing self esteem. High quality music with appeal to the students and to the community is used. Performance venues have included the state capitol, local hospital and other health care facilities, social functions, and schools. The students perform and interact with elderly residents in local assisted-living facilities and often spend time singing, talking, and personally sharing with the individual residents. They also perform in schools for developmental disabilities and act as role models and music mentors for their peers. The group is often involved in community events and has performed with well known local artists. The choral ensemble has generated many positive benefits for the students and their school program.

Program Settings

District music therapists provide music experiences for students with special needs in many different program settings. Music therapy is provided for students in programs for infants/toddlers, pre-kindergarten, elementary, secondary, and adult education. Music therapy services may occur in large groups, small groups, and individually, and in self-contained or inclusive settings.

Prekindergarten and Younger

EXAMPLE 13

The first year in an infant's life is crucial to his or her cognitive, physical, emotional, and social growth and development. Stimulating infant brain development is an area in which music therapy can be very effective. The following example illustrates a music therapist working with a small, inclusive infant group in a local daycare facility.

Service Provider: Music therapist
Course: Infants (ages 2–12 months)
Infants: 7
Targeted Infants: 2 (visual tracking difficulties and delays in child development)

Problem: One infant with special needs was very fussy throughout the day; however, when music was played the baby would often become calm and attentive. The teachers used music daily with the babies but were looking for new resources, materials, and activities to do with very young children. The daycare teachers contacted the music therapist and music therapy services were provided.

Strategies: 1. Provide a variety of appealing age appropriate music activities (singing, playing, moving, and creating).
2. Use eye-catching visual aids (puppets, stuffed animals, small colorful streamers, etc.).
3. Present many different sound sources (be sensitive to young ears).
4. Limit the use of recorded music. Infants need to hear unaccompanied singing as well.

Outcomes: Music therapy sessions occurred once a week for one-half hour. Two daycare teachers, three foster grandparents and occasionally parents, and volunteers from local universities and the community assisted the music therapist. Some babies sat on the laps of the staff while others sat next to staff members in the circle in bouncer chairs. The infants responded well to music and many times did not want the music to stop. The staff enjoyed receiving new music resources and activities and subsequently shared the babies' favorite music selections/activities with their parents.

EXAMPLE 14

Earliest childhood is a time of total exploration and continuous learning, and toddlers respond to everything in their environment with great curiosity and energy. Music offers a captivating avenue of learning and music therapy is considered a valuable compliment to learning programs for young children. In this example music therapy occurred in a small room once a week for 20–25 minutes. The teacher, two foster grandparents, three paraprofessionals, a vision specialist and often a physical therapist, parent, and/or university professor or student participated in the sessions led by a music therapist.

Service Provider: Music therapist
Course: Toddlers (ages 12–24 months)
Children: 16
Targeted Children: 4 (developmental, visual, hearing and physical disabilities and pervasive developmental disorder.)

Problem: Too many toddlers and adults for a small space strewn with toys and obstacles on the floor. Some of the adults talked aloud and were generally insensitive to the sound environment. The children focused on initial sounds but were unable to sustain attention. Music was not conducive to learning and often led to physical aggression resulting in unhappiness.

Strategies: Music therapist collaborated with the teacher to (1) eliminate unrelated clutter, (2) train the staff to listen and to assist in nonverbal ways when music is heard, and (3) plan effective developmentally appropriate activities for toddlers' learning and fun.

Outcomes: Everyone in the room increased their listening skills and participation became wholehearted and joyous. The music itself structured learning experiences as children used speech and language, moved, dramatized, played instruments, created sound effects for favorite books, and transitioned successfully from physically active to calming activities.

EXAMPLE 15

Preparing children for success in school has been a major focus in school systems throughout the United States. A national goal has been that all children will start school ready to learn (U.S. Department of Education, 1995). Music therapists and early childhood educators can work collaboratively toward accomplishment of this goal. They need to plan activities that will prepare young children academically, socially, and musically for successful educational experiences. Music therapy services are provided for students with special needs in self-contained classrooms, integrated classroom settings, and inclusive early intervention classes. The effect of integrating exceptional and nonexceptional students through music has been described in the professional literature (Hughes, Robbins, McKenzie, & Robb, 1990; Humpal, 1991).

The early intervention classes prepare 4-year-old children for readiness to become successful learners in the kindergarten classroom and are comprised of typically developing children and children with varying exceptionalities (Standley & Hughes, 1996, 1997). Below are examples of pre-K music therapy programs.

Service Provider: Music Therapist
Course: Early intervention class (pre-K)
Ages: Four and Five Years
Students: 21
Targeted Students: 10 (varying exceptionalities)

Problem: 1. Social: increasing acceptable group interaction, following classroom and music rules.
2. Academic: increasing attending, group participation and basic skills (e.g., colors, numbers, letters).
3. Music: maintaining a steady beat, recognizing differences-same and different (form), developing singing voices and song repertoire, increasing expressive music performance.

Strategies: The music therapist worked with the entire class once a week for 30 minutes. The classroom teacher and a paraprofessional participated with the children in all activities. The music therapist provided the classroom teacher with lesson plans and any other materials necessary to enable the teacher to continue the activities later.

Outcomes: All students enjoyed singing, playing instruments, listening, moving, and creating music. Having weekly music therapy sessions enhanced the students' positive social interactions. The typical children were good role models for the children with special needs as they all engaged in appealing music activities. The students not only improved social and academic skills but music skills as well, thus increasing the possibility for successful music experiences in kindergarten music. The classroom teacher voiced appreciation having new music activities to use. It was evident by a consistent increase in students' participation levels that the teacher was presenting the materials effectively between sessions.

EXAMPLE 16

In this example 3- and 4-year-olds attend school four half-days per week in classrooms not usually grouped homogeneously by disability. Because teaching children with hearing impairments requires specialized teaching skills, a program was developed for children with hearing impairments together with children whose hearing was typical but who had other developmental delays. This class also ran longer than the typical 3-hour pre-kindergarten session, so teachers were looking for interventions that would be educational and therapeutic, as well as appropriate to a young child's attention span.

Service Provider: Music therapist or music therapy intern
Course: Pre-kindergarten children with hearing impairments and/or developmental delays
Students: 8
Targeted Students: 5 with hearing impairments, 3 with developmental delays

Problem: While all children in the classroom had goals for increasing attending, appropriate social interaction, turn taking and basic pre-academic skills, the children with hearing impairments also needed interventions focused on developing their residual hearing.

Strategies: 1. A session structure appropriate to all of the classroom children was put in place to provide predictability and familiarity. Signed vocabulary associated with this structure was used consistently throughout.
2. Musical activities involving stop/start, sound/silence, moving to a beat, and distinguishing among different sounds were developed that also incorporated pre-academic concepts such as color identification, animal identification and counting.
3. All children were encouraged to make sounds with their voices, bodies, and rhythm instruments within an appropriate group structure. Students were also invited to respond physically to each other's sounds and to sound events created by the service provider.

Outcomes: The children with hearing impairments grew in their abilities to respond to their aural environments as evidenced by increased ability and accuracy in following directions. All children benefited from the use of sign language in language acquisition. The teacher developed a similar structure for use in nonmusic therapy circle time.

Elementary

EXAMPLE 17

The music classroom is considered one of the most positive general education environments for combining students with special needs with others of their own age (Atterbury, 1989). Generally, the music activities can be designed to include a wide range of abilities and rates of learning in students. Students with special needs engage in music learning activities with others through singing, listening, reading and notating music, playing instruments, moving to music, creating, and evaluating.

This example illustrates consultant services in a mainstreamed elementary general music classroom. Music therapists sometimes provide assistance through university music students assigned to work with music educators and students who need additional support in the music classroom. In this example, a university music education practicum student worked with seven students in grades four and five. These students were chosen by the music educator as needing extra practice in rhythmic coordination and reading notation. (Refer to a previous section describing preservice experiences for university music students.)

Service Provider: University music education practicum student
Course: Fourth and fifth grade general music
Students Enrolled: 36
Targeted Students: 7 (learning disabilities and moderate mental handicaps)

Problem: 1. Rhythmic coordination
             2. Reading notation
             3. Off-task behavior

Strategies: Targeted students met with the university music student once each week in a small room to practice skills in identified problem areas through singing, clapping, marching, and playing percussion instruments. The practicum student also came once a week to the music classroom to assist the teacher and students needing additional assistance. Small group sessions were organized around the overall task of producing a music video to demonstrate the students' improved skills. A token system was introduced which allowed the students to purchase parts, instruments, and costumes for the music video.

Outcomes: Once the students had an opportunity to get more individualized attention, they increased their level of participation. With additional assistance in the music classroom and individual practice sessions, the students showed much improvement in rhythmic coordination skills, notation reading skills, and social behavior. Making the video was a rewarding experience for the students. Even though several had received academic warnings in music in the past, not one student received a warning during this particular marking period.

EXAMPLE 18

Music therapy is provided for students in total inclusion elementary schools. The school district defines inclusive education as an approach to education that allows all students with disabilities to attend their home schools, working in a regular education class, while receiving individualized support.

The following example illustrates the effectiveness of music therapy in a total inclusion setting. Twenty-four to 28 children were in each of the four classes served. Sessions were conducted twice a week for 3 months and lasted for 30 minutes each. Each week, the sessions alternated between small groups and entire classes. Fifteen children with special needs in grades kindergarten through five were chosen by their teachers to participate in the small groups.

Service Provider: Music therapy intern
Course: Four total inclusion classes
                      (kindergarten–second, first, third, third–fifth)
Students Enrolled: 24–28 in each class
Targeted Students: 15 (learning disabilities, attention deficit disorder, hyperactive behavior and severe speech deficiencies)

Problem: For targeted students with special needs:
             1. Socialization skills: increasing self control, extending on-task behavior, building self confidence, developing leadership abilities.
             2. Speech/Language and academic skills: increasing vocalizations and letter/sounds, word recognition.
             For the entire class:
             1. Working together as a group, increasing positive responses, following directions, taking turns, improving on-task behavior, and developing positive attitudes to increase class unity.

Most of the children had not been participating appropriately within classroom group activities, lacked confidence in their own abilities, and were not well respected by their peers. Several of the classes had severe morale problems due to children not getting along together.

Strategies: The music therapy intern worked separately once a week with a small group that included targeted students and classroom peers. The students selected for the small sessions were chosen by the classroom teachers. The small group setting was used as a means to develop rapport and trust with each child, to give positive reinforcement, to offer a safe environment for response, to practice skills before participating with the whole class, and to assess the ability of each child and how to best initiate leadership roles within the larger group.

Outcomes: By the end of the 3-month period, the targeted children were standing before the entire group leading successful and exciting activities with confidence and much enthusiasm. Comments by the classroom teachers were very supportive of music therapy in the inclusive classroom. The following are typical examples:
"The targeted children gained self confidence and are becoming contributing members in a group."
"I feel that strides were taken in terms of whole-group cooperation."
"This experience with the entire class has been very encouraging to me because it has brought unity among my children."

EXAMPLE 19

Children with orthopedic impairments receive music therapy in groups at the elementary and middle school levels. Typical goals include increased fine and gross motor dexterity, increased willingness to engage in motor activities, increased independence in motor tasks, development of decision making skills, and reinforcement of classroom academic themes.

Service Provider: Music therapist or music therapy intern
Course: Orthopedic Impairments Program (elementary level)
Students: 7

Problem: In an elementary school class of children with orthopedic impairments, the teacher reported that with the inclusion of a new student in the classroom, students demonstrated difficulty with group unity and decision-making skills.

Strategies: 1. Students were given the goal of a group performance at the Very Special Arts Festival.
2. The music therapist led discussion and interactive movement experiences about student music preferences and types of performance modes open to them.
3. Students were offered choices among interpreting a song using sign language; developing a routine using scarves, streamers, or a parachute; and creating an instrument ensemble as activities that would be appropriate in a public performance. Each of these would involve fine and gross motor development.
4. Samples of carefully chosen music were presented for discussion and decision-making.
5. The music therapist helped in structuring student suggestions into a performance routine.

Outcomes: The students choreographed, practiced and performed an age-appropriate routine involving IEP mandated fine and gross motor skills for more than 300 typically developing and special needs peers at the Very Special Arts Festival. Group acceptance of the new student improved, and the students expressed ownership and pride in the performance.

EXAMPLE 20

Students in a behavioral disorder program are frequently excluded from music education experiences due to behaviors that keep them and others from learning in the typical educational environment. Therefore, in addition to working on goals such as group unity, following rules and directions, and appropriate expression of emotions, district music therapists often include music education elements in the therapeutic session. Musical skills learned can then be used for personal expression and group projects such as drumming and other instrumental ensembles.

Service Provider: Music therapist or music therapy intern
Course: Behavioral Disorders Program (elementary level)
Students: 12

Problem: A class of students with behavioral disorders were invited to attend a professional percussion ensemble performance at a local university. Behavior exhibited by students in the class during past performances caused teachers to be leery about agreeing to such a trip. The music therapist was asked to work with the class on appropriate audience behaviors and to prepare them as fully as possible for the experience.

Strategies: 1. A token system involving behavioral expectations during music therapy was developed so that students could earn the right to attend the concert.
2. Students listened to samples of percussion ensembles from various cultures and discussed similarities and differences.
3. Audience skills (listening quietly, keeping still bodies, and clapping at the end of performances for appropriate amounts of time) were discussed and practiced for each recorded sample heard and for student-contrived performances.

Outcomes: All students behaved in such a way during music therapy as to earn the privilege of attending the concert, and student behavior during the trip was much improved over previous trips. Follow-up work was completed after the concert in which small groups of students developed their own percussion ensembles and performed for each other using their new skills as good audiences.

EXAMPLE 21

Students with Severe Emotional Behavior Disorder (SEBD) receive services through a specialized program. This program includes behavior intervention plans (BIP) for students that are established and monitored by a county behavior specialist. Students in this population need remediation in establishing satisfactory interpersonal relationships with peers and/or teachers, increasing the ability to learn, management of inappropriate types of behavior or feelings, and overall elevation of mood. Due to the engaging and interactive nature of music, music therapy interventions have proven successful with this population.

Service Provider: Music therapy intern
Course: Beginning level guitar instruction (second–fifth grade)
Students: 6
Targeted Students: 6 with SEBD as primary diagnosis

Problem: Students in the SEBD classroom had difficulties working together on group projects. Students often made rude comments to their fellow students and to school staff creating an overall negative classroom environment. The SEBD teacher requested that the music therapy intern develop a program to promote a more positive classroom environment and promote group functioning.

Strategies: 1. After conducting music therapy sessions with the SEBD students, the music therapy intern identified an interest in learning to play the guitar. A guitar training program was developed to teach basic strumming and finger position for three chords.

2. Upon initiating the guitar training program, the music therapy intern led a classroom discussion focused on teamwork and making positive remarks while learning the guitar together. The class decided to work together in order to perform one song at the school-wide holiday program.

3. The music therapy intern established a point system to record appropriate and positive behavior skills exhibited during guitar training sessions. Appropriate skills included complimenting fellow students, following directions, exhibiting good listening skills and handling the guitar appropriately. A reward was given at the end of each session for receiving a total of 10 points during guitar training sessions.

Outcomes: The music therapy intern reported a dramatic improvement in student behavior during guitar training sessions. The point system and interest in learning to play the guitar contributed to an increased positive classroom environment. Students successfully performed a song together on the school-wide holiday program. Students reported feelings of accomplishment and pride following their performance.

EXAMPLE 22

Students with speech and language disorders exhibit problems with articulation, fluency, voice projection and language skills (Blumberg, 1975). Students in this population often struggle in the area of reading skills and comprehension. Research has proven that music can be an effective tool in improving reading skill and language abilities (Hoskins, 1988; Madsen, 1991; Roskam, 1979; Shunk, 1999; Towell, 2000).

Service Provider: Music therapist
Course: Speech and Language Disorders Program (first–third grade)
Students: 7

Problem: Due to delays in the receptive/expressive communication process and basic reading skills, students expressed frustration with reading books, stories, poems, or song lyrics and struggled to discuss content with teacher, speech pathologist, and music therapist.

Strategies: 1. Sound effects were used and created by the students to accompany stories.

2. Short songs were integrated within the telling of stories in an effort to provide repetition of important story content.

3. Interactive materials were used in conjunction with stories and song activities such as: story boards, a storyteller vest, song cards, and puppets.

4. Students participated in songwriting activities in which they created songs telling an original story or songs about a story they had read individually or in class.

Outcomes: Students exhibited increased on-task behavior when music was integrated with reading activities. Students also improved their ability to comprehend and relate information about stories and song activities following music therapy strategies. The classroom teacher, speech pathologist and music therapist all reported a rise in overall student ability to answer questions about story and song content following.

Secondary and Older

EXAMPLE 23

Students with autism often demonstrate self-stimulating behavior in an effort to organize their surrounding environment. Activities promoting sensory stimulation and integration help to decrease these behaviors and enhance interactions. This example demonstrates how sensory integration can be used during music therapy sessions.

Service Provider: Music therapist
Course: Autism Program (secondary level)
Students: 9
Targeted Students: 3 students with disruptive self-stimulating behavior

Problem: During music therapy sessions with a group of students with autism, targeted students exhibited numerous self-stimulating behaviors. Self-stimulating behaviors included rocking, hand flicking, and off-task verbalizations. One student perseverated by repeating song titles over and over, past the end of activities. The music therapist struggled to maintain interest and interaction during music activities due to this behavior.

Strategies: 1. Music therapy structured to provide sensory input to students. Activities included the use of massagers, scarves, and textured objects for tactile stimulation; picture cards and props for visual stimulation; and fine and gross motor movement to provide proprioceptive and vestibular stimulation.
2. A choice board was created with three sections: "choices," "now playing," and "all done." A picture of each song or activity was placed in the "choices" section. Following a musical greeting, students took turns choosing an activity and placing it in the "now playing" section. Upon conclusion, the picture for the activity was placed in the "all done" section of the choice board by the student who chose it.

Outcomes: Increased sensory input led to a successful reduction of self-stimulating behavior in two of the three students targeted. The third student continued to verbalize at all times and often rocked or touched students around him. The "all done" section on the choice board was highly successful in making the conclusion of an activity more concrete for the student who had previously perseverated in this area. Interestingly, allowing the students to choose activities and steer the course of the session often led to student choices deemed appropriate at that time by the music therapist. As an example, if the students had just done an activity with a high level of movement and energy the next student would often choose a calming and quieting activity to follow just as the music therapist would have chosen.

EXAMPLE 24

Service Provider: Music therapy team
Course: Inclusive Annual Holiday Play (middle school level)
Students: 18 selected from 4 schools
Targeted Students: 12 (intellectual disabilities)

Problem: Given the large scope and inclusive nature of the Annual Holiday Play (see Example 10), ways to incorporate more than just elementary school students was preferred and sought.

Strategies: 1. Explore options for involving middle schoolers. Music for the Holiday Play comes from popular recordings, pieces performed by a live elementary school choir, and recordings made by students at a professional recording studio. Plan ways to involve middle schoolers at the studio.

2. Teach students with moderate intellectual disabilities at the middle school level three to five songs from the script. Arrange a trip to the recording studio with typically functioning peers.

3. Encourage classes from which the students were chosen to attend the play to hear and recognize their contribution and to see it interpreted by classes of children with special needs.

Outcomes: The middle school students learned standard child and adult music repertoire. They displayed appropriate skills in following directions, self control and vocal performance skills in order to participate in the recording. Attending the play performance was particularly meaningful to the middle school singers because many of them had participated in the Holiday Play productions during their elementary school years.

EXAMPLE 25

Service Provider: Music therapy intern
Course: High school general music
Students Enrolled: 10
Targeted Students: 10 (severe emotional handicaps)

Problem: The students were referred to this center school for behavior disturbances too severe to be handled in a traditional public school setting. A behavior program was strictly enforced throughout the day. Student behaviors were closely monitored and a point system was used which enabled the students to gain and lose points for academic and social behaviors. All students exhibited difficulty working together as a group, following directions, and speaking appropriately to one another.

Strategies: The music class met once a week for one-half hour. Several students had above average music skills, especially excelling in rhythmic activities. Students studied music from other cultures (Africa, Latin America, Israel, and Indonesia). Visual aids, video tapes and live music performances effectively enhanced the music experience. Many Orff chants were utilized so that the students could read written notation and play individual parts on various instruments.

Outcomes: The students enjoyed making music and performed well as an ensemble. They learned to analyze group performances, using appropriate music and critiquing vocabulary, in a positive way while respecting others opinions. During the holiday season, the students performed for the entire school. The performance was a big success, not just in the enjoyment of the audience, but in the manner in which the students presented themselves to their peers with great confidence.

EXAMPLE 26

Students in the Severe and Profound Intellectual Disability (SID/PID) populations are often socially withdrawn because of limited, if any, verbal skills. When addressing student participation in the school environment, assistive and augmentative technology can be helpful for professionals working with students with Severe and Profound Intellectual Disabilities. This example suggests how technology can be included in the music therapy setting.

Service Provider: Music therapist or music therapy intern
Course: Mixed-Model Intellectual Disabilities Program (High School Level)
Students: 7
Targeted Students: 3 students (nonverbal, SID, PID)

Problem: Issues around group interaction and student participation arose in a music therapy group containing students with moderate, severe and profound intellectual disabilities. The music therapist, intern, and classroom teacher agreed that the nonverbal students were being left out of some activities because they could not interject answers or communicate thoughts or ideas independently. Goals in common for the music therapy environment and the classroom environment with this student group included making choices and appropriately interacting with peers. These goals were complicated to address with nonverbal students because of their limited abilities.

Strategies: 1. Augmentative devices were provided for nonverbal students during a group greeting activity at the beginning of each music therapy session. The device had an age-appropriate peer voice recorded on it singing the words, "Hello, Everybody!" When it was a nonverbal students turn to sing hello. the student activated the device with or without assistance.
2. The music therapist and music therapy intern used voice output devices to have nonverbal students sing song phrases with the group and to make instrument choices.
3. Assistants were instructed to allow several seconds of response time to students given assistive devices in an effort to have students respond independently.
4. Where appropriate and with guidance, students with moderate intellectual disabilities served as partners to nonverbal students to enhance overall participation.

Outcomes: The best outcome of these strategies was that the use of augmentative and assistive technology in the music therapy setting generalized to the classroom environment and other school environments. Augmentative and assistive devices were sent with these students to mainstreamed settings. Students targeted by these strategies appeared more alert during music therapy when devices were used. One of the three students targeted gained independence in activating voice output devices. At the end of treatment, this student could sing song phrases with the class and make an instrument choice without assistance.

EXAMPLE 27

Service Provider: Music therapist or music therapy intern
Course: Intellectual Disabilities Program (secondary level)
Students: 30

Problem: A middle and high school curriculum focusing on functional recreation and leisure skills was developed for students with intellectual disabilities. A portion of this curriculum deals with operation of stereo equipment. Students at the secondary level often have access to their preferred recordings and stereo equipment at home, but do not have the functional skills to operate this equipment.

Strategies: 1. Teach sight word and symbols to students using visuals with songs, raps, and chants that include singing, body percussion and instruments.
2. Teach students the stereo functions associated with each word and symbol through discussion and interaction with a portable stereo system. When students make appropriate choices that cause their preferred music to play, encourage them to dance and sing to the music as reinforcement.

3. Teach transfer from one stereo system to similar but different systems by bringing various equipment into the classroom.

4. Conclude with a trip to a local stereo sales room, where students may demonstrate their skills on many types of equipment with music therapist, intern, teacher, and paraprofessional guidance.

Outcomes: Students reported being better able to play music for themselves at home and in the car, making them more independent and giving them more choices that affect their environments.

EXAMPLE 28

Service Provider: Music therapist or music therapy intern
Course: Intellectual Disabilities Program (high school level)
Students: 30

Problem: At the high school level, a key component of the music therapy curriculum is learning standard adult repertoire. As each new song is learned, places where students might hear the song are discussed. The county's overall academic curriculum for special education emphasizes functional use of skills in the community and real life settings. However, discussion of standard adult repertoire had taken place primarily within the classroom setting.

Strategies: 1. Discuss options for performance of such skills outside the classroom.
2. Discuss alternatives with classroom teachers at the high school level.
3. Prepare students for three performances: the "Star Spangled Banner" at Special Olympics, holiday carols at various school district and community venues, and standard campfire songs at Scouting Outing (see Example 11).

Outcomes: These performances have become annual events. Middle school students look forward to seeing the performance of the "Star Spangled Banner" by the high school students as a rite of passage. All students experience the reinforcement of performance before a warm and appreciative crowd.

EXAMPLE 29

An innovative secondary general music class was initiated and coordinated by music therapists at the high school level. The course, Introduction to Music Performance, was offered at a local high school to students in grades 9 through 12 as a mainstreamed collaborative model. It addressed the nine content standards in the National Standards for Arts Education (1994) and the concepts and intended outcomes specified in the state's course Introduction to Music Performance (Florida Department of Education, 1989). Special features of this class included guest appearances by various performing artists from the community and universities, and collaborative teaching by the music teacher, music therapists, music therapy interns, and university secondary music education students. Funds for this collaborative model were provided by a state Arts in Education Grant.

Service Providers: Music therapists, music teacher, music therapy interns, secondary music education practicum students
Course: Introduction to Music Performance
Students Enrolled: 26
Targeted Students: 10 (CBI)

Problem: Few music courses of a truly inclusive nature are currently available in regular high schools. High school general music classes offer the rare exception.

Strategies: The class met daily for 50 minutes in the high school choral room. The student enrollment included general students with little music background, advanced music students from choral and instrumental backgrounds, and students enrolled in community-based instruction. Approximately one third of the class members were from ESE. A variety of performing artists from the community were responsible for teaching two classes each. Presentations were given in the following areas: Folk and Commercial Music; African Dance and Music; Latin American Music; Choral Styles; Technology: Arranging and Composing for TV; Dance/Movement; Concert Percussion; Opera and Music Theater; and Asian Music. Sessions included artists' performances and related participatory activities led by the artists themselves. Between artists' visits, the music teacher, music therapists, and other instructional team members reviewed and prepared for the artists' visits. They also led the class in other music learning activities: exploring sound; organizing sound; defining music; and illustrating melody, rhythm, harmony, and form. The intended student outcomes for the class were:

1. Play or sing simple musical works in a performance situation.
2. Identify common instruments visually and aurally.
3. Create and play simple melodic and rhythmic passages.
4. Identify major music ensembles (e.g., band, orchestra, chorus, jazz combo, swing choir).
5. Name major music eras and composers in each.
6. Identify varied ethnic or cultural musical styles.
7. Explain the importance of music in everyday life.
8. Express personal music tastes with appropriate vocabulary.
9. Identify career opportunities in music.

Outcomes: The intended student outcomes were met in varying degrees for all members of the class (Hughes, 1992). Students as a whole developed a great amount of enthusiasm for the performing artists' presentations. In addition, they indicated increased awareness of arts opportunities available to them in the community and in the media. They could name a variety of career opportunities in the arts. Perhaps the most pleasing aspect of their growth was evidenced through their spoken words in class. Analysis of their comments indicated that the students (especially the ones with advanced intellectual and musical skills) were broadening their attitudes of open-mindedness toward different kinds of music and different kinds of experiences. The mainstreamed class provided an opportunity for students to participate together through the activities. It allowed some of the students from the CBI class the opportunity to "shine" through their music abilities. Students were asked to evaluate the impact of the community artists on their feelings about music and the course. The written evaluations were quite positive in most respects. Some of the students expressed their feelings better in conversation. A girl from the CBI class told an instructor that "this was the best, most fun class I have ever had!" A girl with advanced skills made a memorable comment during a class discussion on specific types of choral music. When another student said, "Gospel is music sung by black people," this student said, "I don't care if you are black, white, or Chinese. Anyone can sing gospel music! It's the style of the music that makes it gospel, not the singer's color!"

EXAMPLE 30

Service Provider: Music therapy intern
Course: Introduction to Music Performance
Student Enrolled: 1 (homebound)

Problem: A high school junior was diagnosed with acute scleroderma and was subsequently enrolled in homebound education in order to continue her course work. She had been a member of her school's gospel choir and was referred for music therapy because of her expressed interest in music.

Strategies: Music therapy was provided once a week to address goals developed by the student, her homebound teachers and a music therapy intern. She was then engaged in a variety of music experiences to address the goals set in the skill areas of motor, social, music, and academics.

Outcomes: By the end of the school year she had successfully mastered all music therapy goals and objectives. Due to her progress, she continued to receive music therapy at home the following year when she returned to school half-time. Through music therapy services, she completed requirements for Introduction to Music Performance and received an "A" for the course. She also earned course credit needed to graduate with her class.

EXAMPLE 31

Music therapists in the district provide support upon request to high school choral directors. They work as consultants or directly with the music teacher in the high school mainstreamed choral class. Music therapists also act as liaisons between the choral and special education teachers, and observe and support students in the choral class setting.

In this example, a music therapy intern developed and field tested curriculum materials to provide support for students and teachers in choral classes. The materials were designed for students on functional curriculums such as CBI. They could also be used in other music courses such as piano and general music.

Service Provider: Music therapy intern
Course: High school chorus
Students Enrolled: 50
Targeted Students: 4 (CBI)

Problem: At least 30 minutes of choral class time each week was devoted to written work on music fundamentals. The music teachers reported that students from the CBI class were either doing nothing or were drawing pictures while the rest of the class worked in their music theory workbooks. The teachers wanted music related materials that were age appropriate and within the students' ability.

Strategies: A 90-page music theory workbook was developed by a music therapy intern. Before writing the materials, she observed in the choral class and in the CBI class, consulted with all of the teachers involved, and did an extensive review of beginning keyboard theory books and other literature sources.

Outcomes: Four students used the materials successfully during field testing. High school choral teachers have continued to use the adaptive workbook materials with students who need to work at that level. The workbook has also been successfully used in middle school choral and general music classes.

EXAMPLE 32

Music therapists, music therapy interns, and trained musicians from the local universities and community are available to provide support upon request to high school students and teachers in mainstreamed instrumental programs. In this example, a music therapy intern provided support for students and the music teacher in a beginning keyboard class. The teacher had experienced teaching small numbers of students with disabilities in the past and had developed a caring and supportive attitude toward ALL learners. She also had engaged in university study in special education.

Service Provider: Music therapy intern
Course: Beginning Keyboard
Students Enrolled: 20
Targeted Students: 9 (severe disabilities)

Problem: Too many students with very special needs were in one class. Most of the nine students were unable to work independently or to perform together with the rest of the class at functional levels. Due to the nature of piano study, all of the students in the class needed some individual assistance during independent practice times. Adequate assistance for all of the students could not be provided by one teacher and a special education paraprofessional who was sometimes present. In addition, there were instances of inappropriate social behavior on the part of some students.

Strategies: Extra support in the piano classroom was provided two days per week for one semester by the music therapy intern. She helped any of the students needing assistance, but most of the time was spent working with the students with special needs on social and piano skills. She and the special education paraprofessional developed strategies for use by the paraprofessional on days when the intern was not present. She also collaborated with the piano teacher regarding lesson planning and occasionally consulted with special education personnel.

Outcomes: The music teacher expressed gratitude for the assistance offered by the music therapy intern. It not only provided help for the students and relief for the teacher, but also a line of communication between teacher and special education support personnel. This enabled the teacher to specify her needs, especially as they pertained to scheduling in the best interest of all the students.

Adult Education

EXAMPLE 33

Students with special needs attend public school until the age of 21. Following graduation many students find full or part-time employment, while others may attend adult job training/placement programs. Music therapy can assist in improving job related socials skills such as working together, discussing and analyzing within a group setting, and leadership skills which are all necessary skills for employment. Music therapists may also work toward increasing an awareness of leisure time activities for personal enjoyment and facilitating integration into the community. Below is an example of music therapy in an adult education facility.

Service Providers: Music therapist
Course: Adult education (ages 21–55)
Students Enrolled: 32 (developmental disabilities, hearing impairments, physical impairments)

Problem: Classroom teachers were concerned that the adults were not spending their leisure time constructively. During the school day some of the students had part-time jobs, while others studied basic job coping skills, reading, writing, and computer skills at the education center. However, at home many students simply watched television or listened to music.

Strategies: 1. Provide a monthly calendar of activities and current music events going on in the community.
2. Present music from featured events in the community to familiarize students with that particular style of music, thus inspiring the students to attend.
3. Introduce a wide variety of styles of music.
4. Discuss ways in which to incorporate music into everyday life (during work break or weekend leisure activities).

Outcomes: Music therapy sessions occurred once a week for 45 minutes. The students enjoyed experiencing many different styles of music (classical, jazz, folk, multicultural, musical theater). Following each session, the music therapist presented to each student a list of music selections studied in class. Many made purchases from the list at local music stores, thus increasing their home music libraries. Several students attended local concerts, musicals, and festivals in the community and discussed their experiences with enthusiasm. For some, transportation problems hindered eager students from attending local concerts, especially evening performances. Classroom teachers and the music therapist made contacts pertaining to transportation needs. The music therapist suggested additional contacts such as the local Commission for Transportation of the Disadvantaged. The classroom teachers indicated that the students were beginning to explore new ways to use leisure time at home and in the community. They thanked the music therapist for this service and were pleased to see their students involved more in arts events in the community.

Working as a music therapist in a district-wide public school setting can be demanding, challenging, and definitely rewarding. It is also a job that is very comprehensive and full of professional opportunity. It is essential that music therapists stay abreast of current research and other professional literature dealing with issues pertaining to the public schools in order to find new and exciting ways to educate students with special needs. For the latest information on school related issues, it is recommended that music therapists not only consult music therapy research and clinical publications, but also those of other organizations such as The Council for Exceptional Children, The Music Educators National Conference, and The National Association for the Education of Young Children. Readers are invited to contact the authors of this chapter for additional information on music therapy in their individual school districts.

References

Alley, J. M. (1979). Music in the IEP: Therapy/Education. *Journal of Music Therapy, 16,* 111–127.

Atterbury, B.W. (1986). A survey of present mainstreaming practices in the southern United States. *Journal of Music Therapy, 23,* 202–207.

Atterbury, B.W. (1989). *Mainstreaming exceptional learners in music.* Englewood Cliffs, NJ: Prentice Hall.

Blumberg, H.(1975) *A program of sequential language development.* Springfield, IL: Charles C. Thomas.

The Consortium of National Arts Education Associations. (1994). *National Standards for Arts Education.* Reston, VA: Music Educators National Conference.

Darrow, A. A. (1999) Music educators' perceptions regarding the inclusion of students with severe disabilities in music classrooms. *Journal of Music Therapy, 36*(4), 254–273.

Florida Department of Education, Division of Public Schools. (1989). *Introduction to music performance: A secondary school guide for Florida schools.* Tallahassee, FL: Author.

Ford, A., Schnorr, R., Meyer, L., Davern, L., Black, J., & Dempsey, P. (Eds.). (1989). *The Syracuse community-referenced curriculum guide for students with moderate and severe disabilities*. Baltimore: Paul H. Brookes.

Frisque, J., Niebur, L., & Humphreys, J. T. (1994). Music mainstreaming: Practices in Arizona. *Journal of Research in Music Education, 42*, 94–104.

Gfeller, K., Darrow, A. A., & Hedden, S. K. (1990). On the ten-year anniversary of P.L. 94-142. The perceived status of mainstreaming among music educators in the states of Iowa and Kansas. *Journal of Research in Music Education, 38*, 90–101.

Graham, R. (1972). Seven million plus need special attention. *Music Educators Journal, 58*(8), 22–25.

Groene, R. (2001). The effect of presentation and accompaniment styles on attentional and responsive behaviors of participants with dementia diagnoses. *Journal of Music Therapy, 38*, 36–50.

Hoskins, C. (1988). Use of music to increase verbal response and improve expressive language abilities of preschool language delayed children. *Journal of Music Therapy, 25*(2), 73–84.

Hughes, J. E. (1991). Sing, everyone. *General Music Today, 4*, 8–9.

Hughes, J. E., & Robbins, B. J. (1992). *Mainstreaming in school music, K–12: A model program guide for school districts*. Tallahassee, FL.

Hughes, J. E., Robbins, B. J., & King, R. J. (1988). A survey of perception and attitudes of exceptional student educators toward music therapy services in a county-wide school district. *Journal of Music Therapy, 4*, 26–32.

Hughes, J. E., Robbins, B. J., McKenzie, B. A., & Robb, S. S. (1990). Integrating exceptional and non-exceptional young children through music play: A pilot program. *Music Therapy Perspectives, 8*, 52–55.

Hughes, J. E., Robbins, B. J., Smith, D. S., & Kincade, C. F. (1987). The effect of particiation in a public school choral music curriculum on singing abilitiy in trainable mentally handicapped adolescents. *Music Education for the Handicapped, 2*, 1–35.

Hughes, W. O. (1992). Two programs for high-risk students. *General Music Today, 5*, 20.

Humpal, M. E. (1991). The effects of an integrated early childhood music program on social interaction among children with handicaps and their typical peers. *Journal of Music Therapy, 27*(3), 166–177.

Johnson, F. L. (1996). Models of service delivery. In B. L. Wilson (Ed.), *Models of music therapy interventions in school settings: From institution to inclusion* (pp. 48–77). Silver Spring, MD: National Association for Music Therapy.

Madsen, S. (1991). The effect of music paired with and without gestures on the learning and transfer of new vocabulary: Experimenter-derived nonsense words. *Journal of Music Therapy, 28*(4), 222–230.

McGinnis, E., & Goldstein, A. P. (1990). *Skillstreaming in early childhood: Teaching prosocial skills to the preschool and kindergarten child*. Champaign, IL: Research Press.

McGinnis, E., & Goldstein, A. P. (1997a). *Skillstreaming the elementary school child: A guide for teaching prosocial skills*. Champaign, IL: Research Press.

McGinnis, E., & Goldstein, A. P. (1997b) *Skillstreaming the adolescent: New strategies and perspectives for teaching prosocial skills*. Champaign, IL: Research Press.

Riegel, R. H., Mayle, J. A., & McCarthy-Henkel, J. (1988). *Beyond maladies and remedies: Suggestions and guidelines for adapting materials for students with special needs in the regular class*. Novi, MI: Author.

Robbins, B. J. (1989). *Florida music educators' attitudes toward mainstreaming*. Unpublished master's thesis, University of Kansas, Lawrence, KS.

Roskam, K. (1979). Music therapy as an aid for increasing auditory awareness and improving reading skill. *Journal of Music Therapy, 16*(1), 31–42.

Shunk, H. (1999). The effect of singing paired with signing on receptive vocabulary skills of elementary ESL students. *Journal of Music Therapy, 36*(2), 110–124.

Standley, J., & Hughes, J. (1996). Documenting developmentally appropriate objectives and benefits of a music therapy program for early intervention: A behavioral analysis. *Music Therapy Perspectives, 14*, 87–94.

Standley, J., & Hughes, J. (1997). An early intervention music curriculum for enhancing prereading/writing skills. *Music Therapy Perspectives, 15*, 79–86.

Towell, J. (2000). Motivating students through music and literature. *Reading Teacher, 53*(4), 284–287.

U. S. Department of Education. (1995). *A teacher's guide to the U.S. Department of Education.* Washington, DC: Author.

Appendix

Strategies

The strategies presented here address special needs of individuals in public school music settings. They were compiled by the authors from their own professional experiences with students, music therapy colleagues, music teachers, special educators, music therapy interns, practicum students, parents, and others working with students with special needs. The strategies have all proven to be effective in school music settings and specifically address the learning needs of students. This section can be used as a quick reference guide by music therapists working in school music settings.

Music Skills

Skill Area: Singing

Suggested Strategies

- Explore ways in which the voice moves up and down (e.g., compare the voice to an elevator)
- Produce sounds such as sirens, ghosts, owls.
- Use pictures, graphs, physical gestures and instruments to visually and/or aurally display movement of sound
- Use physical gestures (moving arms from high to low and vice versa)
- Provide good vocal models (peers, teachers, paraprofessionals)
- Echo sing phrases or individual tones within the appropriate vocal register
- Listen, think, and hum pitches before singing
- Use a minimum of accompaniment to focus on the vocal line
- Teach ostinatos, echo songs and rounds
- Discuss and demonstrate the differences between the speaking and singing voice
- Explore ways in which to use the voice (whisper, speak, scream, cry, laugh, hum, sing)
- Vocalize using vowel and consonant sounds
- Model deep breathing techniques
- Have the students take deep breaths in and out, laugh, yawn. Feel the muscular action and expansion of the rib cage
- Emphasize the relaxed jaw and open mouth position
- Whisper and speak words clearly
- Emphasize soft singing

- Have students hold an imaginary candle and slowly blow out the flame to improve breath control
- Sing phrases staccato, marcato, legato
- Use songs that elicit free vocalization on open syllables
- Allow the student time to respond vocally
- Use some songs with melodic and rhythmic repetition (e.g., repeated phrases, words or refrain after every verse)
- Find songs within the vocal range of the student having difficulty matching pitches
- Provide outside assistance to practice specific music skills such as solfege syllables and Curwen hand signs used in the Kodaly philosophy of teaching
- Have students put solfege syllables to favorite songs
- Provide several opportunities for students to hear the melody (sing it, outline the melody with your hand, use Curwen hand signs, play it on instruments)
- Incorporate sign language into song activities
- Practice matching pitches using kazoos, step bells, xylophone

Skill Area: Playing Instruments

Suggested Strategies

- Place instruments, visuals (charts, posters, flash cards) and yourself directly in front of the student's line of vision
- Use color coding or braille markings on instruments

- Have mallets in a variety of sizes available so that the student may find one that feels comfortable in his/her hand
- Remove wheelchair trays to enhance physical contact between students during instrument and action song activities
- Allow students with physical limitations to choose their manner of participation (they usually will tell you the successful way)
- Have a peer hold the instrument while the other student plays with his/her dominant hand
- Adapt instruments only after the student has demonstrated that he/she has difficulty manipulating it correctly
- Design rhythm activities that allow the student to respond in his/her own tempo or pattern
- Provide outside assistance to practice rhythm skills
- Echo clap rhythms
- Incorporate movement activities to develop a sense of basic beat and rhythm
- Practice using a variety of percussion instruments
- Use a variety of activities to develop rhythm skills (singing, clapping patterns, moving, playing the recorder and barred instruments, i.e., xylophones)
- Practice verbal and visual cues such as "ready," "begin," and "stop" during all activities
- Model correct playing techniques (peers, paraprofessionals, and teachers)
- Provide several opportunities for students to hear the rhythm patterns (clap it, sing it, play it on instruments)
- Provide outside assistance to practice playing barred instruments
- Use flash cards to teach the letter names on xylophones and other melodic instruments

Suggested Strategies for Recorder
(A wooden or plastic woodwind instrument)

- Provide outside assistance to practice recorder skills
- Use a variety of creative games, notation exercises and familiar songs when practicing recorder
- Provide much repetition

- Use appealing visuals (posters, flash cards, large music staff)
- Use Suzuki precorders for beginning recorder players

Skill Area: Listening

Suggested Strategies

- Keep directions simple—give a series of directions one step at a time (e.g., 1. "Open book"; 2. "Turn to page 1")
- Use movement to reinforce listening to form
- Provide several opportunities for students to hear the melody and rhythm patterns (sing it, clap it, play it on instruments)
- Play a familiar song; have students identify the "mystery tune"
- Sing a portion of a song and stop on a specific word. Students identify that word
- Sing a song. Students listen and sing silently (mouth words)
- Teach rhythm echo activities
- Use call and response songs
- Provide several visuals illustrating form, melody, rhythm, harmony, timbre
- Use activities that are short and simple with much repetition
- Use a multisensory approach (provide movement, visual aids, auditory cues, singing, playing creating)
- Place student closer to the sound source
- Provide visual cues through facial expressions, signs, movements, lights flicking, etc.
- Check with students wearing hearing aids to determine the optimum levels needed for music
- Use a variety of appealing sound sources to capture attention and motivate participation and musical growth

Skill Area: Moving

Suggested Strategies

- Provide sufficient space for wheelchairs
- Design activities that emphasize the students' motor strengths
- Provide activities for the student to develop body skills to move about the classroom with ease and safety

- Allow the student an opportunity to experience movement at his/her own level (moving eyes, fingers, head, hands, etc.)
- Train peers to assist students
- Remove wheelchair trays to enhance physical contact between students during activities
- Develop ways for all students to participate in activities involving dancing and moving through space. Wagons, tricycles, scooterboards, and other devices could be used if wheelchairs are not feasible
- Say and do all movements when first teaching a dance (step right, tap, tap)
- Partners perform side-to-side or face-to-face rather than pushing the wheelchair. Use two peers if necessary—one to push and one to be the partner
- If necessary, design alternative strategies so that all students participate in the same movement activities and reinforce music learning
- Move creatively with scarves, streamers, paper, parachutes, masks, puppets and other motivators

Skill Area: Creating/Composing

Suggested Strategies

- Have students create their own rhythm patterns and accompaniments
- Encourage exploration and improvisation
- Provide a comfortable environment in which students are free to risk sharing new ideas
- Encourage and ensure peer respect
- Design activities where the students can develop their own creative movements
- Use dramatization in the classroom to act out favorite songs, listening selections or environmental events
- Create sound pieces
- Use appealing stories and poems and have students create sound effects
- Use props such as colorful scarves, paper hats and articles from nature

Skill Area: Reading/Writing

Suggested Strategies

- Pair reading notation with visual and auditory cues (pair sound with symbol)
- Sing songs that will assist the student in remembering and understanding note values
- Practice various rhythms by using the verbal music concepts of Kodaly and Orff or any other consistent manner of counting
- Practice the names of the lines and spaces by using an oversized music staff
- Play word association games
- Provide opportunities for repetition with fun ways to practice
- Provide outside assistance to practice reading and notation skills
- Break down the steps into the simplest form possible
- Use a variety of learning and response modes
- Demonstrate and model correct written response first
- Find alternative ways to evaluate the students
- Use repetition and visuals to teach musical language concepts
- Provide rote learning when reading is not possible
- Use clear and uncluttered charts
- ESE teacher provide magnified or braille materials if needed
- Adapt written worksheets if necessary
- Be aware that some students may need to be placed closer to written words and symbols to process the material

General Skills

Skill Area: Participating

Suggested Strategies

- Use a wide range of appealing activities to ensure success
- Have a peer or paraprofessional model appropriate responses
- Have a paraprofessional physically assist the student
- Use a variety of learning and response modes

- Vary classroom groupings (large groups, small groups)
- Place a "peer/buddy" next to the student to model correct responses
- Accept all efforts as praiseworthy
- Assign the student a "buddy" who can spend time with the student in other activities outside of the music class
- Provide individual praise within the group when the student participates
- Provide outside assistance to practice music skills
- Place student between two good role models

Skill Area: Staying On Task

Suggested Strategies

- Use positive reinforcement when the student is on task
- Teach small amounts of materials at a time and gradually increase the number and length of activities
- Provide outside assistance to practice music skills
- Use a multisensory approach (presenting information in many diverse ways)
- Present small tasks to accomplish and reinforce upon completion
- Seat student near teacher or paraprofessional
- Assign a student to be a "buddy/partner"
- Paraprofessional physically assist the student if necessary
- Teacher physically assist student if possible
- Place student in front of the room
- Give verbal cues to encourage the student to attend
- Upon completion of the music class, send a behavior sheet back to the ESE teacher
- ESE teacher reminds student just prior to the class what is expected of him/her in the music class
- ESE teacher provide positive reinforcement in the classroom for good progress at the conclusion of the music class
- Reinforce with verbal praise
- Give directions in multisensory ways (say it, point to it, write it)
- Provide a structured classroom environment

- Give directions more than once during an activity
- Reduce the number of distractions
- Look directly at the student when giving instructions
- Simplify tasks to the level of the student to ensure success
- Assign the student a "buddy" who can also spend time with the student in other fun activities outside of the music class
- Use appealing visual aids
- Provide a variety of fun and appealing activities (singing, moving, playing, creating)

Skill Area: Following Directions

Suggested Strategies

- Look directly at student when giving directions
- Limit the number of new ideas presented at one time
- Demonstrate while giving directions
- Have the student repeat step-by-step instructions as they are given to ensure understanding
- Simplify the tasks to ensure success
- Make your directions simple
- Model correct behaviors and responses
- Give directions in multisensory ways (say it, point to it, write it)
- Give directions more than once during an activity

Skill Area: Reducing Behavior Problems

Suggested Strategies

- Review the rules of appropriate social behavior in the music classroom prior to the class
- Model correct behaviors and responses
- Be firm and always positive
- Be consistent with student expectations, classroom rules, teaching routines and classroom environment
- Have paraprofessional sit next to student to provide assistance if necessary
- Instruct paraprofessional in nonverbal prompting techniques to prevent distractions or interruptions

- Place student next to a good peer role model
- Assign the student a "buddy" who can spend time with the student in other activities outside of the music class
- Recognize student success (social and musical)
- Provide much positive reinforcement for appropriate behavior
- Explain consequences for behaviors
- Use school-wide classroom warnings and time-out procedures
- Send the student back to the classroom only if he/she is very disruptive, making it difficult for other students to learn
- Place student in the front of the room
- Give directions more than once during an activity
- Discreetly use the same positive reinforcement program used in the ESE classroom to achieve the desired behavior in the music classroom
- Find the students' strengths and plan opportunities for success
- Through your own language model, encourage and ensure respect among peers

Skill Area: Improving Motivation

Suggested Strategies

- Place student next to a good role model and friend
- When doing small group work, assign a good role model and friend to that group
- Find the student's strengths and plan chances for small successes
- Provide much positive reinforcement when the student shows an interest
- Provide outside assistance to practice music skills
- Make the student feel comfortable when participating in class activities
- Provide a variety of fun and appealing activities
- Let the student know it is all right to make mistakes
- Relate music concepts to the student's interests and favorite music selections

Skill Area: Increasing Understanding

Suggested Strategies

- Present tasks slowly to allow for success, then gradually increase the level of music difficulty
- Model correct music responses
- Provide outside assistance to practice music skills
- Teach small amount of material at a time
- Place student closer to the teacher
- Provide a variety of activities
- Provide concrete examples
- Use dramatization to increase understanding by acting out song text and listening to musical selections
- Emphasize for the student specific music skills learned in all activities
- Provide much repetition in many fun ways
- Use several appealing visuals
- Provide immediate positive reinforcement
- Give directions clearly

Skill Area: Discussion/ Oral Expression

Suggested Strategies

- Have discussions about the songs
- Accept all efforts as praiseworthy
- Provide praise when student shows interest in the discussion
- Ask questions that require short "yes/no" responses
- Find the student's interest to encourage a greater feeling of comfort
- Use call and response songs
- Use visual aids (posters, rhythm flash cards)

16

MUSIC THERAPY FOR LEARNERS IN A COMMUNITY EARLY EDUCATION PUBLIC SCHOOL

Amelia Greenwald Furman

IN updating this chapter, it is clear that a discussion of music therapy in public schools must now include the importance of adaptability as an essential job skill. It is difficult to convey the tremendous but dispassionate changes that regularly take place in a large urban school system. Continuity is a tremendous challenge as the average length an urban superintendent remains in a district is 28 months. In the Minneapolis Public Schools, for example, there have been three district superintendents and four principals at the Longfellow Community School over the past 10 years. Over the years, my job has flexed and included a wide variety of titles and duties but I have been full time in one building for the last 7 years. Being in a single building means I am part of the overall school climate as well as part of an exceptional early childhood special education (ECSE) team. During the 2001–2002 school year, music therapy evaluations were funded for the first time at the district level and to be completed across the district.

New legislation passed by the state and implemented by several districts including Minneapolis brings another change. As of this writing, Minnesota is the only state utilizing an Interagency Individual Intervention Plan (known as the triple I-P [IIIP]) for students 4 and older. This extends the interagency cooperation of an Individual Family Service Plan (IFSP). The first part of this chapter will cover changes in public school settings with suggestions for maintaining programs, while the second part will cover options for services.

Background

Federal laws such as Public Law 94-142 and the Individuals with Disabilities Education Act (IDEA) impact education in every state. The federal mandates, however, are implemented differently in individual states and school districts. Each state sets requirements within the federal framework and each school district then sets its own policies and procedures to meet the requirements. Every school district negotiates a contract with a teachers union, which also impacts the delivery of services to children. Further, if the school district has implemented site-based management, then each individual school building designates how services and resources are utilized. This tidy flow chart is then impacted by the reality of the people who hold key positions. The goals and climate set by the district superintendent, the head of special education and finally the building principal all affects the programming the students receive. Additional changes in a school district are driven by a multitude of factors including change in the composition and needs of the community (new immigrants, low income housing, increase or decrease in students), a budget impacted by the federal lack of fully covering special education mandates, changing state budgets and mandates, city referendum funding, aging buildings and the cost of maintaining them, and, finally, the people interpreting and implementing the budget.

In some of the previous chapters, the music therapy programs described have been district-wide services. This means the music therapist is responsible to a program director and travels to different schools to provide services to specific special education classrooms. This chapter describes a program that has developed and changed over 10 years in an individual school within a large urban school district.

Minneapolis Public Schools

The largest district in Minnesota, the Minneapolis Public Schools provides educational services for about 50,000 students. At the present time, 68 of the 102 schools in the district serve elementary students. Early Childhood Special Education (ECSE) services may begin at birth. While the number fluctuates, there are approximately 235 children birth to 3 years of age currently receiving home-based services in the district. There are 25 ECSE classrooms throughout the district providing services for 400 students, age 3 to 5, depending upon enrollment.

Longfellow School

Longfellow was built in 1911 as an elementary school in the Minneapolis Public School System. Throughout the 1980s the school served as the primary Early Childhood Special Education (ECSE) site for the district. During this time all the classrooms in the building were self-contained and only for children who were receiving special education services. All students transferred to other schools when they reached kindergarten age. In 1991, several factors influenced a major change in settings where ECSE services were provided: (a) the realization that the least restrictive environment (LRE) did not mean simply being in a "regular" school building with only other special needs students, (b) the growing recognition of the positive impact that inclusion with peers as role models has for special education students (Falvey, Forest, Pearpoint, & Rosenberg, 1994), and (c) the move toward having special needs children attend schools in their own neighborhoods. The Early Childhood Special Education classes were dispersed throughout the district. At the present time, there are 25 classrooms in 17 sites. Longfellow School became an Early Education Center offering regular education classes for students in pre-kindergarten through the second grade. Three ECSE classes remained as part of the Longfellow program. As new superintendents implemented initiatives, listened, and reflected community concerns, district programs continued to change. Increased family involvement became a district focus, and programming was changed to support community schools, ensuring students were closer to their homes. Schools were reconfigured to reduce transitions and develop longer relationships with families. Many larger schools became kindergarten through eighth grade (K–8), while the small buildings were kindergarten through fifth. In order to accommodate more grade level classrooms, the special education programs continued to be dispersed to more schools. At the present time, almost every school has one or perhaps two classrooms providing different special education programs.

In 1999 two additional changes impacted the student population at Longfellow. First, the growing awareness and recognition of autism spectrum disorder (ASD) and the need for early intervention resulted in the development of ECSE autism specific classrooms (Scott, Clark, & Brady, 2000). Longfellow currently has two of the five ECSE-ASD classrooms in the district. Secondly, with the influx of Somalian refugees to the Minneapolis area, Longfellow was designated an English Language Learner (ELL) site in year 2000 to help meet the growing needs of the surrounding neighborhood.

Current Student Composition

The 370 current students represent the diversity found in the urban setting. The student population is approximately 30% African American, 4% Asian, 30% Caucasian, 4% Hispanic, 12% Native American, and 20% Somalian or other ELL. The entire school qualifies for Title 1 funds since about 76% of the students receive free or reduced cost lunches. This federal program, Improving America's Schools, provides partial funding for additional staff, parent programming, and materials. The focus of the Title 1 program is to improve children's learning.

Longfellow currently houses two ECSE-ASD classes and eight ECSE students who are part of the High-Five Inclusion Program. As part of the "regular education" program, there are 1.5 High Five rooms, each providing two sessions a day. This is a readiness program for children who turn 5 years of age after September 2 and before December 31. These children go to kindergarten the following year. There are 1.5 kindergarten rooms, and then a total of 10 classrooms of first through fifth grades complete the academic program. Approximately 10% of students between kindergarten and fifth grade have an Individualized Education Program (IEP). These students qualify for and receive special education services in the full inclusion setting. Full inclusion refers to those classrooms where a child with special needs spends the school day with their peers. There is also a before-and-after school child care program in the building.

Management Framework

The Longfellow program began operating with a *shared leadership team,* sometimes referred to as site-based management, in 1990 and continues with this management style today. This is part of an education reform movement leading to a restructured system trying to meet the changing demands of families and the community (Dettmer, Thurston, & Dyck, 1993). The leadership team includes the principal, teacher representatives, staff representatives (clerks, custodian, paraprofessionals), and parent representatives. Some teams also include community business representatives. The purpose of the shared leadership team is to support and refine the goals and mission of Longfellow Community School within the Minneapolis Public School District by:

1. serving as advocates for the students, parents, staff;
2. supporting the attainment of the school's improvement plan;
3. monitoring and evaluating the progress made toward the achievement of these goals; and
4. communicating the progress toward goals to the district administration, parents, staff, and community.

The mission of Longfellow Early Education Center is to promote in each child a love of learning, a respect for others, and a feeling of self-worth that will enable students to acquire a strong foundation of academic skills and challenge them to meet their intellectual, social, emotional, and physical potential. We strive to empower children to be responsible, contributing, and cooperative participants in their community.

Programming

Individual schools no longer have the responsibility to determine what curriculum, texts, and programming they wish to use. Reflecting the demand for accountability and test score improvement, there are once again district-wide curriculums, newly revised state graduation standards, and tests. However, it is still up to each school to determine the staffing and what subjects will be taught during classroom teacher preparation time. According to the Agreements and Policies section of the 1997–1999 Minneapolis Public School Contract, the normal workday of an elementary teacher includes 55 minutes of preparation time within the defined student day. The contract further states:

> It is the intent of the Minneapolis Elementary Schools to continue to employ specialists in vocal music instruction, art, physical education, media and other areas to serve the elementary schools. The intent of employing these specialists is to provide quality instruction in specialized areas for elementary age children, and relieve elementary teachers of the necessity for preparation in some subject areas. (p. 187)

Because each site determines its own programming, there is a great deal of difference between elementary schools. For example, some schools do not have a music program but may offer physical education, media, and science as the classes provided by specialists. One school provides sign language training as a specialist period for students. Longfellow's current principal feels strongly about consistency and the benefits of having people be full-time in one building. Discussion about and changes in specialist options no longer occurs each year. Whenever possible, jobs are combined to keep people in the building full-time. Longfellow has art, music, physical education, and media as the specialist classes.

Music Therapy

Music therapy, provided by a registered music therapist (RMT) or a board certified music therapist (MT-BC), has been part of the Minneapolis ECSE program since the mid 1970s. Music therapy has given students positive learning experiences and has been an integral part of the excellence in programming for ECSE students. This position is highly valued by teachers, administrators, and parents within the Longfellow setting. The ECSE staff and principals at Longfellow have consistently supported the use of music therapy for providing the teacher preparation time for the ECSE classes. During the first two years after Longfellow became an Early Education Center, all ECSE students were seen four times a week by the music therapist, and the High Five students were seen twice a week. Initially, the regular education students did not receive music.

Longfellow has children at many developmental stages in each classroom and this often creates challenges for staff. The classroom teachers who transferred to Longfellow to teach in the early education program were interested in hiring a music specialist who understood developmentally appropriate practices with young children (Music Educators National Conference, 1992). Since music therapists have been trained to work with diversity in both age and development, a second music therapist was hired for this position. When the building was reconfigured to add upper grade classrooms, music therapists continued to be hired for the position. Under site-based management, the individual schools determine the license required for the job postings. After being part of so many changes, the current music therapist completed a music education license to ensure job security. The job currently consists of .4 in the autism program, .5 in "regular" music education, and this year a new .1 which is 2½ hours a week at the district level for music therapy evaluation and consultation.

Music Therapy or Music Education or Both

At the same time parents and teachers were requesting music for the upper grades, there were fewer ECSE classes in the building. With each building staff setting their own hiring requirements and scheduling, it was difficult to work across buildings in special education. The music therapists began working with what was anticipated would be "regular classrooms." Included in this composition of classrooms were a kindergarten class with 8 children in the ELL program (4 Somalian and 4 Ethiopian), 2 children in foster placements, and 4 being assessed for special education services out of a total of 19. The fifth grade class had 25 students, 3 of whom had been in the Longfellow ECSE program 8 years earlier. The reading skills of the class ranged from second to eighth grade. By the end of the year, there were 6 Somalian students, 2 of whom had never before been to school. Three students were in and out of a homeless shelter and/or foster placements throughout the year. This diversity of students presents constant challenges to a music therapist working in the urban setting. In my particular case, by being in one building I have been able to write grants to pull in additional resources for all the students. This has also provided the opportunity to improve communication between special education and regular education personnel.

Music Therapy Evaluation at the District Level

The addition of a new district-funded position speaks to the increased visibility of music therapy as a profession. The position was created as a result of parents inquiring about and requesting music therapy services for their children. The increased publicity and documentation of the effectiveness of music therapy by the American Music Therapy Association has also been a factor in producing results. Parents of students with Autism Spectrum Disorder, Rett Syndrome, or William Syndrome have been especially vocal in requesting services, partly as a result of their national associations endorsing the advantages of music therapy. The letter from the Dr. Kenneth Warlick, Director of the Office of Special Education and Rehabilitative Services in the United States Department of Education, clarifying music therapy as a related service has been an important resource to further support the availability of music therapy services in the public schools (see Chapter 1). In addition, having special education staff from different schools across the district advocate for music therapy services has been a very effective tool.

After doing a number of evaluations for the district in exchange for some release time, this author requested a meeting with the head of ECSE. At that meeting a list of the districts in Minnesota that had music therapists, as well as copies of the Department of Education letter, was disseminated. It is important to have a serious conversation about the potential cost to the district especially since the initial evaluations are likely to be children who strongly respond to music. At the present time, there is a part-time music therapist covering three schools to meet students' IIIP objectives.

The networking and support generated along the way can be an important resource in support of expansion of music therapy services. Individuals who have worked with or observed a music therapist often become advocates for their services later on. In my particular case, a parent became a teacher, an educational assistant became a special education teacher, an ECSE parent joined the district level finance committee, an early childhood family education (ECFE) staff is now a principal, a coordinator became the assistant of special education, and a principal became head of district special education. All of these people have moved into positions where they have been able to speak to the value of music therapy services. The experience each one had previously with music therapy will impact their handling and response to future situations. Therefore, every interaction you have should be professional, positive, and as helpful as possible.

Recommendations for Creating Positions

Do some research so you know about the district:
- Find out how funding is handled in the district. Are services district-wide or site-based?
- How is the preparation time covered for special education teachers?
- Who makes the hiring determinations and sets the job postings?
- What is the history regarding music therapy and music in the district?
- Music educators can be some of the best allies. Are they currently being expected to provide preparation time for students with special needs?
- Talk with state music therapy members for any background on the district, but remember many changes will have occurred.

Expand the knowledge into understanding how it *really* works:

- Find someone who is positive and can help explain both the politics and people with whom you need to work.

What are the possibilities of having music therapy on the IEP as a related service?

- Is there a program where students are already receiving music therapy before attending the public schools? This can be an excellent lead in for services.

Find a way to even briefly be in the schools:

- Look for a grant through local arts organizations such as VSA-Arts, or State Arts Boards.

Recommendations for Maintaining a Position

Welcome and encourage visitors:

- Always be willing to have visitors observe you or your classroom. One of the best ways to network and provide a clear understanding of music therapy is letting the students demonstrate your skills. Do *not* expect advanced warning of visitors. Encourage the psychologist, pediatrician, or the superintendent to drop in. Be sure that the visitor knows you are a credentialed music therapist and the objectives of your session.
- It does not matter what you did for the previous people. You must start and build a relationship from the beginning with each change. Determine what is valued by the new staff so your skills and work will be considered essential.
- Remember you are a guest in the classroom, building, and hallways. You want to be a guest who is invited back. That means you pitch in and assist with toileting, dressing, and family communication in a way that lets each teacher be comfortable. Are the special education teachers your only contact with the building staff and principal? What is their relationship with the building? Are they representing you well or do you need to forge additional relationships?

Administrative Framework

Assessment

Interagency collaboration between the Public Health Department, Hennepin County Human Services and the Minneapolis School District, as required by Part H of P.L. 99-457, provides the central intake and referral system for children and families. After an initial screening, the child is referred to the public school Early Childhood Evaluation Team.

As shown in Figure 1, the student must first meet criteria in one of three categories: disability, medical diagnosis, or standardized assessment. The final determination is made by considering eligibility plus need for special education services and is based on a recommendation by a team that includes the parent. The assessment team establishes initial goals for children receiving services in the Minneapolis Public Schools.

Individual Plans

Parents, teachers, and other service providers develop a plan to meet the educational, social, and emotional goals of each child and family. For children birth until 3 years of age receiving services, the plan is called an Individual Family Service Plan (IFSP). (See Table 1 for a comparison of the Individual Family Service Plan and the Individualized Education Program.) The trend in Minnesota five years ago was to extend the IFSP rather than change to the IEP at 2.11 years. Some of the reasons for this include: (a) the right to coordinated, interagency family directed services does not end at 3 years of age; (b) as children move into center based programs, it is important to maintain family participation; and (c) duplication of services by agencies is reduced as a result of interagency agreements and better coordination of services. This trend reflected the family focus and emphasis on collaborative planning between organizations that is felt to be in the best interest of the student (Bradshaw, 1996).

In 1998, the Minnesota Legislature passed the Interagency Services for Children with Disabilities Act (Minnesota Statutes 125A.023 and 125A.027) for children and youth with disabilities ages 3–21. This is an example of the state setting more stringent standards within the federal requirements. Minneapolis Schools is one of the districts currently implementing the Interagency Individual Intervention Plan (IIIP) with children

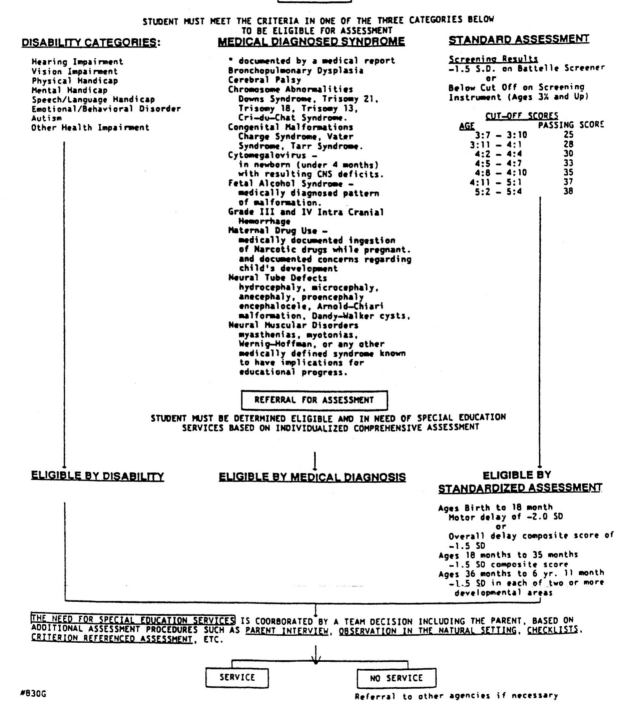

Figure 1. Entry Criteria, Minneapolis Public Schools, Special Education Department

Table 1

Comparison of Individual Family Service Plan (IFSP) and Individualized Education Program (IEP)

Individual Family Service Plan	Individualized Education Program
Addresses the needs of the family as well as the needs of the child.	Addresses the needs of the child and is implemented in the classroom.
Identifies medical and social service needs as well as educational strengths and needs.	Identifies educational strengths and needs.
Ways to meet the school, medical, and social service needs of the child and family are agreed to and written on the plan.	Ways to meet the school needs of the child are agreed to and written on the plan.
Service Coordinator available to help obtain school and non-school services needed.	The school team (teacher, therapists, social worker) available to provide information about different services.
Service Coordinator attends planning meetings and periodic reviews with parent or guardian.	Family attends planning meetings and periodic reviews on their own, but may invite an advocate to attend also.

up to age 5. As of January 2001, no more IEPs were to be written for students 3 to 5 years of age. The next phase includes students 5 to 7 years of age with a rolling implementation until all students age 3–21 have IIIPs.

The actual goals and objectives written in the academic setting are very similar for an IFSP, IEP, or IIIP. The IFSP and IIIP emphasize the family and the partnership between the family and professionals. The needs of the entire family are considered. Although the IFSP and IIIP contain the same information, the format is slightly different. The family thoughts page provides family members an opportunity to think about and share their hopes and concerns for their child as well as family needs and strengths (see Figure 2). This can be completed before the meeting but usually is handwritten at the meeting to reflect the family's current situation.

The team and summary sheet (see Figure 3) emphasizes one of the driving forces behind the IFSP and IIIP, that is, that all the agencies and personnel involved with a family work together to ensure the needs of the entire family are being met. The family should leave the IFSP or IIIP meeting with the names and phone numbers of all the people working with their child. This is a major difference from the IEP, where the focus is primarily on educational needs and the services that are provided only in the school setting.

Action plans help the family create a list of the information, changes, and tasks that need to be documented but do not require an outcome (see Figure 4).

The IFSP and IIIP outcome pages include the goal and objectives. There is little difference between the forms in terms of the information included (see Figures 5 and 6).

The families always decide whom they would like involved in the school conferences whether an IFSP, IIIP or an IEP is used. Families are welcome to include medical providers, county social workers or case managers, friends, or any person significant in the life of the child to assist in determining appropriate goals for the child and family.

Family Considerations and Concerns for the Individualized Family Service Plan

1. Please describe how you see your child. Tell what you most like, any concerns or needs. (Please use the back or additional paper if desired.)

loves music, TV credits, loves his little creatures, seems to be comprehending speech
concerns - basic communication
peer interaction, attention span, toileting

2. Which of the following do you or other family members feel are important concerns or areas about which you would like more information?

for your child

- [ ] getting around
- [x] communicating
- [x] learning
- [x] eating, nutrition
- [x] sleeping
- [x] toilet learning
- [x] having fun w/other children
- [ ] challenging behaviors/emotions
- [ ] equipment or supplies
- [x] health or dental care
- [ ] pain or discomfort
- [ ] vision
- [ ] hearing
- [x] other *hair cuts helping attend Sunday School*

for your family

- [ ] meeting other families whose child has similar needs
- [x] planning/expectations for future
- [ ] finding a support group
- [ ] information/ideas for brothers, sisters, friends, relatives, others
- [ ] finding or working with doctors/other specialists
- [ ] coordinating child's medical care
- [ ] coordinating/making appointments, dealing with agencies
- [x] learning about different services and how they work
- [x] information about available resources
- [ ] information about specific special needs
- [ ] explaining professional terms/roles
- [ ] help with transportation (to school, appointments, or vehicle adaptation)
- [x] finding child care *for J. or all 3 Kids*
- [ ] people who help in your home/care for your child so you can have a break
- [ ] assistance with housing, clothing, jobs, food, telephone
- [ ] assistance in obtaining funds for extra cost of child's special needs

- [ ] help with insurance
- [ ] information about recreational opportunities
- [ ] interpreter – language:
- [ ] other

notes

3. What type of help would you want for your child and family in the months or year ahead?

communicate basic needs, interact with peers, siblings share mutual toys, increase attention span in group, toileting information/contact people in the field of autism

4. What else do you think would be helpful for others to know about your child? ...about your family?

Figure 2. Family Thoughts

Service Delivery Models

Integrated Therapy Approach

At Longfellow, as much as possible and appropriate, the therapists spend time in the classroom. They assist the children in developing functional skills within the classroom routines and work collaboratively with other staff (McWilliam, 1995). Again, change is occurring as the school speech, occupational, and physical therapists began working in 2000 with third party reimbursement. There are requirements under which they can bill for their services and those standards must be meet. As part of the integrated therapy approach, teachers and support staff meet once a week to facilitate communication thereby improving services and teaching for students (Fullan & Hargreaves, 1991). At Longfellow, the support staff includes the teachers, speech clinician, social worker, occupational therapist, music therapist, and district autism lead. At the present time, none of the students have physical therapy on their plans. The meeting time helps to ensure that the entire team is aware of changes in the child's life and any modifications in their program.

The IFSP, IIIP, and IEP are all binding, legal documents. Any services written in must be provided as specified. Not all the schools in the district have music therapy programs. Some students move frequently

Child's Name: _____ TEAM & SUMMARY

A. IFSP Team Membership
Although team membership may change, the initial team is determined BEFORE the IFSP meeting.

B. IFSP Service Summary
If a Team Member provides service, summarize the service information.
This section should be filled out at the END of the meeting.

Name / Position / Agency / Address / Phone / Availability	Attend?	Service / Location / Amt / Frequency	Min/Wk ** Dir—Ind	Start Date	Duration
	Y ☐ N ☐	payment arrangements: .... authorized signature:			
	Y ☐ N ☐	payment arrangements: .... authorized signature:			
	Y ☐ N ☐	payment arrangements: .... authorized signature:			
	Y ☐ N ☐	payment arrangements: .... authorized signature:			
	Y ☐ N ☐	payment arrangements: .... authorized signature:			
	Y ☐ N ☐	payment arrangements: .... authorized signature:			
	Y ☐ N ☐	payment arrangements: .... authorized signature:			

** Minutes per week is a requirement used for administrative reporting, and does NOT reflect scheduling

Team and Summary Sheet
Figure 4

Figure 3. IFSP Team and Summary Sheet

Child's Name:

ACTION - 1

ACTION PLANS for the Child / Family / Team

Date	Activity or Desired Change	People who can help	Notes

Action Plan
Figure 5

TRANSITION PLANNING CHECKLIST
☐ Discussed transition with families. ☐ Notified child study team of transition. ☐ Reviewed child's program options from 3rd birthday to end of school year.
☐ Obtained parental consent. ☐ Convened transition conference. ☐ This IFSP includes one or more Transition Outcomes.

Figure 4. Action Plan

Child's Name Jane OUTCOME # 1

Where do we want to be? *(Major Outcome or Goal)*		Periodic Review Date: _____
Jane will sit on her chair without adult help and stay on task for longer periods of time.		Please provide a description of the degree of progress written in the same format as the objective. You should also indicate whether to continue (C), modify/revise (M) or discontinue (D) the objective.

What steps do we need to take? *(Objectives or Subgoals)* Include criteria, procedures, and timelines used to determine progress	Service and Person Responsible	
1. During group time, Jane will sit on her chair with the adult only sitting near her (participating independently) for 4 consecutive days by May 1996. 2. During group time Jane will independently stay on task for 15 minutes, for 4 consecutive days, by May 1996.	Mary ECSE teacher Cathy Speech/Language Amy Music Therapist	

Steps the county will take to develop service if unavailable.

Child's Name Jane OUTCOME # 2

Where do we want to be? *(Major Outcome or Goal)*		Periodic Review Date: _____
Jane will begin to express some wants and needs using picture schedules, picture choice boards and verbal imitation.		Please provide a description of the degree of progress written in the same format as the objective. You should also indicate whether to continue (C), modify/revise (M) or discontinue (D) the objective.

What steps do we need to take? *(Objectives or Subgoals)* Include criteria, procedures, and timelines used to determine progress	Service and Person Responsible	
1. When present with an array of food pictures, Jane will indicate a choice by pointing to a picture, 2/3 opportunities for 3 days. 2. When presented with an array of song pictures, Jane will indicate a choice by pointing to a picture then participating verbally or physically 2 times during the song 2/3 opportunities for 3 days.	Cathy speech/language intervention in the classroom Amy music therapy sessions in the classroom	

Steps the county will take to develop service if unavailable.

Figure 5. IFSP Goal Sheet

Right form (Learner: R.)

Page 3c of IEP

ED-1878 0.

Learner Name: R.

F. ANNUAL GOALS, SHORT-TERM INSTRUCTIONAL OBJECTIVES

Use one PAGE 3 for each goal. Thoroughly state the goal. List objectives for the goal, including attainment for each objective GOAL # ___ OF ___ GOALS

GOAL:

During structured time, R will use the Introtalker to choose activities and make requests.

Short-Term Instructional Objectives

OBJECTIVES:

During music, grp, and Ind. 1:1 time, R will participate & request activities relating to the structured activity by using the Introtalker with an 8 picture overlay; choosing her desired item given 1 verbal cue 3/4 opport. for 2 consecutive days

During music, grp, and Ind. 1:1 time, R will participate & request activities relating to the structured activity by using the Introtalker with an 8 picture overlay; choosing her desired item given 1 verbal cue 4/5 opport. for 3 consecutive days by the IEP.

G. IEP PERIODIC REVIEW

Date Reviewed: ___ Progress made toward this goal and objectives:

NOTE TO PARENT(S): You are entitled to request a meeting to discuss the results of this review.

Left form (Learner: Tom)

Page 3c of IEP

ED-1878 02

Learner Name: Tom

F. ANNUAL GOALS, SHORT-TERM INSTRUCTIONAL OBJECTIVES

Use one PAGE 3 for each goal. Thoroughly state the goal. List objectives for the goal, including attainment for each objective GOAL # 2 OF 5 GOALS

GOAL:

Tom will go from inconsistent on-task behavior in structured situations to consistent on-task behavior in structured situations.

Short-Term Instructional Objectives

OBJECTIVES:

1. Tom will attend and participate in structured group activities i.e. music, language groups for 10 minutes with 1 verbal prompt 3 out of 4 Days per week for 1 month by periodic review.

2. Tom will attend and participate in structured table activities for 1-3 minutes 3 out of 4 days per week for 1 month by periodic review.

G. IEP PERIODIC REVIEW

Date Reviewed: ___ Progress made toward this goal and objectives:

NOTE TO PARENT(S): You are entitled to request a meeting to discuss the results of this review

Figure 6. IEP Goal Sheet

during a year attending several programs. It is a district administration's decision as to whether specific music therapy goals are written into the service plans. For the ECSE-ASD classrooms at Longfellow, music therapy is part of the services offered to all of the students. Many of the goals and objectives that are written are collaborative, involving more than one discipline, or they can be integrated into the child's whole program. Goals and objectives are written that include music therapy such as: (a) "Bob will continue to increase his participation during structured group activities from responding with 1 action and 1 word to responding with 4–5 words and imitating 4 of 5 actions during songs," or (b) "Tashawna will sit, focus, and participate in structured activities and groups for 10–15 minutes each of 2 days in 1 week without screaming, touching, or hitting another child." Data to determine whether the objectives have been met are collected from groups facilitated by the music therapist, speech clinician, and classroom teacher.

Some examples of the integrated approach include:

1. In one class the occupational therapist came regularly to music group and adjusted positioning during the session. The child's goal was to increase appropriate sitting during activities. Working together, the O.T. and music therapist combined services and the child was able to participate to the fullest extent. The presence of an additional adult ensured that any responses made by the child were reinforced immediately. The use of music as a motivator to set the occasion to practice appropriate skills is utilized over and over again in this age group.
2. A physical therapist doing an assessment identified a child who was resistive to jumping in the P.T. area but was very willing to participate in jumping during music while "jumping on board a sailing ship" from the song "Going Over the Sea" (Fowke, 1969). This provided an *authentic assessment* that evaluated the child's functioning within a real situation.
3. The speech and language pathologist regularly observes music therapy sessions to obtain information on students' ability to imitate as well as to use spontaneous language.

The above examples all reflect times where the music therapist created an opportunity for children to practice and to generalize skills developed in therapy and classroom settings.

Role of Music Therapy in the ECSE Autism Classes

Music therapy sessions provide a motivating environment to work on social, emotional, motor, and cognitive needs of children with autism spectrum disorder. Incorporating or generalizing into the music group the skills which the occupational therapist, speech clinician, and classroom teacher are currently working on with students is part of the ongoing collaboration between team members. Developing and demonstrating activities that allow all the students to participate at their individual level and yet function as part of the group is a key responsibility of the music therapy position. A list of the students and all objectives that relate to skills addressed during the music therapy group is kept in the group area. At the completion of group, the music therapist updates the information.

The classroom make up is six students with a classroom teacher and two educational assistants. Students are seen four times a week. The length of time the music therapist covers the classes is slightly different each day and ranges from 30 to 45 minutes. A group lasts approximately 20 to 25 minutes. This extra time allows for a more gradual transition to and from group. It also means that some days the music therapist may cover snack, art experiences, toileting, or whatever part of the daily routine falls during the time.

One of the other functions of the music therapist is that of a resource for what skills are necessary for successful participation in school. The music therapist's experience across grade levels for regular classrooms becomes invaluable as ECSE classes work to prepare students for full inclusion classrooms or to make determinations about programs that would best meet the needs of students. Additional information about music therapy approaches for young children with autism spectrum disorder is available in *Early Childhood Connections* (Furman, 2001).

Previous Service Delivery Models

Toddler Services

Children who turn 3 between September 1 and December 31 and meet the ECSE criteria are eligible for a toddler program. This school-based class met two times a week for 2½ hours. Six children, a teacher, and a paraprofessional, with additional one-to-one assistants as required (for example, a medically fragile child who must be monitored continually) comprised the class. The music therapist provided a group music session once a week. This was often the first group experience for these students. The main focus of the sessions was exposing the children to the concept of coming to an area, sitting down, focusing on a leader, and using language. The classes were multi-categorical so a wide range of skills and needs were present in each class. The songs were simple and involved movements and sign language. For instance, the music therapist set the occasion by using small puppets, pictures, or instruments. The words *me, my turn,* and *more,* or the sign language equivalents, are prompted as the children take turns doing the activity. The children use the same skill later in the day to respond to the question, "Who wants a snack?" This prepares the students for important survival skills for use later in academic settings, such as volunteering and offering answers.

One aspect of the Toddler program that has been especially effective is having "older" helpers during music time. First and second graders are able to cue and encourage the small children. The older students are more likely to understand than a same age peer if a toddler plays inappropriately with a toy or does not understand the concept of sharing. Additionally, they act as models for appropriate language and behavior.

Case Example

One first grader, who was on a behavioral IEP himself, really enjoyed coming and helping with the Toddler group. He would regularly call attention to his special friend: "Hey look, Chuckie's clapping by himself!" His dismay was apparent one day when he tried to get his partner to come to group. "Hey—he's not listening to me! I told him to come—what'll we do—he's walking away! He's making me mad!" Since the music therapist also saw the older child in his full inclusion music class, the event could be discussed privately in relation to his own inappropriate behaviors. "Do you always listen? How do you think it makes your teachers feel? What should teachers do to help you follow directions?" The first grader and the music therapist then talked with his classroom teacher about his experience and what he wanted to try and do differently to change his own behavior.

3- and 4-Year-Old Special Education Services

The 3- and 4-year-old ECSE classrooms provided services four days a week for 2½ hours. Eight students, a teacher, and paraprofessional, with additional one-to-one paraprofessionals as required make up each classroom. These classrooms were primarily self-contained and multi-categorical (i.e., children of widely varying abilities and needs; it is not uncommon to have a child who is blind and nonambulatory in the same class as a child who is autistic and can read). These students participated in 25-minute music therapy groups two times a week. In order to have the children ready for full inclusion at the kindergarten year, a variety of integrated activities and experiences were structured to assist the students in transferring their skills to new classroom situations (Furman & Furman, 1993).

Longfellow currently utilizes a *whole language approach* where literacy is taught through natural and meaningful context, much like learning to talk. Children are exposed to words, sounds, and stories through listening, chanting, speaking, singing, reading, and writing. The teacher, music therapist, and speech clinician usually plan ECSE classroom themes and activities. Planning together works well and follows the school model of integrated curriculum. A book or several books and poems are often used as the basis for the 3- and 4-year-old classroom themes. For example, instead of using farm animals as a theme, specific children's stories such as *The Big Red Barn* by M. Wise Brown (1989) and *Rosie's Walk* by Pat Hutchins (1968) are used to create an opportunity to study and learn about the characters and events included in the books. In the small ECSE groups the children learn to look at a book, to label pictures, answer questions, sing songs, and participate in music activities related to the story. The use of children's literature can help a child understand what is being sung or talked about (Fallin, 1995; McCoy, 1994).

Classroom themes are often child-directed and reflect their interests such as dinosaurs, frogs, or, as in the case of one child whose father was a truck driver, trucks. This is an *emergent curriculum,* where teachers highlight and extend lessons in response to children's interests.

Integration Techniques

Reverse Mainstreaming

Many ECSE students are very attuned to adults. Their primary learning experiences have occurred in settings with very high adult-to-child ratios. It is important to help the child be ready for the stimulating environment of a classroom full of active students. Reverse mainstreaming, where several students from the High Five program or kindergarten come and participate in the small ECSE music therapy group, is utilized as a first step to help the ECSE children adjust to larger groups. The students come and participate, providing additional models for the ECSE students. It helps the music therapist and other staff have a sense of how much prompting and support the ECSE student is requires. The additional wait for turns and or the ability to share provides information as to the child's readiness. The visiting children have the opportunity to meet the ECSE staff and students with a teacher they already know and trust. Usually after several music times, the children stay and play in the ECSE room.

(Note: Remember to check with the social worker regarding the least restrictive environment (LRE) interpretation in your district. You must be sure appropriate protocol is followed, such as rotating the students who go to the ECSE classroom and informing the parents.)

Mainstreaming

An important part of ECSE music therapy sessions is mainstreaming experiences in the music classes with High Five or kindergarten students. The ECSE students participate in a music class taught by the music therapist. This allows the children the security of a known teacher, the music therapist, and the familiar activities. The visiting child has time to adjust to a new room and more students during the music group where most of the expectations placed on them are familiar and within their capabilities. Through the careful preparation and selection of music and activities, the music therapist can ensure the successful participation of each child. The classroom teacher has the chance to see and meet the child in a comfortable situation where they are not trying to limit or require appropriate behavior. The students have the opportunity to meet each other through structured music activities. The purpose of the mainstreaming experiences is to enable the child to practice making a transition to new situations.

High Five Inclusion Program

A self-contained ECSE classroom is too restrictive for some students, yet they are not ready to be in a High Five classroom without significant support. The Longfellow High Five Inclusion Program was developed to meet this need. Four ECSE students are placed in each of the High Five classrooms with 15 regularly enrolled students. An ECSE teacher or paraprofessional is also in the classroom with the teacher. This model was selected because, when strategies to promote interaction between students are facilitated by teachers, special needs students often make the most gains (Humpal, 1991; Jellison, Brooks, & Huck, 1984).

Case Example

The ECSE-ASD and High Five rooms are connected by a vent, so that even though the rooms are not next to each other, the students could hear one child who engaged in a lot of screaming. The High Five students were concerned about this child. The classroom teacher talked to the music therapist about how to reassure her students the ECSE child was all right. Since this child enjoyed music and did very well in structured situations, the music therapist invited him to a High Five music class. After the music group, the class gave a spontaneous and excited report to their teacher: "Hey, he can talk and take turns—he only screamed one time! He's going to come back again and try to use his words the whole time." The music visits gradually extended into invitations to stay and play in the High Five classrooms.

Because many of these students were previously in the ECSE program, they have a base of knowledge as well as security and familiarity with the music therapist. This familiarity with the structure of coming and sitting for music, knowing the hello song, turn taking, means skills are being generalized from a small group to the large group, instead of trying to learn entirely new skills in a new setting.

Kindergarten and Primary Inclusion in the Music Classroom

As students move into the primary grades, the music therapist functions in a different role. In a primary setting, the amount of teaming time is different. The student is one of 20 or more in a classroom. A special education resource teacher provides additional academic support as specified in the student's IEP. The music therapist who sees the child as part of music for the class often functions as a resource to the classroom teacher regarding behaviors and/or skills. Signs of regression or failure to use skills previously demonstrated can be quickly noted. The music therapist's familiarity with the students and their social skills is helpful as placement for classrooms, small group services, or programs are considered.

Case Example

In trying to determine the correct placement for a child who had been in the ECSE program and for whom English was not the native language, the music therapist strongly suggested he be placed in a High Five classroom. (At the time, there was no inclusion model.) The teacher and music therapist had collaborated regarding several students with great success, and she readily agreed to accept the child (Furman, Adamek, & Furman, 1993). After three days during which the child had not said anything and had mainly stood and observed, the teacher said she felt concerned that perhaps she was not the right teacher for this child. As the class lined up and headed outside for the bus, the rain matched her mood. Then, a little voice started singing "Rain, rain go away" and she thought, "What a good idea to sing—and WHO was that singing?" When she turned around, there was "Juan," the target child, smiling while singing and signing the song. Soon all the children were singing with Juan. At the bus, the teacher asked how he knew the song and without hesitating, the child replied "Amy teach me—want me to teach *you* tomorrow?"

Developing ongoing relationships with teachers leads to a willingness to try new things. This initial experiment led to the development of the High Five Inclusion Program, which was piloted at Longfellow and is now a district-wide program. The music therapist who goes into classrooms and sees students across grade levels provides accurate information about what skills are needed.

Individual/Special Sessions

Individual music therapy sessions are not usually scheduled. There is latitude, however, to develop programming that helps meet individual needs.

Case Example

A child who was a former ECSE student began to misbehave during afternoon language times in the spring of first grade. It appeared he was tired by the afternoon and frustrated at how difficult recognizing letters continued to be for him. A program was set up where he could come and be a music therapy "helper" every afternoon if he had met his behavioral objectives in the morning. He came and assisted in an ECSE classroom where the students were working on pre-academic skills such as sizes, shapes, and colors. He enjoyed being part of a group where he was the successful role model. He was able to go back to his class after 25 minutes as a music therapy helper, more relaxed and ready to work.

Case Example

A Title V Indian Education Grant (Furman, 1993) was used to provide music therapy sessions to help children develop key skills to ensure a more successful school experience. Fourteen first and second grade students, all of whom had difficulty sitting, listening, following directions, and maintaining interpersonal relationships, participated in music therapy groups. Teacher referral and classroom observations showed that the students were on-task and participating in activities less than 50% of the time. Social and classroom skills emphasized in the music groups included taking turns, attending to a task visually, following directions, interacting with peers, and participating actively in games, including trying new ones. The music sessions worked extremely well in motivating all of the students. Singing and rhythm activities, using a variety of familiar and ethnic instruments, were used to set up the learning situations. By the end of the academic year, the students were able to make verbal choices about what instrument they wanted to play, wait their turn, play in combination with different peers, and listen and echo back rhythms and words to songs. Songs and activities were chosen that required problem solving and presented opportunities for discussion. All of the tasks required concentration and focus on the activity at hand. On the average, all the students were on-task and participated appropriately in the music activities between 70–100% of the time. Final group performances were prepared for the classrooms. These were presented and videotaped. The tapes were given to the classrooms to watch at a later date. The classmates were observed singing along with the tapes and making positive comments to the performers about their respective roles in the music group. The performers gave stickers to their peers at the end of the performance; this was also videotaped. This experience gave the classmates and performers an opportunity to acknowledge and to relive some positive interactions, instead of the commonly observed negative interactions. Certificates and pictures were given to all of the participants to set the occasion for them to tell others about their successes.

Generalization: Preparing Students for the Full-Inclusion Music Class

The following suggestions have been useful as the staff works with students coming from other programs into Longfellow inclusion classes, and in preparing our current students for new experiences:

1. Observe the classroom and music groups of the public schools, day cares, or preschools to ensure you are familiar with the musical, social, behavioral, and academic skills required of successful group members. If the students with whom you work are going to (or coming from) a classroom where the teacher has everyone sit in chairs, for example, it is helpful if the students have experienced that. Some typically expected group skills include sitting with the group, facing the leader, starting and stopping with the music, naming instruments, raising hands, and waiting turns.

2. Teach the children's songs that are popular for the geographical area as well as basic folk songs (e.g., "Row, Row, Row Your Boat," and "Mary Had a Little Lamb").

3. Review the music curriculum series used locally and try to use songs from that series. Special education students typically do much better with activities and songs that are familiar to them. Thus, "Little Red Caboose" and "Down at the Station" are two songs taught in ECSE so that when the students are in kindergarten and sing those songs with their class, they may be seen as successful and capable (Cassity, 1981). Many of the routines and basic formats utilized in the music education classes have been part of the therapy sessions. The ECSE students know how to hold instruments properly, how to pass instruments, take turns, look at pictures in order to choose songs, and so on.

4. Encourage flexibility! Often children with special needs require repetition for learning to occur, but may become locked into a routine which becomes difficult to change. If a teacher decides to sing "*3 Little Monkeys Jumping on the Bed*" instead of the more typical "*5 Little Monkeys...*" the student needs to be able to adjust to the change. If bells are always used to accompany a certain song, it may be beneficial to try it with some different instruments. Taking turns with different people being first each time and using different orders besides going around the circle right to left helps keep students flexible. Try drawing names, or giving verbal prompts such as "people who are wearing stripes," or "everyone who walked to school today" for designating leaders, or for turn taking. This can help the students be ready for the demands future teachers will make upon them.

5. Maintain perspective. In working with and consulting for regular education teachers, always keep in mind that 20 to 30 other children are part of the classroom, needing and deserving the time and attention of the teachers. It is easy to develop too complex a plan that works effectively for meeting the needs of the special education child, forgetting that 25 other children have needs to be met simultaneously (Furman & Furman, 1993).

Summary

The music therapist in the public school must be flexible and proactive in watching trends and changes in education and special education programming. In addition, the therapist must be alert to building and district issues, both political and financial, that may impact services to students. By anticipating change and developing model programming, a music therapy program can be nurtured and maintained.

Longfellow Early Education Center has developed a music therapy program that allows children to begin receiving services as 2-year-olds in an ECSE-ASD classroom. The students then have the opportunity to generalize and transfer these skills throughout their early school career as part of inclusion classes. Within the building, the teachers collaborate to structure smooth transitions using reverse mainstreaming, mainstreaming, and special groupings to maximize each child's readiness for successful inclusion. The success that inclusive programming provides, with a familiar environment and consistent teachers over time, is regularly observed firsthand. Through interdisciplinary teaming and individualized programming, the support services and classroom teachers from both special and regular education work together, and with families, to ensure successful educational experiences for all children.

References

Bradshaw, R. (1996). *Use of the IFSP beyond the age of three.* Focus/Discussion Meeting, Minnesota Department of Children, Families and Learning.

Brown, M. W. (1989). *The big red barn.* New York: Harper & Row.

Cassity, M. D. (1981). The influence of a socially valued skill on peer acceptance in a music therapy group. *Journal of Music Therapy, 18,* 148–154.

Dettmer, P., Thurston, L. P., & Dyck, N. (1993). *Consultation, collaboration, and teamwork for students with special needs.* Needham Heights, MA: Allyn and Bacon.

Fallin, J. F. (1995, March). Children's literature as a springboard for music. *Music Educators Journal,* 24–28.

Falvey, M. A., Forest, M., Pearpoint, J., & Rosenberg, R. L. (1994). Building connections. In J. S. Thousand, R. A. Villa, & A. I. Nevin (Eds.), *Creativity and collaborative learning: A practical guide to empowering students and teachers* (pp. 347–368). Baltimore, MD: Paul H. Brookes.

Fowke, E. (1969). *Sally go round the sun.* Toronto: McClelland and Stewart.

Fullan, M., & Hargreaves, A. (1991). *What's worth fighting for? Working together for your school.* Andover, MA: The Regional Laboratory for Educational Improvement.

Furman, A. G. (1993). *Using music therapy to increase socialization and classroom skills with Native American children in a multicultural setting.* Title V Grant Report, Minneapolis Public Schools.

Furman, A. G. (2001). Young children with autism spectrum disorder. *Early Childhood Connections Journal of Music- and Movement-Based Learning, 7*(2), pp. 43–49.

Furman, A. G., Adamek, M. S., & Furman, C. E. (1993, November). *Music therapy with Native American children to increase communication, socialization, and classroom skills.* Paper presented at the Joint North American Music Therapy Conference, Toronto.

Furman, A. G., & Furman, C. E. (1993). Music for children with special needs. In M. Palmer & W. Sims (Eds.), *Music in prekindergarten: Planning and teaching.* Reston, VA: Music Educators National Conference.

Humpal, M. (1991). The effects of an integrated early childhood music program on social interaction among children with handicaps and their typical peers. *Journal of Music Therapy, 28*(3), 161–175.

Hutchins, P. (1968). *Rosie's walk.* New York: Macmillan.

Jellison, J. A., Brooks, B., & Huck, A. M. (1984). Structuring small groups and music reinforcement to facilitate positive interactions and acceptance of severely handicapped students in the regular music classroom. *Journal of Research in Music Education, 32,* 243–264.

McCoy, C. W. (1994, Spring). Music and children's literature natural partners. *General Music Today,* 15–19.

McWilliam, R. (1995). Integration of therapy and consultative special education: A continuum in early intervention. *Infants and Young Children, 7*(4), 29–38.

Minneapolis Public Schools. (1997). *Teacher Contracts, Agreements, & Policies* July 1, 1997–June 30, 1999, p. 187.

Music Educators National Conference. (1992). Position statement on early childhood education. *Soundpost,* 21–22.

Scott, J., Clark, C., & Brady, M. (2000). *Students with autism: Characteristics and instruction programming.* San Diego, CA: Singular.

17

MUSIC THERAPY FOR LEARNERS IN AN EARLY CHILDHOOD COMMUNITY INTERAGENCY SETTING

Marcia E. Humpal

THE Cuyahoga County Board of Mental Retardation and Developmental Disabilities (CCBMR/DD) located in Cleveland, Ohio serves children and adults with mental retardation or developmental disabilities. CCBMR/DD's William Patrick Day Early Childhood Center, East Cleveland Early Childhood Center and several satellite centers provide comprehensive, collaborative, prenatal, and early childhood services to families and their children. The early childhood program emphasizes coordinated services through a true partnership of agencies dedicated to meeting the needs of the entire family unit. Music therapy is one of the services that is part of this team effort.

Background

History

In each of Ohio's counties, boards were established to serve individuals with special needs. These boards have operated schools and adult training centers for individuals with varying levels or ranges of developmental disabilities and multihandicapping conditions. Local school districts initially referred individuals to these boards if they or the individual's family felt that the student could be best served in a separate educational setting. As time passed, county boards began taking on a more collaborative role in Ohio's educational system. Now their personnel often are being used as teachers or consultants within the local school or community setting.

County boards were impacted by the passage of Public Law 99-457 (Education for All Handicapped Children Act Amendments, 1986). In addition to expanding school programs to young children, the law recognizes that some infants and toddlers will need early intervention services because they either have or are at risk for delays that may impact future learning. A major emphasis is placed on serving the needs of the entire family unit. Furthermore, collaboration between agencies, schools and professionals is highly encouraged to best serve the needs of both the children and their families in a least restrictive environment (Hanline & Hanson, 1989; Ludlow, 1987). P.L. 102-119, the Individuals with Disabilities Education Act (IDEA, 1992), and P.L. 105-17 (IDEA Amendments, 1997) further specify services, collaboration, reevaluation procedures and clarify prior laws.

In 1992, CCBMR/DD, reflecting and supporting the mandates of these laws, opened its first center dedicated to early intervention. This facility, the William Patrick Day Early Childhood Center, offers a model program with a holistic approach to providing health, nutrition, parenting and education services to over 400 young children and their families. Several agencies have programs at the facility including CCBMR/DD (Early Childhood Division), Cleveland Public Schools, the Council for Economic Opportunities in Greater Cleveland Head Start, Interlink, WIC (nutrition information for women, infants, and children), Cuyahoga County Early Intervention Collaborative Group, the CCBMR/DD Instructional Media Center and United Cerebral Palsy (Adaptive Computer Technology Program). These agencies provide a range of services that promote inclusion and are accessible, culturally sensitive, and affordable to families (Robertson, 1992).

At its inception, William Patrick Day Early Childhood Center was awarded a five-year federal grant to study how Developmentally Appropriate Practices could be applied to the young child with special needs. Labeled the Transactional Inclusive Program (TRIP), the grant embodied an alternative process that emphasized a play-based, child-initiated approach (Mahoney & Powell, 1984). TRIP was a guiding force behind the developmentally appropriate practices model central to the center's philosophy.

Working within this framework in an inclusive setting, the center's personnel came to realize that although all children were making gains, a subgroup of children with significant needs might make greater progress if initially served in specialized environments. Policymakers looked at methodologies and models of instruction that might allow blending developmentally appropriate practices suitable for all young children with additional support and instruction needed by children with severe involvement (Sandall, Schwartz, & Joseph, 2001). The center now provides some classrooms that have a specific curriculum focus. Staff do not teach isolated skills, but use a curriculum that best meets the unique needs of the child, thus developing independence and internalizing skills that will allow the children to eventually function in an inclusion setting (Welch & Cook, 2001).

It is widely accepted that learning is a life-long commitment for early childhood educators (Vander Ven, 1994) and that these professionals must continue to be good planners, thinkers, and collaborators and be nurturing to the children in their classrooms. Before children arrive at an educational setting, preparation should include thorough plans for human interactions among the children, adults, and between children and adults. Putting this in perspective, early childhood educators need a personal sense of self-understanding in relation to their work. For this reason, professional growth and planning days are vital parts of the Center's schedule. These regularly scheduled opportunities help staff stay abreast of current trends and explore best practices for young children.

Role of Music Therapy

For many years, CCBMR/DD has encouraged integrating children with and without developmental delays into typical early childhood activities. In 1979, its early childhood music mainstream program was developed. A pilot program combined early childhood classes from a separate school for students with disabilities and a class from another preschool for typically developing children. This model has grown into a permanent part of the music curriculum (Dimmick & Humpal, 1989, 1990; Humpal, 1990, 1991; Humpal & Dimmick, 1993) and is at the core of the Early Childhood Division's integrative philosophy.

CCBMR/DD currently employs three full-time music therapists to serve its early childhood population. In addition to their music therapy credentials, all three hold teaching certificates from the State of Ohio. Music therapy is considered a part of the interdisciplinary team approach. The music staff meet with others (such as the classroom teacher or early intervention specialist, speech/language pathologist, occupational therapist, physical therapist and adapted physical education instructor) to determine goals and procedures that best meet the individual needs of the children and their families.

Music classes are provided once each week for all students. Service is delivered in inclusion, integrated, reverse mainstream, small group or individual settings as determined by the individual needs of the child. Service may be conducted jointly with other related services or integrated into playtime. In addition, music therapists direct sessions for families, provide consultation for classroom teachers and ancillary personnel, conduct in-services and public relations seminars, and supervise music therapy practicum students.

Preparation

How Children Learn

While working with young children may look easy, those who understand children know that they learn in their own specific ways. Children often distort statements made by an adult or erroneously interpret what they see. They think very concretely and in the present and often make comparisons that are not true. For example, a child may see a redheaded girl sitting in a wheelchair. The child may conclude that she will someday need to be in a wheelchair because she also has red hair. Since children do not always verbalize what they are thinking or do not know how to express their fears, they should be asked questions to find out exactly what connections they are making. In so doing, the adult may alleviate many of the child's unnecessary fears.

Awareness Training

When CCBMR/DD's original music mainstreaming projects were initiated, two main purposes were identified: to provide positive peer role models for young students with disabilities and to provide for the acceptance and understanding of differences among individuals (Dimmick & Humpal, 1989). With the opening of William Patrick Day Early Childhood Center, music therapy became one of several opportunities for integration. Children now play and learn together in inclusionary, integrated or reverse mainstreamed classes or at least come together for music, physical education, lunch, and play times. Yet, the need to initially facilitate the ideas of acceptance and understanding is still evident. Therefore, the music therapy department delivers a multi-faceted program to prepare students, staff, and parents for inclusionary activities.

There are two basic guidelines that direct this preparation process. First, the awareness training must be carefully planned and geared directly towards the *child's* level of understanding. Furthermore, teachers, parents, and other community agency personnel who will be directly or indirectly involved with the Center should participate in the process.

Before children view the music therapy presentation, teacher preparation packets are distributed to all staff. The packets contain inservice training information, program specifics and activities to use with children prior to and following the disability awareness program itself. Teachers are expected to participate in the complete process, actively assisting the music therapists whenever needed, to help decrease any anxiety the children may have. In addition, parents are notified of the program and are given an overview of the entire process. If they so desire, they may attend the presentation *with* their children. It is very important to keep parents informed; when the child asks questions at home, the parent should feel comfortable and able to give correct information.

The main event of the presentation is a puppet show that stresses similarities and differences among individuals. Songs and signing reinforce these concepts. Also included are opportunities for children to try out the actual equipment that the children with disabilities may use to enhance their abilities to function in society. Actual, child-size examples of wheelchairs, crutches, walkers, communication devices, adapted toys or medical apparatus may be demonstrated. The equipment reflects situations the children will most likely encounter in their particular class setting.

Children at this young age generally have short attention spans. Therefore, particular attention is paid to the length of time spent on the entire presentation as well as the length and type of each activity. The total session should not exceed 45 minutes. Teachers and parents are encouraged to maintain an ongoing, open dialogue.

Framework

Team Approach

The Early Childhood Center represents a collaborative venture where teamwork is of utmost importance. Whether at home or in the school setting, the child is served by a team that is comprised of several people: the classroom teacher or early intervention specialist, teacher assistant, speech/language pathologist, occupational therapist, physical therapist, adapted physical education instructor, and the music therapist. Other ancillary staff such as the outreach worker, psychologist, or nurse may be included. The parents are an essential part of the team; their wants and needs are always solicited and addressed. Good developmentally appropriate music therapy and music education practices take into account the ways in which children acquire musical information, organize and process it, and use it in musical experiences (Briggs, 1991; McDonald & Simons, 1989; Morin, 2001; Neeley, 2001.). This process does not occur independently of other areas of intellectual growth and development. Musical skill development in children has many correlations to learning; it provides opportunities to enhance listening skills, communication, academic challenges, social experiences, motor planning and also creativity (AMTA, 1999; Colwell, 1994; Humpal, 1990, 2001; Jellison, 2000; Loewy, 1995; Standley & Hughes, 1997; Wolfe & Horn, 1993). Music is *not* a separate entity unto itself. Therefore, assessment information is shared with and by the team; goals are developed to address the "total child." All team members try to work together while implementing service delivery. Music therapy really shines in this treatment approach because it may facilitate the goals of all of the other therapies.

Assessment

Since no standard music therapy assessment was available for use in the early childhood setting for children with special needs, a tool was developed by Dimmick and Humpal (1994) to use at CCBMR/DD (see Appendix A). The authors recognized the normalizing effect of music experiences for the young child and examined musical characteristics of, and program goals for, typically developing young children (Andress, 1989; Andress & Walker, 1992; Bayless & Ramsey, 1991; Boswell, 1984; McDonald & Simons, 1989; Overby, 1991; Palmer & Sims, 1993). From this background, a hierarchy of competencies within each musical area as well as non-musical skills and stages of play was developed. This multi-year assessment and evaluation checklist examines how the child explores his/her environment through such musical means as singing, sound play, moving, and listening. Creativity is noted throughout each area as well as how participation and engagement levels reflect the child's stage of social play. Space is also provided for anecdotal information considering the child's social, medical, sensory, communication and motor abilities and/or needs. Additional room is given for team notes regarding such areas as progress made or adaptations needed, and recording of the IFSP outcome or IEP objective and its attainment status. Input is gathered by direct observation, interactive play, and from the entire interdisciplinary team (including the family).

In many cases, a specific music therapy assessment is not conducted because the team decides to obtain information via a formal play-based assessment conducted independently by the main service provider. Team members also share their observations after informally evaluating the child at play or in a more structured setting. Such assessments help the team determine holistic goals that address the needs of the whole child through developmentally appropriate practices.

The underlying philosophy of the Center promotes inclusion and builds on the strengths of all children and their families (CCBMR/DD, 2000). Therefore, every effort is made to serve children in integrated settings. Assessment and team discussions help determine what settings or adaptations might be necessary to structure success for the child with special needs. Assessment also may indicate that a child could benefit from individual music therapy service or that he or she might require additional adult assistance in order to adequately function in an inclusive music class. Flexibility of scheduling and cooperation among staff is essential in order for inclusive programming to run smoothly and effectively.

The Center's music therapists occasionally are asked to consult with early childhood classrooms in local school districts. When an assessment is requested to determine if music therapy should be added to a child's IEP, the music therapists also utilize the Special Education Music Therapy Assessment Process (SEMTAP) tool (Coleman & Brunk, 1999).

Individualized Family Service Plan (IFSP)

The first documentation that the early childhood team uses is the Individualized Family Service Plan (IFSP). This document is used for children from birth to 3 years of age who have or are at risk for developmental delay(s). Public Law 99-457 addresses this plan. However, a collaborative effort among early childhood caregivers and experts developed guidelines to meet the federal mandate of this law long before it became a reality (McGonigel & Johnson, 1991).

The IFSP clearly emphasizes a planning process between the family and professionals. It describes informal and formal resources that may help families meet their goals for their child and themselves. It is dynamic in the sense that changes in outcomes, activities and participants are added to the plan as they are needed and always with the family as ultimate decision-makers. The IFSP is initiated during the first contact with the family and travels with the family should they change services or service coordinators. It continues to be reviewed and modified throughout the family's involvement with early intervention services.

The IFSP is written in actual parent language and terminology to reflect their contribution to the process. The content of the IFSP includes:

1. The child's present level of development based on an assessment that includes professionally acceptable objective criteria and/or informed clinical opinion (see Figure 1).
2. Parent description of the child's current functioning (may be done in a variety of formats).
3. With the concurrence of the family, a statement of the family's resources, priorities, and concerns related to enhancing the development of the child (see Figure 2).
4. A statement of the major outcomes expected to be achieved for the child and family, with the concurrence of the family (see Figure 3).
5. The criteria, procedures, and timelines used to determine progress toward achieving the outcomes and whether modifications or revisions of the outcomes or services are necessary (see Figures 3 and 4).
6. The specific early intervention services necessary to meet the unique needs of the child and the family to achieve the outcomes (see Figures 3 and 4):
   a. The frequency, intensity, method, initiation, and anticipated duration of service delivery.
   b. The natural environments in which early intervention services will be provided as determined by the IFSP team, including the parents. Note that, to the maximum extent appropriate to the needs of the child, early intervention services must be provided in the home and in community settings in which children without disabilities participate.
   c. The payment arrangements, if any.
   d. The name of the person the family has chosen to provide service coordination.

(CCBMR/DD, 1999)

Each IFSP contains a 90-day review. At that time all data and notes are shared with the family and a determination is reached as to whether or not an outcome has or has not been achieved by the child. Outcomes may be continued if they have not been achieved. Those that have been achieved may be continued with an increase in the criteria level, or an altogether new outcome may be added to the IFSP.

As the toddler reaches preschool age, a transitional interim IEP is written by the early childhood and the family team and is forwarded to the new preschool setting. This temporary IEP gives the new school/preschool teacher vital information in determining future objectives for the permanent, yearly IEP.

[IFSP: 12/98]

Summary of _Chloe A's_ _____ Development

Health & Medical Information (including vision & hearing)

- Born at Southwest Hospital (2wks. early) -
  5# 5 oz.
- Diagnosed Williams Syndrome @ 3 mos.
- Vision
- Reflux
- Heart murmur
- Sensitive to loud sounds
- Vision appears normal
- M.D. wants Pediaure 2x per night.

Understanding & Expression (communication development)

- Cries
- Smiles
- Says "da da", "ba ba"

Movement (motor development)

- Sits
- Rolls
- Gets up on hands & knees/rocks

Getting Along with Others (social-emotional development)

- Lifts arms to mom
- Needs to change activities often
- Trouble with transitions (screams)
- Loves to be sung to.
- "Lights up" when to hears music

Thinking & Learning (cognitive development)

- Imitates
- Plays with paper
- Likes sound-producing toys
- Likes "Barney" on TV

Doing Things for Him/Herself (adaptive development)

- Likes bath
- Holds bottle
- Tolerates baby cereal via spoon

Summary Page

Figure 1. IFSP Present Level Summary Page

[IFSP: 12/98]

Conversations About _Child A_ **and Family**

For my family, I am most concerned about:

- motor development
- eating/nutrition
- sleep
- medical coverage

For my child, I am most interested in:

- information/suggestions related to above concerns
- keeping him happy and occupied

I would like more information about:

- Williams Syndrome
- Music therapy

Changes/transitions that are coming:

- New baby expected in May

Conversation Page

Figure 2. IFSP Family Conversation Page

IFSP: 12/98]

Outcome #1

What do we want for _Child A_ **& family?**

Help Child A do better (developmentally) by attending toddler class and getting strategies for use at home.

Date: _day/mo/yr._

What will we do to get there? (strategies/activities)	Who will do it? (services/supports/ resources)	Payment Arrangement	When will we start? How often? Where? How long will it take?	How are we doing? (progress review)
1) Help Child A participate in the Toddler Program.	Mon, Classroom teacher + team	ECBMH/DD	9/2000. 2 days per wk. Wm. Patrick Day ECC 1 yr. (through 9/2001)	See Review Pages dated :
2) Informal and formal assessments of progress + of effective strategies.	Family + team	ECBMH/DD	9/2000 – 9/2001	11/30/00 3/2/01 5/18/01
3) Determine future outcomes with corresponding strategies.	Family + team	ECBMH/DD	9/2000 – 9/2001	See Home Visit Reports dated: 6/15/01
4) Provide opportunities for practice of strategies with Child A.	Family + team	ECBMH/DD	9/2000 – 9/2001	8/24/01

Natural environment(s) _Home and school._

Outcome Page

Figure 3. IFSP Outcome Page

[IFSP: 12/98]

EI ✓ ___ ES

OHIO
Individualized Family Service Plan (IFSP)

for the family of ___Child A___ who was born on ___ ID# ___

Address ___ Phone ___

Parent(s)/Guardian ___ County ___ **Cuyahoga**

___ School Dist./LEA ___

Who Is Helping With This Plan:

CCBMR/DD –

___Teacher's name___
Service Coordinator ___ Agency ___ Phone ___

Supports & Services:
Name ___ Role ___ Phone ___

pediatrician – Kaiser

speech-language pathologist – CCBMR/DD

registered dietician – Dept. of Health

music therapist – CCBMR/DD

☐ CCBMR/DD Home Services ___ Home Visits per Month for ___ hours until ___

☑ CCBMR/DD Toddler Program ___ 2 ___ 1/2 days per week plus ___ 2 ___ home visits until ___9/01___

Initial Plan Date: _9/1/ 00_ Review Dates: _11/30_ _3/2_ _5/18_ _8/24_
            1   2   3   4   5   6   7

Cover Page

Figure 4. IFSP Cover Page

Individualized Education Program (IEP)

Objectives for children over age three are incorporated into the child's Individualized Education Program (IEP). The intent of the IEP is similar to that of the IFSP; however, it differs greatly from the IFSP in style, format, and dissemination of information

Prior to determining an individual plan, the entire team assesses the child through direct observation, family survey or interview, and criterion referenced assessment tools. The parents, team members and local school representatives then come together for a conference. Three issues are discussed at these meetings: (a) educational placement, (b) nature and degree of special education and related services, and (c) specific instructional objectives that will be addressed. Adhering to the Center's philosophy, the team develops goals that will stimulate the child to:

- Become actively and pleasurably engaged in the adult/child interaction.
- Become actively engaged in the exploration and understanding of his/her environment, constructing understanding through participation and manipulation.
- Become active communication partners with adults and peers to express, request, question, and comment via various communicative models.
- Become as independent as possible in self-help areas.
- Become as independent as possible in self-management of daily routines and transitions.
- Interact with peers and adults in a variety of settings.
- Develop self-confidence and an eagerness to learn.
- Represent ideas and feelings through pretend play, dance and movement, music, art, and construction.
- Construct his/her own understanding of relationships among objects, people, and events.
- Increase competence in management of his/her body and acquire basic physical skills.

(Welch & Cook, 2001)

The child's strengths, interest, and needs are assessed in various settings prior to determining goals. The child's present level of performance is discussed with the family at the IEP meeting, as is the vision the family has for the child's future (see Figure 5). The team discusses possible target areas and strategies and then develops a program for the child that emphasizes the positive aspects of his or her repertoire. Specific goals are agreed upon by the family and the team in *cognitive/play, self-help, communication, social/emotional, and gross/fine motor* curricula areas.

The IEP lists date of initiation, anticipated duration and frequency as well as types of related service. Children who attend CCBMR/DD classes have music therapy listed as a related service on their IEP. The child may have a separate music therapy goal (direct instruction format), but more often will have a goal that is being jointly implemented by several members of the team (collaborative consultation format). For instance, a child may have a specific classroom play objective that can be carried over to the music therapy setting. This objective could be written by the music therapist in direct instruction format (see Figure 6).

The same objective could be co-signed with the classroom teacher using the collaborative consultation format (see Figure 7). Using this format, the teacher would address the child's performance level in the classroom setting, briefly mentioning the child's behavior during music play. To encourage a holistic approach to serving children and to make the IEP more succinct, supervisors have encouraged teams to combine or share goals whenever possible. Therefore, the majority of music therapy goals are now implemented via the collaborative consultation model. Services and supports that are provided by related service personnel are further described on a separate form (see Figure 8) that becomes part of the IEP.

The language of the IEP in the early childhood setting is intended to be "reader friendly." The framework of the child's program assumes that:

- Intervention considers the whole child.
- Intervention is family-focused.

IEP-607

Page _____ of _____

**Cuyahoga County Board of Mental Retardation
and Developmental Disabilities**

INDIVIDUALIZED EDUCATION PROGRAM (IEP)

(after hand-written)

Name ___Child B_____ Date of Birth ____/____/____ Grade Level _____ ☐ Male ☐ Female

Student Identification Number _____

Child/Student Address _____

Parent Address _____ Parent/Guardian _____

Home Phone _____ Work _____

Effective Dates From: ___10/2000___ To: ___10/2001___ Meeting Date ___10/29/00___ ☒ Initial IEP ☐ Periodic Review

District of Residence _____ District of Service _____

Step 1 | Discuss Vision: *Future Planning.*

Family would like Child B to be able to communicate. They also would like him to be as typical as he can be. Family also wants him to be challenged and to explore his interest in music. They want him to be in an inclusion class to aid in his social development.

Step 2 | Discuss Present Levels of Performance

Child B has been diagnosed with Williams Syndrome. He stays busy through the school day. He is very interested in the activities presented and joins a group of peers in their activities. He often takes objects from the fine motor cupboard or from the music center during free play time. Child B has trouble transitioning from activity to activity and often tantrums when he does not get his own way, though he does understand the word, "No". Child B is often unaware of where his body is in space, and has difficulty staying on task. He is very curious and is energetic and happy.

IEP I

White - CCBMR COPY   Yellow - PARENT/GUARDIAN COPY   Pink - PUBLIC SCHOOL DISTRICT COPY   Goldenrod - TEACHER/SPECIALIST COPY

Figure 5. IEP Vision and Present Level Page

**Cuyahoga County Board of Mental Retardation
and Developmental Disabilities**

IEP-607

INDIVIDUALIZED EDUCATION PROGRAM (IEP)

Page ____ of ____

Discuss Present Levels of Performance. Domain/

Curricular Area: ___Music___

Child B follows the routine during his music therapy session when given
verbal cues. He is highly motivated by music and responds to group directions
given via song. He often needs to have verbal prompting given to him
specifically. Child B is easily distracted by what is going on around
him and has difficulty focusing on the activity that is taking place.

Objectives

1) Child B will follow group directions
in music therapy sessions.

Annual Goals
**Step 4 - Identify Measurable Goals, Objects, and
Assessment Procedures**

Child B will improve his
ability to follow directions
given to the group.

**Step 4 (continued)
Assessment of Student Progress**

Procedures	Who	Criteria	Schedule	Progress
- Observation - Data Collections Music Therapist		4x per music therapy session (4/5 trials) over 10 sessions.	2 progress reports per yr.	(progress made or date objective met is noted at the IEP Review)

Services - Step 5 Identify Needed Services	Initiation/Duration	LRE - Step 6 Determine Least Restrictive Environment (LRE)
Large group music therapy	School calendar year	Inclusive preschool; Wm. Patrick Day

Instructional Personnel/Title(s) _____   Signed by Music Therapist

Figure 6. IEP Direct Instruction Objective

Cuyahoga County Board of Mental Retardation and Developmental Disabilities

INDIVIDUALIZED EDUCATION PROGRAM (IEP)

IEP-607

Page _____ of _____

Discuss Present Levels of Performance. Domain/

Curricular Area: Social/music/play

Child B follows daily routines with adult help. He imitates peer

activity appropriately but needs prompts to follow directions given to

group. He is beginning to accept limits more readily, though often is

so interested in all that is going around him that he does not pay attention

to directions or the task at hand.

Annual Goals
Step 4 - Identify Measurable Goals, Objects, and Assessment Procedures

Child B will improve his ability to follow directions.

Objectives

1). Child B will follow group directions throughout the school day in a variety of settings.

2) Child B will follow the daily preschool routine each day.

Services - Step 5 Identify Needed Services	Initiation/Duration	LRE - Step 6 Determine Least Restrictive Environment (LRE)
-Special Education	School Calendar yr.	Wm.Patrick Day CCBMR/DD pre-school class;
- Music Therapy (individual, small and large groups)		Inclusive setting

Step 4 (continued)
Assessment of Student Progress

Procedures	Who	Criteria	Schedule	Progress
- Observation			2 progress reports per yr.	(NOTED AT IEP REVIEW)
- Data Collection	-Instructor			
	- Instructor Assistant			
	- Music Therapist			
		4x per session 3 days per wk. over 10 days; 4/5 trials per sesison over 10 days.		

Instructional Personnel/Title(s) __Signed by Instructor, Instructor Assistant, Music Therapist__

IEP III

Figure 7. IEP Collaborative Consultation Objective

CUYAHOGA COUNTY BOARD OF MENTAL RETARDATION
AND DEVELOPMENTAL DISABILITIES

STEP 4: IEP SERVICES AND SUPPORTS

Name _____ Child B _____   Effective Date _____

RELATED SERVICES

___ Employment Training ___ Physical Therapy ___ Psychology ___ Adapted Physical Education ___ Speech-LanguagePathology __x__ Music therapy
___ Occupational Therapy ___ Other

Service (needed to implement educational goal): See *social* music page
Music is an enjoyable, preferred motivator for children to reach objectives across all domains. - Music provides multi-sensory experiences which
stimulate communication, gross and fine motor movement, intellectual development and socialization. - Music is a vehicle for inclusion across all
disciplines.

Service Provider Name(s)/Title: _____ Marcia Humpal , Music Therapist - Board Certified
Initiation/Duration of Service: Throughout school calendar year Grouping: Large/small group, individual

Supplementary Aids and Services and/or Consultative Services: Consultation to families, staff and community for : - disability awareness training
- family/child/community programs - center special events - resources, supplementary enrichment ideas and strategies for using music throughout
the child's day.

Service Provider Name(s)/Title: Same as above

Initiation/Duration: same as above _____ Grouping: Individual, small group, large group

Amount of Service: 2 hours per month provided weekly

STEP 5: LRE-DETERMINE SETTING IN WHICH TO DELIVER THE SERVICE

In the music room, classroom and/or community, in an inclusive setting

Figure 8. IEP Supports and Services Page

- Intervention supports the family's integration into the community.
- Intervention services are coordinated between agencies.
- Curriculum is guided by the belief that all children learn best by becoming actively involved in their play, environments and in interactions with other children and adults.

(CCBMR/DD, 1995; Welch, 2000)

Because of time constraints, it is usually impossible for the music therapist to attend IEP conferences. However, since the music therapist is part of the team that develops the IEP, he or she must sign the IEP, marking "NA" for "not attending" (see Figure 9).

When implementing the IEP, the music therapists take anecdotal notes after sessions. Progress notes addressing each objective are sent home twice per school year. The IEP is valid for one school year but may be amended at any time.

Philosophical Considerations and Methodologies

The music therapist who works in an early childhood setting is presented with both an interesting and yet challenging mission. One must keep abreast of current "best practice" philosophical approaches towards working with young children. For example, a trend in early childhood education is towards using encouragement rather than praise (Hitz & Driscoll, 1988) when attempting to facilitate play or meet an objective. The child's efforts are therefore being affirmed rather than judged. What the child *can* do is encouraged and built upon in an educative rather than an eliminative strategy. These tactics often seem foreign to music therapists who have been firmly entrenched in behavioral programming. Actually, music therapists have an edge in this type of methodology because of their musical training in improvisation and their therapeutic expertise regarding adaptation.

Educating children is a dynamic process. Best practices undergo constant scrutiny. The American Music Therapy Association's Music and the Young Child Fact Sheet (1999) affirms that music therapy does make a difference with young children (see Appendix B). Music therapy students need to become familiar with child development and current practices in the field. Behavioral and psychoanalytical approaches to music therapy appear to be the predominate strategies taught in college programs; perhaps more exposure to specific early childhood philosophical beliefs and methodology would be beneficial.

When working in a collaborative inclusion setting, music therapists may be called upon to coordinate the educational approaches of the different agencies. It is extremely important, therefore, to understand the similarities and differences of philosophy and methodology espoused by experts in early childhood education and how these affect the music therapy process (Davis, 2001; Furman, 2001; Humpal, 2001). It should also be noted that although terminology may be different, intent may be similar. At the Center, the following theories predominate.

Developmentally Appropriate Practices

The National Association for the Education of Young Children (NAEYC) is a leader among organizations that follow, research, develop and disseminate information on and for young children. Presently *Developmentally Appropriate Practice in Early Childhood Programs Serving Children From Birth Through Age 8* (Bredekamp, 1987) represents the basis for teaching strategies with young children. These Developmentally Appropriate Practices (D.A.P.) guidelines inform educators, parents, administrators, policy makers, and others who are involved in the child's program, that current research indicates young children learn best in a concrete, play-based atmosphere. NAEYC, in its 1986 Policy Statement, includes these suggestions:

IEP-607

Cuyahoga County Board of Mental Retardation and Developmental Disabilities

INDIVIDUALIZED EDUCATION PROGRAM (IEP)

Page _____ of _____

Name ___Child B___　　IEP Summary for Effective Dates _____

IEP Meeting Participant's Signatures

_____　Parent　　　_____ ld/Student's Special Education Teacher/Provider

Child/Student's Regular Education Teacher　　District Representative　　Child/Student

Other Titles　(music therapist signs here)　Other Titles　　Other Titles
　　　　　*notes "NA" if applicable

Other Titles　　　　　　Other Titles

Asterisk (*) Chairperson on IEP Team

Date of next IEP review _____

Consent (For initial placement or change in special education services/placement only)

☐ I give consent to initiate special education and related services specified in this IEP. (the IEP serves as prior notice if there is agreement)

☐ I give consent to initiate special education and related services specified in this IEP except for _____

☐ I do not give consent for special education services at this time.

Parent Signature: _____ Date: _____

**If there is not agreement, the district must provide prior notice (PS 401) to the parents.

Reevaluation (State and federal rules and regulations mandate that every child/student with a disability be reevaluated at least every three years.

Your child's last MFE was _____

The next MFE shall occur by _____

You will be invited to participate in this meeting as part of the team. Parent permission is required for reevaluation on PS 402.

Parent Notice of Procedural Safeguards

☐ I have received a copy of the parent notice of procedural safeguards; or
☐ I have a current copy of the parent notice of procedural safeguards.
☐ I waive my right to notification of special education and related service by certified mail.

Parent Signature: _____ Date: _____

☆ *Note: The student receives notice of procedural safeguards at least one year prior to his/her 18th birthday.*

Student Signature: _____ Date: _____

☆**When and How Parents will be Informed of Progress:**

Reason for Placement in Separate Facility (if applicable)
Having considered the continuum of services and the needs of the student, this IEP team has decided that placement in a separate facility is appropriate because:

White - CCBMR COPY　　Yellow - PARENT/GUARDIAN COPY　　Pink - PUBLIC SCHOOL DISTRICT COPY　　Goldenrod - TEACHER/SPECIALIST COPY

IEP IV

Figure 9. IEP Signature Page

- Provide for all areas of a child's development through an integrated approach.
- Base planning on observations and recordings of each child's special interests and developmental progress.
- Plan the environment to facilitate learning through interactive play with adults, peers, and a variety of materials.
- Provide for a wide range of interests and abilities.

Music therapists may find the following strategies helpful when attempting to work within the D.A.P. guidelines:

- Use a multi-sensory approach (visual, auditory, tactile, vestibular, proprioceptive)
- Use a variety of modalities (e.g., props, puppets, pictures)
- Use repetition (repeat the song/activity, but also do it "another way")
- Use adapted or augmentative equipment if needed (e.g., switches, modifications to instruments)
- Use gestures or signs
- Help the child EXPERIENCE the music (via active involvement—moving, singing, playing, exploring).

Furthermore, the music therapy program must match the developmental level of the child. Within the framework of a play-based approach, the teaching strategies will change as the child grows and matures. Music therapy conducted in a play-based setting may take the form of guided group instruction or individual exploration of an arranged musical environment. There are many possibilities and many components in this process; each plays an important role in the child's growth and development.

Music typically is an important part of every young child's day (Bayless & Ramsey, 1991; MENC, 1992, 2000). When implementing D.A.P. procedures, music becomes an essential part of the daily classroom environment. Therefore, the music therapist must understand the basic premise and philosophy of D.A.P. and develop new strategies using the music guidelines listed above to prepare service delivery models, assessments and evaluations that fall within the play-based child-directed program. Although teachers are required by law to take data on the progress of the child, a strict behavioral approach really is not compatible with D.A.P. programming. Music therapy practices in the early childhood setting may fit very nicely within D.A.P. if the therapist can relinquish traditional styles and strategies often associated with service delivery.

Play-Based Approach

The Transdisciplinary Play-Based Approach (TPBA) by Toni Linder (1990) presents a succinct and understandable overview of this method. "Play" can be defined as an active engagement that is voluntary, spontaneous and fun. The TPBA guidelines note six types of play. These are listed below. An application for music therapists is expressed within the parentheses.

1. *Exploratory*—discovering one's environment; includes repetitive motor movements (making noises with mouth or instruments; mouthing instruments; random exploration of instruments, using some or all of the senses).
2. *Relational*—using objects in play for the purpose for which they were intended (playing an instrument according to function; using music equipment such as a tape recorder correctly).
3. *Constructive*—manipulating objects for the purpose of constructing or creating something. The child has an end goal in mind and is thinking at a concrete level, but with a sense of order (sings song that tells a story with a beginning and an end; can play instruments in a consistent sequence [e.g. drums with a cymbal crash finale]).
4. *Dramatic play*—child pretends to do something or be someone (movement activities involving creative depiction of animal/object/person; using props such as a rhythm stick to depict a flute for representational play).

5. *Games with rules*—play involves child in activity with accepted rules or limits (songs with rules/expectations such as "Ring Around the Rosy" or "Farmer in the Dell").
6. *Rough and tumble play*—boisterous and physical, often group related (parachute play to music, creative movement, dancing). Remember that an adult needs to monitor this type of play for safety reasons.

It is important to recognize that play skills do not just happen. There are definitive facilitation and procedural skills used in the play-based curriculum that lead to successful learning. This is a critical component of the play-based approach, yet it is one that is often overlooked. Be aware that free play within this framework may look the same as free play without facilitation, yet there is a crucial difference in the outcome.

Facilitating Play With Music

Linder (1990) suggests that the following six skills are necessary for facilitating play-based instruction (music examples have been added):

1. *Follow the child's level and the child's choices.* (Put out instruments and allow total freedom in playing. Imitate the actions of the child.)
2. *Parallel play with the child; occasionally comment about the play action.* (Play an instrument next to the child then intermittently sing or comment about what is taking place. This demonstrates how to play and gives the child the opportunity to play as he or she pleases. Indirectly the therapist is helping the child learn to label actions and objects. This is *adult* facilitated parallel play and far different from peer parallel play.).
3. *Encourage any mode of communication the child may have (eye gaze, gestures, words, etc.) by imitating or responding in a turn-taking manner.* (Play instruments and imitate both motor and vocal actions, echoing dynamic, pitch and tempo levels. Offer the child a turn and encourage response via various modes.).
4. *Let the activity govern the interaction and limit talking.* (Hum along with the instrumental play or sing a nonsense syllable to attract attention to the play.).
5. *Limit questioning and pause long enough to convey that the child's comments are valued.* (Insert a comment or a musical phrase such as "You're playing the blue bells." This is simply an affirmation of the child's play.)
6. *Once the child is comfortable interacting and playing, try to "bump up" the level of play. Model and expand upon his/her verbal or creative play ideas.* (Whatever music skill the child has been performing, model the next step on the task analysis or show the child another way of doing the skill.).

This "bumping up" step is crucial and is often overlooked by those who do not fully understand the techniques used in D.A.P. If the child's level of play is not showing progress, this is a clue that "bumping up" may be needed.

The results of the interactions and progress in music should correlate to those seen by the interdisciplinary team in other environments. When the music therapy approach is play-based and child-directed in nature, there is a purpose, structure and intent built into the planning and implementation of the session. It is not just play for the sake of play. The *children* are playing but the music therapist has enabled the play by adhering to the above guidelines and responding to the needs of the child.

High/Scope

The Head Start classes in the Center subscribe to the High/Scope curriculum that is guided by the belief that all children learn best by becoming actively involved in their play, environments, and interactions with other children and adults. Overall, the High/Scope philosophy calls for a thoughtfully chosen balance of individual, small, and large group activities that include child-initiated, child-directed as well as adult facilitated and adult structured activities that support children's development across all domains.

At the heart of this curriculum is a meta-cognitive strategy referred to as "Plan–Do–Review." This design supports the development of children's self-management, management of the environment, construction of knowledge and communication about that knowledge. In the "Plan" stage, children think, rehearse and make choices. In the "Do" phase, they act on choices, participate, and interact. In "Review," they recall, reflect, and evaluate (Hohmann & Weikart, 1990).

The High/Scope video *The Daily Routine* (1990) lists components of a typical classroom's day. How selected elements are addressed in inclusion, integrated, and reverse mainstreamed preschool music therapy classes has been added in parentheses:

- *Greeting circle*—lets children know session is beginning; offers a sense of security and consistency (each music session begins with a consistent "Hello" song or activity).
- *Planning time*—a group experience that lets children orient to schedule and make choices ("Today in Music" chart shows a picture schedule of activities of the day; children supplement the schedule by selecting pictures from the "Choices" poster that offers a variety of songs/instruments).
- *Work time*—children carry out their choices at centers/stations and through play (music centers offer choices for exploratory play).
- *Clean up time*—a transition time that is part of the "doing" stage (transition songs help children close one activity and transition to the next while being a responsible part of the group).
- *Circle*—provides group and meeting time. May emphasize themes, music or game. May be part of both the "Do" and the "Review" stage (as the music session draws to a close, children refer back to the "Today in Music" poster and recall what took place).

Curriculum Focus Opportunities

Children who have specifically diagnosed or severe needs may be initially served in classes that have a specific curriculum focus. Available options include:

- A cognitive development approach (the Miller Method®), for children who have autism spectrum disorders.
- An emerging academics approach that uses some Montessori methods and ERIN (Early Intervention Recognition Network) Assessment information.
- An activity-based program designed to teach independence in sitting, standing, and walking for children with motor disabilities (Mobility Opportunities Via Education or MOVE®).

A large grant from The Cleveland Foundation enabled the Center to become a certified model site for MOVE® in May 2002.

Though the above types of classrooms emphasize specific curricula, they all blend in components of other methodologies to achieve a developmentally appropriate instruction model that best meets the needs of each child in the class.

CCBMR/DD has provided training to all staff who are assigned to these classrooms. All music therapists work closely with their teams to provide music therapy direct service that is in alignment with each curriculum. Developing resources that support the curriculum and sharing music strategies that may be used throughout the week is an important function of the music therapy department. Furthermore, ancillary staff are encouraged to develop supplemental curriculum materials and carry out collaborative programming to meet the specific needs of individuals or classes.

Service Delivery Models

Service delivery of music therapy in the early childhood division of CCBMR/DD takes many forms. The music therapists see regularly scheduled classes that may be somewhat structured or may be quite improvisational and child-directed. Music therapists also serve as consultants for teachers, other specialists, parents, and the community and assist in the coordination of special events.

Regularly Scheduled Classes

There are many types of classroom models throughout the center and its satellites. Several nonmusical variables affect how music therapy service is delivered. These include: the specific needs of the children in each class, the number of children in each class, the play levels of the children (and the potential for tolerating a group setting), and the availability of times for integration. Staffing and the spirit of cooperation among available team members present additional considerations. The classroom teacher or teacher assistant always attends each music session. These are conducted either in the music room or in the classroom depending upon the needs of the children and the schedules of the music therapists. The music room is large enough to be set up for either station play or for group activity.

Types of Classes

Inclusion Model. Two full inclusion kindergarten classes are housed at the Center. Eight young children with special needs and 16 typically developing children are in each class that is jointly taught by teachers from the Cleveland Public Schools and CCBMR/DD. These classes receive music therapy once a week. If time permits, the classes are divided into two sections to allow for necessary attention to adapting and enhancing activities. The sessions often follow theme ideas that are being explored concurrently in the classroom setting. Music therapists support the emphasis on emerging literacy and design music activities to accompany books and stories. Elements of music education (in the categorical areas of *singing, listening, playing, and moving*) are always stressed. At times, music and adapted physical education classes are combined into a longer time slot, affording greater opportunities for movement exploration.

Many preschool classes follow an inclusion model, with teachers being hired by both CCBMR/DD and Head Start. Ideally, these groups are split into two sections that receive music therapy one half hour per week. Children are brought together for an opening circle and then experience music through a variety of avenues. The preschool classes are less structured than the kindergarten classes, yet both musical and nonmusical goals are implemented.

Integrated Model. Other preschool classes follow an integrated model, with CCBMR/DD children and Head Start students being housed in separate classrooms. The classes share specific activities or play time throughout the day. These classes often come together for music therapy and adapted physical education classes. Many of the students in the CCBMR/DD classes have significant special needs, yet music time offers a time for playing with typical children who serve as excellent role models and peer tutors. This type of service delivery model often is used in the satellite sites thereby giving CCBMR/DD classes the opportunity to share experiences with other agencies within the community. Music sessions often stress social goals and interaction.

Reverse Mainstream Model. CCBMR/DD offers some reverse mainstream classes for both preschool and toddler students. These are CCBMR/DD classes that have eight students with identified needs and up to four children without disabilities. These typical children often are siblings of other children in the building, children from the neighborhood, or those whose parents have expressed interest in this type of experience. The preschool music classes are conducted in a manner similar to the integrated or inclusion models. Toddler classes, however, are much more child-directed. For instance, the music therapist prepares the environment to encourage various levels of play. Often the activities present and expand upon a theme (e.g., *snow* or *ducks*), using manipulatives and props that call upon many different senses. Music therapists may also enter the child's play, using music to interact with the child or comment about the activity.

Self-contained Model. A few classes (such as those for children with severe delays, autism or pervasive developmental disorder, or motor problems) are fully segregated. Music therapy for these classes may address goals in a more traditional behavioral approach or via a more individualized mode (such as one-on-one therapy with the assistance of the occupational or physical therapist). In some cases, such classes may follow a specialized curriculum unique to the type of disability. Nevertheless, activities are conducted with an emphasis on play and engagement.

Individual Treatment Model. Upon referral from a classroom teacher or team member, a child may qualify for individual music therapy. A limited number of time slots are available for this type of service delivery. This therapy is in addition to the child's regularly scheduled weekly music therapy class. It is reserved for the students who have difficulty with groups, who are highly motivated by music or who show unusual musical talent.

Session Structure

Exploring the (Musical) Environment. The needs of some children who come to the music room are best met by exploring and discovering. These classes may come from any of the previously described classroom models. In the music room, stations are set up before the students enter the room. The children are free to choose which station they wish to enter and they have the freedom to move from one station to another.

Each station is designed by the music therapist to relate to the children's IFSP/IEP outcomes/objectives. The stations may also incorporate the school's themes, seasons, or suggestions elicited from the staff. One station is always a quiet sensory area with adapted instruments and instruments or objects that vibrate, switch-activated lights and equipment, and a tape player and books to go along with available music. Another corner utilizes the "Instrument of the Month" (e.g., cube chairs set around a bass drum, with a wide variety of mallets). A drum table and Orff instruments are available for improvisation and constructive play. Yet another station may be an open area where the children play some type of cooperative musical game or sing or play a song using a chart with picture icons they can read.

One picture board (titled "Today in Music") shows the general schedule of activities while another ("Choices") portrays songs, instruments and props that can be selected. Pictures are laminated and backed with Velcro for quick and easy modifications.

Promoting interaction. Music therapists at the Center generally follow a child-directed mode of service delivery that emphasizes play facilitation. If interaction is the prime focus, music session components for integrated preschool and inclusive kindergarten classes additionally may adhere to the following guidelines.

First, each session begins with a song that brings the children together and establishes the start of the class. The activities that follow are planned to provide avenues for children to *experience* music across several cultures through singing, playing instruments, moving, listening, and creating. Though the music activities may foster classroom survival skills (such as taking turns and following directions), they should be mainly geared towards an integrated theory of play. In an effort to expand the children's responses, activities typically vary by type and length and include both familiar and new songs. A portion of each session is devoted to some aspect of social interaction. Finally, a good-bye song helps to focus the children as a group and add closure to the session. Though the therapist plans the activities, there are some elements of choice for the children. Spontaneity is never discouraged and often presents a springboard for creative group endeavors and improvised play.

The development of social skills may be considered of highest priority by early childhood educators (Katz, 1988). Research indicates that young children with special needs gain more appropriate play skills and interact more readily in a socially integrated setting than in a separate setting (Guralnick & Groom, 1988; Jenkins, Speltz, & Odom, 1985). However, it appears that interaction is best obtained if teachers employ specific interaction strategies to promote play between children with special needs and their typical peers (Cavallaro, Haney, & Cabello, 1993; Jenkins, Odom & Speltz, 1989; Jenkins, Speltz & Odom, 1985; McLean & Odom, 1988; Odom et al., 1988).

Music therapy has been found to be an effective strategy for achieving such interaction (Gunsberg, 1988, 1991; Hughes, Robbins, McKenzie, & Robb, 1990; Humpal, 1991; Jellison, Brooks, & Huck, 1984). Furthermore, music therapy can foster socialization in a manner that is consistent with developmentally appropriate practice (Standley & Hughes, 1996). Music therapists at the Center encourage interaction by asking the staff to join in a circle formation, take part in the opening song, and mingle freely. Directions are given within a musical context to structure spontaneous and nonthreatening interaction. As social play progresses, the music therapist may facilitate interaction at the following levels:

- By issuing a directive (e.g., "Caryn, please dance with Lisa.")
- By issuing an indirect request (e.g., "Greg, find a friend who has another cymbal.")
- By providing a song that has a cue for choosing a partner (e.g., the lyric instructions for the musical game "Rig-a-Jig-Jig"; "...a friend of mine I happened to *meet*")
- By spontaneous selection or by a nondirective facilitation (e.g., "Everyone find a partner!")

(Dimmick & Humpal, 1990).

Staff and peer tutors assist those children who are less able to independently participate.

Consultation

Because music therapy functions as part of a team approach, teachers and other related service personnel may request ideas for the use of music beyond the scheduled music sessions. The music therapy staff offer assistance through several avenues.

Music activity packets that include songs, artwork, and implementation ideas for holidays and general theme concepts (e.g., "transportation" or "animals") plus suggestions for their use in both structured and unstructured play have been developed for use in the classrooms. The music therapists record the songs contained in the packets and make the tapes available to the staff. Props made to enhance the songs may also be signed out from the music lending library. One page "Musical Moments" offer simple musical activity ideas for adult/child interaction. These are posted regularly outside the music room.

Supplementary enrichment ideas are displayed on a "Staff Notes" bulletin board located in the music room. This bulletin board lists tapes (both audio and video), CDs, and resources that are available for use. Upcoming cultural events, both at school and in the community, are posted. These may be a source of possible field trips for students and their families.

Families may borrow music resources to use in their homes. A grant from the Baby Einstein Company provided video and audio classical musical selections for a music lending library for families. The music therapy department added to the resources by producing tapes of its *Top Ten for Little People* and *Transition Songs for Young Children*. Songbooks accompanied each tape. All of these resources are contained in the *Music for My Baby and Me* tote bags. When they are checked out, families are also given a guide for using music with their little ones (see Figure 10). A kit for families in the Hispanic community includes materials translated into Spanish (see Figure 11).

A major aspect of music consultation is helping teachers use music throughout their day in the classroom (such as facilitating relaxation in quiet time or enhancing station play). A music therapist may also demonstrate, build, or adapt equipment. Such topics often are presented at group inservice training sessions. The music therapists have block times in their schedules where they work with the teacher and children in the classroom setting. This allows for musical play and improvisation through a child-directed approach. By directly observing and interacting within the classroom, the music therapist is better able to offer specific suggestions to teachers for using music in various aspects of their particular classroom routine.

The Music Educators National Conference, in its Position Statement on Early Childhood Education (1992), calls for a combined effort among parents, music specialists, and early childhood professionals to ensure that music becomes a natural and important part of every young child's growth and development. The *Start the Music* initiative (MENC, 2000) and *Sesame Street Music Works* (Sesame Workshop, 2001) project are examples of corporate and professional organization partnerships whose mission statements reiterate that music is a vital component in early childhood education and that all children and families can and should make music together (MENC, 2000). (It should be noted that both of the aforementioned groups solicited input from music therapists when developing their projects.) Music for young children is not an option, but is a part of the curricula "best practices" (Bayless & Ramsey, 1991). Therefore, music therapists need to provide the experiences that will ensure that music is used as part of the daily classroom routine. Music will enrich the lives of the children; hopefully, it will be a rewarding, effective part of the teacher's day, too.

To initiate this philosophy, the music therapy staff surveyed the entire staff of the Center to determine the *Top Ten for Little People*. The music therapists taped their renditions of the survey's results and distributed the tapes to each teacher and related service personnel who requested them. Teachers were then able to sing along with a tape that was representative of the typical child's repertoire, thereby promoting normalization and using music in a nonthreatening way. Initially not every staff member was at ease using music, and each individual had different abilities and interests in this area. The music therapy staff needed to accommodate the teacher's abilities and increase their comfort level in utilizing music.

Consultation may also become part of a team strategy for goal implementation. The development of transition songs is representative of this concept. For instance, the speech/language pathologist may request a song to pair with an object as a cue for communicating an upcoming event :

Event: *Going Home on the Bus*
Object cue: Small plastic bus
Tune: "Happy Birthday"

It's time to go home,
It's time to go home.
Our school day is over,
To the bus we will go.

This next transition song prepares a child for handwashing. It was written to facilitate an occupational therapy goal for a child with tactile defensiveness:

Tune: "I'm Gonna Wash That Man Right Out of My Hair"
We're gonna wash that *dirt right off of our hands,
We're gonna wash that dirt right off of our hands,
We're gonna wash that dirt right off of our hands
And get real squeaky clean!

*paint, food, etc.

Music and Your Baby

All babies love music. They experience music by *hearing* it, by *moving* to it, by *banging* to it, and by *playing with their voices*.

Little ones enjoy:
Being sung to:
♪   With a quiet lullaby at nap time and bedtime as you rock. Keep the beat slow and steady. Many babies will find this special time very calming.
♪   About activities of her day --no need to use the same words each time. Making up words that describe her activity is fun for both of you.
♪   With children's songs that are familiar to him (such as "Row, Row, Row Your Boat"). Sing them over and over. Babies love repetition!
♪   With your favorite songs. She will enjoy seeing you enjoy music, too.
♪   As you change activities. The music will help the baby accept and anticipate change.

Little ones enjoy:
Fingerplays, finger wiggles, tickles, and bounces:
♪   While holding onto your finger and feeling the beat as you bounce them on your lap.
♪   Or hearing you sing simple finger play songs (like "Eency Weency Spider").
♪   Or being part of chanting and rhyming games or songs that end with a tickle.

Little ones enjoy:
Sounds:
♪   That have surprises (like "Pop! Goes the Weasel!).
♪   That rattle or ring.
♪   That come from music boxes or musical toys.
♪   That they can make on small instruments such as bells or rattles...
♪   Or from things found around the house (such as pots and pans).
♪   That are in their environment - such as trains or birds singing.
♪   That they can make with their bodies (like clapping, tapping or patting).

A few tips for using music with your baby:

♪   Don't be shy about singing - your child will respond to the rhythm, melody and the joy with which *you* sing...and he will welcome the chance to share this time with you.
♪   Make music a part of the whole day.
♪   Match your child's energy level - upbeat songs when she's ready for play and lullabies when she's tired.
♪   Repeat, repeat, repeat....do it again, and again, and again. Children learn through repetition.
♪   Expose your baby to many different types of music. Borrow tapes and CDs from the library before purchasing them to find the ones that you and your baby like most.
♪   By making music with your baby, you can share traditions of your culture.
♪   Relax and enjoy this special time for interacting and sharing with your child.

Compiled by the CCBMR/DD Early Childhood Music Therapy Department

Figure 10. *Music for My Baby and Me,* **Guide for Caregivers**

La Música y Su Bebé

Todos los bebes aman la música. Ellos disfrutan de la música *escuchandola*, *golpeando*, *moviéndose* y *jugando con sus voces*.

Los mas pequeños disfrutan:
Cuando les cantan:
* Una canción de cuna durante la siesta o al acostarlos durante la noche mientras Usted se mueve en una mecedora. Muchos bebes encontraran este momento muy especial y muy calmante.
* Acerca de las actividades del bebé durante el día —no necesita usar las mismas palabras en cada momento. Será divertido para ambos inventar palabras que describan esas actividades.
* Canciones que sean familiares para el bebé (como por ejemplo "Tortitas"). Cántelas una y otra vez. A los bebes les gusta la repetición. .
* Con sus canciones favoritas, Al bebé le gustará ver que Usted también disfruta de la música.
* Cuando Usted cambia de actividades, La música ayudara a su bebé a anticipar y aceptar los cambios.

Los mas pequeños disfrutan:
Juegos y movimientos, cosquillas y rebotes con los dedos:
* Mientras agarra los dedos de su bebé y los hace seguir el ritmo hágalos rebotar también en su falda.
* O escuchandole a Usted cantar una simple canción para mover los dedos (como "La Arañita")
* O participando en juegos rítmicos o canciones que terminan con un cosquilleo.

Los mas pequeños disfrutan:
Sonidos:
* Que tienen sorpresas (de adentro de una caja salta un payaso).
* De un sonajero o de una campanilla.
* Que provienen de cajas musicales o juguetes con música.
* Que ellos pueden hacer con pequeños instrumentos como campanillas, cascabeles o sonajeros
* O con otros objetos que encuentran en la casa como cacerolas o cacharros.

Algunos consejitos para usar música con su bebé:

* No tenga verguenza de cantar, su bebé respondera al ritmo, a la melodía y al gusto que Usted pone al cantar y agradecera la posibilidad que tiene de compartir ese tiempo con Usted.
* Haga que la música forme parte de su día.
* Observe el nivel de energía de su bebé. Ritmos ligeros cuando su bebé esta listo/a para jugar y canciones lentas cuando esta cansado/a.
* Repita, repita, repita..., hágalo una y otra vez. Los niños aprenden a través de la repetición.
* Hágale descubrir a su bebé los diferentes tipos de música. Saque cassettes y C.D. prestados de la biblioteca para escucharlos y descubrir cuales son los que mas le gustan a su bebé antes de comprarlos.
* Haciendo música con su bebé Usted podrá compartir tradiciones de su cultura.
* Relájese y disfrute de ese tiempo especial para interaccionar y compartir con su niño/niña.

Recopilado por el CCBMR/DD Departamento de Terapia Musical para la Niñez Temprana

Figure 11. Spanish Translation of *Music for My Baby and Me*

These transition songs became so popular that the music therapy department wrote examples for a variety of situations. Furthermore, all staff members were asked to submit an example of a transition song that worked successfully in their settings. These were made into a booklet and the music therapists also recorded the examples. The resources were made available to everyone in the early childhood program.

Family/Child Programs

Not all children served by CCBMR/DD are enrolled in classes at the centers or satellite sites. Some come to these facilities with their families or are served mainly in the home. An early intervention specialist and supportive home services personnel work with the family to develop an IFSP for these children. There are actually two components to music therapy service delivery in this model. First, parents may be advised how to use music in play with their infants or children within the home setting. The second component involves providing a group experience for young children and their parents or families.

Therapists may conduct an inservice to model activities that show families how to utilize music at home. Simple suggestions for converting common household items into instruments or ways to inexpensively make instruments from boxes, paper plates, cereal, etc. are always welcomed. Parents may be asked to provide a blank tape prior to the session. The music therapist will sing the songs from the lesson and often will offer written activity ideas, picture cues, and possible adaptations for use by the parents. If professionally recorded songs are incorporated in the guide, parents should be given a reference/resource list and addresses of where these items may be purchased. (Remember to keep abreast of the copyright laws!)

Often home-based students come to the centers, to one of the satellites, or to a site within the community for weekly group sessions. These experiences enable parents to share concerns and experiences, expose children to socialization with peers, and provide participants with the expertise of many specialists. Parks (1986) believes that parent participation and interaction with the child during the early years can significantly effect the child's growth and development in later years. Parents can be helped to enhance the developmental skills and behaviors of their child by using key parent interaction strategies. Music activities furnish enjoyable means for such interaction. Likewise, families frequently ask for ways to use music to make play, or occupational, physical, or speech therapy exercises more interesting and motivating. This is truly collaboration in action.

Additional early childhood groups may be established to serve families within the community. Such groups provide enrichment opportunities and are open to any interested families. Children with a wide range of abilities have time to play together as their families make new friends and learn strategies for parenting. Music, story time, crafts, creative movement, and snack time are designed around central themes. An early intervention specialist coordinates the group and utilizes support staff on a rotating schedule. Music therapists often direct music activities on a regular basis. Since some of these groups reflect the Cleveland area's rich multicultural heritage, it is important for the music therapists to be familiar with music from a wide range of ethnic influences and to sing some songs in the families' native language.

At the Center, the music therapy and adapted physical education departments work together to provide a "Movement and Music" class for families and their young children. Conducted in the gym, this weekly program is geared towards educating parents how to purposely play with their child using both motor and music strategies.

As the 21st century unfolds, many types of early childhood music opportunities are becoming available to the general public. CCBMR/DD's music therapists have worked together with early intervention specialists to create community music programs for young children and their families. These classes are appropriate for children of all abilities and have been enthusiastically received by families of both children with disabilities and those who are typically developing. Music has provided an arena where all children can be successful.

Miscellaneous

Center Special Events. The music therapy department takes advantage of the tremendous wealth of cultural diversity in the Cleveland area. Performing groups and individual artists come to the Center. Classes take field trips that introduce children to a wide array of enrichment opportunities. Care is taken to ensure that these events are appropriate for young children.

Believing that young children learn best by experiencing, the music and adapted physical education departments co-direct "Music and Movement" days. All children in the center attend these festive occasions during assigned 20–30 minute slots. As a group enters the gym, children come together for a few short songs. They are then introduced to the various stations within the area. Children explore these arranged environments while all staff members assist. As selected background music plays, children may discover a pumpkin patch obstacle course or a cardboard box "sleigh"—complete with numerous and diverse bells. Much thought and preparation go into determining station ideas and coordinating efforts of the two departments. "Music and Movement" days are enthusiastically lauded by students, families, and staff personnel.

Public Relations. CCBMR/DD's music therapy department is often called on to represent the mission of its employer. Each year the group devotes one week in March to promoting "Music in Our Schools Month." The music therapists become performers and present a musical revue that incorporates representative selections from MENC's World's Largest Concert program, vocal and instrumental solos, and large ensemble numbers. Audience participation is always solicited. This troupe takes its program to all CCBMR/DD sites and is often asked to perform for community events, such as headlining at the Cleveland area Very Special Arts Festival.

Music therapists are frequently recruited to speak to professional or civic organizations, to guest lecture at local colleges and universities, to share adaptation ideas with other agencies, to write for professional publications or to present at conferences. CCBMR/DD encourages this professional involvement and recognizes the positive effects of such endeavors in the area of public relations.

Coda

William Patrick Day Early Childhood Center in Cleveland, Ohio has been operating as part of an early intervention interagency collaborative since September of 1992. Innovative change has developed over time. The program is continually being fine-tuned; this process definitely has had its effects upon students, families, and staff of all agencies involved therein. The staff and administration of William Patrick Day Early Childhood Center constantly monitor current trends and have been deciphering which do and which do not transfer from theory into practice. Modifications and re-evaluation are ongoing. Unquestionably, child-initiated and play-based experiences appear to be beneficial to the education of the young child. Likewise, music is a very important part of the early childhood world of play and is gaining much publicity for its positive effects on young children. Therefore, it would seem that music therapists could benefit from learning more about early intervention and how music therapy may be utilized within such a setting. The profession may indeed play a major role in the quickly expanding realm of early childhood education.

Sample Letter to Classroom Teachers

". . . music allows for all levels of responses on the part of all children. It is a universal language and is an effective tool in bringing children of various abilities together. It can be structured or unstructured, based upon the needs of the participants. Music is a fun experience and provides a stimulus for communication and verbalization."

(from CCBMR/DD's Policy Statement regarding the music mainstreaming program)

WHO: Head Start and CCBMR/DD preschool classes
WHAT: Integrated music classes
WHEN: See your individual schedule
WHERE: Usually in the music room (check with your music therapist)

A few "notes" to make our classes more harmonious:

• *Please be on time.*
• *Help the children put on their name tags.*
• *Keep the children in the same group each week* (even if some are absent).
• *Help the children mingle.*
• *Sit within the group and help any child who needs assistance.*
• *Participate in all activities* (this should be fun for **you**, too!).
• *Notify your music therapist in advance if your class will not be attending its music session.*

What you can expect from us:

• *We will facilitate weekly music sessions and center special events.*
• *We will notify you in advance of any canceled sessions.*
• *We will make resources available for you to check out.*

. . . and most important:

We will strive to assist you in any way we can to help you share the gift of music with your children. **PLEASE** feel free to come to us with any suggestions, comments or questions you many have. We look forward to working with you and your classes!

(Signed) Your Music Therapists

Tips

- Communicate expectations to other personnel involved in joint programming.

- Make a poster for each class that lists the children's names and IEP or IFSP objectives or outcomes. Hang this at the back of the room prior to each session for a quick visual reference.

- Keep a folder or notebook for each class. Record anecdotal information immediately following each session.

- Keep a notebook of lesson plans. Plans should list equipment, music, and brief procedure for each activity. Catalogue these plans by date and/or theme.

- Use a multisensory approach and be aware of various learning modalities.

- Repeat activities, but also do them "another way"—*expand* upon the child's experience bank.

- Monitor the pace of the session—and be ready to follow the child's lead.

- Make classroom sets of props—enough for each child to have one (laminate these to preserve them for future use).

- Check out books, CDS, and tapes from the local library to preview before purchasing.

- Encourage parent participation and support. Send home examples of songs, activities, and resources that families can share with their child.

References

American Music Therapy Association. (1999). *Music therapy and the young child.* Silver Spring, MD: Author.

Andress, B. (1989). *Promising practices: Prekindergarten music education.* Reston, VA: MENC.

Andress, B., & Walker, L. M. (1992). *Readings in early childhood music education.* Reston, VA: MENC.

Bayless, K. M., & Ramsey, M. E. (1991). *Music: A way of life for the young child.* New York: Macmillan.

Boswell, J. (1984). The young child and music: Contemporary principles in child development and music education. *Proceedings of the Music in Early Childhood Conference.* Provo, Utah. Reston, VA: MENC.

Bredekamp, S. (1987). *Developmentally appropriate practices in early childhood programs serving children from birth through age eight.* Washington, DC: National Association for the Education of Young Children.

Briggs, C. (1991). A model for understanding musical development. *Music Therapy, 10*(1), 1–21.

Cavallaro, C. C., Haney, M., & Cabello, B. (1993). Developmentally appropriate strategies for promoting full participation in early childhood settings. *Topics in Early Childhood Special Education, 13*(3), 293–307.

CCBMR/DD. (1995). *Early childhood program philosophy, curriculum guidelines, and operational standards.* Cleveland, OH: CCBMR/DD.

CCBMR/DD. (1999). *The Cuyahoga County Board of Mental Retardation and Developmental Disabilities Early childhood program: Individualized Family Service Plan process and procedures.* Cleveland, OH: Author.

CCBMR/DD. (2000). *William Patrick Day Early Childhood Center* [Brochure]. Cleveland, OH: Author.

Coleman, K., & Brunk, B. (1999). *SEMTAP Special Education Music Therapy Assessment Process handbook.* Grapevine, TX: Prelude Music Therapy.

Colwell, C. (1994). Therapeutic application of music in the whole language kindergarten. *Journal of Music Therapy, 31*(4), 238–247.

Davis, R. (2001). Taking first steps in preschool together: A hierarchical approach to group music therapy intervention. *Early Childhood Connections, 7*(2), 33–43.

Dimmick, J. A., & Humpal, M. E. (1989). *A musical bridge: A guide to mainstreaming.* Cleveland, OH: CCBMR/DD.

Dimmick, J. A., & Humpal, M. E. (Authors), & Quill, M. (Director). (1990). *Together as friends* [Videotape]. Cleveland, OH: CCBMR/DD.

Dimmick, J. A., & Humpal, M. E. (1994). *Music Therapy Assessment and Evaluations Checklist: Early childhood.* Cleveland, OH: CCBMR/DD.

Education for All Handicapped Children Act Amendments of 1986, Public Law 99-457. U.S. Congress.

Furman, A. G. (2001). Young children with autism spectrum disorder. *Early Childhood Connections, 7*(2), 43–49.

Gunsberg, A. S. (1988). Improvised musical play: A strategy for fostering social play between developmentally delayed and nondelayed preschool children. *Journal of Music Therapy, 25*(4), 178–191.

Gunsberg, A. S. (1991). A method for conducting improvised musical pay with children both with and without developmental delay in preschool classrooms. *Music Therapy Perspectives, 9,* 46–51.

Guralnick, M. J., & Groom, J. M. (1988). Peer interactions in mainstreamed and specialized classrooms: A comparative analysis. *Exceptional Children, 54*(5), 415–425.

Hanline, M. F., & Hanson, M. J. (1989). Integration considerations for infants and toddlers with multiple disabilities. *JASH, 14*(3), 178–183.

Hitz, R., & Driscoll, A. (1988, July). Praise or encouragement? New insights into praise: Implications for early childhood teachers. *Young Children,* 6–13.

Hohmann, M., & Weikart, D. (Producers). (1990). *The daily routine* [Videotape]. Ypsilanti, MI: High/Scope Press.

Hughes, J., Robbins, B., McKenzie, B., & Robb, S. (1990). Integrating exceptional and nonexceptional young children through music play: A pilot program. *Music Therapy Perspectives, 8,* 52–56.

Humpal, M. E. (2001). Music therapy and the young child. *Early Childhood Connections, 7*(2), 9–15.

Humpal, M. E. (1991). The effects of an integrated early childhood music program on social interaction among children with handicaps and their typical peers. *Journal of Music Therapy, 37*(3), 166–177.

Humpal, M. E. (1990). Early intervention: The implications for music therapy. *Music Therapy Perspectives, 8,* 30–35.

Humpal, M. E., & Dimmick, J. A. (1993). Music at William Patrick Day early childhood center. *Triad, 60*(6), 17–18.

Individual Disabilities Education Act of 1992, Public Law 102-119.

Individual Disabilities Education Act Amendments of 1997, Public Law 105-17.

Jellison, J., Brooks, B., & Huck, A. (1984). Structuring small groups and music reinforcement to facilitate positive interactions and acceptance of severely handicapped students in the regular music classroom. *Journal of Research in Music Education, 32*(4), 243–264.

Jellison, J. (2000). A content analysis of music research with disabled children and youth (1975–1999): Applications in special education. In *Effectiveness of music therapy procedures: Documentation of research and clinical practice* (pp. 199–264). Silver Spring, MD: AMTA.

Jenkins, J. R., Odom, S. L., & Speltz, M. L. (1989). Effects of social integration on preschool children with handicaps. *Exceptional Children, 55*(5), 420–428.

Jenkins, J. R., Speltz, M. L., & Odom, S. L. (1985). Integrating normal and handicapped preschoolers: Effects on child development and social interaction. *Exceptional Children, 52*(1), 7–17.

Katz, L. (1988). *Early childhood education: What research tells us.* Bloomington, IN: Phi Delta Kappa Educational Foundation.

Linder, T. (1990). *Transdisciplinary Play-based Assessment: A functional approach for working with young children.* Baltimore, MD: Paul H. Brankes.

Loewy, J. (1995). The musical stages of speech: A developmental model of pre-verbal sound making. *Music Therapy, 13*(10), 47–73.

Ludlow, B. L. (1987). *Preschool programs for handicapped children.* Bloomington, IN: Phi Delta Kappa Educational Foundation.

McDonald, D. T., & Simons, G. M. (1989). *Musical growth and development, birth through six.* New York: Schirmer Books.

McGonigel, M. J., & Johnson, B. H. (1991). An overview. In B. H. Johnson, M. J. McGonigel, & R. K. Kaufmann (Eds.), *Guidelines and recommended practices for the Individualized Family Service Plan* (2nd ed., pp. 1–5). Bethesda, MD: Association for the Care of Children's Health.

McLean, M., & Odom, S. (1988). *Least restrictive environment and social integration.* Division for Early Childhood White Paper. Reston, VA: Division for Early Childhood of the Council for Exceptional Children.

Mahoney, G. J., & Powell, A. (1984). *Transactional Inclusive Program: Teachers' guide.* Farmington, CT: Pediatric Research and Training Center.

Music Educators National Conference. (1992, Winter). Position statement on early childhood education. *Soundpost,* pp. 21–22.

Music Educators National Conference. (2000). *Proceedings of the June 2000 Summit Meeting, "Start the Music."* Reston, VA: Author.

Morin, F. (2001). Cultivating music play: The need for changed teaching practice. *General Music Today, 14*(2), 24–29.

Neeley, L. (2001). Developmentally appropriate music practice: Children learn what they live. *Young Children, 56*(3), 32–37.

Odom, S. L., Bender, M., Stein, M., Doran, L., Houden, P., McInnes, M., Gilbert, M, DeKlyen, M., Speltz, M., & Jenkins, J. (1988). *Integrated preschool curriculum.* Seattle, WA: University of Washington Press.

Overby, L. Y. (1991). Early childhood creative arts. *Proceedings of the International Early Childhood Creative Arts Conference,* Los Angeles, CA. Reston, VA: American Alliance for Health, Physical Education, Recreation, and Dance.

Palmer, M., & Sims, W. (1993). *Music in prekindergarten: Planning and teaching.* Reston, VA: MENC.

Parks, S. (1986). *Make every step count: Birth to 1 year: Developmental parenting guide.* Palo Alto, CA: VORT Corporation.

Robertson, L. H. (Ed.) (1992, Fall/Winter). One-stop service shopping is the hallmark at our new W.P. Day Early Childhood Center. *Insight.* Cleveland, OH: CCBMR/DD.

Sandall, S., Schwartz, I., & Joseph, G. (2001). A building blocks model for effective instruction in inclusive early childhood settings. *Young Exceptional Children, 4*(3), 3–9.

Sesame Workshop. (2001). *Sesame Street Music Works.* New York: Author.

Standley, J., & Hughes, J. (1996). Documenting developmentally appropriate objectives and benefits of a music therapy program for early intervention: A behavioral analysis. *Music Therapy Perspectives, 14*(2), 87–94.

Standley, J., & Hughes, J. (1997). Evaluation of an early intervention music curriculum for enhancing prereading/writing skills. *Music Therapy Perspectives, 15*(2), 79–86.

Vander Ven, K. (1994). Professional development: A contextual model. In J. Johnson & J. B. McCracken (Eds.), *The early childhood career lattice: Perspectives on professional development* (pp. 79–88). Washington, DC: National Association for the Education of Young Children.

Welch, M. (2000). *CCBMR/DD early childhood program, early childhood IEP manual.* Cleveland, OH: CCBMR/DD.

Welch, M., & Cook, C. (2001). *Early childhood classroom curriculum guidelines and operational standards.* Cleveland, OH: CCBMR/DD.

Wolfe, D., & Horn, C. (1993). Use of melodies as structural prompts for learning and retention of sequential verbal information by preschool students. *Journal of Music Therapy, 30*(2), 100–118.

Appendix A

Music Therapy Assessment and Evaluations Checklist

Name _____

MUSIC THERAPY ASSESSMENT and EVALUATIONS CHECKLIST

- Early Childhood -

Description

The following tool has been developed for use by music therapists who work in an early childhood setting. A description of the child can be noted under CONSIDERATIONS. *where specific information may be inserted. In the* CATEGORY *section, general music education categories (Singing, Playing, Listening, and Moving) and their component parts are arranged so that the therapist may check the child's highest level of mastery and the date of attainment. A* CODE *affords an abbreviated means of addressing other aspects and levels of the child's musical play.*

This Assessment and Evaluation Checklist *is meant to be used in conjunction with a general play-based assessment to determine global goals that address the needs of the whole child through developmentally appropriate practices. Thus, the child's* PARTICIPATION AND ENGAGEMENT *levels will reflect his/her stage of social play (i.e. Onlooker, Solitary, Parallel, Associative, or Cooperative). The levels sytem of the CAT-EGORIES helps verify the child's stage of cognitive play (i.e. Exploratory/ Sensorimotor, Manipulative, Constructive, Pretend, or Dramatic).* TEAM NOTES *can be incorporated into determining general programming and specific interdisciplinary strategies.*

The final page of this instrument lists the IFSP / IEP OUTCOME / OBJECTIVE *that has been selected by the music therapist. In addition, space is provided for describing the child's interests and repertoire (positive reinforcers / motivators and present level). This page serves a dual purpose. It can be duplicated and used as a* PROGRESS NOTE *that can be sent home, with a copy attached to the child's file.*

MUSIC THERAPY ASSESSMENT AND EVALUATION CHECKLIST
- *EARLY CHILDHOOD* -

CHILD'S NAME: _____ FACILITY: _____

Music Therapist: _____

CONSIDERATIONS	CATEGORY	Date:

CONSIDERATIONS

___ HEARING

___ VISION

___ COMMUNICATION

___ MOTOR

___ MEDICAL

___ SENSORY

___ PLAY

___ OTHER

CODE:

+ = child initiated

    facilitated by:

p = physical cue

g = gestural cue

v = verbal cue

a = adapted

CATEGORY

A. SINGING

1. Vocalizes by:

  a. Babbling

  b. Speaking

  c. Whispering

  d. Shouting

  e. Humming

2. Uses inflection in vocal play

3. Imitates

4. Sings on pitch

5. Sings responses

B. SOUND PLAY

1. Uses body sounds in musical play by:

  a. Clapping

  b. Stamping

  c. Patting

  d. Other _____

2. Reaches for sound source

3. Plays instruments by:

  a. Swiping

  b. Scratching

  c. Shaking

  d. Striking with palm of hand

  e. Striking with mallet

CATEGORY	Date:			
B. SOUND PLAY (cont.)				
4. Uses sounds / inst. in play				
5. Chooses sounds / inst. to accompany song / story				
6. Labels sound / inst.				
7. Plays inst. in sequence				
8. Categorizes sounds / inst.				
9. Keeps steady beat				
10. Imitates simple rhythm				
11. Stops on cue				
12. Plays ensemble part				
C. LISTENING				
1. Alerts to sound				
2. Attends to sound (how?_____)				
3. Improvises to sound (how?_____)				
4. Listens quietly as music plays				
5. Responds to changes in: a. dynamics				
b. tempo				
c. rhythm				
d. timbre				
e. form				
f. texture				

CATEGORY	Date:			
D. MOVING				
1. Enjoys moving to music				
2. Creates own actions				
3. Moves to personal beat				
4. Expresses feelings through movement				
5. Aware of body's position in space when moving				
6. Imitates actions				
7. Uses simple concepts during movement activities (e.g. "up")				
8. Uses dance steps, following directions of therapist / song				
PARTICIPATION & ENGAGEMENT				
1. Responds to music across different environments				
2. Watches others play				
3. Chooses music station / instrument independently a. Stays in chosen area _____ (e.g. "flits")				
b. Completes activity				
4. Engages with adult during musical play				
5. Plays next to another child				
6. Plays with another child				
7. Plays in group music activity				
8. Engages in independent functional music routine				
9. Uses music to transition				

TEAM NOTES

Music Therapy IFSP/IEP Outcome/Objective
PROGRESS NOTE
Early Childhood

Child's name _____

Music Therapist_____ Facility _____

Year:	Music Therapy IFSP/IEP Outcome/Objective

Progress Note 1:	Date:

Progress Note 2:	Date:

CHILD'S REPERTOIRE / CHOICES

Appendix B

AMTA Fact Sheet: Music Therapy and the Young Child

AMERICAN
MUSIC
THERAPY
ASSOCIATION

American Music Therapy Association, Inc.

8455 Colesville Road, Suite 1000, Silver Spring, MD 20910   (301) 589-3300   fax (301) 589-5175
email: amta@musictherapy.org   website: www/musictherapy.org

MUSIC THERAPY AND THE YOUNG CHILD

What is Music Therapy?
Music Therapy is an established health profession similar to occupational therapy and physical therapy. It consists of using music therapeutically to address physical, psychological, cognitive, behavioral and/or social functioning. Because music therapy is a powerful and non-threatening medium, unique outcomes are possible. With young children, music therapy provides a unique variety of music experiences in an intentional and developmentally appropriate manner to effect changes in a child's behavior and facilitate development of his/her communication, social/emotional, sensori-motor, and/or cognitive skills.

Music therapy enhances the quality of life. It involves relationships between a qualified therapist and child; between one child and another; between child and family; and between the music and the participants. These relationships are structured and adapted through the elements of music to create a positive environment and set the occasion for successful growth.

How does music therapy make a difference with young children?
- Music stimulates all of the senses and involves the child at many levels. This "multi-modal approach" facilitates many developmental skills.
- Quality learning and maximum participation occur when children are permitted to experience the joy of play. The medium of music therapy allows this play to occur naturally and frequently.
- Music is highly motivating, yet it can also have a calming and relaxing effect. Enjoyable music activities are designed to be success-oriented and make children feel better about themselves.
- Music therapy can help a child manage pain and stressful situations.
- Music can encourage socialization, self-expression, communication, and motor development.
- Because the brain processes music in both hemispheres, music can stimulate cognitive functioning and may be used for remediation of some speech/language skills.

The following case study was written in 1996:
A music therapist working in a community music school refers to one of her students as a "musical child." The six-year old girl, who has physical and developmental delays, is somewhat verbal and interacts in a limited way with others. When she began music therapy at age three, it quickly became obvious that she had exceptional innate musical ability. She could play the piano by ear when she was two, although her hands have only four fingers each. And even though she rarely spoke, she sang – and in tune.

The last three years have resulted in significant growth. Through weekly individual 45-minute and then 60-minute music therapy sessions, the child has made progress in the length of her attention span, degree of independence and ability to follow directions. She now speaks one and two word phrases spontaneously, and there is also marked improvement in her social skills. In addition to singing and playing keyboard and piano, the child now plays the omnichord, autoharp, bells, chimes, xylophones, drum set and various small percussion instruments. In her initial stages of music therapy, when she played the keyboard and piano, she would not allow anyone else to play with her. Now, however, she plays the melody and the therapist plays the accompaniment. The child's preschool teacher has asked her to play for other children in her class, thereby using her musical strength to draw her into the group.

What do music therapists do?

Music therapists involve children in singing, listening, moving, playing, and in creative activities that may help them become better learners. Music therapists work on developing a child's self-awareness, confidence, readiness skills, coping skills, and social behavior and may also provide pain management techniques. They explore which styles of music, techniques and instruments are most effective or motivating for each individual child and expand upon the child's natural, spontaneous play in order to address areas of need.

Often working as a part of an interdisciplinary team, music therapists may coordinate programming with other professionals such as early intervention specialists, medical personnel, child-life specialists, psychologists, occupational and physical therapists, speech/language pathologists, adapted physical education specialists and art and dance/movement therapists. Music therapists may also furnish families with suggestions and resources for using music with the child at home.

Music therapists develop a rapport with children. They observe the child's behavior and interactions and assess communication, cognitive/academic, motor, social/emotional, and musical skills. After developing realistic goals and target objectives, music therapists plan and implement systematic music therapy treatment programs with procedures and techniques designed specifically for the individual child. Music therapists document responses, conduct ongoing evaluations of progress, and often make recommendations to other team members and the family regarding progress. Music therapists will also often make recommendations to team members and the family regarding ways to include successful music therapy techniques in other aspects of the child's life.

Who are music therapists?

Music therapists are college graduates who have earned a minimum of a bachelor's degree from one of seventy approved music therapy degree programs. The approved curriculum for entry level study in music therapy includes coursework in music therapy; psychology; music; biological, social and behavioral sciences; disabilities and general studies. Study includes practical application of music therapy procedures and techniques learned in the classroom through required fieldwork in facilities serving individuals with disabilities in the community. As students, music therapists learn to assess the needs of clients, develop and implement treatment plans, and evaluate and document clinical changes. Those who pass the national certification examination in music therapy become board certified and earn the right to use the credential MT-BC (Music Therapist – Board Certified).

What can one expect from a music therapist?

Since music therapy may be listed on the child's IEP (Individual Education Plan) as a "related service" or may be provided to children under the age of three as part of the IFSP (Individual Family Service Plan), music therapists must be able to assess the needs of the young child as well as those of the family. They design individualized programming, monitor progress, evaluate, and provide documentation related to the child's goals and objectives.

A music therapist who works with young children should possess a strong knowledge of relevant music and materials, early childhood development, specific special needs of the child, and developmentally appropriate practices. A music therapist is accomplished in the use of instruments and voice. He/she is able to adapt strategies to a variety of settings and across disciplines, thus individualizing music therapy interventions to meet children's specific needs. In addition, he/she may provide structured or semi-structured opportunities for children with and without disabilities to interact together in a music setting. Music therapists are creative, energetic, and positive. They demonstrate strong oral and written communication skills and work well with families and other professionals.

Where do music therapists work?
- Early Intervention Centers
- Preschools and Schools
- Hospitals
- Hospice Programs
- Community-based Facilities (such as community music schools and out-patient clinics)
- Home-based Programs
- Daycare Settings
- Group Homes or Residential Treatment Centers
- Private Practice

How does music therapy help families?
Music therapy can provide enjoyable yet purposeful activities and resources for families to share with their children. Families can learn to use music through meaningful play and nurturing experiences. Music therapy may serve as a positive outlet for interaction, providing fun activities that can include parents, siblings, and extended family. Often music therapy allows a family to see a child in a new light as the child's strengths are manifested in the music therapy environment.

What research and resources are available to substantiate and support music therapy?
Through *Music Therapy, Journal of Music Therapy, Music Therapy Perspectives,* and other resources, AMTA has promoted much research exploring the benefits of music therapy with young children. Furthermore, AMTA has established an Early Childhood Network that disseminates additional information to interested parties.

Why music therapy?
Music therapy may address several needs simultaneously in a positive and exciting medium: it may provide pleasurable learning that promotes success. Furthermore, music therapy can greatly enhance the quality of life of the young child and his/her family. Music is often the first thing to which a child relates. It is a "universal language" that crosses all cultural lines. Music occurs naturally in our environment in many settings and is a socially appropriate activity and leisure skill. Music provides a predictable time-oriented and reality-oriented structure while offering opportunities for participation at one's own level of functioning and ability. It should be noted that children with disabilities are not necessarily disabled in their musical skills. Not only may music activities be opportunities for a child to "shine," but also they may be used to reinforce nonmusical goals. Most people, especially children, enjoy music – therefore, music therapy can be the therapy that reinforces all other therapies.

A Director of Educational Services for a public school system affirms:
"The inclusionary preschool music therapy sessions gave children an opportunity to make new friends and learn things about themselves and others. I saw major gains in the children's social skills and in their attention spans. I wholeheartedly endorse the program and think that every child could benefit from music therapy."

An occupational therapist writes:
"I love having a music therapist on our interdisciplinary team. When we co-lead sessions, I notice that the children are much more motivated to push themselves when working with such things as fine motor control and range of motion activities."

The father of a 5 year old diagnosed with Attention Deficit/Hyperactivity Disorder observes:
"Music therapy has helped my son to increase his concentration and attending. His eye contact has increased since participating in music therapy. Moreover, I believe that in part his increased use of language may be attributed to attending music therapy. Finally, he has developed an interest in music." (Child has participated in individual music therapy for 1 1/2 years.)

The mother of a 6 1/2-year-old with Down Syndrome states:
"Music therapy has helped my son to learn turn-taking, sharing, listening skills and some colors, animals, parts of the body and clothes." (Child participated in group music therapy for 2 years in preschool and then in individual music therapy for 1year in kindergarten.)

The mother of twin sons, aged 7 years, one with Tourette Syndrome and one with Pervasive Developmental Disorder, comments:
"For one son music therapy seems to have reduced an extreme sensitivity to sound. For both boys, the therapy has been a catalyst for improved sociability. Much of the time the boys seem to exist on parallel universes, but on the drive home from therapy they usually have a conversation." (The boys have participated in small group or partner music therapy sessions for two years.)

The mother of an 8-year-old with Apert Syndrome and Attention Deficit Behaviors notes:
"Music therapy has (1) helped with my daughter's spontaneous speech; (2) allowed her to use her hands with many different textures and independently of each other; (3) expanded on her natural musical ability; and (4) helped her learn to focus and develop patience with music as the motivator." (Child participated in small group music therapy for 1 1/2 years in preschool and in individual music therapy for 4 years.)

The parent of a hospitalized child undergoing treatment for cancer relates:
"Music therapy has been a tremendous benefit not only for my child, but also for our family. During music therapy time, my child is able to do fun things that help him forget about his pain. We are grateful to share some time with him doing things that bring back a smile to his face."

How can you find a music therapist?
American Music Therapy Association
8455 Colesville Road, Suite 1000
Silver Spring, MD 20910
(301) 589-3300 Fax (301) 589-5175
Email: info@musictherapy.org
Web: http://www.musictherapy.org

Glossary

Adaptation. Any procedure intended to meet an educational situation with respect to individual differences in ability and purpose.

Adaptive behavior. Addresses self-help, independent functioning, and personal and social responsibility as is appropriate for a same-age peer and according to one's culture group.

Age appropriate. Experiences and/or a learning environment that support predictable growth and development in the physical, social, emotional, and cognitive domains that are typical for children at specific chronological ages.

Appropriate education. A standard, required by IDEA, which guarantees that students with disabilities receive an educational program individually tailored to their abilities and needs.

Appropriate environment. Surroundings that are suited to both the age and individuality of all children present.

Appropriate practice. Techniques or a style used with children that is age and individually appropriate.

Assessment. The process of determining the presence of a disability and students' current functioning levels through observation and testing procedures.

Assistive listening devices (ALDs). Equipment, like hearing aids, that help individuals with hearing impairments use their residual hearing.

Associative play. A type of play in which a child plays with others in a group and subordinates individual interests to those of the group.

At-risk. Students that have a greater chance of experiencing difficulties developmentally or at school due to social, economic, environment, or biological factors.

Best practices. Refers to the kinds of content, formats and delivery models that best meet the needs of participants.

Center-based services. Educational services that are provided at a central location, typically through a classroom type format.

Consultant service delivery. A model in which the member of a specific discipline provides service indirectly to the student by working with the professionals who are in direct contact with the student. Services may include on-site assistance, in-service training, and team teaching.

Continuum of services. A wide selection of services that are available so an appropriate education can be provided to each student with special needs.

Cross-categorical. Classes available to students with a variety of disabilities usually according to level of severity.

Curriculum. A systematic grouping of content, activities, and instructional materials.

Device. Any specific aid, tool, or piece of equipment used to assist a student with a disability.

Direct services delivery. A model in which the educational service is provided to a student by a professional member of the discipline.

Early childhood programs. Preschool, day care, and early infant school programs that involve students with disabilities and their families, designed to improve the speech, language, social and cognitive skills of the students attending.

Education for All Handicapped Children Act (EHA). See PL 94-142.

Eligibility. Determination of whether a child meets the criteria to receive special education services.

Evaluation. A comprehensive term which includes screening, assessment, and monitoring activities.

Free appropriate public education (FAPE). A major standard set forth in PL 94-142, now called the Individuals with Disabilities Education Act (IDEA), which states that students with disabilities are entitled to a free appropriate public education which often includes supportive services and highly individualized educational programs.

Full inclusion. All students with disabilities are placed in their neighborhood schools in general education classrooms for the entire day often with greater emphasis on social adjustment than academic improvement.

Functional skill. A skill or task that will be used in the individual's normal environment.

Inclusion. See mainstreaming.

Individualized Education Program Committee (IEPC). A meeting of appropriate persons in order to: (a) review the multifactored evaluation team report; (b) determine the nature and degree of special education and related services needed by the child, if any; (c) develop an IEP for a child determined to be in need of special education in accordance with all the Administrative requirement code; (d) determine the least restrictive environment in which to deliver educational services in accordance with IEP.

Individual Transition Plan (ITP). A written plan that identifies the skills and supportive services that an individual needs to function in the community after schooling is completed.

Individualized Family Service Plan (IFSP). A written plan required by IDEA for children under the age of three who receive special preschool programs; identifies and organizes services and resources to help families reach their goals for their children.

Individuals with Disabilities Education Act (IDEA). See PL 101-476.

Inservice. A developmental activity that a teacher undertakes singly, or with other teachers, after receiving his or her initial teaching certificate, and after beginning professional practice. It is a process designed to foster personal and professional growth for individuals within a respectful, supportive, positive climate having as its aim both learning for students and continuous, responsible self-renewal for educators and schools.

Integration. See mainstreaming.

Intermediate Care Facilities for the Mental Retarded (ICF/MR). Federally funded community-based living centers or group homes where individuals with mental retardation reside.

LEA (Local Education Agency). The public school district which is responsible for a student's education.

Learning disability. A disorder where the individual possesses average or above intelligence but is substantially delayed in academic achievement. It may result in an imperfect ability to listen, think, speak, read, write, spell, or to do mathematical calculations. The term includes such conditions as perceptual disabilities, brain injury, minimal brain dysfunction, dyslexia, and developmental aphasia.

Least restrictive environment (LRE). To the maximum extent appropriate, children with disabilities, including children in public or private institutions or other care facilities, are educated with children who are not disabled, and that special classes, separate schooling, or other removal of children with disabilities from the regular educational environment occurs only when the nature or severity of the disability is such that education in regular classes with the use of supplementary aids and services cannot be achieved satisfactorily.

Mainstreaming, integration, inclusion. While mainstreaming does not necessarily always mean full day, complete instructional and social placement in a regular classroom, for the purposes of this text, mainstreaming, integration, and inclusion will refer to the placement of children with disabilities with typically developing peers into general and music education settings.

Multidisciplinary team approach. Service delivery model in which communication among team members is unidirectional and limited. In this model, the focus of service delivery is discipline-centered and assessment of students is done in isolation from other disciplines.

Multiple disabilities. Concomitant impairments (such as mental retardation-blindness, mental retardation-orthopedic impairment etc.) the combination of which causes such severe educational problems that they cannot be served in special education programs solely for one of the impairments. The term does not include deaf-blindness.

Parallel play. A situation in which a child plays independently with materials similar to those used by children playing in close proximity. Social contact is minimal.

Paraprofessionals. Paid (sometimes volunteer) workers who provide direct instructional and support services to students as classroom aides and teacher assistants.

Physical play. Action that is frequently social, may be competitive, and includes rough-tumble activities.

Preservice. College courses and training taken prior to obtaining a baccalaureate degree.

Preservice teachers. College and university students who have not received a baccalaureate degree.

PL 94-142. Also known as the Education for All Handicapped Children Act, this law required school districts to provide a "free and appropriate public education" to children ages 6-21, to develop an IEP for each child with a disability, and mandated that students with disabilities must receive educational services in the least restrictive environment. The law was originally passed in 1975 (to be implemented in 1977), amended in 1986 by PL 99-457 to include infants and toddlers, amended and reauthorized again in 1990 (under PL 101-476) and in 1997 (under PL 105-17).

PL 101-476. Also known as the Individuals with Disabilities Act (IDEA), this update of PL 94-142 included new categories of disabilities (autism and traumatic brain injury), required all IEPs to include a statement of needed transition services no later than age 16, and expanded the definition of related services.

PL 105-17. Also known as IDEA-1997, this reauthorization of the original federal legislation restructured IDEA from nine subchapters into four parts and added several major provisions including the requirement that the regular education teacher must be a member of the IEP team and that students with disabilities must have access to the general education curriculum.

Regular Education Initiative (REI). A position held by some special educators that students with disabilities should be served in regular education classrooms and not be "pulled out" to attend special classes; an attempt to reform regular and special education so they are a combined system that maximizes mainstreaming.

Related service. Any discipline that contributes to education progress for a student with special needs.

Self-contained classroom. One placement option on the continuum of least restrictive environments, students within a special education class typically have limited opportunity for interaction with their regular education peers.

Transdisciplinary team approach. Service delivery model in which communication among team members is multi-directional and frequent. Parents are an integral part of the team and decisions regarding the student are reached by consensus. The focus of service delivery is child-centered; therefore, assessment, IEP planning and service delivery are integrated and holistic.

Typically developing child. A child who is not identified as having a disability.

Resources

Music Therapy/Music Education

American Music Therapy Association (AMTA)
8455 Colesville Road, Suite 1000
Silver Spring, MD 20910
Phone: (301) 589–3300
Fax: (301) 589–5175

Music Educators National Conference (MENC)
1806 Robert Fulton Drive
Reston, VA 22091
Phone: (800) 336–3768
Fax: (703) 860–1531

Disabilities – General

Council for Exceptional Children (CEC)
1920 Association Drive
Reston, VA 22091
Phone   (703) 620–3660
Fax: (703) 264–9497

National Council on Disability (NCD)
1331 F Street, NW, Suite 1050
Washington, DC 20004
Phone: (202) 272–2004
Fax: (202) 272–2022

National Easter Seal Society
230 West Monroe Street, Suite 1800
Chicago, IL 60606
Phone: (312) 726–6200
Fax: (312) 726–1494

National Organization for Rare Disorders (NORD)
P.O. Box 8923
New Fairfield, CT 06812–8923
Phone: (800) 999–6673

Autism

Autism Research Institute
4182 Adams Avenue
San Diego, CA 92116
Phone: (619) 281–7165
Fax: (619) 563–6840

Autism Society of America
7910 Woodmont Avenue, Suite 650
Bethesda, MD 20814
Phone: (800) 328–8476

More Advanced Autistic People (MAAP)
P.O. Box 524
Crown Point, IN 46307
Phone: (219) 662–1311

The Autism Network for Hearing and Visually Impaired Persons
c/o Dolores and Alan Bartel
7510 Oceanfront Avenue
Virginia Beach, VA 23451
Phone: (804) 428–9036

Deaf/Hard of Hearing

Alexander Graham Bell Association for the Deaf
3417 Volta Place NW
Washington, DC 20007–2778
Phone: (202)337–5220
            (800) HEAR–KID

American Society for Deaf Children
2848 Arden Way, Suite 210
Sacramento, CA 95825–1373
Phone: (800) 942–2732

National Association of the Deaf (NAD)
814 Thayer Avenue
Silver Spring, MD 20910–4500
Phone: (301) 587–1789

Early Childhood

National Association for the Education of the Young Child (NAEYC)
1834 Connecticut Avenue, NW
Washington, DC 20009

Early Childhood Music Newsletter
c/o School of Music, University of Oregon
1225 University of Oregon
Eugene, OR 97403–1225

Early Childhood Music Association
2110 27th Avenue
Greeley, CO 80631

Early Childhood Connections
(a publication of Early Childhood Music Association)
Foundation for Music-Based Learning
P.O. Box 4274
Greensboro, NC 27404–4274

AMTA Early Childhood Information Network
Co-Chairpersons:

Ronna Davis
22450 Douglas Road
Shaker Heights, OH 44122

Marcia Humpal
26798 Mangrove Lane
Olmsted Falls, OH 44138

Juvenile Justice

Juvenile Justice Resource Center/Clearinghouse
1600 Research Blvd.
Rockville, MD 20850
Phone: (800) 638–8736

National Council on Crime and Delinquency (NCDC)
685 Market Street
Suite 620
San Francisco, CA 94105
Phone: (415) 896–6223

National Institute on Juvenile Justice and Delinquency Prevention (NIJJDP)
(U.S. Department of Justice)
633 Indiana Ave. NW
Suite 800
Washington, DC 20531
Phone: (202) 307–2942

Office of Juvenile Justice and Delinquency Prevention (OJJDP)
(U.S. Department of Justice)
633 Indiana Ave. NW
Suite 742
Washington, DC 20531
Phone: (202) 307–0751

Learning Disabilities

Children and Adults with Attention Deficit Disorders (CHADD)
499 Northwest 70th Avenue, Suite 109
Plantation, FL 33317
Phone: (305) 587–3700

Council for Learning Disabilities (CLD)
P.O. Box 40303
Overland Park, KS 66204
Phone: (913) 492–8755

Learning Disabilities Association of America (LDA)
4156 Library Road
Pittsburgh, PA 15234
Phone: (412) 341–1515 *or* (412) 341–8077

National Center for Learning Disabilities
99 Park Avenue
New York, NY 10016
Phone: (212) 687–7211

Orton Dyslexia Society
Chester Building, Suite 382
8600 LaSalle Road
Baltimore, MD 21286–2044
Phone: (410) 296–0232 *or* (800) 222–3123

Mental Retardation

The Association for Persons With Severe Handicaps (TASH)
29 W. Susquehanna Avenue, Suite 210
Baltimore, MD 21204
Phone: (800) 828–8274
E-mail: tashbalt@aol.com

National Down Syndrome Society
666 Broadway, 8th floor
New York, NY 10012–2317
Phone: (800) 221–4602

National Down Syndrome Congress
1605 Chantilly Drive, Suite 250
Atlanta, GA 30324
Phone: (800) 232–6372

National Fragile X Foundation
1441 York Suite, Suite 303
Denver, CO 80206
Phone: (800) 688–8765

The ARC
500 E. Border Street, Suite 300
P.O. Box 1047
Arlington, TX 76010
Phone: (800) 433–5255

International Rett Syndrome Association
9121 Piscataway Road, Suite 2B
Clinton, MD 20735
Phone: (800) 818–7388
E-mail: irsa@paltech.com

Physical Disabilities

United Cerebral Palsy Associations
1660 L Street NW, Suite 700
Washington, DC 20036–5602
Phone: (800) 872–5827

Muscular Dystrophy Association
3300 E. Sunrise Drive
Tucson, AZ 85718–3208
Phone: (800) 572–1717

Spina Bifida Association of America
4590 MacArthur Blvd. NW, #250
Washington, DC 20007–4226
Phone: (800) 621–3141

Visual Impairments

American Foundation for the Blind
11 Penn Plaza
New York, NY 10001
Phone: (800) 232–5463

Blind Children's Center
4120 Marathon Street
Los Angeles, CA 90029
Phone: (800) 222–3566

National Association for Parents of the Visually Impaired
P.O. Box 317
Watertown, MA 02272–0317
Phone: (800) 562–6265

National Organization of Parents of Blind Children
1800 Johnson Street
Baltimore, MD 21230
Phone: (410) 659–9314

MATERIALS FOR PLANNING INCLUSIVE MUSIC EDUCATION/MUSIC THERAPY SESSIONS

Adair, A. J. (1984). *Ready-to-Use Music Activities Kit*. West Nyack, NY: Parker.

Adair, A. J. (1992). *Start With Song: 201 Ready-to-Use Interdisciplinary Activities for Young Learners*. West Nyack, NY: Parker.

Ardley, N. (1989). *Eyewitness Books—Music*. New York: Alfred Knopf.

Bayless, K. M., & Ramsey, M. E. (1991). *Music: A Way of Life for the Young Child*. New York, NY: Merrill-Macmillan.

Benderly, B. L. (1980). *Dancing Without Music: Deafness in America*. Garden City, NY: Anchor Press/Doubleday.

Birkenshaw-Fleming, L. (1989). *Come On Everybody Let's Sing!* Toronto, Canada: Gordon V. Thompson Music.

Chastain, L. D. (1983). *A Handbook on the Use of Songs to Teach Autistic and Other Severely Handicapped Children*. White Oak Press, P.O. Box 123, Route 3, Goodhue, MN 55017.

Clark, C., & Chadwick, D. (1980). *Clinically Adapted Instruments for the Multiply Handicapped*. St. Louis, MO: MMB Music.

Clarkson, G. (1985). *Stop, Look and Listen*. San Diego, CA: Kjos West.

Coleman, K., McNairn, P., & Shioleno, C. (1996). *Quick Tech Magic: Music-Based Literacy Activities*. Solana Beach, CA: Mayer Johnson.

Elliott, B. (1982). *Guide to the Selection of Musical Instruments with Respect to Physical Ability and Disability*. St. Louis, MO: MMB.

Estabrooks, W., & Birkenshaw-Fleming, L. (1994). *Hear & Listen! Talk & Sing!* Toronto, Canada: Arisa.

Farnan, L., & Johnson, F. (1988). *Everyone Can Move*. Hal Leonard.

Farnan, L., & Johnson, F. (1988). *Music Is for Everyone*. Hal Leonard Publications.

Fiarotta, N., & Fiarotta, P. (1993). *Music Crafts for Kids: The How-To Book of Music Discovery*. New York, NY: Sterling.

Freeman, A. (1960). *Ring Along Old Favorites*. Long Beach, CA: Cantabile Press.

Freeman, A. (1989). *Ring Along Christmas Favorites*. Long Beach, CA: Cantabile Press.

Gibson, D., & Scruggs, J. (1984). *Songs to Brighten Your Day*. Austin, TX: Educational Graphics Press.

Ginglend, D. R., & Stiles, W. E. (1965). *Music Activities for Retarded Children*. Nashville, TN: Parthenon Press.

Grant, R. (1977). *A Developmental Music Therapy Curriculum for the Mildly Mentally Retarded*. University of Georgia. Order from: University Microfilms, #77–29, 760.

Gray, C. (1993). *The Sound Story Book* [Series]. Arlington, TX: Future Education.

Hoermann, D., & Bridges, D. (1988). *Catch A Song*. Nashville, TN: Incentive.

Hunt, B. (1984). *Count Me In*. London, England: A & C Black.

Janiak, W. C. (1978). *Songs for Music Therapy*. St. Louis, MO: MMB Music.

Jeunesse, G., & Delafosse, C. (1994). *Musical Instruments: A First Discovery Book*. New York: Scholastic.

Jones, J. (1987). *I Feel Good All Over*. 1845 Bromilow, Las Cruces, NM 88001. Phone: (505) 521–3416.

Jones, J. (1987). *Spread A Little Sunshine*. 1845 Bromilow, Las Cruces, NM 88001. Phone: (505) 521–3416. Theodore Presser.

Lehman, P. (Ed.). (1994). *Teaching Examples: Ideas for Music Educators*. Reston, VA: Music Educators National Conference.

Levin, G., & Levin, H. (1977). *A Garden of Bell Flowers*. Bryn Mawr, PA: Theodore Presser.

Levin, G., & Levin, H. (1981). *Learning Songs.* Bryn Mawr, PA: Theodore Presser.

Lindeman, D. A. (Ed.) (1995). *Strategies for Teaching.* Reston, VA: Music Educators National Conference.

Michel, D. E., & Jones, J. L. (199). *Music for Developing Speech and Language Skills in Children.* St. Louis, MO: MMB Music.

Mitchell, L. (1991). *One, Two, Three . . . Echo Me!* West Nyack, NY: Parker.

Moss, J., & Raposo, J. (1992). *The Sesame Street Songbook.* New York, NY: Macmillan.

Musselwhite, C. R. (1985). *Signs and Symbols for Children.* Asheville, NC.

Nash, G. C., Jones, G. W., Potter, B. A., & Smith, P. F. (1977). *The Child's Way of Learning.* Sherman Oaks, CA: Alfred.

Nelson, E. (1989). *Everybody Sing and Dance.* Cleveland, OH: Instructor Books.

Nocera, S. (1979). *Reaching the Special Learner Through Music.* Morristown, NJ: Silver Burdett. (Currently out of print)

Nordoff, P. (1972). *Spirituals for Children to Sing and Play.* Bryn Mawr, PA: Theodore Presser.

Nordoff, P. (1977). *Folk Songs for Children to Sing and Play.* Bryn Mawr, PA: Theodore Presser.

Nordoff, P. (1979). *Fanfares and Dances.* Bryn Mawr, PA: Theodore Presser.

Nordoff, P., & Robbins, C. (1962). *The First Book of Children's Play Songs.* Bryn Mawr, PA: Theodore Presser.

Nordoff, P., & Robbins, C. (1968). *Fun for Four Drums.* Bryn Mawr, PA: Theodore Presser.

Nordoff, P., & Robbins, C. (1968). *The Second Book of Children's Play Songs.* Bryn Mawr, PA: Theodore Presser.

Nordoff, P., & Robbins, C. (1969). *Pif-Paf-Poltrie.* Bryn Mawr, PA: Theodore Presser.

Nordoff, P., & Robbins, C. (1973). *Songs for Children.* Bryn Mawr, PA: Theodore Presser.

Nordoff, P. & Robbins, C. (1980). *The Fifth Book of Children's Play Songs.* Bryn Mawr, PA: Theodore Presser.

Nordoff, P., & Robbins, C. (1980). *The Fourth Book of Children's Play Songs.* Bryn Mawr, PA: Theodore Presser.

Nordoff, P., & Robbins, C. (1980). *The Third Book of Children's Play Songs.* Bryn Mawr, PA: Theodore Presser.

Palmer, H. (1981). *Hap Palmer Favorites.* Sherman Oaks, CA: Alfred.

Pinson, J. (1983). *Handbells for Special Populations.* Sellersville, PA: Schulmerich Carillons.

Pliska, G., & Madelaine, G. (1993). *Praise for the Singing: Songs for Children.* Boston, MA: Little, Brown.

Powell, H. (1983). *Game Songs with Professor Dogg's Troupe.* London, England: A & C Black.

Raffi. (1984). *The Raffi Singable Songbook.* Ontario, Canada: Chappell.

Raffi. (1986). *The 2nd Raffi Songbook.* New York, NY: Crown.

Robbins, C., & Robbins, C. (1980). *Music for the Hearing Impaired and Other Special Groups.* St. Louis, MO: MMB Music.

Rosene, P. E. (1984). *Making Music with Choirchime Instruments.* Carol Stream, IL: Agape.

Sacks, O. (1989). *Seeing Voices.* Berkeley, CA: University of California Press.

Schmitt, C. (1987). *Music and Dance.* Little Falls, MN: St. Francis Music Center.

Sebba, J. (1986). *Playalong Songs.* London, England: Hamish Hamilton.

Sharon, Lois & Bram. (1980). *Elephant Jam.* San Francisco, CA: McGraw-Hill Ryerson.

Smith, R. B. (1984). *Music Dramas for Children with Special Needs.* St. Louis, MO: MMB Music.

Walden, D. E., & Birkenshaw, L. (1980). *The Goat with Bright Red Socks.* Toronto, Canada: Berandol Music.

Walters, C., & Totten, D. (1991). *Sing A Song All Year Long.* MN: T. S. Denison.

Warren, J. (1983). *Piggyback Songs.* Everett, WA: Warren Publishing House.

Warren, J. (1984). *More Piggyback Songs.* Everett, WA: Warren Publishing House.

Warren, J. (1988). *Holiday Piggyback Songs.* Everett, WA: Warren Publishing House.

Warren, J. (1990). *Animal Piggyback Songs.* Everett, WA: Warren Publishing House.

Warren, J. (1990). *Piggyback Songs for Infants and Toddlers.* Everett, WA: Warren Publishing House.

Williams, S. (1985). *Round and Round the Garden.* Oxford, England: Oxford University Press.

Wirth, M., Stassevitch, V., Shotwell, R., & Stemmler, P. (1983). *Musical Games, Fingerplays and Rhythmic Activities for Early Childhood.* West Nyack, NY: Parker.

Witt, B. (1984). *TOTAL Tunes.* Communication Skill Builders, 3130 N. Dodge Blvd., P.O. Box 42050, Tucson, AZ 85733.

West Music Company
P.O. Box 5521
1212 5th Street
Coralville, IA 52241
Web site: www.westmusic.com
Phone: 800-397-9378
Representative: Kirsten Nelson, MT–BC

This company carries high quality small percussion instruments, as well as inexpensive guitars. They also carry autoharps, a selection of electronic keyboards, and a wide variety of activity and resource books. Informed consultants at West Music will be happy to answer questions about items in their catalog.

Music in Motion
P.O. Box 869231
Plano, Texas 75086
Web site: www.musicmotion.com
Phone: 800-445-0649

This company carries music education items and musical gifts for all ages. They offer an excellent assortment of books that illustrate lyrics of familiar songs.

Peripole
P.O. Box 12909
Salem, Oregon 97309-2909
Web site: www.peripolebergerault.com
Phone: 800-443-3592

This company sells basic rhythm and percussion instruments useful for working with early childhood and elementary aged students.

Music for Little People
P.O. Box 757
Greenland, New Hampshire 03840
Web site: www.mflp.com
Phone: 800-409-2457

This company carries a wide assortment of children's cassette tapes and CDs, as well as videotapes and some books. They are an excellent source for multi-cultural music.

Sing 'n Learn
2626 Club Meadow
Garland, Texas 75043-1102
Web site: www.singnlearn.com
Phone: 800-460-1973

This company offers a variety of tapes and CDs which teach information such as geography, spelling, knowledge of state capitals, Spanish, science, history and many other topics.

National Educational Network
Materials for the Whole Language Classroom
P.O. Box 426
Hilmar, California 95324
Web site: www.n-e-n.com
Phone: 209-668-4142

This company is a source for "Big Books" based on different songs. Some of the many titles available include: Wheels on the Bus, All I Really Need, I Am A Pizza, Octopus Song and Mr. Sun. The "Big Books" are printed on black and white cards, and the teacher or therapist must do the coloring and laminating.

Nellie Edge Resources and Seminars, Inc.
P.O. Box 12399
Salem, Oregon 97309-0399
Web site: www.nellieedge.com
Phone: 800-523-4594

This company carries large black and white "Big Books" which illustrate familiar children's songs. Each large book comes with a master that can be used to make small "mini" books for the students. You will have to color and laminate the "Big Books" yourself.

Tom Hunter
The Song Growing Company
1225 E. Sunset Dr., #518
Bellingham, WA 98226
Web site: http://www.nas.com/sgc
Phone: 360-738-0340

Tom Hunter offers a variety of tapes and CDs including familiar folk and children's songs, and songs dealing with positive attitudes about disabilities and life struggles. He offers workshop and keynote presentations on music and literacy, building lively communities and expressing feelings.

The Learning Workshop
3000 8th Street SE
East Wenatchee, Washington 98802
Web site: www.learningworkshop.com
Phone: 800-752-0663

This company is an additional source for "Big Books" based on mainly original songs. Each "Big Book" can also be purchased with an activity kit or extension packet that offers a variety of written and experiential activities for the students. The company regularly offers "make it/take it" workshops around the United States.

Miss Jo Publications
6131 Royal Crest Drive
Dallas, Texas 75230
Web site: www.missjo.com
Phone: 214-692-1658

This small business is run by a woman who has developed her own, original "sing-along" Big Books and accompanying tapes. Topics include social skills, understanding and caring for animals and citizenship. Books are available in two different sizes. The owner is available for presentations at workshops or as a keynote speaker for conferences.

Prelude Music Therapy
3360 Spruce Lane
Grapevine, Texas 76051
Web site: http://preludetherapy.home.att.net
Phone: 817-481-2323

This company sells inexpensive songbooks and materials for music based learning. Materials are appropriate for use by pre-school teachers, music therapists, music educators, special educators and parents. The company also offers workshops on the use of music to facilitate learning for children and adolescents with disabilities.

Folkmanis Puppets
1219 Park Avenue
Emeryville, California 94608
Phone: 510-658-7678

This company sells their high quality puppets wholesale to educational or therapeutic organizations. The wholesale prices are much less than the retail prices in stores across the United States. Write for a catalog using agency or school letterhead, as the company does not sell to individuals. There is a minimum order amount of $200.

Early Childhood Direct
P.O. Box 369
Landisville, Pennsylvania 17538
Phone: 800-477-5075

This company sells a variety of products related to movement activities, including records and tapes, as well as items such as hoops, balls, ribbons, and other manipulative items.

Lakeshore Learning Materials
2695 E. Dominguez Street
P.O. Box 6261
Carson, California 90749
Phone: 800-421-5354

This company carries a wide variety of durable and high quality educational toys and learning materials for pre-school through elementary developmental levels.

Props & Bags, Etc.
521 S. Warren Avenue
Springfield, Missouri 65806
Web site: www.pbetc.com
Phone: 417-866-8741

This company makes movement props, puppets, bean bags and a variety of useful bags and totes for the professional who is traveling from agency to agency.

Different Roads to Learning
12 West 18th Street, Suite 3 East
New York, New York 10011
Web site: www.difflearn.com
Phone: 800-853-1057

This company carries materials to teach basic language and cognition skills. Useful items include sets of photo cards that illustrate basic nouns and verbs, as well as cards that illustrate categories, spatial relationships and sequencing.

Sammons Preston
An AbilityOne Company
P.O. Box 5071
Bolingbrook, Illinois 60440-5071
Web site: www.sammonspreston.com
Phone: 800-323-5547

This company carries all types of Velcro including: Velcro in two parts (hook and latch) as well as one wrap Velcro. The company is also a source for foam to make built up mallet handles and other instrument adaptations.

Ablenet
1081 Tenth Avenue S.E.
Minneapolis, Minnesota 55414-1312
Web site: www.ablenetinc.com
Phone: 800-322-0956

This company makes various types of basic augmentative communication devices including pressure switches, and simple communication devices including the "Big Mack." Before using pressure switches or simple communication devices, be sure to consult with either the student's physical, occupational or speech therapist.

Enabling Devices
385 Warburton Avenue
Hastings-on-Hudson, New York 10706
Web site: www.enablingdevices.com
Phone: 800-832-8697

This company sells a variety of simple communication devices including the "Cheap Talk," the "Rocker Switch," etc., as well as a number of adapted toys for students with severe physical limitations.

Mayer-Johnson Company
P.O. Box 1579
Solana Beach, California 92075-7579
Web site: www.mayer-johnson.com
Phone: 800-588-4548

This company is the source for books and software containing the Picture Communication Symbols. They also carry a variety of resource books that emphasize the teaching of language and cognitive skills using picture symbols. Consult with a speech therapist for additional information about products from this company.

Crestwood Company
6625 N. Sidney Place
Milwaukee, Wisconsin 53209-3259
Phone: 414-352-5678

This company is a source for a variety of adapted toys and simple augmentative communication devices.

The Little Warehouse, Inc.
4705 Ban Epps Road
Brooklyn Heights, Ohio 44131
Phone: 216-398-0022

This company sells cassette tapes of various lengths, beginning with the 5-minute length.

World Class Tapes
670 Airport Blvd., Suite 1
Ann Arbor, Michigan 48108
Web site: www.worldclasstapes.com
Phone: 800-365-0669

This company sells cassette tapes of varying lengths; including ten minute tapes which are handy for recording just one or two songs or activities.

Future Horizons, Inc.
721 West Abram Street
Arlington, Texas 76013
Web site: www.futurehorizons-autism.com
Phone: 800-489-0727

This company offers high-quality autism workshops around the United States, featuring well known speakers in the field. They also have an extensive catalog of books about autism, covering all levels of autism—from low functioning to those with Asperger syndrome.

Deaf Culture

Benderly, B. L. (1980). *Dancing without music: Deafness in America.* Garden City, NY: Anchor Press/Doubleday.

Gannon, J. R. (1981). *Deaf heritage: A narrative history of deaf America.* Silver Spring, MD: National Association of the Deaf.

Garretson, M. (1990). *Communication issues among deaf people.* Silver Spring, MD: National Association of the Deaf.

Garretson, M. (1991). *Perspectives on deafness.* Silver Spring, MD: National Association of the Deaf.

Kannapel, B. (1980). Personal awareness and advocacy in the deaf community. In W. C. Stokoe, *Sign language and the deaf community.* Silver Spring MD: National Association of the Deaf.

Lane, H. (1984). *When the mind hears: A history of the deaf.* New York: Random House.

Neisser, A. (1983). *The other side of silence.* Washington, DC: Gallaudet University.

Padden, C. (1980). The deaf community and the culture of the deaf people. In W. C. Stokoe, *Sign language and the deaf community.* Silver Spring, MD: National Association of the Deaf.

Padden, C., & Humphries, T. (1988). *Deaf in America: Voices from a culture.* Cambridge, MA: Harvard University Press.

Sacks, O. (1989). *Seeing voices.* Berkeley, CA: University of California Press.

Stokoe, W. C. (1980). *Sign and culture.* Washington, DC: Linstock Press.

Music and the Deaf

Amir, D., & Schuchman, G. (1985). Auditory training through music with hearing impaired preschool children. *Volta Review, 87,* 333–343.

Baird, S. (1979). A technique to assess the preference for intensity of musical stimuli in young hard-of-hearing children. *Journal of Music Therapy, 6,* 6–11.

Bang, C. (1986). A world of sound and music. In E. Ruud (Ed.), *Music and health* (pp. 19–36). Oslo, Norway: Norsk Musikforlag.

Bang, C. (1977). *A music event.* Hicksville, NY: M. Hohner, Inc.

Birkenshaw-Fleming, L. (1990). Music can make a difference. In A. A. Darrow (Ed.), *Proceedings from the Second National Conference on Music and the Hearing Impaired at Gallaudet University* (pp. 14–20). Lawrence, KS: The University of Kansas.

Buechler, J. (1982). *Music for handicapped children: Hearing impaired.* Washington, DC: National Association for Music Therapy.

Coffman, D., Gfeller, K., Coffman, S., & Darrow, A. A. (1992). A computer-assisted comparison of melodic and rhythmic discrimination skills in hearing impaired and normally hearing children. *The Arts in Psychotherapy, 18,* 449–454.

Dalgarno, G. (1990). A computer-based music system for the hearing impaired. In A. A. Darrow (Ed.), *Proceedings from the Second National Conference on Music and the Hearing Impaired at Gallaudet University* (pp. 31–42). Lawrence, KS: The University of Kansas.

Dalgarno, G. (1990). Technology to obtain the best musical sound for hearing impaired listeners. In A. A. Darrow (Ed.), *Proceedings from the Second National Conference on Music and the Hearing Impaired at Gallaudet University* (pp. 43–59). Lawrence, KS: The University of Kansas.

Darrow, A. A. (1979). The beat reproduction response of subjects with normal and impaired hearing: An empirical comparison. *Journal of Music Therapy, 16*, 6–11.

Darrow, A. A. (1984). A comparison of the rhythmic responsiveness in normal hearing and hearing impaired children and an investigation of the relationship of the rhythmic responsiveness to the suprasegmental aspects of speech perception. *Journal of Music Therapy, 21*, 48–66.

Darrow, A. A. (1985). Music for the deaf. *Music Educators Journal, 71*(6), 33–35.

Darrow, A. A. (1987). *A comparison of vocal ranges of hearing impaired and normal hearing children.* Unpublished manuscript, The University of Kansas, Lawrence.

Darrow, A. A. (1987). Exploring the art of sign and song. *Music Educators Journal, 74*(1), 32–35.

Darrow, A. A. (1987). An investigative study: The effect of hearing impairment on the music aptitude of young children. *Journal of Music Therapy, 24*, 88–96.

Darrow, A. A. (1988). Music and the hearing impaired: A review of the research with implication for music educators. *Update: Applications of Research in Music Education, 7*(2), 10–12.

Darrow, A. A. (1989). Music therapy in the treatment of the hearing impaired. *Music Therapy Perspectives, 6*, 61–70.

Darrow, A. A. (1990). The effect of frequency adjustment on the vocal reproduction accuracy of hearing impaired singers. *Journal of Music Therapy, 27*, 24–33.

Darrow, A. A. (Ed.). (1990). *Proceedings from the Second National Conference on Music and the Hearing Impaired at Gallaudet University.* Lawrence, KS: The University of Kansas.

Darrow, A. A. (1990). The role of hearing in understanding music. *Music Educators Journal, 77*(4), 24–27.

Darrow, A. A. (1991). An assessment and comparison of hearing impaired children's preference for timbre and musical instruments. *Journal of Music Therapy, 28*, 48–59.

Darrow, A. A. (1992). The effect of vibrotactile stimuli on the identification of pitch change by hearing impaired children. *Journal of Music Therapy, 29*, 103–112.

Darrow, A. A. (1993). The role of music in deaf culture: Implications for music educators. *Journal of Research in Music Education, 41*, 93–110.

Darrow, A. A. (1995). Music therapy and the hearing impaired. In T. Wigram, R. West, & B. Saperston (Eds.), *A handbook of music therapy.* Chichester, West Sussex: Carden Publications Limited.

Darrow, A. A., & Bolton, B. (1988, April). *A comparison of rhythmic performances by hearing and mainstreamed hearing impaired children.* Paper presented at the Music Educators National Conference, Indianapolis, Indiana.

Darrow, A. A., & Cohen, N. (1991). The effect of programmed pitch practice and private instruction on the vocal reproduction accuracy of hearing impaired children: Two case studies. *Music Therapy Perspectives, 9*, 61–65.

Darrow, A. A., & Gfeller, K. (1987, November). *Verbal identification of music concepts by hearing impaired children.* Paper presented at the National Association for Music Therapy Annual Conference, San Francisco, California.

Darrow, A. A., & Gfeller, K. (1988). Music therapy with hearing impaired children. In C. A. Furman (Ed.), *Effectiveness of music therapy procedures: Documentation of research and clinical practice* (pp. 137–174). Silver Spring, MD: National Association for Music Therapy.

Darrow, A. A., & Gfeller, K. (1991). A study of public school music programs mainstreaming hearing impaired students. *Journal of Music Therapy, 28*, 23–39.

Darrow, A. A., & Goll, H. (1989). The effect of vibrotactile stimuli via the SOMATRON™ on the recognition of rhythmic concepts by hearing impaired children. *Journal of Music Therapy, 26*, 115–124.

Darrow, A. A., & Heller, G. N. (1985). William Wolcott Turner and David Ely Bartlett: Early advocates of music education for the hearing impaired. *Journal of Research in Music Education, 33*, 269–279.

Darrow, A. A., & Starmer, G. J. (1986). The effect of vocal training on the intonation and rate of hearing impaired children's speech: A pilot study. *Journal of Music Therapy, 23,* 194–201.

Edwards, E. (1974). *Music education for the deaf.* South Waterford, ME: The Merriam Eddy Co.

Fahey, J., & Birkenshaw, L. (1972). Bypassing the ear: The perception of music by feeling and touch. *Music Educators Journal, 58*(8), 44–49.

Fisher, J. (1991). *The effect of three selected sensory presentation conditions on the pitch matching accuracy of normal hearing and hearing impaired children.* Unpublished master's thesis, The University of Kansas, Lawrence, KS.

Fisher, J., Baker, B., & Darrow, A. A. (1989, November). *The effect of two selected variables on the tonal perception of hearing impaired children.* Paper presented at the National Association for Music Therapy Annual Conference, Kansas City, Missouri.

Ford, T. A. (1985). *The effect of musical experiences and age on the ability of deaf children to discriminate pitch of complex tones.* Unpublished doctoral dissertation, University of North Carolina, Greensboro.

Ford, T. A. (1990). Development of rhythmic concepts and skills. In A. A. Darrow (Ed.), *Proceedings from the Second National Conference on Music and the Hearing Impaired at Gallaudet University* (pp. 21–30). Lawrence, KS: The University of Kansas.

Ford, T. A., & Shroyer, E. H. (1987). Survey of music teachers in residential and day programs for hearing impaired students. *Journal of the International Association of Music for the Handicapped, 3,* 16–25.

Galloway, H. F., & Bean, M. F. (1974). The effects of action songs on the development of body-image and body-part identification in hearing impaired preschool children. *Journal of Music Therapy, 11,* 125–134.

Gengel, R. W. (1969). Practice effects in frequency discrimination by hearing impaired children. *Journal of Speech and Hearing Research, 12,* 847–855.

Gfeller, K. (1986). Music as a remedial tool for improving speech rhythm in the hearing impaired: Clinical and research considerations. *Music Education for the Handicapped Bulletin, 2,* 3–19.

Gfeller, K. (1987). Songwriting as a tool for reading and language remediation. *Music Therapy, 6*(2), 28–38.

Gfeller, K. (1988, April). *A comparison of hearing aids and tactile aids in facilitating accuracy of profoundly deaf children on rhythm subtest of the PMMA.* Paper presented at the Music Educators National Conference, Indianapolis, Indiana.

Gfeller, K. (1990). A cognitive-linguistic approach to language development for preschool children with hearing impairments. *Music Therapy Perspectives, 8,* 47–51.

Gfeller, K. E. (1992). Music therapy in the treatment of sensory disorders. In W. B. Davis, K. E. Gfeller, & M. H. Thaut (Eds.), *An introduction to music therapy theory and practice* (pp. 209–233). Dubuque, IA: Wm. C. Brown Publishers.

Gfeller, K., & Baumann, A. (1988). Assessment procedures for music therapy with hearing impaired children: Language development. *Journal of Music Therapy, 25,* 192–205.

Gfeller, K., & Darrow, A. A. (1987). Music as a remedial tool in the language education of hearing impaired children. *The Arts in Psychotherapy, 14,* 229–235.

Gfeller, K., Lansing, C., Fryauf-Bertschy, H., & Hurtig, R. (1990, November). *Rhythmic perception by hearing impaired children using assistive devices.* Paper presented at American Speech and Hearing Association National Conference, Seattle, Washington.

Gray-Thompson, H. (1985). *The use of picture song books on the vocabulary development of hearing impaired children.* Unpublished masters thesis, The University of Kansas, Lawrence.

Klajman, S., Koldej, E., & Kowalska, A. (1982). Investigation of musical abilities in hearing-impaired and normal-hearing children. *Folia Phoniatrica, 34,* 229–233.

Korduba, O. M. (1975). Duplicated rhythmic patterns between deaf and normal hearing children. *Journal of Music Therapy, 12,* 136–146.

Leach, K. (1982). *Discrimination of musical elements made by hearing impaired residential school children.* Unpublished masters thesis, University of Kansas, Lawrence.

Madsen, C. K., & Mears, W. G. (1965). The effect of sound upon the tactile threshold of deaf subjects. *Journal of Music Therapy, 2,* 64–68.

Rickard, P., Robbins, C., & Robbins, C. (1990). Experiences in developing a creative language arts program. In A. A. Darrow (Ed.), *Proceedings from the Second National Conference on Music and the Hearing Impaired at Gallaudet University* (pp. 11–13). Lawrence, KS. The University of Kansas.

Rileigh, K. K., & Odom, P. B. (1972). Perception of rhythm by subjects with normal and deficient hearing. *Developmental Psychology, 7,* 54–61.

Robbins, C., & Robbins, C. (1980). *Music for the hearing impaired: A resource manual and curriculum guide.* St. Louis, MO: Magnamusic-Baton.

Robbins, C., & Robbins, C. (1990). Musical activities with young deaf children. In A. A. Darrow (Ed.), *Proceedings from the Second National Conference on Music and the Hearing Impaired at Gallaudet University* (pp. 8–10). Lawrence, KS: The University of Kansas.

Schatz, V. (1990). Using percussion to teach music concepts and enhance music and movement experiences. In A. A. Darrow (Ed.), *Proceedings from the Second National Conference on Music and the Hearing Impaired at Gallaudet University* (pp. 85–92). Lawrence, KS: The University of Kansas.

Sheldon, D. C. (in press). The Illinois School for the Deaf band: An historical perspective. *Journal of Research in Music Education.*

Shroyer, E. H., & Ford, T. A. (1986). Survey of music instruction and activities in residential and day schools for hearing impaired students. *Music Education for the Handicapped Bulletin, 2,* 28–45.

Solomon, A. L. (1980). Music in special education before 1930: Hearing and speech development. *Journal of Research in Music Education, 28,* 236–242.

Spitzer, M. (1984). A survey of the use of music in schools for the hearing impaired. *The Volta Review, 86,* 362–363.

Squires, V. L. (1982). *The beat maintenance and beat reproduction response of hearing-impaired and normal hearing children on sustained and percussive temporal intervals.* Unpublished master's thesis, University of Kansas, Lawrence.

Staum, M. J. (1987). Music notation to improve the speech prosody of hearing impaired children. *Journal of Music Therapy, 24,* 146–159.

Sterritt, G. M., Camp, B. W., & Lipman, B. S. (1966). Effects of early auditory deprivation upon auditory and visual information processing. *Perceptual and Motor Skills, 23,* 123–130.

Weibe, J. (1989). *The effect of adjusted frequency on the tonal perception of older hearing-impaired adults.* Unpublished masters thesis, The University of Kansas, Lawrence.

Woike, D. O. (1987). *Preferred audio response equalization in the hearing impaired.* Unpublished manuscript, Ohio State University, Columbus.

Juvenile Justice

Howell, J., Krisberg, B., Hawkins, J., & Wilson, J. (Eds.) (1995). *A sourcebook on serious, violent, and chronic juvenile offenders.* London: Sage Publications, Inc.

Watts, E. (Ed.). (1992). *Juvenile caseworker: Resource guide.* Laurel, MD: The American Correctional Association.

Learning Disabilities

Ingersoll, B. D., & Goldstein, S. (1993). *Attention deficit disorders and learning   disabilities.*New York: Doubleday.

Pierangleo, R., & Jacoby, R. (1996). Parents' complete special education guide. West Nyack, NY: Simon & Schuster.

Trace. R. (1994). Aphasia: New directions in research, treatment and service. *Advance for Speech-Language Pathologists & Audiologists, 4*(5), 12.

Music Research: Individuals With Disabilities

Cognitive Disabilities

Atterbury, B. W. (1983). A comparison of rhythm pattern perception and performance in normal and learning-disabled readers, age seven and eight. *Journal of Research in Music Education, 31*(4), 259–270.

Bixler, J. (1968). Musical aptitude in the educable mentally retarded child. *Journal of Music Therapy, 5*(2), 41–43.

Bruscia, K. E. (1981). Auditory short-term memory and attentional control of mentally retarded persons. *American Journal of Mental Deficiency, 85*(4), 435–437.

Buker, G. (1966). *A study of the ability of the educable mentally retarded to learn basic music rhythm reading through the use of a specified structured classroom procedure.* Unpublished doctoral dissertation, University of Oregon, Eugene.

Cohen, N. S. (1992). The effect of singing instruction on the speech production of neurologically impaired persons. *Journal of Music Therapy, 29*(2), 87–102.

Davis, W. B., Wieseler, N. A., & Hanzel, T. E. (1983). Reduction of rumination and out-of-seat behavior and generalization of treatment effects using a non-intrusive method. *Journal of Music Therapy, 20,* 115–131.

Decuir, A. A., & Braswell, C. E. (1978). A musical profile for a sample of learning-disabled children and adolescents: A pilot study. *Perceptual and Motor Skills, 46,* 1080–1082.

DiGiammarino, M. (1990). Functional music skills of persons with mental retardation. *Journal of Music Therapy, 27*(4), 209–220.

DiGiammarino, M. (1994). Functional music leisure skills for individuals with mental retardation. *Music Therapy Perspectives, 12*(1), 15–19.

Dorow, L. G. (1976). Televised music lessons as educational reinforcement for correct mathematical responses with the educable mentally retarded. *Journal of Music Therapy, 13,* 77–86.

Edenfield, T. N., & Hughes, J. E. (1991). The relationship of a choral music curriculum to the development of singing ability in secondary students with Down syndrome. *Music Therapy Perspectives, 9,* 52–55.

Eisenstein, S. R. A. (1974). Effects of contingent guitar lessons on reading behavior. *Journal of Music Therapy, 11,* 138–146.

Eisenstein, S. R. A. (1976). A successive approximation procedure for learning music symbol names. *Journal of Music Therapy, 13,* 173–179.

Ellis, D. (1982). *Differences in music achievement among gifted and talented, average, and educable mentally handicapped fifth- and sixth-grade students.* Unpublished doctoral dissertation, University of North Carolina, Greensboro.

Freeman, I. A. (1986). *Rhythmic beat perception in a Down's syndrome population: A computerized measure of beat accuracy and beat interval response.* Unpublished doctoral dissertation, The University of North Carolina, Greensboro.

Garwood, E. C. (1988). The effect of contingent music in combination with a bell pad on enuresis of a mentally retarded adult. *Journal of Music Therapy, 25*, 103–109.

Gfeller, K. E. (1982). *The use of melodic-rhythmic mnemonics with learning disabled and normal students as an aid to retention.* Unpublished doctoral dissertation, Michigan State University, East Lansing.

Gfeller, K. E. (1983). Musical mnemonics as an aid to retention with normal and learning-disabled students. *Journal of Music Therapy, 20*, 179–189.

Gfeller, K. E. (1984). Prominent theories in learning disabilities and implications for music therapy methodology. *Music Therapy Perspectives, 2*, 9–13.

Gilbert, J. P. (1983). A comparison of the motor music skills of non-handicapped and learning disabled children. *Journal of Research in Music Education, 31*(2), 147–155.

Grant, R., & LeCroy, S. (1986). Effects of sensory mode input on performance of rhythmic perception tasks by mentally retarded subjects. *Journal of Music Therapy, 23*(1), 2–9.

Hauck, L. P., & Martin, P. L. (1970). Music as a reinforcer in patient-controlled duration of time-out. *Journal of Music Therapy, 7*, 43–53.

Holloway, M. S. (1980). A comparison of passive and active music reinforcement to increase preacademic and motor skills in severely retarded children and adolescents. *Journal of Music Therapy, 17*, 58–69.

Hughes, J. E., Robbins, B. J., Smith, D. S., & Kinkade, C. F. (1987). The effects of participation in a public school choral music curriculum on singing ability in trainable mentally handicapped adolescents. *Music Education for the Handicapped Bulletin, 2*(4), 19–35.

James, M. R., Weaver, A. L., Clemens, P. D., & Plaster, G. A. (1985). Influence of paired auditory and vestibular stimulation on levels of motor skill development in a mentally retarded population. *Journal of Music Therapy, 22*, 22–34.

Jellison, J. A., & Duke, R. A. (1994). The mental retardation label: Music teachers' and prospective teachers' expectations for children's social and music behaviors. *Journal of Music Therapy, 31*(3), 166–185.

Jorgenson, H. (1971). Effects of contingent preferred music in reducing two stereotyped behaviors of a profoundly retarded child. *Journal of Music Therapy, 8*, 139–145.

Kaplan, P. R. (1977). *A criterion-referenced comparison of rhythmic responsiveness in normal and educable mentally retarded children.* Unpublished doctoral dissertation,

Kleckley, D. M. (1989). *The effects of stress and music on test performance for the learning-disabled and students in remedial classes.* Unpublished doctoral dissertation, University of South Carolina.

Lehr, J. K. (1977). *An investigation of music in the education of mentally and physically handicapped children in the United Kingdom, with particular reference to the course, Music for Slow Learners, at Dartington College of Arts.* Unpublished doctoral dissertation, Ohio State University, Columbus.

Madsen, C. K. (1979). The effect of music subject matter as reinforcement for correct mathematics. *Bulletin of the Council for Research in Music Education, 59*, 54–58.

Madsen, C. K., Dorow, L. G., Moore, R. S., & Wemble, J. U. (1976). Effect of music via television as reinforcement for correct mathematics. *Journal of Research in Music Education, 24*, 51–59.

McCarty, B. C., McElfresh, C. T., Rice, S. V., & Wilson, S. J. (1978). The effect of contingent background music on inappropriate bus behavior. *Journal of Music Therapy, 15*, 150–156.

McLeish, J., & Higgs, G. (1982). Musical ability and mental subnormality: An experimental investigation. *British Journal of Educational Psychology, 52*, 370–373.

Miller, D. M., Dorow, L., & Greer, R. D. (1974). The contingent use of music and art for improving arithmetic scores. *Journal of Music Therapy, 11*, 57–64.

Miller, L. K., & Orsmond, G. (1994). Assessing structure in the musical explorations of children with disabilities. *Journal of Music Therapy, 31*(4), 248–265.

Moore, R., & Mathenius, L. (1987). The effects of modeling, reinforcement, and tempo on imitative rhythmic responses of moderately retarded adolescents. *Journal of Music Therapy, 24*, 160–169.

Nocera, S. D. (1981). *A descriptive analysis of the attainment of selective musical learnings by normal children and by educable mentally retarded children mainstreamed in music classes at the second and fifth grade level.* Unpublished doctoral dissertation, University of Wisconsin, Madison.

Orsmond, G. I., & Miller, L. K. (1995). Correlates of musical improvisation in children with disabilities. *Journal of Music Therapy, 32*(3), 152–166.

Pujol, K. K. (1994). The effect of vibrotactile stimulation, instrumentation, and precomposed melodies on physiological and behavioral responses of profoundly retarded children and adults. *Journal of Music Therapy, 31*(3), 186–205.

Reynolds, B. J. (1989). The effect of training on vocal tone and hiss production for mentally retarded adolescents (abstract). *Missouri Journal of Research in Music Education, 26,* 112–113.

Rosene, P. E. (1976). *A field study of wind instrument training for educable mentally handicapped children.* Unpublished doctoral dissertation, University of Illinois, Urbana.

Saperston, B. M. (1986). *The relationship of cognitive, language, and melodic development of normal children and retarded children and adults.* Unpublished doctoral dissertation, University of Texas, Austin.

Shehan, P. K. (1981). A comparison of medication strategies in paired-associate learning for children with learning disabilities. *Journal of Music Therapy, 18,* 120–127.

Steele, A. L. (1968). Programmed use of music to alter uncooperative problem behavior. *Journal of Music Therapy, 5,* 103–107.

Stratford, B., & Ching, E. Y. (1983). Rhythm and time in the perception of Down's syndrome children. *Journal of Mental Deficiency Research, 27,* 23–38.

Strong, A. D. (1991). The relationship between hemispheric laterality and perception of musical and verbal stimuli in normal and learning disabled subjects. *Dissertation Abstracts, 51,* 3663 A–4A.

Talkington, L. W., & Hall, S. M. (1970). A musical application of Premack's hypothesis to low verbal retardates. *Journal of Music Therapy, 7,* 95–99.

Van Camp, D. J. (1990). An investigation of the effects of a researcher-designed string music curriculum on the playing skills of mildly mentally handicapped middle school students grouped in homogeneous and heterogeneous classes. *Dissertation Abstracts, 50,* 3884A.

Walker, J. B. (1972). The use of music as an aid in developing functional speech in the institutionalized mentally retarded. *Journal of Music Therapy, 9,* 1–12.

Zenatti, A. (1975). Melodic memory tests: A comparison of normal children and mental defectives. *Journal of Research in Music Education, 23*(1), 41–52.

Communication Disabilities

Bergendal, B., & Talo, S. (1969). The response of children with reduced phoneme systems to the Seashore Measures of Musical Talents. *Folio Phoniatrica, 21,* 20–38.

Cassidy, J. W. (1992). Communication disorders: Effect on children's ability to label music characteristics. *Journal of Music Therapy, 29*(2), 113–124.

Cohen, N. S. (1995). The effect of vocal instruction and Visi-Pitch™ feedback on the speech of persons with neurogenic communication disorders: Two case studies. *Music Therapy Perspectives, 13*(2), 70–75.

Cohen, N. S., & Ford, J. (1995). The effect of musical cues on the nonpurposive speech of persons with aphasia. *Journal of Music Therapy, 32*(1), 46–57.

Cohen, N. S., & Masse, R. (1993). The application of singing and rhythmic instruction as a therapeutic intervention for persons with neurogenic communication disorders. *Journal of Music Therapy, 30*(2), 81–99.

Kracke, I. (1975). Perception of rhythmic sequences by receptive aphasic and deaf children. *British Journal of Disorders of Communication, 10,* 43–51.

Michel, D. E., & May, N. H. (1974). The development of music therapy procedures with speech and language disorders. *Journal of Music Therapy, 11,* 74–80.

Reid, D. H., Hill, B. K., Rawers, R. J., & Montegar, C. A. (1975). The use of contingent music in teaching social skills to a nonverbal, hyperactive boy. *Journal of Music Therapy, 12,* 2–18.

Seybold, C. K. (1971). The value and use of music activities in the treatment of speech-delayed children. *Journal of Music Therapy, 8,* 102–110.

Sparks, R., Helm, N., & Marin, A. (1974). Aphasia rehabilitation resulting from melodic intonation therapy. *Cortex, 10,* 303–316.

Physical Disabilities

Howell, R. D., Flowers, P. J., & Wheaton, J. E. (1995). The effects of keyboard experiences on rhythmic responses of elementary school children with physical disabilities. *Journal of Music Therapy, 32*(2), 91–112.

Johnson, S. (1989). *Therapeutic use of music in gross motor upper extremity rehabilitation.* Master's thesis, Colorado State University, Fort Collins.

Lehr, J. K. (1977). *An investigation of music in the education of mentally and physically handicapped children in the United Kingdom, with particular reference to the course, Music for Slow Learners, at Dartington College of Arts.* Unpublished doctoral dissertation, Ohio State University, Columbus.

Sato, C. (1960). Survey on vocal pitch range of cerebral palsied children. *Cerebral Palsy Review, 21*(5), 4–5, 8–9.

Thaut, M. H. (1985). The use of auditory rhythm and rhythmic speech to aid temporal muscular control in children with gross motor dysfunction. *Journal of Music Therapy, 22,* 108–128.

Thaut, M. H. (1988). Rhythmic intervention techniques in music therapy with gross motor dysfunction. *Arts in Psychotherapy, 15,* 127–137.

Thaut, M. H., Schleiffers, S., & Davis, W. B. (1990). Analysis of EMG activity in biceps and triceps muscle in upper extremity gross motor task under the influence of auditory rhythm. *Journal of Music Therapy, 26,* 64–88.

Wolfe, D. E. (1980). The effect of automated interrupted music on head posturing of cerebral palsied individuals. *Journal of Music Therapy, 17,* 184–206.

Sensory Disabilities

Amir, D., & Schuchman, G. (1985). Auditory training through music with hearing impaired preschool children. *Volta Review, 87,* 333–343.

Brown, K. R. (1991). Effects of a music-based memory training program on the auditory memory skills of visually-impaired individuals. *Dissertation Abstracts, 52,* 877A.

Bruscia, K. E., & Levinson, S. (1982). Predictive factors in optacon music-reading. *Journal of Visual Impairment and Blindness, 76*(3), 309–312.

Darrow, A. A. (1979). The beat reproduction of subjects with normal and impaired hearing: An empirical comparison. *Journal of Music Therapy, 16*(2), 91–98.

Darrow, A. A. (1984). A comparison of rhythmic responsiveness in normal and hearing-impaired children and an investigation of the relationship of rhythmic responsiveness to the suprasegmental aspects of speech perception. *Journal of Music Therapy, 21*(2), 48–66.

Darrow, A. A. (1987). An investigative study: The effect of hearing impairment on musical aptitude. *Journal of Music Therapy, 24*(2), 88–96.

Darrow, A. A. (1990). The effect of frequency adjustment on the vocal reproduction accuracy of hearing impaired children. *Journal of Music Therapy, 27*(1), 24–33.

Darrow, A. A. (1991). An assessment and comparison of hearing impaired children's preference for timbre and musical instruments. *Journal of Music Therapy, 28*(1), 48–59.

Darrow, A. A. (1992). The effect of vibrotactile stimuli via the SOMATRON™ on the identification of pitch change by hearing impaired children. *Journal of Music Therapy, 29*(2), 103–112.

Darrow, A. A. (1993). The role of music in Deaf culture: Implications for music educators. *Journal of Research in Music Education, 41*(2), 93–110.

Darrow, A. A., & Cohen, N. (1991). The effect of programmed pitch practice and private instruction on the vocal reproduction accuracy of children with hearing impairments: Two case studies. *Music Therapy Perspectives, 9*, 61–65.

Darrow, A. A., & Gfeller, K. (1991). A study of public school music programs mainstreaming hearing impaired students. *Journal of Music Therapy, 28*(1), 23–39.

Darrow, A. A., & Goll, H. (1989). The effect of vibrotactile stimuli via the SOMATRON on the identification of rhythmic concepts by hearing-impaired children. *Journal of Music Therapy, 26*(3), 115–124.

Darrow, A. A., & Starmer, G. J. (1986). The effect of vocal training on the intonation and rate of hearing-impaired children's speech: A pilot study. *Journal of Music Therapy, 23*, 194–201.

Edwards, J. V. (1991). *The relationship of contrasting selections of music and human field motion (hearing impaired).* Unpublished doctoral dissertation, New York University.

Eisenson, J., Kastein, S., & Schneiderman, N. (1948). An investigation into the ability of voice defectives to discriminate among differences in pitch and loudness. *Journal of Speech and Hearing Disorders, 23*(5), 577–582.

Ford, T. A. (1987). Survey of music teachers in residential and day programs for hearing-impaired students. *Journal of the International Association of Music for the Handicapped, 3*(1), 16–25.

Ford, T. A. (1988). The effect of musical experience and age on the ability of deaf children to discriminate pitch. *Journal of Music Therapy, 25*(1), 2–16.

Galloway, H. F., & Bean, M. F. (1974). The effects of action songs on the development of body-image and body-part identification in hearing-impaired preschool children. *Journal of Music Therapy, 11*, 125–134.

Gfeller, K. E. (1986). Music as a remedial tool for improving speech rhythm in the hearing-impaired: Clinical and research considerations. *MEH Bulletin, 2*, 3–19.

Gfeller, K. E. (1987). Songwriting as a tool for reading and language remediation. *Music Therapy, 6*, 28–38.

Gfeller, K. E., & Baumann, A. A. (1988). Assessment procedures for music therapy with hearing-impaired children. *Journal of Music Therapy, 25*, 192–205.

Gfeller, K. E., & Darrow, A. A. (1987). Music as a remedial tool in the language education of hearing-impaired children. *The Arts in Psychotherapy, 14*, 229–235.

Gfeller, K., & Lansing, C. (1992). Musical perception of cochlear implant users as measured by the Primary Measures of Music Audiation: An item analysis. *Journal of Music Therapy, 29*(1), 18–39.

Heim, K. E. (1963). *Musical aptitude of seven high school students in residential schools for the blind as measured by the Wing Standardized Test of Musical Intelligence.* Unpublished master's thesis, University of Kansas, Lawrence.

Jackson, A. L. (1975). *An exploratory study using a group piano approach in an original comprehensive course for the older blind beginner.* Unpublished doctoral dissertation, Northwestern University, Evanston.

Korduba, O. M. (1975). Duplicated rhythm patterns between deaf and normal hearing children. *Journal of Music Therapy, 12*(3), 136–146.

Kracke, I. (1975). Perception of rhythmic sequences by receptive aphasic and deaf children. *British Journal of Disorders of Communication, 10*, 43–51.

Madsen, C. K., & Darrow, A. A. (1989). The relationship between music aptitude and sound conceptualization of visually impaired. *Journal of Music Therapy, 26*(2), 71–78.

Pitman, D. J. (1976). The musical ability of blind children. *American Foundation for Blind Research Bulletin, 11*, 63–79.

Rileigh, K. K., & Odom, P. B. (1972). Perception of rhythms by subjects with normal and deficient hearing. *Developmental Psychology 7,* 54–61.

Sakurabayshi, H. Y., Satyo, Y., & Uehara, E. (1956). Auditory discrimination of the blind. *Japanese Journal of Psychology of the Blind, 1,* 3–10.

Shroyer, E. H., & Ford, T. A. (1986). Survey of music instruction and activities in residential and day schools for hearing-impaired students. *MEH Bulletin, 2*(1), 28–45.

Sposato, M. (1982). *Implications of maximal exploitation of residual hearing on curriculum planning in music education for hearing impaired children.* Unpublished doctoral dissertation, State University of New York, Buffalo.

Stankov, L., & Spilsbury, G. (1978). The measurement of auditory abilities of sighted, partially sighted, and blind children. *Applied Psychological Measurement, 2,* 491–503.

Staum, M. (1987). Music notation to improve the speech prosody of hearing-impaired children. *Journal of Music Therapy, 24,* 146–159.

Sterritt, G. M., Camp, B. W., & Lippman, B. S. (1966). Effects of early auditory deprivation upon auditory and visual information processing. *Perceptual and Motor Skills, 23,* 123–130.

Social Disabilities

Applebaum, E., Engel, A. L., Koegel, R. L., & Imhoff, B. (1979). Measuring musical abilities of autistic children. *Journal of Autism and Developmental Disorders, 9*(3), 279–285.

Buday, E. M. (1995). The effects of signed and spoken words taught with music on sign and speech imitation by children with autism. *Journal of Music Therapy, 32*(3), 189–202.

Edgerton, C. L. (1994). The effect of improvisational music therapy on the communicative behaviors of autistic children. *Journal of Music Therapy, 31*(1), 31–62.

Eidsen, Jr., C. E. (1990). The effect of behavioral music therapy on the generalization of interpersonal skills from session to the classroom by emotionally handicapped middle school students. *Journal of Music Therapy, 26*(4), 206–221.

Frith, U. (1972). Cognitive mechanisms in autism: Experiments with color and tone sequence production. *Journal of Autism and Childhood Schizophrenia, 2,* 160–173.

Giacobbe, G. A., & Graham, R. M. (1978). The responses of aggressive emotionally disturbed and normal boys to selected musical stimuli. *Journal of Music Therapy, 15*(3), 118–135.

Goldstein, C. (1964). Music and creative arts therapy for an autistic child. *Journal of Music Therapy, 1,* 135–138.

Hollander, F. M., & Juhrs, P. D. (1974). Orff-Schulwerk, an effective treatment tool with autistic children. *Journal of Music Therapy, 11,* 1–12.

Kostka, M. J. (1993). A comparison of selected behaviors of a student with autism in special education and regular music classes. *Music Therapy Perspectives, 11(2),* 57–60.

Litchman, M. D. (1976). The use of music in establishing a learning environment for language instruction with autistic children. *Dissertation Abstracts International, 37,* 4992A. (University Microfilms No. AAD93-15947)

Mahlberg, M. (1973). Music therapy in the treatment of an autistic child. *Journal of Music Therapy, 10,* 189–193.

Nelson, D., Anderson, V., & Gonzales, A. (1984). Music activities as therapy for children with autism and other pervasive developmental disorders. *Journal of Music Therapy, 21,* 100–116.

Obrecht, V. L. (1991). The effect of baroque background instrumental music on academic productivity and on-task performance of emotionally behaviorly disordered students. *Dissertation Abstracts, 52,* 1676A.

O'Connell, T. (1974). The musical life of an autistic boy. *Journal of Autism and Childhood Schizophrenia, 4*, 223–229.

Ornitz, E. M. (1974). The modulation of sensory input and motor output in autistic children. *Journal of Autism and Childhood Schizophrenia, 4*, 197–216.

Saperston, B. (1973). The use of music in establishing communication with an autistic mentally retarded child. *Journal of Music Therapy, 10*, 184–188.

Schmidt, D., & Edwards, J. (1976). Reinforcement of autistic children's responses to music. *Psychological Reports, 39*, 571–577.

Sherwin, A. (1953). Reactions to music of autistic children. *American Journal of Psychiatry, 109*, 823–831.

Stevens, E., & Clark, F. (1969). Music therapy in the treatment of autistic children. *Journal of Music Therapy, 6*, 98–104.

Thaut, M. H. (1980). *Music therapy as a treatment tool for autistic children.* Unpublished master's thesis, Michigan State University, East Lansing.

Thaut, M. H. (1983). A music therapy treatment model for autistic children. *Music Therapy Perspectives, 1*, 7–13.

Thaut, M. H. (1987). Visual vs. auditory (musical) stimulus preferences in autistic children: A pilot study. *Journal of Autism and Developmental Disorders, 17*, 425–432.

Thaut, M. H. (1988). Measuring musical responsiveness in autistic children: A comparative analysis of improvised musical tone sequences of autistic, normal and mentally retarded individuals. *Journal of Autism and Developmental Disorders, 18*, 561–571.